Basic Criminal Procedure

gmc

BLACK LETTER OUTLINES

Basic Criminal Procedure

by Stephen A. Saltzburg

Wallace and Beverley Woodbury University Professor
George Washington University Law School

Daniel J. Capra

Philip D. Reed Professor of Law
Fordham University School of Law

Angela J. Davis

Professor of Law
American University, Washington College of Law

FIFTH EDITION

WEST®

A Thomson Reuters business

Mat #40707836

Black Letter Series and Black Letter Series design appearing on the front cover are trademarks registered in the U.S. Patent and Trademark Office.

COPYRIGHT © 1994 WEST PUBLISHING CO.
© West, a Thomson business, 1997, 2003, 2005
© 2009 Thomson Reuters
  610 Opperman Drive
  St. Paul, MN 55123
  1–800–313–9378

ISBN: 978–0–314–19032–1

 PRINTED ON 10% POST CONSUMER RECYCLED PAPER

SAS to Susan Lee

DJC to Hope

AJD to Howard N. Davis

*

Acknowledgment

The authors gratefully acknowledge
the research assistance of

Vanessa Martin

Rita Montoya

Kendra Mullin

Madhuri Singh

Adnan Sultan

*

Preface

This "Black Letter" is designed to help a law student recognize and understand the basic principles and issues of law covered in a law school course. It can be used both as a study aid when preparing for classes and as a review of the subject matter when studying for an examination.

Each "Black Letter" is written by experienced law school teachers who are recognized national authorities on the subject covered.

The law is succinctly stated by the authors of this "Black Letter." In addition, the exceptions to the rules are stated in the text. The rules and exceptions have purposely been condensed to facilitate quick and easy recollection. For an in-depth study of a point of law, citations to major student texts are given. In addition, a Text Correlation Chart provides a convenient means of relating material contained in the "Black Letter" to appropriate sections of the casebook the student is using in his or her law school course.

If the subject covered by this text is a code or code-related course, the code section or rule is set forth and discussed wherever applicable.

FORMAT

The format of this "Black Letter" is specially designed for review. (1) **Text.** First, it is recommended that the entire text be studied and, if deemed necessary, supplemented by the student texts cited. (2) **Capsule Summary.** The Capsule Summary is an abbreviated review of the subject matter which can be used both before and after studying the main body of the text. The headings in the Capsule

Summary follow the main text of the "Black Letter." (3) **Table of Contents.** The Table of Contents is in outline form to help you organize the details of the subject and the Summary of Contents gives you a final overview of the materials. (4) **Sample Examination.** The Sample Examinations in Appendix A give you the opportunity to test yourself with the type of questions asked on an exam and compare your answer with a model answer.

In addition, a number of other features are included to help you understand the subject matter and prepare for examinations:

Perspective: In this feature, the authors discuss their approach to the topic, the approach used in preparing the materials, and any tips on studying for and writing examinations.

Analysis: This feature, at the beginning of each section, is designed to give a quick summary of a particular section to help you recall the subject matter and to help you determine which areas need the most extensive review.

Examples: This feature is designed to illustrate, through fact situations, the law just stated. This, we believe, should help you analytically approach a question on the examination.

Glossary: This feature is designed to refamiliarize you with the meaning of a particular legal term. We believe that the recognition of words of art used in an examination helps you to better analyze the question. In addition, when writing an examination you should know the precise definition of a word of art you intend to use.

We believe that the materials in this "Black Letter" will facilitate your study of a law school course and assure success in writing examinations not only for the course but for the bar examination. We wish you success.

THE PUBLISHER

Summary of Contents

APPENDICES

App.

Table of Contents

APPENDICES

Capsule Summary

■ INTRODUCTORY CONCEPTS

I. INCORPORATION

Virtually all of the protections granted under the Bill of Rights are granted in equal measure against the states through the Fourteenth Amendment's Due Process Clause.

II. STATE COURT ACTIVISM

The Supreme Court determines the minimum amount of protection granted to individuals through the Federal Constitution. State courts cannot grant defendants less protection than that provided by the Federal Constitution. However, a state court can construe its state constitution to give greater protection to a defendant.

A. Clear Statement Requirement

There is a *presumption* that the state constitution provides coextensive protection with the Federal, *unless* the state court makes a *clear statement* that its decision is based solely on the state constitution, regardless of what the Federal constitution may provide.

■ FOURTH AMENDMENT

I. INTRODUCTION

The Fourth Amendment represents a compromise between the need of government officials to gather evidence and the right of citizens to be free from governmental intrusion. Fourth Amendment limitations on governmental investigations are equally applicable to the state and federal governments.

A. Basics of the Fourth Amendment

1. Does Not Apply to Private Activity

The Fourth Amendment regulates state action, but does not limit private individuals acting on their own initiative. Thus, no matter how unreasonable a search may be, the Fourth Amendment is not implicated if the search is conducted by private actors not acting as agents of the government.

a. Applies to All Government Agents, Not Just Police Officers

The Amendment applies to the acts of all government officials, not just to law enforcement officers.

2. Two Clauses

The Fourth Amendment has two clauses. The first clause, the reasonableness clause, provides a general standard that all searches and seizures must be reasonable. The second clause imposes requirements for obtaining warrants.

a. Which Clause Predominates?

The Supreme Court has read the warrant clause to predominate, or to define presumptively whether official conduct is "reasonable". A search or seizure is presumed unreasonable in the absence of a warrant based upon probable cause.

3. The Theory of the Warrant Clause

The preeminence of the warrant clause was the result of early Supreme Court decisions which stressed the importance of imposing an unbiased factfinder as a buffer between the citizen suspected of crime and the officer engaged in the competitive enterprise of ferreting out crime.

a. Prior Record of Probable Cause

A subsidiary benefit of the warrant requirement is that it requires the officer to establish, on the record, the facts allegedly constituting probable cause before the search is conducted. Thus, the warrant requirement prevents post hoc submissions on probable cause.

b. Limitation on the Scope of a Search

Another benefit of the warrant requirement lies in the language of the amendment which requires that the warrant must *particularly describe* the place to be searched and the things to be seized. A warrant defines the scope of a search and thereby limits the discretion of the officers conducting the search.

4. The Rise of the Reasonableness Clause

Even though the warrant clause is still considered the first reference point for the legality of a search or seizure, the Supreme Court has gradually moved to the point where most searches and seizures are in fact governed by a general standard of reasonableness. A general overview of the Supreme Court's Fourth Amendment cases shows that the dual requirement of a *warrant and probable cause are not needed in the following situations:*

a. Where a warrant is *impracticable* to obtain. See the exigent circumstances exception. (Exception to warrant requirement but not an exception to the probable cause requirement).

b. Where the police conduct a *limited* seizure to investigate possible criminal activity and a *limited* search for weapons to protect the investigating officer. See the *Terry* Doctrine. (Exception to both warrant and probable cause requirements).

c. Where the official is searching for evidence, but the search is conducted for purposes *other than criminal law enforcement.* See administrative and other "special needs" searches. (Exception to both warrant and probable cause requirements).

d. Where a search is conducted *incident to a valid arrest.* (Exception to both warrant and probable cause requirements).

e. Where there is *voluntary consent.* (Exception to both warrant and probable cause requirements).

f. Where the citizen is *arrested in public.* (Arrest warrant not required, but police must have probable cause).

g. Where an incriminating object is in *plain view or plain touch,* it may be seized without a warrant. (Probable cause required).

h. Where the officer searches an *automobile* or other form of transportation. (Exception to warrant requirement but not to probable cause requirement).

II. THRESHOLD REQUIREMENTS FOR FOURTH AMENDMENT PROTECTIONS; "SEARCH AND SEIZURE"

The Fourth Amendment prohibits unreasonable searches and seizures. Unless the government activity is either a "search" or a "seizure" it is not regulated by the Fourth Amendment, and therefore it does not have to be reasonable. In contrast, if the Court holds activity to be a search or a seizure, it does not mean that the activity is prohibited, but only that it must be reasonable.

A. The *Katz* Test

In *Katz v. United States,* 389 U.S. 347, 88 S.Ct. 507, 19 L.Ed.2d 576 (1967), the Supreme Court rejected a literal interpretation of the Fourth Amendment, and held that the amendment was designed to protect *legitimate expectations of privacy,* personal security, and possessory interests in property. "The Fourth Amendment protects people, not places."

1. Modern Definitions of "Search" and "Seizure"

After *Katz,* the term "search" is triggered whenever the state intrudes in any way upon the individual's protected interest in privacy. The term "seizure" is triggered whenever the state intrudes in any way on a protectible interest in property or security.

2. Concurring Opinion of Justice Harlan

Justice Harlan's concurring opinion in *Katz* set forth a two-pronged test to determine whether a search has occurred:

a. Manifestation

First, has the citizen *manifested a subjective expectation of privacy?*

b. Reasonable Expectation

Second, is the interest one that *society is prepared to accept as reasonable?*

B. Interests Protected by the Fourth Amendment After *Katz*

1. "Legitimate" Interests

The Fourth Amendment protects only reasonable and legitimate interests in privacy. Thus, the Court has held on several occasions after *Katz* that there is no legitimate privacy interest in illegal activity. However, to protect innocent people with legitimate privacy and security expectations from mistaken assumptions by Government officials, certain interests must be presumed and protected before the intrusion takes place.

a. Physical Disruption and Inconvenience

Citizens have an interest in being free from physical disruption, inconvenience, or terrorization by Government officials.

b. Interest in Secrecy

Citizens have a right to secrecy—a right of protection against disclosure of information which, although not incriminating, may be embarrassing, sensitive, or extremely private.

c. Possessory Interests

The Fourth Amendment regulates not only invasions of privacy and security interests, but also invasions of possessory interests. The Fourth Amendment prohibits unreasonable *seizures* as well as searches.

C. Manifestation of a Subjective Interest in Privacy

How far must a citizen go to protect his privacy interests?

1. Strict Application

Generally speaking, the courts have required citizens to take vigorous measures to protect their claimed privacy interests.

2. Abandonment

Abandonment of property is inconsistent with the retention of any privacy or possessory interests.

D. Legitimacy of the Expectation of Privacy; Access by Members of the Public

After *Katz*, if an aspect of a person's life (such as his trash or public movement) is subject to scrutiny by members of the public, then that person has no legitimate expectation in denying equivalent access to the police. *There is no search if the police obtain information that members of the public could foreseeably obtain.* Examples of situations in which the right of public access indicates that police activity is not a search include: inspection of bank records; inspection of trash left out for the trash collector; information obtained in an aerial overflight; and numbers dialed on a telephone.

E. Investigation Which Can Only Uncover Illegal Activity Is Not a Search

There is no legitimate privacy interest in illegal activity.

1. Dog Sniffs

A dog sniff of a place or container is not a search as it can only tell the officer whether or not contraband is located therein, and there is no legitimate expectation of privacy in contraband.

2. Chemical Tests

If a chemical test merely discloses whether or not a substance is contraband, the test is not a search.

F. Reopening of Packages by Government Officials

If a package has been opened once consistent with the Fourth Amendment, it will not be a search if it is reopened by a Government official, unless there is a substantial probability that the contents of the package have been changed since the original opening. However, if the subsequent official investigation of the package or its contents exceeds the scope of the original search, it may trigger Fourth Amendment protection to the extent that a further intrusion is made.

G. Sensory Enhancement Devices

Generally speaking, the use by officials of devices which aid their investigation by enhancing the senses does not constitute a search, so long as the devices do no more than aid the police in obtaining information that they could have obtained through their own sensory perception. However, the use of a thermal-imaging device to obtain information about the inside of a private home is a search.

H. Open Fields

A person has no legitimate expectation of privacy in property that lies beyond his house and curtilage. The Fourth Amendment does not protect such "open fields."

1. Curtilage Remains Protected

If the property investigated is within the "curtilage," then the open fields doctrine does not apply, and a state intrusion into the curtilage will be a search if the citizen has manifested an expectation of privacy. Structures appurtenant to the home, such as porches and decks, are part of the curtilage, at least so long as the structure is not shared with other homeowners and is restricted from public access.

I. Public School Students

High school students have an expectation of privacy while in school. However, the state interest in promoting school discipline and safety may permit school officials to conduct searches without probable cause or a warrant.

J. Government Employees

Intrusions into the private areas of Government employees, such as a desk or file cabinet, are searches covered by the Fourth Amendment. However, the interest in promoting government efficiency may permit searches without a warrant or probable cause.

III. THE PROBABLE CAUSE REQUIREMENT

Probable cause is a standard of proof of criminal activity that justifies a search or seizure. The probable cause standard strikes a balance between the rights of innocent citizens to privacy and security, and the interest of the state in investigating and prosecuting crime.

A. Standard of Proof Required for Probable Cause to Exist

The standard of proof required for probable cause is: enough particularized facts to lead a common sense person of reasonable caution to believe that there is a *fair probability* of criminal activity. Proof beyond a reasonable doubt is not required; neither is proof by a preponderance of the evidence.

1. Officers Are Allowed to Make Reasonable Mistakes

Because the probable cause standard is lower than a preponderance, it follows that officers need not be correct in their assessment of the facts. Arrests of the wrong person, and searches which uncover no incriminating evidence, are nonetheless permissible if the officer's mistake was reasonable.

2. Totality of the Circumstances

The analysis of probable cause requires a cumulative look at all pertinent factors.

3. Deference to Police Officer's Expertise

The experience and expertise of the officer is also taken into account. A fact which does not look suspicious at all to the untrained eye may be indicative of criminal activity to a person versed in how criminals operate.

4. Collective Knowledge

The particular officer who conducts an arrest or search need not have personal knowledge of all the facts on which probable cause is based. Probable cause can be based on the *collective knowledge* of the police department.

B. Generally Required for All Searches and Seizures

A search or seizure is presumptively unreasonable unless it is supported by probable cause and a warrant. But even if a search or seizure is conducted pursuant to an exception to the warrant requirement, it generally must still be supported by probable cause.

1. Exceptions

The Court has found three exceptional situations where a nonconsensual search or seizure may be conducted in the absence of probable cause:

a. Seizures of Persons or Things Which Constitute a Limited Intrusion

Temporary and minimally invasive detentions of persons and things, which are necessary to conduct a preliminary investigation, are allowed upon a showing of reasonable suspicion, which is a less demanding standard of proof than probable cause.

b. Limited Searches to Protect the Officer From Harm

An officer can, on reasonable suspicion instead of probable cause, conduct a limited search of a person, thing, or premises in order to protect himself from bodily harm while he is conducting a legitimate investigation.

c. Search or Seizure Conducted for Special Needs Beyond Criminal Law Enforcement

If the search or seizure is not conducted for purposes of criminal law enforcement but rather to effectuate some other governmental objective such as a regulatory interest, it can in most cases be conducted on less than probable cause.

2. All Searches for Criminal Law Enforcement Purposes Require Probable Cause

None of the above exceptions apply to a search conducted by law enforcement officers for the very purpose of enforcing the criminal law.

C. Questions of Identity

Probable cause as to identity must be based on specific information tying a suspect to a crime. Probable cause requires a case-by-case approach; nonetheless, since the standard is only one of fair probability, a suspect's correspondence to a relatively specific description will go far toward a showing of probable cause. Furthermore, the state's case on probable cause as to identity is made significantly stronger if the suspect who fits a general description also has a prior criminal record.

D. Equivocal Conduct

A probable cause question arises where it is unclear whether a crime has been committed or is being committed at all.

1. Innocent Explanations

Most courts will find probable cause if there is some conduct which a reasonable person would think highly suspect, even though an innocent explanation for the conduct is also plausible. The real question is whether plausible innocent explanations substantially outweigh the likelihood of criminality.

2. First Amendment Considerations

First Amendment considerations do not require a standard of proof higher than probable cause before a search may be conducted of speech-related material.

E. Location

A probable cause question arises where officials suspect that a person to be arrested, or evidence of a crime, is located in a particular place. If investigation of such a place would be a search, the officers must have probable cause to believe that the person to be arrested or the evidence to be seized is located in the place to be searched.

1. Staleness

The question of staleness arises when the information on which probable cause is based was discovered significantly earlier than when the search is actually conducted. Whether the information has grown stale is dependent upon such facts as the nature of the crime, the type of evidence, and the length of time that has passed.

2. One of Several Locations

When a piece of evidence could be located in one of several places, but could not be in two locations at the same time, there is probable cause to search in each place, even though the locations are mutually exclusive, so long as there is a *logical nexus* between the crime and the location.

F. The Use of Hearsay

An officer is relying upon hearsay information when the officer does not have personal knowledge of the facts, but is instead using information obtained from other parties. A question then arises as to whether the "facts" related by such third parties are reliable enough to be credited in the probable cause determination.

1. Former Two–Pronged Test

To ensure that the magistrate had some way to make an independent determination of the reliability of hearsay information, the Court in *Aguilar v. Texas*, 378 U.S. 108, 84 S.Ct. 1509, 12 L.Ed.2d 723 (1964), and *Spinelli v. United States*, 393 U.S. 410, 89 S.Ct. 584, 21 L.Ed.2d 637 (1969) imposed what came to be known as the *Aguilar–Spinelli two-pronged test* for structuring the magistrate's analysis of probable cause. The two prongs assessed: (1) the informant's *reliability*, and (2) the *source* of the informant's information. The Supreme Court later rejected the two-pronged test in favor of a less structured *totality of the circumstances* approach. *See Illinois v. Gates*, 462 U.S. 213, 103 S.Ct. 2317, 76 L.Ed.2d 527

(1983). However, lower courts still use the two-pronged test as a helpful tool for evaluating an informant's hearsay.

2. Impact of *Gates* Totality of Circumstances Approach

If *Aguilar–Spinelli* is satisfied, it follows that *Gates* is as well, since the *Gates* test is avowedly more permissive than the former test. Moreover, under the new approach, if a tip is especially strong on one prong, and not absolutely deficient on the other, probable cause may be found. More importantly, after *Gates,* if the tip is insufficient to establish probable cause, some corroboration of the tip by police investigation will ordinarily suffice to establish probable cause, even if the activity corroborated could be considered completely innocent.

IV. OBTAINING A VALID SEARCH WARRANT

Generally speaking, the Fourth Amendment requires every search or seizure to be made pursuant to a warrant issued upon probable cause. A warrant is a document issued by a judicial officer, usually a magistrate, authorizing a law enforcement official to make a search or seizure.

A. Neutral and Detached Magistrate

The magistrate must be a neutral official, who will make an unbiased determination of whether probable cause exists. There is no requirement that a magistrate give reasons for finding probable cause or for rejecting a warrant application. There is no requirement that the person who issues the warrant must be legally trained.

B. Probable Cause Based Only on Facts Presented to the Magistrate

The warrant requirement forces the officer to establish a record supporting probable cause before a search occurs. Probable cause must be judged solely by the information presented to the magistrate in the warrant application. This is an *ex parte* proceeding.

1. Affidavits

A warrant is ordinarily obtained by submitting an affidavit to the magistrate setting forth all the facts supporting probable cause.

2. Telephone Warrants

A warrant may be obtained upon oral testimony communicated by telephone or other means. However, the officer must prepare a written "duplicate original warrant," and then read that warrant verbatim to the magistrate.

C. Particular Description of Place to Be Searched

Even if there is probable cause to search a certain location, a search warrant provides no authority to search it if the location is not described with *reasonable particularity.*

1. Reasonable Particularity

The degree of particularity that is reasonable depends on the nature of the place to be searched, and on the information that an officer could reasonably obtain about the location. Technical precision is not required in all cases.

2. Applicability to More Than One Location

If the warrant contains information as particularized as the officer could reasonably be expected to obtain, then it is sufficiently particular even though the warrant could actually apply to more than one location. The Fourth Amendment allows for reasonable mistakes of fact.

3. Incorrect Address

Variances between the actual address and the address specified in the warrant do not per se invalidate the warrant. The warrant remains valid so long as there is sufficient information therein for the executing officer to know where to execute the warrant despite the specification of a wrong address.

D. Particular Description of Things to Be Seized

The things to be seized must be particularly described in the warrant.

1. Reasonable Particularity

The test of whether a description of things to be seized is sufficiently particular is one of reasonableness, determined by the information that police could reasonably be expected to know prior to the search.

2. Catch–All Clauses

When the warrant describes some items in detail, and then includes a catch-all clause e.g., allowing the seizure of "any other evidence of the crimes," courts will generally find such clauses to be overbroad unless they are somehow qualified by the particular descriptions that precede the catch–all clause in the warrant.

3. Severability

If some clauses in a warrant are sufficiently particular and other clauses are not, the overbroad clauses can be severed from those that are sufficiently particular. The warrant, and the search conducted pursuant to it, will then be evaluated on the basis of the valid clauses.

E. Warrant Can Authorize the Seizure of "Mere Evidence"

A warrant may be issued to search for and seize all evidence of a crime. An officer's search power is not limited to the actual fruits and instrumentalities of the crime.

F. Issuing Warrants Against Non–Suspects

Searches can be made on the premises of non-suspects, either pursuant to a warrant or to an appropriate exception to the warrant requirement, so long as there is probable cause to believe that evidence will be found therein.

1. No Special First Amendment Protection

The fact that the non-suspect is protected by the First Amendment creates no special protection against a search of the premises for evidence.

2. Statutory Protection

Congress has provided protections for journalists and others in the Privacy Protection Act.

V. EXECUTION OF SEARCH WARRANTS

The reasonableness clause of the Fourth Amendment imposes limitations on the execution of a validly obtained warrant.

A. Time of Execution

Most jurisdictions provide that a search pursuant to a warrant must occur within a limited time after the warrant is issued. Most jurisdictions prohibit execution of a warrant in nighttime hours, unless special circumstances are shown.

B. Notice Requirement

The Constitution, as well as a federal statute, requires officers to knock and announce their presence before executing a warrant. The knock and announce requirement is excused, however, if the citizen is already aware of the police presence, or if knocking and announcing would create a risk of harm to the police officers or destruction of evidence.

C. Use of Extraordinary Force

Use of such devices as battering rams are permitted where the circumstances require it. If the circumstances do not justify such extraordinary measures, the use of these devices will render the search unreasonable.

D. Scope and Intensity of the Search

Generally, officers can search all areas specified in a warrant, wherever probable cause exists to believe that the object of the search could reasonably be. Occupants of the premises can be detained while the search is being conducted.

■ EXCEPTIONS TO THE GENERAL FOURTH AMENDMENT REQUIREMENTS OF PROBABLE CAUSE AND A WARRANT

I. INTRODUCTION

A search or seizure is *presumptively unreasonable* in the absence of a warrant based upon probable cause and particularly describing the place to be searched and the things to be seized. However, the Supreme Court has established many exceptions to those general requirements.

II. THE PLAIN VIEW DOCTRINE

A. Seizure Without a Warrant

The plain view doctrine allows an officer, during the course of lawful police activity, to seize an object without a warrant if there is probable cause that it is evidence of criminal activity.

B. Limitations

1. Scope of Lawful Activity

The officer must be lawfully located in a place from which the object can be seen, and must also have a lawful right of access to the object.

2. Warrantless Seizures

The plain view doctrine allows a seizure if there is probable cause to believe that there is contraband or evidence in a container. However, the officer must generally obtain a search warrant to open the container, or find some other exception to the warrant requirement.

3. Probable Cause

There must be probable cause that the object in plain view is evidence of a crime.

4. Probable Cause Must Be Immediately Apparent

If the item must be searched and investigated in order to determine whether there is probable cause to seize it, such an investigation is itself a search that requires probable cause.

C. Plain Touch Exception to the Warrant Requirement

If police, in the course of legal activity, touch an object and can determine that there is probable cause that the object is evidence of a crime, that object may be seized without a warrant.

III. WARRANTLESS ARRESTS

A. No Warrant Required for a Public Arrest

The Fourth Amendment does not require an officer to obtain a warrant before making a public arrest for a felony offense or for a misdemeanor committed in the officer's presence. This is so even if the officer could easily have obtained the warrant without jeopardizing the arrest.

1. Post–Arrest Determination of Probable Cause

If a citizen is arrested without a warrant, he has the right to a prompt post-arrest determination of probable cause by a magistrate or judge.

a. Prompt Hearing Is Required

Anything up to a 48 hour delay between arrest and hearing is presumed reasonable. The hearing need not be held at the first practicable opportunity; the state is allowed some flexibility to create efficient pre-trial procedures. However, any delay beyond 48 hours is presumed unreasonable, and the state has to present compelling circumstances to explain the delay.

B. Warrant Required for an In–Home Arrest

The Fourth Amendment prohibits the police from arresting a defendant in his home without a warrant, in the absence of exigent circumstances.

1. Violation Constitutes Illegal Search, Not an Illegal Arrest

When an officer has probable cause and arrests the defendant in his home without a warrant and without exigent circumstances, the officer has conducted an illegal *search of* the home by entering it to seize the arrestee. But the arrest itself is not illegal presuming it was made with probable cause.

C. Search Warrant Required for an Arrest in the Home of a Third Party

An arrest warrant is insufficient to authorize the arrest of a suspect in the home of another person. In the absence of exigent circumstances or consent, a search warrant must be obtained to look for the suspect in the home of a third party. It is important to determine whether the suspect lives at the premises (in which case an arrest warrant is sufficient), or whether he is merely visiting there (in which case a search warrant is required).

IV. EXIGENT CIRCUMSTANCES

A. Introduction

Police are not required to obtain a warrant if exigent circumstances exist. The rationale is that if in the time it would take to obtain a warrant, something harmful to legitimate state interests will occur, then a warrant should be excused. However, officers operating under this exception must still satisfy the probable cause requirement. Generally speaking, the risks that trigger the exigent circumstances doctrine include those stemming from *hot pursuit* of a suspect, risks to *public safety,* and the risk of *destruction or loss of evidence.*

B. Hot Pursuit

If officers are in hot pursuit of a suspect, this will excuse an arrest warrant where one is otherwise required, and it will also excuse a search warrant where a search of an area must be conducted in order to find and apprehend the suspect. The "hot pursuit" exception does not apply where the suspect is unaware that he is being pursued by police officers.

C. Risk to Public or Police Safety

If circumstances exist in which the police or the public would be harmed in the time it takes to obtain a warrant, officers are not required to obtain a warrant before entering a private area.

D. Destruction or Loss of Evidence

The ground of exigency most often invoked is that in the time it would take to obtain a warrant there is an imminent risk of destruction or loss of evidence.

1. Relevant Factors

The following is a non-exclusive list of factors taken into account in determining whether the risk of destruction or loss of evidence is sufficient to excuse the warrant requirement. All of the factors are relevant and none are necessarily dispositive.

— The *degree of urgency* involved and the *amount of time* necessary to obtain a warrant.

— A reasonable belief that contraband or evidence is *about to be removed*.

— *The possibility of danger* to police officers guarding the premises while a search warrant is sought.

— Information indicating that suspects *know that the police are on their trail*.

— The ready *destructibility* of the evidence.

— The *gravity of the offense* of which the suspects are to be charged.

— Whether the suspects are reasonably believed to have *firearms* in their possession.

— Whether *probable cause is clear* or is rather a close question.

— The *likelihood that suspects may escape* in the absence of an immediate entry.

— The *peaceful circumstances* of the entry.

— The amount of time it would take to obtain a warrant. If a *telephone warrant* is available in the jurisdiction, then the time it would take to obtain such a warrant is the benchmark. Telephone warrants are available under federal practice.

2. Narcotics Cases

Most lower courts liberally apply the exigent circumstances exception in drug cases.

Need Not Be in the Process of Destruction

Courts generally do not require narcotics to be in the actual process of destruction before a warrantless entry can be justified.

3. Murder Scene Searches

While the gravity of the crime is a factor in determining exigent circumstances, there is no per se exigent circumstances exception for the search of a murder scene.

4. Minor Crimes

It is more difficult to establish exigency if the crime is a minor one.

E. Impermissible Creation of Exigent Circumstances

The warrant requirement will not be excused where the exigency has been impermissibly created by the police. But most courts hold that exigency is not impermissibly created unless police officers actually violate the Fourth Amendment (e.g., by making an illegal entry) and thereby create exigent circumstances.

F. Prior Opportunity to Obtain a Warrant

If the officers had clear probable cause and a clear opportunity to obtain a warrant for a significant time before an exigency arose, they are not excused from the warrant requirement.

G. Securing Premises While Waiting for the Warrant

Even in the absence of exigent circumstances, officers can protect against the destruction of evidence by securing a premises for a reasonable period of time while a warrant is obtained.

V. STOP AND FRISK

A. *Terry* and the Court's Reliance on the Reasonableness Clause of the Fourth Amendment

In *Terry v. Ohio*, 392 U.S. 1, 88 S.Ct. 1868, 20 L.Ed.2d 889 (1968), the Court held that a stop can be conducted if an officer has *reasonable suspicion* to believe that crime is afoot. The *Terry* Court further held that an officer who makes a legal stop can conduct a *protective frisk* of a suspect if the officer has *reasonable suspicion to fear* that the suspect is armed and dangerous.

1. Three Categories of Police–Citizen Contacts

After *Terry*, there are three categories of police-citizen contact:

a. Arrest and Incident Search

The most serious intrusion is an arrest, and the standard of proof required to justify an arrest is probable cause. An arrest allows a complete search incident to the arrest, for self-protection and to protect against the destruction of evidence.

b. Stop and Frisk

A less serious intrusion is a stop, which is permitted on the lesser standard of proof of reasonable suspicion. Incident to a stop is a frisk, which is a limited search for weapons, *not for evidence.*

c. Encounter

If an officer merely engages the citizen in an encounter, this is not considered an intrusion at all. Since an *encounter is not a seizure*, it does not implicate the Fourth Amendment, and therefore the officer need not satisfy any standard of proof before conducting an encounter.

B. What Is a "Stop?": The Line Between Stop and Encounter

If an officer "stops" a citizen, he must have reasonable suspicion, because a stop is a seizure that requires a justification; but an officer can "encounter" a citizen for any reason or no reason, as an encounter is not a seizure.

1. The *Mendenhall* Reasonable Person Test

In *United States v. Mendenhall,* 446 U.S. 544, 100 S.Ct. 1870, 64 L.Ed.2d 497 (1980), Justice Stewart proposed a definition for "stop" that was later adopted by the Court with certain modifications: if, in view of all the circumstances, a *reasonable innocent person would have believed that he was not free to leave,* then a stop has occurred.

2. Active Coercion Prohibited

Under the *Mendenhall* test, an officer who affirmatively employs coercive tactics will be held to have conducted a seizure, requiring (at least) reasonable suspicion. If, instead, the officer acts politely and the citizen merely responds to the fact that the questioning is conducted by an officer, then the contact will be deemed an encounter.

3. Informing the Citizen of the Right to Terminate an Encounter or to Refuse Consent

An officer is not obligated to tell the citizen that he has the right to leave or to refuse to answer questions or consent to a search. However, if the officer does inform the citizen of these rights, this will go far toward establishing a consensual encounter.

4. Two Modifications to the *Mendenhall* "Free to Leave" Test

a. Not Free to Leave Because of the Suspect's Own Circumstances

If the citizen is confined because of his own circumstances (e.g., the citizen is in a bus, a subway, or an elevator), the question is whether the *police conduct would have communicated to a reasonable person that the person was not free to decline the officers' requests or otherwise terminate the encounter.* The fact that the citizen is not physically free to leave is essentially irrelevant where the condition is not created by the police but by the suspect's own circumstances.

b. If Coercive Tactics Are Non–Physical, There Is No Stop Until the Suspect Submits

In *California v. Hodari D.,* 499 U.S. 621, 111 S.Ct. 1547, 113 L.Ed.2d 690 (1991), the Court separated "seizures" into two types: those in which the officer has *physically touched* the suspect, and those in which the officer has used a non-physical *show of authority* (such as drawing a gun, ordering the suspect to stop, etc.). A stop *automatically* occurs when an officer physically touches a suspect with the intent of restraining him. Where the officer employs a non-physical show of authority, it must be such that a reasonable innocent person would not feel free to leave, *and the citizen must actually submit to the show of authority.*

5. Officer is Not Required to Use an Encounter as a "Less Intrusive Alternative"

If an officer has reasonable suspicion to support a stop, she can seize the suspect even though an encounter may be equally productive. The officer is not required to employ the less intrusive alternative.

C. What Is Reasonable Suspicion? Similar Analysis to Probable Cause

The analysis used to determine whether reasonable suspicion exists to support a stop is similar to that employed in assessing probable cause. The following analytical concepts are applicable to both standards:

— *A common sense* analysis of the facts presented

— *Deference* to the *expertise* of law enforcement officers

— The *totality of circumstances* must be assessed

— *Reasonable mistakes* of fact are permitted

1. Difference in Quantity and Quality of Proof

The difference between reasonable suspicion and probable cause is that reasonable suspicion is a *less demanding* standard of proof—a stop is permissible upon something less than the fair probability standard that defines probable cause. Reasonable suspicion can be usefully referred to as *possible cause.*

2. Questions of Identity of a Perpetrator

Stops are permissible where it is clear that a crime has occurred, and the officer has an articulable suspicion that a particular person is the perpetrator. The case for reasonable suspicion is stronger if the suspect gives implausible answers during an encounter, or if the suspect has a criminal record consistent with the crime being investigated.

3. Suspicious Conduct

A stop is permitted if, considering all the circumstances, an officer could find it reasonably possible that "criminal activity is afoot." The fact that an innocent explanation for the suspect's conduct can be hypothesized does not preclude a finding of reasonable suspicion.

a. Factors Bearing on Reasonable Suspicion

A totality of the circumstances test is employed to determine whether there is reasonable suspicion to believe that a suspect is engaging or about to engage in illegal activity. Some of the relevant factors include: whether there is a pattern of activity; whether the suspect appears unfamiliar with his surroundings; whether the activity occurs in the day or at night; whether the activity occurs in a high crime area; whether the suspect has a criminal record consistent with the expected activity; whether the suspect is attempting to evade police surveillance; and whether the suspect gives implausible answers during an encounter.

b. Non–Cooperation During an Encounter

The mere fact that a person acts somewhat nervously in the presence of a police officer cannot, by itself, be considered suspicious. Further, a suspect's mere failure to consent to requests by a police officer during an encounter can not be a factor which contributes to reasonable suspicion, as a person who is merely encountered has the absolute right to refuse cooperation and terminate the encounter. However, certain out-of-the-ordinary activity designed to avoid or terminate conduct with the police may be considered suspicious.

4. Use of Profiles

A profile is a list of characteristics compiled by a law enforcement agency which have been found through experience to be common to those engaged in a certain type of criminal activity. The most common example is a drug courier profile.

a. Match With Profile Is Not Dispositive

A suspect's correlation with a profile is no guarantee that there is reasonable suspicion to justify a stop; the reasonableness of a stop must be assessed in light of the *particular circumstances.*

b. Officer's Use of Profile Does Not Render the Stop Illegal

On the other hand, the officer's use of a drug courier profile does not somehow taint the stop, assuming reasonable suspicion exists on the facts.

5. Relevance of Suspect's Race

Some courts have considered racial "incongruity" (i.e., that a person of a certain race is unlikely to be in a certain neighborhood or area) as relevant in assessing reasonable suspicion, although such incongruity is not ordinarily dispositive. There is a recent trend towards prohibiting the use of race in the reasonable suspicion calculus, but some courts have permitted its consideration as one of many factors.

6. Use of Informants

An officer's assessment of reasonable suspicion is often based in whole or in part on information from an informant. However, the *Aguilar–Spinelli* reliability and credibility factors, and even the less demanding *Gates* test for probable cause, are considered unnecessarily rigorous for the standard of reasonable suspicion. Reasonable suspicion is not only a less demanding standard, it is also less rigorous in the types of information that can be used as proof. The fact that the informant's tip alleges possession of a gun does not change the reasonable suspicion calculus.

a. Reasonably Correct Prediction of Future Activity Is Crucial

An informant's tip will be an important consideration towards reasonable suspicion if it correctly predicts future activity. The activity predicted need not be criminal in itself. In contrast, corroboration of contemporaneous conditions (e.g., that the suspect is driving a certain car) indicates little about the reliability of the informant's assessment of criminal conduct, since such conditions could be easily observed by one who has no inside information about criminal activity.

D.   The Right to Frisk Incident to a Stop

A stop is a seizure. A frisk is a search, which is an independent intrusion that must be separately justified. There are two critical determinations that must be made in judging the legality of a frisk: 1) whether the officer's action was justified at its *inception,* and 2) whether it was reasonably related in scope to the circumstances that justified the interference in the first place.

1.   Frisk Is Not a Search for Evidence

Terry does not permit a search for evidence. A search for evidence, in the absence of a need to protect the officer, requires probable cause.

2.   Inception of a Frisk; Reasonable Suspicion of Bodily Harm

Terry requires "reasonable, individualized suspicion before a search for weapons can be conducted." Assuming that a stop is justified, the question upon which the legality of a frisk depends is whether there is reasonable suspicion to believe that the suspect is armed and dangerous. The following is a list of relevant factors that may support a frisk:

— Reasonable suspicion that a person is involved in a *crime of violence*

— Suspicion of *large-scale drug distribution*

— *A bulge* on the suspect that appears to be a weapon

— *A sudden movement* by the suspect toward a place where a weapon might be hidden

— *Previous violent activity* on the part of the suspect, which activity is known to the officer

— *Aggressive or violent behavior* on the part of the suspect

— *A large number of suspects compared to the number of police officers*

— The *nature of the surroundings* and the *time of day*

3. Self–Protective Frisk of Those Not Suspected of a Crime

A person cannot be frisked merely because he or she is at a location where criminal activity exists. However, if an officer can point to articulable facts linking that person to the criminal activity, or to a danger to the police officers, then a protective frisk will be permitted.

4. Ordering a Suspect Out of a Car for Self–Protection

An officer has an *automatic* right to order a person to step out of a vehicle where that vehicle has been lawfully stopped. This rule applies to both drivers and passengers.

5. Limitations on the Scope of a Frisk

In conducting a frisk, an officer can be *no more intrusive than is necessary to* protect against the risk of harm posed by the suspect. A detailed touching of all areas of the suspect's body is beyond the scope of a *Terry* frisk.

a. Probable Cause

If an officer feels a soft package, it cannot be taken out and inspected under the *Terry* doctrine; but the fact that the suspect was carrying a soft package may, together with other factors, constitute probable cause that the suspect is carrying contraband. If this is so, then the suspect may be arrested and the package may be searched incident to the arrest.

b. Containers on the Suspect's Person

If the officer reasonably takes a hard object from the suspect's person and it turns out to be a container, generally the officer may open the container if it could contain a weapon; the risk of harm to the officer which justified the initiation of the frisk also serves to justify the opening of any containers that could contain a weapon.

6. Right to Protective Search Beyond the Suspect's Person

Officers are permitted to conduct protective searches of containers carried by the suspect or within the suspect's grab area, if there is a reasonable risk that an accessible weapon could be located in that area.

a. Protective Search of Automobiles

Cursory inspections of the accessible areas of the passenger compartment of an automobile are permitted whenever there is reasonable suspicion to believe that the suspect poses a threat of harm.

b. Protective Sweep

A "protective sweep" is a quick and limited search of a premises, incident to an arrest and conducted to protect the safety of police officers or others. A protective sweep can be conducted if officers have articulable facts that give rise to reasonable suspicion that a search is necessary to protect the officers or others from dangerous people; probable cause is not required. A protective sweep can only be conducted for safety purposes, and not to prevent the destruction of evidence.

E. Brief and Limited Detentions: The Line Between Stop and Arrest

Stops are permitted upon a showing of reasonable suspicion because stops are more limited intrusions than arrests. Using a totality of the circumstances approach, courts generally look at the following factors to determine whether a police intrusion constitutes a stop requiring reasonable suspicion or an arrest requiring probable cause:

1. Forced Movement of the Suspect to a Custodial Area

Generally, the forced movement of suspects for investigative purposes is beyond the scope of *Terry,* and thus requires probable cause. However, if reasonable suspicion exists, it is often permissible to transport the suspect a short distance so that eyewitnesses may attempt to make an identification. Also, a suspect may be moved from one location to another for purposes of safety or security.

2. Investigative Techniques

An officer conducting a *Terry* stop can engage in preliminary investigation designed to clear up or to further develop reasonable suspicion, such as checking identification, plane tickets, etc. Some investigative techniques are themselves so intrusive, however, as to require probable cause (e.g., body cavity searches).

3. **Time Limits on Terry Stops**

There is no absolute time limit after which a stop will automatically become an arrest. While the question of whether the police "diligently pursued" a quick means of investigation is a *factor* in determining the level of seizure that took place, officers are generally given the benefit of the doubt if they are acting reasonably and not wasting time.

a. **Suspect's Refusal to Consent to a Search**

A suspect's refusal to consent to a search cannot be used as a justification for prolonging a stop. However, a detention can be prolonged if the suspect acts *improperly* to subvert the officer's investigation (e.g., by running away).

b. **Detention of Household Occupants During Execution of a Search Warrant**

Police officers with a valid search warrant may order persons on the premises to remain there while a search warrant is being executed— even if the length of the detention exceeds that ordinarily associated with a *Terry* stop.

4. **Show of Force or Use of Restraint**

The use of forceful, coercive tactics—such as the use of handcuffs or a drawn gun—does not automatically transform a stop into an arrest. Stops may be accompanied by force when the circumstances indicate that such measures are reasonably necessary to ensure the safety of the officers. The following factors are relevant in determining whether an officer, in the course of a *Terry* stop, permissibly employed custodial tactics:

— *The number of officers and suspects* involved

— The *nature of the crime* for which reasonable suspicion exists

— Whether there is *reasonable suspicion to believe the suspect might be armed*

— The *strength of the officers' articulable suspicions*

— Whether the *suspect is cooperative*

— The *need for immediate action* by the officers

F. Detentions of Property Under *Terry*

Terry applies both to seizures of property and persons. There are three types of police contact with personal property:

— *Non-material interference,* which does *not implicate Fourth Amendment concerns*

— *Temporary detentions* interfering with possessory or liberty interests, which require at least *reasonable suspicion*

— Detentions *so lengthy* that they require *probable cause*

Relevant Factors

The following factors are relevant in determining whether the detention of property is so prolonged as to require probable cause, or sufficiently limited as to be permissible upon reasonable suspicion:

— Whether the officers were *reasonably diligent in conducting their investigation*

— The *length* of the detention and whether *liberty interests as well as possessory interests are at stake*

— Whether the suspect is given *information concerning the seizure,* e.g., when the property can be retrieved

VI. ADMINISTRATIVE AND REGULATORY SEARCHES AND SEIZURES

If a search or seizure is justified by *special needs beyond criminal law enforcement,* the Court will balance the state interest in conducting the search against the individual privacy interest at stake, under the *reasonableness clause* of the Fourth Amendment. These searches and seizures, unlike those conducted under the *Terry* doctrine, can be directed towards uncovering evidence.

A. Safety Inspections of Homes

A home inspection, arising from an established inspection policy, can be conducted without probable cause but, except in emergency situations or with the homeowner's consent, the inspection does require a search warrant.

B. Administrative Inspections of Businesses

Administrative inspections of businesses usually can be conducted without probable cause. Furthermore, heavily regulated businesses may be searched without a warrant, due to the significant state interest involved as well as the diminished expectation of privacy attendant to participation in a heavily regulated business. However, such warrantless inspections must *necessarily further a substantial governmental interest,* and statutes must provide *constitutionally adequate substitutes for a warrant, which will operate to limit the officer's discretion.* Investigations of areas open to the general public are not considered searches covered by Fourth Amendment protections.

C. Civil–Based Searches of Individuals Pursuant to "Special Needs"

A special needs balancing analysis is used to uphold civil-based searches of individuals in the absence of a warrant and probable cause. Any evidence uncovered from such searches may be used in traditional criminal law proceedings, so long as the search itself was conducted for a regulatory objective.

1. Searches Directed at Students, Government Employees, Parolees, and Probationers

Most searches of the belongings of students (at school), Government employees (at the workplace), parolees, and probationers may be conducted without a warrant and on the basis of reasonable suspicion. Particularly intrusive searches, such as strip searches, may require the higher standard of proof of probable cause.

2. Security Searches at Airports, Courthouses, Military Installations, Prisons, etc.

In order to provide safety and security for the public in various locales where a security risk has been demonstrated, checkpoint security searches are allowed at airports, courthouses, jails, military installations, etc. without warrants or individualized suspicion. People must be given the option to avoid a search by leaving the premises.

3. Drug Testing of Government Employees

As public employers have a regulatory interest in both public safety and job performance, *drug testing of Government employees* may be conducted without use of warrants and, in certain circumstances, without a finding of reasonable suspicion. Even in the absence of a documented problem of drug abuse, *neutral, non-discretionary, suspicionless testing* may be allowed if undetected drug use would impair a *substantial governmental interest.* However, symbolism is not a sufficient interest to support suspicionless testing. Candidates for public office cannot be subject to suspicionless testing.

4. Drug Testing of Students

The Supreme Court has upheld suspicionless drug testing of high school students who participate in extracurricular activities, relying on the unique interest of the state in protecting students who are entrusted to its care, and the students' reduced expectation of privacy.

D. Border Searches and Seizures

Border searches, or searches at the functional equivalent of the United States border, are generally allowed without warrants, and often without any suspicion at all, due to the Government's interest in protecting the American borders and regulating materials flowing in *and out* of the country (e.g., communicable diseases, narcotics, explosives, illegal aliens). Particularly intrusive searches, such as body cavity or full strip searches, require a finding of individualized suspicion.

E. Roadblocks

While stops of vehicles ordinarily require reasonable suspicion, there are certain circumstances in which roadblock seizures at fixed checkpoints are allowed without any suspicion of criminal activity. These checkpoints are conducted for purposes other than criminal law enforcement, such as highway safety and border control. However, if the primary purpose of a checkpoint is criminal law enforcement, the officer must have reasonable suspicion for the stop.

VII. THE ARREST POWER RULE

The "arrest power rule" grants an automatic right to police officers, during a lawful custodial arrest, to secure the suspect and his grab area without reasonable suspicion or probable cause, and without a warrant. This right is based on two grounds: 1. to *protect the officers making the arrest* and 2. to *protect against the destruction of evidence.*

A. Relevant Factors to Determine Arrestee's "Grab Area"

A suspect's grab area is determined on a case-by-case basis, but certain factors are helpful in these determinations:

— Whether the suspect is *cuffed or restrained*

— The *physical characteristics* of the particular suspect

— The *ratio of police officers to suspects*

— Whether the item searched is *reasonably accessible to the suspect*

B. Circumstances That Justify Searches Beyond the Grab Area

While the arrest power rule is subject to spatial limitations, other exceptions might apply during or after an arrest which may permit officers to conduct searches or seizures beyond the area within the arrestee's immediate control.

1. Moving Grab Area

If an arrestee moves to a different location during a lawful arrest, the *grab area automatically moves along with the arrestee;* police officers need not show a case-by-case risk of danger to follow the suspect and inspect the suspect's grab area.

2. Exigent Circumstances

When a person is arrested, a risk may arise that the arrestee's associates will destroy evidence before a warrant can be obtained.

3. Protective Sweep

The fact of arrest may create a risk of harm to the arresting officers from the arrestee's associates, which could justify a *protective sweep* of the premises.

4. Securing Premises

There may be a need to *secure the premises* during the time it takes to obtain a search warrant after a suspect is arrested.

C. Temporal Limitations

Searches "incident to arrest" are allowed slightly before the formal arrest process, as long as the probable cause to arrest is present before such a search is conducted. Also, searches and seizures that could be made at the time of the arrest are allowed slightly *later* in time as long as the arrest process is not yet complete. A search is ordinarily no longer incident to arrest if the suspect has been removed from the arrest scene.

D. Searches of the Person

Police officers have the *automatic* right to conduct a *complete body frisk,* and to pull out and search all objects *on an arrestee's person,* even if there is no factual risk of harm to the officer or likelihood of destruction of evidence. Generally, police may search, as well as seize, all items that are "immediately associated" with the arrestee (e.g., wallets and purses).

Objects in the Grab Area

Most courts allow searches, as well as seizures, of items not immediately associated with the arrestee, but within the arrestee's grab area (e.g., briefcases and book bags). But there is a split in the courts on this point—some courts allow the automatic seizure of such items, but preclude a search of these items in the absence of warrant and probable cause, or some other exception to the warrant requirement.

E. Searches of Automobiles

When the occupant of a car is lawfully arrested, the arrest power rule allows an *automatic* search of the passenger compartment of the car without a warrant or probable cause. The passenger compartment of a car is *always* in the "grab area," even if the arrestee does not have reasonable access to this area at the time of the search. Generally, anything accessible from the interior of the car is considered within the passenger compartment. The police may search and open all containers found in the passenger compartment.

VIII. PRETEXTUAL SEARCHES AND SEIZURES

Generally, if an officer has an *objective* right to make a stop or arrest for a minor infraction, the stop is legal and it makes no difference that the officer might have "subjectively" used the stop or arrest as a pretext to obtain evidence of a more serious crime. Nor does it matter that a reasonable officer would not, under the circumstances presented, have stopped or arrested the defendant for the minor crime. The question is whether the officer had the legal authority to conduct a stop or arrest on the minor offense, and acted consistently with that authority in conducting a further search or seizure.

IX. SEARCHES AND SEIZURES OF AUTOMOBILES AND OTHER MOVABLE PROPERTY

A. Automobile Exception to the Warrant Requirement

The automobile exception allows the police to search a car without obtaining a warrant if there is probable cause to believe that the car contains evidence of criminal activity. The automobile exception may also be applied to airplanes and mobile homes.

1. Distinguishing the Automobile Exception From a Search Incident to Arrest

The search of an automobile incident to arrest does not depend on the existence of exigent circumstances or probable cause to search, but rather it focuses on the *legality of the underlying arrest* and the *area in which the search occurred.*

2. Which Exception Is Preferred?

The state prefers to invoke the *arrest power rule* because once the arrest of a suspect is found lawful, the right to search the passenger compartment of a car is *automatic.* In contrast, searches pursuant to the automobile exception are not permissible unless officers have probable cause to believe that evidence will be found in the car. However, there are at least three situations in which the arrest power rule will not apply and then the state may find it necessary to resort to the automobile exception:

— The arrest is not made *in or near a car*

— The search of the car is *too far removed* from the arrest so that it can no *longer be deemed incident to the arrest*

— Officers wish to search the *trunk* of the car

B. Movable Property—In and Out of Cars

If a car is subject to a warrantless search under the automobile exception, then the police may search any container located in the car, without a warrant, so long as they have probable cause to believe that the container holds evidence of criminal activity. However, in the absence of exigent circumstances, a warrant is required to search a container that is located outside a car; there is no analogy to the automobile exception for movable containers, such as luggage, which are found outside a car.

C. Car Searches and Seizures Pursuant to the Community Caretaking Function

If officers are performing duties apart from those associated with traditional law enforcement, the officers may conduct warrantless searches of vehicles so long as the searches are reasonably conducted for safety purposes. Similarly, the police do not need probable cause or a warrant to impound a car for caretaking purposes.

Inventory Exception

Automobiles and other containers that are lawfully held in police custody may be searched without a warrant or suspicion under the inventory exception to the warrant requirement, so long as standardized inventory regulations are in place to control the discretion of the searching officer, and so long as those standards are complied with in the individual case. Inventory searches are administrative searches conducted for safety purposes, and to protect property from theft or vandalism.

X. CONSENT SEARCHES

If a suspect *voluntarily* consents to a search, the search is permissible even in the absence of a warrant or any articulable suspicion. Consenting to a search is *not* considered a *waiver* of a constitutional right—which must be intelligent, voluntary, and knowing. Rather, a search made pursuant to voluntary consent is considered *a reasonable* search under the Fourth Amendment. The Government must show by a preponderance of the evidence that the consent was *voluntary under the totality of circumstances.*

A. Factors Relevant to Voluntariness

No single factor is dispositive, but the following factors are relevant in assessing whether a consent was voluntarily obtained:

— Whether the person consenting is *in custody*

— The presence of *coercive police procedures*

— The extent and level of the person's cooperation with the police

— The person's *awareness of his right to refuse consent.* Note that the police are not obligated to inform a person of his right to refuse consent or the right to leave an encounter. Furthermore, a person's lack of knowledge regarding this right does not preclude a finding of consent. On the other hand, if a person is informed that he has a right to refuse consent or leave an encounter, a subsequent consent is likely to be found voluntary.

— The person's *education and intelligence*

— The person's *belief that no incriminating evidence will be found*

An officer's threat to obtain a warrant does not vitiate the voluntariness of a consent, unless the warrant could not actually be obtained.

B. Third Party Consent

If a third party has access to or control over a private area, he or she is considered to have an *independent privacy interest,* and the suspect is considered to have *assumed the risk* that the third party may lawfully consent to a search of that area. A third party's access may be limited or conditional, depending on the circumstances.

1. Marital Relationships

Generally, there is a presumption of *common authority* over premises jointly occupied by both spouses.

2. The Third Party Must Possess Actual or Apparent Authority

Third party consent is valid if the third party possesses either *actual or apparent authority.* Apparent authority results when police officers *reasonably believe* that the third party has authority to consent. This reasonable belief does not arise merely from a third party's assertion of common authority; police officers have a *duty* to make *reasonable inquiries* regarding the third party's claim of authority. Apparent authority exists if the third party would have authority if the facts were as the officer reasonably believes them to be.

C. Scope of Consent

A consenting party may place limitations on the scope of the consent. A search is a valid consent search if a *reasonable person* would conclude that it is within the limitations established by the consenting party.

1. Ambiguity Regarding Scope of Consent Is Construed Against the Suspect

If an officer's interpretation of a general or ambiguous consent is a reasonable one, the resulting search will be considered within the scope of the consent. It is up to the *suspect* to clarify the scope of an ambiguous consent. However, a search that requires mutilation or destruction of property or premises is considered beyond the reasonable scope of a general consent.

2. Limiting the Scope of Consent

If a suspect explicitly limits consent (e.g., "you can search my briefcase but not my suitcase"), this limitation cannot be considered suspicious by the officer, since the suspect is merely standing on his rights.

D. Revocation of Consent

A suspect has the right to revoke consent, although it cannot be revoked retroactively after an officer has found incriminating evidence. The mere withdrawal or limitation of consent cannot be considered a factor in an officer's determination of reasonable suspicion or probable cause. Refusal to give written consent does not constitute the revocation of an oral consent.

■ REMEDIES FOR FOURTH AMENDMENT VIOLATIONS

I. THE EXCLUSIONARY RULE

The *exclusionary rule* provides that evidence obtained in violation of a defendant's Fourth Amendment rights must be excluded from trial in both federal and state courts. The exclusionary rule is a *court-made rule* designed to deter future violations of the Fourth Amendment, and a court is *not constitutionally required to* exclude illegally obtained evidence. The Supreme Court has created exceptions to the exclusionary rule for situations where the rule's costs significantly outweigh the deterrent value of the rule.

II. STANDING TO INVOKE THE EXCLUSIONARY RULE

The standing requirement provides that a defendant cannot obtain exclusion of evidence unless his *own personal Fourth Amendment rights* are violated.

A. Reasonable Expectation of Privacy

Standing questions are resolved by determining whether a person has a *legitimate expectation of privacy* in the area or thing that was searched, or a legitimate possessory interest in the thing seized.

1. Burden on Defendant

The *defendant* bears the burden of proving that he had a legitimate expectation that was violated by the challenged search and seizure.

2. Possessory Interest in Items Seized Is Insufficient

A defendant does not automatically have standing to contest the *search* of an area merely because the items *seized* are owned by the defendant. However, he generally does have a right to object to the *seizure* of such property, even if it is being held by a third party. A seizure would implicate a suspect's *personal* Fourth Amendment possessory interest in the item seized.

3. Disassociation With the Object of the Search

Where a defendant disavows any knowledge of or interest in property that is being searched or seized, such an action is inconsistent with a reasonable expectation of privacy, and the defendant will not have standing to object to the police activity.

4. Co-conspirator Status

The mere fact that a search or seizure has occurred with respect to property controlled by a conspiracy does not mean that each co-conspirator has standing to object. There is no joint venture exception to the principle that standing is dependent on a violation of one's own personal Fourth Amendment rights.

III. EXCLUSION OF "THE FRUIT OF THE POISONOUS TREE"

A. Introduction

A defendant often seeks exclusion of the *very evidence* that was found in an illegal search or seizure. Such evidence is termed the "direct" or "primary" evidence of the illegal search. However, the defendant may also challenge the admission of evidence which was *derived from* an initial illegality. Such evidence is termed "derivative" evidence, or "fruit of the poisonous tree." The exclusionary rule generally applies to all *evidence derived* from the evidence obtained in the illegal search—i.e. to all fruits of the illegality. But there are exceptions to this exclusionary principle.

B. Attenuation

In some cases, the link between the illegal search or seizure and the evidence obtained is *so attenuated* that the evidence can no longer be meaningfully considered "tainted" or the "fruit of the poisonous tree." Under those circumstances, the deterrent effect of the exclusionary rule is considered equally attenuated and, therefore, the cost of excluding reliable evidence outweighs the negligible benefit of deterrence. Attenuation is determined on a case-by-case basis.

1. Test of Causation

The Court has rejected a "but for" test for determining whether evidence is the fruit of an illegality. Instead, the test to determine whether there is a sufficient connection between the illegality and the derivative evidence so as to justify exclusion is as follows: whether, under the totality of circumstances, the evidence has been obtained by *exploitation of the illegality* or instead by means *sufficiently distinguishable* to be purged of the primary taint.

2. Relevant Factors in Determining Attenuation

Once an illegal search or seizure is established, the *Government has the burden* of proving that the causal chain is sufficiently attenuated to dissipate the taint of the illegality. Several factors are deemed relevant in this determination:

— The giving of *Miranda warnings.* Note that *Miranda* warnings will *not* per se break the chain of causation, but they are relevant to dissipating the taint of an illegal search or seizure.

— The time between the *illegality and the obtaining of the evidence*

— The presence of *intervening circumstances*

— The *purpose and flagrancy of the official misconduct*

3. Abandonment During the Course of an Illegal Search or Seizure

A suspect's decision to abandon property subsequent to an illegal search or seizure may or may not be tainted by that illegality. Courts determine if abandoned evidence is tainted by looking at whether a defendant had *sufficient time and opportunity* to make a calculated decision to abandon the property (in which case the suspect's voluntary act served to cut off any tainting effect of the illegality), or whether the decision to abandon the property was a *spontaneous reaction* to the illegal activity (in which case the evidence would be fruit of the poisonous tree despite the abandonment).

4. Testimony of Live Witnesses

An illegal search or seizure may lead to the discovery of a witness who can give testimony against the defendant. Generally, a witness' voluntary decision to testify against the defendant will mean that the testimony is attenuated from the illegality.

C. Independent Source

Evidence will not be excluded as the fruit of the poisonous tree if the Government can show that it was derived from an *independent legal source.* The independent source exception admits the fruits of illegally obtained evidence when such fruits are also found by *legal means unrelated to the original illegal conduct.* Under those circumstances, application of the exclusionary rule would impermissibly place the officers in a worse position than they would have been absent any violation.

D. Inevitable Discovery

The *inevitable discovery* exception to the exclusionary rule allows the fruits of illegal activity to be admitted at trial if the Government can show that the challenged evidence would *inevitably* have been discovered through means completely independent of the illegal activity. In essence, the inevitable discovery exception is a "hypothetical" independent source exception.

1. Inevitability Must Be Shown by a Preponderance

The exception is applicable if the Government proves by a *preponderance of the evidence* that the discovery would have inevitably occurred through legal means.

2. Focus on What Would, Not Could, Have Been Done

For the inevitable discovery exception to apply, the question is *not* what the police could *or should* have done, but what they actually *would* have done to reach the evidence by independent legal means.

3. Active Pursuit

Some courts require the police to be *actively pursuing* lawful means *at the time* the illegal search is conducted in order to invoke the inevitable discovery exception. Under the majority view, active pursuit is one way, but not the only way, to meet the state's burden of proof on inevitability.

IV. "COLLATERAL USE" EXCEPTIONS TO THE EXCLUSIONARY RULE

A. Introduction

Use of illegally obtained evidence outside the context of the Government's case-in-chief is generally permitted, though there are some exceptions where the deterrent effect of the rule has been found to outweigh the cost of exclusion.

B. Grand Jury

The exclusionary rule does not apply to grand jury proceedings.

C. Sentencing, Parole or Probation Revocation

The exclusionary rule is generally inapplicable to the consideration of evidence for purposes of sentencing and parole or probation revocation proceedings. However, if a search or seizure is made to *harass* a defendant, or if it has been conducted *expressly for the purpose of obtaining evidence for a parole or probation revocation, or to enhance a sentence,* then the exclusionary rule may apply.

D. Forfeiture Proceedings

The exclusionary rule is applicable to forfeiture proceedings if the property is not *intrinsically illegal in character.* Illegally seized *contraband* need not be returned to the owner.

E. Deportation Proceedings

The exclusionary rule is inapplicable in civil deportation proceedings.

F. Civil Proceedings

The exclusionary rule is inapplicable in a civil proceeding brought by the Government (e.g. a tax collection action), at least where the proceeding falls outside the offending officer's zone of primary interest.

G. Habeas Corpus Proceedings

A habeas petitioner cannot invoke the exclusionary rule to challenge evidence seized in violation of the Fourth Amendment, so long as the petitioner was given a "full and fair opportunity" to litigate the Fourth Amendment claim during his state court proceeding. If a petitioner loses a Fourth Amendment claim in the state courts because of *ineffective assistance of counsel,* habeas review may be allowed, as a violation of the standards of effective assistance is considered a separate constitutional issue.

H. Impeachment

1. Direct Testimony

The exclusionary rule does not prevent the prosecution from using illegally obtained evidence to *impeach* the defendant's direct testimony.

2. Cross–Examination

The prosecutor may use illegally obtained evidence to impeach a defendant's answer to a question put to him on cross-examination, so long as the question is within the scope of the direct examination.

3. Defense Witnesses

However, the exclusionary rule does prohibit the use of illegally obtained evidence to impeach the defendant's *witnesses.* See the full outline for the reasoning behind the distinction.

V. THE "GOOD FAITH" EXCEPTION TO THE EXCLUSIONARY RULE

Where an officer, acting in objective good faith, has obtained a search warrant from a judge or magistrate that is ultimately found to be unsupported by probable cause, any evidence obtained from the resultant search or seizure may generally be used in the Government's case-in-chief, despite the fact that it is illegally obtained. This is because the error was made by the magistrate, not the officer who reasonably relied on the magistrate's action. The exclusionary rule is considered to have a deterrent effect on the conduct of police officers in the competitive enterprise of ferreting out crime, but to have no deterrent effect on the activity of magistrates, who are judicial officers.

A. Reasonably Unreasonable

An officer can "reasonably" rely on an invalid warrant as long as reasonable minds can differ as to whether a particular warrant is valid. Where all reasonable people would agree that a warrant is invalid, then the officer will be in error in relying on that warrant; in those circumstances, the exclusionary rule is presumed to have some deterrent effect in assuring future compliance.

B. Exceptions to the Good Faith Exception

There are *four situations* in which an officer's reliance on a warrant is considered unreasonable:

1. Misleading Information

If the magistrate who issued the warrant was misled by information in an affidavit that the affiant *knew or would have known* was false except for his *reckless disregard* of the truth, then the error in issuing the warrant was that of the officer, not the magistrate, and the exclusionary sanction will apply.

2. Abandonment of Judicial Role

Where the issuing magistrate wholly abandons his judicial role, then no reasonably well-trained officer should rely on the warrant. The officer's reliance on such a warrant is not fatal, however, unless the officer *knew or had reason to know* of this abandonment.

3. Affidavit Clearly Insufficient to Establish Probable Cause

If all reasonable minds would agree that the information set forth in the affidavit did not constitute probable cause, then the officer cannot reasonably rely on the magistrate's issuance of the warrant.

4. Facially Deficient Warrant

If a warrant is *so egregiously deficient* in its particularization, or in comporting with other procedural requirements, that all reasonable people would find it invalid, then an officer who relies on it is in error and the exclusionary rule will apply.

C. Unreasonable Execution of the Warrant

Improper execution of a valid warrant is an error attributable to the officer rather than to the magistrate, and is therefore subject to the exclusionary rule.

D. Reliance on Unconstitutional Legislation

Where the officer reasonably relies on a statute that is subsequently held unconstitutional, the officer has not committed a wrong, and the exclusionary rule will not apply. The exclusionary rule is considered to have no effect on the conduct of legislators.

1. Unreasonable Reliance on Unconstitutional Legislation

If the legislature wholly abandons its responsibility to enact constitutional laws or if a statute is clearly unconstitutional, it would be objectively unreasonable for an officer to rely on such legislation.

2. Misinterpretation of Legislation

The good faith exception does not apply to a police officer's reasonable though mistaken interpretation of the scope of a statute permitting a search. Such a mistake is one that is made by the *officer,* not by the legislature, and the exclusionary rule would apply to this misconduct—assuming that the search itself is in violation of the Fourth Amendment.

E. Reliance on Court Clerical Personnel

Where the officer reasonably relies on recordkeeping by court clerical personnel concerning outstanding arrest warrants, the good faith exception applies where such warrants are in fact invalid or non-existent. The error in such circumstances is by the court personnel, rather than the officer. While the officer can be deterred by exclusion, court clerical personnel cannot.

F. Does Not Apply to Warrantless Searches

Currently, the exclusionary rule applies if an officer conducts an illegal warrantless search, even if the officer had an objective good faith belief that the warrantless search was legal. The good faith exception only applies where an officer has reasonably relied on a magistrate, court clerical personnel, or a legislative act.

■ THE PRIVILEGE AGAINST SELF–INCRIMINATION

I. INTRODUCTION

The Fifth Amendment's privilege against compelled self-incrimination prohibits the Government from compelling individuals to provide incriminating testimony in *any proceeding* if their answers might incriminate them in an *ongoing or future* criminal proceeding. A statement can tend to incriminate even if the offense admitted is rarely, if ever, prosecuted. The state may compel disclosure of information for use in civil or other non-criminal proceedings. Generally, a proceeding is "civil" in nature when denominated as such by the legislature. Also, as a general rule, the Fifth Amendment does not protect against the risk of foreign prosecution.

II. WHAT IS COMPULSION?

A. Use of Contempt Power

The state's *use of the contempt power is compulsion* because it imposes substantial punishment on a witness who claims the privilege, and presents the witness with the classic *"cruel trilemma"* of choosing between *self-accusation, contempt, and perjury—each* of which could lead to imprisonment.

B. Other State–Imposed Sanctions Which May Create Compulsion

1. Custodial Interrogation

See the *Miranda* doctrine, infra.

2. The Threat of Economic Sanctions

If a person suffers a Government-imposed economic sanction for invoking his Fifth Amendment right to silence, the sanction is considered compulsion because it punishes the person for invoking his right. Examples of such compulsion are disbarment and depriving the person of the right to bid on public contracts.

3. Comment by the Prosecutor or Judge on a Defendant's Failure to Testify

Adverse comment to the jury on the criminal defendant's election not to testify constitutes punishment for the invocation of silence and violates the Fifth Amendment. An adverse inference can permissibly be drawn in a civil case, however.

III. IDENTIFYING THE HOLDER OF THE PRIVILEGE

A. The Privilege Is Personal

The privilege against self-incrimination belongs only to the person who would be compelled to incriminate himself by his own testimony.

B. Business Entities; Collective Entity Rule

The Fifth Amendment does not protect partnerships or corporations.

C. Sole Proprietorships

The Fifth Amendment protects a sole proprietorship, as it is not an entity that is legally separate from the individual.

IV. INFORMATION PROTECTED BY THE PRIVILEGE

A. Testimonial Evidence

The Fifth Amendment protects only against compelled disclosure of *testimonial* evidence. If evidence is non-testimonial, the Government can compel its production.

1. The Cruel Trilemma

Evidence is testimonial when it contains an express or implied assertion of fact that can be either true or false; it is only this type of evidence that subjects a compelled individual to the cruel trilemma of truth, falsity and silence that is at the heart of Fifth Amendment protection. In contrast, physical evidence cannot be either true or false, and thus a defendant cannot commit perjury by its compelled production. So for example, the Government can compel the defendant to provide a blood sample or a handwriting exemplar, even though the evidence could incriminate the defendant.

2. Refusal to Supply Physical Evidence

An individual's refusal to supply the state with physical evidence may be used against him at trial.

B. Documents

Generally, the contents of both business and personal documents are not protected by the Fifth Amendment if they were prepared before a Government subpoena was ever served. This is because the *preparation* of such documents is "wholly voluntary" and an act completely independent from the compelled act of *producing* the documents for use by the Government.

1. Act of Production

The act of producing documents communicates that documents exist; that they are under the *control and in the possession* of the person producing the documents; and that the documents are *authentic* (i.e. that they are in fact the documents described by the subpoena). Thus, the act of production could have certain testimonial aspects triggering Fifth Amendment protection, independent of the content of the documents, which are not protected by the Fifth Amendment. While incriminating acts of production are generally protected, the privilege will not apply if existence, control, and authentication can be proven by the government through *independent evidence.* In such cases, the act of production, in context, is not sufficiently incriminating to trigger the privilege.

2. Compelling Agents of Business Entities to Produce Documents: The Collective Entity Rule

If an agent of a business entity produces compelled documents, the act of production may incriminate the agent. However, the agent produces such documents not in a personal capacity, but as a representative of a corporation, and so his act of production is not protected by the Fifth Amendment, though as a matter of evidence the act of production is only relevant as a corporate and not a personal act. The collective entity rule does not allow the Government to force a corporate agent to give personally incriminating oral testimony.

C. Required Records Exception

If the Government requires documents to be kept for a *legitimate administrative purpose,* neither the content nor the act of production of these documents are protected by the Fifth Amendment. However, if the recordkeeping requirement is directed to a class that is inherently suspected of committing criminal activity (e.g., marijuana growers), the required records exception does not apply.

V. PROCEDURAL ASPECTS OF SELF–INCRIMINATION CLAIMS

A. Assertion of the Privilege

Whenever a person is compelled to answer questions that might tend to incriminate him, he has the right to refuse to answer. If he does answer, the privilege is lost with respect to the answer and the answer can be used as evidence.

B. Immunity

Even assuming the testimony tends to incriminate a witness, the Government may compel testimony when the witness has received immunity. There are two *types* of immunity: *transactional immunity and use immunity.*

1. Transactional Immunity

Transactional immunity protects an individual from prosecution for *any transaction* described in his testimony. Transactional immunity gives *greater* protection than is constitutionally required.

2. Use and Derivative Use Immunity

Use and derivative use immunity prevent the use of testimony obtained from a person, or any information directly or indirectly derived from such testimony. A grant of use and derivative use immunity is *coextensive* with the Fifth Amendment privilege, and therefore a person who receives such immunity has no right to refuse to testify.

a. Prosecution Is Still Possible

The Government may grant use immunity and yet still prosecute the witness for the transaction admitted to if there is evidence *independent* of such testimony and the fruits of such testimony.

b. Government's Burden

The burden is on the Government to prove that the evidence it proposes to offer against the witness at trial is derived from a source independent of the immunized testimony.

C. **Waiver of the Privilege**

Individuals can *explicitly waive* the privilege against self-incrimination, and can *also implicitly waive* the privilege by giving testimony that is inconsistent with the retention of the privilege. If a witness testifies, he cannot, under a claim of the privilege, refuse to testify about related subject matter.

■ SELF–INCRIMINATION AND CONFESSIONS

I. CONFESSIONS AND DUE PROCESS

A. A Confession Must Be "Voluntary" in Order to Be Admissible at Trial

The Due Process Clause of the Fifth and Fourteenth Amendments prohibits the admission of "involuntary" confessions, generally defined as confessions obtained *by physical force or psychological coercion.* A court determines the "voluntariness" of a confession under the totality of circumstances by focusing on *three main factors: the actions of the police, the personality of the defendant,* and the *circumstances surrounding the confession.*

B. Judicial Interpretations of "Voluntariness" and "Coercion"

1. Actual Violence Not Required

A credible threat of physical violence is ordinarily sufficient to support a finding of coercion. Police practices that fall short of threats of violence or actual physical force are less likely to establish a claim of "coercion" under the Due Process Clause. In particular, a misrepresentation of fact—e.g., that the suspect's fingerprints were found at the scene when that is not the case—is ordinarily insufficient in and of itself to render a subsequent confession involuntary.

2. Some Police Coercion Required

The Due Process Clause is not implicated unless there is some police misconduct that is causally related to a confession.

3. The Harmless Error Doctrine and Involuntary Confessions

The erroneous admission of an involuntary confession is not per se reversible error but, instead, is reviewed under the "harmless error" standard for constitutional violations—i.e., whether the erroneous admission of the involuntary confession was harmless beyond a reasonable doubt.

4. An Involuntary Confession Is Not Admissible at Trial for Any Purpose

A coerced confession may not be admitted either in the state's case-in-chief or during the state's cross-examination of a defendant.

II. THE SPECIAL FEDERAL STANDARD FOR CONFESSIONS

Congress has codified a test providing for exclusion of involuntary confessions and admission of all voluntary confessions. The legislative provision sets forth a totality of circumstances approach. One of the factors to be considered is whether there was unnecessary delay in presenting the suspect to the magistrate before he confessed. Another factor is whether the suspect has been warned of his right to silence and counsel.

III. CONFESSIONS AND THE FIFTH AMENDMENT

A. *Miranda v. Arizona*

Intimidating police techniques may produce a confession that is not "involuntary" under Due Process standards, but is nonetheless obtained in violation of the privilege against self-incrimination. In *Miranda v. Arizona*, 384 U.S. 436, 86 S.Ct. 1602, 16 L.Ed.2d 694 (1966), the Court established *prophylactic safeguards to* protect a suspect's Fifth Amendment right to remain silent from the *inherently coercive pressures of custodial interrogation.*

1. The *Miranda* Safeguards

a. The Warnings

A suspect must be warned that he has the right to remain silent, and that anything he says can and will be used against him in court. The suspect must also be informed that he has the right to consult with a lawyer and to have the lawyer with him during interrogation, and that if he is indigent, a lawyer will be appointed to represent him.

b. Custodial Interrogation

The warnings about the rights to silence and counsel are *absolute prerequisites to custodial interrogation.* However, the warnings are not required if the police interrogate a suspect who is not in custody, or if the police place a suspect in custody but do not interrogate him. It is the interplay between custody and interrogation that creates the inherent Fifth Amendment compulsion that the warnings are designed to alleviate.

c. Counsel Has No Independent Role to Play

Under *Miranda* the right to counsel must be invoked by the suspect. In the absence of an invocation, counsel has no independent authority to control police interrogation.

2. *Miranda* Is Not a "Constitutional Straightjacket"

Congress and the states may create alternatives for protecting the privilege, so long as they are as effective as the *Miranda* rules. But in the absence of *equally effective* procedures for protecting the rights of suspects, *Miranda* safeguards are constitutionally required and must be observed.

B. *Miranda* and Impeachment

The failure of an officer either to give warnings or to abide by them does not prevent the use of the *Miranda*-defective statements to impeach a defendant at trial. However, the post-arrest statements can only be considered in judging the defendant's "credibility," and not as evidence of guilt.

1. Defense Witnesses

Statements obtained in violation of *Miranda* cannot be used to impeach a defendant's witnesses.

2. Invocation of the Right to Silence

A reference at trial to a defendant's post-warning silence violates the defendant's constitutional right to Due Process. A prosecutor may, however, impeach a defendant about inconsistent omissions in post-warnings statements, as those omissions are not "silences" protected by Due Process.

3. Silence Before *Miranda* Warnings Are Given May Be Used for Impeachment Purposes

The Constitution does not prohibit the prosecution from impeaching a defendant with his pre-arrest or post-arrest silence before receiving *Miranda* warnings, as no governmental action "implicitly induced" the defendant to remain silent.

C. The Fruit of the Poisonous Tree and the *Miranda* Safeguards

The "fruit of the poisonous tree" doctrine—under which all evidence derived from a constitutional violation is excluded—does not generally apply to *Miranda* violations.

1. Subsequent Confessions

Where a defendant makes a *Miranda*-defective confession, and thereafter makes a confession pursuant to *Miranda* warnings, the subsequent confession is ordinarily admissible.

2. The Fruits of Involuntary Confessions Are Excluded

Even when police officers give proper *Miranda* warnings, an involuntary confession, and any fruits of such a confession, are excluded from trial.

3. Physical Evidence as the Fruit of a *Miranda* Violation

Physical evidence obtained as a fruit of a *Miranda* violation is admissible at trial.

D. The "Voluntary, Knowing, and Intelligent" Waiver of *Miranda* Rights

Police must seek a "voluntary, knowing, and intelligent" waiver of rights before interrogating a suspect in the absence of an attorney. A "voluntary, knowing, and intelligent" waiver must be the product of *free and deliberate choice* (which is the same standard as the Due Process voluntariness test), and must be made with a *full awareness* both of the nature of the right being abandoned and the consequences of the decision to abandon it. No waiver can be considered knowing and intelligent in the absence of *Miranda* warnings.

1. The State Has the Burden of Proving Waiver

The state must prove a waiver by a preponderance of the evidence. The state must make an *affirmative* showing of free choice, and must show that the defendant both had the capacity to understand the warnings and, in fact, did understand the warnings imparted by the officer.

2. A "Conditional" Waiver May Be "Knowing and Intelligent"

If a defendant makes a conditional waiver of *Miranda* rights, a subsequent confession is admissible so long as police comply with the suspect's condition.

3. A Waiver Is Valid Even When a Suspect Is Not Informed of Matters That Would Be Useful in Making an Informed Decision

Miranda warnings encompass the sum and substance of all the information required for a defendant to make a knowing waiver. The police need not impart further "useful" information to a suspect that goes beyond the general *Miranda* structure. For example, the police need not inform a suspect that his lawyer wants to speak with him.

4. Revoking a Waiver

A suspect may invoke his rights after answering some questions, and thereby withdraw any waiver given at the outset.

E. Waiver and the Resumption of Questioning After Invocation of Rights

The state has a more difficult case to make on waiver if a defendant first *invokes* either his right to silence or right to counsel, and then later decides to *waive* his rights. Under these circumstances, the state must show that the defendant's rights were given the proper respect, and that no police pressure was responsible for the defendant's change of heart.

1. Police May Obtain a Waiver From a Suspect Following His Invocation of the Right to Remain Silent

Miranda did not create a blanket prohibition of or permanent immunity from police interrogation following a suspect's invocation of the right to remain silent. Instead, *Miranda* requires only that the right to cut off questioning be "scrupulously honored" by the police. This "scrupulous honor" requirement is generally met by giving the suspect a "cooling off" period, after which the suspect can be asked whether he has changed his mind about remaining silent. The "scrupulous honor" requirement is a requirement *in addition to* the suspect knowingly and voluntarily waiving his *Miranda* rights.

2. Waiver Following the Invocation of the Right to Counsel

If a suspect invokes his right to counsel, police officers may not further interrogate him unless the suspect's attorney is present, or unless the suspect *initiates* at least a generalized discussion of the investigation. This rule applies even after a suspect has consulted with an attorney.

a. Bright Line Rule

A confession is *automatically* excluded if the police initiate re-interrogation of the suspect after he has invoked his right to counsel—even if the state can make a convincing argument that the defendant knew his rights and voluntarily waived them.

b. Definition of "Initiation"

Generally, a defendant "initiates" discussion by making an inquiry or statement relating directly or indirectly to the investigation. An inquiry or statement that merely relates to "routine" incidents of the custodial relationship does not constitute initiation.

c. Knowing and Voluntary Waiver Must Still Be Found

The bright-line initiation or presence of counsel requirement is in addition to the general requirement that all *Miranda* waivers must be knowing and voluntary.

3. *Miranda* Right to Counsel Is Not "Offense–Specific"

A suspect's invocation of the right to counsel under *Miranda* is not *offense-specific*. Thus, when a suspect invokes the *Miranda* right to counsel, the police are barred from initiating an interrogation even about a crime different from that for which the suspect was arrested.

a. Distinction From a Defendant's Sixth Amendment Right to Counsel

If a defendant requests counsel at the start of formal proceedings, the defendant is invoking his offense-specific, Sixth Amendment right to counsel. If only the Sixth Amendment right to counsel is involved, officers may subsequently obtain a voluntary waiver from the defendant for a separate investigation, without the presence of counsel or initiation by the defendant.

b. Formal Proceedings

An invocation of counsel during a formal proceeding such as an arraignment is considered an invocation of the Sixth Amendment right to counsel, and not the offense-general right to counsel under *Miranda*. This is because no custodial interrogation occurs at a formal proceeding, and *Miranda* rights cannot be invoked in *anticipation* of a future custodial interrogation.

4. Ambiguous Invocations

Only a clear invocation of the right to counsel triggers the prophylactic "initiation" requirement. If the suspect's reference to counsel is ambiguous, interrogation may continue and a subsequent confession will be admissible so long as a knowing and voluntary waiver is obtained.

F. Incomplete or Ambiguous Miranda Warnings

The *Miranda* warnings merely have to reasonably convey the *Miranda* rights to a suspect; they need not be a verbatim recital of the *Miranda* opinion. However, an officer may not *affirmatively mislead* a suspect through ambiguous wording of the *Miranda* rights.

G. The Meaning of "Custody"

Miranda protections only apply when a defendant is *both* in custody and under interrogation by the police. A defendant is in *custody* when, under the totality of circumstances, he is either under arrest or his freedom of movement is restrained to the degree associated with arrest. A *Terry* stop will never trigger *Miranda* rights because, by definition, a defendant who is stopped is not under arrest.

1. Questioning a Suspect at the Stationhouse

Questioning a suspect at the stationhouse does not per se constitute custody. With stationhouse interrogation, the question of custody will generally depend on whether the suspect came to the stationhouse voluntarily or not. Custody will ordinarily not be found in the former case and ordinarily it will be found in the latter.

2. Relevant Factors

The determination of custody focuses on *objective* factors of police coercion. Some of the relevant factors are:

— The *purpose* of the police investigation

— The *place and length* of the interrogation

— The suspect's *awareness of his freedom to leave*

— The suspect's *actual freedom from restraint*

— The *source of initiation* of the contact with the suspect

— The use of *"coercive stratagems"* by the police

— The similarity of the setting to the *"police-dominated"* atmosphere of the stationhouse

H.   The Meaning of "Interrogation"

Interrogation by police under *Miranda* is defined as express questioning or its functional equivalent.

1. Functional Equivalent

The "functional equivalent" of express questioning includes words or actions that police should have known are *reasonably likely to elicit an incriminating response* from an *average suspect*.

2. Intent of the Officer

Although the definition of interrogation focuses primarily upon the perceptions of the suspect, the intent of the police officers to obtain incriminating information, or the lack of such intent, is an important, though not dispositive, factor in this determination. This is because if an officer intends to obtain information, the tactics that he will employ are more likely to elicit information from an average suspect than if the officer had no such intent.

3. Peculiar Susceptibility

If officers know or have reason to know that a defendant has a peculiar susceptibility, exploitation of that weakness will generally constitute interrogation.

4. Routine Booking Questions Are an Exception

Booking questions for legitimate administrative purposes (such as determining the arrestee's name, address, place of employment, etc.) are an exception to *Miranda's* interrogation prong. A question will come within the booking question exception if it is reasonably attendant to legitimate custodial procedures.

5. Police Procedures

Questions attendant to legitimate police procedures (such as whether the suspect understands what he is supposed to do during a sobriety test) do not fall within the *Miranda* definition of interrogation.

6. Confrontation With Incriminating Evidence May Be a Form of Interrogation

Confronting a suspect with incriminating evidence is ordinarily likely to elicit an incriminating response from the average suspect; however, this is not a per se rule.

I. The Application of *Miranda* to Undercover Police Activity

Miranda warnings are not required when a suspect is unaware that he is speaking to a law enforcement officer, as the "coercive atmosphere" of police interrogation does not exist in these circumstances. Therefore, an undercover agent may validly elicit incriminating statements from a suspect, without warnings, under *Miranda*.

J. Misdemeanors

The *Miranda* protections apply whether the defendant is arrested for a misdemeanor or a felony.

K. The "Public Safety Exception" to *Miranda*

Police may ask questions reasonably prompted by a concern for public safety without first advising a suspect in custody of the *Miranda* warnings. The validity of the public safety "exception" to *Miranda* does not depend upon the motivation of the individual officers involved. Generally, the public safety exception is analogous to the exigent circumstances exception to the Fourth Amendment warrant requirement.

Involuntary Confessions Not Admitted

If a confession is *involuntary*, it is inadmissible even if obtained in response to a public safety problem. The introduction of an involuntary confession at trial violates the Due Process Clause at the time of admission and, thus, exclusion is constitutionally required.

IV. CONFESSIONS AND THE SIXTH AMENDMENT

The Sixth Amendment right to counsel prohibits the police or secret Government agents from "deliberately eliciting" incriminating statements from suspects in the absence of counsel after the initiation of adversary judicial proceedings. Deliberate elicitation does not focus on the subjective intent of the officer but, rather, on whether a *reasonable person would find it likely* that a planned course of conduct would lead to the elicitation of incriminating information from a formally charged defendant. Unlike Fifth Amendment protections which focus upon *police coercion*, the Sixth Amendment focuses on whether the state acted *unethically* by interposing itself between the accused and his counsel after the commencement of adversarial proceedings.

A. Sixth Amendment Waiver

The Sixth Amendment right to counsel *automatically* attaches upon the start of adversarial judicial proceedings. Police officers must then obtain a "voluntary, knowing, and intelligent" waiver from a defendant before an officer's deliberate elicitation of information. A waiver of the Sixth Amendment right to counsel will not be found merely because a defendant was warned of his rights and subsequently confessed. The state must *affirmatively* show that the defendant knowingly and voluntarily waived his rights and confessed.

1. Sixth Amendment Warnings

The *Miranda* warnings generally provide the sum and substance of Sixth Amendment rights. No extra warnings are ordinarily necessary to support a knowing and intelligent waiver of the Sixth Amendment right to counsel. One exception, however, is that the suspect must be told if his counsel wants to see him. Such a warning is not required under *Miranda*.

2. Sixth Amendment "Initiation" Rule

Police officers may seek a waiver of a defendant's Sixth Amendment right to counsel unless the defendant invokes his right to counsel. After an invocation of his rights, officers may only interrogate the defendant absent counsel if the defendant "initiates" a generalized discussion regarding the pending charges. Initiation is a bright-line rule that requires exclusion of any statement obtained through interrogation in the absence of counsel from a defendant who did not seek discussion with officers following an invocation of his rights.

3. Offense–Specific Invocation

The Sixth Amendment right to counsel is *offense-specific*. After an accused has invoked his Sixth Amendment right to counsel, an officer may validly approach the accused and seek a waiver regarding crimes different from that with which the defendant is formally charged. This is so even if the defendant has not initiated further interrogation.

4. Impeachment

The Sixth Amendment bright-line initiation rule is considered a prophylactic safeguard of the right to counsel and, thus, while statements obtained in violation of the rule are excluded from the prosecution's case-in-chief, they may still be used to impeach the credibility of the defendant.

B. "Deliberate Elicitation" and the Passive Ear

If a Government informer "passively listens" to an accused without any affirmative attempt to "elicit" incriminating information, there is no Sixth Amendment violation and the statements may be introduced in court. Similarly, if a private individual obtains information from an indicted defendant, and then unilaterally refers it to the Government, the information is admissible because there is no improper "elicitation" by the Government.

C. Deliberate Elicitation and Continuing Investigations

Statements pertaining to pending charges are inadmissible when obtained absent counsel or waiver of counsel, even if the purpose of the investigation was to obtain information about uncharged crimes. However, statements concerning uncharged crimes, obtained in the absence of counsel, are admissible in subsequent prosecutions for those crimes, at least insofar as the Sixth Amendment is concerned.

■ CONSTITUTIONAL LIMITATIONS ON IDENTIFICATION EVIDENCE

I. POST–INDICTMENT IDENTIFICATIONS

A corporeal, post-indictment line-up conducted in the absence of defense counsel, and without a valid waiver of such counsel, violates the Sixth Amendment's right to counsel, which applies during *critical pre-trial stages* as well as at trial.

A. "Per Se" Exclusion

Post-indictment, corporeal identifications that take place absent counsel are "per se" excluded from trial. Exclusion is required even if the state can show that the identification is in fact reliable.

1. In–Court Identification and Independent Source

The same witness whose out-of-court identification is excluded from trial may make an *in-court identification* if the prosecution proves that, under the totality of circumstances, the in-court identification stems from an *independent source* sufficiently distinguishable from the previous, illegal line-up.

2. Relevant Factors

Certain factors are relevant to a determination of whether an in-court identification is based on a source *independent* from an illegal pre-trial identification:

— The extent of the *prior opportunity to view* the defendant other than at the illegal line-up

— *Discrepancies*, if any, between the witness' description of the suspect before the line-up was conducted, and the defendant's actual appearance

— *The certainty* of the witness' identification at the line-up or, conversely, the witness' failure to identify the defendant on prior occasions

— The *lapse of time* between the criminal act and the line-up identification

— The *degree of suggestiveness* employed in the tainted pre-trial lineup

II. PRE–INDICTMENT IDENTIFICATIONS

The Sixth Amendment does not apply to identifications that occur prior to indictment or formal charge. However, if adversary proceedings are *deliberately delayed* in order to evade the post-indictment rule, the resulting counsel-free identification will be invalidated.

A. Charge–Specific

It is permissible to hold a counsel-free line-up for an indicted defendant as to a different charge, since being indicted on one charge is not a "criminal prosecution" as to any other.

B. Photographic Identification

A defendant has *no right to counsel at a photographic identification* conducted either pre- or post-indictment.

III. DUE PROCESS LIMITATIONS ON SUGGESTIVE IDENTIFICATIONS

Where the Sixth Amendment right to counsel does not apply to an identification procedure, the identification must still satisfy the Due Process Clause, which requires exclusion if *police suggestiveness creates a substantial risk of mistaken identification.*

A. Two–Step Test

The defendant has the burden of proving a due process violation through a two-step test. First, the defendant must show that the identification procedure *was impermissibly suggestive.* If so, the defendant must then show the identification was *unreliable* under the *totality of circumstances.*

1. Exigent Circumstances

Certain exigent or extraordinary circumstances can make suggestive police procedure necessary and, thus, permissible. However, with the exception of street identifications conducted immediately after a crime, courts rarely find the circumstances so exigent as to allow the state to conduct a suggestive identification.

2. The Linchpin of Reliability

An identification may be reliable *despite* police suggestiveness. Suggestive procedures are considered in light of all the circumstances to determine whether an *independent source* exists for a reliable identification. Certain *factors* are relevant in a totality of circumstances determination of the reliability of an identification, although none are dispositive:

— The degree and nature of *police suggestiveness*

— The extent of the witness' *opportunity to view* the suspect prior to the challenged identification (e.g., at the scene of the crime)

— The witness' degree of *attention* to the suspect prior to the challenged identification

— The *accuracy of the description* of the perpetrator given by the witness before the identification

— The witness' *level of certainty* at the time of making the identification

— The *time* between the pre-identification opportunity to view the suspect and the identification itself

— The *character* of the identifying witness

B. If Pre–Trial Identification Is Excluded, At–Trial Identification Is Impermissible

If the pre-trial identification is unreliable because it is caused by police suggestiveness, then the Due Process Clause prohibits an at-trial identification as well. This is because if the prior identification was caused by police suggestiveness, there can *by definition* be no independent legal source for the in-court identification.

■ THE RIGHT TO COUNSEL

I. BASICS OF THE RIGHT TO COUNSEL

The Sixth Amendment's guarantee of *assistance of counsel* encompasses the right of indigent defendants to receive appointed counsel, as well as the qualified right of a non-indigent defendant to use retained counsel of choice. Counsel must provide "effective" assistance, and generally must not labor under conflicts of interest. The right to assistance of counsel and to "effective" assistance may be waived, and the right to self-representation invoked in its stead. These rights apply only at trial or at "critical" pre-trial stages.

A. The Right to Appointed Counsel for Indigent Defendants

Indigent defendants have the right to appointed counsel in all *federal criminal prosecutions*, and in all *state felony* prosecutions. In *misdemeanor* or petty offense cases, counsel must be provided if the defendant receives an actual *jail sentence, even if the sentence is immediately suspended and the defendant is placed on probation.* There is no constitutional right to appointed counsel of choice. Trial courts have broad discretion to decide whether to accept a defendant's preferred choice of counsel.

B.   The Definition of a "Criminal Prosecution" Where Counsel Rights Apply

Right to counsel protections attach after "adversarial judicial proceedings" have begun, and the trial process has reached a "critical stage." A stage in the trial process is considered "critical" if substantial potential prejudice to a defendant's rights inhere in a confrontation, and the presence of counsel may help to avoid that prejudice. Critical stages include a preliminary hearing, a post-indictment lineup, a guilty plea negotiation, and a sentencing hearing. Non-critical stages include photographic identification procedures, handwriting exemplar procedures, probation revocation hearings, and administrative detention of inmates.

C.   The Right to Counsel on Appeal

There is a per se Due Process right to effective counsel on the first appeal. But there is no such right for later appeals, for the certiorari process, or for collateral attack. Thus, even if counsel is representing a defendant past the first appeal, there is no Due Process right to effective assistance of counsel.

D.   Due Process Right to Tools With Which to Prepare an Effective Case at Trial and on Appeal

Besides the right to counsel, there are some circumstances in which the state must provide technical support for counsel so that an effective case can be prepared.

1.   The Right to a Trial Transcript

In order for an indigent defendant to have adequate access to the appellate process, a trial transcript must be provided by the state.

2.   The Right to Obtain Expert Witnesses for Trial

Due Process requires that indigent defendants receive the basic tools of an adequate defense at trial, including expert witnesses where necessary for an effective presentation of the case.

E. The Right to "Effective Assistance" of Counsel

The right to counsel means the right to *effective assistance* of either appointed or retained counsel. Conversely, if there is no right to counsel, there is no right to effective assistance of counsel.

1. Ineffective Assistance Based on Deficient Performance

A defendant's right to effective assistance of counsel is violated when counsel's performance falls below "prevailing professional norms," and when this performance causes "prejudice" because there is a reasonable probability it affected the outcome (i.e., *but for* the attorney's errors, there is a reasonable probability that the case result would be different). Counsel must render effective assistance during the plea bargaining process, as well as during the process of trial preparation and the trial itself, and on the first appeal of right. Claims of ineffective assistance are ordinarily assessed on a case-by-case basis.

2. Per Se Prejudice

There are certain very limited circumstances in which ineffectiveness and prejudice are presumed, because the likelihood that any lawyer, even a fully competent one, could provide effective assistance of counsel is so minimal that a presumption of prejudice is appropriate without inquiry into the actual conduct of the trial.

3. Ineffective Assistance Based on Conflict of Interest

Multiple representation of criminal clients is not a "per se" violation of the clients' right to effective assistance. Rather, there is a *limited and conditional presumption of prejudice* if the defendant establishes that counsel "actively represented conflicting interests," and that "an actual conflict of interest adversely affected" the lawyer's performance. Most courts hold that a defendant may waive his right to conflict-free counsel by making a knowing, intelligent, voluntary, clear and unequivocal waiver. A trial court has discretion whether to accept the waiver.

F. The Right to Self–Representation

In *Faretta v. California,* 422 U.S. 806, 95 S.Ct. 2525, 45 L.Ed.2d 562 (1975), the Court held that a defendant has a right to self-representation, which is derived by implication from the text of the Sixth Amendment. The right to self-representation protects the personal autonomy of the defendant.

1. Self–Representation Requires a Waiver of the Right to Counsel

The right to counsel and the right to self-representation are mutually exclusive. A defendant who is "literate, competent and understanding" may waive the right to counsel, and thereby invoke the right to self-representation. The waiver must be *unequivocal* to ensure that the defendant does not inadvertently waive the right to counsel, and to prevent the defendant from taking advantage of the mutual exclusivity of the two rights by arguing on appeal that he was denied one or the other. A defendant's technical legal knowledge is not relevant to an assessment of his knowing exercise of the right to defend himself.

2. Limitations on the Right to Self–Representation

The right to self-representation is not absolute. A state may impose certain conditions on the defendant's right to proceed pro se, where such conditions are necessary to further legitimate state interests. These conditions include the court's option to appoint standby counsel to assist the pro se defendant—even over the defendant's objections. Self-representation may be precluded altogether if the defendant makes an untimely request to represent himself, or if the defendant is disrupting courtroom proceedings.

3. The Role of Standby Counsel

A "pro se" defendant may be given standby counsel to assist him at trial or to take over the defense if necessary. There is no constitutional right to receive such counsel; nor may a defendant object to the appointment of standby counsel. Standby counsel violates the *Faretta* right when he deprives the defendant of actual control over the case, or destroys the jury's perception that the defendant represents himself. A defendant has the right to claim that standby counsel was ineffective.

4. *Faretta* **Violation Cannot Be Harmless**

A violation of the right to self-representation cannot constitute harmless error. A violation of *Faretta* means that the defendant has been deprived of his *choice* to represent himself; thus, a state may not argue that the counsel imposed upon the defendant against his will did a better job than the defendant could have done.

*

Perspective

■ THE STUDY OF BASIC CRIMINAL PROCEDURE

The basic course in Criminal Procedure concerns the limitations imposed on the State and Federal Governments in investigating and prosecuting crime. These limitations are mainly grounded in the Fourth, Fifth, Sixth and Fourteenth Amendments of the United States Constitution. This outline is intended to provide comprehensive coverage of the scope of constitutional protections ordinarily considered in a basic course in Criminal Procedure.

The Fourth Amendment requires generally that before the police conduct a search or seizure, they must obtain a warrant based upon probable cause that the search or seizure will uncover criminal activity or evidence thereof. As will be seen in the outline, there are many exceptions to this general rule, as the Supreme Court has sought to balance the needs of law enforcement against the privacy rights of the people.

The Fifth Amendment prohibits the state from compelling a citizen to be a witness against himself. This prohibition now comes into play when the police seek to obtain a confession from a suspect. As will be seen in the outline, the Supreme Court in the landmark *Miranda* case sought to protect Fifth Amendment rights by imposing procedural safeguards, such as warnings, when a suspect is subject to custodial interrogation.

The Fifth Amendment also contains a due process clause, which generally protects criminal defendants from the introduction of evidence that is unreliable, or which was obtained by egregious methods. As in other areas of constitutional adjudication, due process protection is applied in a case-by-case approach, with the court looking at the totality of circumstances. The Fifth Amendment also provides protections which are not ordinarily considered in the basic course on Criminal Procedure (and hence are not treated here) such as the right to be free from double jeopardy and the right to grand jury indictment.

The Sixth Amendment guarantees certain fundamental rights to an "accused" in a "criminal prosecution." These terms imply that the Sixth Amendment protections apply only when the state has proceeded from an investigatory stage to an accusatory stage. The Supreme Court has held that the protections of the Sixth Amendment do not attach until the state has begun formal proceedings against the citizen. Usually this is done by way of indictment. Once the Sixth Amendment has attached it provides several protections to a criminal defendant. Most importantly it guarantees a right to effective counsel. This right is applicable not only at trial, but also at certain other critical stages after indictment. For instance, the Supreme Court has held that the accused has an automatic right to counsel whenever the state deliberately elicits a confession from him concerning a charge for which he has been indicted. Also, if the state conducts a line-up post-indictment, the defendant has the right to have counsel present.

The Sixth Amendment also contains important trial rights, such as the right to confrontation, the right to compulsory process, and the right to a jury based on a fair cross-section of the community. These rights are ordinarily not treated in the basic Criminal Procedure course, and hence they are not treated here.

The limitations on Government contained in the Fourth, Fifth and Sixth Amendments were not originally applicable to the states. However, the Fourteenth Amendment's Due Process Clause has been held to incorporate all the protections in these amendments, (with the exception of the right to grand jury indictment) so that they are equally applicable to state and federal actors.

The basic course in Criminal Procedure is generally concerned with Supreme Court jurisprudence interpreting and applying the Fourth, Fifth and Sixth Amendments. A cursory review of any Supreme Court term in the last thirty years will show that the Court has devoted a major part of its docket to Criminal Procedure cases. It is no secret that the area of Criminal Procedure has been largely constitutionalized by the Supreme Court, beginning with the Warren Court in the 1960's. However, nonconstitutional standards are also pertinent to criminal investigation and prosecution, most notably the Federal Rules of

Criminal Procedure and many state counterparts. The obvious thrust of the outline is to provide an understanding of the constitutional standards affecting Criminal Procedure, but non-constitutional standards will be discussed as well.

■ GENERAL PRINCIPLES

The course in basic Criminal Procedure highlights the tension between the Government's interest in investigating and prosecuting crime, and the individual's interest in privacy, dignity, autonomy and fair treatment. A balance inevitably must be struck between these competing interests. On the one hand, it is costly to impose procedural limitations on the state: some crimes may go unpunished if the state is too constricted. On the other hand, if the state is not constricted at all, the rights of all individuals could be in peril. In deciding any issue of constitutional criminal procedure, this general tension is at the heart of Supreme Court decisionmaking. Speaking very generally, the Warren Court expanded procedural protections owed to criminal defendants. Later, the Burger and Rehnquist Courts expanded fewer rights, limited some earlier holdings, and often struck the balance in favor of prosecution of the factually guilty. While there are many exceptions to these general statements, one of the most fascinating aspects of the course in Criminal Procedure is its jurisprudential component: how, within the confines of *stare decisis,* the Supreme Court first recognized and then limited the reach of particular constitutional provisions.

Amidst this tension between claims of individual liberty and the need to prosecute the guilty, there are several factors that influence members of the Court. Each Justice establishes his or her own balance on the basis of these factors. The relevant factors include:

1. **THE PERCEIVED ROLE OF THE COURT IN PROTECTING CIVIL LIBERTIES**

    Our democratic state and federal governments rely heavily on the electoral process and majoritarian rule. In theory, if there is a problem, it can be addressed through the ballot box where the legislative and executive branches are elected. The theory works best when those effected by legislative action or inaction have sufficient political clout to make their voices heard.

The Warren Court decisions of the 1960's, dealing with civil rights issues generally and criminal procedure issues specifically, were based on the proposition that the majoritarian model breaks down when those who suffer from the acts of Government officials are politically powerless. Such is often the case with an individual who claims to be the subject of overreaching investigative or prosecutorial activity. Criminal suspects have no lobbyist in the legislature; they are a highly unpopular minority. Moreover, criminal suspects are often poor and/or people of color, possessing little political influence outside the criminal justice system. The Warren Court exercised a counter-majoritarian influence to address problems that it felt could not be fairly addressed by the majoritarian legislative and executive bodies. In so doing, it frequently took an expansive view of the rights of criminal defendants in the justice system.

In contrast, the Burger and Rehnquist Courts have tended to look at the counter-majoritarian nature of the Supreme Court to be something of a danger to democratic principles. Hence, the Court has in recent years been more willing to defer to legislative and executive action or inaction, and has intervened less often to protect those members of minority groups who would seem to need court protection. This trend is less clear in criminal procedure than in some other areas, however, since in the ordinary criminal procedure case, the Court is analyzing an ad hoc action by a police officer, rather than the constitutionality of legislation or standard executive practice. Judicial deference to the legislative and executive process is not as easily translated to the random act of a police officer.

2.   EMPHASIS ON RELIABILITY AS OPPOSED TO PROTECTION OF THE GUILTY

Some constitutional provisions are specifically designed to assure that a verdict will be reliable. An example is the right to effective assistance of counsel at trial. Without that right, there can be no assurance that the adversary system will work properly to achieve a correct result. However, other constitutional provisions focus on other interests and have little to do with reliability. In fact, they may be responsible for the exclusion of reliable evidence, and make it more likely that an incorrect result will be reached. An example is the Fourth Amendment, which protects the privacy and security rights of innocent and guilty alike.

Some Justices believe that the interest in reliable verdicts is paramount, and take the position that a higher priority should be given to those protections which ensure reliable fact-finding. These Justices concomitantly think that less emphasis should be given to those protections which serve to exclude reliable evidence and protect the factually guilty.

Other Justices take the position that all constitutional provisions bearing on the criminal justice system are to be given high priority. These Justices assert that provisions which protect the guilty in a particular case also serve to protect society at large. For example, the Fourth Amendment might protect a guilty defendant in an individual case, but it also protects the innocent by discouraging the police from making unreasonable searches and seizures against anyone. Thus, the criminal defendant may essentially be a class action plaintiff (though an odious one) protecting the rights of all. Moreover, these Justices argue that even constitutional provisions which protect only the guilty are important, because a society is judged by the way it treats those suspected and charged with crime.

In recent years, the Court has tended to give greater emphasis to reliability in fact-finding as opposed to protection of the factually guilty. This has especially occurred where the issue is not whether the constitution has been violated, but rather whether exclusion of evidence is the appropriate remedy for the constitutional violation.

3. BRIGHT LINE RULES AS OPPOSED TO CASE–BY–CASE ADJUDICATION

The Supreme Court takes cases, and thus decides the applicability of a constitutional protection to a specific fact situation. A case-by-case approach to constitutional adjudication can sometimes lead to unacceptable results. It is, however, possible that lower courts may be reluctant to provide the scope of protection intended by the Supreme Court, and may thus seek to distinguish cases on their facts. Another deleterious effect of the case-by-case approach is that officials may be hard-pressed to apply Supreme Court precedent to different fact situations. Arguably, the officer in the field needs clear guidance in how to follow the law: telling him to be reasonable under the circumstances tells him little. A third cost of the case-by-case approach is that it imposes a burden on the lower courts in having to struggle to apply vague law to the factual circumstances of every case.

On the other hand, establishment of a bright line rule for a generally worded constitutional provision is both overinclusive and underinclusive. The question, then, is whether a bright line rule can be established which will reach the correct result in the vast majority of circumstances. If so, the cost of over-

and under-inclusiveness will be outweighed by the benefits of clear conduct guidance and ease of administration. The Court has adopted several bright-line rules, (such as with custodial confessions in *Miranda* and search incident to arrest in *New York v. Belton*) with varying success. In other situations (such as with the *Terry* stop and frisk doctrine) the Court has usually employed a case-by-case approach.

4. BURDENS ON THE STATE

Rulings which give constitutional protection to criminal defendants are, to a greater or lesser degree, burdensome on the state. There is considerable disagreement among the Justices as to whether and how to consider the burdens imposed on the state by a proposed constitutional ruling. At one end of the spectrum, some Justices argue that if a guarantee is constitutionally mandated, then the burdens it imposes on the state are irrelevant, since the Framers have already considered those burdens in establishing the constitutional guarantee. This argument is more compelling when the constitution clearly provides a protection than when the constitutional language is ambiguous. Where there is ambiguity, the argument that burdens are irrelevant is somewhat question-begging, since the very question is whether the Constitution requires such protection.

At the other end of the spectrum, some Justices believe that burdens on the state should always be considered in determining whether a right should be recognized, and further that in some cases the burdens on the state can be so compelling as to deny the right entirely. Justices who find administrative burdens to be especially relevant may be prone to find substantial burdens on law enforcement where there is a dispute between the Government and an individual as to the extent of the actual burden. For instance, Justices who oppose the exclusionary rule argue that the rule imposes substantial burdens on law enforcement.

■ AN APPROACH TO THIS BOOK

The primary goal of this book is to give comprehensive treatment to Supreme Court cases setting forth the scope of individual rights under the Fourth, Fifth, Sixth, and Fourteenth Amendments. Reference is also made where appropriate to important lower court cases, different approaches taken by state courts, and non-judicial sources such as the Federal Rules of Criminal Procedure. To understand current rules, it is usually necessary to trace the progression from Warren Court rulings to modifications by the Burger and Rehnquist Courts. Therefore, we have tried, where appropriate, to discuss an entire line of cases leading up to the latest Supreme Court ruling. We feel that this will aid an understanding of current law, and raise the important question of whether current law provides an approach which is preferable to its immediate antecedents.

We have found that more than any other course, Basic Criminal Procedure generates heated discussion and debate. The issues brought up in the course go to the heart of how we think about individual rights in America. The issues and the fact situations that generate them are as up-to-date as today's newspaper. Because the cases are controversial, Basic Criminal Procedure runs a danger of confusion of legal and "political" viewpoints. It is a risk, therefore, to discuss the rationale of a case as well as the rule it establishes. But, we believe it is a risk worth taking. We have attempted to provide the rationale for many leading cases, a critique of that rationale, and an analysis of the likely scope of the decision. Our goal is not to persuade anyone to adopt a particular point of view, but is rather to provide some perspective which will help the reader to participate in classroom discussion and to give more full-bodied answers on the examination.

■ EXAMINATIONS IN BASIC CRIMINAL PROCEDURE

Like other examinations, an exam in Criminal Procedure requires you to spot the issues. For this process, there are standard exam-taking techniques that are obvious but helpful.

First, read the entire examination through quickly before you start to write. You may think you spot an issue hidden in question one, but it might be that if you read question four, you will find that it is clearly the main issue in that question. It is rare that a professor wants the same issue discussed fully in two separate questions. Consequently, by reading the entire exam, you can give the issue its due at the place where the professor intended.

Second, answer only the question that is asked. For instance, if the question is whether evidence should be excluded, you must answer both whether a right has been violated and whether exclusion is the appropriate remedy. In contrast, if the question is whether the search is illegal, a thorough discussion of the exclusionary rule is probably not mandated (and thus not credited), since the exclusionary rule presumes that the search is illegal.

Third, avoid long preparatory discussion of lines of precedent. Thus, if the question is whether the exclusionary rule should apply, a long discussion of the history of Supreme Court jurisprudence concerning the exclusionary rule is interesting, but not likely to be given much credit.

Fourth, it is crucial to apply law to fact. Discussing the law of search incident to arrest, the validity of current Supreme Court doctrine, and the scope of that doctrine is fine, but ultimately you must tell the professor in detail how that doctrine is applied to the facts set forth in the exam. While the goal of every exam-taker is to demonstrate how well he or she knows the law, this can be accomplished only by applying the correct law to the fact situation provided.

Fifth, to apply law to fact, you must be clear on what the facts are. The fact situations in Criminal Procedure exams can be more complex and convoluted than in other exams. Mastery of the facts is crucial. Thus, if the agent took the defendant's airplane ticket before he asked the defendant to accompany him to another room, that is a fact that cannot be overlooked. If you miss that fact, your entire analysis may be altered, and may be irrelevant because the pertinence of later facts and questions often depends on what has gone before. Some professors are merciful about such an error if your analysis of the facts as you have misinterpreted them is sound. Other professors believe that mercy is for sentencing, not for grading.

Sixth, if you are stumped, or if you think you have more to say but are just not sure what it will be, move on and come back later. But make sure you leave room in your exam. The use of arrows, directions like "continued at end of exam," writing in margins, etc. are the bane of law professors. No matter how fairly a professor tries to grade, it stands to reason that you do not want to make your exam an ordeal for any professor if that can be avoided. A disorganized paper might suggest a disorganized mind, and that can never reflect well on the test-taker.

Seventh, if the question asks you to, be sure to come to a conclusion and to justify it. It is of course necessary and appropriate to discuss both sides of an argument. But sometimes one argument is more compelling than another, and the two do not deserve equal weight. Other times, the law clearly favors one position over the other, even though you might believe the favored position is wrong. We have seen students, consumed with the need to discuss both sides of an issue, reach out to set forth specious arguments for one side or the other. This wastes time and suggests that you are unable to determine which arguments are strong and which are weak.

Eighth, in preparing for an examination, focus primarily on those issues which have been left open by the courts, or in which there has been recent action. If an issue has been closed by a clear and long-standing Supreme Court ruling, it is less likely to be tested than is newer, developing material. It is also important, of course, to attend classes and note where the professor thinks the most interesting issues are. A review of the professor's prior examinations can give you a clue as to the nature of the questions you may face.

The above "tips" are pretty universal. But there is one more that we give in the belief that it is especially important in many Criminal Procedure courses. We suggest that you pay close attention in class to whether the professor spends time analyzing and critiquing Supreme Court decisions in Constitutional Criminal Procedure. When you read cases, is your professor content when you know the holding? Or, does the professor question the holdings and ask you to think about them? Some thoughts the professor might seek to encourage are: 1. Are the cases well-reasoned? 2. Do they ignore, reject, or improperly distinguish prior precedent? 3. Do they give too much discretion to the police? 4. Do they create intractable problems for law enforcement? 5. Do they do what they set out to do?

While it is hard to generalize, we feel that professors who ask you to think about these questions in class may develop exams that invite and indeed call for a broader approach than merely issue spotting and discussing what the law is. Rather, just as in the classroom, the professor may want to know whether you think a rule is well-reasoned, problematic, insupportable, etc. This requires a deeper understanding of the cases and reasoning than can be provided by hornbook law. It is our hope that, even though this is called a "Black Letter Outline," we can give you some perspective on the deeper questions underlying Supreme Court cases in Criminal Procedure.

*

I

Introductory Concepts: Determining the Effect of a Supreme Court Decision on Criminal Procedure

■ ANALYSIS

I. **Application of Bill of Rights Protections to the States—Incorporation.**
    A. Bill of Rights and Fourteenth Amendment.
    B. Advantages and Disadvantages of Equal Application on Federal and State Level.
    C. Non–Constitutional Protections.

II.   **State Court Activism: Providing Greater Rights to Criminal Defendants by Relying on the State Constitution.**
    A.   Greater Protection Under State Law.
    B.   Two–Step Process.
    C.   Limitations on Activism.

Before addressing the constitutional protection afforded criminal defendants, most courses in basic Criminal Procedure consider two general doctrines which help to put the Supreme Court's Criminal Procedure decisions, and their effects, into context.

1. The first is the *incorporation* doctrine, which established that Supreme Court decisions construing constitutional protections apply on both the state and federal level.

2. The second doctrine is that of *state court independence,* which means that Supreme Court decisions favoring the Government may not be the last word as a matter of state law.

I. Application of Bill of Rights Protections to the States— Incorporation

A. Bill of Rights and Fourteenth Amendment

The Bill of Rights, as originally enacted, imposed limits only on the Federal Government, not on the states. *Barron v. Mayor of Baltimore,* 32 U.S. (7 Pet.) 243, 8 L.Ed. 672 (1833). The Fourteenth Amendment was enacted in 1868, and specifically prevents the states from depriving any person of life, liberty, or property without due process of law.

1. Scope of Protection

It is clear that the Fourteenth Amendment's Due Process Clause imposes some limitations on state criminal procedures. The question is whether the limitations imposed by the Fourteenth Amendment on the states is different in any way from those imposed by the Bill of Rights upon the Federal Government.

2. Incorporating the Bill of Rights

The Supreme Court, in a series of cases, has held that almost all of the protections granted under the Bill of Rights are granted in equal measure against the states through the Fourteenth Amendment's Due Process Clause. In the Court's own terminology, the Fourteenth Amendment *incorporates* most of the Bill of Rights protections. *Duncan v. Louisiana,* 391 U.S. 145, 88 S.Ct. 1444, 20 L.Ed.2d 491 (1968) (Sixth Amendment right to jury trial applies to states through the Fourteenth Amendment).

3. Analysis Employed

The analytical process by which Bill of Rights protections have become applicable to the states has been tortuous at best. At one time or another, three views have been espoused by various members of the Court on the incorporation question.

a.   Fundamental Rights Approach

The fundamental rights approach was the predominant way of looking at the Fourteenth Amendment up until the 1960's. This approach viewed the Fourteenth Amendment as prohibiting only those practices which are inconsistent with the concept of "ordered liberty." *Palko v. Connecticut,* 302 U.S. 319, 58 S.Ct. 149, 82 L.Ed. 288 (1937). According to this view, the Due Process Clause requires a case-by-case, totality of circumstances approach to determine whether a particular state practice so *shocks the conscience* that it is unacceptable in the Anglo–American legal system. Under this view, the Bill of Rights protections are relevant indicators of fundamental rights, but they do not necessarily apply to the states. An action may be prohibited by the Bill of Rights and yet still be consistent with fundamental concepts of ordered liberty. For example, in *Betts v. Brady,* 316 U.S. 455, 62 S.Ct. 1252, 86 L.Ed. 1595 (1942) (overruled by *Gideon v. Wainwright, infra),* the Court held that the "shock the conscience" test did not require the State to appoint counsel to an indigent felony defendant, even though it had previously held that the Sixth Amendment required such an appointment at the Federal level.

b.   Criticism of Case–By–Case Approach

Critics of the fundamental rights approach argued that the test imposed few meaningful limitations on the states. They contended that Supreme Court overview of criminal justice rendered by the states is all but impossible if the applicability of a right, such as the right to jury trial, turns on all the conditions of a case. The result of the fundamental rights approach was that the limitations imposed upon state governments were significantly less than those imposed upon the Federal Government.

c.   Total Incorporation Approach

This view, primarily espoused by Justice Black, holds that the Fourteenth Amendment incorporates the entire Bill of Rights, and makes all Bill of Rights protections applicable to the states. Under this view, the terms "privileges and immunities" and "due process" are convenient shorthand devices used in the Fourteenth Amendment as substitutes for an entire restatement of the Bill of Rights. See *Duncan v. Louisiana, supra* (concurring opinion of Justice Black).

d. Criticism of Total Incorporation Approach

Critics of the total incorporation view argued that there is little in the legislative history of the Fourteenth Amendment which shows that the drafters intended to incorporate all Bill of Rights protections through the terms "privileges and immunities" and "due process." If that were the intent, it could have been clearly stated by providing that "The Bill of Rights protections are hereby applicable to the states."

e. Effect of Total Incorporation View

The total incorporation approach never gained the support of a majority of the Court. Nonetheless, the views espoused by Justice Black and others had a great influence on the ultimate incorporation of most Bill of Rights guarantees under the selective incorporation approach.

4. The Selective Incorporation Approach

This view, originally espoused by Justice Brennan, is a hybrid of the fundamental rights and the total incorporation theory. Selective incorporation theorists agree that the Due Process Clause encompasses rights that are necessary to "ordered liberty" and that the Bill of Rights protections are neither the required nor the exclusive fundamental protections. However, the selective incorporation approach rejects the totality of circumstances, case-by-case analysis of the fundamental rights approach as impermissibly subjective, formless, and inefficient.

a. Generalized Approach

To determine whether a Bill of Rights protection is "fundamental," the selective incorporation approach requires that the Court look at the total right guaranteed by the Bill of Rights provision, not just a single aspect of that right, and not as applied to particular factual circumstances. If a particular Bill of Rights provision is *fundamental to the Anglo–American system of jurisprudence,* it is incorporated into the Fourteenth Amendment *in its entirety.* For example, if the right to jury trial is fundamental (as it is) then it must be applied in every state case to the same extent that it applies to the Federal Government under the Bill of Rights. And that includes "accoutrements" such as the number of jurors, whether they must be unanimous, etc.

b. Criticism of Selective Incorporation

The selective incorporation approach has been criticized as being an artificial compromise between the fundamental rights and the total incorporation approaches, and as having no basis in the language or history of the Fourteenth Amendment. It has also been criticized as being contrary to basic notions of federalism. Critics argue that it is inappropriate to impose nationwide solutions on local problems, and that placing a constitutional strait-jacket on the states will prevent them from experimenting with local solutions.

5. **Selective Incorporation Predominates**

    The selective incorporation approach has been predominant since the 1960's, and is unlikely to be rejected by a majority of the Court at this point. Using selective incorporation, the Court has held that the following Bill of Rights protections are applicable to the states to the same extent as they are applicable to the Federal Government:

    a. The Fourth Amendment right to be free from unreasonable searches and seizures. *Mapp v. Ohio,* 367 U.S. 643, 81 S.Ct. 1684, 6 L.Ed.2d 1081 (1961).

    b. The Eighth Amendment prohibition against cruel and unusual punishment. *Robinson v. California,* 370 U.S. 660, 82 S.Ct. 1417, 8 L.Ed.2d 758 (1962).

    c. The Sixth Amendment right to counsel. *Gideon v. Wainwright,* 372 U.S. 335, 83 S.Ct. 792, 9 L.Ed.2d 799 (1963).

    d. The Fifth Amendment privilege against compelled self-incrimination. *Malloy v. Hogan,* 378 U.S. 1, 84 S.Ct. 1489, 12 L.Ed.2d 653 (1964).

    e. The Sixth Amendment right to confrontation. *Pointer v. Texas,* 380 U.S. 400, 85 S.Ct. 1065, 13 L.Ed.2d 923 (1965).

    f. The Sixth Amendment right to a speedy trial. *Klopfer v. North Carolina,* 386 U.S. 213, 87 S.Ct. 988, 18 L.Ed.2d 1 (1967).

    g. The Sixth Amendment right of compulsory process for obtaining favorable witnesses. *Washington v. Texas,* 388 U.S. 14, 87 S.Ct. 1920, 18 L.Ed.2d 1019 (1967).

    h. The Sixth Amendment right to jury trial. *Duncan v. Louisiana, supra.*

    i. The Fifth Amendment protection against double jeopardy. *Benton v. Maryland,* 395 U.S. 784, 89 S.Ct. 2056, 23 L.Ed.2d 707 (1969).

j. The Sixth Amendment rights to a public trial and to notice of the nature and cause of the accusation. *Gannett Co., Inc. v. DePasquale*, 443 U.S. 368, 99 S.Ct. 2898, 61 L.Ed.2d 608 (1979) (interpreting prior cases as selectively incorporating these rights).

6. Rights Not Selectively Incorporated

Only two Bill of Rights protections bearing upon criminal procedure have not been explicitly incorporated through the Fourteenth Amendment. They are the Fifth Amendment requirement of a grand jury indictment in felony cases, and the Eighth Amendment limitation on excessive bail. The Supreme Court has not directly ruled on the bail clause, but has implied that it is fundamental. *See Schilb v. Kuebel*, 404 U.S. 357, 92 S.Ct. 479, 30 L.Ed.2d 502 (1971). Prosecution by grand jury indictment was found not to be fundamental in *Hurtado v. California*, 110 U.S. 516, 4 S.Ct. 111, 28 L.Ed. 232 (1884), and the Court has continued to follow *Hurtado*. *See Albright v. Oliver*, 510 U.S. 266, 114 S.Ct. 807, 127 L.Ed.2d 114 (1994).

B. Advantages and Disadvantages of Equal Application on Federal and State Level

A central point of incorporation is that once the right is considered fundamental, it is applied to the states in exactly the same way as it is applied to the Federal Government. Thus, if the Fourth Amendment applies to the states, as it does, then the same tests for probable cause, particularity of a warrant, and validity of an arrest, apply on a Federal and state level. Supreme Court cases construing the amendment apply equally at both levels.

1. Efficiency

Incorporation is efficient in terms of case management. The Court does not have to decide both a Federal and a state case since either one will do.

2. Possible Erosion of Federal Protections

However, the incorporation approach, which was originally designed to upgrade state standards by tying them to Federal standards, may in fact erode Federal protections in cases where the Court decides that the states should be allowed to experiment with alternative forms of procedure. The only way to allow the states to experiment with lesser protections, within the confines of incorporation, is to dilute the Federal standard as well.

Example: An example of possible dilution of Federal protection due to incorporation is *Williams v. Florida*, 399 U.S. 78, 90 S.Ct. 1893,

26 L.Ed.2d 446 (1970), where the Court held that the Sixth Amendment did not require twelve jurors in a criminal case. If not for incorporation, the Court may well have allowed the state to experiment with the number of jurors, up to the bounds of "shocking the conscience," while continuing to insist that the Federal Sixth Amendment standard required twelve jurors.

C. Non–Constitutional Protections

It should be noted that even while the Bill of Rights protections generally apply against the states, there remain some non-constitutional limitations which apply only against the Federal Government and its agents. For example, the Federal Rules of Criminal Procedure continue to require twelve jurors, even though the Sixth Amendment does not after *Williams*.

1. Supervisory Power

Federal courts may in some limited circumstances impose standards on the Federal system pursuant to their supervisory power. *See McNabb v. United States*, 318 U.S. 332, 63 S.Ct. 608, 87 L.Ed. 819 (1943) (excluding confessions obtained if arraignment delayed).

2. Limitations

The Court has, however, recently restricted the use of the supervisory power. A Federal court cannot use its supervisory power simply because it believes that a current constitutional protection is insufficient. *United States v. Payner*, 447 U.S. 727, 100 S.Ct. 2439, 65 L.Ed.2d 468 (1980) (court cannot use supervisory power to exclude evidence otherwise admissible under the Fourth Amendment); *United States v. Williams*, 504 U.S. 36, 112 S.Ct. 1735, 118 L.Ed.2d 352 (1992) (Federal court has no supervisory authority to dismiss an indictment on the ground that the prosecutor refused to present exculpatory evidence to the grand jury).

II. State Court Activism: Providing Greater Rights to Criminal Defendants by Relying on the State Constitution

As the Supreme Court in the 1970's and 1980's began to retreat from some earlier decisions which provided significant constitutional rights to criminal suspects, many state courts retained the earlier rules. They did so by providing greater protection under their state constitutions than the Supreme Court provided under the Federal Constitution. The states in the forefront of relying on their own constitutions are Alaska, Connecticut, Hawaii, Mississippi, New York, Oregon, and Washington; many other state courts have invoked their state constitution to protect criminal defendants from time to time.

A. Greater Protection Under State Law

There can be no disagreement about the scope of a federal constitutional protection once the Supreme Court has spoken. However, a state court can construe its state constitution to give greater protection to a defendant than is granted by the Federal Constitution.

No Federal Question

As to state law, the highest court of the state is the supreme arbiter. The United States Supreme Court cannot even review a state court's construction of its state constitution, because such a case does not invoke a federal question. If the Court were to take such a case and hold that the result was not mandated by federal law, its ruling would have no effect, since the state court's decision would still be mandated by state law. Thus, while a state cannot give a suspect less protection than the Federal Constitution provides, it can provide more.

B. Two–Step Process

State courts have generally used a two-step process to determine whether the state constitution gives more protection than the Federal.

1. Different Language

The first step is to determine if there is specific language in the state constitution, different from the Federal, which would show some indication of special protection.

Example: In Washington, Article I, section 7 of the state constitution is analogous to the Fourth Amendment. However, the drafters of the Washington State Constitution rejected the specific language of the Fourth Amendment, in favor of language that specifically protected a citizen's private affairs. This specific mention of privacy has been relied on by the Washington Supreme Court to provide more protection than that given to citizens under the Fourth Amendment. *See State v. Gunwall,* 106 Wash.2d 54, 720 P.2d 808 (1986) (rejecting Supreme Court decision which held that the monitoring of telephone calls by a pen register was not a search).

2. Independent Policy Determination

Even in the absence of differentiating language, a state court may make its own policy determination and its own balance of interests. While there is a presumption that the state constitution is coextensive with the Federal, that presumption can be overcome.

Example: The New York Court of Appeals has rejected Supreme Court cases as unsound, insufficiently protective of citizens, and in conflict with the clear common law and political history of the utmost respect for personal rights in New York. *See People v. Johnson,* 66 N.Y.2d 398, 497 N.Y.S.2d 618, 488 N.E.2d 439 (1985) and *People v. Bigelow,* 66 N.Y.2d 417, 497 N.Y.S.2d 630, 488 N.E.2d 451 (1985) (rejecting the totality of circumstances approach to informant hearsay and the good faith exception to the exclusionary rule).

C. Limitations on Activism

There have been *two recent developments* that have dampened state court activism somewhat.

1. Amendments to State Constitutions

A few states have amended their constitutions in an attempt to prevent greater rights from being granted on the state level.

Example: The Florida constitution now states that United States Supreme Court decisions provide the full extent of protection from search and seizure. After this amendment, the state constitution cannot provide greater protection, ending a trend of several cases in which the Florida courts had granted greater rights against searches and seizures than those provided by the Fourth Amendment.

2. Plain Statement Rule

The Supreme Court has held that it can review state court cases unless the state court makes a *clear statement* that its decision is based solely on the state constitution. *See Michigan v. Long,* 463 U.S. 1032, 103 S.Ct. 3469, 77 L.Ed.2d 1201 (1983). Thus, in the absence of a clear indication that the state court has decided the case solely on state grounds, the Supreme Court *presumes* that the state court decided the case on Federal constitutional grounds and hence that it can review the decision.

a. Decision on Both Federal and State Grounds

To avoid review under *Long,* a state court must make a clear statement that the state constitution requires a certain protection *regardless of* what the Federal Constitution may provide. A state court which bases a ruling on both Federal and state law does not satisfy the clear statement rule of *Long* and its ruling can be reviewed by the Supreme Court. When the state court relies on Federal and state law simultaneously, it may be saying that the state constitution requires a protection *because* the Federal Constitution does. This is not a clear statement that the state constitution grants a right regardless of the limitations of Federal law.

b. Remand to State Court

If there is no clear statement and the Supreme Court decides that a state court erred in giving the defendant too much protection, the state court can nonetheless have the final word on remand. For example, the New York Court of Appeals in several cases held that the state and Federal constitutions were violated. These cases were reversed by the Supreme Court. That Court reached the merits because the New York court had not made a clear statement that it was relying solely on state law. But on remand, the New York court adhered to its views that state law required the protection the court had previously mandated, and thus the defendant eventually prevailed. *See People v. P.J. Video*, 68 N.Y.2d 296, 508 N.Y.S.2d 907, 501 N.E.2d 556 (1986).

*

II

The Fourth Amendment

■ **ANALYSIS**

I. Introduction

The Fourth Amendment represents a compromise between the need of Government officials to gather evidence and the right of citizens to be free from governmental intrusion. The Amendment provides that "[t]he right of the people to be secure in their persons, houses, papers, and effects, against unreasonable searches and seizures, shall not be violated, and no Warrants shall issue, but upon probable cause, supported by Oath or affirmation, and particularly describing the place to be searched and the persons or things to be seized." Fourth Amendment limitations on governmental investigations are equally applicable to the state and Federal governments. *Mapp v. Ohio,* 367 U.S. 643, 81 S.Ct. 1684, 6 L.Ed.2d 1081 (1961).

A. Basics of the Fourth Amendment

From a reading of the Amendment itself and an understanding of general constitutional principles, some basic points can be derived which will apply generally to all Fourth Amendment questions.

1. Does Not Apply to Private Activity

The Fourth Amendment, like other protections in the Bill of Rights and the Due Process Clause, is a limit on state action, but does not limit private actors acting on their own. *See United States v. Jacobsen,* 466 U.S. 109, 104 S.Ct. 1652, 80 L.Ed.2d 85 (1984) (no Fourth Amendment protection where package was opened by Federal Express employees acting on their own). Thus, no matter how unreasonable a search is, the Fourth Amendment is not implicated if the search is conducted by private actors not acting as agents of the Government.

a. Government Can Use the Fruits of a Private Search

If a private party conducts a search and uncovers evidence, the Fourth Amendment does not prohibit the Government from using that evidence in a criminal trial or in any other way. This is because the subsequent Government conduct is not itself a search or seizure—that has already been done by the private party. *See Burdeau v. McDowell,* 256 U.S. 465, 41 S.Ct. 574, 65 L.Ed. 1048 (1921).

b. Not Acting in an Official Capacity

Generally speaking, anyone who is not employed by the Government, and who is acting in the course of their private employment or private life, is a private actor whose actions are not regulated by the Fourth Amendment. Thus, even Government employees are private actors if they are not acting while in the course of employment. *See United States v. McGreevy*, 652 F.2d 849 (9th Cir.1981) (police officer working at second job as security officer is not governed by Fourth Amendment).

c.   Private Actors as Government Agents

If the private actor is making a search at the behest of a state actor or is encouraged to act by a Government official, then state action may be found and the Fourth Amendment will apply. *See United States v. Walther*, 652 F.2d 788 (9th Cir.1981) (airline employee acted as Government agent when he expected a DEA reward for his actions and the agency had encouraged him). Otherwise, Government officials could too easily avoid the strictures of the Fourth Amendment by "deputizing" private actors to do their work for them. The Government need not require or mandate a private party to conduct a search in order for state action to be found. If the facts show significant Government encouragement, endorsement and participation at the outset, then state action will be found and the private party's search will trigger the Fourth Amendment. On the other hand, if the officer is a passive observer to a private search, the Fourth Amendment is not implicated. *See United States v. Leffall*, 82 F.3d 343, 348(10th Cir.1996) (airline employee who decided on his own to search a suspicious package, and sought out police oversight in case the package contained explosives, was a private actor: "Although law enforcement officers may not circumvent the Fourth Amendment by acting through private citizens, officers need not restrain or discourage private citizens from doing that which is not unlawful.")

d.   Applies to All Government Agents, Not Just Police Officers

The Court has rejected the argument that the Fourth Amendment regulates only searches and seizures by law enforcement officers. The Amendment applies to the acts of Government officials generally. *New Jersey v. T.L.O.*, 469 U.S. 325, 105 S.Ct. 733, 83 L.Ed.2d 720 (1985) (school principal governed by Fourth Amendment). However, as will be discussed later in this outline, a search or seizure undertaken by non-law enforcement personnel may be considered reasonable where the same conduct by a police officer enforcing criminal law objectives may not.

2. Protects "The People"

The Fourth Amendment ascribes the right provided to the people, not to a "Person" as the Fifth and Sixth Amendments do. This language lends support to the position that a court enforcing the Fourth Amendment is not necessarily limited to remedying an individual violation.

a. Protects Innocent and Guilty Alike

Most Fourth Amendment questions arise in the context of a criminal proceeding, in which a person who appears to be factually guilty seeks to suppress probative evidence. Courts have recognized that the Fourth Amendment protects innocent "people" as well as the guilty person before the court. Much evidence that is seized is neither contraband nor the fruits of crime and is taken from individuals who are presumed innocent until convicted.

b. Does Not Protect Aliens When the Search Is Conducted Abroad

In *United States v. Verdugo–Urquidez*, 494 U.S. 259, 110 S.Ct. 1056, 108 L.Ed.2d 222 (1990), the Supreme Court held that the Fourth Amendment does not apply to a search of property owned by an alien and located in a foreign country. The Court stated that the Fourth Amendment's reference to "the people," as opposed to a particular person, was a "term of art" intended to refer to a class of persons "who are part of a national community or who have otherwise developed sufficient connection with this country to be considered a part of that community." Thus, the Court looked at the term "the people" as a limiting term. The Court held that the defendant, who had been involuntarily transported to the United States three days before the foreign search was conducted, lacked sufficient connection with the United States to be one of "the people" protected by the Fourth Amendment.

c. Dissent

Dissenting in *Verdugo–Urquidez*, Justice Brennan argued that it was anomalous for the Federal Government to require aliens residing outside the United States to obey Federal laws (through extraterritorial application), and yet for the Government to refuse to obey its own laws in investigating the very extraterritorial activity that it has criminalized.

d. Open Question: Does the Fourth Amendment Apply to Searches Conducted of Illegal Aliens and Their Property in the United States?

In *Verdugo–Urquidez*, the Court specifically refused to decide whether an illegal alien who lived in the United States would be one of "the people" protected by the Fourth Amendment. Presumably, however, the Fourth Amendment would apply, since an illegal alien living in the United States would seem to have the "connection" with this country required to be one of "the people."

3. **Protects "Persons, Houses, Papers and Effects"**

At least on its face, the Fourth Amendment does not draw a distinction in the existence or the scope of protection between a person, his property, or his house. In fact, however, the courts have frequently distinguished among these various interests. In descending order, courts give the greatest protection to the house, then to the person's property, then to the person himself. *See United States v. United States District Court,* 407 U.S. 297, 92 S.Ct. 2125, 32 L.Ed.2d 752 (1972) ("Entry into the home is the chief evil against which the wording of the Fourth Amendment is directed."); *United States v. Chadwick,* 433 U.S. 1, 97 S.Ct. 2476, 53 L.Ed.2d 538 (1977) (providing greater protection to defendant's property than to his person in a search incident to arrest).

4. **Two Clauses**

The Fourth Amendment has two clauses. The first clause, the reasonableness clause, provides a general standard that all searches and seizures must be reasonable. The second clause imposes requirements for obtaining warrants.

a. Which Clause Predominates?

A quick reading of the Amendment would indicate that the reasonableness clause should set the standard for most Government searches and seizures, and that the text of the Fourth Amendment does not require all or even any searches to be made pursuant to a warrant. The warrant clause seems merely to impose limitations on a warrant should a police officer decide to obtain one. These expressed limitations on the warrant process are consistent with the intent of the Framers to control the possibility of officials obtaining a *general warrant* to conduct arbitrary searches.

b. Historical Basis

It was the use of general warrants by British officials that spurred the inclusion of the Fourth Amendment in the Bill of Rights. *See*

United States v. Verdugo–Urquidez, supra ("The driving force behind the adoption of the Amendment, as suggested by Madison's advocacy, was widespread hostility among the former Colonists to the issuance of writs of assistance * * * and general search warrants.") It may seem anomalous that a warrant requirement would be the touchstone of an amendment designed to limit warrants.

c. Predominance of the Warrant Clause

Despite the way the Amendment reads, the Supreme Court has read the warrant clause to predominate, or to define presumptively whether official conduct is "reasonable." That is, a search or seizure is presumed unreasonable in the absence of a warrant based upon probable cause.

d. Rationale

The Court has concluded that without the content and specific limitation that the warrant clause provides, the Fourth Amendment's general command that a search be "reasonable" would be devoid of meaning, and subject to case-by-case balancing approaches of shifting judicial majorities. To the extent that the Framers were concerned with the threat of arbitrary police activity, the warrant clause addresses that concern by requiring the official to obtain authorization from a neutral magistrate before conducting a search.

e. Common Law Approach

There is another method of construing Fourth Amendment protections that is to some people truer to the plain language and historical context of the Amendment. This method is to consider the Fourth Amendment as codifying the protections provided by the common law at the time the Amendment was adopted. The main proponent of this historical approach is Justice Scalia. *See California v. Acevedo*, 500 U.S. 565, 111 S.Ct. 1982, 114 L.Ed.2d 619 (1991) (concurring opinion). Under Justice Scalia's view, if a warrant was not required for a police practice under common law, it is not required by the Fourth Amendment. Justice Scalia does recognize that certain police activities, such as wiretapping and automobile searches, were unheard of in 1791. But he maintains that common law principles can be translated to these activities as well. While Justice Scalia's view has persuaded the Court in only one case

(California v. Hodari D., discussed below), it is possible that his historical approach will become more influential in the coming years.

5. **The Theory of the Warrant Clause**

The preeminence of the warrant clause was the result of early Supreme Court decisions which stressed the importance of imposing an unbiased factfinder as a buffer between the citizen suspected of crime and the officer engaged in the competitive enterprise of ferreting out crime. The thought was that if the question of probable cause was left to the officer, the officer's natural bias may lead him to find that sufficient cause existed and that a search could be conducted. According to this view, the warrant requirement prevents questionable searches from being conducted, and assures that only those as to whom probable cause exists will be subject to an intrusion. *See Johnson v. United States,* 333 U.S. 10, 68 S.Ct. 367, 92 L.Ed. 436 (1948) (Fourth Amendment requires that probable cause must be determined by a neutral and detached magistrate rather than "by the officer engaged in the often competitive enterprise of ferreting out crime.")

a. Prior Record of Probable Cause

A subsidiary benefit of the warrant requirement is that it requires the officer to establish, on the record, the facts allegedly constituting probable cause, *before* the search is conducted. Without an antecedent warrant requirement, an officer questioned about probable cause could work backwards from the search, and fill in the facts as if he knew them before the search was conducted. Thus, the warrant requirement prevents post hoc submissions on probable cause.

b. Limitation on the Scope of a Search

Another benefit of the warrant requirement lies in the language of the Amendment requiring that the warrant must particularly describe the place to be searched and the things to be seized. A warrant defines the scope of a search and thereby limits the discretion of the officers conducting the search.

c. Sign of Authority

Finally, an important function of the warrant requirement is that an officer carrying a warrant "greatly reduces the perception of unlawful or intrusive police conduct, by assuring the individual whose property is searched or seized of the lawful authority of the executing officer, his need to search, and the limits of his power to search." *Illinois v. Gates,* 462 U.S. 213, 103 S.Ct. 2317, 76 L.Ed.2d 527 (1983).

6. The Rise of the Reasonableness Clause

Even though the warrant clause is still considered the first reference point for the legality of a search or seizure, the Supreme Court has gradually moved to the point where most searches and seizures are in fact governed by a general standard of reasonableness. The strict requirement of a warrant based upon probable cause can be dispensed with in a variety of situations. While each situation will be discussed in detail later in this Outline, a general overview of the Supreme Court's Fourth Amendment cases shows that the dual requirement of a *warrant and probable cause are not needed in the following situations:*

— Where a warrant is impracticable to obtain. See the exigent circumstances exception.

— Where the police conduct a *limited* seizure to investigate possible criminal activity and a *limited* search for weapons to protect the investigating officer. See the *Terry* Doctrine.

— Where the official is searching for evidence, but the search is conducted for purposes *other than criminal law enforcement.* See administrative and other "special needs" searches.

— Where a search is conducted *incident to a valid arrest.*

— Where there is *voluntary consent.*

— Where the citizen is *arrested in public.*

— Where an incriminating object is in *plain view.*

— Where the officer searches an *automobile* or other form of transportation.

Some of these exceptions still require probable cause for the search or seizure to be reasonable. Others do not. For a full analysis of each of these exceptions, see the discussion below.

II. Threshold Requirements for Fourth Amendment Protections—"Search" and "Seizure"

The Fourth Amendment prohibits unreasonable searches and seizures. Unless the Government activity is either a "search" or a "seizure" it is not regulated by the

Fourth Amendment, and therefore it does not have to be reasonable. So when the Court holds that a police activity is neither a search nor a seizure, it means that it is not subject to restriction, and the officer has no obligation to explain it. *See Florida v. Riley,* 488 U.S. 445, 109 S.Ct. 693, 102 L.Ed.2d 835 (1989) (aerial surveillance need not be based on any suspicion and does not require a warrant). In contrast, if the Court holds activity to be a search or a seizure, it does not mean that the activity is prohibited, but only that it must comply with Fourth Amendment requirements.

A. The *Katz* Test

1. Government Contentions in *Katz*

In *Katz v. United States,* 389 U.S. 347, 88 S.Ct. 507, 19 L.Ed.2d 576 (1967), Government officials intercepted Katz's telephone conversations by use of an electronic listening and recording device attached to the outside of the public telephone booth from which Katz placed his calls. The Government argued that there was no search of a person, house, paper or effect, as those terms are used in the Fourth Amendment. The Government also contended that there was no seizure, since it was impossible to seize an intangible conversation. The Government argued further that there was no search or seizure because there was no physical intrusion into a private area: Katz was at a public telephone booth when he placed his calls.

2. Court's Response in *Katz*

In *Katz,* the Court rejected the Government's literal interpretation of the Fourth Amendment. Essentially, the Court looked beyond the words of the Fourth Amendment to determine what interests the Amendment was supposed to protect. The Court's answer was that the Fourth Amendment was designed to protect the *legitimate expectations of the people to privacy and security.* After *Katz,* the Fourth Amendment is not to be read literally as protecting only against a physical invasion of certain protected areas.

3. Modern Definition of "Search" and "Seizure"

After *Katz,* the term "search" is triggered whenever the state intrudes in any way upon the individual's protected interest in privacy. And the term "seizure" is triggered whenever the state intrudes in any way on a protectible individual interest in property or security. *See United States v. Mendenhall,* 446 U.S. 544, 100 S.Ct. 1870, 64 L.Ed.2d 497 (1980) (a person is "seized" by an officer when a reasonable innocent person in his position would not feel free to leave). Thus, if Katz were entitled to assume that his telephone conversation would remain private, the intrusion into that privacy by electronic surveillance was a search—even though the invasion was not physical, and even though Katz was in public. As the Court in *Katz* stated: "The Fourth Amendment protects people, not places."

4. Concurring Opinion of Justice Harlan

Justice Harlan's concurring opinion in *Katz* is often quoted and has had as much influence as the majority opinion. Justice Harlan set forth a two-pronged test to determine whether a search has occurred:

— First, has the citizen manifested a subjective expectation of privacy?

— Second, is the interest one that society is prepared to accept as reasonable?

Even though Justice Harlan later expressed reservations about his own test (see his opinion in *United States v. White,* 401 U.S. 745, 91 S.Ct. 1122, 28 L.Ed.2d 453 (1971)), the Supreme Court has adopted the two-pronged test to determine whether a search has occurred. *See California v. Greenwood,* 486 U.S. 35, 108 S.Ct. 1625, 100 L.Ed.2d 30 (1988).

B. Interests Protected by the Fourth Amendment After *Katz*

If the Fourth Amendment protects only reasonable and legitimate interests in privacy, one could question why Katz was entitled to protection. Katz was not talking about his private thoughts; he was engaging in illegal betting transactions.

1. The Fourth Amendment Protects "Legitimate" Interests

The Court has held on several occasions after *Katz* that there is no legitimate privacy interest in illegal activity. *See United States v. Place,* 462 U.S. 696, 103 S.Ct. 2637, 77 L.Ed.2d 110 (1983) (no privacy interest in possession of contraband). However, people such as Katz receive Fourth Amendment protection nonetheless, since it is usually not possible to know in advance of the search that their activity is illegal. To protect innocent people with legitimate privacy and security expectations from mistaken assumptions by Government officials, certain interests must be presumed and protected before the intrusion takes place.

2. If it Is Legitimate, What Is There to Hide?

It could be argued that if the Fourth Amendment is designed to protect legitimate expectations, then the Amendment is unnecessary, since a person engaged in legitimate activity has nothing to hide. In fact this is not true. An innocent person can indeed be harmed by a Government intrusion. The courts after *Katz* have found three separate interests of innocent persons which can be affected by a Government intrusion.

a. Physical Disruption and Inconvenience

All citizens have an interest in being free from physical disruption, inconvenience, or terrorization by Government officials. For the official to say, after an arrest and body search, "no harm done" because nothing was found or seized is not acceptable. Such an "explanation" fails to consider the privacy and security interests of innocent individuals.

b. Interest in Secrecy

Another protectible interest of innocent citizens, one implicated in *Katz,* is the right to secrecy—a right of protection against disclosure of information which, although not incriminating, may be embarrassing, sensitive, or extremely private. Without the Fourth Amendment's protection of innocent people, the state could listen to a private conversation which may disclose illness, love, suffering, and many other types of non-incriminating but nonetheless sensitive information.

c. Possessory Interests

The Fourth Amendment regulates not only invasions of privacy and security interests, but also invasions of possessory interests. The Fourth Amendment prohibits unreasonable seizures as well as searches. *See Soldal v. Cook County,* 506 U.S. 56, 113 S.Ct. 538, 121 L.Ed.2d 450 (1992) (noting that a seizure of property occurs "whenever there is some meaningful interference with an individual's possessory interests in that property.")

3. **Different Intrusions**

A seizure may occur without a search, and a search may occur without a seizure.

Examples: A police officer detains a suspect's luggage pending a canine sniff or the obtaining of a warrant. This is a seizure of the luggage, and triggers the Fourth Amendment even if the luggage is never opened. *See United States v. Place, infra. See also Soldal v. Cook County,* 506 U.S. 56, 113 S.Ct. 538, 121

L.Ed.2d 450 (1992) ("seizures of property are subject to Fourth Amendment scrutiny even though no search within the meaning of the Amendment has taken place.")

In *Katz*, the Government did not seize the defendant or his property. But a search occurred because the Government intruded upon a private conversation.

C. Application of the *Katz* Principle: Manifestation of a Subjective Interest in Privacy

If Katz had been shouting into a telephone, so that his conversation could be heard down the block, officers who heard him would not be engaged in a search since Katz would not have manifested any interest in keeping the conversation private. The question is, how far must the citizen go to protect his privacy interests?

1. Strict Application

Generally speaking, the courts have required citizens to be extremely protective of their claimed privacy interests.

Examples: Defendant's barn has no windows. The door of the barn is six feet high. Above the door is a heavy mesh fabric, which cannot be seen through from any distance. However, if one were to jump up on the door and press one's face to the mesh, one could see inside the barn. The officer did this. The Supreme Court held that this was not a search, since defendant had not sufficiently manifested an expectation of privacy in the interior of the barn. *United States v. Dunn,* 480 U.S. 294, 107 S.Ct. 1134, 94 L.Ed.2d 326 (1987). Compare *United States v. Blount,* 98 F.3d 1489 (5th Cir.1996) ("We conclude and hold that when a police officer walks into the partially fenced back yard of a residential dwelling, using a passage not open to the general public, and places his face within inches of a small opening in an almost completely covered rear window to look into the house and at the inhabitants, that officer has performed a "search" within the meaning of the fourth amendment.")

2. Abandonment

Abandonment of property is inconsistent with the retention of any privacy or possessory interests.

Examples: Courts have held that if a person is questioned by the police and denies that certain property is his (e.g., an unidentified suitcase in the baggage claim area of an airport), he thereby abandons any interest in the property. *See United States v. McBean*, 861 F.2d 1570 (11th Cir.1988); Federal agents seized unopened mail from a private mailbox that defendant had rented. Defendant had not checked mail or paid rent in over a year. The court held that the mail seizure did not violate defendant's fourth amendment rights because he had abandoned the mailbox and unopened mail. *See United States v. Thomas*, 451 F.3d 543 (8th Cir. 2006) (defendant did not have an ongoing reasonable expectation of privacy in abandoned unclaimed mail).

3. Sufficient Manifestation Found Under Some Circumstances

There are some cases, however, where the police conduct has been especially energetic, and the courts have held that the citizen has sufficiently manifested a protected interest.

Example: An officer climbs to the top of a building and peers through louvers of a vented fan in the ceiling. The court found that this was a search, explaining that a citizen does not need to deprive himself of all ventilation in order to retain a privacy interest. *United States v. Amuny*, 767 F.2d 1113 (5th Cir.1985).

D. Application of the *Katz* Principle: Legitimacy of the Expectation of Privacy, Access by Members of the Public

Even if a citizen tries to keep information private (thus having a subjective expectation), it is sometimes the case in society that the citizen will not get her wish. Sometimes we do not get all the privacy we want. One person cannot tell another not to look at him as he walks down the street. Nor can a homeowner demand that planes not fly overhead. Society is not prepared to accept such demands as reasonable and legitimate. After *Katz* the Supreme Court has held in a series of cases that if an aspect of a person's life (such as his trash or public movements), is subject to scrutiny by members of the public, then that person has no legitimate expectation in denying equivalent access to the police. *There is no search if the police obtain information accessible to members of the public.*

1. Bank Records

In *United States v. Miller*, 425 U.S. 435, 96 S.Ct. 1619, 48 L.Ed.2d 71 (1976), the Government served a subpoena on Miller's bank to obtain copies of

Miller's checks, deposit slips and financial statements. The Court held that this activity was not a search (and therefore the Government did not have to obtain a warrant and did not have to have any suspicion of wrongdoing), because Miller had no reasonable expectation of privacy in information which he had conveyed to his bank. Since the bank had access to the information, Miller could not reasonably prevent the Government from equivalent access.

2. Telephone Pen Registers

In *Smith v. Maryland*, 442 U.S. 735, 99 S.Ct. 2577, 61 L.Ed.2d 220 (1979), the police installed a pen register device in the phone company offices. This device recorded the numbers called by the defendant on his home telephone. The Court held that the use of the pen register was not a search, since Smith had no right to expect that the phone numbers he called would remain private. In making the call, Smith gave this information to the phone company; therefore equivalent access by the Government could not be denied.

a. Recordkeeping by Third Party Not Required

In *Smith,* the Government obtained the numbers of local calls, which were not itemized on Smith's monthly bill, and which were not recorded by the phone company as a general matter. The Court found it irrelevant that the phone company kept no records of local phone numbers called. The Court found it controlling that the phone company was given the information by Smith, and that the company could have kept the records if it so desired.

b. Dissents in *Smith* and *Miller*

The dissenters in *Smith* and *Miller* argued that the results in the cases were harsh and unrealistic. The release of information by the citizens in *Smith* and *Miller* was very circumscribed. The defendants in these cases did not grant access to all or most members of the public and then unreasonably seek to exclude the police. The dissenters pointed out that the grant of access to information in these cases was not the product of free choice. It is hard to do without a phone and a bank account.

c. Response

The majority in these cases responded that free choice is not the issue. The issue is whether society is prepared to accept a privacy expectation as reasonable where members of the public have access to the information. It is not always possible in today's society to keep all information totally private. The majority found no reason to create a distinction between access to members of the public and access by the police. Thus, if information is exposed to a third party, it is exposed in equal measure to the police.

3. Trash

In *California v. Greenwood*, 486 U.S. 35, 108 S.Ct. 1625, 100 L.Ed.2d 30 (1988), the police over a two month period rummaged through trash left by the defendant for the local garbage service. Defendant left the trash in opaque bags at the curb in front of his house. The Court held that the rummaging was not a search. It reasoned that since passersby, snoops, scavengers, the trash service, and animals have access to trash left out at the curb, the trash is exposed in equal measure to the police. Hence there is no legitimate expectation of privacy.

a. Lack of Choice Irrelevant

Greenwood was prohibited by city ordinance from disposing of his trash in any way other than leaving it for the trash service. Greenwood argued that he did not voluntarily waive any right to privacy he had in the trash. The Court found, however, that lack of choice was irrelevant to whether a person's expectation of privacy was reasonable, just as it had been in *Smith* and *Miller*. For good or ill, society does force the citizen to put some information at risk of public access; the question is not whether a waiver has occurred, but whether one can reasonably expect to keep information from members of the public. If members of the public could obtain access, the police have equivalent access to the information, because it is unreasonable to expect that the police would be excluded when members of the public are not.

b. Efforts at Concealment

It did not matter in *Greenwood* that the trash was placed in an opaque bag. Nor would it matter if the trash was mingled with the trash of others in a dumpster, because if the public has access to the trash, the defendant would be engaged in the futile activity of trying to manifest a privacy interest that does not in fact exist. *See United States v. Scott*, 975 F.2d 927 (1st Cir.1992) (it made no difference that defendant shredded the paper trash before placing it outside: "What we have here is a failed attempt at secrecy by reason of underestimation of police resourcefulness, not invasion of constitutionally protected privacy.")

c.   Dissent

Dissenting in *Greenwood,* Justice Brennan argued that society is prepared to accept a citizen's expectation of privacy in trash as reasonable. According to Justice Brennan, most members of society would be appalled at the prospect that others would search through their trash to obtain intimate details of how they lead their personal lives.

Justice Brennan further argued that the *mere possibility* that some member of the public may rummage through trash should not preclude a legitimate expectation of privacy. In *Greenwood,* there was no indication that local residents routinely, or ever, had their trash investigated by members of the public. Justice Brennan contended that if the mere possibility of public access is enough to destroy a privacy interest, then there is little privacy left. For example, the mere possibility that a house could be broken into by burglars cannot mean that the homeowner has no expectation of privacy in his home. Yet Justice Brennan found it difficult to draw a principled line between the *Greenwood* "mere possibility" analysis and this hypothetical.

d.   Limitations on *Greenwood*

The majority in *Greenwood* relied on the fact that Greenwood left his trash out on a public street. *Greenwood* does not apply when the police officer, in order to obtain the trash, enters an area from which the public is excluded. This is because, in the process of obtaining the trash, the officer will have conducted a search of a private area. *See New York v. Class,* 475 U.S. 106, 106 S.Ct. 960, 89 L.Ed.2d 81 (1986) (there is no privacy interest in a vehicle identification number, but an officer who entered the automobile to find the number conducted a search of a private area).

e.   Other Kinds of "Waste"

A manufacturer lacked a reasonable expectation of privacy in wastewater discharged from his plant. Environmental Protection Agency (EPA) agents did not violate the Fourth Amendment when they took samples of wastewater without warrant or consent because their conduct did not constitute a "search." The wastewater at manhole from which the samples were taken was irretrievably flowing into public sewer, from which any member of the public could have taken a sample. (*Riverdale Mills Corp. v. Pimpare,* 392 F.3d 55 (1st Cir. 2004)).

f.   Homeless Persons

At least one court has found the *Greenwood* analysis inapplicable to homeless persons. That court found that a homeless person had a reasonable expectation of privacy in a duffel bag and a cardboard box kept on public property. The court reasoned that a contrary result would mean that millions of Americans would be unable to assert a privacy interest in their personal belongings. *See State v. Mooney*, 218 Conn. 85, 588 A.2d 145 (1991).

4.   **Aerial Surveillance**

The Court has applied the public access rationale of *Smith* and *Miller* to aerial surveillance of private areas. In *California v. Ciraolo*, 476 U.S. 207, 106 S.Ct. 1809, 90 L.Ed.2d 210 (1986), police officers used an airplane to conduct aerial surveillance of defendant's backyard, and found marijuana growing there. The police had no warrant or probable cause to conduct the aerial surveillance. The airplane flew over the defendant's yard in navigable airspace at a height of 1,000 feet. The Court held that the Fourth Amendment did not apply to the police conduct because the aerial overflight was not a search.

a.   Rationale

As in *Smith* and *Miller*, the Court reasoned that since members of the public could fly over the defendant's yard and view the activity therein, Ciraolo could not reasonably expect to exclude the police from doing so. The fact that the area was viewed by the use of a police plane rather than a commercial airliner was irrelevant: if two planes pass over, the effect on the privacy interest is the same even though one is being used for investigatory purposes and one is not.

b.   Dissent

Justice Powell, dissenting in *Ciraolo*, contended that aerial surveillance by police is of a different character from that obtained by commercial aircraft. Passengers in a commercial airplane do not generally circle continually over a particular backyard to inspect activity in detail; and even if they do, they do not connect any discovered activity with a specific person, so that the property owner effectively retains a secrecy interest.

c.   Low–Flying Helicopters

The Court extended *Ciraolo* in *Florida v. Riley*, 488 U.S. 445, 109 S.Ct. 693, 102 L.Ed.2d 835 (1989), and held that surveillance of a backyard from a helicopter hovering at 400 feet was not a search. The crucial question in *Riley* was whether the public indeed had access to the information in Riley's backyard by way of aerial surveillance. All members of the Court agreed that if there was sufficient public access to Riley's backyard by way of a helicopter overflight, then the use of a helicopter by police would not be a search. Yet there was significant disagreement as to whether there was sufficient public access in *Riley*.

d. Legally Permissible Access
Justice White wrote a plurality opinion in *Riley* which reasoned that since members of the public *could legally* hover over Riley's property in a helicopter at 400 feet, the police could do so as well. Justice White relied on FAA regulations which allow helicopters to be operated at virtually any altitude so long as they do not pose a safety hazard.

e. Actual Access
Justice O'Connor's opinion concurring in the result in *Riley* disagreed with Justice White's analysis and in fact agreed with the four dissenting justices as to the appropriate test for determining whether helicopter surveillance is a search. A majority of the Court therefore was of the view that the test for a search was whether members of the public *in fact ordinarily hovered* over Riley's yard at 400 feet in helicopters—if so, it would be unreasonable to expect that the police could not do so. According to five justices, the mere fact that it would be legal for a member of the public to hover in a helicopter at 400 feet did not preclude a legitimate expectation of privacy from such activity.

f. Burden of Proof
Justice O'Connor nonetheless concurred in the result in *Riley*. While agreeing with the dissenters as to the appropriate test, Justice O'Connor was of the view that the *burden was on the defendant* to show that members of the public did not regularly hover over his property in helicopters at 400 feet. Since Riley offered no proof on this point in the lower court, she concluded that a search was not shown on the facts in *Riley*. The four dissenters in *Riley* argued that the burden should be on the Government to show that the defendant's Fourth Amendment rights were not violated. They found support in the fact that it is the Government which is moving to admit the evidence.

g. Implications From *Riley*

The actual rule to be derived from *Riley* is not as drastic as the result in the case would make it appear. A majority of the court focused on whether the public would *ordinarily have access* to the defendant's information, not on whether it was physically and legally possible to get the information as a theoretical matter.

5. **Limitations on Public Access Theory**

From time to time the Court finds the Fourth Amendment applicable and rejects the Government's argument that no search occurred because members of the public had access to the information uncovered by police officers. The reasoning in these cases is not always consistent with that of *Smith, Miller,* and *Greenwood,* and it seems that the Court is not prepared to hold that a person *always* surrenders his privacy interests whenever some member of the public has access to information retrieved by police officers.

a. Hotel Room Searches

In *Stoner v. California,* 376 U.S. 483, 84 S.Ct. 889, 11 L.Ed.2d 856 (1964), the Court found that a paying guest had a reasonable expectation of privacy in a motel room—therefore, police entry into that room constituted a search. The Court concluded that a hotel guest pays for the right to privacy and has the right to exclude others, even management. It found that the Fourth Amendment applied even though a hotel tenant implicitly authorizes maids, janitors, and repair personnel to enter his room. The implied grant of public access did not mean that the police were granted equivalent access.

b. Distinction from *Smith* and *Miller*

The distinction between *Stoner* and *Smith* and *Miller* is elusive. In all these cases, the citizen grants access to one or two discrete parties. Yet in *Smith* and *Miller* that limited grant of access renders unreasonable the expectation of excluding the Government. One possible distinction is that in *Smith* and *Miller,* the records were actually the property of the third parties who had access to them, whereas in *Stoner,* the hotel tenant, by paying the bill, is the holder of property and associated privacy rights. A more important distinction is that in *Smith* and *Miller,* the Government access was *equivalent* to that granted to the third party, whereas the access granted to others by the hotel tenant in *Stoner was more limited in nature* than the actual search conducted by the Government authorities. That is, in *Smith* and *Miller,* the bank and the telephone company had an absolute right to inspect the information, so the police officer had the same right. In contrast, in *Stoner,* the maid had the right to enter the hotel room to clean it, but the police officer entered the hotel room to inspect it. Thus, the grant of access in *Stoner* was more limited than that sought to be used by the police officer.

c. Must Have a Current Right to Reside in the Room

Of course, to trigger an expectation of privacy in a hotel room, the tenant must have paid for the right to exclude management, other guests, and hence the police. So for example, if checkout time has passed, and the tenant has not paid for the next day, the tenant loses his expectation of privacy. A subsequent inspection of the room by police officers will not invade the privacy rights of a person who is no longer the tenant. Courts have held that an expectation of privacy in the room is lost even if the defendant has been arrested and thus is unable to keep his hotel bill current. *See United States v. Rahme*, 813 F.2d 31 (2d Cir.1987).

d. Bags in Public Transit

In *Bond v. United States*, 529 U.S. 334, 120 S.Ct. 1462, 146 L.Ed.2d 365 (2000), the Court held that a law enforcement agent conducted an illegal search in violation of the Fourth Amendment when he physically manipulated a canvas bag that a passenger placed in the overhead bin above his seat. The Government argued that Mr. Bond's expectation that members of the public would not physically manipulate his bag on a public bus was not reasonable, relying on the "public access" rationale in *Ciraolo* and *Riley*. The Court rejected the Government's argument, noting that although one would reasonably expect members of the public to handle bags in an overhead bin, one would not expect the type of "probing tactile examination" conducted by the agent in this case. The Court also distinguished the aerial surveillance cases by noting that they involved visual observation rather than tactile manipulation, which the Court found to be inherently more intrusive.

E. Application of *Katz*: Investigation Which Can Only Uncover Illegal Activity Is Not a Search

There is no legitimate privacy interest in illegal activity. Those engaged in illegal activity are ordinarily protected by the Fourth Amendment only because there is no way to tell before an intrusion whether or not the activity being investigated is illegal. However, if a certain mode of investigation can only uncover *whether or not* illegal activity exists, and cannot disclose innocent activity, then the investigation is not a search because it does not implicate any secrecy interest protected by the Fourth Amendment.

1. Dog Sniffs

In *United States v. Place,* 462 U.S. 696, 103 S.Ct. 2637, 77 L.Ed.2d 110 (1983), the Court held that a dog sniff of closed luggage is not a search. A dog sniff can only tell the officer whether the luggage contains contraband or not. There is no protectible privacy interest in contraband, and through the sniff, the officer learns nothing about any personal, innocent information contained in the luggage. The canine sniff is not a search because it can never disclose a protected Fourth Amendment secrecy interest.

a. Implications From *Place*

If a canine sniff is not a search, it means that there are no reasonableness limitations imposed upon it. It follows from *Place* that officers could arbitrarily use dogs to sniff any piece of luggage, or indeed to roam through a neighborhood without justification.

b. Seizure of Luggage in Order to Conduct the Canine Sniff Triggers Fourth Amendment Protections

While the dog sniff in *Place* was not a search, the Court nonetheless held that the cocaine found in Place's luggage had to be suppressed. This was because before conducting the sniff, the police detained the luggage for 90 minutes. This detention was an exercise of dominion and control over Place's property, which implicated the Fourth Amendment because it was a *seizure.* As such, the Fourth Amendment standards were triggered, and the seizure had to be reasonable. The Court in *Place* found that the deprivation of Place's possessory interest in the luggage was lengthy and severe, and that the length of the seizure could have been minimized if the officers had acted with reasonable diligence. Under the circumstances, the Court found that the seizure could only be reasonable if the officers had probable cause to detain the luggage; and probable cause did not exist before the canine sniff on the facts of *Place.* See the further discussion of *Place* in the stop and frisk section, *infra.*

c. Positive Result Does Not Allow Opening the Luggage

Even if a dog sniff of luggage is positive, and the seizure giving rise to the sniff is reasonable, it does not follow that the officers can open the luggage. Even with a positive alert, there may be legitimate secrecy interests contained in the luggage. So, while the sniff is not a search, and the information from the sniff is legally obtained, the *opening is a search,* which triggers the Fourth Amendment and requires a warrant or some exception. The dog sniff is useful to the police, however, because the information therefrom can be freely used for the probable cause determination by either the magistrate, or by the officer who searches pursuant to an exception to the warrant requirement.

A positive result from a canine sniff can also be used as justification to detain the bag pending a warrant. The detention of the bag would of course be a seizure, but it would be reasonable given the positive alert, presuming that the dog could be shown to be reliable and that a positive alert actually indicates that the suspect is carrying drugs. *See United States v. Ludwig,* 10 F.3d 1523 (10th Cir.1993) (positive dog alert suffices for probable cause where it is shown that the dog has a reliable track record); *United States v. United States Currency,* 39 F.3d 1039 (9th Cir.1994) (court notes research indicating that 97% of all currency in the United States is contaminated by trace amounts of cocaine; therefore, a positive canine alert, while probative of drug possession, must be combined with other suspicious facts in order to constitute probable cause).

d. Dog Sniffs of People
    The Supreme Court has never considered whether a canine sniff of a person is a search. The Fourth Amendment guarantees personal security as well as privacy. There was no threat to personal security in *Place* because the dog sniff was conducted without Place even being present. It is possible, then, that a dog sniff of a person implicates the Fourth Amendment.

e. Dog Sniffs of Rooms and Residences
    The lower courts are split as to whether the reasoning of *Place* applies to dog sniffs of residences. The Second Circuit has held that a dog sniff of a house, from the outside, is a search because the area intruded upon is more private than that involved in *Place. See United States v. Thomas,* 757 F.2d 1359 (2d Cir.1985). The District of Columbia Circuit disagrees, reasoning that while a privacy interest in a dwelling is more profound than that in luggage, in neither case does a dog sniff intrude upon a legitimate privacy interest. The sniff

uncovers no innocent secret information, regardless of where the sniff occurs. *See United States v. Colyer*, 878 F.2d 469 (D.C.Cir.1989) (permitting a canine sniff of an Amtrak sleeper compartment in the absence of articulable suspicion). The reasoning of *Place* appears to support the view of the District of Columbia Circuit. It must be remembered, however, that residences have been treated differently from other objects and areas in Fourth Amendment cases. *See, e.g., Payton v. New York*, 445 U.S. 573, 100 S.Ct. 1371, 63 L.Ed.2d 639 (1980) (arrest warrant needed to arrest felony suspect at home).

f. Dog Sniffs During a Routine Traffic Stop
In *Illinois v. Caballes*, 543 U.S. 405, 125 S.Ct. 834, 160 L.Ed.2d 842 (2005), the Court held that a dog sniff conducted during an otherwise lawful traffic stop did not violate the Fourth Amendment. The Court found that while it is true that a seizure valid at inception can turn into one that violates an individual's Fourth Amendment rights, here the dog only sniffed the exterior of the car while Caballes was legally stopped for a traffic violation. The sniff did not prolong the time of the traffic stop nor did it reveal any information other than the location of contraband in which defendant had no legitimate expectation of privacy.

2. Chemical Tests

If a chemical test merely discloses whether or not a substance is contraband, the test is not a search. There is no legitimate expectation of privacy in the information uncovered by such a test if a positive result shows only the existence of contraband (as to which there is no legitimate expectation of privacy), and a negative result uncovers no secret, innocent information. In *United States v. Jacobsen*, 466 U.S. 109, 104 S.Ct. 1652, 80 L.Ed.2d 85 (1984), the Court relied on its rationale in *Place* to hold that a chemical field test of a white powder was not a search, since the test would only indicate whether the powder was contraband or not.

a. Not All Chemical Tests Are Free From Fourth Amendment Scrutiny
The Court in *Jacobsen* did not free all chemical tests from the constraints of the Fourth Amendment. Some chemical tests uncover not only contraband but also innocent private information. For example, a drug test of a urine sample indicates whether or not the subject has taken illegal drugs, but it also may uncover the existence of epilepsy, pregnancy, or the use of prescription drugs. Since such

a test can convey innocent, secret information, a drug test of urine was unanimously held by the Supreme Court to be a search in *Skinner v. Railway Labor Executives' Assoc.*, 489 U.S. 602, 109 S.Ct. 1402, 103 L.Ed.2d 639 (1989).

b. Seizure to Do the Test

As in *Place*, the investigative activity in *Jacobsen was not a search* because it could only uncover the existence of contraband; but a *seizure* was still necessary in order to conduct the test. Arguably, the seizure in *Jacobsen* was more intrusive than that in *Place*, because it was necessary to *destroy* the substance in order to do the field test. However, the Court in *Jacobsen* found that the seizure was reasonable (unlike in *Place*) because only a de minimis amount of property was destroyed, and because the officer had probable cause to believe the substance was cocaine *before he did the field test.*

F. **Application of *Katz*: Re–Opening of Packages by Government Officials**

If a package has once been opened consistent with the Fourth Amendment, it will not be a search if it is reopened by a Government official, unless there is a substantial probability that the contents of the package have been changed since the original opening.

1. **Rationale**

The Court has reasoned that if the original opening of a container was legal, the owner's privacy interest in the package has been lost. The secrecy interest in the contents of the package has already been disclosed; it does not reattach to the very contents already viewed, since once a privacy interest has been lost, it does not return. However, if the contents have been changed, a secrecy interest does reattach. Otherwise, a suitcase once legally opened in, say, a customs search, could be reopened years later without a warrant or probable cause.

2. **Re–Opening After Private Search**

In *United States v. Jacobsen, supra,* a Federal Express employee opened a package, and notified authorities of his suspicion that it contained contraband. He then sealed the package. Then a DEA agent reopened the package while it was still in the custody of Federal Express. The Court held that the DEA agent's reopening of the package was not a search, since the package had by that time already been legally opened; the original opening was not prohibited by the Fourth Amendment since it was done by a private party; and the contents of the package had obviously not been changed since the original opening.

a. Dissent

Justice White, dissenting in *Jacobsen*, could not see the difference between a package opened by a private party, and a house entered by a private party. He argued that if the *Jacobsen* rationale were taken to its logical extreme, police could enter a home after a private party did so, even if the private party entered the home illegally, and yet the subsequent police entry would not be a search. However, the *Jacobsen* rule does not inevitably allow the police to enter a house previously entered by a private person. The Court has often treated the house as deserving of special Fourth Amendment protection.

b. Later Activity Can Be a Search to the Extent That it Exceeds the Scope of the Original Legal Search

If the subsequent official investigation of the package or its contents exceeds the scope of the original search, it may trigger Fourth Amendment protection to the extent that a further intrusion is made. For instance, in *Walter v. United States*, 447 U.S. 649, 100 S.Ct. 2395, 65 L.Ed.2d 410 (1980), a private party opened a package and found that it contained films. Police officers then viewed the films through a projector. The Court held that the viewing of the films was a search, since it exceeded the scope of the private search.

3. Controlled Delivery

The proposition that a privacy interest, once invaded, does not return, has been applied to validate controlled deliveries of packages. A typical delivery works as follows: a package is sent by mail or delivery service, and is legally opened while in transit—for instance, in a customs search or in a search by a private party; the package is then resealed and the police track it to its ultimate destination. When it arrives, the recipient is arrested and the police reopen the package. Reopening a package pursuant to a controlled delivery is *not a search*, provided that the privacy interest in the contents has already been legally disclosed. *Illinois v. Andreas*, 463 U.S. 765, 103 S.Ct. 3319, 77 L.Ed.2d 1003 (1983).

a. Lapse in "Control"

Even if the police conducting a controlled delivery temporarily lose sight of the package, their subsequent reopening of the package will not be a search, so long as there is a substantial likelihood that the contents of the package have been unchanged since the original opening.

Example: In *Andreas*, police officers, posing as deliverymen, delivered a package which had originally been legally opened. The package contained a table with contraband inside. The officers lost sight of the package when it was brought into the defendant's apartment for 35 minutes. Then the defendant exited his apartment, carrying the package. The police then arrested defendant, seized the package, and reopened it. The Court held that the reopening was not a search. The unusual size of the package, its non-generic purpose, and the relatively limited time period of lapsed control, all indicated that there was a substantial likelihood that the contents of the package had not been changed.

b. Dissent

Justice Brennan in dissent proposed that "a reasonable expectation of privacy should reattach if the person has unobserved access to the package and any opportunity to change its contents."

G. Application of *Katz*: Sensory Enhancement Devices

Generally speaking, the use by officials of devices which aid their investigation by enhancing the senses does not constitute a search, so long as the devices do no more than aid the police in obtaining information that they could have obtained through their own sensory perception.

1. Beepers

In *United States v. Knotts*, 460 U.S. 276, 103 S.Ct. 1081, 75 L.Ed.2d 55 (1983), police officers tracked the movements of the defendant's vehicle by using an electronic device which sent out radio "beeping" signals. The Court held that the use of the beeper was not a search in these circumstances. The information obtained consisted only of the defendant's public movements, as to which he had no reasonable expectation of privacy. (See the *Smith* and *Miller* "public access" doctrine, *supra*). The fact that the police tracked the defendant's public movements through an electronic beeper rather than through sensory perception was held immaterial. The Court reasoned that the beeper did no more than what could be done through ordinary sensory perception—i.e., the police could themselves have tracked the defendant's public movements. In essence, the defendant suffered "no prejudice" through the use of an electronic device.

a. Sale of Merchandise Containing a Beeper

The fact that the police have installed a beeper device in merchandise later purchased by a citizen does not itself constitute a search or seizure. This is because the installation of the device does not invade a privacy interest. No information is obtained by the installation. The Fourth Amendment only becomes applicable when the beeper begins to transmit information, and then only if the information transmitted concerns private activity. Nor is the installation of a beeper tantamount to a seizure of the merchandise. It does not significantly change the character of the merchandise, nor does it deprive the owner of the right to possession or control. *United States v. Karo*, 468 U.S. 705, 104 S.Ct. 3296, 82 L.Ed.2d 530 (1984) ("Although the can may have contained an unknown and unwanted foreign object, it cannot be said that anyone's possessory interest was interfered with in a meaningful way.")

b. Entering a Private Area to Install a Beeper

While the use of a beeper is not a search if it conveys public information, police installation of the beeper may itself be a search under certain circumstances. For example, if the police open a car door to place a beeper inside, the entry into the car will be a search. *See New York v. Class, supra* (there is no privacy interest in a vehicle identification number, but an officer who entered the automobile to uncover the number conducted a search of a private area). There was no search on these grounds, however, in either *Knotts or Karo.* In both cases, the beeper was installed on merchandise before it was sold. *See Karo* ("The can into which the beeper was placed belonged at the time to the DEA, and by no stretch of the imagination could it be said that the respondents then had any legitimate expectation of privacy in it.")

c. Obtaining Private Information Through Use of a Beeper

If the police use a beeper to obtain private information that they could not obtain through their own sensory perception, the use of the beeper is a search. This occurred in *United States v. Karo* when officers installed a beeper in a can of ether, and then tracked the movement of the can into the defendant's *house.* The Court held that the defendant had a reasonable expectation of privacy in movements inside the house; and the beeper gave the officers information about the location of the can in the house which they could not have obtained through their own sensory perception.

2. Flashlights

The use of a flashlight to aid an officer in an inspection is not itself a search. The flashlight aids the officer's perception, but it does not provide the officer with information beyond what could be obtained from unaided sensory perception. Essentially, the use of a flashlight does not prejudice the defendant in any way. *See Texas v. Brown*, 460 U.S. 730, 103 S.Ct. 1535, 75 L.Ed.2d 502 (1983) ("The use of artificial means to illuminate a darkened area simply does not constitute a search, and thus triggers no Fourth Amendment protection.")

3. Binoculars

If police use binoculars to see what could otherwise be seen through the naked eye, then the use of binoculars as a sensory aid is not a search under *Knotts*, because it results in exposure only of that information which is otherwise visible. On the other hand, if police use binoculars to discover minute details located in a private area, which information could not otherwise be seen through the naked eye (such as the lettering on bottles on the bedroom bureau) the use of binoculars will be a search under *Karo. See United States v. Taborda*, 635 F.2d 131 (2d Cir.1980) (agents invaded a reasonable expectation of privacy when they used a telescope to see into an apartment at a distance from which the activities viewed would not be visible with the naked eye).

4. Microphones

The use of microphones for auditory enhancement is comparable to the use of binoculars for visual enhancement. If a conversation could be heard with the naked ear, then the use of microphones is not a search. If it could not be heard by ordinary sensory perception, then the use of microphones is a search.

5. High–Tech Cameras

In *Dow Chemical Co. v. United States*, 476 U.S. 227, 106 S.Ct. 1819, 90 L.Ed.2d 226 (1986), Government officials flew over Dow's commercial property, and used a $22,000 camera to take pictures of the areas between the defendant's buildings. The photographs could be enlarged so that objects one-half inch in diameter could be seen. The Court held that the use of the camera was not a search. Relying on the rationale of *Knotts*, the Court stated that Dow had no legitimate expectation of privacy in the area between its buildings—at least not with respect to aerial surveillance. Therefore, aerial surveillance of that area could not be a search.

Since no private information was obtained, the mode of investigation could not be of concern to Dow; it was not prejudiced by the use of the camera.

Limitations on *Dow*

> *Dow* is most fairly read as holding that if the defendant has no privacy interest in information to begin with, the use of an enhancement device is not a search, even if it gives the officer information he could not otherwise gain through personal perception. The mode of investigation can make no difference to the citizen if he or she has no right to privacy protection in the first place. This doctrine carries its own limitation. If the device in *Dow* could pierce through walls and obtain *private* information that could not be obtained through sensory perception, then the use of such an enhancement device would be a search. *See Dow* ("an electronic device to penetrate walls or windows so as to hear and record confidential discussions * * * would raise very different and far more serious questions.")

6. Thermal Imaging Devices

A thermal imaging device is an infrared device which can compare the heat emanating from one object with the intensity of the heat from surrounding objects. This device is often used by police officers who suspect that a person is growing marijuana inside his house. Is the use of this device a search? Before the Supreme Court decided this issue, virtually every lower court declared that the use of a thermal imaging device does not constitute a search. However, the Court decided otherwise in *Kyllo v. United States*, 533 U.S. 27, 121 S.Ct. 2038, 150 L.Ed.2d 94 (2001). Law enforcement agents seated in a car across the street from Mr. Kyllo's home used a thermal-imaging device to determine that the roof over Mr. Kyllo's garage and the side wall of his home were substantially warmer than the rest of his home and neighboring homes. The agents inferred that Mr. Kyllo was using halide lights to grow marijuana in his house, and used this information along with the results of other investigation to obtain a search warrant for the house. The Supreme Court held that the use of the thermal-imaging device was a search protected by the Fourth Amendment because the device obtained information that could not have otherwise been obtained without physical "intrusion into a constitutionally protected area," citing *Silverman v. United States*, 365 U.S. 505, 512, 81 S.Ct. 679, 5 L.Ed.2d 734 (1961). The Court focused on the fact that the device was used to detect information inside the home, distinguishing the enhanced photography of the industrial complex in *Dow Chemical*. The Court also noted that thermal-imaging devices were not in general public use, alluding to the "public access" rationale of the aerial surveillance cases.

H. Application of *Katz*: Prisoners and Jail Cells

In *Hudson v. Palmer*, 468 U.S. 517, 104 S.Ct. 3194, 82 L.Ed.2d 393 (1984), the Court held that a prisoner has no legitimate property or privacy interests in his or her belongings kept in the prison cell. Consequently, the Fourth Amendment did not apply to an officer's intentional destruction of this property. Nor would the officer's arbitrary inspection of such property implicate the Fourth Amendment. Police are not required to be reasonable if their conduct is neither a search nor a seizure.

1. Rationale

The Court analyzed the legitimacy of a prisoner's expectation by considering the societal interests furthered by prison cell searches, and by balancing these interests against the prisoner's privacy and property interests. The Court concluded that the state interests in maintaining prison discipline and controlling crime outweighed the obviously limited privacy and property interests that a prisoner could expect to have.

2. Dissent

The dissenters in *Hudson* argued that the majority had ignored the explicit language of the Fourth Amendment, which is triggered upon the search or seizure of a person, house, paper or effect. The dissenters contended that the majority's balancing analysis was more appropriately applied to determine whether a search is *reasonable*, not whether it is a search at all.

3. Searches of Persons

Even after *Hudson*, the Fourth Amendment probably applies to searches of prisoners, as opposed to their cells. In *Bell v. Wolfish*, 441 U.S. 520, 99 S.Ct. 1861, 60 L.Ed.2d 447 (1979), the Court implicitly held that the Fourth Amendment applied to searches of pretrial detainees—though it found the searches there conducted (body inspections after contact with visitors) to be reasonable. The same result should apply for prisoners as applies to detainees—though whether a search is reasonable under the circumstances may depend in part on the status of the incarcerated person. A search which may be reasonable as applied to a death-row inmate may not be reasonable as applied to a suspected misdemeanant who is about to post bail.

I. Application of *Katz*: Open Fields

In *Oliver v. United States*, 466 U.S. 170, 104 S.Ct. 1735, 80 L.Ed.2d 214 (1984), the Court held that a property owner's fields which lay beyond the house and its curtilage were not protected by the Fourth Amendment. The rule that the Fourth Amendment has no applicability beyond the curtilage has been termed the "open fields" doctrine. But as the Court recognized in *Oliver*, this term is somewhat of a misnomer, since the doctrine permits the search of all property beyond the curtilage, whether or not it is open, and whether or not it is a field. For instance, in *Oliver*, the property searched could not in any way be called "open." It was set back behind fences and gates, "no trespassing" signs were posted, and the area could not be seen from any public vantage point.

1. Rationale

The Court in *Oliver* first looked at the literal language of the Fourth Amendment, found that it only covered "persons, houses, papers and effects," and reasoned that a field outside the curtilage was none of these. The Court also contended that society was not prepared to accept as legitimate an expectation of privacy in the area outside the curtilage. The Court claimed that open fields are not usually the settings for intimate activity, and that they are usually open to public scrutiny.

No Case–By–Case Approach

Responding to the majority's analysis of privacy interests in *Oliver*, the defendant argued that while open fields are *normally* subject to public scrutiny, that may not be so in an individual case—as the facts in *Oliver* demonstrate. The majority rejected the defendant's argument for a case-by-case determination of whether property really is open or closed and private. The Court stated that a case-by-case approach to the problem would be unworkable, because police officers would have to guess in every case whether the citizen had sufficiently closed the field from public scrutiny to establish a right of privacy. The Court's rejection of a case-by-case approach means that there can never be an expectation of privacy in an open field, no matter what the property owner has done to deny public access. Such a property owner would be demonstrating a subjective expectation of privacy which is not reasonable after *Oliver*.

2. Dissent

The dissenters in *Oliver* complained that the majority's literal construction of the Fourth Amendment was without support after *Katz*. In *Katz*, the Court found that wiretapping was a search, even though it was not literally a search of a person, house, paper or effect. The dissenters argued that private activities often occur in areas outside the curtilage of a house.

3. **Curtilage Remains Protected**

If the property investigated is within the "curtilage," then the open fields doctrine of *Oliver* does not apply; a state intrusion into the curtilage will be a search if the citizen has manifested an expectation of privacy. The scope of curtilage must be resolved through a case-by-case approach. The Supreme Court has stated that four factors are pertinent to this determination (*See United States v. Dunn, supra*):

1. The *distance* between the home and the area claimed to be curtilage;

2. Whether the area is within a *fence or enclosure* that surrounds the home;

3. Whether the *uses to which the area is put* correspond to those ordinarily conducted in a home or not; and

4. The *steps taken by the citizen to protect the area* from public view.

Example: In *Dunn*, an entire ranch was enclosed by a perimeter fence, and an interior fence circled the farmhouse alone. A barn was sixty yards from the farmhouse, outside the interior fence. To get to the barn, the officers had to cross the perimeter fence and two other fences. The Court held that the barn was not within the curtilage, and therefore that the officer's action of pressing his face above the gate to the barn to see through mesh material into the interior of the barn was not a search. The Court stated that the distance between the barn and the house was "substantial"; that the house was enclosed by an interior fence which did not include the barn; that the officers possessed objective data that the barn was being used as a place for manufacturing drugs, and thus was not being used for activities associated with the home; and that Dunn did not sufficiently manifest an expectation of keeping the barn private from those standing in the open fields.

a. Porches, Decks, etc. as Curtilage

Courts applying the *Dunn* factors have generally held that structures appurtenant to the home, such as porches and decks, are part of the curtilage, at least so long as the structure is not shared with other homeowners and is *restricted from public access. See State v. Santiago,* 27 Conn.App. 741, 610 A.2d 666 (1992) ("A sheltered porch, attached to a home, is an area intimately tied to the home itself, and an area in which domestic activity commonly occurs.") Compare *United States v. Taylor,* 90 F.3d 903 (4th Cir.1996) (officer who walked up onto a front porch and looked into a window did not make a search, where no fence surrounded the property and so the porch was "as open to law enforcement officers as to any delivery person, guest, or other member of the public.")

b.   Aerial Surveillance

As discussed above, a homeowner's curtilage is not free from aerial observation if members of the public routinely fly overhead and can see into the curtilage with the naked eye. *See Florida v. Riley, supra.*

c.   Industrial Property

In *Dow Chemical Co. v. United States, supra,* the Court held that the area surrounding a commercial or industrial building is not entitled to the same Fourth Amendment protection as the area immediately surrounding the home. Areas outside commercial and industrial buildings have some of the characteristics of open fields, and some of the characteristics of curtilage. The Court concluded that such an area could not be entered from ground level so long as fences excluded the public (as if it were curtilage), but that it could be viewed from the air, even with sophisticated sensory enhancement devices not used by members of the public (as if it were an open field). Thus, the Fourth Amendment does not recognize the concept of industrial curtilage, at least with respect to aerial surveillance.

d.   Other Property

In *Dunn,* the Court implicitly rejected the notion that the barn itself could have curtilage surrounding it. Even though the barn had a fence around it, the Court held that it was permissible for the officer to jump that fence and peer into the barn. Apparently, the barn was neither commercial enough to warrant protection of the areas surrounding it as "industrial curtilage" (protected from ground inspection under *Dow, supra),* nor domestic enough for the area to be treated as curtilage surrounding a home. *See United States v. Pace,* 955 F.2d 270 (5th Cir.1992) ("Whatever *Dow Chemical* may have left open concerning the concept of a curtilage surrounding a business or commercial establishment, *Dunn* indicates that there is no business curtilage surrounding a barn lying within an open field.")

J. Application of *Katz*: Public School Students

In *New Jersey v. T.L.O.*, 469 U.S. 325, 105 S.Ct. 733, 83 L.Ed.2d 720 (1985), the Court held that high school students have some reasonable expectation of privacy while attending school. It declined the invitation to apply the prison case, *Hudson v. Palmer*, to the school context. The Court stated that schools could not yet be equated to prisons in terms of expectation of privacy. Thus, a student does not lose all rights to privacy by bringing personal property into the school.

Search Is Reasonable

Finding that state investigative activity is a search only begins the analysis. The Court in *T.L.O.* held that while the school official's opening of a student's purse was a search, it was conducted consistent with the Fourth Amendment because the search was reasonable under the circumstances. The high state interest in regulating school discipline, even when balanced against a student's expectation of privacy, led the Court to conclude that the search was reasonable even though conducted without a warrant, and on the basis of reasonable suspicion rather than the higher standard of probable cause. See the further discussion of school searches later in this Outline.

K. Application of *Katz:* Government Employees

In *O'Connor v. Ortega*, 480 U.S. 709, 107 S.Ct. 1492, 94 L.Ed.2d 714 (1987), the Court rejected the state's argument that Government employees can never have an expectation of privacy in their place of work. While there was no opinion for the Court, all Justices agreed that where the employee keeps a private container such as a desk or a file cabinet, a Government intrusion into that area will constitute a search. A majority of the Court further held that an employee's office itself would be protected by the Fourth Amendment, unless the office was subject to unrestricted public access. Four members of the Court found it unnecessary to determine whether an employee could have a reasonable expectation of privacy in his office, as distinct from the closed containers therein.

Search Is Reasonable

Like *T.L.O.*, the finding that the conduct in *O'Connor* was a search was only the beginning of the analysis. A majority of the Court balanced the state and the individual interests at stake and found the search of the employee's desk and file cabinets to be reasonable, even though it was conducted without a warrant, and was made with only reasonable suspicion as opposed to probable cause to believe the employee had engaged in misconduct.

III. The Probable Cause Requirement

Probable cause is a standard of proof of criminal activity, which justifies a search or seizure. Even though a citizen may be innocent of wrongdoing, a showing of probable cause is sufficient to permit intrusions into the citizen's interests in privacy and security. The legitimate state interests in investigating and prosecuting crime could be impaired if a standard of proof higher than probable cause were required before a search or seizure could even be conducted. *See Brodnicki v. City of Omaha,* 75 F.3d 1261 (8th Cir.1996) ("The officers were not required to conduct a mini-trial before arresting Brodnicki.") Thus, the probable cause standard strikes a balance between the rights of innocent citizens to privacy and security, and the interest of the state in investigating and prosecuting crime.

A. Standard of Proof Required for Probable Cause to Exist

The standard of proof required for probable cause is: enough particularized facts to lead a common sense person of reasonable caution to believe that there is a *fair probability* of criminal activity. *Illinois v. Gates,* 462 U.S. 213, 103 S.Ct. 2317, 76 L.Ed.2d 527 (1983).

1. No Requirement of Certainty

The Court in *Gates* emphasized that the "fair probability" standard is not especially strenuous. Proof beyond a reasonable doubt is not required; neither is proof by a preponderance of the evidence. Probable cause is a standard that permits investigations of suspects, and investigations are needed to allow the state to obtain proof beyond a reasonable doubt. *See Brodnicki v. City of Omaha,* 75 F.3d 1261 (8th Cir.1996) (There was probable cause to arrest a man for attempted kidnapping, based on the description of a nine-year-old girl, even though the man differed from the description as to weight, facial hair and hair color).

2. Plausible, Innocent Explanations Are Not Dispositive

Because the term "fair probability" is intentionally meant to be less than a preponderance, the fact that a citizen has plausible explanations for his activity does not preclude a finding of probable cause. It is only where the plausible explanations substantially outweigh the probability of criminal activity that the probable cause standard will not be met.

Example: A person sends a small package by way of an airline's "express overnight" service. The package is mailed in November, and on the package is written the message "Do not open until Christmas." The sender exhibits nervousness when arranging for the transport of the package. The sender tells the airline clerk that the package contains watches. But when the agent passes the package through the magnetometer, there is no indication that it contains anything metallic. The airline clerk notifies a law enforcement officer of all this information. The officer opens the package and finds narcotics. The court held that under the totality of circumstances, there was probable cause to open the package. Even though the package may well have contained a fruitcake, or a book, there were suspicious facts which, taken in their entirety, indicated a fair probability that the package was evidence of some criminal activity. These facts included: the nervousness of the sender; the sender's untruthful description of the contents of the package; and the implausibility of sending a package in November by overnight service if it truly was a Christmas present. *See United States v. Sullivan*, 544 F.Supp. 701 (D.Me.1982).

3. Officers Are Allowed to Make Reasonable Mistakes

Because the probable cause standard requires only a fair probability, it follows that officers need not be correct in their assessment of the facts. Arrests of the wrong person, and searches which uncover no incriminating evidence, are nonetheless permissible if the officer's mistake was reasonable.

Example: In *Hill v. California*, 401 U.S. 797, 91 S.Ct. 1106, 28 L.Ed.2d 484 (1971), two men driving Hill's car admitted that they and Hill had committed a robbery. Based upon the description the two gave of Hill, and verified by police records, police went to Hill's apartment and arrested a man who fit the description, but who claimed to be Miller. The arrestee was in fact Miller and not Hill. The Court nonetheless held that there was probable cause to arrest Miller even though he was the wrong man, and even though he protested his innocence. Miller's protestations did not preclude a finding of probable cause, since criminals commonly use aliases, and commonly protest their innocence. The Court stated that "sufficient probability, not certainty, is the touchstone of reasonableness under the Fourth Amendment."

4. Totality of Circumstances

The analysis of probable cause requires a cumulative look at all pertinent factors. Perhaps the defendant could come up with an innocent explanation for each factor, taken individually. But that will not suffice if all the factors taken together are indicative of criminal activity. Probable cause takes into account the cumulative effect of suspicious factors, since each may color the other.

Example: There are many legal reasons for a person to buy dry ice, acetone and a beaker; and there are many reasons for a substantial increase in the electrical bill of that person's house; and it is no crime for that person to associate with people who have been convicted in the past of manufacturing amphetamines. No single one of these factors is enough in itself to constitute a fair probability of criminal activity. But if all the factors are considered together, the entire submission is suspicious enough that probable cause will likely be found.

5. Deference to Police Officer's Expertise

The Supreme Court has stated that probable cause is a common sense standard. But while the Court looks at how a common sense person would evaluate the evidence, the experience and expertise of the officer is also taken into account. A fact which does not look suspicious at all to the untrained eye may be indicative of criminal activity to a person versed in how criminals operate. For instance, if the officer knows that a certain chemical or a certain smell is often associated with the manufacture of an illegal drug, that fact may be taken into account when probable cause is assessed by the officer, even though it is beyond the experience of the common person.

6. Probable Cause for an Arrest Different From the Charge on Which the Defendant Was Arrested

In *Devenpeck v. Alford*, 543 U.S. 146, 125 S.Ct. 588, 160 L.Ed.2d 537 (2004), a police officer believed that respondent had been impersonating a police officer and pulled over his car. The officer's supervisor arrested respondent for violating the state's privacy act after discovering that he had audiotaped their conversation during the stop. There was not probable cause to arrest respondent for violating the privacy act, but there was probable cause that he had impersonated a police officer and obstructed justice. The Supreme Court held that the offense establishing probable cause did not have to be "closely related" to the offense identified by the arresting officer at the time of arrest. The Court held that such a rule was inconsistent with its precedent that the officer's state of mind is irrelevant to probable cause. The Court noted that the "closely related offense" rule would not eliminate sham arrests and would cause officers to cease providing reasons for arrests, or to cite every class of offense for which probable cause could conceivably exist.

7. Collective Knowledge

The particular officer who conducts an arrest or search need not have personal knowledge of all the facts on which probable cause is based. Probable cause can be based on the *collective knowledge* of the police department. Thus, an officer who executes an arrest warrant supported by probable cause is acting legally even if he or she has no personal knowledge of the facts upon which the warrant is based. On the other hand, in order to be relied upon, the collective knowledge of the police must in fact equal probable cause. An officer can thus violate the Fourth Amendment by serving as an arresting or searching functionary, when the collective information of the department as a whole does not constitute probable cause. *See Whiteley v. Warden,* 401 U.S. 560, 91 S.Ct. 1031, 28 L.Ed.2d 306 (1971).

B. Generally Required for All Searches and Seizures

A search or seizure is presumptively unreasonable unless it is supported by probable cause and a warrant. But even if a search or seizure is conducted pursuant to an exception to the warrant requirement—such as the exigent circumstances exception—it must still be supported by probable cause, as a general rule. Otherwise, the officer would have an incentive to invoke an exception to the warrant requirement, and the Fourth Amendment's preference for warrants would be undermined.

1. Exceptions

The Court has found three exceptional situations where the Fourth Amendment does not require probable cause. (All these exceptions will be discussed in detail later in this Outline).

a. Seizures of Persons or Things Which Constitute a Limited Intrusion

Temporary and minimally invasive detentions of persons and things, which are necessary to conduct a preliminary investigation, are allowed upon a showing of reasonable suspicion, which is a lesser standard of proof than probable cause. *Terry v. Ohio, infra* (seizure of person); *United States v. Van Leeuwen, infra* (detention of package). The rationale is that the limited nature of the intrusion, and the legitimate law enforcement objective for making the intrusion, justify the police action on less than probable cause.

b. **Limited Searches to Protect the Officer From Harm**
An officer can, on reasonable suspicion instead of probable cause, conduct a limited search of a person, thing or premises in order to protect himself from bodily harm while he is conducting a legitimate investigation. *See Terry v. Ohio, infra* (frisk of person while conducting stop); *Michigan v. Long, infra* (cursory weapons check of automobile passenger compartment pursuant to traffic stop); *Maryland v. Buie, infra* (protective sweep of premises to search for persons who could injure police officers who are making a legal arrest).

c. **Search or Seizure Conducted for Special Needs Beyond Criminal Law Enforcement**
If the search or seizure is not conducted for purposes of criminal law enforcement but rather to effectuate some other governmental objective such as a regulatory interest, it can in most cases be conducted on less than probable cause. *See New Jersey v. T.L.O., infra* (search of students to maintain school discipline).

2. **All Searches for Criminal Law Enforcement Purposes Require Probable Cause**
None of the above exceptions apply to a search conducted by law enforcement officers for the very purpose of enforcing the criminal law. The Supreme Court has consistently held that such searches must be supported by probable cause. It has rejected arguments, for instance, that a search by law enforcement officers for evidence of a crime could be conducted on less than probable cause so long as it was minimally intrusive. *See Arizona v. Hicks*, 480 U.S. 321, 107 S.Ct. 1149, 94 L.Ed.2d 347 (1987) (lifting turntable to check serial numbers is a search which must be supported by probable cause). *But see U.S. v. Knights, infra.* Some lower courts have failed to follow what appears to be a clear statement from the Court in *Hicks*. *See United States v. Concepcion*, 942 F.2d 1170 (7th Cir.1991) (officers took a key found on the defendant, and inserted it into a lock on a door to an apartment in which drugs had been found; while this was a search, it could be conducted on less than probable cause, because the search was minimally intrusive).

C.   Application of the Probable Cause Standard to Questions of Identity

One circumstance in which a question of probable cause arises is where a crime has been committed, but it is unclear whether the suspect to be arrested is the perpetrator.

1.   Particularized Information Required

Probable cause as to identity must be based on specific information which ties a suspect to a crime.

a.   Statistics

A pure statistical analysis is not determinative of probable cause. For example, statistics may indicate that one out of five people in a certain area is a criminal; but this does not allow the police to randomly arrest every fifth person in the area. *See Wong Sun v. United States*, 371 U.S. 471, 83 S.Ct. 407, 9 L.Ed.2d 441 (1963) (person cannot be arrested on a pure statistical probability). The question is, how particularized must the information be?

b.   Ownership and Control

In *Maryland v. Pringle*, 540 U.S. 366, 124 S.Ct. 795, 157 L.Ed.2d 769 (2003), the Supreme Court unanimously held that it is reasonable for an officer to find probable cause to arrest all of the passengers of a car containing cocaine based on the inference that the occupants had knowledge of and exercised dominion and control over the cocaine. In *Pringle*, a police officer stopped a car for speeding at three o'clock in the morning, and the driver consented to a search of the car. The officer discovered $763 in the glove compartment and five plastic baggies of cocaine in the back seat armrest. Police arrested all three occupants, including Pringle, who sat in the front passenger seat. The Court noted that probable cause justifying the search or seizure of a person must be particularized with respect to that person, quoting *Ybarra v. Illinois, infra*. However, citing *Wyoming v. Houghton, infra*, the Court noted that the money was found directly in front of Pringle and the cocaine was accessible to all of the occupants. Thus the officer's inference that all of the passengers were engaged in the common enterprise of concealing the fruits of their wrongdoing was a legitimate one.

2.   Fitting a Description

Probable cause requires a case-by-case approach, and as such it is difficult to draw conclusions as to the facts necessary to justify an arrest of a person on the ground that he was identified as the perpetrator of a crime. Nonetheless, since the standard is only one of fair probability, a suspect's correspondence to a relatively specific description will go far toward a showing of probable cause.

> *Example:*   An officer reports a drug transaction in the area of 48th Street and Ninth Avenue in Manhattan. This is an area known for drug trafficking, and the residents are predominantly Hispanic. The officer describes one of the perpetrators as "[h]ispanic male in his 20's, black leather jacket, grey pants with a comb in back pocket, and a white v-neck shirt." Ten minutes later, another officer arrests Valez, who is walking in the area. Valez fits the description, and the arresting officer searches Valez and finds cocaine. The officer who originally reported the drug transaction later comes by and states that Valez is not the perpetrator: Valez had facial hair while the perpetrator did not. The court held that the arrest and the resulting search were valid, because the arrest was supported by probable cause. The suspect fit a description that was not impermissibly general, and he was found in the area. *United States v. Valez,* 796 F.2d 24 (2d Cir.1986).

3. Prior Criminal Record

The state's case on probable cause as to identity is made significantly stronger if the suspect who fits a general description also has a prior criminal record. This information adds to the fair probability that the suspect was the perpetrator, especially if the defendant has been previously convicted of a crime similar to that currently being investigated. Rules of evidence (such as the rule excluding from trial some prior crimes of a criminal defendant) do not apply to a probable cause determination.

D. Application of Probable Cause Standard to Equivocal Conduct

Another circumstance in which a probable cause question arises is where it is unclear whether a crime has been committed or is being committed at all. In these instances, the officer has a specific person in mind as a perpetrator, but is not certain whether there is any criminal activity afoot. For example, suppose that an officer on patrol sees a person at 2:00 a.m., in a high crime area, pushing a shopping cart containing a television and a stereo. The question is not the identity of the perpetrator; the question is whether there has been a crime.

1. **Innocent Explanations for Equivocal Activity**

While each case of equivocal conduct depends on a common sense view of the particular facts, this much can be said: the presence of an innocent explanation for the conduct is clearly not enough to eliminate probable cause. Most courts will find probable cause if there is some conduct which a common sense person would think highly suspect, even though an innocent explanation for the conduct is also plausible. The real question is whether plausible innocent explanations substantially outweigh the likelihood of criminality.

Example: Acting on a tip, officers investigated a secluded farmhouse. They detected the odor of phenylacetic acid and of ether, two chemicals commonly used in the manufacture of amphetamines. The next day, they found that the farmhouse had been boarded up, and the only opening other than the doors was a large vent equipped with a fan. A pickup truck entered the driveway of the farmhouse, its driver honked the horn, and the vehicle remained there for five minutes before someone came from the farmhouse and entered the passenger side of the truck. The officers followed the pickup truck for several miles, to a point where it appeared to be leaving the area. They stopped the truck and placed the driver and passenger under arrest. The driver challenged the arrest as lacking probable cause. The court rejected the driver's argument. While there is no probable cause to arrest someone merely because he associates with a criminal, the court found more than mere association in this case. The farmhouse was in an isolated location. The driver drove directly up to the farmhouse in a manner that indicated he knew his destination and was not lost. He did not appear to be seeking directions, or to be engaged in an innocent errand like delivering milk. He blew the truck's horn as if he were expected, and someone came from the house in response. The truck appeared to be leaving the area, and the officer could fairly presume that the truck was loaded with drugs. *United States v. Raborn*, 872 F.2d 589 (5th Cir.1989).

2. **First Amendment Considerations**

In *New York v. P.J. Video, Inc.*, 475 U.S. 868, 106 S.Ct. 1610, 89 L.Ed.2d 871 (1986), the Court held that First Amendment considerations do not require a standard of proof higher than probable cause before a search may be conducted of speech-related material. The warrants at issue in *P.J. Video* authorized the seizure of certain films that were allegedly obscene. The affidavits on which the warrants were based described sex acts occurring in excerpted scenes of the films. The defendant argued that the affidavits merely described the sex scenes, but did not establish probable cause that the film as a whole lacked artistic merit. The Court rejected this argument, reasoning that since so many sex scenes were described in films that lasted from sixty to ninety minutes, there was a fair probability that *there was little other than sex scenes in the films*, and that the *films* therefore as a whole lacked artistic value. An actual assertion in the warrant application as to the lack of artistic value was held not required, given the minimal standard of the "fair probability" test.

E. Probable Cause as Applied to Location

A third situation in which the probable cause question arises is where officials suspect that a person to be arrested, or evidence of a crime, is located in a particular place. If investigation of such a place would be a search, the officers must have probable cause to believe that the person to be arrested or the evidence to be seized is located in the place to be searched. A problem may arise when a piece of evidence could be located in one of several places, but could not be in two locations at the same time. For example, the suspect's murder weapon might be in his car, his office, or his home, but it cannot be in all three places. In this situation, the courts have held that there is probable cause to search in each location, even though they are mutually exclusive, so long as there is a *logical nexus* between the crime and the location. This nexus need not be based on direct observation, but can be based on the type of crime, the nature of the items, and logical inferences as to where evidence would be located. So for example, in a fraud case, where the suspect is a stockbroker, there will generally be probable cause to search for a "smoking gun" document in the suspect's office, home, and briefcase, as well as in other places which have a logical nexus with the fraud. *See United States v. Jones*, 994 F.2d 1051 (3d Cir. 1993)(items taken in robbery were the kinds of things criminals might keep in their homes).

F. The Use of Hearsay in the Probable Cause Determination

Where probable cause is based solely on an officer's observation and the inferences derived therefrom, the only question is whether all the facts known lead to a fair probability of criminal activity. However, where officers do not have personal knowledge of the facts, but are instead relying upon information from other parties, there is also a question of whether the "facts" related by such third parties are reliable enough to be credited in the probable cause determination. Probable cause does not exist if the "facts" related are actually false. If the officer or magistrate relies on other sources, he or she is relying on hearsay information. As in the course on Evidence, hearsay statements, to be credited, must be evaluated to determine whether they are reliable.

1. Former Two–Pronged Test for Evaluating Hearsay

To insure that the magistrate—or the reviewing court if a warrant was not obtained—had some way to make an independent determination of the reliability of hearsay information, the court in *Aguilar v. Texas,* 378 U.S. 108, 84 S.Ct. 1509, 12 L.Ed.2d 723 (1964), and *Spinelli v. United States,* 393 U.S. 410, 89 S.Ct. 584, 21 L.Ed.2d 637 (1969), imposed what came to be known as *the Aguilar–Spinelli two-pronged test* for structuring the analysis of probable cause. The Supreme Court later rejected the two-pronged test in favor of a less structured totality of circumstances approach. *See Illinois v. Gates,* 462 U.S. 213, 103 S.Ct. 2317, 76 L.Ed.2d 527 (1983). However, as the Court in *Gates* recognized, the two-pronged test is still a helpful means by which to evaluate an informant's hearsay, and lower courts have used the structure as a means of evaluation, though not as a dispositive test. Consequently, it is necessary to understand the structure set forth in *Aguilar* and *Spinelli.*

2. First Prong: Reliable Informant

Under *Aguilar–Spinelli,* the person providing the information upon which the warrant is based must be reliable and credible. The person providing information could be found reliable on one of several grounds:

a. Police Officers

Under *Aguilar–Spinelli,* police officers were presumed to be telling the truth when reporting facts based on their own personal knowledge to other officers or to the magistrate.

b. Citizen–Informants

Where police obtain information from non-criminal sources, such as ordinary citizens, or victims or witnesses of crimes, these sources are presumed reliable. It is a reasonable presumption that a law-abiding citizen would tell the truth to a police officer.

c. Informants With Track Records

Criminals and ex-criminals working as police informants are not presumed reliable under either *Aguilar–Spinelli* or the later test of

Gates. Under *Aguilar–Spinelli* and *Gates,* the presumption is that such an informant is prone to lie, and hence was not credible. However, this presumption can be overcome in a number of ways. One way is by a showing that the informant had given reliable information on numerous occasions in the past. An inference of truthfulness in the current case can be drawn from a past record of truthfulness.

d. Declarations Against Interest

Under *Aguilar–Spinelli* and the more permissive *Gates* test, the informant can overcome the presumption of untruthfulness by describing criminal activity in which he participated, which if true would subject him to penal liability. Under these circumstances, courts draw an inference that the informant would not have related such self-inculpatory facts unless they were true. *See United States v. Harris,* 403 U.S. 573, 91 S.Ct. 2075, 29 L.Ed.2d 723 (1971) (informant's statement that he had purchased illegal liquor from Harris was sufficiently disserving to the informant to be deemed reliable).

e. Anonymous Informants

Under both *Aguilar–Spinelli* and *Gates,* if the informant is anonymous, reliability cannot be presumed. There is no way to know whether an anonymous informant is an ordinary citizen, or a person steeped in criminality. Even if the informant is an ordinary citizen, anonymity is a protection against any sanction for lying to the police, and consequently the anonymous informant may tell a lie.

3. Second Prong: Personal Knowledge

Even if the information comes from a reliable source, that source may not have personal knowledge of the facts attested to.

a. Direct Statement of Personal Knowledge

If the informant stated to the police officer that he heard or saw the information he was relating, such a direct statement of knowledge satisfies the personal knowledge prong of *Aguilar–Spinelli,* and goes far toward establishing probable cause under the *Gates* totality of circumstances test.

b. Self–Verifying Detail

Even if there is no direct statement of personal knowledge, a statement containing a wealth of detail can create an inference of personal knowledge. For example, an informant might say: "Joe keeps his drugs in a striped suitcase inside a secret compartment behind his bookshelf, which is opened by pulling out the third book on the top left shelf." The informant has not stated how he came by his information. However, the wealth of detail creates a fair inference of "inside information"—knowledge either from personal observation or from the defendant himself. As stated in *Spinelli,* in order for detail to be considered "self-verifying" and thus to satisfy the personal knowledge prong, the detail must be more than would be imparted by "barroom rumor."

4. Independent Prongs

Under *Aguilar–Spinelli,* the veracity prong and the personal knowledge prong were analyzed as totally separate and independent from each other. Thus, even if an informant had a previous track record of truthfulness, his information could not be credited for a warrant application unless he was speaking from a proper basis of knowledge. Conversely, a statement clearly based on personal knowledge could not be credited if the source of the information was unreliable.

5. Corroboration

Under *Aguilar–Spinelli,* a defect in one or both prongs could be remedied if the police obtained significant independent evidence corroborating the information related by the informant. However, the corroborative evidence had to be *substantial,* or corroborative of *suspicious facts* in order to shore up a defect in one of the prongs.

Example: In *Spinelli,* the officer sought a warrant to search Spinelli's apartment for evidence of a bookmaking operation. The application was based in major part on a tip from an informant, who related that Spinelli was a gambler who had two phone lines in his apartment; the informant gave the phone number for each line. The warrant application did not state how the informant came upon this information, nor on what basis the informant concluded that Spinelli was a gambler. Nor was there a showing that the informant had a previous track record of reliable tips. However, the police determined through independent investigation that the informant was correct as to the two phones and separate phone numbers. The Court, however, found this information to be insufficient corroboration for either prong. The information corroborated was neither substantial nor in any way suspicious or incriminating. The Court contrasted its prior decision of *Draper v. United States,* 358 U.S. 307, 79 S.Ct. 329, 3 L.Ed.2d 327 (1959), in which a reliable informant stated that Draper would be arriving on a certain train wearing distinct clothing; the officers met that train and saw a person disembark with the exact unique clothing that the informant had described in advance. In *Spinelli,* the Court found that the corroboration in *Draper* was substantial enough to shore up a defect in the basis of knowledge prong.

G. Rejection of the Two–Pronged Test and Adoption of the Totality of Circumstances Approach

In *Illinois v. Gates, supra,* the Court rejected the *Aguilar–Spinelli* test as a controlling framework for evaluating hearsay information in determining probable cause. The *Aguilar–Spinelli* two-pronged approach is still used by courts after *Gates* to analyze a hearsay problem, and according to *Gates* the two-pronged test is still relevant. But the Court in *Gates* rejected the notion that the *Aguilar–Spinelli* test had to be satisfied before a hearsay statement could be credited toward probable cause. The Court stated that the correct approach is whether the judge, using common sense, and taking into account the fact that there is a hearsay problem, could find under the totality of circumstances that probable cause exists.

1. Facts of *Gates*

Police in *Gates* received an anonymous letter that Lance and Sue Gates were drug traffickers. The letter alleged that the Gates' were about to obtain drugs in Florida and bring them home to Illinois, and it described their itinerary: Sue would drive their car down to Florida on a certain day; Lance would take a certain flight down to meet her; Lance then would drive back with drugs in the trunk; and Sue would fly back. The police checked out this information. They found that Lance had booked a flight to West Palm Beach.

Lance was followed to a hotel room registered in Sue's name. The next morning, Lance and a woman (later identified as Sue) began to drive northbound on the freeway, in a car registered to Lance. Based upon the above information, the officer obtained a warrant from the magistrate to search the Gates' house and car. When the Gates' got back to Illinois, their house and car were searched pursuant to the warrant, and drugs were found in both places.

2. **Lower Court Analysis**

The Illinois courts excluded the evidence on the ground that the informant's tip, even though corroborated to some extent, failed under *Aguilar–Spinelli*. The informant was anonymous, and so there was no presumption of reliability. Nor did the informant's letter indicate that it was based on personal knowledge. Thus the tip on its face failed both prongs of the *Aguilar–Spinelli* test. The lower courts rejected the Government's argument that the corroboration of the Gates' travel plans was sufficient to shore up the defects in the tip itself. According to the Illinois courts, the corroboration was not substantial, since it merely concerned the Gates' itinerary, and was not even completely correct as to that: the tip stated that Sue would fly back when in fact she did not. Nor were the facts corroborated sufficiently suspicious to shore up the *Spinelli* prongs.

3. **Analysis in *Gates***

The Court in *Gates* rejected the *Aguilar–Spinelli* two-pronged test on the ground that it imposed an unduly rigid, technical and legalistic structure on what ought to be a common sense evaluation. The Court stated that probable cause is a standard to be applied in light of a common sense evaluation of the totality of the circumstances. It followed that information supporting probable cause—even hearsay information—should be evaluated the way that a common sense person would. A common sense person looking at an informant's hearsay information would not separate it out neatly into "prongs;" would not evaluate the sufficiency of corroboration in the same manner as a schooled appellate court; and would not disregard the hearsay upon the mere fact that there was a technical defect in one or the other prong. Rather, a common sense person would look at the totality of information, considering the fact that some of it was hearsay, and make a common sense determination of the reliability and sufficiency of the information supporting probable cause. Thus, the question after *Gates* for informant's hearsay is not "does it satisfy the two-pronged test?" but rather "how would it strike a common sense person?"

4. **Dissent in *Gates***

Justice Brennan contended that the majority had confused the relevant standard of proof—probable cause, which requires a common sense evaluation of the facts—with the *permissible sources of proof,* i.e. whether certain information is even reliable enough to count as a fact toward probable cause. Justice Brennan asserted that there is no "common sense" way to evaluate the reliability of hearsay; rather, legal standards were needed so that the magistrate could properly assess whether the hearsay was sufficiently reliable to count toward probable cause.

H. Impact of *Gates*

To determine the effect of *Gates* on probable cause determinations it is necessary to apply the two-pronged test and see how it differs from the *Gates* test in concrete cases. Most courts still apply the two-pronged test as a non-dispositive guideline to evaluating hearsay from informants.

1. No Change in Many Cases

In many cases since *Gates*, probable cause would be found even under the *Aguilar–Spinelli* two-pronged test. If *Aguilar–Spinelli* is satisfied, it follows that *Gates* is as well, since the *Gates* test is avowedly more permissive than the former test.

Example: An informant whose information has led to convictions on four past occasions tells the officer that "Little Mike" will be carrying illegal weapons to a meeting of the Hells Angels. The informant provides a detailed description of the car, of the weapons in the car, and of "Little Mike's" itinerary. Under these circumstances, probable cause would be found under *Aguilar–Spinelli*. The informant has a track record of reliability, and has given a wealth of detail which creates an inference of personal knowledge. Accordingly, the more permissive common sense standard of *Gates* is automatically satisfied. *See United States v. Lessard,* 720 F.2d 1000 (8th Cir.1983).

2. A Tip Which Fails Both Prongs Cannot Itself Constitute Probable Cause

If an informant's tip fails both of the *Aguilar–Spinelli prongs, and there is no police corroboration of the information,* then the tip is insufficient for probable cause even under the more permissive *Gates* standard.

Example: This is shown by the facts and analysis in *Gates*. The tip was from an anonymous informant, and thus did not of itself satisfy the *Aguilar–Spinelli* veracity prong. Nor did the informant relate his basis of knowledge, and the detail in the tip was not sufficient to be deemed self-verifying. Justice Rehnquist stated that the tip itself would not satisfy probable cause even under the common sense, totality of the circumstances approach mandated by *Gates.* Justice Rehnquist also gave another example of a tip failing both of the *Aguilar–Spinelli* prongs which would be insufficient under *Gates: the barebones affidavit.* An affidavit such as "a reliable informant told me that Joe Smith was selling illegal drugs" provides the magistrate with absolutely no way to determine whether the information is reliable, and consequently fails both *Aguilar–Spinelli* and *Gates. See United States v. Wilhelm,* 80 F.3d 116 (4th Cir.1996) (anonymous informant's conclusory statements that defendants are dealing drugs out of their house held insufficient to establish probable cause).

3. Strong Showing on One Prong Can Make up for a Weak Showing on the Other

The Court in *Gates* stated that a common sense approach would not separate the prongs and require that each be satisfied in all cases; a common sense person could believe hearsay as itself sufficient for probable cause when one prong is especially strong and the other prong is somewhat weak. The strength in one could make up for the weakness in the other. Thus, if the informant has been unusually reliable in the past, his failure to set forth the specific basis for his knowledge or to give minute detail should not necessarily preclude a finding of probable cause. Conversely, even if there is some reason to doubt the informant's reliability, that doubt can be overcome by an especially strong showing that the informant observed the event first-hand. Thus, *even without corroboration,* a tip which is especially strong on one prong, and not absolutely deficient on the other, can itself satisfy probable cause.

Examples: Phillips' estranged wife goes to the police and tells them, in specific and copious detail, about Phillips' drug transaction, including where exactly in the home the drugs are stored. The wife admits that she has "an axe to grind" against Phillips, and it would please her to see him get in trouble with the law. A court after *Gates* found this tip sufficient in itself to constitute probable cause. The court recognized that the informant's reliability was somewhat suspect given her motives for vengeance. However, her credibility was not as questionable as a criminal paid informant, so the tip was found not completely lacking on the veracity prong. To the extent the wife did not satisfy the veracity prong, the court found that the defect was more than offset by the strong showing on the basis of knowledge prong. *See United States v. Phillips*, 727 F.2d 392 (5th Cir.1984). *See also Massachusetts v. Upton*, 466 U.S. 727, 104 S.Ct. 2085, 80 L.Ed.2d 721 (1984) (probable cause found on basis of tip from an informant who wanted to "burn" the defendant).

An informant with a track record of reliable tips informs the police that marijuana is growing on Carter's property. The informant gives the general locations and dimensions of the field, but does not say how he came by his information. After *Gates*, a reviewing court found that this tip, standing alone, established probable cause. The court noted that there was a minor defect in the basis of knowledge prong, since the informant did not say that he had visited the field. However, the informant did give some detail about the field, though perhaps not enough to constitute "self-verifying" detail under *Aguilar–Spinelli*. Still, the court reasoned that any defect in the basis of knowledge prong was overcome by the strong showing of the informant's veracity. The court concluded that a common sense person would credit the informant's tip as true. *See Carter v. United States*, 729 F.2d 935 (8th Cir.1984).

4. The Expanded Role of Corroboration

After *Gates*, even if the tip is insufficient to establish probable cause, some corroboration of the tip by police investigation will ordinarily allow a common sense person to believe the informant's report of criminal activity. This is where the *Gates* totality of circumstances approach has had its largest impact. Under *Aguilar–Spinelli*, corroboration could shore up a defective tip, but only if the corroboration was itself substantial (not just phone numbers as in *Spinelli)* or if the corroborated facts were themselves highly suspicious. Moreover, if there were discrepancies between the tip and the corroborated facts (e.g., the tip indicated travel plans different from the travel which actually occurred) this would count heavily against crediting the tip. After *Gates*, the function of corroboration is simply to help a common sense person determine, without regard to specific defects in specific prongs, whether the informant is telling the truth. The question under *Gates* is: Would the common sense person, suspicious of the tip because it is hearsay, feel sufficiently assured by the fact that police investigation found that the tip was true in at least some respects? The answer to that question after *Gates* is ordinarily "yes."

Example: In *Gates,* the police checked out the travel plans of the Gates. They found that the informant correctly related some aspects of the travel plans: that Sue would drive to Florida by herself and rent a room, and that Lance would fly down to meet her on a certain day, and drive the car back immediately. But the investigation also showed that the tip was incorrect in at least one respect: the informant said that Sue would fly back when in fact she did not. The corroboration in *Gates* would probably not have been sufficient under *Spinelli,* since it did not deal with any obviously suspicious activity, (as the dissenters pointed out, at the time the warrant was issued, the police did not know that the Gates' were driving immediately back to their home), nor did it corroborate a significant portion of the facts related in the tip. Also under *Spinelli,* the discrepancies would weigh heavily against both the veracity and basis of the informant. Nonetheless, in *Gates* the Court concluded that a common sense person, evaluating the tip together with the corroboration, would conclude that the informant knew basically what was going on, and appeared to be telling the truth. The corroboration in *Gates* sufficiently reduced the risk of a total untruth, since, in common sense, the fact that the informant knew some facts made it more likely that he knew the important incriminating fact—that Lance and Sue were transporting drugs. *See also United States v. Murphy,* 69 F.3d 237 (8th Cir.1995) (informant gave tip that a suspect who had just been released from prison after a murder conviction was in possession of a lot of weapons at a certain address; the officer investigated and found that the suspect had in fact just been released from prison, and that he did in fact live at that address; this corroboration was sufficient to constitute probable cause after *Gates*).

a.   Corroboration of Innocent Activity

The Court in *Gates* held that corroboration could be sufficient to support a tip even though the activity corroborated could be considered completely innocent. According to the Court, the innocent nature of the corroborated facts would not prevent a common sense person from concluding that the informant was correct in his assertion about criminal activity. Thus in *Gates* it did not matter that the travel plans corroborated by the officers could well have been made by tourists rather than drug dealers. The function of corroboration is to provide some assurance that the informant is telling the truth and knows what he is talking about; and the *Gates* Court reasoned that this function could be satisfied even if the facts corroborated give no hint that criminal activity is afoot. The tip itself can then explain why the facts, though apparently innocent, are indicative of criminality.

5. Strict Scrutiny of the Magistrate's Determination Is No Longer Permitted

According to *Gates,* one of the defects of the *Aguilar–Spinelli* approach was that reviewing courts reviewed magistrates' determinations in an excessively legalistic and rigid manner. In response, the Court in *Gates* held that a reviewing court is not allowed to strictly scrutinize a magistrate's determination of probable cause. The standard of review after *Gates* is deferential: the reviewing court determines only whether the magistrate had a *substantial basis* for finding probable cause, and for crediting an informant's hearsay. Put another way, the question for the reviewing court is: Could any reasonable person have found that the hearsay was reliable and that the facts indicated a fair probability of criminal activity?

6. Deferential Review in Warrantless Search Cases

Lower courts have read *Gates* to mean that the same deferential standard of review of magistrates' determinations should also apply to a court's review of a police officer's assessment of probable cause, in cases where the officer acts pursuant to an exception to the warrant requirement (e.g., if there are exigent circumstances). Thus, the courts will not second-guess an officer's reliance on an informant's tip, so long as the officer had a substantial basis for crediting the hearsay.

I. *Gates* Rejected by a Number of State Courts

At least eight states have rejected *Gates* as a matter of state law, concluding that its treatment of hearsay is unacceptably shapeless and permissive. These courts argue that the *Spinelli* test, if not applied hypertechnically, is a good structure for solving the legal problem presented when hearsay information is offered to show probable cause. *See, e.g., People v. Johnson,* 66 N.Y.2d 398,

497 N.Y.S.2d 618, 488 N.E.2d 439 (1985). Remember that a state court, construing its own state's constitution, can provide for more protections than are granted by the Federal Constitution.

J. Disclosure of Informant's Identity

Where probable cause is based in whole or in part on an informant's information, the defendant will often seek disclosure of the informant's identity at a suppression hearing. Defendants claim that such disclosure is required in order to assure that the informer was in fact reliable (for instance, that he could have witnessed what he said he did), and indeed to assure that the officer is not just *inventing an informant*.

1. Disclosure Is Not Generally Required

In *McCray v. Illinois*, 386 U.S. 300, 87 S.Ct. 1056, 18 L.Ed.2d 62 (1967), the Court held that disclosure of an informant's identity at a suppression hearing is ordinarily not required. The Court reasoned that it did not matter whether the informant was actually telling the truth to the police officer. The relevant question for probable cause was whether the officer could reasonably believe that the informant was telling the truth. The Court also noted that the state had a legitimate interest in protecting the confidentiality of its informants.

2. Where Officer's Testimony Is Not Credible

If it appears that the officer is not being truthful about whether an informant even existed, the court may in its discretion compel production of the informant. This discretionary power helps to ensure that officers will not simply manufacture probable cause by creating fictional informants.

3. In Camera Proceedings

Many courts protect against the problem of police perjury by requiring disclosure of the informant's identity at an in camera proceeding. The in camera proceeding is conducted outside the presence of defendant and his counsel; however, the judge is given access to the informant. In this way, police perjury can be uncovered while the state's interest in confidentiality is preserved. A court will generally order an in camera proceeding only upon a substantial showing by the defendant that the existence of an informant is in doubt.

K. Police Misrepresentation of Facts Constituting Probable Cause

Even if an affidavit submitted by police officers to the magistrate states facts sufficient to constitute probable cause, there may be a question of whether the "facts" in the affidavit are true or just made up by the officers.

1. *Franks* Hearing

If the defendant makes a substantial showing that a false statement was included in the affidavit, *and that the officer included the information with knowledge or reckless disregard of its falsity,* then the defendant is entitled to a hearing to prove his allegations. If at the hearing, the defendant proves his allegations by a preponderance of the evidence, then the misstatements must be struck from the affidavit, and the court must determine whether the remaining information in the affidavit establishes probable cause. *See Franks v. Delaware,* 438 U.S. 154, 98 S.Ct. 2674, 57 L.Ed.2d 667 (1978).

2. No Relief for Negligent Misstatements

The Supreme Court in *Franks* held that if the misstatement in the affidavit was the result of mere negligence, the defendant is not entitled to relief. Consequently, *Franks* gives a very limited remedy to defendants: they must show not only that a fact in the affidavit is untrue, but also that the officer included it in the affidavit knowing or having reckless disregard for its falsity.

3. Remaining Information May Still Constitute Probable Cause

Even if there are intentional or reckless misstatements in the affidavit, the resulting warrant may still be valid. So long as the remaining information constitutes probable cause, the Fourth Amendment is not violated. In other words, the Court in *Franks* gave protection only as to *material* misstatements.

IV. Obtaining a Valid Search Warrant

Generally speaking, the Fourth Amendment requires every search or seizure to be made pursuant to a warrant issued upon probable cause. A warrant is a document issued by a judicial officer, authorizing a law enforcement official to make a search or seizure. The judicial officer is usually a magistrate, and we will use that term here generically to refer to any judicial officer who issues a warrant. The following section describes the procedural prerequisites for obtaining a valid search warrant.

A. Neutral and Detached Magistrate

The rationale of the warrant requirement is to interpose an unbiased judicial official between the citizen and the police officer, because the police officer is in the competitive enterprise of ferreting out crime, and may, because of that, reach mistaken conclusions about the existence of probable cause.

1. Cannot Be a Law Enforcement Official

In *Coolidge v. New Hampshire,* 403 U.S. 443, 91 S.Ct. 2022, 29 L.Ed.2d 564 (1971), the state Attorney General issued a search warrant, as authorized by state law. The state Attorney General is the highest law enforcement official in the state, and was in fact conducting the investigation at issue in *Coolidge.* The Court held that the warrant was invalid since the state Attorney General could not be considered neutral and detached.

2. Conducting the Search Destroys Neutrality

In *Lo-Ji Sales, Inc. v. New York,* 442 U.S. 319, 99 S.Ct. 2319, 60 L.Ed.2d 920 (1979), the magistrate issued a warrant to seize pornographic books from a store. Then the magistrate accompanied law enforcement officers to the store, and actively participated in the search by examining items in the store to determine whether they should be seized. The Court held that the active participation of the magistrate destroyed his neutrality and thus resulted in an illegal search and seizure.

3. Contingent Fee Destroys Neutrality

In *Connally v. Georgia,* 429 U.S. 245, 97 S.Ct. 546, 50 L.Ed.2d 444 (1977), a magistrate received $5 for every warrant he issued, but nothing for any warrant application he denied. The Court held that such a magistrate was not neutral and detached as required by the Fourth Amendment: his salary was contingent upon issuing warrants, and such a pecuniary interest could impermissibly affect his impartial judgment.

4. "Rubber Stamp"

A magistrate who issues a warrant without reading the warrant or the supporting application is not considered neutral and detached as required by the Fourth Amendment. Such a magistrate has become nothing more than a rubber stamp for law enforcement. *See United States v. Decker,* 956 F.2d 773 (8th Cir.1992) (magistrate loses neutral and detached status when he fails to read a warrant because he was "intrigued" by the manner in which the officer became suspicious of the defendant).

5. Need Not Be a Lawyer

In *Shadwick v. City of Tampa,* 407 U.S. 345, 92 S.Ct. 2119, 32 L.Ed.2d 783 (1972), the Court held that a municipal court clerk, who was authorized by state law to issue warrants but who was not a lawyer, could constitutionally issue arrest warrants for municipal violations.

a. Federal Courts

The ruling in *Shadwick* authorizing non-lawyers to issue warrants has no bearing on Federal practice. In the Federal courts, magistrates are lawyers who are appointed by the district courts under 18 U.S.C.A. § 3060.

6. Must Be Competent to Determine Probable Cause

The magistrate must have the intellectual ability to determine probable cause. However, since probable cause is a common sense standard, there would appear to be no intellectual prerequisite or educational credential that is required as a matter of constitutional law. While *Shadwick* dealt with arrest warrants for minor offenses, the Court in *Illinois v. Gates, supra,* assumed that non-lawyers may issue search warrants for major crimes as well.

7. Magistrate Decisions

There is no requirement that a magistrate give reasons for finding probable cause or for rejecting a warrant application.

B. Probable Cause Based Only on Facts Presented to the Magistrate

One rationale behind the warrant requirement is that it forces the officer to establish a record supporting probable cause *before* a search occurs. This prevents the officer from "working backward:" i.e., having found the evidence, an unscrupulous officer might construct a factual scenario by which one could have obtained probable cause before the search. To protect against this danger, probable cause must be judged solely by the information presented to the magistrate in the warrant application.

1. Affidavits

A warrant is ordinarily obtained by submitting, to the magistrate, an affidavit of all the facts supporting probable cause. Some courts have held that probable cause must be determined solely on the basis of the information submitted in the affidavit. *See* Federal Rule of Criminal Procedure 41(c). Other courts have held that the affidavit can be supplemented by sworn oral testimony before the magistrate.

2. Telephone Warrants

Federal Rule of Criminal Procedure 41(c) authorizes a warrant to be obtained upon oral testimony communicated by telephone or other means, "if the circumstances make it reasonable to dispense with an affidavit." However, a warrant cannot be obtained by mere telephone conversation. The officer must prepare a written "duplicate original warrant," and then read that warrant verbatim to the magistrate. The magistrate then must transcribe what is read in order to prepare an original warrant. A record must be made of the telephone conversation. Those who give testimony over the telephone are sworn by the magistrate. Most states have a rule of criminal procedure permitting telephone warrants as well.

3. Warrant Is Obtained *ex parte*

The defendant is not present at a warrant application, and does not at that point get an opportunity to challenge the police officer's submission on probable cause. However, the validity of the warrant can be attacked at a suppression hearing before trial.

C. Particular Description of Place to Be Searched

Even if there is probable cause to search a certain location, a warrant authorizing a search is invalid if the location is not described with reasonable particularity.

1. Rationale

The colonial experience with general warrants was the major reason for including the Fourth Amendment in the Bill of Rights. The particularity requirement, as applied to the location of a search, is designed to protect against the use of a warrant as a general warrant.

2. Reasonable Particularity

The Fourth Amendment requires that the warrant must set forth the location of the place to be searched with *reasonable particularity*. Technical precision is not required in all cases. The degree of particularity which is reasonable depends on the nature of the place to be searched, and on the information that an officer could reasonably obtain about the location.

Example: In urban areas, a street address and, if applicable, an apartment number reasonably limit the discretion of the executing officer, and are reasonable to obtain. If the officer has probable cause to search a certain apartment as opposed to all apartments on the floor, the warrant should be restricted to the single apartment. If the officer cannot identify a particular apartment, then it is unlikely that there is probable cause to search the apartment in the first place. If the search is to be conducted in a rural area, courts necessarily take a more flexible view of whether a description is sufficiently particular. For instance, "a blue house with a trailer, with a broken mailbox, on highway 23A two miles from Tannersville" would be reasonably particular, whereas "a house two miles from Tannersville" would not be.

3. Applicability to More Than One Location

If the warrant describes a location with information as specific as one could reasonably expect to obtain, then it is sufficiently particular even though the warrant could actually apply to more than one location.

Example: In *Maryland v. Garrison*, 480 U.S. 79, 107 S.Ct. 1013, 94 L.Ed.2d 72 (1987), the warrant authorized a search of the entire third floor of an apartment building. Officers had probable cause to believe that illegal activity was being conducted in an apartment on the third floor, and they undertook an investigation to determine whether there was more than one apartment on the floor. An officer obtained information from the utility company and telephone company which appeared to indicate that the entire third floor consisted of one apartment. A look at the door buzzers outside the apartment building did not indicate how many apartments were on any particular floor. There were seven apartments listed in the four-story building. After entering the apartment building, the officers saw one door on the third floor. They eventually found that there were two apartments behind the single door—the apartments shared an entryway. The Court held that the warrant was sufficiently particular as issued, even though as it turned out it authorized the search of two apartments rather than one. The Fourth Amendment requires reasonable particularity, and accordingly allows for reasonable mistakes of fact. As the Court stated, "the validity of the warrant must be assessed on the basis of the information that the officers disclosed, or had a duty to discover and disclose, to the issuing magistrate."

4. Problems of Execution

In executing the warrant, the police may commit error if it is clear that the warrant, even though sufficiently particular when issued, was not intended to cover a certain area. Thus, in *Garrison*, the officer could not execute the warrant if it was readily apparent before the search that there were two apartments on the floor instead of one. *See Kreines v. United States*, 959 F.2d 834 (9th Cir.1992) (warrant to search a house cannot cover an internally separate living area, marked with a different number, and leased out to a third party). However, under the circumstances of *Garrison*, there was only one door to enter both apartments. The police did not discover that there were two separate apartments until both had been entered and separate kitchens were found in each living area off the common entryway. Up to that point, the warrant was being properly executed since the Fourth Amendment allows for reasonable mistakes of fact. The reasonableness of a searching officer's conduct depends on the information that becomes available as the search proceeds.

5. Incorrect Address

One problem that arises with respect to particularity of location, especially in urban areas, is where the warrant gives the wrong address for the premises to be searched. For example, assume that there is probable cause to search an apartment in a building on the corner of Maple and Elm. The building's entryway faces Maple, and the officer who prepares the affidavit gives the address as Maple Street. But the actual mailing address is Elm Street. Can the warrant satisfy the particularity requirement even though it sets forth the wrong address?

Technical Accuracy Not Required

Variances between the actual address and the address specified in the warrant do not per se invalidate the warrant. The warrant remains valid so long as there is sufficient information therein for the executing officer to know where to execute the warrant despite the wrong address. Thus, if the warrant gives the wrong address, but describes the corner, the building, the color of the building, etc. sufficiently to distinguish it from other buildings, then there is no risk of an official's abuse of discretion, and the warrant will be deemed sufficiently particular as to location.

Example: A warrant authorized the search of defendant's home, and gave the street address as 1601 Marsh. "The premises were described as a light green house trailer, which faces north and has a concrete step and porch structure leading to the front door." The residence to be searched was actually 8300 Karleen. While facially these addresses seem widely disparate, on closer examination they are not. Karleen and Marsh Streets intersect. The defendant's business was on the southeast corner of the intersection, with the street address of 1601 Marsh. The business was located in a single story, cinder block building. Immediately behind and to the east of the business was the defendant's residence, a light green house trailer with a concrete step and porch structure leading to the front door. Thus, while the warrant misdescribed the address, the actual address described in the warrant was contiguous to the trailer, and both the trailer and the business at 1601 Marsh were owned by the defendant. Moreover, nobody could have mistaken the defendant's business for the premises to be searched. In light of the physical arrangement of the properties and the particular description of the defendant's home, the court upheld the warrant as sufficiently particular. *United States v. Ridinger,* 805 F.2d 818 (8th Cir.1986).

D. Particular Description of Things to Be Seized

The things to be seized, like the place to be searched, must be particularly described in the warrant. The rationale of the particularity requirement respecting things to be seized is to control the discretion of the executing officer. A general rummaging could occur unless the officer's goals are specifically delineated in the warrant.

1. Reasonable Particularity

As with other particularity issues, the test of whether a description of things to be seized is sufficiently particular is one of reasonableness, determined by the information that police could reasonably be expected to know prior to the search. In order to have probable cause to seize something, there must ordinarily be some information which reasonably identifies it, although the degree of precision will depend on the facts and circumstances of each case.

In *Groh v. Ramirez,* 540 U.S. 551, 124 S.Ct. 1284, 157 L.Ed.2d 1068 (2004), the Supreme Court held that a search warrant that failed to particularly describe the items to be seized was invalid on its face, notwithstanding the fact that the items were described in detail in both the warrant application and the supporting affidavit. Groh, an ATF agent, prepared and signed a warrant application that described with particularity a large stock of weaponry that he expected to seize at Ramirez's ranch. Groh supported the application with a detailed affidavit. However, he did not include the items on the warrant itself, nor did he incorporate the accompanying documents by reference. The magistrate issued the warrant, and Groh led a search of the property. No weapons were found, and Ramirez sued the agent and others under under *Bivens v. Six Unknown Fed. Narcotics Agents*, 403 U.S. 388, 91 S.Ct. 1999, 29 L.Ed.2d 619 (1971) and U.S.C. § 1983, claiming a Fourth Amendment violation. The Court held that the Fourth Amendment requires particularity in the warrant, not in the supporting documents, and found that this warrant was so obviously deficient that the search was essentially "warrantless" within the meaning of its case law (citing *Maryland v. Garrison, supra* and *United States v. Leon, infra*). The Court specifically declined to decide whether the warrant would have been valid had the agent incorporated the accompanying documents by reference.

2.   Documents

Assuming probable cause to seize documents, a warrant allowing the seizure of "all documents, books and records" is obviously overbroad, since there is no limitation on the executing officer's discretion. On the other hand, especially with complex fraud cases, it is difficult for police to specifically describe all pertinent documents before the search. As a result, courts will generally find a warrant to be sufficiently particular if police have done all they reasonably could to limit the discretion of the officer who executes the warrant. The warrant must contain a substantive, subject matter limitation sufficient to control the discretion of the executing officer.

Example: Police officers have probable cause to believe that a doctor has been prescribing Quaaludes to patients without a proper medical purpose. A warrant authorizing the seizure of "all patient records" is overbroad, since it would cover the doctor's entire medical practice. However, a warrant authorizing seizure of "all patient records where Quaaludes were prescribed" is as particular as can be expected under the circumstances, and gives a clear standard for evaluation, thus limiting the discretion of the executing officer.

a.   Document Searches Will Usually Be Extensive
Even if a search of documents is reasonably limited by a subject matter description in the warrant, the search will often require the

inspection of thousands of documents to determine whether they fit the subject matter described. But this is not a problem under the Fourth Amendment so long as there is probable cause to search the files, and the officer's discretion to search and seize is as limited as reasonably possible. *See, e.g., United States v. Hayes*, 794 F.2d 1348 (9th Cir.1986) (the fact that officers looked through 10,000 patient files is not problematic, since there was probable cause to search for distribution of controlled substances, and officers were allowed to seize only those records concerned with such substances).

b. Pervasive Criminal Activity

Ordinarily, a warrant authorizing the seizure of "all documents and records" or "all property" is patently overbroad. This will not be the case, however, if criminal activity on the premises to be searched is so pervasive that every document or piece of property is in fact connected to a crime. If a business is "permeated with fraud" so that no document is prepared for a legal purpose, a warrant authorizing the seizure of all documents on such premises will be found sufficiently particular.

3. **Catch-All Clauses in the Warrant**

The most difficult particularity problems arise where the warrant describes some items in detail, and then includes a catch-all clause—for example, a clause allowing the seizure of "any other evidence of the crime." These clauses become relevant at a suppression hearing when the Government attempts to uphold the seizure of items not specifically described in the warrant by arguing that the items were covered by the catch-all clause.

a. Catch-Alls Must Be Qualified by Preceding Descriptions

Looked at independently, a catch-all clause in a warrant is no better at controlling police discretion than a warrant which is overbroad in its entirety. Consequently, courts find catch-all clauses to be overbroad unless they are somehow qualified by the particular descriptions that are set forth together with the catch-all clause in the warrant.

b. Qualification by Reference to a General Crime Is Insufficient

Catch-alls are not made sufficiently particular by merely referring to the specific crime for which there is probable cause. Evidence of that crime can be far-ranging and difficult for the executing officer to determine. The executing officer would essentially be left to his or her own devices to determine the scope and meaning of the relevant criminal statute. Thus, catch-all clauses allowing the seizure of "other stolen property," other evidence of "narcotics trafficking" and other "misbranded drugs" have been struck down as over-broad.

Example: A warrant authorized the seizure of certain specified drugs that were cocaine substitutes. The court held that a catch-all clause allowing the seizure of "other cocaine substitutes" would be sufficiently particular, whereas a clause applying to "misbranded drugs" would not. The term "misbranded drugs" could apply to any drug, including, presumably, penicillin. *United States v. Storage Spaces*, 777 F.2d 1363 (9th Cir.1985).

c. **Must Be Qualified by Previously Described Property**
To be sufficiently particular, a catch-all clause must be related to and qualified by previously described property, as opposed to a generalized criminal offense. *Andresen v. Maryland*, 427 U.S. 463, 96 S.Ct. 2737, 49 L.Ed.2d 627 (1976) (the phrase "together with other fruits, instrumentalities and evidence of crime at this [time] unknown" was not fatally general because it referred to a specifically described piece of property).

d. **Searches of Computers**
The Court in *Andresen* noted that in a search for documents, it is inevitable that the police will view innocuous private documents. This same problem occurs when the police conduct computer searches. In *United States v. Adjani*, 452 F.3d 1140 (9th Cir. 2006), FBI agents executed a search warrant at defendant's home to obtain evidence in support of extortion charges. The warrant authorized them to search for documents and a variety of materials and equipment that might contain evidence of the alleged crime, including computers. The agents seized and subsequently searched a computer belonging to defendant's roommate and found e-mails that implicated Adjani and his roommate. The court rejected his claim that the warrant should have restricted the search to a particular email program and specific search terms. The court noted that because of the ease of disguising or renaming computer files, much evidence could escape discovery if police had to limit the

warrant to such a specific search protocol. The court found that "[t]he government should not be required to trust the suspect's self-labeling when executing a warrant."

4. Severability

If some clauses in a warrant are sufficiently particular and other clauses are not, the overbroad clauses can be severed from those that are sufficiently particular. The warrant, and the search conducted pursuant to it, will then be evaluated on the basis of the valid clauses. If an item is covered by one of the valid clauses, then it is properly seized pursuant to the warrant even if the item is also covered by an overbroad clause such as a catch-all.

Example: Defendants were convicted of operating an illegal gambling business and money laundering, and one defendant was also convicted of filing a false income tax return. Defendants claimed that the warrant authorizing the seizure of many documents contained overly-broad clauses in violation of the particularity requirement. The court held that the clause that authorized the seizure of "[b]ooks, records, receipts, bank statements and records, money drafts, letters of credit, money orders and cash checks, money wrappers, pass-books, bank checks, automatic teller machine receipts, Western Union receipts, safety deposit box keys, and other items evidencing the obtaining, secreting, transfer, and/or concealment of assets and the obtaining, secreting, transfer, concealment, and or expenditure of money" was overly broad. However, the court rejected the defendant's argument that all of the evidence seized under the warrant should be excluded. Instead, the court held that the proper remedy was severance of the overly-broad portions of the warrant. Thus, the evidence seized under the clauses that were sufficiently particular was properly admitted. *United States v. Ford*, 184 F.3d 566 (6th Cir.1999).

E. Warrant Can Authorize the Seizure of "Mere Evidence"

It has always been the case that a warrant could authorize the seizure of the instrumentalities of a crime (such as a gun used for an armed robbery), the fruits of a crime (such as the money obtained in an armed robbery) and contraband (materials whose possession is prohibited by law, such as illegal narcotics). However, before 1967, the Court did not permit the seizure of items which were of evidentiary value only, such as a diary containing incriminating information. The rationale was that the Government had no valid property interest in such "mere evidence." In *Warden v. Hayden,* 387 U.S. 294, 87 S.Ct. 1642, 18 L.Ed.2d 782 (1967), the Court discarded the "mere evidence" rule, holding that the right to seize evidence did not rest on the Government's property interest, but rather on the Government's legitimate interest in solving crime. Consequently, the seizure of a robbery suspect's clothing, which had been identified by an eyewitness, was upheld. Federal Rule of Criminal Procedure 41(b) now specifically states that a warrant may be issued to search for and seize all evidence of a crime.

F. Issuing Warrants Against Non–Suspects

Searches can be made on the premises of non-suspects, either pursuant to a warrant or an appropriate exception to the warrant requirement, so long as there is probable cause to believe that evidence will be found therein. This principle is a natural outgrowth from *Warden v. Hayden,* the case allowing the search for and seizure of "mere evidence." The state's interest in enforcing the criminal law and recovering evidence is the same whether the third party is culpable or not. Nothing in the language of the Fourth Amendment limits its scope to the premises of criminals. *United States v. Ponce,* 947 F.2d 646 (2d Cir.1991) (if there is probable cause to believe that evidence of a crime is located on particular property, then a warrant may be issued and it is not necessary that the owner of the property be suspected of crime).

1. No Special First Amendment Protection

The fact that the non-suspect is protected by the First Amendment creates no special protection against a search of the premises for evidence. *Zurcher v. Stanford Daily,* 436 U.S. 547, 98 S.Ct. 1970, 56 L.Ed.2d 525 (1978) (search of newspaper files for photographs of suspects upheld where conducted with a warrant issued upon probable cause).

2. Statutory Protections for the Media

In response to *Zurcher,* Congress provided protection for the press in the Privacy Protection Act of 1980, which limits the Government's authority to conduct a search of journalists and news organizations. 42 U.S.C.A. § 2000aa. Government agents may not search for the work product of the media, unless the news gatherer is involved in the crime, or unless an immediate search is necessary to prevent the death or serious bodily injury of a human being. Documents are subject to search under similar circumstances and also when there is reason to believe that serving notice by subpoena would result in the destruction of the documents, or when the news gatherer has defied a court order to produce the documents.

V. Execution of Search Warrants

The Fourth Amendment does not contain specific language directing law enforcement agents on the correct procedure for executing a warrant. However, the general clauses requiring probable cause and reasonableness have been interpreted as placing constitutional limitations on the manner in which agents perform those duties.

A. Time of Execution

Many jurisdictions have statutes or court rules providing that a search warrant must be executed within a fixed period of time (e.g., ten days). If law enforcement officers execute the warrant after that set time, the prevailing view requires evidence found in that search to be suppressed. *Sgro v. United States*, 287 U.S. 206, 53 S.Ct. 138, 77 L.Ed. 260 (1933).

1. Staleness

One problem that can arise with the location of a search is that there may have been probable cause at one point to believe that evidence or a person to be arrested would be found therein, but the search is actually conducted at a point significantly later in time. This is a question of staleness. For example, the day after a bank robbery, there may be probable cause to believe that the money from the robbery will be located in the robber's house. But that probability is significantly diminished a year after the robbery. Whether the information on which probable cause was originally based has grown stale is dependent upon such facts as the nature of the crime, the type of evidence, and the length of time that has passed.

Examples: The police have probable cause to believe that the suspect ordered and accepted magazines showing sex acts conducted with children. However, the magazines were delivered to defendant's home six months prior to the time the officers obtained a warrant. The defendant argues that the information was stale—that there was no probable cause to believe that the magazines are still in his home at the time the warrant was issued. However, in the affidavit supporting the warrant, the officers included a statement from a psychiatrist who concluded that the facts indicated that the defendant was a pedophile, and that pedophiles are likely to retain such magazines for a long time, rather than destroy or distribute them. Consequently, the court found that the information upon which probable cause was based had not grown stale—there was a fair probability that the magazines were still in the defendant's home. *United States v. Rabe*, 848 F.2d 994 (9th Cir.1988). *See also United States v. Ponce*, 947 F.2d 646 (2d Cir.1991) (information that was two weeks old was not stale where it indicated that the premises were used for an ongoing narcotics trafficking operation).

Similarly, in *United States v. Farmer*, 370 F.3d 435 (4th Cir.2004), defendant had been running a large scale counterfeiting operation. Federal agents obtained a search warrant for his home and confirmed that he had purchased blank t-shirts and sweatshirts and was placing brand name logos on them. Defendant contended that the search warrant of his home was based on stale information and that his indictment failed to allege any violation of the criminal trademark infringement statute. The court found that nine-month old information about the defendant's large scale counterfeiting operation was not stale because it was "unlikely to have been suddenly abandoned" and the information indicated that the operation had been going on for a long time.

2. New Information

A delay in executing the warrant may mean that the probable cause which existed when the warrant was *issued* is gone by the time the warrant is *executed.* In such a case, the search would be unconstitutional.

Example: In *United States v. Bowling*, 900 F.2d 926 (6th Cir.1990), the police conducted a search of premises pursuant to a warrant. Between the time the warrant was issued and the search conducted, the police had already searched the premises pursuant to the consent of the owner. That search had not uncovered any evidence. The court concluded that "where an initial fruitless consent search dissipates the probable cause that justified a warrant, new indicia of probable cause must exist to repeat a search of the same premises pursuant to the warrant." Compare *Wicks v. State*, 552 A.2d 462 (Del.1988) (although defendant informed police prior to search for a stolen gun that he had sold the evidence, probable cause remained as police were "simply not required to believe this statement.")

3. Anticipatory Search Warrants

Many lower courts have upheld search warrants based on "anticipatory" probable cause. The search warrant in such cases is grounded in the magistrate's determination that, if certain expected events happen in the future, probable cause will then exist to execute the warrant. The Supreme Court upheld anticipatory warrants in *United States v. Grubbs*, 547 U.S. 90, 126 S.Ct. 1494, 164 L.Ed.2d 195 (2006). In this case, the warrant would only be issued after a triggering condition, namely the controlled delivery of a child pornography videotape by an undercover agent posing as a postal inspector. The affidavit described the triggering condition and referred to two attachments which described the residence and the items to be seized. The attachments, but not the affidavit, were attached to the warrant. Defendant moved to suppress the evidence because the warrant failed to list the triggering condition and challenged the constitutionality of anticipatory warrants. The Supreme Court held that anticipatory warrants are constitutional and noted that all warrants are anticipatory to a certain degree in that they require the magistrate to determine that it is probable that contraband or evidence will be on the premises at some point in the future when the warrant is executed. The fact that the affidavit describing the triggering conditions was not attached to the warrant was not relevant, according to the Court, since the Fourth Amendment doesn't require that any affidavit or even warrant be shown to the property owner.

4. Execution in the Nighttime

Slightly less than half the states restrict execution of searches to "daylight" hours absent special circumstances; Fed.R.Crim. 41 restricts searches to daytime unless "reasonable cause" is shown. "Daylight" is generally defined by specific hours in the state statutes; it encompasses the hours of 6:00 a.m. to 10:00 p.m. according to local time in the Federal rule. "It is the *entry* of the police in the nighttime, not their mere presence, that is thought to call for particular judicial authorization." *State v. Valenzuela*, 130 N.H. 175, 536 A.2d 1252 (1987).

Constitutional Concerns

Although the Supreme Court has never held that the Fourth Amendment imposes special restraints on nighttime searches, some lower courts have stated that nighttime searches implicate the reasonableness requirement of the Amendment. Many courts require a showing of some form of exigent circumstances before a nighttime search can be authorized. *See, e.g., United States v. Morehead,* 959 F.2d 1489 (10th Cir.1992) (noting that nighttime searches are related to the "reasonableness" issue of the Fourth Amendment but upholding the search as the evidence could have been destroyed during the night).

5. **Execution in the Absence of the Occupant**

The Supreme Court has indicated in dictum that a search is permissible in the absence of the occupant. *Alderman v. United States,* 394 U.S. 165, 89 S.Ct. 961, 22 L.Ed.2d 176 (1969). The lower courts have generally agreed, although a few courts have found it relevant to consider whether officers made any effort to locate the occupants of the premises before conducting a search in their absence. *See Commonwealth v. Prokopchak,* 279 Pa.Super. 284, 420 A.2d 1335 (1980) (noting that officers waited an additional 15 minutes past the time the occupants should have returned to the house before forcibly entering the premises under the reasonable assumption that no one was planning to arrive and voluntarily let the officers inside).

6. **Covert and Surreptitious Entries**

Officers sometimes may wish to enter a premises surreptitiously, so as not to notify the suspects that a search is being or has been conducted. In *United States v. Freitas,* 800 F.2d 1451 (9th Cir.1986), the court held that a warrant allowing surreptitious entry to scrutinize a drug lab operation, without any provision for post-search notice to the occupants, was constitutionally defective. The *Freitas* court reasoned that surreptitious entries should not be authorized except in circumstances of the greatest necessity, because such searches are unusually intrusive: "the mere thought of strangers walking through and visually examining the center of our privacy interest, our home, arouses our passion for freedom as does nothing else." However, Rule 41 of the Federal Rules of Criminal Procedure now permits the issuance of warrants authorizing such surreptitious entries.

B. Notice Requirement

18 U.S.C.A. § 3109 provides that a law enforcement officer may break into premises to execute a search warrant "if, after notice of his authority and purpose, he is refused admittance or when necessary to liberate himself or a person aiding him in the execution of the warrant." This Federal "knock and announce" statute, similar to those in most of the states, codifies the longstanding common law rule of notice conditioning official entry to premises, absent exigent circumstances.

1. Rationale

The concept of requiring law enforcement officers to give notice before entering private premises is grounded in practical realities. Notice decreases the potential for violence as occupants are made aware of law officers' official purpose and presence. Prior announcement decreases the possibility of police mistakenly entering the wrong premises. Notice allows for at least a minimal amount of time to prepare for official entry into the home. Lastly, notice provides occupants with the opportunity to voluntarily admit officers into their home, facilitating and speeding up the search process while, at the same time, minimizing the privacy intrusion and the possibility of property damage. *See generally Ker v. California,* 374 U.S. 23, 83 S.Ct. 1623, 10 L.Ed.2d 726 (1963).

2. Constitutional Basis

In *Wilson v. Arkansas*, 514 U.S. 927, 115 S.Ct. 1914, 131 L.Ed.2d 976 (1995), the Court held that "in some circumstances an unannounced entry into a home might be unreasonable under the Fourth Amendment." Thus, the Fourth Amendment encompasses some aspect of a "knock and announce" requirement. The practical effect of *Wilson* is limited to those few states which have no statute or rule requiring announcement before entry with a warrant.

3. Manner of Entry

The notice requirement generally is triggered when law enforcement officers forcibly enter private premises. The Federal statute requires that notice must be given before an officer can "break open any outer or inner door or window of a house." The Supreme Court has stated that the Federal statute is triggered whenever "officers break down a door, force open a chain lock on a partially open door, open a locked door by use of a passkey, or, as here, open a closed but unlocked door." *Sabbath v. United States*, 391 U.S. 585, 88 S.Ct. 1755, 20 L.Ed.2d 828 (1968).

a. Open Doors

The courts are split on whether entry through an open door is a "breaking" that requires prior notice by police officers. Although the majority view is that an open door does not trigger the statutory requirement, *see United States v. Remigio,* 767 F.2d 730 (10th Cir.1985), some courts have required notice in particular cases. *See People v. Bradley,* 1 Cal.3d 80, 81 Cal.Rptr. 457, 460 P.2d 129 (1969) (although not every entry through an open door will require notice, an officer's entry through an open door at night when the occupant is apparently asleep violates the California statutory requirement).

b. Entry by Ruse

Courts generally agree that an officer's entry by ruse does not constitute a "breaking" requiring prior notice. *See, e.g., United States v. Contreras–Ceballos,* 999 F.2d 432 (9th Cir.1993) (officer did not violate knock and announce statute where he fooled the defendant into thinking that he was a Federal Express deliveryman, and barged in when the defendant opened the door; this was not a breaking); *see also United States v. Alejandro,* 368 F.3d 130 (2d Cir. 2004)(no breaking where officer gained entry into defendant's apartment by misrepresenting himself as a gas company employee investigating a gas leak).

4. Compliance With the Notice Requirement

The notice requirement mandates that the officer "give appropriate notice of his authority and purpose to the person * * * in apparent control of the premises to be searched." Model Code of Pre–Arraignment Procedure § 220.3(2) (1975). As one court noted, the proper focus is not on "magic words" spoken by the police but, rather, on how the policemen's actions are perceived by the occupants. *United States v. One Parcel of Real Property,* 873 F.2d 7 (1st Cir.1989) (officers' pounding on door and yelling out "police" sufficiently informs the occupants that the officers wish to enter either for purposes of search or arrest).

Response by Occupants

Once the officers have knocked and announced their identity and purpose, they are then required to wait for voluntary admittance or constructive refusal of admittance. Courts generally defer to the police assessment as to the amount of time they should wait before assuming that they are being refused admittance; in some cases, a delay of from 5–10 seconds has been found sufficient to permit police to forcibly enter the premises. *See United States v. Bonner*, 874 F.2d 822 (D.C. Cir.1989) (10 seconds sufficient when warrant was executed in a small apartment in the early evening). Sounds from inside the premises are frequently factored into the court's holding that occupants are preparing to keep the officers out. *See, e.g., State v. Ruscoe,* 212 Conn. 223, 563 A.2d 267 (1989) (clicking sound as officers approached was reasonably assumed to be occupants locking the front door).

5. Emergency Exception

Police officers need not "knock and announce" their presence when they are acting to prevent the imminent destruction of evidence. However, in *Richards v. Wisconsin,* 520 U.S. 385, 117 S.Ct. 1416, 137 L.Ed.2d 615 (1997), the Court rejected the state's argument that police officers are *never* required to knock and announce their presence when executing a search warrant in a felony drug investigation. The Court concluded that a per se rule would be overinclusive, and could not be easily limited to drug cases. The *Richards* Court set forth the following test for determining whether the knock-and-announce requirement is excused: "the police must have a reasonable suspicion that knocking and announcing their presence, under the particular circumstances, would be dangerous or futile, or that it would inhibit the effective investigation of the crime by, for example, allowing the destruction of evidence. This standard—as opposed to a probable cause requirement—strikes the appropriate balance between the legitimate law enforcement concerns at issue in the execution of search warrants and the individual privacy interests affected by no-knock entries." Under the circumstances presented in *Richards,* the Court found that the officers had a legitimate excuse for dispensing with notice—the defendant was aware of their presence, and the risk of destruction of drugs was a real one.

There is no requirement that police officers obtain a no-knock warrant, even if they believe conditions at the premises might justify such a warrant. Nonetheless, "if police obtain a no-knock warrant prior to the search, the defendant bears the burden to show that the entry method was not justified. If, however, police execute a general search warrant without knocking and announcing, then the government is required to justify use of the no-knock entry." (*United States v. Esser*, 451 F.3d 1109 (10th Cir.2006)).

a. Destruction of Property

In *United States v. Ramirez*, 523 U.S. 65, 118 S.Ct. 992, 140 L.Ed.2d 191 (1998), the Court upheld the *Richards* standard for a "no-knock" entry, even when the police destroy property in the process. Ramirez argued that although a "mild exigency" might justify a "no-knock" entry, a heightened degree of exigent circumstances is required to justify the destruction of property. The Court rejected this argument, holding that the *Richards* rule did not depend upon whether the police find it necessary to destroy property to enter. The Court noted that the Fourth Amendment reasonableness requirement does impose some limitations on the destructiveness of a search, but found the limited property damage in this case to be reasonable.

b. Forcible Entry After Knocking and Announcing

Police officers may forcibly enter the premises fifteen to twenty seconds after they knock and announce their presence if there is an exigency of possible destruction of evidence, according to the Court in *United States v. Banks*, 540 U.S. 31, 124 S.Ct. 521, 157 L.Ed.2d 343 (2003). In *Banks*, police officers went to an apartment to execute a search warrant for cocaine. They called out "police search warrant" as they tapped loudly on the door. Citing *Richards* and *Ramirez*, the Court noted that the standards governing when a police officer can enter after knocking and announcing are the same as that for a no-knock entry. The reasonableness of the wait time should be governed by the facts as known to the police, and a longer wait may have resulted in the destruction of the cocaine.

C. Use of Extraordinary Force

It is sometimes necessary for police officers to use extraordinary force in order to enter the premises of certain types of suspected criminal enterprises. In *Langford v. Superior Court*, 43 Cal.3d 21, 233 Cal.Rptr. 387, 729 P.2d 822 (1987), the court was asked to enjoin the Los Angeles Police Department from using certain destructive devices to gain entrance to what the police contended were "fortress-like" buildings where drugs were being prepared and sold. The court found that police guidelines were sufficient to control the discretion of officers' employing "flashbangs," described as low-impact explosive devices. The court concluded that such devices caused suspects only momentary disorientation and a minimal risk of physical injury. However, it held that the use of motorized battering rams posed a serious risk of physical injury and excessive property damage, and that battering rams could only be employed when prior judicial authorization is combined with exigent circumstances arising contemporaneously with an attempt to search the premises. *See also United States v. Stewart*, 867 F.2d 581 (10th Cir.1989) (court finds use of steel battering ram unreasonable under the circumstances).

D. Scope and Intensity of the Search

As previously discussed, the discretion of an officer operating pursuant to a warrant is limited by the constitutional requirement of particularity relating both to location and to the items to be seized. Similarly, the scope and duration of a search relate directly to the neutral magistrate's previous determination of probable cause, thus limiting the officers' discretion throughout the search.

1. Search of the "Premises" Described in the Warrant

A warrant authorizing a search of "premises" or a particular street number is generally deemed to cover, not only the basic residence, but also the grounds and other structures that are found within the curtilage of the house. "Curtilage" is defined as "the area to which extends the intimate activity associated with the sanctity of a man's home and the privacies of life." *Oliver v. United States*, 466 U.S. 170, 104 S.Ct. 1735, 80 L.Ed.2d 214 (1984). Courts commonly interpret this definition to include backyards, courtyards, and the acreage and associated buildings of farms and ranches as long as there is some indicia that such outer area is connected to the main dwelling named in the warrant.

2. Vehicles Within Curtilage of Described Premises

If the warrant authorizes a search of premises, the scope of the search will include any vehicles within the curtilage, so long as there is probable cause to believe that the things described in the warrant may be found in the vehicle. *United States v. Evans*, 92 F.3d 540 (7th Cir.1996). But, the reverse is not true. If a warrant limits a search to a car alone, "authority to search a vehicle [will] not include authority to enter private premises to effect a search of a vehicle within those premises." *People v. Sciacca*, 45 N.Y.2d 122, 408 N.Y.S.2d 22, 379 N.E.2d 1153 (1978).

3. Scope of Search Inside the Premises

"A lawful search of fixed premises generally extends to the entire area in which the object of the search may be found and is not limited by the possibility that separate acts of entry or entry or opening may be required to complete the search." *United States v. Ross*, 456 U.S. 798, 102 S.Ct. 2157, 72 L.Ed.2d 572 (1982). Thus, a valid search warrant need not (and likely could not) particularly describe every room, cabinet, or piece of furniture to be searched. Rather, the search of a house authorizes smaller, separate entries into rooms and containers that might feasibly contain the items described in the warrant. Of course, a warrant may restrict a search to certain areas in the house; however, officers are entitled to walk through unnamed parts of a residence if reasonably necessary to gain access to the areas to be searched. *See, e.g., Commonwealth v. Young,* 6 Mass.App.Ct. 953, 383 N.E.2d 515 (1978) (reasonable for officers to walk through first floor apartment in order to reach basement apartment when the only outer entrance to basement was locked and barricaded).

4. Personal Effects in Described Premises

"In general, a warrant authorizing a search of a premises justifies a search of the occupant's personal effects that are plausible repositories for the objects specified in the warrant." *State v. White,* 13 Wash.App. 949, 538 P.2d 860 (1975). *See United States v. Hughes,* 940 F.2d 1125 (8th Cir.1991) (a search of a coat pocket for a necklace is within the scope of a warrant authorizing the seizure of the necklace).

5. Search of Person Described in Warrant

A warrant may validly authorize the search of a person either exclusively or jointly with a search of a particular location. *See United States v. Ward,* 682 F.2d 876 (10th Cir.1982).

6. Search of Person Includes Things Carried by the Person

A warrant authorizing the search of an individual extends to property carried by the individual at the time of the search. *State v. Worth,* 37 Wash.App. 889, 683 P.2d 622 (1984) (purse considered "readily recognizable personal effect" of the defendant such that it became "an extension of her person").

7. Search of Person Not Described in Warrant

"A warrant to search premises does not authorize officers to conduct a personal search of individuals found at the site but not described in the warrant." *State v. Worth,* 37 Wash.App. 889, 683 P.2d 622 (1984). The Supreme Court, in *United States v. Di Re,* 332 U.S. 581, 68 S.Ct. 222, 92 L.Ed. 210 (1948), stated in dictum that a search of a house or car pursuant to a warrant would not permit a search of its occupants.

8. Detention of Individuals While the Premises Is Searched

Officers can prevent individuals from leaving the premises "until the officer[s] can be certain that the detainee is not engaged in removing the property specified in the warrant," assuming that the evidence sought is of a nature to be "easily removed or concealed." *United States v. Festa*, 192 F.Supp. 160 (D.Mass.1960). In *Michigan v. Summers*, 452 U.S. 692, 101 S.Ct. 2587, 69 L.Ed.2d 340 (1981), the Court held that police could seize and detain an *occupant* of premises during the time it takes to properly execute a search warrant. The Court identified three important governmental interests in detaining such individuals: 1. preventing the possible flight of the individual if incriminating evidence is discovered; 2. minimizing the risk of harm to officers as the suspect might leave and then return with the intention of thwarting the success of the search; and 3. facilitating the orderly completion of the search by "open[ing] locked doors or locked containers to avoid the use of force that is not only damaging to property but may also delay the completion of the task at hand." The Court also pointed out that this type of detention was substantially less intrusive than a full-fledged arrest, and only minimally added to the public stigma of the search itself.

In *Muehler v. Mena*, 544 U.S. 93, 125 S.Ct. 1465, 161 L.Ed.2d 299 (2005), the Court upheld the detention of Iris Mena, who was handcuffed and detained in a converted garage, guarded by a member of the SWAT team, during a search of the residence that she and others shared. The officers had reason to believe that at least one member of the gang West Side Locos lived at the residence and that he was armed and dangerous. Before the officers left, Mena was released. Mena filed a § 1983 claim against the officers claiming that they held her for an unreasonable amount of time and in an unreasonable manner in violation of the Fourth Amendment. The Court, applying *Michigan v. Summers*, held that Mena's detention was permissible because a warrant existed to search the residence, and Mena was an occupant of the residence at the time of the search. The Court found that the governmental interests of minimizing the risk of harm to the officers and the residence's occupants outweighed the marginal intrusion on Mena. The Court characterized the search for weapons and a wanted gang member as an inherently dangerous situation in which using handcuffs to detain the residence's occupants was authorized, noting that the need to detain multiple occupants made the use of handcuffs even more reasonable. The Court also noted that Mena's 2–3 hour detention in the garage was reasonable in light of the officers' continuing safety concerns.

9. Arrival While Search Is Conducted

Generally, an individual who enters the premises after the search has begun would be outside the scope of the search authorized by the warrant. However, under some circumstances, courts allow searches of individuals who arrive subsequent to the execution of the warrant. *See Logan v. State*, 135 Ga.App. 879, 219 S.E.2d 615 (1975) (search for gambling paraphernalia allows "search of individuals entering while the search of the house was going on.")

10. Intensity of Search

The scope of a search is limited to places in which items described in the warrant may reasonably be concealed. Thus, it would be unreasonable to search for a handgun nine inches long "inside a utility bill or bank statement envelope, in a flat notebook, or inside any other container too small to hold the weapon." *Miles v. State*, 742 P.2d 1150 (Okl.Crim.App.1987). Within the permissible physical boundaries of a search, the type of procedure utilized is largely left to the discretion of the officers; warrants do not contain specific guidelines that the officers must follow when executing a search warrant.

11. Length of Search and Damage to Premises

Officers may remain on the premises only as long as is reasonably necessary to quickly and efficiently complete the search. Moreover, officers must refrain from committing unnecessary property damage during the course of a search. See Model Code of Pre–Arraignment Procedure § 220(3), (5) (1975) (the scope of a search under a warrant is "only such as is authorized by the warrant and is reasonably necessary to discover the individuals or things specified therein"); *Tarpley v. Greene*, 684 F.2d 1 (D.C. Cir.1982) (officers must avoid unnecessary damage to premises). Although the courts generally give officers a certain amount of latitude as to how a search is conducted, deliberate attempts to widen the scope of a search may result in suppression of the evidence. *Purcell v. State*, 325 So.2d 83 (Fla.App.1976) (fruits of search suppressed when officers almost immediately saw the container described in the warrant but nonetheless proceeded to thoroughly search the rest of the premises before seizing the container). However, if the warrant authorizes a search for an undisclosed amount of evidence such as "narcotics," the police are allowed to search through the entire premises, even if a large amount of contraband has already been found. *Hagler v. State*, 726 P.2d 1181 (Okl.Crim.App.1986) (police allowed to search for more drugs after finding a large amount of drugs, because the "scope of the warrant authorized a seizure of marijuana in general.")

12. The Presence of Private Citizens

a. Assistance by Occupant

While the direction of an occupant might be helpful to the authorities, officers are not required to limit the scope of their search on the basis of an occupant's claims as to location of evidence. *United States v. Hughes*, 940 F.2d 1125 (8th Cir.1991) (although the occupant informed police that the necklace described in the warrant was in a jewelry box, the search of the bedroom was upheld as "the officers were not required to accept the word of [the defendant] and alter the sequence of their search.")

b. Assistance of Private Individuals

Courts will sometimes permit officers to be accompanied by private citizens during a search in order to more quickly and efficiently execute the warrant. For example, in *United States v. Clouston*, 623 F.2d 485 (6th Cir.1980), the court upheld a search conducted with the assistance of two telephone company employees where the warrant authorized seizure of certain electronic devices used in surreptitious interception of wire communications. Warrants may even authorize outside assistance in the execution of a warrant from experts in a particular field. *People v. Noble*, 635 P.2d 203 (Colo.1981) (warrant authorizes observations by an expert on child abuse). However, it is not permissible to allow private persons to participate in a search when they are there only for their own purposes.

c. Media Ride Alongs

In *Wilson v. Layne*, 526 U.S. 603, 119 S.Ct. 1692, 143 L.Ed.2d 818 (1999), the Supreme Court addressed the constitutionality of police officers inviting members of the media to observe the execution of a warrant. Officers brought a reporter and photographer from the *Washington Post* with them when they attempted to execute an arrest warrant for Dominic Wilson at the home of his parents. They entered the Wilsons' home late at night, and Mr. Wilson became upset. He was subdued on the floor at gunpoint, and Mrs. Wilson was present dressed in her nightgown. The *Washington Post* employees observed the entire incident, and the photographer took numerous pictures. The officers left when they realized Dominic Wilson was not present in his parents' home. The Wilsons brought a civil rights action, claiming that the officers violated their Fourth Amendment rights by bringing the newspaper employees along to observe the execution of the warrant. The Supreme Court agreed, holding that police actions in the execution of a warrant must be related to the objectives of the intrusion. Citing its historical recognition of the sanctity of the home, the Court noted that the newspaper employees were not present to assist in the execution of the warrant and held that the general law enforcement purposes claimed by the officers— publicizing the government's efforts to combat crime, facilitating accurate reporting on law enforcement activities, minimizing police abuses, and promoting the officers' safety—were outweighed by the Wilsons' right to privacy in their home.

13. Flagrant Disregard of Warrant Limitations

If officers legally seize evidence pursuant to a warrant, but then continue the search beyond the limitations of the warrant, a question arises whether the previously obtained evidence should be excluded. For example, in *Waller v. Georgia*, 467 U.S. 39, 104 S.Ct. 2210, 81 L.Ed.2d 31 (1984), the defendant objected to the introduction of wiretap evidence, claiming that the officers flagrantly disregarded the scope of the warrants. He argued that because the search so exceeded the warrant limitations, all of the evidence obtained by the officers should be excluded—even the evidence that was admittedly obtained within the scope of the warrant. In rejecting the defendant's claim, the Court distinguished between the conduct of an officer which exceeded the scope of a warrant "in place searched" from that which exceeded the scope of the warrant in the evidence to be seized. Noting that the officer's conduct in *Waller* fell into the latter category, the Court concluded that the lawfully seized evidence should not be suppressed— even presuming that the officers flagrantly disregarded the warrant limitations. Similarly, in *United States v. Decker*, 956 F.2d 773 (8th Cir.1992), the court held that although over 300 items were improperly seized, under *Waller*, the lawfully seized items were still admissible as the officers merely indulged in "excessive seizures."

*

III

Exceptions to the General Fourth Amendment Requirements of Probable Cause and a Warrant

■ **ANALYSIS**

IX. **Searches and Seizures of Automobiles and Other Movable Property.**
   A. The Automobile Exception to the Warrant Requirement.
   B. Movable Property—In and Out of Cars.
   C. Searches and Seizures of Automobiles Pursuant to the Community Caretaking Function.
   D. Impoundment of Vehicles and the Inventory Exception to the Warrant Requirement.

X. **Consent Searches.**
   A. Consent Must Be Voluntary.
   B. Third Party Consent.
   C. Scope of Consent.
   D. Revoking Consent.

I. Introduction

A. Presumptively Unreasonable

A search or seizure is presumptively unreasonable in the absence of a warrant based upon probable cause and particularly describing the place to be searched and the things to be seized. However, the Supreme Court has established many exceptions to those general requirements.

B. Different Requirements for Each Exception

In the discussion of exceptions which follow, you must keep in mind which requirements are being excused by the particular exceptions. Some exceptions, like those for automobiles and for exigent circumstances, excuse the warrant requirement but still require the officer to have probable cause. Other exceptions, such as the stop and frisk doctrine, excuse both probable cause and a warrant. Some exceptions, such as the plain view exception, authorize warrantless seizures but not warrantless searches.

II. The Plain View Doctrine

A. Seizure Without a Warrant

The plain view doctrine is an exception to the warrant requirement, which arises whenever the police are engaged in a legitimate investigative activity, and come across evidence not covered by any warrant. The plain view doctrine allows the police to seize an object in these circumstances if there is probable cause that the object is evidence of criminal activity.

Examples: In executing a warrant to search for and seize guns, the officer walks through a house and sees a bag of white powder on top of the television. The officer can seize this white powder because he is operating in the course of legal activity, the powder is in plain sight, and there is probable cause to believe that the bag of white powder is narcotics.

While making a lawful traffic stop, the officer looks into the defendant's car and sees a sawed-off shotgun on the seat. A warrantless seizure of the gun is permitted under the plain view doctrine. *See United States v. Weatherspoon*, 82 F.3d 697 (6th Cir. 1996) (after a lawful stop of a vehicle, one of the officers saw the barrel of a gun that the driver had just placed under the seat; the gun could be seized under the plain view doctrine).

Justification

A warrant is not needed to make these seizures because the heart of the Fourth Amendment is already complied with; the officer came upon the incriminating object while within the scope of legal activity. Moreover, if the object is incriminating and in plain view, the extra intrusion of seizing it is not that great, and there is little to be gained from requiring a warrant at that point.

B. Limitations on the Plain View Doctrine

The justifications for the plain view doctrine—that the officer is already acting within the scope of permissible police activity and that there is probable cause to seize an object in plain view—suggest the limitations on the scope of the doctrine.

1. Officer Must Be Within the Scope of Lawful Activity

The plain view doctrine can apply to seizures in the course of both warrantless searches and searches conducted pursuant to a warrant. However, the officer must be lawfully located in a place from which the object can be seen, and must also have a lawful right of access to the object in order to seize it. So even though an officer sees contraband through a house window, he is not allowed to enter the house to seize it, unless there is an independent lawful means of access into the house.

Example: Officers enter an apartment in response to a call that a fight is going on and neighbors heard a shot. When they enter the apartment, they see a large brick of white powder on a table in the foyer. They seize the brick without a warrant. This seizure is permissible under the plain view doctrine since the officers were in the course of legal activity when they came upon the brick; the imminent risk to public safety allowed the initial intrusion under the exigent circumstances exception to the warrant requirement. However, if the officers entered the apartment, arrested the two occupants who were fighting in the foyer, and then searched the upstairs bedroom and discovered a large brick of white powder, then the plain view doctrine could not apply. The intrusion into the bedroom would not be justified by a warrant or an exception to the warrant requirement.

2. Plain View Doctrine Allows Warrantless Seizures, Not Warrantless Searches

Just because a briefcase is in "plain view" does not mean it can be *searched* without a warrant—even if there is probable cause to open it.

The plain view doctrine does, however, allow a *seizure* if there is probable cause to believe that there is contraband or evidence in the container. Then the officer must obtain a search warrant to open the container, or find some other exception to the warrant requirement.

Example: Officers investigating the defendant on suspicion of drug dealing, and acting in the course of legitimate activity, come upon a leather camera lens case. They have probable cause to believe that the lens case contains cocaine. Under these circumstances, the plain view doctrine authorizes the *seizure* of the lens case, but not the search. *See United States v. Donnes,* 947 F.2d 1430 (10th Cir. 1991) ("In cases involving closed containers * * * the plain view doctrine may support the warrantless seizure of a container believed to contain contraband but any subsequent *search* of the concealed contents of the container must be accompanied by a warrant or justified by one of the exceptions to the warrant requirement.").

Exception for Containers Which "Bespeak" Their Contents

A search of a container will be permissible under the plain view doctrine where the contents of the container are a "foregone conclusion" because the container "bespeaks its contents." For example, the configuration or the labeling of a container may be so distinctive as to indicate that contraband or an instrumentality of crime is contained therein. *See United States v. Morgan,* 744 F.2d 1215 (6th Cir. 1984) (police may, without a warrant, open a bottle where the label on the bottle made it apparent that the bottle contained contraband).

3. Probable Cause Required for a Plain View Seizure

A third limitation on the plain view doctrine is that there must be probable cause that the object in plain view is evidence of a crime. The question of whether probable cause exists has already been considered in this outline, and the "fair probability" test discussed in that section is fully applicable to the question of whether an object in plain view can be seized.

Nexus to Criminal Activity

In some contexts, objects that would otherwise seem innocent may provide a fair probability of a connection to criminal activity. For example, assume that officers searching through a house used as a narcotics distribution center come upon twenty fur coats hanging in a closet. While there is nothing inherently incriminating in having fur coats, there is a fair probability under these circumstances that the coats are the fruits of drug proceeds, and therefore the coats can be seized without a warrant under the plain view doctrine. This would not necessarily be the case if the officers found only one fur coat in the closet.

4. Probable Cause Must Be Immediately Apparent, Without the Necessity of a Further Search

If the item must be searched and investigated in order to determine whether there is probable cause to seize it, such an investigation is itself a search which requires probable cause.

a. *Arizona v. Hicks*

An example of the requirement that probable cause must be immediately apparent without the necessity of a further search is found in the important case of *Arizona v. Hicks*, 480 U.S. 321, 107 S.Ct. 1149, 94 L.Ed.2d 347 (1987). In *Hicks*, Arizona police entered Hicks' apartment after a bullet was fired through its floor into the apartment below, injuring a man. The officers looked for the shooter, other victims and weapons. The apartment was in squalid condition. The officers noticed two new sets of stereo components in the apartment. Suspecting that the components were stolen, one officer moved a turntable in order to read its serial number. This led to information that the turntable had been taken in an armed robbery. The state conceded that there was no probable cause to seize the stereo components without first looking at the serial number. But it argued that the components could nonetheless be seized under the plain view doctrine.

b. Ruling in *Hicks*

The Supreme Court rejected the state's argument and found the plain view doctrine inapplicable because the officers engaged in a search to determine whether there was probable cause to seize the stereo, and that search was beyond the permissible scope of the initial intrusion into the apartment. The Court held that such a search could not be conducted in the absence of probable cause. The fact that there was some suspicion, short of probable cause, that the stereos were stolen, did not justify the search of the turntable.

c. **Immediately Apparent**

The result in *Hicks* means that in order to seize something under the plain view doctrine, probable cause must be *apparent upon visual inspection*—no search, no matter how cursory, is allowed in order to determine whether probable cause exists. Courts refer to this as a further requirement of the plain view doctrine—that probable cause must be "immediately apparent." This might have been the case in *Hicks* if there had been several brand new stereos in boxes in the squalid apartment. Then there may well have been probable cause to believe that all the stereos were stolen.

C. No Requirement That the Plain View Discovery Be Inadvertent

The Supreme Court, in *Horton v. California*, 496 U.S. 128, 110 S.Ct. 2301, 110 L.Ed.2d 112 (1990), held that the plain view doctrine could apply even if an officer expected in advance to find the object in plain view. There is no requirement that the officer discover evidence in plain view "inadvertently."

1. Facts of *Horton*

The warrant in *Horton* authorized the search of Horton's house and the seizure of the proceeds of a robbery. The officer also had probable cause to believe that the weapons used in the robbery would be found in the search, but the warrant did not authorize their seizure. During the search for the proceeds, the officer, as he had expected, saw the weapons in plain view. The State admitted that this discovery was not inadvertent. The Court held that the weapons were properly seized under the plain view doctrine.

2. Rationale of *Horton*

The Court in *Horton* found the inadvertence requirement to be unsound on two grounds. First, the standard of inadvertence is impermissibly subjective. It would invalidate a seizure based on the state of mind of the officer. The *Horton* Court found that the officer's state of mind is irrelevant, because the question under the Fourth Amendment is whether the search or the seizure is objectively "reasonable."

Second, the Court found unpersuasive the argument that an inadvertence requirement was necessary to prevent warrantless general searches. In order to trigger the plain view doctrine, the officer must be in a lawful place to find the items that are described in a warrant or that are found in the proper scope of warrantless but legal activity. So rejecting the inadvertence requirement would not allow the officer to look in any more places or with any more intensity than he would otherwise be able to do. In fact, the officer would want to include all seizable materials in a warrant, since that could serve to expand the scope of a lawful search.

D. Plain Touch

If an officer, acting in the course of lawful activity, can determine by touch that an object is evidence or contraband, he can seize the object under the "plain touch" doctrine. In *Minnesota v. Dickerson,* 508 U.S. 366, 113 S.Ct. 2130, 124 L.Ed.2d 334 (1993), an officer, in the course of a stop and frisk permitted by the *Terry* doctrine, frisked the suspect and felt a small, hard, pea-shaped object in the suspect's shirt pocket. At the suppression hearing, the officer testified that when he patted Dickerson down, he examined the object with his fingers "and it slid and it felt to be a lump of crack cocaine in cellophane." Since the suspect had left a house known to be a place for drug activity, the officer concluded that there was probable cause to believe that the pea-shaped object was crack cocaine, and pulled the object (which was indeed crack) from the suspect's pocket. This seizure would not have been permitted under the *Terry* doctrine itself, because a *Terry* frisk is only permitted to the extent necessary to uncover weapons.

1. Rationale

The Court in *Dickerson* stated that the plain view doctrine "has an obvious application by analogy to cases in which an officer discovers contraband through the sense of touch during an otherwise lawful search." Like the plain view doctrine, if an officer determines probable cause by sense of touch while within the scope of lawful activity, the seizure of the object should be permissible because "there has been no invasion of the suspect's privacy beyond that already authorized by the officer's search."

2. Touch Cannot Be Beyond the Scope of Legal Activity

Even though there is a plain touch exception to the warrant requirement, it is important to remember that the touching must be within the scope of lawful activity. While the Court in *Dickerson* validated the plain touch exception, it also found that the exception was not applicable under the facts presented. This was because the officer did more than merely touch the object in the course of a lawful *Terry* frisk. Rather, he pushed and prodded the object in order to determine whether it was contraband. Such an aggressive procedure was held to be beyond the limited frisk authorized by *Terry.* Accordingly, the incriminating nature of the object was not immediately apparent under *Hicks, supra,* and the Court therefore found that the cocaine was illegally obtained.

III. Warrantless Arrests

A. No Warrant Required for a Public Arrest

In *United States v. Watson*, 423 U.S. 411, 96 S.Ct. 820, 46 L.Ed.2d 598 (1976), the Court held that the Fourth Amendment does not require an officer to obtain a warrant before making a public arrest. This is so even if the officer could easily have obtained the warrant without jeopardizing the arrest. Thus, for public arrests, the officer can determine for himself whether probable cause exists to support the arrest.

1. What Is at Stake

An illegal arrest does not preclude a prosecution. *See United States v. Crews*, 445 U.S. 463, 100 S.Ct. 1244, 63 L.Ed.2d 537 (1980). Rather, the defendant in a case like *Watson* is arguing that because of the illegal arrest, the evidence that was obtained as a result of the arrest should be excluded as the fruit of the poisonous tree. For example, in *Watson*, the defendant sought to suppress evidence that was obtained from him in a search incident to the arrest. Watson's argument was unsuccessful because the Court held that there was no poisonous tree—that the arrest was permissible without a warrant.

2. Rationale of *Watson*

The majority in *Watson* relied heavily on the premise that warrantless arrests were permissible under the common law. The Court also used a utilitarian analysis and concluded that the benefits of a warrant require-ment (i.e., the protection of citizens' privacy interests) were outweighed by the costs to law enforcement of having to obtain warrants for public arrests.

3. Post–Arrest Determination of Probable Cause

While a warrantless public arrest is permissible upon an officer's determination that probable cause exists, the Supreme Court has recog-nized that the officer's determination of probable cause may be errone-ous because the officer is in "the competitive enterprise of ferreting out crime." Therefore, the Court in *Gerstein v. Pugh*, 420 U.S. 103, 95 S.Ct. 854, 43 L.Ed.2d 54 (1975), held that if a citizen is arrested without a warrant, he has the right to a prompt post-arrest determination of probable cause by a magistrate or judge.

a. Much Like a Pre–Arrest Warrant Procedure

The Court in *Gerstein* stressed that the Government was not required to provide a full-blown adversary hearing for a post-arrest determination of probable cause. Thus, protections such as the right to counsel or the right to confrontation are not required. The intent in *Gerstein* is to provide the citizen with essentially the same protection after an arrest as the citizen would have received if the officer had obtained an arrest warrant.

b. Prompt Hearing Is Required

The function of a post-arrest determination of probable cause is to keep the damage from an erroneous arrest to a minimum. The Court in *Gerstein* therefore held that a citizen is entitled to a "prompt" post-arrest determination of probable cause if the citizen was arrested without a warrant. In *County of Riverside v. McLaughlin*, 500 U.S. 44, 111 S.Ct. 1661, 114 L.Ed.2d 49 (1991), the Court defined "prompt" as "reasonably prompt." The Court stated that a 48 hour delay between arrest and a *Gerstein* hearing would be presumed reasonable. Any delay beyond 48 hours would be presumed unreasonable, and the state would have to present compelling circumstances to explain the delay.

c. Arrests for Minor Offenses

In his concurrence in *Gustafson v. Florida*, 414 U.S. 260, 267, 94 S.Ct. 488, 492, 38 L.Ed.2d 456, 462 (1973), Justice Stewart suggested that a custodial arrest for a minor traffic violation might violate the Fourth and Fourteenth Amendments. However, the Court decided otherwise in *Atwater v. City of Lago Vista*, 532 U.S. 318, 121 S.Ct. 1536, 149 L.Ed.2d 549 (2001), holding that an officer does not violate the Fourth Amendment if he arrests an individual for a very minor criminal offense, as long as he has probable cause to believe that the individual has committed the offense in his presence. See discussion of *Atwater, infra.*

B. Warrant Required for an In–Home Arrest

In *Payton v. New York*, 445 U.S. 573, 100 S.Ct. 1371, 63 L.Ed.2d 639 (1980), the Court held that the Fourth Amendment prohibited the police from arresting the defendant in his home without a warrant, in the absence of exigent circumstances.

1. Distinguished From *Watson*

The essential distinction between *Payton* and *Watson* is that an in-home arrest is a greater intrusion on privacy than a public arrest. In the course of making an in-home arrest, the officer must enter into an area which has traditionally been accorded the highest protection. As the Court has stated, entry into the home is the "chief evil" at which the Fourth Amendment is directed. The warrant requirement in *Payton* is not intended to protect the citizen from being wrongly arrested; rather, it is intended to protect the citizen from having his home searched in the absence of probable cause to arrest him. In *Kirk v. Louisiana*, 536 U.S. 635, 122 S.Ct. 2458, 153 L.Ed.2d 599 (2002), the Court affirmed *Payton* in a per curiam opinion.

2.   *Payton* Violation Constitutes Illegal Search, Not an Illegal Arrest

It follows that when an officer has probable cause and arrests the defendant in his home without exigent circumstances, the officer has conducted an illegal *search* of the home by entering it to seize the arrestee. But the arrest itself is not illegal, presuming it was made with probable cause. This was made plain in *New York v. Harris,* 495 U.S. 14, 110 S.Ct. 1640, 109 L.Ed.2d 13 (1990), where the officer arrested the defendant in his home without a warrant. Harris was subsequently taken down to the police station, where he confessed. He moved to suppress the confession as "the fruit of the poisonous tree." But the Supreme Court held that the confession was properly admitted, because there was no connection between the *Payton* violation and the subsequent confession. The Court stated that "the rule in *Payton* was designed to protect the physical integrity of the home." It was not intended to protect defendants who are arrested with probable cause.

3.   Reason to Believe the Suspect Is at Home

In *Payton*, the Court made it clear that a valid arrest warrant authorizes police officers to enter a suspect's dwelling when there is reason to believe the suspect is at home. *Payton* leaves it to the officer executing the warrant to make that determination. Some courts have held that the "reason to believe" standard means something less than probable cause. *See United States v. Thomas,* 429 F.3d 282 (D.C. Cir. 2005) ("the Supreme Court in *Payton* used a phrase other than 'probable cause' because it meant something other than probable cause"). Other courts equate "reason to believe" with "probable cause" ("the 'reason to believe' standard directly echoes the underlying definition of probable cause." *United States v. Pruitt,* 458 F.3d 477 (6th Cir. 2006)).

4.   When Is an Arrest Made in the "Home"?

Given the bright-line distinction between home arrests, which require a warrant, and public arrests, which do not, it becomes important to determine whether an arrest is made in the home or in public.

a. Doorway Arrests

Where the defendant is arrested upon answering the door to his home, courts have split on whether the arrest occurs in the home or in public. Some courts have stated that if the defendant is ordered to open the door under a claim of authority, and is arrested upon opening the door, then the arrest occurs in the home and a warrant is required. *See United States v. Winsor*, 846 F.2d 1569 (9th Cir. 1988). Other courts hold that if the officers remain outside the doorway and inform the defendant that he is under arrest, then the arrest is made in public. This view leads to difficult fact questions where the officer subsequently enters the home; if the arrest was made before the physical entry, then the entry can be justified as incident to the arrest and information discovered during the incident search will be considered legally obtained. However, if the arrest is made after the entry, then there has been a *Payton* violation, and the information discovered during the entry is illegally obtained. *See United States v. Berkowitz*, 927 F.2d 1376 (7th Cir. 1991) (remanding to determine whether the officers informed the defendant that he was under arrest before or after entering his home). The courts which hold that a doorway arrest constitutes an arrest in the home do not have to deal with such fine-line distinctions.

b. Common Hallways

If the arrest is made in a common hallway outside the defendant's apartment, then the arrest is treated as a public arrest that does not require a warrant. *See United States v. Holland*, 755 F.2d 253 (2d Cir. 1985) (public arrest where the defendant answers the buzzer at the outside door to his apartment building, while standing in a common hallway).

c. Homeless Persons

Some courts have held that the arrest of a homeless person cannot violate *Payton*, even if the arrest occurs in a place which the person calls "home." *See United States v. Ruckman*, 806 F.2d 1471 (10th Cir. 1986) (warrantless arrest of defendant in a cave on Government-owned property did not violate *Payton*). Increasingly, however, courts have been sympathetic to the privacy interests of homeless persons, and have begun to hold that the term "home" must be flexibly applied to include a public area in which a homeless person has established a living space. *See, e.g., Community for Creative*

Non–Violence v. Unknown Agents of U.S. Marshals Service, 797 F.Supp. 7 (D.D.C. 1992) (*Payton* applies to arrests conducted in a homeless shelter).

d.   Hotels and Motels

The protections against warrantless intrusions into the home announced in *Payton* apply with equal force to a properly rented hotel or motel room during the rental period. *United States v. Morales*, 737 F.2d 761 (8th Cir. 1984). However, this is only the case so long as the person has rightful possession of the room. If the rental period has terminated, or if the person has been rightfully ejected from the premises, then the premises can no longer be considered a "home." *United States v. Larson*, 760 F.2d 852 (8th Cir. 1985).

e.   Houseboats, Mobile Homes, etc.

Relying on cases dealing with searches of motor vehicles and boats, the courts have held that *Payton* does not require officers to obtain an arrest warrant before entering a houseboat, car, or motor home to effectuate an arrest. *United States v. Hill*, 855 F.2d 664 (10th Cir. 1988).

5.   Arrest in the Course of Executing a Search Warrant

If an officer has a valid search warrant, an arrest of the defendant in his home during the course of that search is valid even though the officer does not also have an arrest warrant. The rationale is that the evil with which *Payton* is concerned (the warrantless search of the home in the course of effectuating an arrest) is nullified by the officer having obtained a valid search warrant. *See Mahlberg v. Mentzer*, 968 F.2d 772 (8th Cir. 1992).

C.   Search Warrant Is Required for an Arrest in the Home of a Third Party

An arrest warrant authorizes an arrest of a particular person, but it does not specify the particular places in which the arrest can be effectuated. In *Payton*, the Court noted that an arrest warrant affords less protection than a search warrant, because a search warrant must describe a particular place in which the search is to be conducted. The Court did hold, however, that officers armed with an arrest warrant could only enter the suspect's home if "there is reason to believe that the suspect is within." But this factual standard need not be demonstrated to a magistrate. As noted above, *Payton* leaves it to the officer executing the arrest warrant to determine whether there is "reason to believe the suspect is within the home."

1. **Arrest Warrant Not Sufficient if the Suspect Is Temporarily in the Home of Another**

   In *Steagald v. United States,* 451 U.S. 204, 101 S.Ct. 1642, 68 L.Ed.2d 38 (1981), the Court held that in the absence of exigent circumstances or consent, a search warrant must be obtained to look for a suspect in the home of a third party if the suspect is not a resident of the premises. That is, a magistrate must determine whether there is probable cause to believe that the suspect is located in the home of a third party.

2. **Rationale of *Steagald***

   The Court reasoned that an arrest warrant could not protect the privacy interests of a third-party homeowner, since the arrest warrant was not based on any judicial determination that there was probable cause to search for the suspect in the third-party's home. The Court was concerned that a contrary rule would invite abuse: "Armed solely with an arrest warrant for a single person, the police could search all the homes of that individual's friends and acquaintances."

3. **Distinction From *Payton***

   In a case like *Payton,* there is a risk of error in the execution of an arrest warrant, i.e., that the officers may determine that there is reason to believe the suspect is at home when in fact he is not. The Court determined that this risk of error did not justify review by a magistrate. In *Steagald,* there was the same risk of error—that officers may determine there is probable cause that the suspect is in the home of a third party when in fact he is not. However, the risk of error is more grave in *Steagald* because the error could be made in any and every house that the officer chooses to search. In *Payton,* the risk of erroneous entry is limited to a discrete number of places; in *Steagald,* there is a risk that an arrest warrant can be used as a general warrant to search any house in the community in which the suspect might be. Consequently, this much greater and more pervasive risk of erroneous entry required a magistrate's review.

4. **Is the Suspect Living at or Visiting the Premises?**

   After *Steagald,* it is important to determine whether the suspect lives at the premises (in which case an arrest warrant is sufficient), or whether he is merely visiting there (in which case a search warrant is required). Courts have looked to how long and how consistently the suspect has stayed at the premises, whether the suspect is responsible for utilities, and other indicia of permanent residence. *See United States v. Risse,* 83

F.3d 212 (8th Cir. 1996) (police officers reasonably believed that suspect named in arrest warrant was living at her boyfriend's residence, where suspect told police she was staying at that residence and could be contacted there).

5. Who Has Standing to Object to the Lack of a Search Warrant?

In *Steagald*, the officers entered Steagald's home with a warrant to arrest the suspect Lyons. In the course of effectuating the arrest, the officers discovered evidence which was used against Steagald at trial. The Court held that the evidence should have been suppressed because Steagald's Fourth Amendment rights were violated in the absence of a search warrant. It follows from this reasoning that Lyons, the suspect, would have no standing to object to the lack of a search warrant, since *Steagald* was concerned with the privacy rights of the third-party homeowner. *See United States v. Underwood*, 717 F.2d 482 (9th Cir. 1983) (*Steagald* addressed only the right of a third party not named in the arrest warrant to the privacy of his or her home; this right is personal and cannot be asserted vicariously by the person named in the arrest warrant).

a. Anomaly

It would be anomalous to allow the suspect to challenge the lack of a search warrant when he is arrested in a third party's home. Such a rule would mean that the suspect would be entitled to demand a search warrant when arrested in the home of another, while he could only demand an arrest warrant when arrested in his own home. *See United States v. Kaylor*, 877 F.2d 658 (8th Cir. 1989) ("Kaylor cannot claim any greater Fourth Amendment protection in the Lindgren home than he possessed in his own home.").

b. Can a Visitor Object to the Lack of an Arrest Warrant When Arrested in a Third Party's Home?

In *Minnesota v. Olson*, 495 U.S. 91, 110 S.Ct. 1684, 109 L.Ed.2d 85 (1990), the Court held that a defendant had standing to object to his warrantless arrest where it occurred in an apartment in which he was an overnight guest. However, what if the suspect is not an overnight guest, but is rather merely temporarily visiting the premises of a third party? Can he object to a warrantless arrest under *Payton*, or is it as if he is being arrested in a public place, wherein he has no expectation of privacy? In *Minnesota v. Carter*, discussed *infra* in the section on standing, the Supreme Court decided that such a temporary visitor has no legitimate expectation of privacy.

IV. Exigent Circumstances

A. Introduction

Police are not required to obtain a warrant if exigent circumstances exist. However, while exigent circumstances provide an exception to the warrant requirement, officers operating under this exception must still satisfy the probable cause requirement. For example, if exigent circumstances exist, officers can enter a person's home to arrest him without a warrant. But the officers still must have probable cause for the arrest.

1. Rationale

The exigent circumstances exception is based on the fact that it takes time to obtain a warrant, and in some cases, some type of harm might well occur during the delay caused by the warrant process. Certain risks resulting from the delay in obtaining a warrant are so severe that in order to avoid them, the Fourth Amendment's preference for obtaining a warrant is excused.

2. Types of Risks Which Excuse the Warrant

Generally speaking, the risks that trigger the exigent circumstances doctrine include those stemming from *hot pursuit* of a suspect, risks to *police or public safety,* and the risk of *destruction or loss of evidence.*

B. Hot Pursuit

If officers are in hot pursuit of a suspect, this will excuse an arrest warrant where one is otherwise required, and it will also excuse a search warrant where a search of an area must be conducted in order to find and apprehend the suspect. The rationale is that it is unrealistic to expect police officers to stop in the middle of a chase and resort to the warrant process. To do so could allow the suspect to get away and thus render the warrant meaningless. The delay of obtaining a warrant could also allow the fleeing suspect to destroy evidence or to create a dangerous situation for police officers or members of the public.

Example: The leading hot pursuit case in the Supreme Court is *Warden v. Hayden*, 387 U.S. 294, 87 S.Ct. 1642, 18 L.Ed.2d 782 (1967). Officers pursued a robbery suspect into what was subsequently determined to be the suspect's house. The suspect's wife answered the door, and the police entered the house to search for the suspect. In the course of looking for him, they also looked for weapons which he might have concealed during the pursuit. The officers found incriminating clothing in a washing machine. The Court held that the warrantless search was justified by the "hot pursuit" exception. The fact that the officers found clothing as opposed to weapons in the washing machine was not problematic, since the officers had the right, in these emergency circumstances, to search the washing machine to look for weapons, and thus the seizure of the clothing was permissible under the plain view doctrine.

Suspect Must Be Aware of Pursuit

The "hot pursuit" exception is based on the fact that the suspect, knowing that he is being pursued, may seek to escape, or to destroy evidence or create a threat to public safety. It follows that the "hot pursuit" exception cannot apply where the suspect is unaware that he is being pursued by police officers. If the "hot pursuit" exception were based only on how "hotly" the officers were "pursuing" a suspect, then it could apply in virtually every case.

Example: In *Welsh v. Wisconsin,* 466 U.S. 740, 104 S.Ct. 2091, 80 L.Ed.2d 732 (1984), officers were called to the scene of a car that had been driven into a ditch. Eyewitnesses told the officers that the driver had been driving erratically, and had walked away from the scene. The officers immediately went to the address listed on the vehicle registration, and arrested Welsh in his home for driving while intoxicated. The Court held that the "hot pursuit" exception could not apply in these circumstances, since Welsh was never aware until he was arrested that he was being pursued by police officers. There was no semblance of a chase.

C. Risk to Public or Police Safety

Even in the absence of hot pursuit of a suspect, there may be circumstances in which the police or the public would be harmed in the time it takes to obtain a warrant. If so, the police are excused from obtaining one. For example, if officers hear screams and shooting from an apartment, or if officers have reason to believe that the health and safety of a child is in imminent danger, they are not required to obtain a warrant before entering the premises.

1. Government Must Show an Imminent Risk to Public or Police Safety

The warrant requirement will not be excused unless the Government can establish facts which indicate that the officers faced an imminent risk to public or police safety. The Government must show that the risk was substantial, and was likely to arise during the delay attendant to obtaining a warrant. Broad, conceptual arguments that "public safety" was at stake will not do.

Example: In *Welsh v. Wisconsin, supra,* the State argued that the officers' warrantless arrest of Welsh in his home was required because Welsh represented a threat to public safety, in that he was intoxicated and had recently left his car in a ditch. Essentially, the State made the broad argument that intoxicated drivers present a risk to public safety, which should excuse the warrant requirement. The Court rejected this broad argument and noted that on the facts, Welsh presented no *imminent risk* to public safety. At the time of his arrest, he was sitting in his home and there was no indication that he was going out to drive while intoxicated. *See also Richards v. Wisconsin, supra* (rejecting the argument that there is an automatic risk to police safety during the search of a large-scale drug creation).

2. Public Safety and the Officer's Motives

In *Brigham City v. Stuart,* 547 U.S. 398, 126 S.Ct. 1943, 164 L.Ed.2d 650 (2006), police officers responded to a call at 3 a.m. regarding a loud party at a residence. Upon arriving at the house, they heard shouting from inside and observed two juveniles drinking beer in the backyard. They entered the backyard, and saw, through a screen door and windows, an altercation taking place in the kitchen of the home. Four adults were attempting to restrain a juvenile who eventually struck one of the adults in the face. The officers observed the victim of the blow spitting blood into a nearby sink. They arrested three of the adults and charged them with contributing to the delinquency of a minor, disorderly conduct, and intoxication. The defendants argued that the warrantless entry violated the Fourth Amendment because the officers were motivated by a desire to make arrests rather than save lives. They further argued that their conduct was not serious enough to justify the warrantless entry of the home. The Supreme Court held that the officers' state of mind was irrelevant as long as the circumstances, viewed objectively, justified their actions. The Court stated that the officers had an objectively reasonable basis for believing both that the injured adult might need help and that the violence in the kitchen was just beginning. Nothing required them to wait until someone was "unconscious" or "semi-conscious" or worse before entering. Thus, the entry did not violate the Fourth Amendment.

3. Fire Scenes

When a building is on fire, firefighters may enter without a warrant in the name of public safety. In *Michigan v. Tyler*, 436 U.S. 499, 98 S.Ct. 1942, 56 L.Ed.2d 486 (1978), the Court extended this principle and held that firefighters and inspectors could remain on the premises for a reasonable time in order to investigate the cause of the fire. However, the Court held that subsequent entries made days and weeks after the fire required a warrant, because these entries were "detached from the initial exigency."

D. Destruction or Loss of Evidence

The ground of exigency most often invoked is that in the time it would take to obtain a warrant, there is an imminent risk of destruction or loss of evidence.

Example: In *United States v. Riley*, 968 F.2d 422 (5th Cir. 1992), officers were aware that a drug deal had been arranged from a certain house. They placed the house under surveillance. They observed a person leaving the house carrying a white bag. Two officers followed this person as he drove to a hotel where the drug deal was to be consummated. The person who was followed, subsequently determined to be Terry Moore, was arrested on a drug charge. The white bag contained cocaine. Moore informed the officers that there was a large sum of money, a gun, and another person at the house from which he came. Officers also discovered that Moore was carrying a cellular phone. The commanding officer then dispatched nine officers to the house. They forced open the door, and discovered Riley, and incriminating evidence, in the house. The court held that the warrantless entry was justified. It stated that "the presence of a cellular phone indicated to the officers that Moore was going to report back and failure to call back or return would alert the other occupant that something had gone wrong." The court also emphasized that the evidence, narcotics, could be quickly and easily destroyed.

1. Factors Relevant to Whether an Imminent Risk of Destruction of Evidence Exists

Courts have set forth several factors which are considered relevant to whether the officers faced an imminent risk of destruction of evidence. None of these factors are dispositive and the list is not exclusive. As the courts have stated, the essential question is whether officers were faced with an *"urgent need"* to take action. In determining whether this "urgent need" existed, the following factors are relevant:

— The *degree of urgency* involved and the *amount of time* necessary to obtain a warrant. For example, in *Riley, supra,* the court took account of the fact that the arrest of the drug dealer took place on a Sunday night, and concluded that "the warrant would not be fast coming."

— A reasonable belief that contraband or evidence is *about to be removed.* For example, if officers become aware that the suspect is about to wash clothing that may contain incriminating forensic evidence, this may be a reason to enter the premises in the absence of a warrant.

— The *possibility of danger* to police officers guarding the premises while a search warrant is sought.

— Information indicating that suspects *know that the police are on their trail. See United States v. Scroger,* 98 F.3d 1256 (10th Cir. 1996) (exigent circumstances found where it was apparent that persons suspected of drug distribution were aware of police presence).

— The ready *destructibility* of the evidence. This is obviously an important factor in drug cases. *See Riley, supra* ("The need to invoke the exigent circumstances exception is particularly compelling in narcotics cases because of the ease with which they may be destroyed."). *Compare United States v. Holzman,* 871 F.2d 1496 (9th.Cir. 1989) (no exigency where, among other things, the evidence of stolen credit cards was not easily destroyed).

— The *gravity of the offense* of which the suspects are to be charged. See the discussion of minor offenses and searches of a murder scene, below.

— Whether the suspects are reasonably believed to have *firearms* in their possession. If so, it may be necessary to enter immediately before the suspects become aware of police surveillance and decide to arm themselves. *See United States v. MacDonald,* 916 F.2d 766 (2d Cir. 1990) (exigent circumstances found in a drug case, in part because "the defendant and at least one of his associates were armed with loaded, semi-automatic weapons").

— Whether *probable cause is clear* or is rather a close question. The stronger the showing of probable cause, the less crucial the need to obtain a magistrate's review, and the more likely it is that a court will accept the argument that emergency circumstances excused the failure to bring the facts before a magistrate.

— The *likelihood that suspects may escape* in the absence of an immediate entry.

— The *peaceful circumstances* of the entry.

2. Narcotics Cases

Relying upon the seriousness of a narcotics offense and the ready destructibility of narcotics, most lower courts liberally apply the exigent circumstances exception in drug cases. *See Riley, supra.* This is despite the Supreme Court's ruling in *Vale v. Louisiana*, 399 U.S. 30, 90 S.Ct. 1969, 26 L.Ed.2d 409 (1970). Officers arrested Vale outside his home after they had seen him engage in a narcotics sale. The officers then entered Vale's home to prevent the destruction of evidence. The Court held that the exigent circumstances exception did not apply, because there was no indication that Vale's accomplices were in *the process of destroying evidence.*

a. Need Not Be in the Process of Destruction

Most courts after *Vale* have not required narcotics to be in the actual process of destruction before a warrantless entry can be justified. Thus, there may be an imminent risk of destruction of evidence even though no evidence has yet been destroyed. *See United States v. MacDonald*, 916 F.2d 766 (2d Cir. 1990) (risk of destruction of evidence found after undercover officer made a drug buy, even though the suspects were not aware that the buyer was an undercover agent and there was no indication that police surveillance has been discovered). The court in *MacDonald* noted that due to the severity of the crime and the destructibility of the evidence, "ongoing retail narcotics operations often confront law enforcement agents with exigent circumstances."

b. Not an Automatic Rule

While the exigent circumstances exception is applied liberally in drug cases, the presence of drugs does not *per se* give rise to exigency. *See Richards v. Wisconsin, supra* (rejecting a "blanket rule" and requiring a showing of a risk of destruction of the drugs under the circumstances).

3. Murder Scene Searches

While the gravity of the crime is a factor in determining exigent circumstances, it is not a per se factor. In *Mincey v. Arizona*, 437 U.S. 385,

98 S.Ct. 2408, 57 L.Ed.2d 290 (1978), the Court held that there is no per se exigent circumstances exception for the search of a murder scene. A police officer was shot and killed in Mincey's apartment. Mincey was arrested and detectives undertook an extensive search of the apartment. The search lasted four days, during which Mincey was in the hospital and no person other than police officers attempted to enter the apartment. The officers never tried to obtain a warrant. The Court held that an immediate warrantless search of a murder scene is permissible to determine whether perpetrators or victims remain at the scene. However, the extensive four-day search of Mincey's apartment was illegal, because there was no factual indication that there was an imminent risk of destruction of evidence during that time.

4. Minor Crimes

Since the gravity of the crime is a factor in determining exigent circumstances, it follows that it is more difficult to establish exigency if the crime is a minor one. This principle was applied in *Welsh v. Wisconsin, supra*. Officers arrested Welsh in his home without a warrant. They had probable cause to believe that Welsh had been driving while intoxicated. Under Wisconsin law, this was a noncriminal, civil forfeiture offense for which no imprisonment was possible. The Court recognized that in the time it would have taken to obtain an arrest warrant, evidence of Welsh's intoxication probably would have been lost. But it held that in light of the state's expression of minimal interest in the substantive offense, "a warrantless in-home arrest cannot be upheld simply because evidence of the petitioner's blood-alcohol level might have dissipated while the police obtained a warrant." The Court concluded that application of the exigent circumstances exception "should rarely be sanctioned when there is probable cause to believe that only a minor offense, such as the kind at issue in this case, has been committed."

No Misdemeanor/Felony Distinction

The Court in *Welsh* specifically rejected the suggestion that an offense is "minor" (and thus an insufficient basis for excusing the warrant requirement on the ground that evidence of the crime is at risk), merely because it is classified as a misdemeanor. It appears that after *Welsh,* the exigent circumstances doctrine will be unavailable only when the evidence at risk pertains to offenses similar to that in *Welsh:* noncriminal offenses for which no imprisonment is authorized.

E. Impermissible Creation of Exigent Circumstances

The warrant requirement will not be excused where the police have, through impermissible conduct, created exigent circumstances. For example, officers cannot goad a suspect into running away in order to engage in a "hot pursuit." However, as the courts have noted, "in some sense the police always create the exigent circumstances that justify warrantless entries and arrests." For example, by arresting one member of a drug conspiracy, other members may become aware that something is wrong and may begin to destroy evidence. It is important to distinguish police activity which constitutes impermissible creation of exigent circumstances from police activity which is legitimate.

1. No Impermissible Creation of Exigency Where Officers Act Lawfully

Most courts refuse to find impermissible creation of exigent circumstances where the officers' activity is objectively lawful—even if it is apparent that the officers acted with the intent to create a situation in which the suspects would attempt to destroy evidence. For example, in *United States v. Acosta*, 965 F.2d 1248 (3d Cir. 1992), officers entered an apartment building to execute an arrest warrant for Carlos Santiago, who had previously lived in the building. Officers began knocking on the doors of the apartments in the building, announced that they were the police and that they had a warrant, and ordered the occupants to open the door. When they conducted this procedure at Acosta's apartment door, officers heard scuffling and commotion, and toilets flushing. Officers stationed in the back of the building informed the officers at the door that the people in the apartment were throwing "stuff" out the back window. At that point, the officers at the front door broke down the door and entered the apartment. A search of the premises revealed contraband and related items. Acosta argued that while there may have been an imminent risk of destruction of evidence at the time the officers entered the apartment, the exigency was impermissibly created by the officers having knocked on the door and announcing their presence. The Court held, however, that the officers' act of simply knocking on the door and ordering it to be opened was not itself unlawful: such conduct was not itself a search or seizure, and therefore it did not matter that the officers had no search warrant for Acosta's apartment and no probable cause to believe that Santiago was in the apartment. The Court in *Acosta* concluded that "exigent circumstances are not to be disregarded simply because the suspects chose to respond to the agents' lawful conduct by attempting to escape, destroy evidence, or engage in any other unlawful activity." *See also United States v. MacDonald*, 916 F.2d 766 (2d Cir. 1990) (exigency was not impermissibly created where officers knocked on the door of an apartment used for an ongoing drug operation, and announced their presence, ostensibly to seek consent to search the apartment; the court found it irrelevant that the officers were carrying a battering ram with them when they were seeking "consent").

Initial Search or Seizure Must Itself Be Illegal for "Impermissible Creation" Doctrine to Be Applicable

In the view of the courts discussed above, there is no such thing as impermissible creation of exigency if the officer's activity which creates the exigency is not itself an illegal search or seizure. Under this view, the doctrine of impermissible creation of exigency is no different from the standard rule that evidence which is the fruit of an illegal search or seizure is generally excluded from trial. Thus, the police can knock on any door and announce their presence in the hopes of creating exigent circumstances.

2. Another View—Impermissible Creation Is Found When the Officer's Sole Intent Is to Create Exigent Circumstances

A few courts have held that police activity not illegal in itself can nonetheless constitute impermissible creation of exigent circumstances. According to these courts: "even when the conduct of Government agents may be termed lawful, we must not countenance deliberate efforts to circumvent the warrant requirement." These courts equate "deliberate" creation of exigency with "impermissible" creation of exigency. For example in *United States v. Timberlake*, 896 F.2d 592 (D.C. Cir. 1990), officers, who had no warrant, knocked on the door to an apartment and shouted "police, open up." They then heard sounds which made it apparent that evidence was being destroyed in the apartment; they broke down the door and entered. The court held that the exigent circumstances exception could not apply, because the officers had "deliberately" created exigent circumstances. The court explained that there was "no evidence that the police, when they knocked on the door, intended anything other than a warrantless search of the apartment." *See also United States v. Duchi*, 906 F.2d 1278 (8th Cir. 1990) ("deliberate" and thus impermissible creation of exigency where police drastically altered a package of drugs being sent to the defendant and then conducted a controlled delivery to the defendant's home).

a.   Intent–Based Test

Under the "deliberate creation" view, the exigent circumstances may be impermissibly created (and a warrantless search found illegal) even though the officer's conduct leading up to the emergency situation was legal and objectively reasonable.

b.   Supreme Court's Emphasis on Objectivity

The intent-based test appears inconsistent with the Supreme Court's emphasis on objective standards in construing the Fourth Amendment. In *Whren v. United States*, 517 U.S. 806, 116 S.Ct. 1769, 135 L.Ed.2d 89 (1996), the Court, in a related context, declared that subjective intentions of a police officer "play no role" in Fourth Amendment analysis. (See the discussion of *Whren* in the section on pretextual searches and arrests, *infra)*. Similarly, in *Brigham City v. Stuart, supra*, the Court emphasized that the officer's intent is not relevant. The Supreme Court, in light of *Whren* and *Brigham City*, would probably hold that exigent circumstances are not created impermissibly, if the officer's conduct is objectively lawful.

F.   Prior Opportunity to Obtain a Warrant

If the officers had probable cause and an opportunity to obtain a warrant for a significant time before an exigency arose, then the exigency does not excuse them from the warrant requirement. To take an easy example, assume that on Monday morning, officers obtain reliable information that stolen goods are being stored in a warehouse, and that the goods will be sold on Thursday afternoon. On Thursday afternoon, there is a risk of loss of evidence because the buyers will be taking delivery of the stolen goods. But the exigent circumstances exception does not permit a warrantless entry into the warehouse on Thursday afternoon. This is because the officers had three days to obtain a warrant before the exigency arose, and this exigency was foreseeable.

1.   Probable Cause and Opportunity to Obtain a Warrant Must Be Clear

Officers are not required to go to the magistrate for a warrant immediately upon determining that probable cause could arguably exist. Officers are permitted to strengthen doubtful cases on probable cause by taking more time and conducting further investigation. Moreover, even if there is a strong case on probable cause, officers may find that reporting to the magistrate could interrupt the flow of a continuing investigation. Therefore, courts have held that a prior opportunity to obtain a warrant will be found (and hence the exigent circumstances exception will be inapplicable) only if the officers had *clear probable cause* and an *obvious opportunity* to obtain a warrant.

Example: In *United States v. Miles,* 889 F.2d 382 (2d Cir. 1989), a reliable informant arranged a cocaine buy in Miles' apartment. Officers monitored a telephone call between Miles and the informant indicating Miles' willingness to make the deal later that day. The officers did not obtain a warrant. They entered Miles' apartment after the transaction was consummated between Miles, the informant, and the drug supplier, and after the informant had left the apartment ostensibly to obtain money for the buy. At that point, exigent circumstances existed because the informant's absence "for an extended period of time while the agents sought a warrant would create a substantial risk of alerting" the suspects to the imminence of an arrest. Miles argued that the officers should not have been allowed to take advantage of that exigency because they had an opportunity to obtain a warrant at any time after they monitored the telephone call. But the court responded that "law enforcement officers may delay obtaining a warrant until events have proceeded to a point where agents are reasonably certain that the evidence would ultimately support a conviction" and that it was not until the transaction actually took place that such a reasonable certainty existed. *See also United States v. Samboy*, 433 F.3d 154 (1st Cir. 2005) (no evidence that police delayed getting a warrant in order to manufacture the exigency).

2. Litigation Anomaly

Note that at a suppression hearing the issue of whether the officers had a prior opportunity to obtain a warrant before an exigency arose leads the parties to make arguments that appear contrary to arguments that they would make in other contexts. Thus, it is the defendant who must argue that the officers had a clear case of probable cause, and it is the State which must argue that the officers had no probable cause or at best a weak case before the exigent circumstances arose.

G. Telephone Warrants

The doctrine of exigent circumstances is invoked when deleterious consequences would occur within the time it takes to obtain a warrant. The length of time necessary to obtain a warrant is thus crucial to the inquiry. Federal Rule of Criminal Procedure 41 authorizes officers to obtain warrants by telephone, and such warrants are available in many states as well. Courts have accordingly held that where one is available, exigent circumstances must be determined in light of the time it takes to obtain a telephone warrant. *See United States v. Cuaron,* 700 F.2d 582 (10th Cir. 1983) ("Courts should consider the amount of time required to obtain a telephone warrant in assessing the urgency of the situation.").

Telephone Warrants Can Be Time–Consuming

Under Rule 41 and similar telephone warrant requirements in the states, a duplicate original warrant must be prepared by the officer, and must be read verbatim over the phone to the magistrate, who must physically transcribe it and prepare an original warrant for the record. Thus, obtaining a telephone warrant can be a time-consuming process, although it obviously involves less time than that required to obtain a warrant in person. Generally speaking, if an exigency would arise within a few minutes, courts will find the danger to be so imminent as to prevent the officers from obtaining even a telephone warrant. *Compare United States v. Berick,* 710 F.2d 1035 (5th Cir. 1983) (risk of destruction of evidence resulting from arrest of drug seller was so immediate as to render it impracticable to obtain a telephone warrant) with *United States v. Patino,* 830 F.2d 1413 (7th Cir. 1987) (agent could have obtained a telephone warrant during a 30–minute wait for back-up assistance).

H. Securing Premises While Waiting for the Warrant

Even in the absence of exigent circumstances, officers can protect against the destruction of evidence by securing a premises for the reasonable time it takes to obtain a warrant. By seizing the premises, officers can prevent people from going in and out, thus eliminating the risk of destruction of evidence while a warrant is being sought. In *Segura v. United States,* 468 U.S. 796, 104 S.Ct. 3380, 82 L.Ed.2d 599 (1984), Chief Justice Burger, joined by Justice Stevens, stated that "securing a dwelling, on the basis of probable cause, to prevent the destruction or removal of evidence while a search warrant is being sought is not itself an unreasonable seizure of either the dwelling or its contents." A majority of the Court found it unnecessary to reach the question of whether the seizing of the premises in *Segura* was reasonable. However, the principle established by Chief Justice Burger in *Segura* was adopted by the Court in *Illinois v. McArthur.*

1. *Illinois v. McArthur*

In *Illinois v. McArthur*, 531 U.S. 326, 121 S.Ct. 946, 148 L.Ed.2d 838 (2001), the Court firmly established the authority of police officers to seize and secure a home while a warrant is being obtained. In *McArthur*, police officers accompanied Tera McArthur to the trailer where she had lived with her husband while she removed her belongings. She went in to the trailer while the officers waited outside. After she came out, she informed the officers that she had seen her husband place illegal drugs under the couch. The officers knocked on the door, told Charles McArthur what Tera had said and asked for permission to search the trailer. Charles denied permission. At this point, Charles was on the porch of the trailer. One officer went to get a search warrant while another officer waited with Charles and informed him that he could not re-enter the trailer unless a police officer accompanied him. While they waited for the warrant, Charles entered the trailer two or three times (to get cigarettes and make phone calls). Each time, the police officer stood just inside the door to observe Charles while he was in the trailer. The officer returned with a warrant within two hours and, along with the other officers, conducted a search. The officers found marijuana and drug paraphernalia in the trailer.

2. The Court's Rationale

The Court found the warrantless seizure reasonable, in light of the facts and circumstances of the case. The police had probable cause to believe that the trailer contained evidence of a crime and good reason to believe that McArthur would destroy the evidence if they did not keep him under surveillance. They also used the least intrusive method to fulfill their law enforcement goals. They didn't search the trailer or attempt to arrest or otherwise restrain McArthur while waiting for the warrant, and only entered the trailer enough to keep McArthur within view. Finally, the seizure was only two hours long. The Court cited *Segura*, noting that in that case, the majority and minority agreed that officers with probable cause to believe an apartment contained drugs could have secured the apartment from the outside and restricted entry while waiting for a warrant. The Court also cited other circumstances where the Court has upheld temporary restraints to preserve evidence until police could obtain a warrant.

V. Stop and Frisk

A. *Terry* and the Court's Reliance on the Reasonableness Clause of the Fourth Amendment

In *Terry v. Ohio,* 392 U.S. 1, 88 S.Ct. 1868, 20 L.Ed.2d 889 (1968), Terry and two others walked several times back and forth past a store. Officer McFadden, an experienced policeman, saw this activity and suspected that the three men were casing the store in preparation for a robbery. Officer McFadden approached the suspects and identified himself, and asked them to identify themselves and explain their conduct. When the suspects mumbled something that he couldn't hear, Officer McFadden grabbed Terry, patted down the outside of his clothing, felt a pistol in Terry's pocket, and confiscated the pistol. Terry was convicted on charges of carrying a concealed weapon, and he challenged the search and seizure of the pistol. In the Supreme Court, it was undisputed that McFadden lacked probable cause when he spun Terry around and frisked him. The question was whether the seizure and search were justifiable on a standard of proof less demanding than that of probable cause.

1. Stop and Frisk Permissible if Reasonable Suspicion Exists

The Court in *Terry* found that Officer McFadden had both seized and searched Terry, and therefore that the Fourth Amendment applied to the officer's conduct. The Court, however, rejected Terry's argument that both a warrant and probable cause were required for a search and seizure such as that conducted by Officer McFadden. The Court held that a stop can be conducted if an officer has *reasonable suspicion* to believe that crime is afoot. The *Terry* Court further held that an officer who makes a legal stop can conduct a *protective frisk* of a suspect if the officer has *reasonable suspicion to fear* that the suspect is armed and dangerous. Although the majority in *Terry* never used the term "stop and frisk," this term has become a well-recognized description of the intrusions upheld in *Terry.*

2. Inapplicability of the Warrant Clause

In a typical stop and frisk situation, there is no serious argument that the officer should have obtained a warrant. For example, in *Terry,* if Officer McFadden had left the scene to obtain a warrant, the suspects would probably have been gone when he returned. Yet under the Court's warrant clause jurisprudence, probable cause is still required for a search or seizure even if exigent circumstances excuse the warrant requirement. The chief innovation of *Terry* is the Court's holding that the warrant clause (and its concomitant requirement of probable cause) was inapplicable to the stop-and-frisk conducted by Officer McFadden. Rather, Officer McFadden's conduct was reviewed to determine whether it was a *reasonable* search and seizure. Contrary to its previous jurisprudence which held the warrant clause predominant over the reasonableness clause, the Court in *Terry* held that the reasonableness clause provided the benchmark for assessing the constitutionality of a stop and frisk.

3. Importance of Reasonableness Clause Analysis

An analysis based on reasonableness is obviously more flexible than an analysis which assumes that a search or seizure requires probable cause in all circumstances. What is reasonable depends on a balance of interests. In the Fourth Amendment context, reasonableness depends on the nature of the state interest involved in conducting the search or seizure, as balanced against the nature of the intrusion on the individual. It may be that requiring probable cause for a certain intrusion would give too much weight to the individual interest at the expense of the state interest. An analysis based on reasonableness could take account of this and conclude that a certain intrusion could be conducted on a standard of proof less demanding than probable cause.

4. Application of Reasonableness Balancing to Stop and Frisk

The Court in *Terry* balanced the nature of the intrusion involved in a stop and frisk with the state interest involved in conducting such an intrusion, and concluded that probable cause was not required for a stop and frisk. Rather, a stop and frisk was reasonable if conducted on the lesser standard of proof of reasonable suspicion. The Court's rationale was that the individual interest at stake in a stop and frisk was less serious than that involved when a suspect is arrested and/or when a full-scale search is conducted. Unlike an arrest, a stop is a momentary, small-scale intrusion. And unlike a full-scale search for evidence, a frisk is a cursory inspection for weapons. Balanced against these lesser intrusions was the high state interest in conducting a stop and frisk. A stop is often necessary to investigate crime on a preliminary basis, and is an essential tool of crime prevention as well as detection. A frisk effectuates the strong state interest of protecting the safety of police officers. The Court in *Terry* concluded that if a stop and frisk required probable cause, the interests of the state and the individual would not be in appropriate balance. An unacceptable number of crimes would go undetected or unprevented, and police officers would face an unacceptably high level of risk.

5.   Application of Reasonable Suspicion Standard to the Facts of *Terry*

The Court concluded that the stop of Terry was reasonable because it would have been "poor police work" to allow the suspicious activity to have gone uninvestigated. The Court further concluded that the frisk of Terry was reasonable because the suspects appeared to be involved in planning an armed robbery and therefore the officer had reasonable suspicion to believe that Terry was armed. The Court also noted that the frisk was no more intrusive than necessary to find and seize a weapon.

6.   Reasonableness Balancing Not Limited to Stop and Frisk

The Court in *Terry* took pains to note that its rejection of the warrant clause in favor of a reasonableness balancing approach was limited to the unique area of stop and frisk. Justice Douglas, in dissent, was unconvinced, and predicted the demise of the probable cause requirement in favor of a more flexible and more permissive ad hoc balancing approach. For better or worse, Justice Douglas' predictions have come true, at least in part, as the Court has extended its reasonableness analysis well beyond the context of stop and frisk. *See* the discussion of reasonableness searches, *infra* in this outline. *See also* Justice Marshall's dissent in *Skinner v. Railway Labor Executives' Ass'n,* 489 U.S. 602, 109 S.Ct. 1402, 103 L.Ed.2d 639 (1989) (decrying the rejection of the probable cause standard and the employment of reasonableness balancing in a drug-testing case).

7.   Three Categories of Police–Citizen Contacts

In light of *Terry,* the Court has defined three categories of police-citizen contact, and has set forth the appropriate standard of proof for each:

a.   Arrest and Incident Search

The most serious intrusion is an arrest, and the standard of proof required to justify an arrest is probable cause. An arrest allows a complete search incident to the arrest, for officer self-protection and to protect against the destruction of evidence.

b.   Stop and Frisk

A less serious intrusion is a stop, which is permitted on the lesser standard of proof of reasonable suspicion. Incident to a stop is a frisk, which is a limited search for weapons, *not for evidence.* The permissibility and scope of a frisk is limited to its rationale of protecting the officer in the course of a lawful stop. *See Sibron v. New*

York, 392 U.S. 40, 88 S.Ct. 1889, 20 L.Ed.2d 917 (1968) (*Terry* does not permit a search for evidence on less than probable cause; frisk must be justified by the need for self-protection).

c. Encounter

If an officer merely engages the citizen in an encounter, this is not considered an intrusion at all. Since an *encounter is not a seizure,* it does not implicate the Fourth Amendment, and therefore the officer need not satisfy any standard of proof before conducting an encounter. Obviously no incident search or frisk is allowed pursuant to an encounter.

8. **Standard of Proof Must Accord With the Intrusion**

It is crucial for the state to match its intrusion with the correct standard of proof. Otherwise, a subsequent search or seizure is likely to be excluded as the fruit of the poisonous tree. For example, in *Florida v. Royer,* 460 U.S. 491, 103 S.Ct. 1319, 75 L.Ed.2d 229 (1983), the officers obtained consent from Royer to search his luggage. However, this consent was held tainted since Royer had been subjected to such a serious intrusion that the Court found that he was under arrest at the time he gave his consent; and at that time the officers had only reasonable suspicion, not probable cause, to believe that Royer was involved in drug trafficking. If the officers had had probable cause, Royer's consent would probably have been valid. Likewise, if the officers had not exceeded the limitations of a stop and escalated the intrusion into an arrest without probable cause, the consent would probably have been valid. *See United States v. Taylor,* 956 F.2d 572 (6th Cir. 1992) (consensual search of bag held permissible where consent was obtained in an encounter; therefore it did not matter that the officers had no reasonable suspicion to believe that defendant was involved in drug activity).

B. **What Is a "Stop"?—The Line Between Stop and Encounter**

If an officer does not have reasonable suspicion that a citizen is involved in illegal activity, he cannot "stop" the citizen, because a stop is a seizure which requires a justification; but an officer can "encounter" a citizen for any reason or no reason, because an encounter is not a seizure. *See United States v. Taylor,* 956 F.2d 572 (6th Cir. 1992) (since officers conducted an encounter rather than a stop, it was irrelevant under the Fourth Amendment that the officers approached the defendant because he was African–American). It is therefore important to delineate stops from encounters.

1. The *Mendenhall* Reasonable Person Test

In *United States v. Mendenhall,* 446 U.S. 544, 100 S.Ct. 1870, 64 L.Ed.2d 497 (1980), Justice Stewart proposed that a stop be defined as follows: if, in view of all the circumstances, a *reasonable innocent person would have believed that he was not free to leave,* then a stop has occurred. While the majority of the Court in *Mendenhall* found it unnecessary to employ this test in that case, the "free to leave" test was subsequently adopted by the Court (*See INS v. Delgado,* 466 U.S. 210, 104 S.Ct. 1758, 80 L.Ed.2d 247 (1984)), though it has subsequently been modified for some situations, as discussed below.

2. Does a Reasonable Person Ever Feel Free to Leave From an Officer's Presence?

If the *Mendenhall* test were applied literally, it is arguable that *every* police-citizen contact would constitute a stop. Very few citizens feel free to walk away from an officer who approaches them to ask questions. Even if an officer does not act coercively, there is an inherent coercive power in the status of an officer, which renders most citizens reluctant to leave the scene. It is clear, however, that the Court has never intended that the *Mendenhall* test be applied literally, since the Court has specifically held that an officer needs no justification to approach a citizen and ask a few questions. *See INS v. Delgado, supra* ("Police questioning, by itself, is unlikely to result in a Fourth Amendment violation. While most citizens will respond to a police request, the fact that people do so * * * hardly eliminates the consensual nature of the response.").

3. Active Coercion Prohibited

The *Mendenhall* test is an attempt to balance the need of an officer to conduct a preliminary inquiry without having to justify it, and the interests of ordinary citizens in being free from police coercion. Therefore, as applied, the test has come to mean that an officer who affirmatively employs coercive tactics will be held to have conducted a seizure, requiring (at least) reasonable suspicion. If, instead, the officer acts politely and the citizen merely responds to the fact that the questioning is conducted by an officer, then the contact will be deemed an encounter.

4. Factors Considered Under the *Mendenhall* Test

While each case varies on its facts, courts have established and applied a variety of factors to determine whether an officer has employed coercive tactics sufficient to constitute a stop. On the one hand, it is clear that simply approaching a citizen and asking a few questions is not a stop. On the other hand, drawing a gun and placing the citizen in the back of a police car is at least a stop. In between these two situations is a gray area, in which the following factors are relevant.

— *Physical Obstruction of Movement*

If officers block the suspect's forward movement, this will go far toward showing that a stop has occurred. *See Brower v. County of Inyo*, 489 U.S. 593, 109 S.Ct. 1378, 103 L.Ed.2d 628 (1989) (use of roadblock to force a suspect to stop constitutes a seizure).

— *Show of Force*

A show of force, such as drawn guns, or other menacing activity, is a strong indication that a stop has occurred.

— *Retaining Identification, Airplane Tickets, and the Like*

An officer can, without reasonable suspicion, approach a suspect and politely ask him for identification, or for his airplane ticket in an airport encounter. The suspect is considered free to reject the request. However, if the suspect complies with the request, the officer is not permitted, in the absence of reasonable suspicion, to retain the identification or the ticket in order to prolong the inquiry. A reasonable person is not likely to feel free to leave when his identification or his airplane ticket would be left behind. *See United States v. Jordan*, 958 F.2d 1085 (D.C. Cir. 1992) ("police withholding of a person's identification conveys a definite message that the person is not free to leave"); *Florida v. Royer, supra* (stop occurs where officers retain Royer's airplane ticket).

— *Threatening Tones or Coercive Orders*

While polite questioning is permissible, the officer's use of threatening language or tone of voice is relevant to whether a seizure has occurred. For example, courts have been more likely to find that a stop has occurred if the officer threatened the suspect with detention or accused the suspect of criminal activity. *See United States v. Alarcon–Gonzalez*, 73 F.3d 289 (10th Cir. 1996) (Police order to "freeze" communicates that suspects are not free to leave and is sufficient to effect seizure).

— *Brevity*

Even polite questioning must be brief; otherwise it could appear to the reasonable person that the officer will not be satisfied no matter what answers are given.

— *Polite Requests to Consent to Search or to Move the Questioning*

If the officer politely asks the citizen whether he would consent to a search of his person or of a piece of luggage or the like, this will be considered a consensual encounter in the absence of other coercive factors. Likewise, if the officer politely asks the citizen to continue the conversation in a different place (such as to move the questioning from an airport concourse to an investigative office), the citizen's compliance with this request will not itself indicate that a stop has occurred.

— *Informing the Citizen of the Right to Terminate an Encounter or to Refuse Consent*

An officer is not obligated to tell the citizen that he has the right to refuse to answer questions or consent to a search. However, if the officer does inform the citizen of these rights, this will go far toward establishing a consensual encounter.

— *Coercive Surroundings*

If the police-citizen contact occurs in closed surroundings, that setting may be indicative of coercion, though not dispositive. Thus, in *Florida v. Bostick*, 501 U.S. 429, 111 S.Ct. 2382, 115 L.Ed.2d 389 (1991), the Court recognized that if questioning occurs in the cramped confines of a bus, it is more likely to be coercive than if it occurs in a more open area such as an airport concourse—though the Court held that a seizure does not *automatically* occur merely because the questioning occurs in close physical surroundings. Likewise, if questioning occurs in an area away from public view, it is more likely to be coercive than if the questioning occurs in an area visible to the public—though again this factor is not dispositive. *See United States v. Rodriguez*, 69 F.3d 136 (7th Cir. 1995) (court finds encounter and not a stop: "Nor were the physical surroundings isolating or restraining. The encounter took place in a busy public concourse at O'Hare airport, surrounded by travelers.").

5. Two Modifications to the *Mendenhall* "Free to Leave" Test

The Court has modified the *Mendenhall* test in two important cases. Both cases expand the authority of officers to investigate free from the strictures of the Fourth Amendment.

a. *Bostick*: Not Free to Leave Because of the Suspect's Own Circumstances

In *Florida v. Bostick,* 501 U.S. 429, 111 S.Ct. 2382, 115 L.Ed.2d 389 (1991), two officers boarded an interstate bus on which Bostick was a passenger. They boarded during a stopover in Fort Lauderdale. The officers moved through the bus and, without articulable suspicion, picked out Bostick and asked to inspect his ticket and identification. Bostick complied. Bostick's ticket matched his identification and both were returned to him as unremarkable. The officers then told Bostick that they were on the lookout for illegal drugs and requested Bostick's consent to search his luggage. Bostick consented and the officers found drugs in his luggage. Bostick argued that he was seized without reasonable suspicion at the time he gave his consent, and that therefore the consent was tainted and the evidence was illegally obtained. He contended that he was not "free to leave" because the bus was soon scheduled to depart.

i. Literal Application Rejected

The Court concluded that the "free to leave" test could not be applied literally in cases like Bostick's. The Court stated that the term "free to leave" should be construed in accordance with "the principle that those words were intended to capture." In this case, Bostick had no desire to leave, because the bus was about to depart. Therefore the "free to leave" test, as applied to these circumstances, was "not an accurate measure of the coercive effect of the encounter" since Bostick would not have felt free to leave even if the police had not been present.

ii. Freedom to Terminate the Encounter

The question, therefore, in cases where the citizen is confined because of his own circumstances (such as in a bus, a subway, or an elevator) is whether *the police conduct would have communicated to a reasonable person that the person was not free to decline the officers' requests or otherwise terminate the encounter.* The *Bostick* court remanded the case to determine whether the officers' conduct constituted a seizure under that modified standard.

iii. No Per Se Rule Requiring that Passengers be Warned

In *United States v. Drayton*, 536 U.S. 194, 122 S.Ct. 2105, 153 L.Ed.2d 242 (2002), the Supreme Court applied *Bostick* in another "bus sweep" case involving similar facts. In *Drayton*, three plainclothes police officers entered a Greyhound bus at a scheduled stop. One remained at the front, one remained at the back, and a third worked his way toward the front of the bus, asking questions of the passengers, including Drayton and his companion Brown. Drayton and Brown argued that they were seized and that their consent to the search that revealed illegal drugs was involuntary. The Court of Appeals for the Eleventh Circuit agreed, holding that the consent of passengers during a bus sweep is involuntary unless the officers advise them of their right not to cooperate and to refuse consent. The Supreme reversed, rejecting this per se rule and holding that the Fourth Amendment did not require police officers to inform bus passengers of these rights, citing *Schneckloth v. Bustamonte* and *Ohio v. Robinette, infra*.

iv. Passengers Seized During Traffic Stops

In *Brendlin v. California*, ___ U.S. ___, 127 S.Ct. 2400, 168 L.Ed.2d 132 (2007), the Supreme Court held that a passenger is considered seized during a traffic stop. In *Brendlin*, police officers saw a parked car with expired registration tags. They later saw the car on the road and stopped it. One of the officers recognized the front passenger as one of the Brendlin brothers and recalled that he was a parole violater. After verifying this fact, the officer ordered Brendlin out of the car at gunpoint and arrested him. The officer conducted a search incident to the arrest and found evidence. Brendlin was charged with possession and manufacture of methamphetamine. He moved to suppress the evidence, claiming that the car was stopped without probable cause or reasonable suspicion and that the evidence was the fruit of an illegal seizure. The motion was denied and Brendlin appealed. The California Supreme Court held that the stop was illegal but that Brendlin was not seized. The United States Supreme Court reversed, citing *Mendenhall, supra,* and other seizure cases, noting that no reasonable person in that situation would believe he was free to leave. A contrary ruling, according to the Court, would allow police officers to stop cars with passengers without probable cause or reasonable suspicion, understanding that any evidence recovered in connection with the passengers would be admissible.

b. *Hodari:* If Coercive Tactics Are Non–Physical, It Is Not a Stop Until the Suspect Submits

In *California v. Hodari D.*, 499 U.S. 621, 111 S.Ct. 1547, 113 L.Ed.2d 690 (1991), officers encountered a group of youths who were huddled around a car and who fled when they saw the officers. The officers pursued Hodari. In the course of the chase, Hodari discarded a rocklike object. One officer tackled Hodari and handcuffed him. Subsequently, the officer discovered that the discarded rock was crack cocaine. Hodari argued that the police pursuit was a seizure, since a reasonable person would have considered it so coercive as not to feel free to leave.

i. Two Types of Seizures

The *Hodari* Court separated seizures into two types: those in which the officer *has physically touched* the suspect, and those in which the officer has used a non-physical *show of authority* (such as drawing a gun, ordering the suspect to stop, etc.).

ii. Physical Touching Is a Seizure

The Court concluded that a stop *automatically* occurs when an officer physically touches a suspect with the intent of restraining him—a seizure "is effected by the slightest application of physical force." The Court noted, however, that such a seizure would not be permanent if the suspect breaks away from the officer's control.

iii. Non-physical Show of Authority Is Not a Stop Until the Suspect Submits

The physical touching aspect of the seizure definition was not at issue in *Hodari*, since the parties agreed that Hodari was stopped when he was tackled and handcuffed. The question was whether he was "seized" when he was being pursued. The Court concluded that the *Mendenhall* test, when read "carefully," says that a person has been seized "only if," not "whenever" the officer employs a show of authority. Thus, where the officer employs a non-physical show of authority, it must be such that a reasonable person would not feel free to leave, and *the citizen must actually submit to the show of authority.*

iv.   Application to the Facts of *Hodari*

As applied to *Hodari,* there would have been a stop if Hodari had stopped running in response to the police activity; but he did not. Therefore the stop did not occur until Hodari was physically subdued by the officer. The pursuit did not require articulable suspicion because a seizure had not yet occurred. *See also United States v. Washington,* 12 F.3d 1128 (D.C. Cir. 1994) (no seizure where officer orders a suspect to stop his car, suspect stops momentarily, but then speeds off before the officer can reach the car).

6.   Officer Is Not Required to Use an Encounter as a "Less Intrusive Alternative"

In *United States v. Sokolow,* 490 U.S. 1, 109 S.Ct. 1581, 104 L.Ed.2d 1 (1989), officers stopped Sokolow in an airport on suspicion that he was trafficking in narcotics; he gave consent to a search of his luggage and narcotics were found. The Court rejected Sokolow's argument that the officers did not have reasonable suspicion to support the stop. Sokolow argued further, however, that even if the officers had reasonable suspicion, their seizure of Sokolow in the airport was illegal because they could have obtained the same results (consent to search Sokolow's luggage) if they had merely encountered him rather than seized him. The Court held that agents are not obligated to use the least intrusive means available to verify or dispel their suspicions. The Court reasoned that a rule requiring a "least intrusive alternative" approach would unnecessarily penalize the police for making objectively reasonable, on-the-spot decisions.

C.   What Is Reasonable Suspicion?

The degree of suspicion required to make a stop is referred to as "reasonable suspicion" by the courts. Since *Terry,* courts have struggled with the meaning of reasonable suspicion and with how the reasonable suspicion standard differs from that of probable cause. It is clear, however, that the standards are materially different. There are many cases in which the courts have held that reasonable suspicion existed but probable cause did not; the consequence of the distinction would be the exclusion of any evidence obtained if the officer's intrusion constituted an arrest rather than merely a stop. *See Florida v. Royer,* 460 U.S. 491, 103 S.Ct. 1319, 75 L.Ed.2d 229 (1983) (consent tainted where it was obtained while Royer was under arrest and officers had only reasonable suspicion and not probable cause to believe that Royer was involved in drug activity).

1. Nature of the Analysis Is Similar

The analysis employed by the courts in assessing reasonable suspicion is similar to that employed in assessing probable cause. The following analytical concepts are applicable to both standards:

— A *common sense* analysis is employed to evaluate the facts presented.

— *Deference* is given to the *expertise* of law enforcement officers, who may know through experience that certain facts are indicative of criminal activity. *See United States v. Michael R.*, 90 F.3d 340 (9th Cir. 1996) (substantial weight given to experienced officer's deduction that suspects, who were staring the officer down, were "mad-dogging" him as a prelude to a gang attack).

— *The totality of circumstances* must be assessed. While each fact may seem innocent if considered individually, the factors considered in their totality may not be so easily explained away.

— *Reasonable mistakes of fact* do not preclude a finding of either reasonable suspicion or probable cause. Certainty is not required for either standard.

2. Difference in Quantity and Quality of Proof

The difference between reasonable suspicion and probable cause is that reasonable suspicion is a less demanding standard of proof—a stop is permissible upon something less than the fair probability standard which defines probable cause. Some courts have defined reasonable suspicion as a fair *possibility* (as opposed to probability) of criminal activity. Reasonable suspicion can be usefully referred to as *possible cause.*

Example: A probabilistic example of the difference between reasonable suspicion and probable cause is presented by the facts of *United States v. Winsor*, 846 F.2d 1569 (9th Cir. 1988). Officers chased suspected bank robbers fleeing from the bank into a hotel. The hotel had approximately 40 guest rooms. The question was whether there was probable cause to search each of the rooms for the suspects. The court found that a one-in-forty probability was too small to establish probable cause, but that it did establish reasonable suspicion: "The odds on discovering the suspect in the first room upon whose door the police knocked were high enough to support a founded suspicion. The odds favoring discovery increase as rooms are searched. At some point, perhaps at the last two or three unsearched rooms, probable cause may be said to exist." Conversely, at some point of improbability, even reasonable suspicion would not have existed. For example, if the hotel had 600 rooms, there would clearly have been no reasonable suspicion to believe that the suspects were in any particular room. Because there was only reasonable suspicion and not probable cause in *Winsor*, the court held that the search of the hotel room in which the suspects were found was illegal. A search for law enforcement purposes requires probable cause and cannot be justified under *Terry. See also United States v. Gonzalez*, 70 F.3d 1236 (11th Cir. 1995) (mere presence at the scene of an illegal transaction does not provide probable cause, but it can constitute reasonable suspicion).

3. Quantum of Suspicion Required for Reasonable Suspicion

The Supreme Court's definition of the appropriate quantum of suspicion to support a stop was articulated in *United States v. Cortez*, 449 U.S. 411, 101 S.Ct. 690, 66 L.Ed.2d 621 (1981): "Based upon the whole picture the detaining officers must have a particularized and objective basis for suspecting the particular person stopped of criminal activity * * *. The process does not deal with hard certainties, but with probabilities."

4. Questions of Identity of a Perpetrator

The Court in *Terry* and in *Cortez* dealt with questions of reasonable suspicion in the context of an identifiable suspect who was engaged in ambiguous activity. But stops are also permissible where it is clear that a crime has occurred, and the question for the officer is whether a particular person is the perpetrator. In *United States v. Hensley*, 469 U.S. 221, 105 S.Ct. 675, 83 L.Ed.2d 604 (1985), the Court approved the use of *Terry* stops where "police have a reasonable suspicion, grounded in specific and articulable facts, that a person they encounter was involved in or is wanted in connection with a completed felony." The question in these cases is whether the officer has enough articulable facts as to the identity of the perpetrator to match with the suspect.

a. "Stop and Identify" Statutes

The Supreme Court upheld the constitutionality of a "stop and identify" statute in *Hiibel v. Sixth Judicial District Court of Nevada, Humboldt County*, 542 U.S. 177, 124 S.Ct. 2451, 159 L.Ed.2d 292

(2004). A police officer stopped Hiibel based on reasonable suspicion and asked him to identify himself pursuant to Nevada's "stop and identify" statute. When Hiibel refused to comply, the officer arrested him. The Court rejected Hiibel's claim that the statute violated the Fourth Amendment. It noted that its prior decisions clearly established a police officer's right to ask a suspect to identify himself during the course of a Terry stop (citing *Hensley* and *Adams v. Williams, infra*) but left open the question of whether the suspect could be arrested and prosecuted for refusing to answer. The Court noted that language in Justice White's concurrence in *Terry* that "the person stopped is not obliged to answer, answers may not be compelled, and refusal to answer furnishes no basis for an arrest," was not controlling. It held that the Nevada statute satisfied the standard established in *Delaware v. Prouse, infra*, of balancing the intrusion on the person's Fourth Amendment interests against the promotion of legitimate government interests.

b. **General Description Can Support a Stop**
As discussed above, reasonable suspicion is a minimal standard. Therefore, a stop may be justified even though the suspect merely accords with a general description. *See, e.g., United States v. DeBerry*, 76 F.3d 884 (7th Cir. 1996) (suspect could be stopped where his clothing matched the clothing of a person described as illegally carrying a gun).

c. **Descriptions Can Be Incorrect in Certain Particulars**
When there are several points of comparison between the suspect and the description of the perpetrator, it may be permissible to stop the suspect even though there is a discrepancy on some points. The question is whether there are enough specific factors which do match up so that, when weighed against the discrepancies, it is reasonably possible that the suspect is the person described as the perpetrator. For example, in *United States v. Wantland*, 754 F.2d 268 (8th Cir. 1985), an eyewitness reported that a bank robber fled in a gold 1971 Dodge Dart with license number 104–819. The officer stopped a Plymouth Duster leaving the town in which the bank robbery occurred; the Duster's license number was 104–849. The court held that there was reasonable suspicion to stop the car, given the similarity of the two vehicles and the license plate numbers, and the fact that an eyewitness description, under the circumstances, could not be expected to be exact.

d. **Changed Circumstances May Be Taken into Account**

An officer assessing a description can take into account the fact that circumstances may have changed between the time of the description and the point at which the officer discovers a person whom he suspects as the perpetrator. The concept of reasonable suspicion accommodates the possibility that a perpetrator may try to conceal his identity or avoid detection. For example, suppose three people are seen leaving a bank robbery, and an officer comes across two people who fit the description of two of the robbers. The officer must obviously be allowed to take into account the fact that the group may have split up—or that some members may be concealed from view. *See Williams v. State*, 261 Ind. 547, 307 N.E.2d 457 (1974) (officer knew that two robbers had fled by car; he stopped a car fitting the general description, even though there was only one person visible in the car; the other robber was found hiding in the rear seat). Likewise, if a perpetrator is described as having a beard, an officer may be permitted to stop a person with no facial hair. The reasonable possibility may exist that the beard is a disguise.

e. **Size of the Area Is Relevant**

If the description of the perpetrator is so general as to cover a large number of persons (such as "a white male in his 30's") then it will be important to assess the distance between the stop and the scene of the crime. For one thing, the stop must be within the range of possible flight. *See State v. Smith*, 9 Wash.App. 279, 511 P.2d 1032 (1973) (stop held proper in part because it was reasonably within appropriate driving distance from the crime scene, considering the time of the robbery). More importantly, the size of an area also helps to determine the universe of potential suspects. A general description may support a stop within a two block radius of a shooting incident, but not within a five mile radius.

f. **Number of People in the Area Is Relevant**

A description must be more particular if the stop is made in a location where there are many people about (such as a crowded urban area), and it can be less particular if the relevant area of inquiry is sparsely populated at the time of the stop. *See United States v. Basey*, 816 F.2d 980 (5th Cir. 1987) (stop based on description that perpetrator was driving a "1980 yellow Ford Sedan" held permissible; court stresses the minimal number of persons and cars about in a rural area). In fact, there have been cases in which the number of people in the vicinity of a crime was so few that a stop of a person in that area was upheld even though the officer had no description of the perpetrator whatever. *See United States v. Crittendon*, 883 F.2d 326 (4th Cir. 1989) (call to police about burglary in progress made at 3 a.m.; defendant and his companion were "the only persons encountered in the vicinity of the reported crime"). *Compare Cauthen v. United States*, 592 A.2d 1021 (D.C. App. 1991) (call to police about drug transactions on the street made at 2 a.m.; stop not permissible without any description, since police response time was 20 minutes and there was much street activity in the area).

g. Suspicious Activity of a Person Fitting a General Description

While some descriptions may be too general to support reasonable suspicion, the police, through further investigation, may stop a person fitting that description if the person is in fact acting suspiciously. The suspicious conduct, together with the general description, may make it reasonably possible that the suspect is the perpetrator. It will be relevant, for example, if the suspect is acting as if he is trying to avoid detection, or if he appears inordinately nervous. *See United States v. Danielson*, 728 F.2d 1143 (8th Cir. 1984) (suspect was leaving the area at an unusually fast speed, and tried to duck out of sight when police officers approached).

h. Suspect "Fails" the Encounter

A police officer can encounter a citizen, and ask a few preliminary questions, even without reasonable suspicion. Officers working with an overly general description will often encounter, rather than stop, a person who fits that description. If the citizen gives implausible answers to the preliminary questions, or acts suspiciously in any other sense, then the suspect's conduct may be sufficiently suspicious to support a stop. *See, e.g., United States v. Morgan*, 725 F.2d 56 (7th Cir. 1984) (suspect stated during an encounter that he was travelling alone, though officers knew that he was travelling with a companion); *United States v. Blanco*, 844 F.2d 344 (6th Cir. 1988) (suspects state that they drove 1000 miles to Cincinnati to see a Reds baseball game, even though the Reds were at that time on an extended road trip; officer could consider it suspicious that "two gentlemen who had driven from Miami to Cincinnati to take in a baseball game should not have known that the team was going to be out of town").

i. **Prior Record of Criminal Activity**

There may be reasonable suspicion to support a stop if a general description is coupled with the officer's knowledge that a suspect who fits the description has previously engaged in similar crimes. *See United States v. Morgan*, 936 F.2d 1561 (10th Cir. 1991) (description of "three black males" as bank robbers held sufficient to stop a car with three black males where, in addition, officer recognized the car as having been reported leaving the scene of a different bank robbery, and recognized one of the men as having previously been charged with bank robbery).

j. **At Some Point, the Totality of Factors Remains Too General to Support a Stop**

The standard of reasonable suspicion is minimal, and the use of a totality of circumstances approach will often lead to a finding that a stop was permissible on the basis of the suspect's matching a general description together with other relevant factors. Nonetheless, there are cases in which a stop was found invalid due to the lack of suspicious circumstances and the generality of the description.

Example: In *People v. Miller*, 121 A.D.2d 335, 504 N.Y.S.2d 407 (1st Dep't 1986), officers responded to a call stating that a short, black Jamaican man wearing a tan leisure suit had taken a gun out of a case and placed it in his waistband; that he ran with two other black men into the basement of 277 Edgecombe Avenue; that one of the other men was dressed all in grey and was a little taller than the gunman; and that the man carrying the gun looked like he was going to shoot someone. Officers were at the address within a minute. In front of the building, they saw defendant, who was 6'1" tall, wearing an open gray shirt with a black tank top underneath, and black pants; they also saw a man about 5'3" tall, in a brown uniform, sweeping the sidewalk; and a third man was sitting on the stoop of the building with defendant. All three men were black. No one else was on the street. The officers observed the defendant remove his hand from inside the front waistband area of his pants, consistent with either tucking in his shirt or, in the officers' experience, the act of a gun carrier pushing the weapon down to make sure that it does not slip out. The officers seized the defendant, and a subsequent frisk uncovered a gun. Defendant was convicted on a weapons charge and argued on appeal that the officers had no reasonable suspicion to seize him. The appellate court agreed with the defendant. The court noted that the defendant was taller than the description given to the police officers of the gunman's companions, and that the clothes he was wearing did not match the description. The court also emphasized that all three men were acting naturally and calmly in front of the building when the police arrived. The court found the defendant's hand movement to be "innocuous" in light of all the circumstances, and noted that the officers never testified that they saw a bulge or protrusion in the area of the gesture.

5. Suspicious Conduct

A different situation in which the reasonable suspicion standard is applied is where the officer sees or knows about conduct that the officer views as suspicious.

The question in these cases is not the identity of the perpetrator of a crime, but rather whether any crime has been committed at all. A stop is permitted if, considering all the circumstances, an officer could find it reasonably possible that, as the Court in *Terry* put it, "criminal activity is afoot."

a. Case-by-Case Approach—Relevant Factors

There is obviously a wide variety of circumstances in which an officer might stop a suspect on the basis of suspicious activity. This makes it difficult to state clearly exactly what situations indicate a sufficient level of suspicion to justify a stop. As the Supreme Court stated in *United States v. Sokolow*, 490 U.S. 1, 109 S.Ct. 1581, 104 L.Ed.2d 1 (1989), "the concept of reasonable suspicion, like probable cause, is not readily or even usefully reduced to a neat set of legal rules." However, some factors arise frequently enough in the cases to indicate that they will ordinarily be relevant to a finding of reasonable suspicion. The more these factors accumulate, the stronger the case on reasonable suspicion will be. It must be kept in mind, however, that ordinarily, no single factor is a dispositive indicator of reasonable suspicion. *See Sokolow* (finding reasonable suspicion that defendant was a drug courier, on the basis of several suspicious factors, while recognizing that "any one of these factors is not by itself proof of any illegal conduct and is quite consistent with innocent travel"). Conversely, the fact that several suspicious factors can be individually explained away is not dispositive. As the Court stated in *Sokolow,* the relevant inquiry "is not whether particular conduct is innocent or guilty, but the degree of suspicion that attaches to particular types of noncriminal acts."

Example: In *Sokolow,* the defendant travelled round-trip from Honolulu to Miami, a known source city for drugs, over a 48–hour period. He paid $2100 for two airplane tickets with cash from a roll of $20 bills. He travelled under a name that did not match the name under which his telephone number was listed. He had appeared nervous during the trip. He had not checked any luggage. Each of these factors was consistent with innocent activity. The Court found, however, that these factors taken together made it reasonably possible that the defendant was a drug courier.

b.   *Sokolow* Approach Affirmed

The Court affirmed this "totality of the circumstances" approach in *United States v. Arvizu,* 534 U.S. 266, 122 S.Ct. 744, 151 L.Ed.2d 740 (2002). In *Arvizu,* border patrol agent Stoddard observed a minivan driving on an unpaved road near the Mexican border frequently traversed by smugglers trying to avoid a nearby border patrol checkpoint. As Stoddard approached the minivan, it slowed down dramatically. He observed two adults in the front seat and three children in the back. The driver had a rigid posture and avoided looking at the agent. Stoddard noticed that the knees of the two children in the back seat were unusually high, as if they were propped up on something. Stoddard followed the van, and shortly thereafter, all of the children simultaneously began to mechanically wave at Stoddard in an abnormal pattern. The waving continued on and off for four or five minutes before Arvizu turned suddenly onto the last road that would have permitted him to avoid the checkpoint. Stoddard radioed for a registration check and learned that the minivan was registered to an address in an area known for alien and narcotics smuggling. He then decided to stop the minivan. He asked for permission to search, Arvizu agreed, and he discovered over 100 pounds of marijuana in the van.

Arvizu argued that Stoddard did not have reasonable suspicion to stop him but the District Court ruled otherwise. The Court of Appeals for the Ninth Circuit reversed the District Court, holding that seven of the ten factors Stoddard considered carried little or no weight in the reasonable suspicion calculus. These factors included Arvizu's slowing down, the raised position of the children's knees, and their odd waving pattern. The Ninth Circuit concluded that the remaining factors were not sufficient to constitute the requisite reasonable suspicion. The Supreme Court reversed, rejecting the Ninth Circuit's "divide and conquer" approach of considering each factor separately. The Court cited *Terry* and *Sokolow*, *supra*, in affirming the "totality of the circumstances" approach and rejecting the Ninth Circuit's approach of assigning no weight to individual factors that appeared innocent when considered piecemeal.

c. Patterns of Activity

Activity that appears repetitious may indicate that the suspect may be checking out whether a crime can be successfully completed. For example, if a person looks into the interior of one or two cars in a parking lot, this will not ordinarily seem suspicious. However, if a person walks down a line of thirty cars in a parking lot, and looks into the interior of each one, an inference may be drawn that the person may be looking for a car to break into. Indeed, the suspects in *Terry* were stopped by Officer McFadden because they repeatedly passed back and forth and peered into a store—this activity was suspicious because it was consistent with that of a person "casing" the premises for a robbery.

d. Demonstrated Unfamiliarity

If the suspect's activity indicates that he is unfamiliar with either his surroundings or with the things he is carrying or operating, this may be some indication that crime is afoot. For example, if a person has a set of keys and tries several of them in a door lock, an officer may reasonably suspect that the keys are stolen. Likewise, if a person has difficulty operating a car with a standard transmission, or has difficulty finding the lights or the emergency brake, this demonstrated unfamiliarity is relevant to whether the car has been or is being stolen. Unfamiliarity with the area in which the suspect is found may be suspicious, though it will rarely be dispositive, since it may be that the suspect is, simply and innocently, lost. *Compare United States v. Holland,* 510 F.2d 453 (9th Cir. 1975) (reasonable suspicion found where, among other things, the suspects were in a car driving slowly in a rural area, as if they were unfamiliar with the areas and looking for a particular residence) with *United States v. Pavelski,* 789 F.2d 485 (7th Cir. 1986) (no reasonable suspicion to stop car with out of state license plates, after car took an abrupt turn down a country road; this single factor is not enough to establish reasonable suspicion).

e.   Time of Day

Activity which is completely unremarkable at one time of day may be suspicious at another. For example, it is not suspicious to push a rack of clothing down the street in the Garment District of New York City at midday. But it is suspicious to do so at 3 a.m. Courts take account of the fact that most criminal activity occurs at night rather than in broad daylight. *See United States v. Kerr,* 817 F.2d 1384 (9th Cir. 1987) (no reasonable suspicion where defendant was "loading boxes into a vehicle on residential property at mid-afternoon, a time of day not raising an inference of criminal activity"); *People v. Allen,* 50 Cal.App.3d 896, 123 Cal.Rptr. 80 (1975) (reasonable suspicion found where defendant was standing in a used car lot at 2:35 a.m.). However, the fact that activity occurs at night is not itself sufficient grounds for a stop; there must be some other suspicious circumstances. *See, e.g., State v. Phipps,* 429 So.2d 445 (La. 1983) (stop not permissible merely because defendants were out on the street at 3 a.m.; Mardi Gras parade had taken place a few hours previously).

f.   Location of Activity; High Crime Area

The location in which an act occurs may have some bearing on whether it is suspicious. For example, an overloaded truck near the border is more suspicious than an overloaded truck on an interstate highway in the middle of the country. Shaking hands and passing a small plastic bag in an area known for drug activity is more suspicious than if the same activity occurred in a suburban backyard. Courts frequently rely on the fact that a suspect's conduct occurred in a high crime area, and that the conduct was consistent with the type of crime pervasive in the area. *See United States v. Garrett,* 959 F.2d 1005 (D.C. Cir. 1992) (stop permissible where defendant was observed exchanging money for a small object in an area rife with drug activity). However, as with time of day, the fact that a person is simply found in a high crime area is not itself sufficient to justify a stop. *See Brown v. Texas,* 443 U.S. 47, 99 S.Ct. 2637, 61 L.Ed.2d 357 (1979) ("The fact that appellant was in a neighborhood frequented by drug users, standing alone, is not a basis for concluding that appellant himself was engaged in criminal conduct.").

g. Known Criminal Record

A suspect's activity may take on a more suspicious color if it is consistent with criminal activity for which the suspect has already been arrested or convicted. *See United States v. Barnes*, 496 A.2d 1040 (D.C. App. 1985) (defendant's previous arrest for armed robbery, when considered with the fact that he was loitering outside a store while his companion entered several times, gave rise to reasonable suspicion). Again, however, the mere fact that a person has prior arrests or convictions is not itself sufficient to justify a stop; a seizure may not be based solely on the suspect's past record. *See People v. Johnson,* 64 N.Y.2d 617, 485 N.Y.S.2d 33, 474 N.E.2d 241 (1984) (the fact that defendant had previously been arrested for burglary and was found in an alley looking at houses did not constitute reasonable suspicion: "It can hardly be regarded as unusual that defendant was looking at houses, for there is little else to look at in a residential neighborhood.").

h. Evasion in a High Crime Area

In *California v. Hodari D., supra*, the Court implied that a person's flight from approaching police officers could itself constitute reasonable suspicion but found it unnecessary to decide the issue. In *Illinois v. Wardlow*, 528 U.S. 119, 120 S.Ct. 673, 145 L.Ed.2d 570 (2000), the Court held that unprovoked flight, at least when it occurs in a high crime area, constitutes reasonable suspicion. Wardlow ran upon seeing a caravan of police cars approaching in an area known for narcotics trafficking. A police officer stopped him and frisked him for weapons. The officer discovered a handgun, and placed Wardlow under arrest. The Court stressed that presence in a high crime area alone would not justify the stop, but that location is a relevant factor. Here, the Court found the location combined with Wardlow's evasion sufficient.

i.   Dissent in *Wardlow*

The State suggested that the Court adopt a per se rule that flight from police officers would *always* constitute reasonable suspicion, while Wardlow pressed for the opposite per se rule—that flight would *never* equal reasonable suspicion. Justice Stevens concurred in the Court's rejection of both per se rules and agreed that flight is a relevant factor to be considered in the totality of the circumstances. However, he dissented from the Court's holding that flight in a high crime area is sufficient. Stevens pointed out that many innocent explanations for flight from the police are often concentrated in high crime areas and minority communities, citing studies that document the prevalence of police brutality, harassment, and racial profiling of minorities. Stevens noted that an inference of guilt from flight in these locations may be less appropriate, rather than more so.

j.   Some Reactions Are Not Evasive

The mere fact that a person acts somewhat nervously in the presence of a police officer is not suspicious. It is an ordinary reaction to the presence of the police. So, for example, if a driver slows down below the speed limit so as not to pass a police car on the road, this will not be considered suspicious. *See State v. Johnson,* 444 N.W.2d 824 (Minn. 1989) (no grounds for a stop if a driver "merely appears startled at the sight of a police officer passing him and then slows down a bit"); *United States v. Pavelski, supra* (no reasonable suspicion where driver and occupants of a car stare straight ahead and avoid eye contact with police when being passed by a police car). Also, evasive action will not be considered suspicious where the officers are not identifiable as police officers. *See People v. Allen,* 109 A.D.2d 24, 489 N.Y.S.2d 749 (1st Dep't 1985) (no reasonable suspicion where defendant merely stepped back from an elevator and put his hand to his pocket upon seeing eight men step out of the elevator, in a high crime area; defendant had no way of knowing that the men were plainclothes officers). As stated above, however, a person who breaks into a run at the sight of police may be considered suspicious. Such conduct is more than ordinary nervousness.

k.   Failing an Encounter

As with questions of identity, a person whose activity may not be suspicious enough to permit a stop may nonetheless be approached and asked preliminary questions. Then, if the answers to the questions are implausible or demonstrably false, the suspect's "failure" may raise the level of suspicion to that required for a stop. *See United States v. Lanford*, 838 F.2d 1351 (5th Cir. 1988) (disheveled-looking driver in a fancy car, driving in New Mexico; when asked what he was doing, he stated that he was "just driving around"; this was implausible because the car had Louisiana license plates; the answer, together with other factors already known, constituted reasonable suspicion to believe that the car was stolen).

l. **Non-cooperation During an Encounter**
A suspect's mere failure to consent to requests by a police officer during an encounter cannot be a factor which contributes to reasonable suspicion. For example, if a suspect refuses to produce identification, or refuses to consent to a search of his bag, or refuses to answer questions, such refusals are not relevant to reasonable suspicion. This is because a person who is merely encountered has the absolute right to refuse cooperation and terminate the encounter. It would be anomalous if officers could term the police-citizen contact an encounter because it was completely consensual, and then, in the course of that encounter, consider it suspicious that the citizen refused to cooperate, thereby permitting a stop. *See United States v. Davis*, 94 F.3d 1465 (10th Cir. 1996) ("Davis' failure to stop when asked by the officer cannot justify his detention.").

m. **Non-cooperation Distinguished From Evasion**
While a citizen has an absolute right to terminate an encounter, it is nonetheless true that certain out-of-the-ordinary activity designed to avoid or terminate conduct with the police may be considered suspicious. It is one thing to walk away from an encounter; it is another to run away at full speed. It is one thing to refuse consent. It is another to slap the officer. *See People v. Vasquez*, 108 A.D.2d 701, 485 N.Y.S.2d 1008 (1st Dep't 1985) (reasonable suspicion found when, together with other suspicious facts, defendant slapped at the officer's hand when he approached: "Ordinarily, a person addressed by a police officer does have an equal right to ignore his interrogator and walk away. This should not, however, be read to mean that one can strike out at an officer in doing so.").

n. **Nervousness During an Encounter**
Simple nervousness during an encounter cannot itself give rise to reasonable suspicion, since that is an ordinary reaction to direct contact with the police. *United States v. Erwin*, 71 F.3d 218 (6th Cir.

1995) (fact that suspect was nervous and sweating "was not particularly unusual for someone stopped by police officers in the middle of summer"). However, extreme nervousness or unusually erratic behavior in the presence of police officers can be considered suspicious.

6. Examples of Cases in Which Reasonable Suspicion Was Found

The best way to get a handle on the case-by-case analysis of reasonable suspicion is to apply the above factors to a real case. A close case on reasonable suspicion is found in *United States v. Weaver*, 966 F.2d 391 (8th Cir. 1992). Officer Hicks was at the Kansas City airport, awaiting the arrival of an early morning flight from Los Angeles. As Weaver disembarked from the flight, he caught the officer's attention because he was a "roughly dressed" young African–American male who was carrying two bags and walking rapidly, almost running, down the concourse toward a door leading to a taxi stand. Hicks was aware that a number of young African–American males from street gangs in Los Angeles frequently brought drugs into the Kansas City area. He also testified that narcotics couriers commonly leave an airport by walking quickly towards a taxi. Hicks approached Weaver and asked Weaver if he would answer some questions. Weaver said "o.k." In response to Hicks, Weaver stated that he had been in Los Angeles trying to find his sister who had been missing for several years. Hicks requested to see Weaver's airline ticket, but after searching his pockets, Weaver said that he must have left it on the plane. Nor could Weaver provide any identification, though he did give his correct name and Kansas City address. Hicks testified that while it is extremely uncommon for adults to be without identification, it is common for drug couriers not to have any. Hicks also testified that Weaver appeared to be very nervous; his voice was unsteady, his speech was rapid, his hands shook, and his body swayed. Hicks testified that although people often became nervous when approached by a police officer, Weaver exhibited "more nervousness than innocent people usually do." Weaver declined Hicks' request to search his bags, and began to walk out of the terminal. At this point, Hicks decided to seize the bags, and so informed Weaver. Weaver nevertheless got into the back seat of the taxi with both bags. Hicks grabbed one of the bags and tried to take it out of the taxi. When Weaver began to hit Hicks' hand in an attempt to pry it loose from the bag, he was placed under arrest. Drugs and money were found on Weaver pursuant to a search incident to the arrest. On the basis of all of this information, Hicks obtained a warrant to search the bags. A subsequent search of the bags uncovered more than six pounds of crack cocaine.

The court first held that Weaver was not seized until the point where Hicks decided to seize Weaver's bags. Up to that point, it was a consensual encounter. The question then was whether there was reasonable suspicion to stop Weaver at the time that Officer Hicks seized the bags. If not, the subsequent search of Weaver's person, and even the search of the bags pursuant to a warrant, would be considered "fruit of the poisonous tree" and the evidence could be excluded. The court held that reasonable suspicion existed for a seizure. It relied most heavily on the facts that Weaver was walking briskly, lacked identification, had no plane ticket, and was exceedingly nervous. As the Supreme Court has done, the court in *Weaver* emphasized that while each of the factors could be viewed as innocent, non-suspicious details, a reasonable suspicion was raised when all the factors were considered together.

The dissent in *Weaver* assailed the court's consideration of the race of the suspect as a relevant factor in the reasonable suspicion calculus. *See* "Relevance of Suspect's Race," *infra.*

Another case in which reasonable suspicion was found is *United States v. Dennison*, 410 F.3d 1203 (10th Cir. 2005). In *Dennison,* a police officer observed two men sitting in a Ford truck in a high crime area at 3 a.m. with the engine turned off. They told the officer that they were waiting for a tow truck for a Chevy pickup that was parked some distance away. Shortly after this encounter, the officer returned and found the men still in the truck with the engine running and closer to the Chevy. The officer frisked the men and found a machine gun. The court held that the stop was supported by reasonable suspicion based on the totality of the circumstances: 1) It was 3 a.m.; 2) it was an area known for nighttime car theft; 3) at the first encounter, the Ford was parked far away from the Chevy and in a location unlikely to be seen by a tow truck; and 4) shortly after the first encounter, they had moved the Ford, and the engine was running.

7. Example of Case in Which Reasonable Suspicion Was Not Found

In *United States v. Davis*, 94 F.3d 1465 (10th Cir. 1996), two Tulsa police officers were patrolling at night an area where complaints had been received that gunshots had been fired. One building in the area was known as a "juice joint"—a business that sells liquor without a license; legal activities such as dominoes also took place in that building. The officers were in a marked police car and observed a brown Monte Carlo with four occupants parked just north of the "juice joint." Upon the officers' arrival, one of the occupants, defendant Davis, exited the Monte Carlo. As he did so, he made eye contact with Officer Yelton, then broke eye contact and walked toward the "juice joint" with his hands in his pockets. Officer Yelton knew that Davis was an ex-convict who had been acquitted of a gang-related homicide. The officers told Davis to stop and take his hands out of his pockets, but Davis kept walking toward the "juice joint." The officers then each took one of Davis' arms, and a gun was discovered on Davis.

The Court held that the officers did not have reasonable suspicion to stop Davis. The Court reasoned as follows: 1. Davis' criminal record was not in itself sufficient to justify a stop; 2. The fact that Davis was walking at night with his hands in his pockets was not suspicious at all; 3. The parking of the car outside the "juice joint" was hardly suspicious, especially given the fact that legal activity took place there as well; 4. That Davis was in a neighborhood frequented by criminals was not enough, in itself to justify the stop; 5. Looking at a police officer and then looking away is not suspicious, but rather expected; 6. Refusing to cooperate in an encounter cannot be used against the suspect; and 7. Even looking at all the factors cumulatively, there was simply not enough to indicate anything more than a "hunch" that Davis was up to no good. Reasonable suspicion requires more than a "hunch."

8. **Use of Profiles**

    Officers often use profiles to determine whether the conduct of citizens is sufficiently suspicious to justify a stop. A profile is a list of characteristics compiled by a law enforcement agency, which have been found through experience to be common to those engaged in a certain type of criminal activity. The most common example is a drug courier profile, but officers also employ such profiles as gang member profiles.

    a. Match With Profile Is Not Dispositive

        The suspect's correlation with a profile is no guarantee that there is reasonable suspicion to justify a stop. Partly this is because the profile used will vary among law enforcement agencies, and partly it is because the courts adhere to the principle of *Terry* that the reasonableness of a stop must be assessed in light of the *particular circumstances. See United States v. Berry,* 670 F.2d 583 (5th Cir. 1982) (because a case-by-case approach is mandated, "a match between certain characteristics listed on the profile and characteristics exhibited by a defendant does not automatically establish reasonable suspicion"). The suspect's correlation with a drug courier profile is not dispositive because many profiles are obviously over-inclusive. Profiles have been used to find it suspicious that a person was the first to deplane, that another was among the last to deplane, and that another deplaned in the middle of the crowd. Correlation with a profile has been found when a person was carrying luggage and when a person was carrying no luggage. Therefore, the courts have generally concluded that "we will assign no characteristic greater or lesser weight merely because the characteristic happens to be present on, or absent from, the profile." *United States v. Berry, supra.*

b. **Officers' Use of Profile Does Not Render the Stop Illegal**
On the other hand, the officer's use of a drug courier profile does not somehow taint the stop, assuming reasonable suspicion exists on the facts. In *United States v. Sokolow, supra,* the Court concluded that a court "sitting to determine the existence of reasonable suspicion must require the agent to articulate the factors leading to that conclusion, but the fact that these factors may be set forth in a profile does not somehow detract from their evidentiary significance as seen by a trained agent." In other words, a profile can be used as an investigative tool by the officer, but the actual existence of reasonable suspicion must be determined on the facts. The suspect's correlation with a profile is, in itself, irrelevant.

9. **Relevance of Suspect's Race**
For questions of identity, the suspect's race must obviously be considered relevant. For example, if the perpetrator is described a black male in his 20s, an officer assessing reasonable suspicion must necessarily take into account that the person he decides to stop is black. More difficult questions arise, however, when the suspect's race is a factor in the reasonable suspicion calculus in cases where identity is not an issue.

a. **Racial Incongruity**
For example, is it appropriate to consider it suspicious that an African–American male is walking down the street of an affluent suburb at 11 p.m., where the same conduct from a white male would not be suspicious? Courts have considered such racial "incongruity"

as relevant in assessing reasonable suspicion—although such incongruity is not ordinarily dispositive. *See State v. Ruiz,* 19 Ariz.App. 84, 504 P.2d 1307 (1973) (Hispanic person properly stopped where it was officers' experience that it was unusual for other than black people to frequent the area except for the purpose of buying drugs). However, other courts have invalidated stops that have been based in material part on the fact that it may have been unusual for a person of the suspect's race to be in a certain place at a certain time. One court has referred to a stop on the basis of racial incongruity as "invidious discrimination." *See City of St. Paul v. Uber,* 450 N.W.2d 623 (Minn. App. 1990) (invalidating a stop made on the basis that a white male from the suburbs was driving in an area with mostly African–American residents: "We would not tolerate the blatant discriminatory proposition that any member of a minority group found on a public street in [an affluent suburb] had better live there, or be required to stop and justify his or her presence to the authorities."); *see also State v. Barber,* 118 Wash.2d 335, 823 P.2d 1068 (1992) ("[R]acial incongruity, i.e., a person of any race being allegedly out of place in a particular geographic area, should never constitute a finding of reasonable suspicion of criminal activity.").

b. Racial Profiling

Police officers sometimes consider a suspect's race as a relevant factor in the reasonable suspicion calculus out of a belief that people of certain races are more inclined to commit certain types of crimes. This practice, known as racial profiling, is most commonly employed in the investigation of drug offenses. Some courts permit police officers to consider the race or ethnicity of a suspect as one factor in the total reasonable suspicion calculus. *United States v. Weaver, supra,* was one such case. The dissent in *Weaver* strongly objected to the court's consideration of race:

> Finally, a word about the reliance placed on Weaver's race. This factor is repeated several times in the Court's opinion. I am not prepared to say that it could never be relevant. If, for example, we had evidence that young blacks in Los Angeles were more prone to drug offenses than young whites, the fact that a young person is black might be of some significance, though even then it would be dangerous to give it much weight. I do not know of any such evidence. Use of race as a factor simply reinforces the kind of stereotyping that lies behind drug-courier profiles.

When public officials begin to regard large groups of citizens as presumptively criminal, this country is in a perilous situation indeed.

The Supreme Court examined the constitutionality of a stop by roving patrols looking for illegal aliens in *United States v. Brignoni–Ponce, supra.* There the Court held that the Mexican ancestry of the occupants of a vehicle was a relevant factor, but could not stand alone as the basis for the stop.

Racial profiling has been widely criticized, as numerous studies continue to reveal its fallibility. National and local legislative bodies and law enforcement agencies have attempted to ban the practice through legislation and policies. However, enforcement of these laws and policies is difficult since police officers may subconsciously consider race or fail to acknowledge their consideration of race in the reasonable suspicion calculus. Since the bombing of the World Trade Center and the Pentagon on September 11, 2001, racial profiling has been directed towards men and women who appear to be of Middle Eastern descent. Some prior critics of racial profiling have attempted to justify racial profiling of Middle Eastern men after September 11th, while others maintain that it continues to be an unjustifiable and ineffective practice.

10. Officers Can Rely on Collective Knowledge

An officer involved in making a stop need not be personally aware of all the facts justifying the intrusion. The officer may rely on the knowledge of another officer or officers. This "collective knowledge" concept was endorsed by the Supreme Court in *United States v. Hensley,* 469 U.S. 221, 105 S.Ct. 675, 83 L.Ed.2d 604 (1985), where officers who stopped Hensley in Kentucky acted solely in reliance on a flyer issued by Ohio police stating that Hensley was wanted for criminal investigation in connection with a felony committed in Ohio. The Court held that a stop based on such a flyer was permissible so long as the officers who issued the bulletin themselves had an adequate basis for making a stop.

Limitation

If the officers who have personal knowledge do not in fact have sufficient information to support a stop, then the stop is illegal. The stopping officer is not entitled to plead his lack of personal knowledge as an excuse for stopping a citizen where reasonable suspicion does not in fact exist.

11. Use of Informants

As with probable cause, an officer's assessment of reasonable suspicion is often based in whole or in part on information from an informant. In *Alabama v. White*, 496 U.S. 325, 110 S.Ct. 2412, 110 L.Ed.2d 301 (1990), the Court held that an anonymous tip which was partially corroborated could constitute reasonable suspicion to support a *Terry* stop.

a. Facts of *White*

Police received an anonymous tip that White would be leaving a particular apartment in a brown Plymouth station wagon with the right taillight lens broken, and would be driving to Dobey's Motel with a brown attaché case containing cocaine. The officers went to the apartment and saw White enter a brown Plymouth station wagon with a broken right taillight. She was not carrying an attaché case. The police followed the station wagon as it took the most direct route to Dobey's Motel. White was stopped just short of Dobey's Motel, and consented to the search of a brown attaché case that had been placed in the car before police began surveillance. The officers found marijuana in the attaché case, and three milligrams of cocaine in White's purse, which was searched during processing at the station. The issue for the Court was whether there was reasonable suspicion to make the stop, given that the tip was from an anonymous informant and that none of the activity corroborated was in any way suspicious.

b. Analysis in *White*

The Court relied on the totality of circumstances approach to informants' tips as supporting probable cause, originally established in *Illinois v. Gates, supra.* As discussed in the section on probable cause, the Court in *Gates* looked to the two traditional "prongs" of veracity and basis of knowledge in assessing the informant's reliability, and also considered the extent to which the officers corroborated the informant's tip. But the fact that a tip has been corroborated receives more consideration under *Gates* than previously.

The Court in *White* found that the factors of basis of knowledge and veracity are also relevant in the reasonable suspicion context. But the Court reasoned that these factors must be applied even more permissively than under the *Gates* approach, since reasonable suspicion is a less rigorous standard of proof than probable cause.

c. **Application of the More Permissive Standards to the Facts of _White_**

Even given the lesser showing required, the majority in _White_ acknowledged that the anonymous tip did not itself provide reasonable suspicion, since it did not show that the informant was reliable, nor did it give any indication of the informant's basis for predicting White's activities. However, that did not end the analysis. While the tip did not stand on its own, even for reasonable suspicion, the majority found that as with probable cause, corroboration of the tip could lead to a finding of reasonable suspicion.

d. **Corroboration Not as Substantial**

The majority determined that the corroboration in _White_ was not as substantial as that in _Gates_. In _Gates,_ for instance, the officers corroborated relatively unique travel plans, with more details than those given by the informant in _White_. Also, the defendants in _Gates_ were observed to engage in somewhat suspicious travel activity. There was nothing unique, suspicious, or detailed about the travel activity in _White_. White merely got in the car and drove a direct route toward Dobey's Motel; the route could also have taken her to a wide variety of places, and even if she was going to Dobey's Motel, there was nothing inherently incriminating or suspicious about that fact.

However, the fact that the corroboration was less than that necessary to satisfy probable cause was held not fatal in _White_. The Court reasoned that since reasonable suspicion is a less stringent standard than probable cause, the degree of corroboration required to support reasonable suspicion could be correspondingly less. The lesser standard is a reduction in both quantity and quality of proof.

e. **Corroboration Sufficient to Support a Stop**

The Court found that the stop of White was based on reasonable suspicion, even though the corroboration of the tip was not complete, and in fact the tip was not correct in some details. The majority acknowledged that the corroboration of the mere existence of the car was insignificant, since "anyone could have predicted that fact because it was a condition presumably existing at the time of the call." What was important was the caller's ability to predict White's _future behavior, i.e._ the travel plans. According to the Court, the correct prediction of itinerary (incomplete though the itinerary was at the time of the stop) demonstrated that the informant had inside knowledge about White's activity. Unlike the facts about the car, the general public would have had no way of knowing White's future travel plans. The Court found it reasonable for police to believe that a person with access to innocent inside information is likely to also have access to reliable information about that individual's illegal activities—at least it is an inference strong enough to support the minimal, lesser standards of reasonable suspicion.

f.   Dissent in *White*

The dissenters in *White* found it dangerous that an anonymous informant, with the barest knowledge of a person's innocent future activity, could generate a police intrusion. They concluded that "an anonymous neighbor's prediction about somebody's time of departure and probable destination is anything but a reliable basis for assuming that the commuter is in possession of an illegal substance—particularly when the person is not even carrying the attaché case described by the tipster."

g.   Reasonably Correct Prediction of Future Activity Is Strong Corroboration

After *White*, a very important form of corroboration will be evidence showing an informant's substantially correct prediction of future activity. It need only be substantially correct, since reasonable suspicion is such a minimal standard. *See United States v. Thompson*, 906 F.2d 1292 (8th Cir. 1990) (where informant predicted defendant would be robbing certain banks, and defendant was parked outside one of the banks, there was reasonable suspicion to make a stop, even though description of car and license plate were wrong).

h.   Reliability of a Tip Is Irrelevant if Police Investigation Uncovers Sufficient Facts

If the investigation made to corroborate the tip uncovers articulable facts that independently support a reasonable suspicion of criminal activity, then it does not matter whether the tip is reliable or not. For example, in *United States v. Lane*, 909 F.2d 895 (6th Cir. 1990), the police received an anonymous tip that drug dealing was going on in an apartment hallway in a building known to police for drug activity. When uniformed officers entered the building, the defendants fled at the sight of them. The court held that the flight, "along with the background facts," supplied the officers with a reasonable basis for conducting an investigative stop and made it "unnecessary to decide whether the anonymous tip in this case was sufficiently corroborated."

i.   No "Firearm Exception"
In *Florida v. J.L.*, 529 U.S. 266, 120 S.Ct. 1375, 146 L.Ed.2d 254 (2000), the government urged the Court to adopt a "firearm exception" to the rule that anonymous tips must be accompanied by specific indicia of reliability in order to form the basis for reasonable suspicion. In *J.L.*, police officers received an anonymous tip that a young black male standing at a particular bus stop wearing a plaid shirt was carrying a gun. Two officers went to the bus stop minutes later and saw three black males, one wearing a plaid shirt. Without any additional information, one of the officers ordered the male wearing the plaid shirt to put his hands up on the bus stop. The officer then frisked him and seized a gun from his pocket. The Supreme Court held that the anonymous tip in this case lacked the indicia of reliability as required in *White.* There was no prediction of future activity or other information that would show that the tipster had knowledge of concealed criminal activity. The Court rejected the government's suggestion that police officers be permitted to stop and frisk based on an anonymous tip without the standard indicia of reliability in cases involving firearms. The Court left open the possibility that there may be some cases where the potential danger is so great as to justify a search without the requisite showing of reliability (cases involving bombs, for example).

But see United States v. Heard, 367 F.3d 1275 (11th Cir. 2004) which also involved an anonymous tip about a firearm. In *Heard*, an officer saw a man and a woman arguing loudly at a train station. The woman accused the man of owing her money. The officer intervened and encouraged the man to pay her. After paying the woman, the man walked away. The woman then told the officer that the man had a weapon. The officer told the woman to stay at the train station so she could make a statement, but she got on a train and was never seen again. The officer approached the man, frisked him, and found a firearm. The court held that the tip was reliable because it was relayed face-to-face and the officer had the opportunity to observe the anonymous tipster's demeanor and assess her credibility. The officer stated that the unknown woman seemed frightened. Furthermore, he reasonably concluded that she knew the man since they were arguing about money, making it more likely that she would have knowledge that he possessed a weapon.

D. The Right to Frisk Incident to a Stop

A stop is a seizure. A frisk is a search, which is an independent intrusion that must be separately justified. The justification for a frisk is to protect the officer who is making the stop. In *Terry*, the Court reasoned that if an officer has the right to make a stop, he should be able to protect himself in the course of a lawful seizure. It therefore held that if police officers are justified in believing that the individuals whose suspicious behavior they are investigating at close range are armed and presently dangerous, they may conduct a limited protective search for weapons. As one court applying *Terry* has stated: "The Fourth Amendment does not require police to allow a suspect to draw first." *United States v. Rideau*, 969 F.2d 1572 (5th Cir. 1992).

The Court in *Terry* stated that there are two critical determinations that must be made in judging the legality of a frisk: "whether the officer's action was justified at its *inception,* and whether it was reasonably related in scope to the circumstances which justified the interference in the first place."

1. Frisk Is Not a Search for Evidence

Since the justification for a frisk is to protect the officer who is making a stop, it follows that *Terry* does not permit a search for evidence. A search for evidence of crime, in the absence of a need to protect the officer, requires *probable cause.* In *Arizona v. Hicks*, 480 U.S. 321, 107 S.Ct. 1149, 94 L.Ed.2d 347 (1987), the Court refused to permit a search for evidence where the officers had only reasonable suspicion and not probable cause to believe that the search would be successful. The Court in *Hicks* squarely rejected the Government's argument that reasonable suspicion was sufficient to justify a search for evidence beneath a stereo turntable; the Government argued that the search was so limited as to be merely a "cursory inspection" rather than a full-blown search. But the Court stated that "a search is a search" and refused to distinguish between extensive searches and cursory inspections. Thus, even cursory inspections *for evidence of crime* require probable cause.

a. Plain View

While a frisk for evidence is not permissible, it will often occur that an officer, in the course of a self-protective frisk, will uncover evidence of crime. For example, an officer who has reasonable suspicion of bodily harm may frisk and pull out a hard object on the suspect's person if it may be a weapon. If the object turns out to be tightly bundled drugs, this evidence can be lawfully seized under the plain view doctrine.

b. *Terry* Applied Outside the Stop and Frisk Context—Probationers and Parolees

i. Probationers

The Supreme Court extended the *Terry* reasonableness analysis to the search of a probationer's residence in *United States v. Knights*, 534 U.S. 112, 122 S.Ct. 587, 151 L.Ed.2d 497 (2001). Knights was placed on probation for a drug offense and signed an order agreeing to the conditions of his probation, including submitting his "person, property, place of residence, vehicle, personal effects, to search at anytime, with or without a search warrant, warrant of arrest or reasonable cause by any probation officer or law enforcement officer." A sheriff's deputy had reasonable suspicion that Knights was involved in an arson offense and decided to conduct a full-blown search of Knights' residence. He did so without a warrant based on Knights' probation order. Knights was subsequently arrested and charged with conspiracy to commit arson and related offenses. Knights argued that the search of his residence violated the Fourth Amendment because the condition of probation only permitted searches with a "probationary purpose." The District Court granted Knight's motion to suppress the evidence and the Court of Appeals for the Ninth Circuit affirmed.

The Supreme Court reversed, holding that the search was reasonable under a general "totality of the circumstances" analysis. The Court deemed Knights' probationary status to be the most significant circumstance, noting that probation is a form of criminal sanction along the continuum of punishments ranging from community service to imprisonment in a maximum-security facility. The Court explained that a probationer, like others convicted of criminal offenses, may be deprived of the freedoms enjoyed by law-abiding citizens and that Knights' probation conditions diminished his reasonable expectation of privacy. The Court limited its holding to cases where there is reasonable suspicion of criminal activity and specifically declined to address the constitutionality of a suspicionless search based on a probation order. The Court also declined to decide whether Knights' acceptance of the probation order constituted voluntary consent to the search under *Schneckloth, infra.*

Knights is significant in that it was not a "special needs" search like the search of the probationer's home in *Griffin v. Wisconsin*, discussed *infra*, where the search was based on the state's special interest in rehabilitation. *Knights* is an exception to the Court's rule that reasonable suspicion does not justify a full-blown search for law enforcement purposes.

ii.   Parolees

The *Knights* analysis was extended to parolees in *Samson v. California*, 547 U.S. 843, 126 S.Ct. 2193, 165 L.Ed.2d 250 (2006). Samson was on parole in California. A police officer recognized him and knew he was a parolee. The officer proceeded to search Samson under the authority of California Penal Code § 3067(a), which provided that every parolee must agree in writing to be subject to a search or seizure by either a parole officer or law enforcement officer at any time of the day or night, with or without a search warrant, and with or without cause. The officer did not suspect Samson of any criminal activity when he searched him. The officer found drugs in Samson's possession. The Supreme Court, relying heavily on *Knights*, held that the suspicionless search was a reasonable condition of parole which advanced state interests. The Court emphasized that parolees have a substantially diminished expectation of privacy. As in *Knights*, the Court specifically declined to characterize the search as a "special needs" search, relying entirely upon and extending the analysis in *Knights*.

Although the Court in *Knights* limited its holding to searches of probationers based upon reasonable suspicion, in *Samson*, the Court upheld searches of parolees that were entirely suspicionless, reasoning that parolees have "fewer expectations of privacy than probationers, because parole is more akin to imprisonment than probation is."

2.   Inception of a Frisk—Reasonable Suspicion of Bodily Harm

Terry requires "reasonable, individualized suspicion before a search for weapons can be conducted." *Maryland v. Buie*, 494 U.S. 325, 334, 110 S.Ct.

1093, 1098, 108 L.Ed.2d 276 (1990). Thus, the same standard of proof is required for a frisk as is required for a stop. However, the question to which the standard is applied is somewhat different. The question upon which a frisk depends is whether there is reasonable suspicion to believe that the suspect is armed and dangerous. Such reasonable suspicion must be based on articulable facts specific to the suspect, and not on mere hunches.

a. **Automatic, Immediate Right to Frisk a Person Suspected of Violent Crime**

If an officer reasonably suspects that a person is involved in a crime of violence, that same reasonable suspicion will ordinarily justify an officer in believing that the suspect may be armed and dangerous. *See Adams v. Williams*, 407 U.S. 143, 92 S.Ct. 1921, 32 L.Ed.2d 612 (1972), where the officer had reasonable suspicion to believe that the suspect was involved in a violent crime, and the Court upheld an immediate protective frisk. Lower courts have held that the right to frisk is automatic for such crimes as robbery, burglary, rape, and assault with a deadly weapon.

b. **Drug Distribution**

If a person has been stopped on suspicion of large-scale drug distribution, most courts will find that the officer has an automatic right to a self-protective frisk. The rationale is that large-scale drug dealers are likely to be armed, even though drug dealing is not per se a crime of violence. *See United States v. Brown*, 913 F.2d 570 (8th Cir. 1990) ("[S]ince weapons and violence are frequently associated with drug transactions, the officers reasonably believed that the individuals with whom they were dealing were armed and dangerous."). *But see Richards v. Wisconsin, supra* (rejecting the argument that *all* drug dealers are presumed to be armed and dangerous).

c. **Non-violent Crimes**

For other types of crimes, such as shoplifting, public drunkenness, prostitution, or bookmaking, there must be articulable circumstances present other than the suspicion of the crime itself, in order to justify a protective frisk. Examples of some common factors include: a *bulge* on the suspect that appears to be a weapon; a *sudden movement* by the suspect toward a place where a weapon might be hidden; *previous violent activity* on the part of the suspect, known to the officer; *aggressive or violent behavior* exhibited by the suspect to the officer or others; the *number of suspects compared to the number of police officers;* and *the nature of the surroundings and the time of day.*

Example: In *United States v. Rideau,* 969 F.2d 1572 (5th Cir. 1992), officers were patrolling a high crime area, where people often carried weapons and transacted drug deals on the street, and where public drunkenness was a recurring problem. Officer Ellison saw a man wearing dark clothing standing in the road. Ellison flashed his bright lights to see the man better and to encourage him to get out of the road. The man stumbled as he moved toward the shoulder. Ellison suspected he was drunk. He pulled over, got out of the car, and approached the man to investigate. Ellison asked the man his name. The man seemed nervous; when he did not answer but began to back away, Ellison immediately closed the gap and reached out to pat the man's outer clothing. The first place he touched was the man's right front pants pocket, where he felt a firearm. Ellison removed the gun and placed the man under arrest. The man, Rideau, was subsequently charged with illegal possession of a firearm, and he moved to exclude the gun.

The court held that the gun was legally obtained as a result of a permissible *Terry* frisk. The court relied on the following facts: 1. Rideau backed away from the officer, so "it was not unreasonable under the circumstances for Ellison to have feared that Rideau was moving back to give himself time and space to draw a weapon"; 2. Rideau's moves took place at night; and 3. the confrontation occurred in a high crime area. The court recognized that the mere fact that a person is in a high crime area at night is not in itself enough to support either a stop or a frisk. But the court concluded that "when someone engages in *suspicious activity* in a high crime area, where weapons and violence abound, police officers must be particularly cautious in approaching and questioning him."

3. Self–Protective Frisk of Those Not Suspected of a Crime

Can an officer frisk a person who is not himself suspected of a crime, but who is in the vicinity of a police officer acting in the course of lawful police activity? This question arose in *Ybarra v. Illinois*, 444 U.S. 85, 100 S.Ct. 338, 62 L.Ed.2d 238 (1979), where officers arrived at a bar to conduct a search pursuant to a search warrant. They decided to frisk everyone who was in the bar. The Supreme Court declared that Ybarra's *mere presence* in the bar was not enough to constitute reasonable suspicion of bodily harm, and therefore that the frisk of Ybarra was illegal. The Court emphasized that *Terry* mandated a *case-by-case* approach, and that an officer cannot conduct a frisk unless he or she has *articulable* facts supporting reasonable suspicion that the suspect presents a risk of harm.

Automatic Companion Rule

Some courts have held that an officer who is conducting an arrest has an *automatic right* to conduct a weapons frisk on any companion of the arrestee. *See United States v. Berryhill*, 445 F.2d 1189 (9th Cir. 1971) (upholding the frisk of a person who was a passenger in a car driven by the arrestee: "it is inconceivable that a peace officer effecting a lawful arrest of an occupant of a vehicle must expose himself to a shot in the back from defendant's associate because he cannot, on the spot, make the nice distinction between whether the other is a companion in crime or a social acquaintance."). Other courts have rejected the automatic companion rule on the ground that it is inconsistent with the case-by-case approach to reasonable suspicion mandated by *Terry*. In these courts, a companion or associate can only be frisked upon articulable facts establishing reasonable suspicion to believe that the person is armed and dangerous. *See United States v. Whitfield*, 907 F.2d 798 (8th Cir. 1990) (rejecting automatic companion rule, but upholding the frisk on the ground that the companion of the arrestee was wearing a bullet-proof vest and there was a suspicious bulge underneath the vest).

4. Ordering a Person Out of a Car for Self–Protection

In *Pennsylvania v. Mimms*, 434 U.S. 106, 98 S.Ct. 330, 54 L.Ed.2d 331 (1977), an officer stopped a vehicle for the purpose of issuing a traffic citation. The officer lacked grounds to conduct a frisk, but he nonetheless ordered the driver, Mimms, to step out of the car. When Mimms got out of the car, the officer noted a bulge under his jacket, which *then* gave the officer grounds to conduct a frisk, and a gun was uncovered. Mimms did not challenge the stop itself; he argued that the officer acted unreasonably in ordering him out of the car, in the absence of reasonable suspicion to believe that Mimms was armed and dangerous. The Supreme Court held that an officer has an *automatic right* to order a driver to step out of a vehicle where that vehicle has been lawfully stopped. The Court found this to be merely a "de minimus" incremental intrusion, given the fact that the driver has already been legally stopped. This minimal intrusion was justified as a "precautionary measure to afford a degree of protection to the officer."

a. Bright–Line Rule

The *Mimms* Court implicitly determined that its automatic rule for de minimus intrusions was not prohibited by the case-by-case approach to reasonable suspicion mandated by *Terry.*

b. Passengers

In *Maryland v. Wilson,* 519 U.S. 408, 117 S.Ct. 882, 137 L.Ed.2d 41 (1997), the Court held that an officer has an automatic right to order a passenger out of a lawfully stopped vehicle. It found the rationale of *Mimms* to be equally applicable to passengers.

5. Limitations on the Scope of a Frisk

In conducting a frisk, an officer can be no more intrusive than is necessary to protect against the risk of harm posed by the suspect. Ordinarily, a pat-down is sufficient to determine whether the suspect is carrying weapons that could be used effectively by the suspect during the course of the stop. A detailed touching of all areas of the suspect's body is beyond the scope of a *Terry* frisk. *See Minnesota v. Dickerson, supra* (Supreme Court invalidates a search where it was more intrusive than necessary to determine whether an object carried by the defendant was a weapon).

a. Feeling an Object During a Pat–Down

If an officer feels an object during a pat-down, the question is whether the officer can take the object from the suspect's person in order to determine whether it may be a weapon. This depends on whether there is reasonable suspicion to believe that the object could be a weapon. Generally speaking, an inspection of the object is not permissible if it is *soft to the touch. See Ellis v. State,* 573 So.2d 724 (Miss. 1990) (officer who pulls out object which turns out to be a bag of marijuana has acted beyond the permissible scope of a *Terry* frisk). If the object feels hard to the touch, then the question is whether it could be a weapon in light of *its size or contours;* because the operative standard is reasonable suspicion, the officer need not be certain that the object is a weapon. *See United States v. Quarles*, 955 F.2d 498 (8th Cir. 1992) (large hard lump "might have been a firearm").

b. Probable Cause

If an officer feels a soft package, it cannot be taken out and inspected under the *Terry* doctrine; but the fact that the suspect was carrying a soft package may, together with other factors, constitute probable cause to believe that the suspect is carrying contraband. If this is so, then the suspect may be arrested and the package may be searched incident to the arrest. *See United States v. Salazar*, 945 F.2d 47 (2d Cir. 1991) (officer who conducted legal pat-down of suspected drug dealer and felt a soft package had probable cause under the circumstances to arrest and search the suspect for drugs). See the discussion of the "plain touch" doctrine, *supra*.

c. Containers on the Suspect's Person

If the officer takes a hard object from the suspect's person and it turns out to be a container, the question arises whether the officer can open the container under *Terry*. Assuming that up to this point there has been and remains reasonable suspicion that the suspect is armed and dangerous, does the need to protect the officer extend to opening a container that the officer is currently holding? Of course a search of the container is impermissible if it could not reasonably contain a dangerous weapon. *See People v. Roth*, 66 N.Y.2d 688, 496 N.Y.S.2d 413, 487 N.E.2d 270 (1985) (where hard object turned out to be a roll of papers, officer was not justified in unwrapping and examining the papers). But even if it could reasonably contain a weapon, one might question whether opening it is necessary in light of the fact that the officer has custody of the container.

The Supreme Court, however, has held that the officer may open a container that may contain a weapon, on the ground that the suspect is only being stopped and not arrested. Since the stop is a momentary intrusion, and the suspect must eventually be released (if arrested because probable cause subsequently develops, the container may be searched incident to arrest), the officer will have to return the container to the suspect. Under these circumstances, an officer may reasonably fear the possibility of harm if he returns the container unexamined at the conclusion of the stop—especially considering the fact that the officer's back may be turned after the stop is concluded. *See Michigan v. Long,* 463 U.S. 1032, 103 S.Ct. 3469, 77 L.Ed.2d 1201 (1983) (noting the risk to officers after a stop if the suspect is not arrested and regains access to weapons).

6. **Right to Protective Search Beyond the Suspect's Person**

As with containers found on the person, courts have permitted protective searches of containers carried by the suspect or within the suspect's grab area. Again, the courts reason that such a search is permitted even if the suspect is denied access to the container during the course of the stop. Thus, in *United States v. Johnson,* 932 F.2d 1068 (5th Cir. 1991), the court upheld a cursory inspection of a pair of overalls located a few feet away from a suspect who appeared to be attempting to burglarize a house. The court reasoned that the mere separation of the suspect from his effects during the stop would not be a sufficient protection, since if the stop was terminated, the officers would have to return the property to the suspect. An officer could reasonably conclude that the property should be examined before returning it to the suspect.

a. Protective Search of Automobiles

In *Michigan v. Long,* 463 U.S. 1032, 103 S.Ct. 3469, 77 L.Ed.2d 1201 (1983), the Court upheld a protective search of the passenger compartment of a car during the course of a *Terry* stop. The Court held that where police reasonably suspect that a person is dangerous, *Terry* permits a limited examination of any area from which that person might gain a weapon that could be used against the officers. The Court found that there could be a risk of harm to the officers where, "if the suspect is not placed under arrest, he will be permitted to reenter his automobile, and he will then have access to any weapons inside." *See also United States v. Holifield,* 956 F.2d 665 (7th Cir. 1992) (search of locked glove compartment permissible where keys were in car, suspect was about to re-enter car, and suspect had exhibited "erratic driving and aggressive and boisterous behavior"). However, a search will not be permitted under *Long* if there is no reasonable suspicion in the first place to believe that the suspect poses a risk of harm to the officer or others. *See United States v. Lott,* 870 F.2d 778 (1st Cir. 1989) (search of passenger compartment impermissible where the police were not in fear for their own safety, as indicated by the fact that the suspects were not frisked upon exiting the car; *Long* does not permit a search for evidence).

See also United States v. Wallen, 388 F.3d 161 (5th Cir. 2004). In *Wallen,* a police officer stopped the defendant's truck for speeding. The officer observed what appeared to be two rifles and a handgun on the passenger side of the car. The defendant hesitated in complying with the officer's instruction to move to the rear of the truck. The officer put defendant in handcuffs and placed him in the patrol car. The officer searched the interior of defendant's vehicle and found numerous illegal weapons. The court held that the search was a valid protective sweep for weapons under the Fourth Amendment. Although defendant was in handcuffs, the possibility that the officer might release defendant to his truck provided grounds for the protective search.

b. **Protective Sweep**

A "protective sweep" is a quick and limited search of a premises, incident to an arrest and conducted to protect the safety of police officers or others. In *Maryland v. Buie*, 494 U.S. 325, 110 S.Ct. 1093, 108 L.Ed.2d 276 (1990), the Court held that a protective sweep could be conducted if officers have reasonable suspicion to believe that it is necessary to protect police officers or the public; probable cause is not required.

  i. **Facts of *Buie***

  Following an armed robbery, police obtained arrest warrants for Buie and his accomplice, and went to Buie's house. Buie was arrested upon emerging from the basement. The officers did a cursory search of the basement to see if anyone else was there, and in the course of that search, they found incriminating evidence in plain view.

  ii. **Analysis in *Buie***

  Relying on *Long*, the *Buie* Court held that the reasonable suspicion standard was an appropriate balance between the arrestee's remaining privacy interest in the home and the officer's safety-based interest in conducting a protective sweep. The Court noted that while even a cursory inspection of a home was a severe intrusion, the state has a heavy interest in protecting officers who are in the course of making an arrest.

  iii. **Protective Sweep Not Permitted to Protect Against Destruction of Evidence**

  A protective sweep can only be conducted for safety purposes, and not to prevent destruction of, or to search for, evidence. The majority in *Buie* specifically refers to protective sweeps as justified to "protect the safety of officers or others." This is consistent with its derivation from *Terry*. A *Terry* search, of which the protective sweep is just an example, is justified by the need to protect the officer; it cannot be invoked to justify a search for evidence. *See United States v. Noushfar,* 78 F.3d 1442 (9th Cir. 1996) (search of a box containing business receipts cannot be justified as a protective sweep).

iv. **Arrests Outside the Home**

In *Buie*, the defendant was arrested in the home. Courts have upheld protective sweeps where the suspect is arrested outside the house, so long as there is reasonable suspicion that someone within the house presents a risk of harm to the officers. *See United States v. Oguns,* 921 F.2d 442 (2d Cir. 1990) (protective sweep of home permissible where defendants arrested outside house at twilight and police have reasonable suspicion to believe that individuals inside house observed arrest, posed a danger to the officers, and might destroy evidence).

v. **Articulable Facts Must Indicate a Risk of Harm**

A protective sweep is not permissible unless the officers have reasonable suspicion that it is necessary to conduct a sweep to neutralize the risk of harm to the officers or others. *See United States v. Colbert,* 76 F.3d 773 (6th Cir. 1996) (protective sweep improper where officers had no information that there was anyone other than the arrestee on the premises).

vi. **Protective Sweep Other than During an Arrest**

Courts have held that police officers may do protective sweeps even when no arrest is involved. *See United States v. Miller,* 430 F.3d 93 (2d Cir. 2005) (Officer assisting with the service of a protective order in a domestic dispute involving defendant and his cousin was justified in conducting a protective sweep when he followed the defendant into a rear bedroom. The officer knew that defendant had threatened to shoot his cousin in the head and believed defendant might be a threat if allowed to go into the bedroom alone.).

E. Brief and Limited Detentions: The Line Between Stop and Arrest

It is often difficult to distinguish between an arrest, which requires probable cause, and a stop, which requires only reasonable suspicion. Both are seizures. An "arrest" is more intrusive than a "stop," which is why a higher standard of proof is required to effect one. Generally speaking, the following factors have been considered relevant in distinguishing an arrest from a stop: whether the suspect has been *forced to move to a custodial area for investigative purposes*; whether investigative techniques employed are *so intrusive as to exceed those identified with a stop*; whether the suspect has been detained for a *lengthy period of time*; and whether the officers *use custodial procedures—such as handcuffs or drawn guns—that are unnecessary for their protection during a stop.*

1. Forced Movement of the Suspect to a Custodial Area

In *Florida v. Royer*, 460 U.S. 491, 103 S.Ct. 1319, 75 L.Ed.2d 229 (1983), officers moved Royer from the public area of an airport to a small room, where they sought and obtained Royer's consent to a search of his luggage. The Court held that the consent was invalid because it was obtained during the course of an arrest without probable cause. In determining that Royer had been arrested, as opposed to merely stopped, the Court found it crucial that officers had transferred the site of the encounter from the airport concourse to a small interrogation room, solely for the purpose of obtaining Royer's consent to a search of his luggage. The Court concluded that "at the time Royer produced the key to his suitcase, the detention to which he was then subjected was a more serious intrusion in his personal liberty than is allowable on mere suspicion of criminal activity."

a. Police Cars

A suspect who is detained in a police car, for purposes of questioning or other investigation, is ordinarily found to be under arrest. *See United States v. Thompson*, 906 F.2d 1292 (8th Cir. 1990) (placing suspect in squad car was not within the scope of a *Terry* stop, where it was done to prolong the investigation and not to ensure the safety of the officers).

b. Transporting the Suspect to the Station for Interrogation or Fingerprinting

In *Kaupp v. Texas*, 538 U.S. 626, 123 S.Ct. 1843, 155 L.Ed.2d 814 (2003) (per curiam), the Supreme Court held that forced transportation and interrogation of a suspect constitutes an arrest for which probable cause is required. Detectives suspected that 17–year-old Kaupp was involved in a murder but did not have probable cause to arrest him. They went to Kaupp's home at 3 a.m. on January 27th, awakened him, and one detective said, "we need to go and talk." When Kaupp responded "Okay," the detectives handcuffed him, took him outside and placed him in the patrol car. Kaupp was shoeless and dressed only in his underwear. The detectives drove him to the site where the victim's body was found, and then to the sheriff's headquarters where he was questioned. He eventually confessed to involvement in the crime. Citing *Dunaway v. New York*, 442 U.S. 200, 99 S.Ct. 2248, 60 L.Ed.2d 824 (1979), the Court noted that this case presented even stronger evidence of an arrest and that no reasonable person in Kaupp's situation would have thought that he was in that interrogation room as a matter of choice.

c.   **Forced Movement in Order to Obtain an Immediate Identification**
Despite the Supreme Court cases holding that the forced movement of suspects for investigative purposes is beyond the scope of *Terry*, many courts have found that, if reasonable suspicion exists, it is permissible to transport the suspect a short distance so that eyewitnesses may attempt to make an identification. Courts reason that the only other alternative would be to bring the witnesses to the suspect, and that this alternative might be so time-consuming as to be even more inconvenient to the suspect. *See People v. Hicks*, 68 N.Y.2d 234, 508 N.Y.S.2d 163, 500 N.E.2d 861 (1986) ("Securing the defendant and his companion and securing transportation for the witnesses would have been a more time-consuming process than that chosen.").

d.   **Forced Movement for Purposes of Safety or Security**
The Court in *Royer* recognized that "there are undoubtedly reasons of safety and security that would justify moving a suspect from one location to another during an investigatory detention, such as from an airport concourse to the interrogation room." So for example, a suspect may be placed in a police car, even though the officers are operating on only reasonable suspicion and not probable cause, if the suspect cannot safely be left in his own vehicle and detention outside the car is impractical. *See United States v. Manbeck*, 744 F.2d 360 (4th Cir. 1984) (suspect cannot be left in his car for safety reasons, and cannot be detained outside of car due to weather conditions).

2. **Investigative Techniques**
It is clear that an officer conducting a *Terry* stop can engage in preliminary investigation designed to clear up or to further develop

reasonable suspicion. Some preliminary investigative techniques found permissible under *Terry* include: a request for identification, airplane tickets or vehicle registration; a request for an explanation of the suspicious circumstances giving rise to the stop; and a request for consent to search. *See United States v. Hunnicutt*, 135 F.3d 1345 (10th Cir. 1998) (officer conducting routine traffic stop may request driver's license and vehicle registration and run a computer check). The officer may also verify the information obtained from the suspect by communicating with others, or by conducting a vehicle registration check or a computer search for outstanding warrants. *See United States v. Glover*, 957 F.2d 1004 (2d Cir. 1992) (permissible within the confines of a *Terry* stop to conduct a computer check to verify the accuracy of the suspect's "rather dubious" proof of identification); *United States v. Lego*, 855 F.2d 542 (8th Cir. 1988) (proper within the confines of a *Terry* stop to check for outstanding warrants). Courts have also permitted officers to detain suspects on reasonable suspicion in order to conduct a canine sniff or to conduct a preliminary investigation of other suspicious circumstances. *See United States v. Hardy*, 855 F.2d 753 (11th Cir. 1988) (proper to detain suspects while canine brought to scene to sniff vehicle); *People v. Contreras*, 780 P.2d 552 (Colo. 1989) (examination of visible portions of a car to see if it had been stripped, as anonymous caller had asserted).

Overly Intrusive Investigation Techniques

Some investigative techniques are themselves so intrusive as to require probable cause. The most obvious example is a search for evidence, which, as stated above, goes beyond the scope of a *Terry* stop. But other techniques may be overly intrusive even if they cannot be labeled a "search." So for example, some courts have held that a suspect cannot be subjected to a series of demanding physical tests to determine sobriety, in the absence of probable cause. *See People v. Carlson*, 677 P.2d 310 (Colo. 1984) (holding that the full battery of tests employed was so intrusive as to constitute an arrest). Roadside sobriety tests that are less demanding may be permissible under *Terry*, however. *See State v. Wyatt*, 67 Hawaii 293, 687 P.2d 544 (1984) (limited field sobriety test permissible on reasonable suspicion). Other courts have held that probable cause is required if the officer wishes to conduct an extensive investigation beyond the scope of the matter for which the suspect was stopped. *See United States v. Walker*, 933 F.2d 812 (10th Cir. 1991) (where the suspect was stopped for speeding and established that he had license and registration, it was improper to detain him further to question him extensively about guns and drugs). It is permissible, however, for the officer to ask a suspect for consent to search even after the justification for the stop has terminated. *Ohio v. Robinette,* 519 U.S. 33, 117 S.Ct. 417, 136 L.Ed.2d 347 (1996).

3. Time Limits on *Terry* Stops

In *United States v. Sharpe,* 470 U.S. 675, 105 S.Ct. 1568, 84 L.Ed.2d 605 (1985), the Supreme Court refused to impose an absolute time limit on *Terry* stops, though it recognized that "if an investigative stop continues indefinitely, at some point it can no longer be justified as an investigative stop." The test for assessing whether the time limits for a stop have been violated is "whether the police diligently pursued a means of investigation that was likely to confirm or dispel their suspicions quickly, during which time it was necessary to detain the defendant."

a. Reasonable Diligence Test

In *Sharpe,* a DEA officer trailed two vehicles, one a camper which was riding low, and one a Pontiac. He radioed for help, and a Highway Patrol trooper came to his assistance. The officers motioned for both vehicles to pull over. The driver of the Pontiac obeyed, but the camper sped away. The trooper followed the camper and eventually overtook it several miles down the road. Being unversed in drug interdiction, the trooper decided to detain the camper until the DEA agent arrived. The DEA agent had to wait for local police to arrive to "maintain the situation" where the Pontiac had been stopped. The DEA agent then drove to where the camper had been stopped. He smelled marijuana, opened the rear of the camper and discovered a number of bales of marijuana, then proceeded back to the Pontiac to arrest its occupants.

The occupants of the Pontiac had been detained between 30 and 40 minutes before they were arrested. They argued that, if the officers had been diligent, the DEA officer would have followed the camper, since that was the more likely storage vehicle for the drugs. The Court in *Sharpe* rejected this argument, stating that a court "should not indulge in unrealistic second-guessing" of the officer's conduct. The Court stated that "the question is not simply whether some other alternative was available, but whether the police acted unreasonably in failing to recognize or pursue it." The Court concluded that the officers had not exceeded the confines of a *Terry* stop, because they were confronted with a "swiftly developing situation" and were engaged in reasonably diligent activity designed to clear up or develop the suspicious facts which justified the stop. After *Sharpe*, lower courts have tended to give officers the benefit of the doubt in assessing whether their conduct was "reasonably diligent." *See, e.g., United States v. Davies*, 768 F.2d 893 (7th Cir. 1985) (forty minute detention did not exceed limits of *Terry* stop, where officers were inexperienced and were awaiting advice from superiors as to how to proceed).

b. Suspect's Actions May Justify a Lengthier Detention
    The Court in *Sharpe* also relied on the fact that the delay in detaining the suspects was caused, at least in part, by their own actions, i.e., by the refusal of the driver of the camper to stop even though he was ordered to do so. So for example, if a suspect gives a fictitious name or address, resulting in an inconclusive warrant or identification check, the consequent delay will not count against the officers. *See United States v. Knox*, 839 F.2d 285 (6th Cir. 1988) (two suspected drug couriers were lawfully detained for thirty minutes; investigation took longer than usual because the suspects falsely claimed not to know each other).

c. Suspect's Refusal to Consent to a Search
    The suspect's refusal to consent to a search cannot be used as a justification for prolonging the stop, since the suspect has a constitutional right to refuse to give consent to a search. In *Sharpe*, the people in the truck sped away even though they were ordered to stop. They had no right to do so. Thus, a detention can be prolonged if the suspect acts improperly to subvert the officer's investigation, but not if the suspect lawfully invokes his constitutional rights.

d. Detention of Household Occupants During Execution of a Search Warrant
    In *Michigan v. Summers*, 452 U.S. 692, 101 S.Ct. 2587, 69 L.Ed.2d 340 (1981), the Court held that police officers with a valid search warrant could order persons on the premises to remain there while a search warrant is being executed—even if the length of the detention exceeded that ordinarily associated with a *Terry* stop. The Court declared that such a detention would always be reasonable even though it may take a significant period of time to execute the warrant. The Court reasoned that the detention of an occupant in his home is less serious than the public stops approved in *Terry*, that the

search warrant protected against the risk of overreaching by the officers, and that the state had a legitimate interest in preventing flight and the destruction of evidence.

The Court upheld even more intrusive seizures of household occupants in *Muehler v. Mena*, 544 U.S. 93, 125 S.Ct. 1465, 161 L.Ed.2d 299 (2005) and *Los Angeles County v. Rettele*, 550 U.S. 609, 127 S.Ct. 1989, 167 L.Ed.2d 974 (2007). In *Mena*, the Court cited *Summers* in upholding the handcuffing, detention, and questioning of a person during the warranted search of the home of a suspected gang member believed to be armed and dangerous. Similarly, in *Rettele*, the Court upheld police officers' decision to order a couple out of bed and hold them at gunpoint while they executed a search warrant in the home of suspects believed to be armed. In both cases, the Court emphasized that the detentions were relatively brief and noted that they were reasonable under the circumstances to minimize the risk of harm to the officers.

e. **When an Extended Detention Becomes an Arrest**
   In *United States v. Washington*, 387 F.3d 1060 (9th Cir. 2004), six officers, five of whom were uniformed and visibly carrying weapons, were outside defendant's hotel room when defendant responded to a knock at the door. The officers asked the defendant for consent to search his room and the defendant declined. The officers detained the defendant in the hallway while they continued to question him and request consent. The court held that the officers' actions were calculated to circumvent the requirement that a warrant be obtained to search an individual's home and were beyond the scope of a permissible detention under the Fourth Amendment.

4. **Show of Force or Use of Restraint**
   An arrest is often accompanied by the use of handcuffs and drawn gun. It does not follow, however, that every use of such coercive tactics will constitute an arrest. Courts have upheld the use of handcuffs, drawn guns and similar tactics when the circumstances indicate that they are reasonably necessary to assure the safety of the officers conducting the stop. *See, e.g., United States v. Jackson*, 918 F.2d 236 (1st Cir. 1990) (police did not exceed the scope of a *Terry* stop when they approached a vehicle with weapons drawn, where there was reasonable suspicion to believe that the suspects were armed, and where the defendant was a convicted

felon and a suspected drug trafficker); *People v. Allen*, 73 N.Y.2d 378, 540 N.Y.S.2d 971, 538 N.E.2d 323 (1989) (proper, within the confines of a *Terry* stop, for officers to handcuff suspect who matched the description of an armed bank robber, after chasing him down a dark alley in a high crime area). On the other hand, the use of a gun or other forceful tactics (such as ordering the suspects to lie prone on the ground) cannot be justified under *Terry* if the suspects are cooperative, and there is no reason to think that such tactics are necessary to protect the officers. *See Washington v. Lambert*, 98 F.3d 1181 (9th Cir. 1996) (not permissible under *Terry* to draw guns and employ handcuffs where suspects are cooperative and not suspected of a violent crime).

Relevant Factors

Factors to consider in determining the reasonableness of the officers' use of a show of force or other restraining activity during the course of a stop include: 1. the number of officers involved; 2. the nature of the crime for which reasonable suspicion exists; 3. whether there is reasonable suspicion to believe the suspect might be armed; 4. the strength of the officers' articulable suspicions; 5. whether the suspect is cooperative; and 6. the need for immediate action by the officers.

Example: In *United States v. Raino*, 980 F.2d 1148 (8th Cir. 1992), officers responded to a report of a drive-by shooting, and reports that other shots had been fired in the area. When they arrived, they observed a group of people mingling on the street and several people fighting in a nearby yard. They saw a BMW double-parked, with two females leaning into the driver's side, talking to the driver. The officers approached with their marked car, and the BMW began to pull away. The officers shined a spotlight on the driver, got quickly out of their car, and one officer pointed his gun at the driver and ordered him to stop. The driver was ordered out of the car, and the officers saw a gun in plain view behind the driver's seat. A subsequent search uncovered drugs. Raino, the driver, contended that the show of force elevated the initial detention into an arrest. The court held that there was reasonable suspicion and that the officer's show of force was justified under the circumstances. The court noted that the officers were responding to a late night call in an area where several shots had been fired; that there was a considerable amount of activity in the area; that people were fighting; and that only two officers were present on the scene.

F. Detentions of Property Under *Terry*

Terry concerned seizures of the person, but its principles have been applied to seizures of property as well. In *United States v. Place*, 462 U.S. 696, 103 S.Ct. 2637, 77 L.Ed.2d 110 (1983), the Court stated that "the limitations applicable to investigative detentions of the person should define the permissible scope of the person's luggage on less than probable cause." So there are three types of police contacts with a person's property, just as there are three types of police contacts with a person: that which is so minimal as not to constitute a seizure; that which is short-term and requires reasonable suspicion; and that which is so serious as to require probable cause. And as in *Terry*, the courts balance the interest of the state against the nature and severity of the intrusion to determine the level of suspicion required to justify the detention of the property.

1. Personal Interests at Stake

Where property is detained, an individual obviously has a possessory interest at stake. During the time that the state detains the property, the citizen is deprived of the use of it. But in some cases, the citizen may also have a *personal liberty interest* at stake when his property is detained. For example, in *Place, supra*, officers detained Place's luggage as he deplaned in New York City from Miami. He was told that he was free to leave but that his luggage would remain with the authorities. The Government in *Place* argued that seizures of property are generally less intrusive than seizures of the person. The Court responded that this assertion was "true in some circumstances" but that the Government's premise was "faulty on the facts we address in this case." The Court noted that the seizure of a traveler's property "can effectively restrain the person since he is subjected to the possible disruption of his travel plans in order to remain with his luggage or to arrange for its return." Accordingly, a seizure of property will be more strictly scrutinized when it is tantamount to the seizure of the person as well, and less strictly scrutinized if it results only in the deprivation of a possessory interest.

See United States v. LaFrance, 879 F.2d 1 (1st Cir. 1989) (detention of Federal Express package for over two hours pending a dog sniff was permissible where officers had reasonable suspicion to believe the package contained drugs: "While the police are not free to dispossess an individual at will, they are subject to fewer restraints where they trammel no other recognized interest apart from possession alone"; court contrasts luggage cases, which implicate "dual concerns"). *See also United States v. Va Lerie*, 424 F.3d 694 (8th Cir. 2005) (no seizure where officers removed checked luggage from bus and moved it inside a bus terminal to obtain consent to search; the removal of the luggage did not delay the passenger's travel or affect his freedom of movement in any way).

2. No Suspicion Required if There Is No Material Interference With Property

If the officer's detention of the property is so insignificant that there is no meaningful interference with the citizen's possessory or liberty interest, then the detention will not constitute a seizure. As such, the police activity need not be justified by any articulable suspicion.

Example: In *United States v. England*, 971 F.2d 419 (9th Cir. 1992), England deposited two packages for Express Mail delivery from California to Alabama. Officers had a hunch that the packages contained narcotics. Each package was set aside and presented to a narcotics-sniffing dog. The dog reacted positively, and the packages were subsequently opened pursuant to a warrant. It was not disputed that had the sniffs been negative, the packages could have been placed on their regularly scheduled flight to Alabama. The court found it unnecessary to determine whether reasonable suspicion existed to detain the packages, because no seizure had occurred.

3. Reasonable Suspicion Is Sufficient for Certain Temporary Detentions of Property

Even if a possessory or liberty interest is impaired by a detention of property, the seizure may be permissible upon reasonable suspicion rather than probable cause. Illustrative is *United States v. Van Leeuwen*, 397 U.S. 249, 90 S.Ct. 1029, 25 L.Ed.2d 282 (1970), where postal inspectors detained two packages, having reasonable suspicion to believe the packages contained illegally imported coins. They delayed the packages for nearly 30 hours in order to conduct an investigation. They ultimately got enough information to reach the level of probable cause, and obtained a warrant. The Court held that the 30 hour detention on the basis of reasonable suspicion was permissible under *Terry.* The Court noted that the officers conducted their investigation diligently and promptly.

Justification for Lengthy Detention of Property

It is extremely unlikely that the Court would uphold a 30–hour detention of a person if the officer had only reasonable suspicion and not probable cause. *See Place, supra* (noting that the Court had never approved a 90–minute detention of a person under *Terry*). Yet the 30–hour detention of the mailed package was unanimously upheld in *Van Leeuwen.* This result is explained by the fact that Van Leeuwen was deprived of a possessory interest only; he had no personal liberty interest at stake when the package was seized. Moreover, even the possessory interest was minimal during the time the package was detained. Van Leeuwen was receiving a package through the mails. As such, he had no assurance that his package would arrive precisely on a certain day. The package may well have been delayed independently of a police investigation. As such, the 30–hour delay was not a very substantial intrusion on Van Leeuwen's legitimate possessory interest in the package—only intrusive enough to require reasonable suspicion rather than probable cause. *Compare United States v. LaFrance, supra* (where package is sent by Federal Express and delivery is guaranteed at noon, the individual's possessory interest is implicated precisely at noon).

4. Detentions of Property That Require Probable Cause

A detention of property may in some circumstances be so lengthy and intrusive as to require probable cause. Illustrative is *United States v. Place, supra.* Officers had reasonable suspicion to believe that Place was a drug courier. They knew he was traveling into LaGuardia Airport in New York City on a flight from Miami. When Place deplaned, his luggage was seized in order for a dog sniff to be conducted. However, there was no narcotics detecting dog at LaGuardia at that time. It was only after Place's plane arrived that the officers decided to summon a dog from Kennedy Airport. Because of this last-minute decision, Place's luggage was detained for 90 minutes, with only reasonable suspicion and not probable cause to believe that the luggage contained drugs.

a. Holding in *Place*

The Court in *Place* held that the 90–minute detention of the luggage violated the Fourth Amendment. It concluded that the intrusion was severe in length, and tantamount to the seizure of Place under these circumstances.

b. Relevance of Notice

The Court in *Place* noted that the seizure was "exacerbated by the failure of the agents to inform the respondent of the place to which they were transporting his luggage, of the length of time he might be dispossessed, and of what arrangements would be made for return of the luggage if the investigation dispelled the suspicion."

c. Diligence of the Investigation

Most importantly, the Court in *Place* concluded that the officers *had not diligently pursued the investigation,* because they had not called for a dog until Place's plane had already arrived.

5. Relevant Factors Determining Whether a Seizure of Property Requires Probable Cause

After *Place*, courts assess three factors to determine whether a seizure of property is so intrusive that it requires probable cause. The relevant factors are: 1) the diligence of the investigation; 2) the length of the detention and whether liberty interests as well as possessory interests are at stake; and 3) information conveyed to the suspect concerning the seizure.

a. Reasonable Diligence Required

As with seizures of the person, officers are not required to be perfect or even very efficient in the course of their investigation attendant to the seizure of property. If the officers are *reasonably diligent,* their detention of property for even a lengthy period of time is likely to be held permissible, even though there is only reasonable suspicion and not probable cause to believe that there is anything incriminating with respect to the property. For example, despite *Place*, there is no requirement that officers have a narcotics sniffing dog immediately at hand for every detention of a package. *See United States v. Tavolacci*, 895 F.2d 1423 (D.C. Cir. 1990) (15–minute delay while seeking drug-detecting dog at train station was proper, even though "the dog would have been waiting on the platform in a world where the time of dogs and their handlers was cost-free"). The reason why the officers' conduct was unreasonable in *Place* was not because the dog was unavailable at the very first moment, but rather because the officers did not bother to summon the dog until after Place's plane arrived—even though they could have anticipated the need for a dog from the moment Place got on the plane in Miami. *Compare State v. Jerome,* 69 Hawaii 132, 736 P.2d 438 (1987) (30–minute delay in bringing dog to area was not unreasonable where the officers received their tip only 10 minutes before the suspect's arrival at the airport).

b. Relevance of Notice to the Property Owner

According to *Place,* an intrusion becomes more serious if the owner is not notified of the fate of his property and the amount of time he will be dispossessed. This is because, without such information, the owner of the property is likely to wish to remain with the property, and therefore the seizure of the property will also be a deprivation of the owner's liberty interest. Also, the deprivation of a possessory interest is more serious if it appears to the owner that the property may never be returned. Accordingly, courts after *Place* have upheld fairly lengthy seizures where the owner has been informed of the relevant detention procedures. *See United States v. Hooper,* 935 F.2d 484 (2d Cir. 1991) (30–minute detention permissible, in part because "the agents exchanged phone numbers with Hooper so that arrangements could be made for the return of the suitcase in the event their suspicions were not confirmed").

VI. Administrative and Regulatory Searches and Seizures

The Supreme Court has applied the reasonableness clause of the Fourth Amendment to searches and seizures conducted for purposes other than traditional criminal law enforcement. The Court has reasoned that the traditional requirements of a warrant and probable cause, while usefully applied to searches and seizures of evidence by law enforcement officials, are not well-suited to searches made by government officials for a legitimate administrative or regulatory purpose. Therefore, if a search or seizure is justified by *special needs other than traditional criminal law enforcement,* the Court engages in a balance of interests under the reasonableness clause to assess the minimum requirements for such a search or seizure. Under this reasonableness analysis, as in *Terry,* the Court balances the need for a particular search or seizure against the degree of intrusion upon personal rights which the search or seizure entails. If the probable cause standard and/or the warrant requirement takes insufficient account of the state interests at stake (i.e., unduly subjugates the state interest in light of the intrusion imposed), then the Court will find it reasonable to dispense with such requirements in favor of lesser standards such as reasonable suspicion, area warrants, or other controls on official discretion. If there is no special need beyond criminal law enforcement at stake, then a search is considered one to obtain evidence for law enforcement purposes, and it presumptively requires probable cause and a warrant, or another exception to the warrant requirement.

A. Safety Inspections of Homes

Inspections of homes by housing inspectors, such as for building code violations and other safety conditions, promote special needs beyond criminal law enforcement. The Court balanced the need for such searches against the intrusion suffered by homeowners in *Camara v. Municipal Court*, 387 U.S. 523, 87 S.Ct. 1727, 18 L.Ed.2d 930 (1967).

1. Probable Cause Not Required

If the traditional probable cause requirement were applied to administrative safety inspections, then a right of entry would arise only if there was a fair probability that certain specific conditions in a specific building constituted a violation of a safety code. The traditional probable cause requirement would thus preclude area-wide safety inspections and periodic safety inspections. In *Camara*, the Court rejected the homeowner's claim that the right of inspection was limited to instances where there is probable cause to believe that there is a violation in a specific building. The Court held that a valid entry could be made on other grounds, such as the *passage of time*, the *nature of the building*, or the fact that an *area-wide inspection* is being conducted.

Rationale

The Court in *Camara* reasoned that periodic and area-wide inspections are crucial to the effectiveness of a safety inspection scheme, and that to require probable cause would undermine the legitimate state interest in building safety. The Court noted that many safety hazards "are not observable from outside the building and indeed may not be apparent to the occupant himself"; these hazards would go unremedied if probable cause were required. Against the state's heavy interest in building safety, the Court weighed the individual interests at stake, and found that home safety inspections "involve a relatively limited invasion of the urban citizen's privacy." The Court reasoned that such inspections are not personal in nature and do not involve a full-scale search of the home. Accordingly, the

Court concluded that the probable cause standard was not an appropriate balance of the state and individual interests.

2. Search Warrant Required

The Court in *Camara* held that, except in emergency situations or where the homeowner consents, the safety inspector must have a search warrant to enter the home. Again balancing the interests at stake, the Court concluded that the burden of obtaining a warrant was not likely to frustrate the governmental purpose behind the home safety inspection. It reasoned that "in the enforcement of housing codes immediate searches are almost never necessary" because, if the inspector is turned away and then proceeds to get a warrant, no significant state interest will be impaired. At worst, the homeowner will attempt to make "hasty reparation" before a delayed inspection, which reparation will itself fulfill the objectives of the safety inspection. The Court further reasoned that a warrant requirement would impose only a minimal burden on the state because most homeowners would voluntarily comply with an initial request to conduct the inspection without a warrant; the homeowner would have little to gain by triggering the displeasure of the inspector, who would only return with authority to inspect the premises and with the power to cite the homeowner for code violations.

a. Role of the Judicial Officer

A judicial officer issuing a warrant for a home safety inspection under *Camara* necessarily performs a different function than the magistrate assessing a search warrant application in a criminal investigation. This is because, as discussed above, the standard of proof required for a home safety inspection is different from the traditional probable cause standard. A home inspection can be conducted on the basis of such generalized facts as passage of time, nature of the building, and as part of an area-wide inspection.

The Court in *Camara* stressed that judicial review of the reasons for a safety inspection should occur "without any reassessment of the basic agency decision to canvass an area." Thus, the magistrate is not charged with evaluating the legislative and administrative policy decisions as to frequency of inspection, resource expenditures, and the like. The magistrate need only decide whether *an established inspection policy exists* and whether the inspection for which a warrant is sought *fits within that program.*

b. Benefit of the Warrant Requirement

The Court in *Camara* assumed that the magistrate, by determining whether the proposed search fits within an established inspection program, would protect the privacy interests of the homeowner. For example, a warrant sought for personal spite, or for purposes of a "shakedown" by administrative inspectors, may well not fit within the frequency limitations of the established inspection policy. Thus, the warrant process in this setting is intended as a limitation upon arbitrary and abusive searches.

c. Post–*Camara* Limitation on the Use of Warrants Without Probable Cause

The *Camara* Court imposed a rather unique requirement for home safety inspections—that a warrant would be required, but that the warrant would be issued upon some objective standard other than probable cause. Subsequently, in *Griffin v. Wisconsin*, 483 U.S. 868, 107 S.Ct. 3164, 97 L.Ed.2d 709 (1987), the Court again addressed the question whether a warrant which is not based upon particularized probable cause can be mandated. Justice Scalia, writing for the Court, contended that such a warrant would violate the specific language in the Fourth Amendment that "no warrant shall issue, but upon probable cause." He distinguished *Camara* as a case where the Court "arguably came to permit an exception to that prescription for administrative search warrants, which may but do not necessarily have to be issued by courts." He emphasized that the *general rule for judicial search warrants is that they can only be issued upon particularized probable cause.*

B. Administrative Inspections of Businesses

As with housing safety inspections, safety and regulatory inspections of businesses fulfill a special need beyond ordinary criminal law enforcement. As with housing inspections, there are two questions which are pertinent to Fourth Amendment limitations on administrative inspections of businesses: 1. whether the search may be conducted on some standard less than the particularized probable cause required for a search for evidence by criminal law enforcement; and 2. whether the inspection, in the absence of consent, may be conducted without a warrant.

1. Same Basic Analysis

In *See v. City of Seattle*, 387 U.S. 541, 87 S.Ct. 1737, 18 L.Ed.2d 943 (1967), the Court concluded that the reasoning of *Camara* was equally applicable to administrative inspections of commercial structures. Therefore, *See* could not be convicted for refusing to permit a warrantless fire inspection of his locked commercial warehouse. The Court reasoned that "a businessman, like the occupant of a residence, has a constitutional right to go about his business free from unreasonable official entries upon his private commercial property."

More Searches May Be Permitted

The Court in *See* cautioned that it was not holding that businesses would be treated exactly the same as homes with respect to administrative searches. It merely concluded that the analysis—a balance of the state and individual interests at stake—would be the same. In particular, the Court stated that "we do not in any way imply that business premises may not reasonably be inspected in many more situations than private homes."

2. May Not Be a Search at All

If the inspector enters and investigates an area that is open to the general public, the inspection will not be a search at all and no Fourth Amendment limitations will apply. For example, in *Donovan v. Lone Steer, Inc.*, 464 U.S. 408, 104 S.Ct. 769, 78 L.Ed.2d 567 (1984), the Court held that the Fourth Amendment did not apply where a fire inspector walked through a hotel lobby and checked for fire exits. The Court reasoned that the proprietor had no expectation of privacy in an area open to the public.

3. Balance of Interests at Stake

The Court applied the *Camara* standards to businesses in *See*, but it is apparent that administrative searches of businesses often involve different issues and interests than those presented in home safety inspections. An administrative search of a business may implicate more complex regulatory concerns; the state has an interest not only in the safety of a business structure, but also in whether the business itself is being properly, safely and legitimately conducted. Also, it may well be that a businessperson may have a diminished expectation of privacy in the area to be searched, given the nature of the business conducted. This means that the state interest involved in administrative business searches may be stronger than in home safety inspections, and the individual interest may be weaker.

4. Heavily Regulated Businesses

In a series of cases, the Court has held that the *See* warrant requirement is not applicable if the business to be searched is part of a "heavily regulated industry." The rationale is that with such businesses, unannounced and frequent inspections are necessary to effectuate the state interest in the proper operation of the business. *See United States v. Biswell,* 406 U.S. 311, 92 S.Ct. 1593, 32 L.Ed.2d 87 (1972) (warrantless inspection of licensed gun dealer's storeroom: "If inspection is to be effective and serve as a credible deterrent, unannounced, even frequent, inspections are essential. In this context, the prerequisite of a warrant could easily frustrate inspection."). The Court also reasons that a businessperson who operates in a heavily regulated industry has a diminished expectation of privacy. *See Biswell* ("It is also plain that inspections for compliance with the Gun Control Act pose only limited threats to the dealer's justifiable expectations of privacy. When a dealer chooses to engage in this pervasively regulated business and to accept a federal license, he does so with the knowledge that his business records, firearms and ammunition will be subject to effective inspection.").

a. Examples of Heavily Regulated Businesses

Some of the industries held by the courts to be pervasively regulated, and thus not entitled to the protections of the warrant requirement, include: *sales of liquor (Colonnade Catering Corp. v. United States,* 397 U.S. 72, 90 S.Ct. 774, 25 L.Ed.2d 60 (1970)); *sales of firearms (Biswell, supra); mining (Donovan v. Dewey,* 452 U.S. 594, 101 S.Ct. 2534, 69 L.Ed.2d 262 (1981)); *trucking (United States v. Dominguez–Prieto,* 923 F.2d 464 (6th Cir. 1991)); *horseracing (Shoemaker v. Handel,* 795 F.2d 1136 (3d Cir. 1986)); *public utilities (Rushton v. Nebraska Public Power District,* 844 F.2d 562 (8th Cir. 1988)); the *production and sale of veterinary drugs (United States v. Argent Chemical Laboratories, Inc.,* 93 F.3d 572 (9th Cir. 1996)); and *railroads (Skinner v. Railway Labor Executives' Ass'n,* 489 U.S. 602, 109 S.Ct. 1402, 103 L.Ed.2d 639 (1989)).

b. OSHA Searches

In *Marshall v. Barlow's, Inc.,* 436 U.S. 307, 98 S.Ct. 1816, 56 L.Ed.2d 305 (1978), the Court considered the constitutionality of a provision of the Occupational Safety and Health Act (OSHA), which permitted inspectors, without a warrant, to enter any business premises subject to OSHA for the purpose of conducting a safety inspection. The Court held that the provision for warrantless searches violated the Fourth Amendment. It rejected the contention that the "heavily regulated industry" exception to the warrant requirement was applicable; it reasoned that OSHA applied *across the board to a wide variety of* industries, rather than to any discrete, pervasively regulated industry. *See also V–1 Oil Co. v. Wyoming Dept. of Environmental Quality,* 902 F.2d 1482 (10th Cir. 1990) (statute authorizing warrantless inspection of any commercial property suspected of causing pollution was unconstitutional, because the statute was of "general application," not targeted toward a specific heavily regulated industry).

Relying on *Camara,* the Court in *Barlow's* held that while a warrant was required to search for OSHA violations, particularized probable cause was not; a search could be conducted pursuant to neutral legislative criteria, as determined by the judicial officer. The Court concluded that a "warrant showing that a specific business has been chosen for an OSHA search on the basis of a general administrative plan for the enforcement of the Act derived from neutral sources such as, for example, dispersion of employees in various types of industries across a given area, and the desired frequency of searches in any of the lesser divisions of the area, would protect an employer's Fourth Amendment rights."

5. Expansion of Heavily Regulated Industries Exception

The Court has expanded the "heavily regulated" industry exception to the warrant requirement, in a way that is likely to permit warrantless inspections of a large number of businesses. In *New York v. Burger,* 482 U.S. 691, 107 S.Ct. 2636, 96 L.Ed.2d 601 (1987), the Court held that a vehicle-dismantling business was pervasively regulated, and thus that the legislative provision for frequent warrantless inspections did not violate the Fourth Amendment. The scope of the regulation at issue in *Burger* consisted of the following: 1. the operator of the business was required to obtain a license and pay a fee; 2. the operator was required to maintain an inventory list; 3. the operator was required to display his registration number prominently at his place of business, on business documentation, and on inventory that passed through the business.

a. Dissent

The application of the "heavily regulated" industry exception to the business in *Burger* led Justice Brennan to comment in dissent that "if New York City's administrative scheme renders the vehicle dismantling business closely regulated, few businesses will escape such a finding." Justice Brennan noted that no regulation governed the condition of the premises, the hours of operation, the personnel employed, or the equipment utilized. *See S & S Pawn Shop Inc. v. City of Del City,* 947 F.2d 432 (10th Cir. 1991) (finding pawn shops to be closely regulated under *Burger* criteria).

b. Relevance of Historical Regulation

Many of the industries held to be "heavily regulated" have been subject to a history of regulation, which would tend to diminish the expectation of privacy of any person who chose to enter such an industry. Examples include sales of liquor, sales of firearms, and mining. The Court in *Burger* held, however, that an "ancient history of government oversight" is *not required* for a finding that a particular industry is heavily regulated. Otherwise, such new industries as nuclear power could not be considered heavily regulated for a long period of time, even though the scope of regulations on such an industry may be pervasive and the state interest in surprise warrantless inspections may be critical.

6. **Regulatory Statute Must Be an Adequate Substitute for a Warrant**

The Court in *Burger* held that even in the context of a pervasively regulated business, there must be some substitute for a warrant. The Court stated that the inspection program itself must "provide a constitutionally adequate substitute for a warrant" in order to protect the privacy interests of the businessperson from the risk of arbitrary searches by Government officials who are unconstrained by a warrant requirement. In particular, the Court stated that the regulatory statute must perform "the two basic functions of a warrant." First, it must advise the citizen that the search is being conducted pursuant to the law and that it has a properly defined scope. Second, it must limit the discretion of the officers by carefully controlling the time, place and scope of the search.

Examples: The Court held that the inspection scheme in *Burger* provided a constitutionally adequate substitute for a warrant. The Court relied on the following factors: 1. the statute informed the operator that inspections would be made on a regular basis—so that when the inspection did occur, the operator would know that it was being conducted pursuant to a statute and not as a result of "discretionary acts by a government official"; 2. the scope of the inspection was reasonably limited to the records and the inventory; 3. the statute notified the operator as to who is authorized to conduct the inspection; 4. the statute targeted only vehicle-dismantling and related industries; and 5. inspecting officers were allowed to conduct an inspection only during regular business hours. *See also United States v. Castelo*, 415 F.3d 407 (5th Cir. 2005) (administrative scheme limiting weighing and inspection of trucks to commercial trucks and only when the trucks were operating on the state highways imposed sufficient limits on officer discretion).

Limitations on Frequency of Inspection

The statutory scheme upheld in *Burger* placed no limitation on the frequency of inspecting any particular vehicle-dismantling business. Under the statute, an inspector could theoretically conduct a search of a particular business several times a day for several days or weeks. The defendant in *Burger* argued that the statute therefore left open a significant possibility of harassment and unconstrained discretion by inspecting officers. But the Court rejected the defendant's argument. It recognized that limitations on the frequency of inspection were "a factor in the analysis of the adequacy of a particular statute." However, the existence or lack of limitations on frequency would not be "determinative of the result so long as the statute, as a whole, places adequate limits upon the discretion of the inspecting officers." The Court noted that with some industries, frequent inspections may be required to fully effectuate the state interest in assuring that businesses are properly conducted. Particularly was this true of the vehicle-dismantling industry, where inventory flows in and out very quickly.

7. Enforcing the Criminal Law

Since *Camara*, administrative inspections have been subject to more flexible standards than those applied to searches for evidence by law enforcement officers. The traditional standards of a warrant issued upon particularized probable cause have been considered ill-suited to searches which effectuate "special needs" beyond ordinary criminal law enforcement.

a. Argument in *Burger*

In *New York v. Burger, supra,* the defendant argued that the statute authorizing searches of vehicle dismantling businesses had no truly administrative purpose but was "designed to give the police an expedient means of enforcing penal sanctions for possession of stolen property." He noted that under the statute, inspecting officers could conduct an inspection for stolen vehicle parts even if an operator failed to produce his records; from this he concluded that the statute was not directed at appropriate recordkeeping, as was, for example, the statute applied to sales of firearms. The defendant therefore asserted that the traditional standards of a warrant and probable cause ought to apply.

b. Analysis in *Burger*

The Court rejected the defendant's contentions and held that a state can address a problem (in this case car theft) both by way of an administrative scheme and through penal sanction. According to the Court, "administrative statutes and penal laws may have the same ultimate purpose of remedying the social problem, but they have different subsidiary purposes and prescribe different methods of addressing the problem." Thus, under *Burger,* a search is administrative if it *uses administrative methodology* (e.g., the officers are inspecting business records and operating conditions, rather than specifically looking for evidence of criminal activity) and if it is used to *enforce regulatory standards* such as proper recordkeeping and maintenance of the business.

c. Application of Analysis in *Burger*

The Court found that the statute permitting inspection of records and inventory in *Burger* was administrative in nature, because it served the regulatory goals of "seeking to ensure that vehicle dismantlers are legitimate businesspersons and that stolen vehicles and vehicle parts passing through automobile junkyards can be identified." The Court reasoned that these regulatory objectives were met by allowing a search of the inventory as well as the records of the proprietor: the inventory would have to be compared with the records to determine whether the records were properly kept. The fact that the statute allowed a search of the inventory even if the proprietor failed to produce any records was also held properly within an administrative interest; otherwise an illegitimate vehicle dismantler could "thwart the purposes of the administrative scheme" simply by refusing to produce records. *See also United States v. Hernandez,* 901 F.2d 1217 (5th Cir. 1990) (search of goods carried in commercial truck to check whether bill of lading produced by driver was accurate; search uncovered drugs, held valid administrative search).

d.   Administrative Search Can Lead to Evidence of a Criminal Violation
A search that is properly administrative in its subsidiary objectives does not become a search for law enforcement purposes merely because it uncovers evidence of a criminal violation. As the Court in *Burger* stated:

> "The discovery of crimes in the course of an otherwise proper administrative inspection does not render that search illegal or the administrative scheme suspect."

e.   Use of Police Officers to Conduct an Administrative Search
In *Burger*, the administrative search of the defendant's vehicle-dismantling business was in fact conducted by New York City police officers. The defendant argued that the search was, therefore, a criminal law enforcement search, and as such could not be conducted in the absence of a warrant and probable cause. But the Court rejected this contention. The Court noted that police officers have "numerous duties in addition to those associated with traditional police work" and that many states and localities do not have sufficient administrative personnel to enforce a particular administrative scheme. The Court concluded that, "so long as a regulatory scheme is properly administrative, it is not rendered illegal by the fact that the inspecting officer has the power to arrest individuals for violations other than those created by the scheme itself."

C.   Civil–Based Searches of Individuals Pursuant to "Special Needs"
The Supreme Court has used its special needs balancing analysis in a series of cases to uphold civil-based searches of individuals in the absence of a warrant and probable cause.

1.   Searches Directed at Students
In *New Jersey v. T.L.O.*, 469 U.S. 325, 105 S.Ct. 733, 83 L.Ed.2d 720 (1985), the Court held that a warrantless search of a student's handbag was reasonable where the school administrator had reasonable suspicion, but not probable cause, to believe that the student was carrying cigarettes in the handbag. The Court found that the traditional requirements of a warrant and probable cause did not apply in light of the state's *special need to maintain discipline and an educational environment* in its schools.

a.   Balance of Interests Does Not Justify a Warrant Requirement
The Court in *T.L.O.* weighed the student's interest in privacy against the state interest in maintaining discipline and an educational

environment and concluded that a warrant was not a prerequisite for a search of a student by an administrator. The Court reasoned that the warrant process is ill-suited to the context in which school searches arise. For one thing, school searches are ordinarily conducted by administrators or teachers unfamiliar with the warrant process. The Court also noted that requiring a teacher or administrator to obtain a warrant would "unduly interfere with the swift and informal disciplinary procedures needed in the schools."

b. Balance of Interests Allows a Search on the Basis of Reasonable Suspicion

The Court in *T.L.O.* held that application of the probable cause requirement to the school search at issue would give undue weight to the student's interest at the expense of the state's interest. If the school official was required to wait until probable cause developed, then many essential searches could never be conducted (or they would be conducted too late to be useful in correcting a problem), and school discipline and the educational environment would suffer. Searches of suspicious circumstances that do not rise to the level of probable cause were thought by the Court to be necessary to nip potential disciplinary problems in the bud.

c. Distinction From *Terry*

Note that the search conducted in *T.L.O.* could not have been conducted under the *Terry* doctrine. It is true that *Terry* allows searches upon reasonable suspicion, but not if those searches are directed toward uncovering evidence. Rather, *Terry* permits only those searches necessary to protect the officers or others. The school administrator in *T.L.O.* was not concerned with his safety. Rather, he had reasonable suspicion that T.L.O.'s purse contained evidence of a violation of school rules against smoking. The reason that the search for evidence could be conducted on the basis of reasonable suspicion was not that *Terry* applied, but because the search was in furtherance of special needs beyond traditional criminal law enforcement.

d. More Intrusive Searches

The Court in *T.L.O.* stressed that in assessing the reasonableness of a search, a court must take into account the intrusiveness of the search employed. It follows that a search which is significantly more intrusive than the handbag search in *T.L.O.* may require a greater justification than the reasonable suspicion standard approved by the Court in *T.L.O.* For example, a strip search of a student, because of its intrusiveness, may well require probable cause. *See Konop v. Northwestern School District*, 26 F. Supp. 2d 1189 (D.S.D. 1998) (strip search of eighth grade students by principal and teacher for allegedly stealing $200 without reasonable basis to believe particular student had committed crime was not objectively reasonable).

e. Suspicionless Searches

In *T.L.O.*, the Court noted that it did not have to decide whether individualized suspicion is an essential element of the reasonableness standard as applied to searches of students. The Court implied, however, that a school search without individualized suspicion might be reasonable if the "privacy interests implicated by a search are minimal and where other safeguards are available to assure that the individual's reasonable expectation of privacy is not subject to the discretion of the officer in the field." Subsequently, in *Vernonia School District v. Acton* and *Board of Education of Independent School District No. 92 of Pottawatomie County v. Earls*, *infra* the Court upheld suspicionless drug-testing of high school students who participate in extracurricular activities. *Acton* and *Earls* are discussed later in this section.

f. Searches by Law Enforcement Officials

In *T.L.O.*, the search was conducted by a school administrator. The Court cautioned that the case did not present "the question of the appropriate standard for assessing the legality of searches conducted by school officials in conjunction with or at the behest of law enforcement agencies." If the search of the student is conducted by law enforcement officials, a strong argument can be made that the traditional Fourth Amendment requirements should apply, since such a search does not effectuate "special needs" beyond ordinary criminal law enforcement. It is true that in *New York v. Burger*, the Court held that a search of a vehicle-dismantling business did not lose its administrative character simply because it was conducted by law enforcement officials. But the Court's rationale on this point was that states and localities might not have the resources to employ specialized administrative officials to conduct the searches. This is hardly the case in the school context, where teachers and school administrators are employed for the very purpose of maintaining school discipline and an educational environment. Accordingly, lower courts have generally held that if the police conduct the search of a student, then the traditional requirements of a warrant and probable cause must be met. *See M. v. Board of Education,* 429 F.Supp. 288 (S.D.Ill. 1977) (invalidating a search of a student by a police officer). *Compare Cason v. Cook,* 810 F.2d 188 (8th Cir. 1987) (*T.L.O.* standard applies where the search of the student's purse and locker was conducted by the vice principal, while police officer who was liaison officer with the school was standing by, for at most "this case represents a police officer working in conjunction with school officials.").

g. **Use of Evidence Obtained**

If the search is conducted by a school administrator and is thus a special needs search, any evidence uncovered can later be used for criminal law enforcement and adjudication. For example, in *T.L.O.*, the school official suspected a violation of school rules against smoking; a search of T.L.O.'s handbag uncovered marijuana, which was subsequently used against T.L.O. in a juvenile proceeding. Yet this was permissible, because, as the Court in *Burger* put it, the "discovery of evidence of crimes in the course of an otherwise proper administrative inspection does not render that search illegal or the administrative scheme suspect."

h. **Searches of Students in Private Schools**

If a search is conducted by a private school official, it is not subject to even the flexible *T.L.O.* requirements. This is because such a search does not constitute state action, and the Fourth Amendment only regulates the conduct of public officials. *See Duarte v. Commonwealth,* 12 Va.App. 1023, 407 S.E.2d 41 (1991) (search by dean of students at private college, even if without articulable suspicion, is not illegal because the "Fourth Amendment is not implicated").

2. **Employer Inspections of Government Offices**

The Court applied the *T.L.O.* balancing analysis to a search of the office of a government employee in *O'Connor v. Ortega,* 480 U.S. 709, 107 S.Ct. 1492, 94 L.Ed.2d 714 (1987). *O'Connor* involved a work-related search for files by the government in its capacity as employer. The employer had reasonable suspicion, but not probable cause, to believe that the employee had engaged in various acts of mismanagement. No warrant was obtained. As in *T.L.O.*, the Court found that the search was conducted in furtherance of "special needs" beyond ordinary criminal law enforcement, and therefore that the relevant interests could be balanced to determine the reasonableness of the search. The special need at stake in this case was to ensure "that the work of the agency is conducted in a proper and efficient manner."

a. Balance of Interests Does Not Justify a Warrant Requirement

The Court in *O'Connor* held that a warrant is not required for an inspection of a government employee's office for employment-related purposes. Relying on *T.L.O.*, the Court reasoned that a warrant requirement was ill-suited to the informal searches conducted by Government employers. Work-related searches run the gamut from the search of a person's office for a file needed by another worker, to a search conducted to safeguard government property. None of these searches could be efficiently conducted if the "unwieldy" warrant process were imposed.

b. Balance of Interests Allows a Search on the Basis of Reasonable Suspicion

The Court in *O'Connor* examined two types of searches into the effects of a government employee: 1. a non-investigatory work-related intrusion; and 2. (as occurred in *O'Connor*) an investigatory search for evidence of work-related malfeasance. The Court held that both types of searches can be conducted if there is "reasonable grounds to suspect" that the search is necessary for a civil-based purpose such as to retrieve a file (in the former situation), or to uncover evidence that the employee is guilty of work-related misconduct (in the latter situation).

c. Non–Investigative Work–Related Searches

As to searches conducted for non-investigative reasons, the Court stated that the work of Government agencies would suffer "if employers were required to have probable cause before they entered an employee's desk for the purpose of finding a file or piece of office correspondence." The Court reasoned that the concept of probable cause, rooted as it is in the criminal investigatory context, had little meaning when applied to a non-investigatory work-related search.

d. Searches to Investigate Suspicion of Work–Related Misconduct

On the more difficult question of whether investigatory searches to uncover work-related misconduct should require probable cause, the *O'Connor* Court, as in *T.L.O.*, reasoned that government interests would be unduly impaired if officials had to wait for probable cause to develop before such a search could be conducted. As with *T.L.O.*, the Court expressed concern that a probable cause requirement would mean that a search would have to be delayed until it was too late to correct the administrative problem. Under these circumstances, a probable cause requirement would give insufficient consideration to the state interest and undue weight to the individual interest, especially since, according to the Court in *O'Connor*, an employee may often have a diminished expectation of privacy in an office, desk or file cabinet, due to office procedures and legitimate regulation.

e.   Search for Evidence of Criminal Activity Which Is Not Work–Related

The Court in *O'Connor* stressed that the "special needs" balancing analysis was being employed for purposes of regulating work-related conduct. The Court pointedly distinguished cases in which the Government conducted the search of an employee to investigate criminal misconduct unrelated to the work environment. Such law enforcement-based searches are outside the "special needs" analysis and must therefore satisfy the traditional requirements of warrant and probable cause, or some other exception to these requirements (such as exigent circumstances). *See United States v. Taketa*, 923 F.2d 665 (9th Cir. 1991) (video surveillance of employee "was not an investigation of work-related employee misconduct that could benefit from the reasonableness standard of *O'Connor*. It was, rather, a search for evidence of criminal misconduct.").

3.   **Searches Directed at Parolees and Probationers**

The *T.L.O.* "special needs" balancing test was again used by the Court in *Griffin v. Wisconsin*, 483 U.S. 868, 107 S.Ct. 3164, 97 L.Ed.2d 709 (1987), to uphold a warrantless search of a probationer's home. The search was conducted by a probation officer, who had reasonable suspicion, but not probable cause, to believe that Griffin had engaged in an act that violated the terms of his probation. The Court held that a state's operation of its probation system, like its operation of a school or Government office, "presents special needs beyond normal law enforcement that may justify departures from the usual warrant and probable cause requirements." The special needs cited were the state's interest in rehabilitation, and the interest in assuring that "the community is not harmed by the probationer's being at large."

a. Balance of Interests Does Not Justify a Warrant Requirement
After finding the special needs necessary to justify resort to a
reasonableness balancing test, the Court in *Griffin* balanced the
relevant interests at stake and concluded that a warrant requirement
would not sufficiently accommodate the state interest in conducting
a search of a probationer's home. The Court found the warrant
requirement would "interfere to an appreciable degree with the
probation system," because it would substitute the magistrate for
the probation officer as the judge of how close the supervision of
any particular probationer should be. The Court also stated that the
delays inherent in the warrant process would make it more difficult
for probation officers to quickly intervene where the probationer is
encountering difficulty in adjusting to society, and would "reduce
the deterrent effect that the possibility of expeditious searches
would otherwise create." Against these state interests, the Court
balanced the possible protection that a warrant requirement would
provide to a probationer. The Court found that the protection was
minimized by the fact that a probation officer, while not a magistrate, is charged by law to take account of the welfare of the
probationer; therefore, the risk of arbitrariness that might be posed
by a police officer in the competitive enterprise of ferreting out
crime is lessened when the search is conducted by a probation
officer. Also, the individual privacy interest at stake was minimized
because the citizen was a probationer, whose liberty was conditional.

b. Balance of Interests Allows Search Upon Reasonable Suspicion
The Court in *Griffin* held that the special needs of a state's probation
system justified the replacement of the traditional probable cause
requirement with the less demanding standard of reasonable suspicion. As in previous cases, the Court concluded that the probable
cause standard would require the state to wait too long before it
could intervene to rectify a civil-based problem. As the Court put it
in *Griffin*, "the probation agency must be able to act based upon a
lesser degree of certainty than the Fourth Amendment would
otherwise require in order to intervene before a probationer does
damage to himself or to society."

c. Search by Police Officers
The Court in *Griffin* justified its use of the "special needs" analysis
(and its rejection of the warrant and probable cause requirements) in

large part on the ground that the search was conducted by a probation officer, who is not "the police officer who normally conducts searches against the citizen." The Court also noted that "we deal with a situation in which there is an ongoing supervisory relationship—and one that is not, or at least not entirely, adversarial—between the object of the search and the decisionmaker." In light of this reasoning, it is unlikely that an investigatory search of a probationer, by a police officer and without any participation by probation officers, could be justified as a "special needs" search. In fact, the Supreme Court upheld just such an investigatory search under ordinary Fourth Amendment analysis in *United States v. Knights, supra,* by expanding the reasonable suspicion analysis beyond the "stop and frisk" context. In *Knights,* the state never argued that the police search fell under the "special needs" analysis. Similarly, in *Samson v. California, supra,* the Court upheld suspicion-less searches of parolees, relying on *Knights.*

d. Participation by Police Officers

On the other hand, the search in *Griffin* itself was conducted by probation officers who were *accompanied* by three policemen present at the probation officers' request; the Court found nothing improper in this arrangement. *See State v. Burke,* 235 Mont. 165, 766 P.2d 254 (1988) ("Police cooperation with probation officers is to be encouraged as an important aid to effective administration of the probation system."). Likewise, courts have held that if a search is conducted by police officers *at the request* of probation officers, the search does not lose its character as a "special needs" search. *See United States v. Richardson,* 849 F.2d 439 (9th Cir. 1988) (The Court in *Griffin* "approved the concept that the decision to authorize the search was more important than who was present when the search was made."). Under some circumstances, however, a court may find that the probation officer is acting as a mere *"stalking horse"* for law enforcement officers. If that is the case, the search will lose its character as a "special needs" search. *Shea v. Smith,* 966 F.2d 127 (3d Cir. 1992) (evidence excluded where parole officers conducted a search solely to retrieve evidence for the police).

e. Application to Parolees

Griffin dealt with a search by a probation officer, but its principles apply equally to a search of a parolee conducted by or at the behest of a parole officer to investigate a possible parole violation. Like a search of a probationer, a search of a parolee is conducted at least in part to effectuate state interests in rehabilitation. Like the probationer, the parolee has a diminished expectation of privacy. *See United States v. Hill*, 967 F.2d 902 (3d Cir. 1992) ("[T]here is no constitutional difference between probation and parole for purposes of the Fourth Amendment."). *But see Samson, supra* (suspicionless searches of parolees authorized by statute upheld under Fourth Amendment analysis).

4. **Security Searches at Airports, Courthouses, Military Installations, Prisons, etc.**

Suspicionless searches at airports were first implemented after an escalation of airplane hijacking in the 1960's. At that time, the FAA ordered air carriers to implement a hijacker detection system. The detection system was a preflight screening program that employs magnetometers and other electronic screening devices. Similar concerns with security resulted in checkpoint security searches in places such as courthouses, jails, military installations, and even some schools. Some of these searches use electronic screening devices. Others employ visual inspection. These security searches are conducted without suspicion and are justified as administrative searches which effectuate "special needs" beyond ordinary criminal law enforcement. The special need asserted is the need to provide safety and security for the public in various locales where a safety risk has been demonstrated. *See United States v. Davis*, 482 F.2d 893 (9th Cir. 1973) ("Screening searches of airline passengers are conducted as part of a general regulatory scheme in furtherance of an administrative purpose, namely, to prevent the carrying of weapons or explosives aboard aircraft, and thereby to prevent hijackings. The essential purpose of the scheme is not to detect weapons or explosives or to apprehend those who carry them, but to deter persons carrying such material from seeking to board at all.").

After the terrorist attacks on the World Trade Center in New York and the Pentagon on September 11, 2001, suspicionless searches at airports and other public places are more intrusive than ever before. The Supreme Court has not yet reviewed the reasonableness of these searches, but they have been upheld uniformly by lower courts.

a. No Requirement of Particularized Suspicion
Balancing the state interest in promoting security against the individual interest in privacy and the degree of intrusion imposed

by the security search, the courts have held that searches with electronic screening devices, as well as other cursory inspections, can be conducted even in the absence of individualized suspicion, so long as four conditions are met: 1. the search is conducted in response to a *documented security problem* or to address a *serious risk of harm* to the public; 2. all *persons who pass the security checkpoint must be searched,* to prevent the risk that, in the absence of particularized suspicion, officers would subject certain people to arbitrary and harassing searches; 3. the security screening search is *no more intrusive than necessary* to satisfy the security interests that justify the search; and 4. people must be given the *option to avoid a search* by leaving the premises.

Examples: In the 1970's, the lower courts upheld suspicionless magnetometer searches at airports, and these cases have been cited favorably by the Supreme Court. Suspicionless screening was found permissible because:

1.   The possibility of airplane hijacking or terrorism presents a significant risk to human lives and to property. *See United States v. Edwards,* 498 F.2d 496 (2d Cir. 1974) ("When the risk is the jeopardy to hundreds of human lives and millions of dollars of property inherent in the pirating or blowing up of a large airplane, that danger alone meets the test of reasonableness."). Because of the grave consequences of hijacking or terrorism, the courts found that it did not matter that only an infinitesimal fraction of prospective passengers are likely to be hijackers or terrorists. As the Supreme Court has stated, "when the government's interest lies in deterring highly hazardous conduct, a low incidence of such conduct, far from impugning the validity of the scheme for implementing this interest, is more logically viewed as a hallmark of success." *National Treasury Employees Union v. Von Raab,* 489 U.S. 656, 109 S.Ct. 1384, 103 L.Ed.2d 685 (1989).

2.   All prospective passengers are subject to the search procedures. This eliminates the possibility of arbitrary

searches, and also makes the searches less intrusive than they would otherwise be. Part of the intrusiveness of a search for law enforcement purposes is that the person who is searched suffers a stigma and perhaps public ridicule. But there is no stigma suffered when all persons must pass through a magnetometer.

3. The electronic screening is no more intrusive than necessary to address the security problem. The search does not involve a detailed visual inspection, or a substantial inconvenience. Also, there is no real alternative to suspicionless searches of all prospective travelers. Requiring particularized suspicion would undoubtedly permit some hijackers or terrorists to get through. As the court in *Davis* noted, "there is no foolproof method of confining the search to the few who are potential hijackers." Finally, if something suspicious is found in the electronic screening, a subsequent search is conducted in a minimally intrusive fashion: in the case of a bag, the passenger is asked to open his bag for a quick visual inspection; in the case of a person, the passenger merely displays the contents of his pockets, or submits to a more specific magnetometer or, when that fails, to a frisk.

4. Passengers are notified that the search will be conducted and are given the option to avoid the search by choosing not to travel. *See United States v. Davis, supra* ("Since a compelled search of persons who elect not to board would not contribute to barring weapons and explosives from the plane, it could serve only the purpose of apprehending violators of * * * some criminal statute. Such searches would be criminal investigations subject to the warrant and probable cause requirements of the Fourth Amendment.").

b. More Intrusive Searches Upheld After 9/11
In *United States v. Marquez*, 410 F.3d 612 (9th Cir. 2005), Marquez was randomly selected for a more thorough airport search. The "additional procedure involved a full-body wanding with a hand held magnetometer that used technology similar to, but more sensitive

than, the walkthrough magnetometer." Once Marquez was selected, a Transportation Security Administration (TSA) agent directed Marquez to a secondary inspection area and proceeded to waive the hand held magnetometer over Marquez' body. The magnetometer alerted at Marquez' hip. The TSA agent and his supervisor moved Marquez into a private screening room and eventually retrieved four bricks of cocaine from Marquez' person. Marquez moved to suppress the evidence arguing that the search procedures were unreasonable because they were not based on an individualized suspicion of wrongdoing. Citing *Davis, supra*, the court found the search reasonable since the procedure used was aimed at the detection and deterrence of airborne terrorism. The court stressed the randomness of the search and its limited duration and scope.

See also United States v. Hartwell, 436 F.3d 174 (3rd Cir. 2006). In *Hartwell*, an individual set off a metal detector at an airport and proceeded to empty his pockets. He passed through again and was removed from the line by a TSA agent. The agent then conducted a wand inspection. The court upheld the search, noting that it was minimally intrusive and "well-tailored to protect personal privacy, escalating in invasiveness only after a lower level of screening disclosed a reason to conduct a more probing search." The court also noted that the searches were void of social stigma since every airport passenger must pass through security checkpoints and passengers are on notice that they will be searched prior to boarding the plane.

In *MacWade v. Kelly*, 460 F.3d 260 (2d Cir. 2006), the court upheld a search program of the New York City subway system. The program involved daily inspection checkpoints at selected subway stations. Passengers were randomly selected for a search of their bags and other effects before they entered the station. If they refused the search, they were not permitted to enter the station. The targeted stations changed from day to day. MacWade and others sued, arguing that the search program violated their Fourth Amendment rights. The court found that the government interest in searching was "immediate and substantial" in light of terrorist threats on the subway system and bombings of commuter trains elsewhere. The Court also noted that the searches were minimally intrusive.

5. Drug–Testing of Government Employees and Officials

Because of the drug crisis, a growing number of employers are requiring employees to submit to urinalysis testing. Where the testing is conducted by private employers, the Fourth Amendment does not apply. However, when government employees are tested, or where the government requires private employees to be tested, Fourth Amendment concerns are implicated. *See Skinner v. Railway Labor Executives' Ass'n*, 489 U.S. 602, 109 S.Ct. 1402, 103 L.Ed.2d 639 (1989) (Fourth Amendment applies to drug-testing by private railroad companies where there are "clear indices of the Government's encouragement, endorsement, and participation" in the testing process).

a. Drug–Testing Is a Search

The Court in *Skinner* held that urine-testing was a search because it invaded an employee's legitimate expectation of privacy. The Court noted that a chemical analysis of urine could disclose private information such as whether the employee was pregnant, diabetic, or was taking prescription drugs. The Court also stressed that the testing *procedures* intruded upon privacy interests, because they required either visual or aural monitoring of the obviously private act of urination.

b. Special Needs Analysis Applies

In *Skinner* and the companion case of *National Treasury Employees Union v. Von Raab*, 489 U.S. 656, 109 S.Ct. 1384, 103 L.Ed.2d 685 (1989), the Court held that drug-testing by government employers effectuates special needs beyond ordinary criminal law enforcement, and therefore that such testing schemes are not necessarily regulated by the traditional requirements of a warrant and probable cause. Rather, the relevant interests could be balanced to determine what requirements complied with general Fourth Amendment standards of reasonableness. *Skinner* involved urinalysis of all railroad employees involved in a railroad accident. *Von Raab* concerned drug-testing of all Customs Service employees upon their promotion to or application for various sensitive positions. In each case, the Court found that the employers had a legitimate regulatory interest in assuring that the tested employees remained drug-free. The Court noted that drug use could impair the employee's job performance and put the public at risk. Also, in *Skinner*, the railroads were found to have an interest in testing after an accident to determine whether or not drug use may have been a contributing factor in the accident.

c. Dissent

Justice Marshall, joined by Justice Brennan, dissented from the Court's use of "special needs" analysis in *Skinner* and *Von Raab*. He argued that the warrant and probable cause requirements were necessary to provide a benchmark against which to assess the validity of searches and seizures; a balancing test based on reasonableness was, to him, "virtually devoid of meaning, subject to whatever content shifting judicial majorities, concerned about the problems of the day, choose to give to that supple term."

d. Balance of Interests Does Not Justify a Warrant Requirement

A finding of "special needs" beyond ordinary criminal law enforcement allows a court to depart from the usual Fourth Amendment standards and to determine whether the balance of relevant interests actually justifies the application of a warrant requirement. With drug-testing of government employees, the courts have uniformly held that a warrant requirement would skew the balancing process in favor of the employee at the expense of the government. For one thing, the warrant would be sought in an employment context and, as in *O'Connor*, employers who conduct searches for work-related purposes are not law enforcement officers familiar with the warrant process. Also, the formalities of the warrant process are in tension with the need for flexibility in employer-employee relationships. Finally, and most importantly, most drug-testing procedures are implicated by triggering events or are conducted at random. For example, in *Von Raab*, drug-testing was mandated only when the employee sought promotion or transfer to certain jobs; in *Skinner*, drug-testing was mandated after an accident occurred. Many drug-testing plans are random and are implemented at regular intervals. *See Dimeo v. Griffin*, 943 F.2d 679 (7th Cir. 1991) (random drug-testing of jockeys and starters at frequent intervals). Where the search is based on a random plan or an obvious triggering event, there is no contestable issue for a magistrate to review.

e. Balance of Interests May Allow Suspicionless Drug-Testing in Some Cases

Before *Von Raab* and *Skinner*, the lower courts had regularly held that drug-testing of government employees could be conducted on reasonable suspicion rather than probable cause. The courts found that the important state interests at stake could not be sufficiently accommodated if the government had to wait for probable cause to develop—by that time, much of the damage caused by drug use could already have occurred. *See Fraternal Order of Police v. City of Newark*, 216 N.J.Super. 461, 524 A.2d 430 (1987) (upholding drug-testing of police on reasonable suspicion) (overruled by *New Jersey Transit PBA v. New Jersey Transit Corp.*, 151 N.J. 531, 701 A.2d 1243 (1997) where court applied *Skinner* balancing test). The question presented by *Von Raab* and *Skinner* was whether drug-testing plans could ever be reasonable *in the absence of individualized suspicion*. In both cases, the Court answered in the affirmative. The Court stated: "In limited circumstances, where the privacy interests implicated by the search are minimal, and where an important Government interest furthered by the intrusion would be placed in jeopardy by a requirement of individualized suspicion, a search may be reasonable despite the absence of such suspicion."

f. **Diminished Expectation of Privacy**

The Court in both cases found the privacy interest minimal. While the monitoring of the act of urination was intrusive, the Court noted in both cases that steps were taken to minimize the intrusion as much as possible: the testing was conducted in a medical environment, and aural rather than visual monitoring was employed. Also, the privacy interests of the employees were found diminished in both cases. In *Skinner*, the employees were found to have voluntarily entered into a pervasively regulated industry. In *Von Raab*, the privacy interest of the employees was minimized by the fact that drug-testing only occurred when the employee sought transfer or promotion to a certain position. Thus, as in the airport magnetometer cases, the citizen could control the search to some extent by refusing to submit to it and engaging in some alternative form of conduct (e.g., not asking for promotion). *See also Dimeo v. Griffin*, 943 F.2d 679 (7th Cir. 1991) (rule requiring jockeys and other participants in horse races to submit to random, suspicionless drug-testing was reasonable under the Fourth Amendment; the privacy interest implicated by urine-testing is minimal when applied to persons who are subject to frequent medical examinations, and horse-race participants voluntarily enter a profession where frequent medical exams are required).

g. **Government Interest Placed in Jeopardy by Requirement of Individualized Suspicion**

Before *Skinner* and *Von Raab*, the Court used "special needs" analysis to allow searches based on reasonable suspicion on the ground that important state interests would suffer if the government had to wait for probable cause to develop. In *Skinner* and *Von Raab,* the Court used the same analysis, but determined that the interests at stake were such that the government should not even have to wait for reasonable suspicion to develop. Therefore, suspicionless searches were found reasonable. One reason given by the Court in both cases is that it would be *too difficult to obtain reasonable suspicion* in the cases presented. In *Skinner,* the Court noted that the scene after a train accident is chaotic and that it would obviously be difficult to determine in those circumstances whether there was reasonable suspicion to believe that any of the employees to be tested were drug-impaired. In *Von Raab,* the Court noted that the employees subject to testing were generally field employees, whose *activity could not be closely monitored.*

Furthermore, in both cases, the Court found the interest at stake so crucial that, even if suspicious circumstances could be detected, the state interest would be impaired during the time it had to wait for the facts to develop. For example, *Von Raab* dealt with employees who sought transfer or promotion to jobs on the front-line level of narcotics interdiction. The Court reasoned that, by the time reasonable suspicion developed as to such an employee, the employee may already have been compromised, or may have, while impaired, allowed drug dealers to get away.

h. Deterrence Factor Is Relevant
    In deciding whether suspicionless testing was reasonable, the Court in *Skinner* and *Von Raab* relied on the fact that a suspicionless testing scheme may be a more effective *deterrent* to drug use than a scheme triggered by individualized suspicion. As the Court put it in *Skinner*, the suspicionless testing was reasonable in part because it was "an effective means of deterring employees engaged in safety-sensitive tasks from using controlled substances in the first place."

i. Documented Problem of Drug Abuse Not Absolutely Required for Suspicionless Testing
    In *Skinner,* the Government justified the need for a suspicionless testing plan in part on the ground that many previous train accidents had been caused by drug-impaired employees. But there was no such record of drug abuse in *Von Raab* as to customs employees. The Court in *Von Raab* found the lack of a documented

drug problem to be not dispositive of whether random, suspicion-less drug-testing could be reasonable. The Court held that it was reasonable to impose a suspicionless testing plan, even in the absence of a documented drug problem, if undetected drug use would impair a *critical government interest.* In other words, the question is not only whether there is a drug problem, but rather the nature and gravity of the harm that would ensue if a problem eventually arises and goes undetected. The Court relied on the airport magnetometer cases, discussed *supra,* and noted that such searches are reasonable even though the vast majority of persons subject to the searches pose no danger to airline safety. The Court stated that "where the Government's interest lies in deterring highly hazardous conduct, a low incidence of such conduct, far from impugning the validity of the scheme for implementing this interest, is more logically viewed as a hallmark of success." *See also Rushton v. Nebraska Public Power District,* 844 F.2d 562 (8th Cir. 1988) (suspicionless testing of nuclear power employees even in the absence of a documented drug problem); *Dimeo v. Griffin,* 943 F.2d 679 (7th Cir. 1991) (state interests in drug-testing of jockeys and starters include assuring the safety of participants, and preserving the integrity of parimutuel betting in order to ensure state revenues; the fact that there have been no proven cases of serious horse-racing accidents caused by drug use is not dispositive after *Von Raab).*

j. Dissent

Justice Scalia dissented in *Von Raab,* though he joined the majority in *Skinner.* The difference, for him, was that in *Von Raab* there was not "even a single instance in which any of the speculated horribles actually occurred: an instance, that is, in which the cause of bribe taking, or of poor aim, or of unsympathetic law enforcement, or of compromise of classified information, was drug use." He distin-guished cases allowing suspicionless searches of airplane passen-gers and nuclear power plant employees as cases where a violation could cause "such catastrophic social harm that no risk whatever is tolerable." He declared that if the majority considered the threat from drug-impaired Customs officials to be equivalent to that presented by drug-impaired nuclear power employees, "then the Fourth Amendment has become frail protection indeed."

k. Not All Suspicionless Drug–Testing Is Reasonable

The Court in *Von Raab* clearly expanded the circumstances in which random, suspicionless drug-testing could be permissible. Even in the absence of a documented drug problem, suspicionless testing can be reasonable if drug use could cause *some significant social harm* and if having to *wait for individualized suspicion would impair that government interest.* However, *Von Raab* does not support the proposition that all random, suspicionless drug-testing of government employees will be reasonable. Indeed, the Court in *Von Raab* found itself unable to assess the reasonableness of suspicionless testing as applied to all employees at the Customs Service who had access to "classified" documents. The Court was concerned that some of the employees subject to testing would not in fact have access to truly sensitive information (given the number of government documents routinely labeled "classified"), and therefore that drug use by these employees would not create so great a risk of harm if undetected as to justify suspicionless testing. Courts after *Von Raab* have held that suspicionless testing, in the absence of a documented drug problem in the work force, is not reasonable if drug use by the employees would do no more than affect the generalized efficiency of government services.

In *Chandler v. Miller,* 520 U.S. 305, 117 S.Ct. 1295, 137 L.Ed.2d 513 (1997), the Court invalidated suspicionless drug-testing of candidates for public office. The Court relied on two major considerations:

1. *No documented drug problem was shown.* In the absence of a drug problem, the State must show that a suspicionless plan of testing is necessary to protect against a *public hazard of critical proportions.* The plan in *Von Raab* met this standard because there was a risk that customs agents with guns could create serious harm if they were under the influence of narcotics. No such critical risk was presented by candidates for public office who might use narcotics.

2. *Candidates can be monitored for evidence of drug use.* Unlike the customs agents in *Von Raab,* who worked in the field and whose activities could not be monitored, candidates for public office are subject to intense and pervasive scrutiny. Therefore, a plan based on reasonable suspicion would be workable.

Essentially, the Court in *Chandler* limited *Von Raab.* Suspicionless testing in the absence of an existing drug problem will only be permissible where it protects against a critical hazard to the public, and then only if a plan based on reasonable suspicion is unworkable.

l.   Suspicionless Drug–Testing Plan Must Be Neutral to Be Reasonable

Presuming that suspicionless drug-testing can be reasonable, the Fourth Amendment requires that it must be conducted pursuant to some neutral, non-discretionary standard. A neutral standard substitutes for individualized suspicion; without either reasonable suspicion or a neutral standard, the government official's decision to test a particular employee would be completely unrestrained and arbitrary. So for example, the drug-testing plan in *Skinner* subjected every employee involved in an accident to drug-testing. *See also National Treasury Employees Union v. Yeutter*, 918 F.2d 968 (D.C. Cir. 1990) (upholding drug-testing of government drivers when conducted on a random basis); *Dimeo v. Griffin, supra* (rule requiring jockeys and other participants in horse races to submit to random, suspicionless drug-testing was reasonable under the Fourth Amendment).

6.   Drug-testing of Students

In *Vernonia School District v. Acton*, 515 U.S. 646, 115 S.Ct. 2386, 132 L.Ed.2d 564 (1995), the Court upheld suspicionless drug-testing of high school athletes.

a.   Rationale

The Court relied on the following factors to justify suspicionless drug-testing: 1. High school students have a diminished expectation of privacy while attending school; 2. School athletes have an especially diminished expectation of privacy, since they usually dress and shower in front of others, and since they have voluntarily chosen to "go out for the team"; 3. The state has a unique interest in preventing drugs in the schools, because students "have been committed to the temporary custody of the State as schoolmaster"; 4. There was documentation of a drug problem among student-athletes in the district; and 5. Requiring reasonable suspicion might actually be worse than suspicionless testing, because testing on the basis of individualized suspicion could impose a "badge of shame" on those tested, and could allow teachers to impose drug-testing "arbitrarily upon troublesome but not drug-likely students."

b. Preference for Suspicionless Searches?

The analysis in *Acton* is notable for its implication that suspicionless testing might actually be *preferable* to testing on the basis of reasonable suspicion, since suspicionless searches do not impose a "badge of shame" on those intruded upon. This implication caused Justice O'Connor to dissent, arguing that individualized suspicion should be the benchmark of Fourth Amendment analysis, and that suspicionless searches should be permitted in "unusual" cases where an individualized suspicion standard would be impracticable.

Acton Extended to Participants in All Extracurricular Activities

The Supreme Court expanded the rationale of *Acton* to a policy requiring the drug testing of all students who participate in competitive extracurricular activities in *Board of Education of Independent School District No. 92 of Pottawatomie County v. Earls*, 536 U.S. 822, 122 S.Ct. 2559, 153 L.Ed.2d 735 (2002). The School District in *Earls* adopted such a policy, which applied to activities such as the Academic Team, Future Farmers of America, Future Homemakers of America, band, choir, pom pom, cheerleading and athletics. Unlike in *Acton*, there was no documented problem of drug abuse among the targeted groups, nor was drug abuse identified as a major problem in the school district. Instead, the school adopted the policy in support of its general interest in detecting and preventing drug use among students. The method of testing and limitations on use of the test results were almost the same as in *Acton*. The Supreme Court upheld the constitutionality of the policy and cited *Von Raab, supra*, noting that in that case it had not required the demonstration of a pervasive drug problem before permitting suspicionless drug testing. It also rejected the argument that the testing of non-athletes did not implicate the safety concerns discussed in *Acton*, noting that the safety concerns furthered by drug testing were substantial for all students, including non-athletes. The Court's rationale was the same as in *Acton*, particularly its focus on the limited privacy interests of public school students and the government's special responsibility for maintaining their health and safety. *But see Doe v. Little Rock School District*, 380 F.3d 349 (8th Cir. 2004) (general concerns about weapons and drugs did not justify random suspicionless searches of students' belongings, especially since evidence found was routinely turned over to the police).

7. Drug Testing of Pregnant Mothers

In *Ferguson v. City of Charleston*, 532 U.S. 67, 121 S.Ct. 1281, 149 L.Ed.2d 205 (2001), the Court struck down a state hospital policy requiring drug testing of pregnant mothers suspected of cocaine use.

a. Rationale

In *Ferguson*, the Court held that the drug tests were not "special needs" searches because "the central and indispensable feature of the policy" was fulfillment of the State's law enforcement goals. The Medical University of South Carolina (MUSC) instituted a policy that required the drug testing of urine samples from maternity patients suspected of using cocaine. If the patient tested positive, she was required to undergo subsequent tests and was ultimately arrested and prosecuted if subsequent tests were positive. The policy was developed and administered with the assistance of police and prosecutors, as evidenced by the inclusion of information about chain of custody, the range of criminal charges and the logistics of police notification and arrests. Since the evidence was collected for the specific purpose of incriminating the patients, the Court held that the Fourth Amendment's prohibition against nonconsensual, warrantless, and suspicionless searches applies in the absence of consent. The Court did not reach the issue of the sufficiency of the evidence with regard to consent and assumed, for purposes of the decision, that the searches were conducted without the patient's consent.

b. Distinguishing Previous Drug–Testing Cases

The Court distinguished this case from its previous cases upholding drug tests as fulfilling legitimate "special needs" (*Skinner, Von Raab*, and *Acton*). Here, the invasion of privacy was much more substantial because the test results were disseminated to third parties, namely the police and prosecutors. However, the Court found the most critical difference between its previous cases and this one to be the nature of the "special need" asserted by the State. In each of the earlier cases, the "special need" advanced was totally divorced from the State's general interest in law enforcement while the purpose of the MUSC policy was indistinguishable from that goal. The Court noted that while the ultimate goal of the policy may have been to help addicted patients, the immediate objective was "to generate evidence for law enforcement purposes in order to reach that goal."

c. Dissent

Justice Scalia dissented, joined by the Chief Justice and Justice Thomas. Scalia contended that the urine tests were not protected by the Fourth Amendment because they were obtained with the patients' consent. He noted that the urine samples were not extracted forcibly, and that under established Fourth Amendment law, the hospital was not required to inform the patients that the urine would be tested for drugs and the results turned over to the police.

D. Border Searches and Seizures

Border searches are considered administrative "special needs" searches. The special need beyond ordinary criminal law enforcement is the interest in protecting American borders, and regulating the goods which flow into the country. As the Court stated in *United States v. Montoya de Hernandez*, 473 U.S. 531, 105 S.Ct. 3304, 87 L.Ed.2d 381 (1985), officials regulating the border "have more than merely an investigative law enforcement role." They are charged with "protecting this Nation from entrants who may bring anything harmful into this country, whether that be communicable diseases, narcotics, or explosives."

Because a border search serves special needs, it is evaluated under the reasonableness clause of the Fourth Amendment. Given the heavy state interest in protecting the border, as well as the diminished expectation of privacy attendant to a border crossing, border searches are ordinarily found reasonable without a warrant and probable cause, and often without any suspicion at all.

1. Routine Border Searches

In *United States v. Ramsey*, 431 U.S. 606, 97 S.Ct. 1972, 52 L.Ed.2d 617 (1977), the Court held that routine border searches "are reasonable simply by virtue of the fact that they occur at the border." So for example, a person wishing to enter the country by international flight may be required to submit to a search of his outer clothing, his pockets, and his luggage, even though the officers have no warrant and no reason to suspect that the person is bringing contraband or some other prohibited item into the country. *See United States v. Charleus*, 871 F.2d 265 (2d Cir. 1989) ("routine border searches of the personal belongings and effects of entrants may be conducted without regard to probable cause or reasonable suspicion"). In *Ramsey*, the Court opined that incoming international mail could be opened without a warrant and without any suspicion of a criminal violation. Technically, however, the Court was not required to decide the legality of suspicionless searches of incoming mail, because the governing statute in *Ramsey* required reasonable suspicion.

a.   Minimally Intrusive

Courts have upheld suspicionless routine border searches by balancing the previously discussed substantial state interest against the fact that routine border searches are less intrusive than searches by law enforcement officers for evidence of crime. Courts reason that routine border searches are minimally intrusive for two reasons. First, the citizen has *prior notice* that he or she is subject to such a search; this makes the search, when it is conducted, less surprising and humiliating. Also, because the citizen controls the timing of the search, he can limit its intrusiveness by controlling the nature and character of goods which he brings with him. Second, the search is directed at a *class of travelers* as opposed to any person, and thus lacks the quality of insult, humiliation and stigma associated with the search of a particular person for evidence of a criminal violation.

2.   **Searches Beyond the Routine**

Under the reasonableness balancing test, the level of intrusiveness of a search will have an effect on the level of suspicion required to justify the search. That is, the more intrusive the search, the more suspicious the articulable facts must be for the search to be reasonable. It therefore follows, and all courts have held, that searches more intrusive than a "routine" border search must be justified by some level of individualized suspicion.

a.   Definition of "Routine"

What factors distinguish routine from non-routine border searches? A good rule of thumb is that if the search is *typical of that conducted* at the border—such as a simple inspection of luggage—then it is a routine search that can be conducted without suspicion. *See United States v. Sandoval Vargas*, 854 F.2d 1132 (9th Cir. 1988) (routine search where border officials referred the defendant's car to a secondary inspection area and conducted a thorough search of the passenger compartment and the trunk; the search was "typical of those conducted at the border").

However, it is important to note that in *United States v. Flores–Montano, infra*, the Supreme Court cautioned against a literal interpretation of the word "routine." The real distinction, according to the Court, is the level of intrusiveness of a particular search. The Court, in describing the actions of the lower court in *Flores–Montano* stated "The Court of Appeals took the term "routine," fashioned a new balancing test, and extended it to searches of vehicles. But the reasons that might support a requirement of some level of suspicion in the case of highly intrusive searches of the person—dignity and privacy interests of the person being searched—simply do not carry over to vehicles. Complex balancing tests to determine what is a "routine" search of a vehicle, as opposed to a more "intrusive" search of a person, have no place in border searches of vehicles."

b. Dismantling Property

In *United States v. Flores–Montano*, 541 U.S. 149, 124 S.Ct. 1582, 158 L.Ed.2d 311 (2004), the Supreme Court held that the dismantling and subsequent search of a car's gas tank was a routine border search and did not require any level of suspicion. The Court held that the rationale for requiring some level of suspicion for overly intrusive searches of the person does not apply in the case of automobiles. In *Flores-Montano*, a customs inspector tapped the gas tank of a station wagon and noted that it sounded solid. He then arranged for the removal and disassembly of the gas tank and found 37 kilograms of marijuana bricks. The entire process took 15 to 25 minutes and did not involve destruction of property. The Court held that such a search did not require any level of suspicion, specifically declining to rule on searches involving drilling or other types of destructive disassembly. *See United States v. Ickes*, 393 F.3d 501 (4th Cir. 2005) (thorough inspection of Ickes' computer and computer disks did not require reasonable suspicion because they were located in the car he was driving into the United States and thus subject to the lower standard applied to border searches).

c. Strip Searches

A "strip" search is clearly more intrusive than the routine border search. But the line between a "strip" search and a routine border search is sometimes difficult to draw. Questions arise when the defendant is forced to simply lift a piece of clothing, or to take off only one piece of clothing for inspection. Most courts have held, for example, that simply requiring the defendant to lift his shirt, or to take off his shoe, does not constitute a strip search and therefore is within the realm of a routine border search. *See United States v. Charleus*, 871 F.2d 265 (2d Cir. 1989) (discussing cases finding such activity as removal of shoes, pulling down a girdle in a private room, and lifting up a skirt to be routine border searches, and concluding that "since the potential indignity resulting from a pat on the back followed by a lifting of one's shirt simply fails to compare with the much greater level of intrusion associated with a body cavity or full strip search, we decline to hold that reasonable suspicion was here required"). *Compare United States v. Sanders*, 663 F.2d 1 (2d Cir. 1981) (forcing the defendant to take off his artificial leg for inspection was tantamount to a body cavity search, and therefore more intrusive than a routine border search; reasonable suspicion required).

d. Drilling or Dismantling

If the border official drills into or dismantles the property of the entering citizen, this is considered a search that is more intrusive than a routine border search. Courts have consequently demanded that the official have reasonable suspicion before such a search can be conducted. *See United States v. Puig*, 810 F.2d 1085 (11th Cir. 1987) (reasonable suspicion required before Customs Service official may drill a hole into the hull of a boat); *United States v. Carreon*, 872 F.2d 1436 (10th Cir. 1989) (agent's use of electric drill to find marijuana within a camper shell installed on a truck was permissible only because agent had reasonable suspicion of drug smuggling). *But see United States v. Chaudhry*, 424 F.3d 1051 (9th Cir. 2005) (reasonable suspicion not required where border agents drilled a 5/16–inch hole in the bed of pickup truck during border search. A single hole with a diameter of 5/16 of an inch was not "so destructive as to require a different result" as it did not significantly damage the car so as to hinder its operation or affect its safety.).

e. Extended Detentions

A traveler crossing the border who is subject to a search is also, of course, seized during the course of that search. Such a seizure if routine is, like the routine search, permissible without individualized suspicion. However, if a traveler is detained for an extended period of time, then the seizure will require individualized suspicion even if a search is never conducted. Illustrative is *United States v. Montoya de Hernandez*, 473 U.S. 531, 105 S.Ct. 3304, 87 L.Ed.2d 381

(1985), where the defendant was suspected of being an internal carrier of drugs (a balloon swallower), and was detained for 16 hours until she made a bowel movement; eventually she passed 88 balloons containing 528 grams of 80% pure cocaine. The Court in *Hernandez* did not doubt that the long-term detention was far more serious than a routine border seizure, and held that individualized suspicion was required before such a seizure could occur. On the other hand, a momentary detention of a citizen by a border official, so that the official can ask a few questions or inspect identification, travel arrangements and the like, is permissible without individualized suspicion. *See United States v. Pierre*, 958 F.2d 1304 (5th Cir. 1992) (seizure for purposes of questioning occupants of a vehicle about citizenship and travel plans was permissible without reasonable suspicion).

3. Search or Seizure Beyond the Routine Requires Reasonable Suspicion—Sliding–Scale Approach Rejected

In *Montoya de Hernandez, supra,* the lower court had found that the extensive delay was so severe that it had to be justified by a "clear indication" of criminal activity. This was a standard of proof somewhere between reasonable suspicion and probable cause. On review, the Supreme Court held that such a sliding scale approach, matching a variety of intrusions to a variety of standards of proof, was not permissible under the Fourth Amendment. The Court reasoned that "subtle verbal gradations may obscure rather than elucidate the meaning" of reasonableness.

a. Reasonable Suspicion Sufficient

The Court in *Montoya de Hernandez* held that the detention of the defendant for 16 hours until she made a bowel movement was permissible because officers had *reasonable suspicion* to believe that she was an internal carrier. The Court rejected a requirement of probable cause under these circumstances, concluding that this more demanding standard of proof would unduly subjugate state interests in controlling the border. The Court noted that alimentary canal smuggling "gives no external signs and inspectors will rarely possess probable cause to arrest or search, yet governmental interests in stopping smuggling at the border are high indeed."

b. Distinction From *Terry*

Of course, a 16–hour detention such as occurred in *Montoya de Hernandez* would be impermissible under the *Terry* doctrine if the officer had only reasonable suspicion and not probable cause to believe that the defendant was smuggling drugs. However, *Montoya de Hernandez* is not *a Terry* case; it is a border seizure case. The detention was reasonable as a border seizure, where it would not have been under *Terry*, because of the heavy state interest and diminished expectation of privacy unique to a border crossing.

c. No Warrant Requirement

The Court in *Montoya de Hernandez* held that the Customs officials did not need a warrant to detain the defendant for over 16 hours while waiting for nature to take its course. This has led some lower courts to conclude that no warrant is ever required for a border detention, regardless of how long that detention may be, until the defendant is actually arrested and then entitled to a post-arrest determination of probable cause. *See United States v. Esieke*, 940 F.2d 29 (2d Cir. 1991) (36–hour detention until bowel movement: "an extended border detention of a suspected alimentary canal smuggler does not implicate the Fourth Amendment's warrant clause and, accordingly, does not require judicial approval * * * The length of an extended border detention is governed by the detainee's bodily processes, not by a clock."). Other courts have imposed procedural safeguards requiring judicial supervision of extended detentions, without specifically stating that such safeguards are required by the Fourth Amendment. *See United States v. Adekunle*, 2 F.3d 559 (5th Cir. 1993) (concerned with the "incommunicado" nature of a long-term detention, the court held that the government is required to obtain judicial determination of reasonable suspicion within 48 hours of detention of a suspected alimentary canal smuggler).

4. **Two Types of Intrusions**

After *Montoya de Hernandez*, there are apparently two types of intrusions that can occur at the border. One is a routine border search or seizure; it can be conducted without suspicion. The other is a non-routine border search or seizure; it requires reasonable suspicion.

a. Probable Cause Not Required

It could be argued that some intrusions occurring at the border could be so severe as to be permissible only upon probable cause. However, after *Montoya de Hernandez*, and given the substantial state interest in controlling the border, it is unlikely that probable cause is required for *any* border search or seizure, no matter how intrusive. It is hard to conceive of an intrusion much greater than the long-term detention and monitored bowel movement in *Montoya de Hernandez;* and yet that intrusion did not require probable cause. *See United States v. Adekunle,* 980 F.2d 985 (5th Cir. 1992) (probable cause not required where suspect is subject to 100 hour incommunicado detention, forced use of laxatives, and monitored bowel movement); *United States v. Odofin,* 929 F.2d 56 (2d Cir. 1991) (24–day detention before bowel movement does not require probable cause).

b. **Some Standard Less Than Reasonable Suspicion Is Not Appropriate**

The Court in *Montoya de Hernandez* rejected the use of a standard of proof somewhere between reasonable suspicion and probable cause to regulate searches and seizures somewhere between non-routine and extremely intrusive. The Court reasoned that such a sliding scale approach was unacceptably indeterminate. The same reasoning should preclude the use of a standard of proof somewhere between no suspicion and reasonable suspicion for a search or seizure somewhere between a routine border search or seizure and one that is somewhat more intrusive. So, for example, in *United States v. Charleus,* 871 F.2d 265 (2d Cir. 1989), the court rejected a proposed standard of "some suspicion" for a search which "straddles the line between the two categories of border search" and concluded that a traveler could be forced to lift his shirt even though the Customs official had no individualized suspicion. The court reasoned that the Supreme Court's rejection in *Montoya de Hernandez* of a standard of proof somewhere between reasonable suspicion and probable cause "applies equally to the creation of new standards based on levels of suspicion between no suspicion and reasonable suspicion." For a contrary view, see *People v. Luna,* 73 N.Y.2d 173, 538 N.Y.S.2d 765, 535 N.E.2d 1305 (1989) ("some" suspicion required before a patdown border search can be conducted).

5. **Functional Equivalent of the Border**

A search may be considered as a border search (and thus subject to a balance of interests under the reasonableness clause of the Fourth Amendment) even if it is not undertaken at the geographical point at which a border is crossed. The right to search at the border has been extended to searches conducted at the functional equivalent of the border. The Supreme Court has cited, as examples of a functional equivalent, "searches at an established station near the border, at a point marking the confluence of two or more roads that extend from the border" and "a search of the passengers and cargo of an airplane arriving at a St. Louis airport after a non-stop flight from Mexico City."

6. **Recent Border Crossings—Extended Border Search**

Even if the search or seizure is not conducted at a border checkpoint or other port of entry that can be considered the functional equivalent of the border, an intrusion may be justified as a border search or seizure if it can be established that a border crossing has been made and that no material circumstances have changed since the border crossing. A typical case is *United States v. Moore*, 638 F.2d 1171 (9th Cir. 1980), where agents monitoring a radar screen detected a plane crossing the border from Mexico. The plane was tracked by radar, and tower personnel at the airport kept the plane in view as it landed. Even though the plane was far from the border when the officers searched it, the search of the airplane was upheld as an "extended border search" because it was clear that the plane had crossed the border, and that no material conditions had changed since the border crossing.

a. Suspicion Not Required for Routine Extended Border Search or Seizure

In order to justify a search or seizure under the "extended border" doctrine, the government must have a clear indication that the person or thing has recently crossed the border and that material conditions have not been changed by the time of the government intrusion. But if the actual search or seizure is routine (i.e., typical of an ordinary border search), then the government need not have an independent suspicion that a violation of law has occurred. Thus, a search or seizure under the "extended border" doctrine can be conducted under the same standards as if it were made at an actual port of entry. The standard of proof that must be met pertains to whether the border has been crossed, not to whether the search will be successful.

b. Change of Conditions

Obviously, the "extended border" doctrine does not permit a Customs official to search a person's suitcase on the ground that the person traveled abroad with the suitcase three years earlier. The government must show an absence of changed conditions to justify an extended border search or seizure. *See United States v. Anderson,*

509 F.2d 724 (9th Cir. 1974) (search not justified as an extended border search where car stops after crossing border and a passenger gets out of the car, retrieves a package from behind a tree, and re-enters the car).

7. Roving Patrols in the Interior

In an effort to deal with the flow of illegal aliens into the United States, immigration officials have undertaken investigative techniques at areas removed from the border. One technique is the roving patrol. The constitutionality of roving patrols was first considered by the Supreme Court in *Almeida-Sanchez v. United States,* 413 U.S. 266, 93 S.Ct. 2535, 37 L.Ed.2d 596 (1973), where the defendant's car was stopped 25 miles from the Mexican border. A subsequent search uncovered contraband. No claim was made that there was probable cause to search the car or that there was probable cause to believe that the car had crossed the border. Nonetheless, the government argued that the search was a routine border search and was therefore reasonable, particularly in light of a statute permitting roving stops within 100 miles of the border. The Court rejected this argument, and stated that the search "by a roving patrol on a California road that lies at all points at least 20 miles north of the Mexican border, was of a wholly different sort" from a border search. Thus, traditional Fourth Amendment standards applied to the search, and it was therefore declared illegal in the absence of probable cause.

a. Reasonable Suspicion

Thereafter, in *United States v. Brignoni–Ponce,* 422 U.S. 873, 95 S.Ct. 2574, 45 L.Ed.2d 607 (1975), the Court considered "whether a roving patrol may stop a vehicle in an area near the border and question its occupants when the only ground for suspicion is that the occupants appear to be of Mexican ancestry." The Court held that the mere fact of Mexican ancestry would not support a stop and that, as in *Almeida-Sanchez,* a stop by an officer on roving patrol could not be justified as a border seizure. However, invoking the *Terry* doctrine, the Court held that an officer on roving patrol could stop a person or vehicle if there is reasonable suspicion to believe that the person is an illegal alien or that the vehicle contains illegal aliens. The Court concluded that "except at the border and its functional equivalents, officers on roving patrol may stop vehicles only if they are aware of specific articulable facts, together with rational inferences from those facts, that reasonably warrant suspicion that the vehicles contain aliens who may be illegally in the country." Since the stop was made on the basis of Mexican ancestry alone, the Court concluded that the reasonable suspicion test had not been satisfied. *See also United States v. Garcia*, 732 F.2d 1221 (5th Cir. 1984) (reasonable suspicion found where occupants of overloaded camper, driving near the border, ducked down when a patrolman shined a light into the vehicle).

8. "Reverse" Border Searches and Seizures

Courts have unanimously held that border officials have the same broad power to search and seize outgoing persons and things as they have with respect to persons and things entering the country. Thus, a "routine" search of the luggage of a departing traveler is permissible without a warrant and without any suspicion of illegality. As the court explained in *United States v. Berisha*, 925 F.2d 791 (5th Cir. 1991), "both incoming and outgoing border searches have several features in common; for example, the government is interested in protecting some interest of United States citizens, there is a likelihood of smuggling attempts at the border, and the individual is on notice that his privacy may be invaded when he crosses the border." The court in *Berisha* upheld a warrantless, suspicionless patdown search of a departing traveler, which uncovered $17,000 of domestic currency. For a dissenting view on the "reverse" border exception, see *United States v. Nates*, 831 F.2d 860 (9th Cir. 1987) (Kozinski, J., dissenting) (noting that exit searches are "quite uncommon" and therefore that departing travelers have no diminished expectation of privacy when crossing the border to exit the country; also noting that intrusions are more serious because luggage searches of departing passengers are ordinarily conducted secretly, after the passenger has checked his bags with the airline).

E. Roadblocks

Under *Terry*, the police are ordinarily required to have reasonable suspicion before stopping an automobile. *See Delaware v. Prouse*, 440 U.S. 648, 99 S.Ct. 1391, 59 L.Ed.2d 660 (1979) (holding that an officer's random, suspicionless decision to stop a car for a vehicle registration check violated the Fourth Amendment). However, in two cases the Supreme Court has applied the *Terry* balancing test and upheld roadblock seizures of automobiles even though the officers had no suspicion that the drivers were engaged in criminal activity.

1. Permanent Fixed Checkpoints

In *United States v. Martinez–Fuerte*, 428 U.S. 543, 96 S.Ct. 3074, 49 L.Ed.2d 1116 (1976), the Court upheld suspicionless stops of motorists at permanent fixed checkpoints several miles from the U.S. border. These stops could not be justified under the doctrine allowing suspicionless border searches and seizures (see *infra* for a discussion of border searches), since the checkpoint at issue was so far from the border that it was clear that most of the motorists who were stopped at the checkpoint had not recently, if ever, crossed the border.

a. Balance of Interests

Using the *Terry* balancing analysis, the Court in *Martinez–Fuerte* reasoned that the state interest in investigating and deterring the flow of illegal aliens outweighed the interests of the motorists in being free from suspicionless seizures. The Court asserted that if articulable suspicion was required before a stop, the effectiveness of the fixed checkpoint system would be nullified. The Court relied heavily on the fact that the individual interest at stake was minimal, because of the nature of the permanent fixed checkpoint: motorists could not be surprised by the checkpoint, the detention was very brief, and all motorists were stopped and thus *none could be singled out for arbitrary treatment* without any individualized suspicion. The risk of unconstrained and standardless police discretion was eliminated by the fact that all cars were stopped at the checkpoint. As the Court put it, "the regularized manner in which established checkpoints are operated is visible evidence, reassuring to law-abiding motorists, that the stops are duly authorized and believed to serve the public interest."

b. Location of a Permanent Fixed Checkpoint

In *Martinez–Fuerte,* the Court emphasized that "the location of a fixed checkpoint is not chosen by officers in the field, but by officials responsible for making overall decisions as to the most effective allocation of limited enforcement resources." The Court also noted that the reasonableness of a particular exercise of discretion as to the location of the checkpoint is subject to post-stop judicial review. Presumably, then, the location of a permanent fixed checkpoint could in some cases be deemed unreasonable—for example, if it were placed in an area where the expressed state interest could not possibly be implemented (e.g., an "immigration checkpoint" in the middle of Kansas).

2. Temporary Fixed Checkpoints

In *Michigan Department of State Police v. Sitz*, 496 U.S. 444, 110 S.Ct. 2481, 110 L.Ed.2d 412 (1990), the Court, relying heavily on *Martinez–Fuerte*, upheld suspicionless stops of motorists at *temporary,* fixed sobriety checkpoints.

a. Analysis in *Sitz*

The Court in *Sitz* concluded that a suspicionless stop at a temporary sobriety checkpoint was a reasonable balance of the state interest at stake and the nature of the intrusion suffered by the motorist. The Court relied upon the fixed (albeit temporary) nature of the checkpoint to conclude that there was no risk of arbitrariness or abuse of authority, no surprise or humiliation in the stop itself and no long-term seizure. The Court emphasized that the checkpoints were selected pursuant to department guidelines, and that uniformed police officers stopped every car. The Court concluded that "the intrusion resulting from the brief stop at the sobriety checkpoint is for constitutional purposes indistinguishable from the checkpoint stops we upheld in *Martinez–Fuerte.*"

Against this limited intrusion, the Court balanced the heavy state interest in eradicating drunken driving. Respondents in *Sitz* argued that sobriety checkpoints did not effectively advance this undeniable state interest, and that other methods, such as roving patrols, would be more effective. But the Court responded that it would not "transfer from politically accountable officials to the courts the decision as to which among reasonable alternative law enforcement techniques should be employed to deal with a serious public danger." The Court concluded that "the choice among such reasonable alternatives remains with the government officials who have a unique understanding of, and a responsibility for, limited public resources."

b. Controls on Locating a Temporary, Fixed Checkpoint

The Court in *Sitz* imposed no time, place or manner restrictions on the use of a temporary, fixed checkpoint. This is not to say, however, that the decision as to where to place a temporary checkpoint is *totally* beyond judicial review. The Court in *Martinez–Fuerte* emphasized that the decision as to the location of a permanent checkpoint is subject to post-stop judicial review; there is no reason to think that the result would be different with respect to temporary checkpoints.

Accordingly, some courts after *Sitz* have sought to limit the discretion of field officers in choosing checkpoint sites. For example, in *Hall v. Commonwealth*, 12 Va.App. 972, 406 S.E.2d 674 (1991), the court invalidated a plan which gave field officers discretion to place a checkpoint on any one of 54 sites throughout the county, at any time. The court was concerned that an officer who had already decided to stop a particular person "could do so within these guidelines by ascertaining at what time that person would travel through a particular intersection and set up a roadblock accordingly."

On the other hand, while judicial review of the placement of a checkpoint is possible, the clear deference given by the Court to the guidelines in *Sitz* indicates that it is only the rare case in which the decision to place a checkpoint at a certain location will be deemed unreasonable.

c. Roadblocks for Drug Detection Invalidated

In *City of Indianapolis v. Edmond*, 531 U.S. 32, 121 S.Ct. 447, 148 L.Ed.2d 333 (2000), the Court invalidated a checkpoint program whose primary purpose was discovery and interdiction of illegal drugs. The Indianapolis Police Department established checkpoints to interdict unlawful drugs pursuant to directives issued by the chief of police. The policy permitted a predetermined number of cars to be stopped at each roadblock. One officer informed the driver that he or she was being stopped at a drug checkpoint and asked for the driver's license and registration. That officer also looked for signs of impairment and examined the exterior of the car. A drug-sniffing dog walked around the outside of each stopped car. Further detentions or searches were authorized only by consent or based on the appropriate level of particularized suspicion. The individual officers had no discretion to stop cars out of sequence or otherwise vary from the authorized procedure. Each stop was to last no more than five minutes or less, in the absence of reasonable suspicion or probable cause. Signs were posted warning approaching drivers of the purpose of the checkpoint.

i. Rationale

The Court held that the drug detection checkpoints violated the Fourth Amendment because their primary purpose was "indistinguishable from the general interest in crime control." It distinguished *Martinez–Fuerte* and *Sitz*, noting that although there was a law enforcement component in each of these cases, the primary purpose of the checkpoints in these cases were border control and highway safety, respectively. In *Edmond*, however, the State conceded that the primary purpose of the checkpoint was narcotics detection. Interestingly, in a footnote, the Court specifically declined to decide the constitutionality of a checkpoint program with the primary purpose of checking licenses or driver sobriety and a secondary purpose of interdicting narcotics.

ii. Dissent

Chief Justice Rehnquist dissented, joined by Justice Thomas and, in part, by Justice Scalia. Chief Justice Rehnquist saw no meaningful distinction between *Martinez–Fuerte* and *Sitz* on the one hand, and *Edmond* on the other, accusing the majority of creating a new "non-law-enforcement primary purpose test." He found the primary vs. secondary purpose distinction irrelevant, citing *Whren, supra*, for the proposition that an officer's subjective intent would not invalidate an otherwise objectively justifiable stop of an automobile. Since *Sitz* legitimized the secondary purposes of the stop, the primary purpose was irrelevant, according to the dissent. The only difference in the *Edmond* checkpoint program was the presence of the drug-sniffing dog. Since the dog sniff neither constituted a search nor lengthened the time of the otherwise legitimate stop, the dissent found that the checkpoint program complied with the Court's prior decisions.

d. Information–Seeking Checkpoints Upheld

The Court distinguished *Edmond* in *Illinois v. Lidster*, 540 U.S. 419, 124 S.Ct. 885, 157 L.Ed.2d 843 (2004), upholding a checkpoint at which police sought information about a recent hit-and-run accident on the same highway. In *Lidster*, police officers established a checkpoint to obtain information from motorists about a fatal hit-and-run accident that occurred at the same location and time a week earlier. Each stop lasted about 10 to 15 seconds, during which officers asked the occupants whether they had seen anything happen there during the previous weekend and handed them a flyer describing and requesting information about the accident. The Court held that *Edmond* was not controlling because here the officers were not seeking to determine whether the occupants themselves were committing a crime but were seeking the voluntary cooperation of members of the public in the investigation of a crime in all likelihood committed by others. Furthermore, the stops were much briefer and less intrusive than in *Edmond* and much less likely to provoke anxiety.

3. Suspicionless Seizures, Not Searches, Are Authorized

It is important to note that *Martinez–Fuerte, Sitz,* and *Edmond* are *seizure* cases. They do not allow a *search* for law enforcement purposes on less than probable cause. The Court has permitted searches on less than probable cause in only three circumstances: 1. a search for weapons and dangerous people, not evidence, made for purposes of self-protection (*Terry*); 2. a search for evidence, where there are special needs beyond mere law enforcement; and 3. in certain circumstances, a search of a probationer's residence (*Knights*).

4. Longer Detentions and Interrogations Not Permitted Without Suspicion

The detentions upheld in *Martinez–Fuerte* and *Sitz* were momentary intrusions suffered by all motorists at the checkpoint. If an officer decides to single out a motorist for a more prolonged detention or for interrogation, the officer must have at least an articulable suspicion to justify this more serious intrusion. *See United States v. Walker,* 941 F.2d 1086 (10th Cir. 1991) (*Sitz* distinguished where officer singles out a motorist for prolonged stop and questioning about contraband; "the lack of any constraint on an officer's decision to detain some individuals and to let others go creates a situation ripe for abuse").

F. Inventory Searches

The community caretaking function of police officers focuses on the policeman's role as "jack-of-all-emergencies." The doctrine encompasses the wide range of responsibilities that police officers must discharge aside from law enforcement duties. If such caretaking activities are justified "either in terms of state law or sound police procedure," they can be conducted without a warrant or probable cause and do not violate the Fourth Amendment. *Cady v. Dombrowski,* 413 U.S. 433, 93 S.Ct. 2523, 37 L.Ed.2d 706 (1973).

1. Justifying Searches

In performing searches pursuant to their community caretaking function, the police do not have to possess a warrant. The search, however, must be performed pursuant to a community caretaking duty. In *Cady v. Dombrowski*, 413 U.S. 433, 93 S.Ct. 2523, 37 L.Ed.2d 706 (1973), the police searched a car of a police officer that was towed to a garage after the officer was involved in a car accident. The police claimed that they conducted the search because they believed the car contained the officer's gun. The Supreme Court held that the search was reasonable as part of a community caretaking function "to protect the public from the possibility that a revolver would fall into untrained or perhaps malicious hands."

Must Be a Public Safety Interest

To justify a search under the community caretaking function, the Government must show that the police conducted the search for safety purposes. For example, in *United States v. Lugo*, 978 F.2d 631 (10th Cir. 1992), a police officer, during a search of a car, bent back the corner of a vent in a door panel and reached inside the cavity between the door panel and door to retrieve a paper sack. Because the defendant had told the officer where a weapon in the car was located and the officer had already found that weapon and did not suspect the presence of any other, the court held that the search was not within the community caretaking function and was thus illegal.

2. Justifying Seizures of Vehicles

The community caretaking function also justifies the initial seizure of vehicles in a variety of circumstances. Thus, the police do not need probable cause or a warrant to impound a car if done for caretaking purposes.

Example: In *United States v. Rodriguez–Morales*, 929 F.2d 780 (1st Cir. 1991), the police stopped the defendants' car on the highway for reckless driving. Due to the failure of the driver to produce accurate identification, the police transported the defendants to the police barracks for further questioning. The police then impounded the vehicle and allowed a narcotics trained dog to perform a canine sniff around the perimeter of the car. The court found that the seizure of the car was reasonable under the "community caretaking function." The court noted that "it is important to recognize that the community caretaking function is totally divorced from the detection, investigation, or acquisition of evidence relating to the violation of a criminal statute." Thus, as long as the police act reasonably in carrying out their community caretaking duties, the police may impound a vehicle even though they do not have probable cause to search the car or probable cause to arrest the driver.

a. Impoundment of Vehicles and the Inventory Exception to the Warrant Requirement

If automobiles are lawfully held in police custody, the police may inventory the contents of the automobiles pursuant to established standardized procedures. Inventory searches are not searches for law enforcement or evidentiary purposes. These searches are based on special needs beyond law enforcement and thus are justified as *administrative searches.*

i. When Impoundment Is Justified

To conduct an inventory search, the car must lawfully be in police custody. The police may impound a car to protect it from theft or vandalism, provided they make their impoundment decision "according to standard criteria and on the basis of something other than suspicion of evidence of criminal activity." *Colorado v. Bertine,* 479 U.S. 367, 107 S.Ct. 738, 93 L.Ed.2d 739 (1987). Authority to impound is provided by statute in most states. The Court in *Bertine* upheld an impoundment of an arrestee's car, based on police regulations requiring a car to be impounded if it could not be safely parked and locked.

ii. Requirements for Inventory Searches

Assuming a car is lawfully impounded, the police may conduct an inventory search of the car without suspicion and without a warrant. But in the absence of any requirement of suspicion, regulations must exist which control police discretion. Otherwise there would be too great a risk of arbitrary searches. In *South Dakota v. Opperman,* 428 U.S. 364, 96 S.Ct. 3092, 49 L.Ed.2d 1000 (1976), the Court upheld an inventory search of an impounded vehicle conducted pursuant to standardized procedures. The Court emphasized the diminished expectation of privacy attendant to automobiles, and concluded that inventory searches are reasonable when performed to protect certain state interests.

b. **Special Needs Beyond Law Enforcement That Are Effectuated by Inventory Searches**

The Court in *Opperman* identified three interests that are furthered by a proper inventory search. First, the owner of the vehicle needs protection against the *threat of theft or damage* to the vehicle. Second, the police need protection from *claims of lost or stolen property.* Third, the police and the public need protection from the *potential danger* that the vehicle or its contents may cause. Inventory searches of vehicles protect against these risks and are valid, therefore, when properly conducted, even in the absence of a warrant or suspicion of criminal activity.

c. **Warrant Not Required**

The Court in *Opperman* held that where inventory searches are performed according to departmental procedures, a warrant is not required. Because inventory searches are conducted pursuant to standardized procedures and not for purposes of a criminal investigation, there are no facts for a neutral magistrate to review.

3. **Must Conduct Inventory Search Pursuant to Standardized Regulations**

For an inventory search to be valid, the police must act pursuant to standardized regulations. In *Colorado v. Bertine,* 479 U.S. 367, 107 S.Ct. 738, 93 L.Ed.2d 739 (1987), the Supreme Court upheld the inventory search of a van which included the search of a backpack, a nylon bag, and other containers within the van. The Court found that "reasonable police regulations relating to inventory procedures administered in good faith satisfy the Fourth Amendment, even though courts might as a matter of hindsight be able to devise equally reasonable rules requiring a different procedure." In *Bertine,* regulations required the police to open every container found in a car during an inventory search.

a. **Regulations Concerning Treatment of Containers Found in Cars During the Course of an Inventory Search**

In *Florida v. Wells,* 495 U.S. 1, 110 S.Ct. 1632, 109 L.Ed.2d 1 (1990), an officer opened a locked suitcase in a car after impounding the car and arresting the driver. The police department, however, had promulgated no regulations concerning whether a container could be opened in an inventory search. The Court invalidated the search, stating that it could not be classified as an inventory search in the absence of inventory regulations which control the discretion of the officer. Since inventory searches can be conducted without suspicion, the Court stressed that there must be some substitute for a standard of articulable suspicion, which will prevent the officer from conducting arbitrary searches. Inventory regulations are thus a necessary substitute for a standard of articulable suspicion.

b. Some Discretion Permitted

Although the Court in *Wells* found the search to be insufficiently regulated, the Court disagreed with the Florida Supreme Court's finding that "the police under *Bertine* must mandate either that all containers will be opened during an inventory search, or that no containers will be opened." Chief Justice Rehnquist, writing for the majority, stated that police standards controlling inventory searches could give officers some discretion to decide whether or not to open impounded containers. An all-or-nothing rule was not required. For example, a standard could require police officers to open only containers that reasonably appear to contain valuables, or to open containers only when they cannot discern the contents. Both of these directives permit only a limited use of discretion, and are in accordance with the objectives of an inventory search.

c. Police Must Follow Regulations

When conducting an inventory search, the police must follow the standardized regulations for such searches. If they do not, the search is deemed a search for evidence and not an inventory search. Inventory searches will only pass Fourth Amendment scrutiny if they are performed to protect property, not to search for evidence. If officers comply with the regulations, however, the existence of law enforcement motives becomes irrelevant. Thus, courts will uphold searches performed by officers with pretextual motives if the search is objectively reasonable. So for example, if an officer purports to conduct an inventory search of a car, and discovers drugs, the drugs are subject to exclusion if the officer violated inventory regulations, or failed to file an inventory form, or seized the drugs but left other valuables in the car. On the other hand, the drugs would be admissible if the officer follows all the inventory rules and makes the search look like an inventory search, even if the officer's dominant intent is to search for evidence.

4. Alternative "Less Intrusive" Means

As in other areas of Fourth Amendment analysis, officers are not required to employ the least intrusive means to effectuate the state interests involved in an impoundment or an inventory search. Rather, the question is whether the actions taken are reasonable under the Fourth Amendment. So for example, it could be argued that instead of opening a container to inventory its contents, the officer could merely seal the container. Arguably, this would protect the property from theft and protect the police from false claims, and yet would be less intrusive of the defendant's privacy interest in the contents of the container. However, in *Illinois v. Lafayette,* 462 U.S. 640, 103 S.Ct. 2605, 77 L.Ed.2d 65 (1983), the Court squarely rejected the notion that this less onerous alternative was constitutionally required. The Court stated that "even if less intrusive means existed of protecting some particular types of property, it would be unreasonable to expect police officers in the everyday course of business to make fine and subtle distinctions in deciding which containers or items may be searched and which must be sealed as a unit." Likewise, in *Bertine,* the Court rejected the defendant's claim that the police violated the Fourth Amendment by impounding his car instead of permitting Bertine to make alternative arrangements for its disposition. The Court found that "while giving Bertine an opportunity to make alternative arrangements would have undoubtedly have been possible * * * the reasonableness of any particular governmental activity does not necessarily or invariably turn on the existence of alternative less intrusive means." Thus, defendants cannot prevail by arguing that the police could have protected property interests and public safety interests in ways other than through impoundment of their vehicle. Defendants could claim, however, that impoundment of the vehicle was unreasonable because it was unnecessary. *See, e.g., Sammons v. Taylor,* 967 F.2d 1533 (11th Cir. 1992) (noting that although appellant cannot argue that the police should have employed alternative means, appellant can claim that the impoundment and inventory search of his car was unreasonable).

5. Inventory Searches of Other Property

In *Illinois v. Lafayette, supra,* the Supreme Court upheld the inventory search of a shoulder bag of a suspect arrested for disturbing the peace. The Court stated that the police need to protect the property of arrestees, to protect themselves against claims of lost or stolen property and to remove dangerous instrumentalities from arrestees.

6. Immediately Bailable Offenses

In *Lafayette,* the Court stated that an inventory search may be unreasonable if the defendant is not going to be incarcerated. If, for example, the defendant can and will immediately post bail after being booked, there is no legitimate state interest in inventorying his property; there is, under these circumstances, no risk of loss of property or false claims. *See United States v. Mills*, 472 F.2d 1231 (D.C. Cir. 1972) (inventory not permissible where the arrestee has a right to release without incarceration).

7. Seizure and Inventory Under Forfeiture Laws

In *Florida v. White*, 526 U.S. 559, 119 S.Ct. 1555, 143 L.Ed.2d 748 (1999), the Court considered the constitutionality of a warrantless seizure of a car that is subject to forfeiture. The Florida Contraband Forfeiture Act authorized the seizure of any contraband, including any "vehicle of any kind . . . used . . . as an instrumentality in the commission of, or in aiding or abetting in the commission of, any felony." Police officers observed White using his car to deliver cocaine. Months later, he was arrested on unrelated charges, and the arresting officers seized his car without a warrant under the forfeiture law. During a subsequent inventory search, police discovered cocaine in the car. White later moved for its suppression on grounds that the warrantless seizure of the car violated the Fourth Amendment and that the cocaine was the "fruit of the poisonous tree." The Court held that the seizure and subsequent search were legal because the officers had probable cause to believe that the car itself was contraband. The Court noted that no privacy interests were implicated since the car was seized in a public place. Citing *Carroll v. United States*, *infra*, the Court further justified the warrantless seizure by noting the readily movable nature of the vehicle.

VII. The Arrest Power Rule

Police have historically possessed powers incident to arrest that allow them the automatic right to further intrude upon the arrestee. This right is based on two grounds: 1. to *protect the officers making the arrest*; and 2. to *protect against the destruction of evidence*. At one time, the *arrest power rule* allowed the police to search a suspect's entire house if they arrested the suspect on the premises. *See United States v. Rabinowitz*, 339 U.S. 56, 70 S.Ct. 430, 94 L.Ed. 653 (1950). But then the Supreme Court in *Chimel v. California*, 395 U.S. 752, 89 S.Ct. 2034, 23 L.Ed.2d 685 (1969), imposed spatial limitations on the use of the arrest power, to accord with the reasons underlying the exception.

A. Spatial Limitations

In *Chimel*, the Court limited the geographical scope of the arrest power rule. The Court confined the scope of a search incident to arrest to areas which in fact are accessible to the arrestee. Justice Stewart, writing for the Court, stated that "[t]here is ample justification * * * for a search of the arrestee's person and the area within his immediate control—construing the phrase to mean the area from within which he might gain possession of a weapon or destructible evidence." Thus, a search incident to arrest is confined to the search of the suspect and the search of his or her "grab area" or "wing span."

1. Arrest Power Rule Is Automatic

Although *Chimel* limited the scope of a search incident to arrest, it stressed that the police have the *automatic right* to secure everything within the grab area. Therefore, the police may, incident to a lawful arrest, secure the person and the grab area of the arrestee without reasonable suspicion or probable cause, and without a warrant. Because the rule is automatic, there is no case-by-case approach as to whether in fact the arrestee poses a risk of harm, or whether in fact there is destructible evidence within the grab area.

2. Determining the Grab Area

Courts use a case-by-case approach to determine whether a certain place or object is within the arrestee's grab area.

a. Determination of Grab Area at Time of Arrest

Some courts determine the grab area by focusing on where the defendant could have reached when arrested, even though the search or seizure occurs *after the defendant has been moved*. Such a result, however, seems contrary to *Chimel* and the rationale behind the exception, which is concerned with neutralizing the arrestee. An example of this questionable approach is *United States v. Turner*, 926 F.2d 883 (9th Cir. 1991), where the police searched the defendant's room and closet after the defendant was handcuffed and removed from the room. The court upheld the search under the arrest power rule, reasoning that the evidence was within Turner's immediate control when he was arrested, and contending that subsequent events did not diminish the risks to such an extent as to make the search unreasonable.

b. Determination of Grab Area at Time of Search

Most courts determine the grab area by analyzing where the defendant could have reached at the time of the search. Some of these courts, however, find the grab area to be remarkably broad under the circumstances.

3. Factors Helpful in Defining the Area Within the Immediate Control of the Arrestee

Although a determination of the grab area depends on the facts of the case, some factors that are helpful in determining this area include: 1. whether the suspect is *cuffed or restrained*; 2. the *physical characteristics* of the particular suspect—a young, agile arrestee will have a more expansive grab area than an older, infirm arrestee; 3. the *ratio of police officers to suspects*—the higher the ratio, the less likely it would be for the suspect to leap a long distance to grab a weapon; and 4. whether the item searched is *reasonably* accessible—a locked safe may be very near to the arrestee, but it is not within the grab area under *Chimel*. *See United States v. Currence*, 446 F.3d 554 (4th Cir. 2006) (police stopped defendant while he was on his bicycle, placed him under arrest, and searched handlebars of bicycle while defendant stood nearby in handcuffs. Court upheld search, noting that because police were able to remove the handlebar end cap by simply sliding it off "with very minimal intrusion," there was no basis to treat the handlebar differently from other items within the immediate control of an arrestee that could be opened during a search incident to an arrest).

4. Movable Grab Area: No Risk of Danger Needed to Trigger the Arrest Power

To protect the integrity of an arrest, police officers may accompany an arrestee to a different location without having to prove a risk of danger. With post-arrest movement, the grab area moves along with the arrestee.

Example: In *Washington v. Chrisman*, 455 U.S. 1, 102 S.Ct. 812, 70 L.Ed.2d 778 (1982), a police officer approached a student who was carrying liquor and appeared to be underage. The officer placed him under arrest. Chrisman was not carrying identification, so the officer accompanied him to his dormitory room to retrieve it. Upon entering the room, the officer found evidence of marijuana. Although the officer had no fear of bodily harm or destruction of evidence, the Court held that "the absence of an affirmative indication that an arrested person might have a weapon available or might attempt to escape does not diminish the arresting officer's authority to maintain custody over the arrested person." According to the Court, "every arrest must be presumed to present a risk of danger to the arresting officer." Therefore, a police officer may monitor an arrestee's movements and if, during the course of such activity, the officer observes evidence of criminal activity, he may seize it pursuant to the plain view exception.

a. Application of *Chrisman* in the Lower Courts

A question arising after *Chrisman* is whether officers can demand that an arrestee dress in a certain way to go down to the station, and consequently monitor the arrestee's movements while he changes. For example, in *United States v. Butler,* 980 F.2d 619 (10th Cir. 1992), the police arrested the defendant in front of his trailer pursuant to an arrest warrant. The ground outside of the trailer was covered with litter and broken glass. Because the defendant was barefoot, the arresting officer told the defendant to enter the trailer to retrieve his shoes. When the officer entered the trailer to monitor the defendant's movements, he saw a shotgun in plain view in the defendant's bedroom. The court found that the search was a valid exercise of the arrest power, reasoning that "police may conduct a limited entry into an area for the purpose of protecting the health or safety of the arrestee." The court noted that this extension of *Chrisman* "in no way creates a blank check for intrusion upon the privacy of the sloppily dressed."

5. Other Exceptions That Justify Searches Beyond the Grab Area

Even though the arrest power rule has spatial limitations, other exceptions to the warrant requirement could apply during or after the arrest of a person, that would allow police officers to conduct searches or seizures beyond the area within the arrestee's immediate control. The three possibilities justifying a search or seizure beyond the grab area are: 1. *exigent circumstances* arising due to an arrest; 2. the need to perform a *protective sweep* to protect the safety of the arresting officer; and 3. the need to *secure the premises* during the time it takes to obtain a warrant.

a. Exigent Circumstances

Justice White, dissenting in *Chimel,* argued for a bright line rule allowing the police to search the entire premises upon an arrest because an arrest most often gives rise to exigent circumstances and probable cause to search the premises. This bright line rule was rejected as overbroad because not every arrest gives rise to these factors. But when an arrest situation also leads to probable cause to believe that evidence is in a certain place, and also triggers a risk of destruction of that evidence by the arrestee's cohorts, then the police may conduct a search of that place even though it is beyond the grab area.

In many cases, the fact of an arrest will create a risk of destruction of evidence by the arrestee's associates and will thus give rise to exigent circumstances. *See, e.g., United States v. Socey*, 846 F.2d 1439 (D.C. Cir. 1988) (holding that exigent circumstances existed where arrest was made outside a house containing a large-scale drug operation). *See also United States v. Hill*, 430 F.3d 939 (8th Cir. 2005). A task force of state police officers and FBI agents raided Hill's home to execute an arrest warrant for aggravated robbery. As they arrested Hill on the doorstep, one officer saw an unidentified man run into the house. The officer entered the home and saw weapons and ammunition in plain view. The court held that exigent circumstances justified the entry of the home.

b. Protective Sweeps

Another justification for searching beyond the grab area in an arrest situation is illustrated in *Maryland v. Buie*, 494 U.S. 325, 110 S.Ct. 1093, 108 L.Ed.2d 276 (1990), discussed *supra* in the section on *Terry*. The Court in *Buie* defined a protective sweep as a "quick and limited search of a premises, incident to an arrest and conducted to protect the safety of police officers or others." In *Buie*, the Court held that police may conduct a protective sweep based on reasonable suspicion that persons who might harm the officers or others are present. Thus, where circumstances justifying a protective sweep are present, the police may search beyond the grab area of the arrestee. While conducting a search pursuant to a protective sweep, the police may seize evidence of criminal activity by invoking the plain view exception.

c. Seizing the Premises

Although the arrest power rule may not allow the police to search the premises beyond the arrestee's grab area, the police may *seize* the entire premises under certain conditions. If the police must leave the premises to obtain a warrant but wish to protect against the destruction of evidence during that time, they may secure the premises when they have probable cause to believe it contains evidence of criminal activity. *Illinois v. McArthur*, 531 U.S. 326, 121 S.Ct. 946, 148 L.Ed.2d 838 (2001). Although securing the premises is a seizure (because it is an exercise of dominion and control over the property), the seizure is considered reasonable where police have probable cause and need to preserve the status quo while they obtain a warrant. See the discussion of *McArthur* in the section on exigent circumstances.

B. Temporal Limitations

A search incident to arrest usually occurs immediately after the arrest. But it is permissible for the search to precede the arrest, when both are nearly simultaneous, and probable cause to arrest existed before the police conducted the search. *See Rawlings v. Kentucky,* 448 U.S. 98, 100 S.Ct. 2556, 65 L.Ed.2d 633 (1980) ("Where the formal arrest followed quickly on the heels of the challenged search of petitioner's person, we do not believe it particularly important that the search preceded the arrest rather than vice versa."). A search, therefore, may immediately precede an arrest. But the police cannot use evidence discovered during the search to provide probable cause to make the arrest. *See Smith v. Ohio,* 494 U.S. 541, 110 S.Ct. 1288, 108 L.Ed.2d 464 (1990) (While the arrest power rule can justify a search which immediately precedes an arrest, that search cannot be used to provide the probable cause necessary to make the arrest.).

1. When Is the Search Too Late or Too Far Removed to Be "Incident to" an Arrest?

A search "incident to" an arrest implies that a search conducted too long after or too far removed from the arrest will not satisfy the exception. In *Chambers v. Maroney,* 399 U.S. 42, 90 S.Ct. 1975, 26 L.Ed.2d 419 (1970), the police searched an automobile after they arrested the occupants and impounded the car and brought it to the police station. The Court stated that "once an accused is under arrest and in custody, then a search made at another place, without a warrant, is simply not incident to the arrest." *See also United States v. Chadwick,* 433 U.S. 1, 97 S.Ct. 2476, 53 L.Ed.2d 538 (1977) (holding that the search of a footlocker at the police station, after the defendant was arrested and incarcerated, "cannot be viewed as incidental to the arrest or as justified by any other exigency").

In *United States v. Edwards,* 415 U.S. 800, 94 S.Ct. 1234, 39 L.Ed.2d 771 (1974), a suspect was arrested for attempting to break into a post office and was jailed after midnight. The next morning, police seized Edwards' shirt and pants and subjected them to forensic analysis, which linked Edwards to the crime. The Court upheld the search of the clothing as incident to arrest, stating that "searches and seizures that could be made on the spot at the time of arrest may legally be conducted later when the accused arrives at the place of detention." The Court noted that "the normal processes incident to arrest and custody had not yet been completed when Edwards was placed in his cell." *See also United States v. Johnson*, 445 F.3d 793 (5th Cir. 2006) (gunpowder residue test of defendant's hands after he was taken to the police station was a permissible search incident to arrest since residue could have been destroyed by Johnson or the passage of time).

a. Distinction Between *Edwards and Chambers*

Arguably there is a conflict between *Edwards,* where a search was found to be incident to the arrest even though the arrestee had been incarcerated for several hours, and *Chambers,* where the Court held that the search was not incident to the arrest because the defendant was in jail at the time of the search. These cases can be reconciled on two grounds, however. First, the officers in *Edwards* seized the arrestee's clothing, which he was wearing at the time of the arrest *and at the time of the seizure*; in contrast, the officers in *Chambers* searched the defendant's car, from which he was obviously far removed in both time and place at the time of the search. Second, because of the late hour of Edwards' incarceration, the arrest process—including taking Edwards' clothing and giving him institutional garb—had not yet been completed. In contrast, in *Chambers,* the process of arrest had been fully completed by the time the search of the car was conducted. Thus, *Edwards* does not by any means eliminate all temporal limitations on the arrest power rule.

C. Searches of the Person Incident to Arrest

The search incident to arrest exception has always permitted a search of the person of the arrestee. In *United States v. Robinson*, 414 U.S. 218, 94 S.Ct. 467, 38 L.Ed.2d 427 (1973), the Supreme Court addressed questions concerning the scope of such a search.

1. *United States v. Robinson*

In *Robinson,* a police officer conducted a body search of the defendant incident to an arrest for a traffic violation. During this search, the officer felt an object on the defendant's person and although he could not identify whether it was evidence of criminal activity, he pulled it out of Robinson's pocket. The object was a crumbled cigarette package. The officer opened the package and found heroin. The officer had no probable cause or even reasonable suspicion to believe that Robinson was carrying narcotics, nor was the officer concerned with self-protection when he arrested Robinson. The Court held that a valid arrest supplies police officers with the *automatic power* to neutralize an arrestee in order to protect against danger to the officer and destruction of evidence, whether or not such risks exist on the facts. The Court further held that police officers have the automatic right to conduct a complete body frisk, and to pull out and to search all objects on an arrestee's person, even if there is no factual risk of harm to the officer or destruction of evidence. In *Robinson,* there was clearly no likelihood of destruction of evidence, as the defendant was arrested for a traffic violation. But the Court found that "[i]t is the fact of the lawful arrest which establishes the authority to search, and * * * in the case of a lawful custodial arrest a full search of the person is not only an exception to the warrant requirement of the Fourth Amendment, but is also a 'reasonable' search under the Amendment." *Robinson* establishes the automatic right to search containers found on an arrestee.

a. Distinguishing a Search of a Person Incident to Arrest From a *Terry* Frisk

    The Court in *Robinson* distinguished a search pursuant to the arrest power from a *Terry* frisk. A search incident to arrest allows an officer the automatic right to perform a full body search and to remove, as well as to open, all objects found during such a search. Under *Terry,* on the other hand, the frisk must be based on reasonable suspicion of bodily harm. The difference between a stop and an arrest justifies the distinction in the search power. An arrest is a more serious event in which the arrestee may act more desperately than a suspect who is subject to a stop. Although the actual facts in an arrest situation may not show a risk of harm or destruction of evidence, arrests in general create an increased possibility that harm to the police officer or destruction of evidence could occur. Therefore, the Court in *Robinson* found that an *automatic rule* in arrest situations was necessary.

b. Arrests for Traffic Violations: Police Discretion

    In *Gustafson v. Florida,* 414 U.S. 260, 94 S.Ct. 488, 38 L.Ed.2d 456 (1973), which was decided along with *Robinson,* a police officer arrested the defendant for driving without a valid driver's license, and then conducted a full scale body search of the defendant. Unlike the case in *Robinson,* however, no police department regulations required the officer to take the defendant into custody. Also unlike

Robinson, there was no departmental policy establishing the conditions under which a full scale search should be conducted. Gustafson argued that these differences created an unacceptable risk of arbitrary searches and thus distinguished his case from *Robinson*. But the Court held that these distinctions were not "determinative of the constitutional issue." Thus, there is no requirement that a custodial arrest must be mandated, only that it must be authorized.

i.   Custodial Arrests for Minor Traffic Offenses Held
     Constitutional

In his concurrence in *Gustafson*, Justice Stewart noted that a custodial arrest for a minor traffic offense might be in violation of the Fourth and Fourteenth Amendments. The Supreme Court addressed this precise issue in *Atwater v. City of Lago Vista*, 532 U.S. 318, 121 S.Ct. 1536, 149 L.Ed.2d 549 (2001), holding that it is not a violation of the Fourth Amendment for a police officer to arrest an individual if he has probable cause to believe that the person has committed even a very minor criminal offense in his presence. In *Atwater*, a police officer arrested a woman in Lago Vista, Texas, who was driving without wearing her seatbelt and without buckling the seatbelts of her two children. The seatbelt violations are misdemeanors that carry a maximum penalty of a $50 fine. Atwater was handcuffed, searched, and detained in a jail cell for an hour before posting bond. Her 3 and 5 year old children witnessed the arrest before they were picked up by a family friend. Atwater and her husband filed suit under section 1983, claiming that the arrest was an unreasonable seizure under the Fourth Amendment. The Supreme Court held that it was not, rejecting Atwater's proposed rule forbidding custodial arrests for offenses that could not carry jail time and when there is no compelling need for immediate detention. The Court noted that this proposal would be too complicated to administer, as it would require police officers to make an on-the-spot determination of the penalty for each offense, sometimes requiring them to predict facts impossible to know at the time of the arrest. Instead the Court affirmed the probable cause standard as clear, simple, and easy to apply on the spur of the moment.

ii.   Dissent in *Atwater*

Justice O'Connor dissented, joined by Justices Stevens, Ginsburg and Breyer. O'Connor found the seizure unreasonable, pointing out the exacting toll on liberty and privacy imposed by a custodial arrest, including a full search of the person, confiscation of her possessions, search of the passenger compartment of the car and all of its packages, detention of the person for 48 hours before a determination of probable cause by a magistrate, and a permanent arrest record. Justice O'Connor conceded that there may be some instances requiring a custodial arrest, even when the punishment for the offense is only a fine, such as instances involving a risk of flight or impending criminal conduct. However, she maintained that "justifying a full arrest by the same quantum of evidence that justifies a traffic stop— even though the offender cannot ultimately be imprisoned for her conduct—defies any sense of proportionality and is in serious tension with the Fourth Amendment's proscription of unreasonable seizures." Extracting language from *Terry v. Ohio*, Justice O'Connor proposed a requirement that when there is probable cause to believe that a fine-only offense has been committed, the officer should issue a citation unless he can point to "specific and articulable facts which, taken together with rational inferences from those facts, reasonably warrant the intrusion" of a full custodial arrest. Justice O'Connor also stressed the dangers of leaving such unbounded discretion in the hands of police officers, noting the potential for abuse.

In *Hedgepeth ex rel. Hedgepeth v. Washington Metropolitan Area Transit Authority*, 386 F.3d 1148 (D.C. Cir. 2004), a twelve year old girl was arrested for eating a single French fry in a subway station pursuant to the Washington Metro Area Transit Authority's "zero tolerance" policy on eating in metro rail stations. The girl's mother ultimately filed a § 1983 claim alleging that her daughter's arrest constituted an unlawful seizure under the Fourth Amendment. The court, relying on *Atwater*, found no violation of Hedgepeth's Fourth Amendment rights.

c. Arrests Based on Probable Cause Constitutional Even if in Violation of State Law

In *Virginia v. Moore*, ___ U.S. ___, 128 S.Ct. 1598, 170 L.Ed.2d (2008), the Supreme Court held that police did not violate the Fourth Amendment when they arrested Moore based on probable cause and searched him incident to the arrest even though the arrest was in violation of Virginia law. In Moore, the officers arrested Moore for driving with a suspended license. They then searched him incident to the arrest and found cocaine and cash. Under Virginia state law, the officers should have issued Moore a summons instead of arresting him. Moore argued that the arrest, and thus the search, violated the Fourth Amendment.

The Supreme Court held that if an officer has probable cause to believe that a person committed even a minor crime, the arrest is constitutional, even if state law prohibits such an arrest. The Court also held that the search incident to arrest was constitutional. The Court noted that "the Fourth Amendment's meaning did not change with local law enforcement practices" and that "linking Fourth Amendment protections to state law would cause them to vary from place to place and from time to time," citing *Whren v. United States, supra.*

2. Search of Objects in the Grab Area

Robinson holds that officers can pull out and search objects on *the person* of the arrestee. *Robinson* did not address whether police officers may search, as well as seize, objects that are in the grab area but not on the arrestee's person, e.g., a briefcase or book bag.

a. Effect of *Chadwick*

The Supreme Court's decision in *United States v. Chadwick,* 433 U.S. 1, 97 S.Ct. 2476, 53 L.Ed.2d 538 (1977), further clouds this issue. In *Chadwick,* police officers arrested the defendant at a railroad station, and then brought his footlocker to the police station and searched it there without a warrant. Holding that the search could not be justified as a search incident to arrest, the Court noted that "[u]nlike searches of the person, searches of possessions within an arrestee's immediate control cannot be justified by any reduced expectations of privacy caused by the arrest." Because the footlocker was not "immediately associated" with the arrestee, it retained a privacy interest greater than any object on the arrestee's person. The Court also noted, however, as previously discussed, that the search was too far removed in time to be justified as an exercise of the arrest power rule at any rate. That is, the Court in *Chadwick* gave two reasons for why the search of the footlocker could not be justified under the arrest power rule. It is therefore unclear from *Chadwick* whether the Court would prohibit a search (rather than a seizure) of an object within the suspect's grab area if the search were to occur contemporaneously with the arrest.

b. Searches of Objects "Immediately Associated" With the Arrestee

Relying on *Robinson* and distinguishing *Chadwick*, almost all lower courts hold that the police may search, as well as seize, items that are immediately associated with the arrestee, such as wallets and purses. For example, in *United States v. Passaro,* 624 F.2d 938 (9th Cir. 1980), the court upheld the warrantless seizure of an arrestee's wallet, the search of its contents, and the photocopying of documents contained in the wallet. Distinguishing the case from *Chadwick,* the court in *Passaro* stated that "[u]nlike a double-locked footlocker, which is clearly separate from the person of the arrestee, the wallet found in the pocket of Mr. Passaro was an element of his clothing, his person."

c. Searches of Objects Not "Immediately Associated" With the Person of the Arrestee

Lower courts differ on whether police officers can search, as well as seize, items in the grab area that are not immediately associated with the arrestee. Some lower courts have interpreted *Chadwick* as forbidding an automatic search of items in the grab area that are not immediately associated with the arrestee. According to these courts, police officers can automatically *seize* these items, to protect against harm to the officer and against the risk of destruction of evidence, but cannot search them. Thus, these courts would allow the seizure, but not the search, of objects such as bookbags and briefcases, while permitting both the search and seizure of items immediately associated with the arrestee, such as wallets and cigarette packs. *See, e.g., United States v. Gorski,* 852 F.2d 692 (2d Cir. 1988) (holding that search of bag during arrest must be justified by exigent circumstances, otherwise seizure is all that is permitted). Thus, in *United States v. Six Hundred Thirty–Nine Thousand Five Hundred and Fifty–Eight Dollars in United States Currency,* 955 F.2d 712 (D.C. Cir. 1992), the court considered whether a warrantless search of the arrestee's luggage could be justified as a search incident to arrest. The arrestee was handcuffed to a chair when the officers searched his luggage. Holding that such a search violated the Fourth Amendment, the court stated that "*Chadwick* rejected the argument that because an immediate search without a warrant could have been justified as incident to arrest, that exception would justify a warrantless search of a closed container conducted later, *after the exigency had ended.*"

Most courts, however, have applied the automatic arrest power rule of *Robinson* to searches of items in the grab area, such as briefcases, etc. *See, e.g., United States v. Morales,* 923 F.2d 621 (8th Cir. 1991) (distinguishing *Chadwick* as a case involving a search which occurred too long after the arrest was completed).

D. The Arrest Power Rule Applied to Automobiles

In *New York v. Belton,* 453 U.S. 454, 101 S.Ct. 2860, 69 L.Ed.2d 768 (1981), the Supreme Court clarified the application of the arrest power rule to automobiles. The *Belton* rule must be distinguished from the automobile exception to the warrant requirement. (See the discussion of the automobile exception to the warrant requirement *infra*). Under the automobile exception, the police can search a car without a warrant, but they must have *probable cause* to believe that there is evidence of criminal activity in the car. In contrast, the arrest power rule as applied to cars allows an *automatic intrusion* into the grab area, without probable cause or a warrant, so long as there is probable cause to make a custodial arrest. The distinction between probable cause to arrest (the relevant issue under the arrest power rule) and probable cause to search (the relevant issue under the automobile exception) is most pronounced when the defendant is arrested for a traffic offense. In such a case, there is probable cause to arrest, but no probable cause to believe (in the absence of other information) that evidence will be found in the car.

1. *New York v. Belton*

In *Belton*, the Supreme Court determined the scope of the arrest power rule when an occupant of an automobile is subjected to a lawful arrest.

a. Passenger Compartments of Cars Are Always in the Grab Area

The *Belton* Court held that "when a policeman has made a lawful custodial arrest of the occupant of an automobile, he may, as a contemporaneous incident of that arrest, search the passenger compartment of the automobile." The Court determined that the passenger compartment of a car is *always* within the arrestee's grab area, even if the arrestee does not have access to this area at the time of the search. The Court thus rejected the case-by-case determination of an arrestee's grab area that was established in *Chimel*. The *Belton* Court reasoned that a bright-line rule was appropriate because the passenger compartment of an automobile "is generally, even if not inevitably, within the area into which an arrestee might reach in order to grab a weapon or evidentiary item." *See United States v. Karlin,* 852 F.2d 968 (7th Cir. 1988) (after *Belton*, the passenger compartment is within the arrestee's grab area even if he is in the squad car and handcuffed).

b. **Does Not Apply to the Trunk**

The Court in *Belton* held that the automatic grab area rule applied only to the passenger compartment of the car, and not to the trunk. Presumably, the trunk could be within the arrestee's grab area in a specific case, but the state would have to show this to be the case on *the facts*. Thus, wherever the *Belton* bright-line rule does not apply, the court must resort to the *Chimel* case-by-case approach to determine whether a certain place is within the arrestee's grab area.

c. **The Police May Search All Containers Found in the Passenger Compartment**

The Court in *Belton* further held that "the police may also examine the contents of any containers found within the passenger compartment, for if the passenger compartment is within reach of the arrestee, so also will containers in it be within his reach." The Court noted that a rule giving the officer an automatic right to open containers in the grab area was consistent with *Robinson*.

2. Aftermath of *Belton*

Although *Belton* established some bright-line rules, some questions remain unanswered.

a. **Temporal Limitations**

One question concerns the amount of time that can occur between the arrest of the defendant and the search of the passenger compartment. For example, if a search of the passenger compartment occurs an hour or two after the arrest of the defendant, the defendant may argue that such a search is not "incident to" the arrest. Some post-*Belton* courts have held that searches pursuant to the *Belton* rule are valid so long as the defendant remains at the scene, irrespective of the amount of time between the search and the arrest. *See, e.g., United States v. Fiala*, 929 F.2d 285 (7th Cir. 1991) (search of the passenger compartment conducted 90 minutes after the arrest was still "incident to" the arrest, where the arrestee remained on the scene). *But see United States v. Vasey*, 834 F.2d 782 (9th Cir. 1987) (holding that a search conducted between 30 and 45 minutes after the arrest of the defendant lacked the "contemporaneity" requirement of a search incident to arrest). The Supreme Court has focused both on the location and the time interval of the search to determine whether the search is still incident to arrest. *See United States v. Chadwick*, 433 U.S. 1, 97 S.Ct. 2476, 53 L.Ed.2d 538 (1977) (search cannot be justified as incident to arrest "either if the search is remote in time or place from the arrest").

b. **What Is the "Passenger Compartment"?**

The Court in *Belton* noted that the passenger compartment includes only the interior of the car and does not encompass the trunk of the automobile. But with some vehicles it is difficult to determine whether a certain area is within the passenger compartment or the trunk. Most courts have held that the passenger compartment constitutes anything *accessible from the interior of the car. See United States v. Pino*, 855 F.2d 357, 364 (6th Cir. 1988) (holding that the rear section of a mid-size station wagon was part of the passenger compartment); *United States v. Russell*, 670 F.2d 323 (D.C. Cir. 1982) (holding that the hatchback area of a car was part of the passenger compartment).

c. **Containers in the Passenger Compartment**

The Court in *Belton* specifically held that the police can automatically open all containers in the passenger compartment. This raises the question of what is a container? Are the door panels considered containers because they have an empty space in which something can be stored? Lower courts have limited searches under *Belton* to areas in the passenger compartment that can be investigated without causing serious damage to the vehicle. *See, e.g., United States v. Diaz–Lizaraza*, 981 F.2d 1216 (11th Cir. 1993) (holding that the search of defendant's truck was within the scope allowed by *Belton*, where the officer "looked under the seats on the floor of the truck, but did not rip the upholstery, look under the hood, or damage the truck in any way"). As the *Belton* court noted in a footnote that a container found within the passenger compartment "includes closed or open glove compartments," the courts have held that *Belton* allows the search of a locked glove compartment. *See United States v. Holifield*, 956 F.2d 665 (7th Cir. 1992).

d. **"Recent Occupants" of a Vehicle**

In *Thornton v. United States*, 541 U.S. 615, 124 S.Ct. 2127, 158 L.Ed.2d 905 (2004), the Court extended *Belton* to "recent occupants" of a vehicle. In *Thornton*, the defendant pulled into a parking lot and got out of his vehicle before the police officer had the opportunity to pull him over. The police officer accosted Thornton just after he exited his car and placed him under arrest. Incident to the arrest, the officer searched Thornton's car and found a handgun under the driver's seat. The Court stated that the same concerns of officer safety and destruction of evidence presented by a suspect inside a vehicle applied to a suspect next to a vehicle. The Court furthered reasoned that while the defendant's status as a recent occupant may depend on temporal or spatial factors, it does not turn on whether he was inside or outside the car at the moment that the officer first initiated contact with him.

e. **Are the *Belton* Bright–Line Rules Applicable Outside of the Automobile Context?**

The Court in *Belton* took pains to note that its bright-line rules were applicable only to the "particular and problematic" context of the search of an automobile incident to arrest, and that the decision "in no way alters the fundamental principles established in the *Chimel* case regarding the basic scope of searches incident to lawful custodial arrests." Nonetheless, some courts have applied *Belton's* bright-line rules in other areas. For example, in *United States v. Palumbo*, 735 F.2d 1095 (8th Cir. 1984), the court held that a search of a drawer in a motel room was within the arrestee's control area, even though the arrestee was handcuffed. Relying on *Belton*, the court found that the arrest power rule "is not constrained because the arrestee is unlikely at the time of the arrest to actually reach into an area." *See also United States v. Johnson,* 846 F.2d 279 (5th Cir. 1988) (relying on *Belton* to hold that containers within the grab area could be immediately searched, even though the arrest did not occur in or near a car).

f. **No Arrest, No Search**

In *Knowles v. Iowa*, 525 U.S. 113, 119 S.Ct. 484, 142 L.Ed.2d 492 (1998), the Court struck down an Iowa statute that permitted police officers to conduct a full-blown search of an automobile and driver in cases where the officer elected to issue a citation instead of making a custodial arrest. The statute gave officers the discretion to either issue a citation or make an arrest in cases involving violations of any traffic or motor vehicle equipment law. Knowles was stopped for speeding and the officer issued a citation. He then conducted a full search of Knowles' car and found marijuana and drug paraphernalia under the driver's seat. In a unanimous decision, the Court noted that the Iowa statute permitting a search incident to the issuance of a citation fulfilled neither of the purposes set forth in *Robinson*—disarming a suspect before taking him into custody or preserving evidence for later use at trial.

VIII. Pretextual Searches and Seizures

The arrest-power rule, as we have seen, allows an officer considerable search powers upon the making of a custodial arrest. The *Terry* doctrine allows the officer more limited, but still significant, investigatory power upon the making of a stop. A leading case on the arrest-power rule, *United States v. Robinson, supra,* involved the search of a person incident to arrest for a traffic violation. Although *Knowles* forbids searches in the absence of an arrest or some other exception to the warrant requirement, *Atwater v. City of Lago Vista, supra*, permits arrests for even minor traffic offenses. Therefore, the current state of the law is that these search powers can be used to investigate even minor crimes.

A. The Pretext Problem

It is now clear that it is possible for an officer to invoke the arrest-power rule or *Terry* as to a minor crime, in order to stop or arrest the suspect in circumstances in which a reasonable officer would not have made the stop or arrest for a minor offense. Suppose a driver is driving at 60 miles an hour where the speed limit is posted at 55. He is breaking the laws against speeding, and is technically subject to a stop or arrest; but in reality most officers would not stop or arrest the driver for this conduct. But what if the officer wishes to use such a stop or arrest to search for drugs, in the absence of probable cause or reasonable suspicion as to a drug offense? Assume that an officer has merely an inarticulable hunch that a driver is a drug courier, and decides to follow the driver for miles in the hope that the driver will commit a traffic violation. When the driver exceeds the speed limit by even a few miles per hour, the officer places the driver under arrest and conducts an automatic search of the passenger compartment of the car under *Belton*. If the officer has a legal right to stop or arrest the driver, as he has in this example, does it make a difference that no reasonable officer would exercise that right if the speeding violation were the only issue?

This is the pretext problem that Justice Marshall warned of in his dissent in *Robinson*. Marshall maintained that "an arrest may not be used as a pretext for a search for evidence." His view was not upheld in the Court's subsequent jurisprudence.

1. Supreme Court View

In *Whren v. United States,* 517 U.S. 806, 116 S.Ct. 1769, 135 L.Ed.2d 89 (1996), the Supreme Court held that a police officer may stop an individual if he has probable cause to believe that a traffic offense has been committed, regardless of the officer's subjective motivations for the stop. The effect of *Whren* was to permit an officer to use *Terry* or the arrest power for a minor crime as a pretext to investigate a more serious crime. The Court in *Whren* upheld the seizure of evidence made by plainclothes police officers who stopped the defendant for a traffic violation. The fact that these officers did not ordinarily make traffic stops (indeed, it was against local police regulations for plainclothes officers to make traffic stops) was considered irrelevant since the defendant had violated a traffic law.

2. Rationale

The *Whren* Court reasoned that the Fourth Amendment requires a police officer's conduct to be *objectively reasonable*. It therefore does not matter that an officer has a subjective intent to use an otherwise lawful stop or arrest as a pretext. The only question is whether the officer had the *legal right* to do what he did. *But see City of Indianapolis v. Edmond, supra,* where the Court considered subjective intent to determine whether a suspicion-less stop was valid under the Court's "special needs" analysis or whether it was an ordinary stop requiring reasonable suspicion.

a. *Whren* Reaffirmed

In *Arkansas v. Sullivan,* 532 U.S. 769, 121 S.Ct. 1876, 149 L.Ed.2d 994 (2001), the Court reaffirmed its holding in *Whren,* reversing the Arkansas Supreme Court's holding that the search of Mr. Sullivan's car was illegal because it was based on a pretextual arrest. Justice Ginsburg, joined by Justices Stevens, O'Connor and Breyer, concurred in the decision, "given the Court's current caselaw." Ginsburg referred to the majority opinion in *Atwater,* where the Court claimed a "dearth of horribles demanding redress." Justice Ginsburg expressed a hope that the Court would reconsider *Atwater* if experience demonstrates "anything like an epidemic of unnecessary minor-offense arrests." On remand, the Arkansas Supreme Court ultimately again affirmed the trial court's suppression of the evidence in Mr. Sullivan's case, holding that the pretextual arrest was illegal, this time basing its opinion on state law grounds, *Arkansas v. Sullivan,* 348 Ark. 647, 74 S.W.3d 215 (2002).

B. The Selectivity Problem

The fact that a traffic stop or arrest can be used as a pretext for a more serious investigation that could not otherwise be conducted raises the possibility that these stops or arrests can be used to single out members of a minority group. The petitioners in *Whren*, who were both black, contended that "police officers might decide which motorists to stop based on decidedly impermissible factors, such as the race of the car's occupants." The *Whren* Court agreed that this was a danger, but held that this danger could not be regulated by the Fourth Amendment, with its objective standard of reasonableness. The Court declared that "the constitutional basis for objecting to intentionally discriminatory application of laws is the Equal Protection Clause, not the Fourth Amendment." According to the Court, subjective intentions play no role in ordinary, probable cause Fourth Amendment analysis.

C. Stop or Arrest for Minor Offense Must Itself Be Legal

While officers are permitted to stop or arrest a person for a minor infraction and then use the detention to obtain evidence of a more serious crime, this option is open to officers only if they have reasonable suspicion to stop or probable cause to arrest the suspect for the minor crime. Otherwise, the stop or arrest is itself illegal, pretextual or not. For example, in *United States v. Sanders*, 954 F.2d 227 (4th Cir. 1992), officers suspected Sanders of bank robbery, but had insufficient articulable suspicion to justify a search or seizure as to that crime. They found Sanders' car in a parking lot. Then they saw Sanders get into his car, start it and back it up to the other side of the parking lot. They arrested him for having an expired license tag, and an uninsured vehicle. A subsequent search uncovered evidence of a bank robbery. The court held that the arrest was illegal and the evidence inadmissible, because the traffic offenses for which Sanders was arrested required the operation of a vehicle upon the state's highways, and the officers "lacked any evidence that Sanders' car was driven on a public road."

Search Must Be Within Confines of Minor Offense

It follows from the above that if the officer ostensibly investigating a minor offense goes beyond the scope of a permissible search for that offense, the search will be illegal without regard to the question of pretext. For example, assume that an officer suspects that a driver is a drug courier, but that his suspicion does not rise to the level of probable cause. The officer follows the driver, who changes lanes without signaling, and the officer arrests him for a traffic violation. If the officer searches the passenger compartment and finds drugs, this evidence is legally obtained under *Whren* even if the officer used the traffic arrest as a pretext to search for drugs. However, if the officer searches the *trunk* and finds drugs, this evidence is *illegally* obtained even under *Whren*. This is because the officer, by searching the trunk, exceeded the scope of the search permitted for the traffic violation; *New York v. Belton* allows a search of the passenger compartment incident to a traffic arrest, but does not allow a search of the trunk. The *Whren* analysis on pretext thus does not permit a search unless the officer is acting in accordance with the Fourth Amendment when conducting a search and seizure with respect to a minor offense.

D. *Whren* Extended to Parking Violations

Whren was extended to parking violations in *United States v. Choudhry*, 461 F.3d 1097 (9th Cir. 2006). In *Choudhry*, the defendant was charged with being a felon in possession of a firearm and filed a pretrial motion to suppress evidence seized during an investigatory stop. The defendant argued that a civil parking offense that was enforced through an administrative process could not, standing alone, justify the stop. The court held that because parking infractions constituted traffic violations under California's Vehicle Code, a civil parking violation under the Code fell within the scope of *Whren v. United States*. Accordingly, the parking violation provided the officers with reasonable suspicion to conduct the investigatory stop that ultimately led to the search of the vehicle.

IX. Searches and Seizures of Automobiles and Other Movable Property

A. The Automobile Exception to the Warrant Requirement

The automobile exception allows the police to search an automobile without obtaining a warrant if they have probable cause to believe that the car contains evidence of criminal activity. *Carroll v. United States*, 267 U.S. 132, 45 S.Ct. 280, 69 L.Ed. 543 (1925). This exception does not depend upon probable cause to arrest the driver or any particular individual; the issue instead is whether there is probable cause to believe that evidence is somewhere in the car.

1. The *Carroll* Doctrine

In *Carroll,* the Supreme Court created the automobile exception, upholding a search of a car where the police had probable cause to search the car but had no time to obtain a warrant. The Court emphasized that, in the time it would have taken to obtain a warrant, the car could easily have been moved out of the area.

2. Distinguishing *Carroll* From Search Incident to Arrest

The automobile exception is distinct from the search incident to arrest exception as applied to automobiles. *See New York v. Belton*, discussed *supra.* Under the automobile exception, courts must look at whether the police had probable cause to believe that the car contained evidence of criminal activity. In contrast, the search incident to arrest exception, also referred to as the arrest-power rule, does not depend on the existence of probable cause to search but focuses on the legality of the underlying arrest and the area in which the search occurred.

a. When the Automobile Exception Is Used

The arrest power rule is preferred by the state over the automobile exception, because the state must only establish that there was probable cause to arrest the defendant—at that point the right to search the passenger compartment of the car is *automatic.* In contrast, the automobile exception will not apply unless there is probable cause that evidence will be found in a particular place in the car. Especially with respect to minor offenses such as traffic arrests, the arrest power rule is easier for the state to invoke than is the automobile exception.

However, there are at least three situations in which the arrest power rule will not apply and then the state must try to resort to the automobile exception: 1. Where there is *no arrest* or where the arrest is *not made in or near a car*; 2. Where the search of the car is *too far removed* from the arrest so that it can no longer be deemed incident to the arrest; and 3. Where the officers wish to search the *trunk* of the car.

3. **Warrantless Searches and Seizures of Automobiles**

Carroll seems to be based on the mobility of the car—by the time the officers went to get a warrant, the car would be gone. But this does not explain why a *search* can be conducted without a warrant. It could be argued, instead, that the *Carroll* doctrine could be used only to permit an officer to *seize* a vehicle pending the issuance of a warrant. Seizure would take care of the mobility problem and yet preserve the citizen's privacy interest in the vehicle.

a. *Chambers v. Maroney*

The Supreme Court in *Chambers v. Maroney*, 399 U.S. 42, 90 S.Ct. 1975, 26 L.Ed.2d 419 (1970), rejected the argument that the automobile exception permitted only the warrantless seizure, rather than the warrantless search, of a car. In *Chambers*, the Court upheld the warrantless search at the police station of a car that was seized upon the arrest of the occupants. The Court found that as far as the Fourth Amendment was concerned, there was "no difference between on the one hand seizing and holding a car before presenting the probable cause issue to a magistrate and on the other hand carrying out an immediate search without a warrant."

b. **Justification for the Automobile Exception**

The Court in *Chambers* shed new light on the justification for the automobile exception. Proceeding from the unassailable assumption that the mobility of the car justifies a warrantless seizure (pending the obtaining of a warrant), the Court reasoned as follows: If a warrantless seizure is justified, then a warrantless search is equally justifiable so long as it is no more intrusive than a warrantless seizure would be. The Court concluded that in many cases, the delay involved in seizing a car pending a warrant would be even more intrusive than an immediate search—as to which, if no evidence were uncovered, the citizens could immediately proceed on their way. Therefore, the Court found no reason for police to have to choose between a warrantless seizure and a warrantless search of the car. Since they were basically equal intrusions, the fact that one was justified by the car's mobility meant that either could be done.

c. **Dissent**

Justice Harlan in dissent stated that "a warrantless search involves the greater sacrifice of Fourth Amendment values * * * [because] in the circumstances in which this problem is likely to occur, the lesser intrusion will almost always be the simple seizure of the car for the period—perhaps a day—necessary to enable the officers to obtain a search warrant." He argued that in most cases where probable cause existed to search the car, the driver would be arrested, and would therefore suffer "minimal further inconvenience from the temporary immobilization" of the car pending a warrant. Justice Harlan also found it ironic that "the Court, unable to decide whether search or temporary seizure is the lesser intrusion, in this case authorizes both."

d. **Difference Between Searches and Seizures**

Searches and seizures invade different interests. Searches invade privacy interests while seizures invade possessory interests. In most cases, one would think that a search of a car would be a greater intrusion than the temporary detention of the car pending a warrant—especially since, as Justice Harlan noted, the owner of the car is often incarcerated and cannot use the car at any rate. However, after *Chambers*, the Court explained its equation of automobile searches and seizures by asserting that the search of a car was not in fact a very serious intrusion, due to the fact that a citizen has a *diminished expectation of privacy in a car*. As a result, the search and seizure are equally intrusive, since neither is considered very serious. *See United States v. Chadwick*, 433 U.S. 1, 97 S.Ct. 2476, 53 L.Ed.2d 538 (1977) (distinguishing a car search (not requiring a warrant) from a search of a footlocker (requiring a warrant) on the ground that citizens have a diminished expectation of privacy in cars).

e. Reasons for Diminished Expectation of Privacy in Cars
    According to the Court, individuals have a lesser privacy interest in cars than in other personal containers, such as suitcases, for three reasons. First, a car is a means of *transportation*, in contrast to containers which are used to keep things private. Second, an individual *drives a car in plain view* and other people can see inside the car. Third, a car is *heavily regulated*. Thus, because the search of a car causes a lesser intrusion than, for example, a search of a house or a suitcase, this minimal intrusion is equivalent to that caused by a seizure of the car pending a warrant. The automobile exception therefore allows both the warrantless search and the warrantless seizure of a car, if there is probable cause to believe that there is evidence in the car.

4. **Dual Justification for the Automobile Exception**
    The Supreme Court clarified the basis for the automobile exception to the warrant requirement in *California v. Carney*, 471 U.S. 386, 105 S.Ct. 2066, 85 L.Ed.2d 406 (1985). The Court in *Carney* stated that there are *two justifications* for the automobile exception. Although the mobility of the automobile, as expressed in *Carroll*, remains one basis for the exception, the Court found that the automobile exception is also justified by the diminished expectation of privacy in automobiles. The Court noted that "[e]ven in cases where an automobile was not immediately mobile, the lesser expectation of privacy resulting from its use as a readily mobile vehicle justified application of the vehicular exception." *See United States v. Chadwick*, 433 U.S. 1, 97 S.Ct. 2476, 53 L.Ed.2d 538 (1977) (noting that the Court has upheld warrantless searches of cars "in cases in which the possibilities of the vehicle's being removed or evidence in it destroyed were remote, if not non-existent").

5. Exigency Not a Requirement

Although the mobility of the automobile was a justification for the exception in *Carney*, the Court has explicitly disavowed exigent circumstances as a requirement for the applicability of the automobile exception. In *Pennsylvania v. Labron*, 518 U.S. 938, 116 S.Ct. 2485, 135 L.Ed.2d 1031 (1996) and *Maryland v. Dyson*, 527 U.S. 465, 119 S.Ct. 2013, 144 L.Ed.2d 442 (1999), the Court upheld warrantless searches of automobiles where there was no risk of destruction of evidence or any other exigency that would have prevented the police from obtaining a warrant. In *Dyson*, the Court specifically stated that "the automobile exception has no separate exigency requirement."

6. Application of the Automobile Exception to Mobile Homes

In *Carney*, the Court held that the automobile exception justified a warrantless search of a mobile home. Rejecting the argument that mobile homes are necessarily different from other vehicles, the Court reasoned that such a distinction "would require that [the Court] apply the exception depending on the size of the vehicle and the quality of its appointments." The Court did not address whether the automobile exception would apply to a mobile home "that is situated in a way or place that objectively indicates that it is being used as a residence." In *Carney*, this was clearly not the case, since the mobile home was parked in a parking lot and was not hooked up to utilities or plumbing. It was thus more like a car than a house.

7. The Automobile Exception as Applied to Airplanes

In *United States v. Nigro*, 727 F.2d 100 (6th Cir. 1984), the court extended the automobile exception to airplanes. Although the plane was immobilized when the warrantless search occurred, the court held that "[t]he automobile exception has always depended on the inherent mobility of the vehicle to be searched, not on whether it could in fact be used immediately to effect a removal of evidence once existing officers have determined that they have probable cause to search it and have taken steps to prevent its departure."

B. Movable Property—In and Out of Cars

Because the automobile exception is based on the diminished expectation of privacy in vehicles as well as on their mobility, the exception does not permit warrantless searches of other containers, even if these containers are mobile. The Supreme Court distinguished between cars and other containers in *United States v. Chadwick*, 433 U.S. 1, 97 S.Ct. 2476, 53 L.Ed.2d 538 (1977).

1. *Chadwick*

In *Chadwick,* the police, having probable cause but no warrant, seized a footlocker, brought it to the police station, and then searched it and discovered drugs. Although the footlocker was found in the trunk of a defendant's car, the Government did not argue that the footlocker's brief contact with the car made it part of an automobile search. Rather, the Government argued that since the container was mobile, it should be treated the same as a car. The Supreme Court held that the mobility of the footlocker permitted a *seizure* pending a warrant, but that the police needed a warrant to *search* the footlocker unless exigent circumstances were present (such as if the footlocker contained an explosive).

Distinguishing between cars and other containers, the Court stated that "[t]he factors which diminish the privacy aspects of an automobile do not apply to respondents' footlocker." According to the Court, luggage and other similar containers are not open to public view, in contrast to a car. In addition, luggage functions to keep things private, while cars are a means of transportation. Thus, expectations of privacy are substantially greater in luggage than in an automobile. Because of the diminished expectation of privacy in a car, the Court in *Chambers* considered a warrantless search to be no more intrusive than a seizure pending a warrant. But the same could not be said of a container. The Court in *Chadwick* refused to equate a search of a container with its seizure, on the ground that the search would invade a significant expectation of privacy in the contents of the container. Under *Chadwick,* the police may seize containers if they have probable cause to believe the container holds evidence of criminal activity, but they must generally obtain a warrant before searching them, unless exigent circumstances are actually present.

2. **Containers in Cars**

Because a warrant is required to search a container but not a car, it was unclear after *Chadwick* whether the container rule or the car rule applied to containers found in cars.

a. Clash Between Container Rule and Car Rule in *Sanders* and *Ross*

In *Arkansas v. Sanders,* 442 U.S. 753, 99 S.Ct. 2586, 61 L.Ed.2d 235 (1979), the police observed Sanders exit an airport carrying a green suitcase after they received an informant's tip that he would do so and that the suitcase would contain marijuana. Sanders' companion placed the suitcase in a trunk of the taxi. In *Sanders,* the Court held that the police needed a warrant to search the suitcase found in the trunk of the taxi. In *United States v. Ross*, 456 U.S. 798, 102 S.Ct. 2157, 72 L.Ed.2d 572 (1982), however, the Court held that the warrantless search of a bag found during the search of a car did not violate the Fourth Amendment.

b. **The *Ross* Rule**

The Court in *Ross* stated that if probable cause is focused particularly on a container within the car, but no probable cause exists to search the car generally, the container rule applies and the police must obtain a warrant before searching the container. This was the case in *Sanders*, where the officers had probable cause to search the suitcase but not the taxi. But the Court in *Ross* further stated that if the police have probable cause to search the car and, in the course of the search, discover a container, the police may search the container. This type of probable cause was called "car-wide" probable cause. Because the officers in *Ross* had probable cause to search the car, as opposed to specific probable cause to search the container, the warrantless search was upheld. The *Ross* Court found that "the practical consequences of the *Carroll* decision would be largely nullified if the permissible scope of a warrantless search of an automobile did not include containers and packages found inside the vehicle * * * [as] [c]ontraband goods rarely are strewn across the trunk or floor of a car."

c. **The *Ross* Anomaly**

The *Ross* distinction between car-wide probable cause and container-specific probable cause created difficulty. It meant that a warrant was not required if officers had general knowledge about criminal activity, but a warrant was required if the officer's information was more specific. Thus, under *Ross*, if the officer received a reliable tip that the suspect was dealing drugs out of his car, the officer could search the car without a warrant and he could open all the containers in the car which could contain drugs. However, if the officer received a reliable tip that the defendant had a suitcase full of drugs in his car, then the officer would need a warrant to open the suitcase, because the probable cause would be specific to the suitcase rather than car-wide. Officers actually had an incentive to know less rather than more.

d. ***California v. Acevedo:* Resolving the Anomalies**

The Supreme Court in *California v. Acevedo*, 500 U.S. 565, 111 S.Ct. 1982, 114 L.Ed.2d 619 (1991), found that the *Ross* distinction of

Sanders (i.e., the distinction between car-wide and particularized probable cause) was unsupportable in logic and practice. Thus, the Court overruled *Sanders* and held that the police may search any container located in a car, without a warrant, so long as they have probable cause to believe that it holds evidence of criminal activity. The *Acevedo* Court held that "the Fourth Amendment does not compel separate treatment for an automobile search that extends only to a container within the vehicle." Thus, the Court concluded that "it is better to adopt one clear-cut rule to govern automobile searches and eliminate the warrant requirement for closed containers set forth in *Sanders*."

Critique of *Acevedo* Rule

Justice Stevens, joined by Justice Marshall, dissented in *Acevedo*, stating that "[t]o the extent there was any anomaly in our prior jurisprudence, the Court has cured it at the expense of creating a more serious paradox. For, surely it is anomalous to prohibit a search of a briefcase while the owner is carrying it exposed on a public street yet to permit a search once the owner has placed the briefcase in the locked trunk of his car." Thus, after *Acevedo*, an officer needs a warrant to open a container—until the container is placed in a car. Moreover, there is still the need to determine whether probable cause exists to search a container found in a car.

e. ### Search of a Passenger's Property

In *Ross* and *Acevedo*, the containers clearly belonged to the drivers of the cars. In *Wyoming v. Houghton*, 526 U.S. 295, 119 S.Ct. 1297, 143 L.Ed.2d 408 (1999), the Court addressed the issue of whether police officers may search containers in a car that clearly belong to a passenger. In *Houghton*, a police officer stopped a car for a traffic violation, noticed a hypodermic syringe in the driver's shirt pocket, and ordered the driver out of the car. After the driver admitted that he used the syringe to take drugs, the officer ordered the two passengers out of the car and searched the passenger compartment of the car for contraband. He found a purse on the back seat, and one of the passengers, Sandra Houghton, informed the officer that it belonged to her. The officer searched the purse and found drugs and paraphernalia. Houghton was arrested. The Wyoming Supreme Court reversed Houghton's conviction, finding that the officer knew that the bag did not belong to the driver and that there was no probable cause to search Houghton's bag. The Supreme Court reversed, holding that the officer had probable cause to search the car and any containers in the car that might contain the object of the search. Citing *Zurcher v. Stanford Daily, supra,* the Court stated, "The critical element in a reasonable search is not that the owner of the property is suspected of crime but that there is reasonable cause to believe that the specific 'things' to be searched for and seized are located on the property to which entry is sought." The Court also found that passengers, like drivers, have a reduced expectation of privacy in property that they carry in cars and that passengers "will often be engaged in a common enterprise with the driver, and have the same interest in concealing the fruits or the evidence of their wrongdoing."

i.   Dissent in *Houghton*

Justices Stevens, Souter and Ginsburg dissented, noting that the Wyoming Supreme Court concluded that there was no probable cause to search Houghton's purse. They agreed with that conclusion, pointing out that the spatial association between a passenger and a driver does not provide an acceptable basis for presuming that they are partners in crime. The dissent noted that under the Court's ruling, if a police officer had probable cause to believe a cabdriver had a syringe somewhere in his cab, he would be permitted to search the briefcase of a passenger in the cab who clearly has no connection to the driver.

X. Consent Searches

When police officers obtain consent to search, they need not possess a warrant or any articulable suspicion. A search based on valid consent is reasonable and thus does not violate the Fourth Amendment.

A. Consent Must Be Voluntary

In order to be reasonable, consent to search must be voluntarily obtained. The Supreme Court addressed this issue in *Schneckloth v. Bustamonte,* 412 U.S. 218, 93 S.Ct. 2041, 36 L.Ed.2d 854 (1973).

1. *Schneckloth v. Bustamonte*

In *Bustamonte,* a police officer stopped a car due to a traffic infraction. Six people were in the car. The officer asked an occupant if he could search the car. The man agreed and opened the trunk for the officer. Later, he objected that his consent was involuntary because he never knew that he had a right to refuse the officer's request.

a. Test for Voluntariness of Consent

The Court in *Bustamonte* stated that "the question whether a consent to search was in fact voluntary or was the product of duress or coercion, express or implied, is a question of fact to be determined from the totality of the circumstances." The Court distinguished the traditional concept of waiver from consent to search. The question of waiver is determined by whether the defendant knew his right, and, knowing the consequences of a waiver, voluntarily decided to forego his right. A waiver cannot be obtained in the absence of knowledge of the right. In contrast, where the issue is consent to search, the proper test focuses not on whether the defendant waived his Fourth Amendment rights but instead on whether the consent to search was voluntary under the totality of the circumstances. The Court concluded that "[w]hile knowledge of the right to refuse consent is one factor to be taken into account, the government *need not establish such knowledge* as the sine qua non of an effective consent." Although defendants need not know of their right to refuse in order for consent to be voluntary, such consent cannot be "coerced, by explicit or implicit means, by implied threat or covert force."

2. Burden of Proof

The state has the burden of showing that consent was voluntary by a preponderance of the evidence. *See Bumper v. North Carolina*, 391 U.S. 543, 88 S.Ct. 1788, 20 L.Ed.2d 797 (1968) (holding that the burden of proving that consent was "freely and voluntarily given" rests with the prosecution and "[t]his burden cannot be discharged by showing no more than acquiescence to a claim of lawful authority").

3. Factors Relevant to Voluntariness

According to *Bustamonte*, consent need not be knowing or intelligent but must only be voluntary to support a valid search. To determine whether consent is voluntary, courts must analyze whether a person's free will to refuse consent was overborne by police coercion. In *United States v. Gonzalez–Basulto*, 898 F.2d 1011 (5th Cir. 1990), the Fifth Circuit listed some of the factors that are relevant in determining whether consent is voluntarily obtained. These factors are: 1. the voluntariness of the defendant's *custodial status*; 2. the presence of *coercive police procedures*; 3. the extent and level of the defendant's *cooperation* with the police; 4. the defendant's *awareness of his right to refuse consent*; 5. the defendant's *education and intelligence*; and 6. the defendant's *belief that no incriminating evidence will be found.* No single factor is dispositive. *See, e.g., United States v. Watson,* 423 U.S. 411, 96 S.Ct. 820, 46 L.Ed.2d 598 (1976) (finding consent voluntary even though the defendant was under arrest). The court in *Gonzalez-Basulto* found that the defendant voluntarily consented to the search of his trailer by relying on the following facts: the border patrol agents did not use any force or threaten the defendant; the defendant was not under arrest when the consent was obtained; the evidence was well-hidden so the defendant may have expected that it would not be found; and the defendant cooperated with the agents when they requested his consent.

a. **The Right to Refuse Consent**

The police do not have to inform the suspect of his right to refuse consent, and the suspect's lack of knowledge regarding this right does not in itself vitiate consent. *Schneckloth v. Bustamonte,* 412 U.S. 218, 93 S.Ct. 2041, 36 L.Ed.2d 854 (1973). The lack of a warning informing the suspect that he may refuse consent is simply a factor to be considered in the "totality of the circumstances." Although such a warning is not required, the presence of a warning strongly indicates that the consent was voluntarily obtained.

b. **Consent After Completion of a Stop**

In *Ohio v. Robinette,* 519 U.S. 33, 117 S.Ct. 417, 136 L.Ed.2d 347 (1996), a police officer stopped a driver for speeding. After checking the driver's license and finding no violations, he gave the driver, Robinette, a verbal warning. When the officer gave Robinette his license back, the officer asked him whether he had weapons or drugs in his car. When Robinette said no, the officer asked for, and received, permission to search the car. The search turned up drugs. Robinette argued that the consent was not voluntary, because the officer never told him that the stop was over and he was free to go. But the Court found that it was "unrealistic to require police officers to always inform detainees that they are free to go before a consent search may be deemed voluntary." The voluntariness of consent is dependent on the totality of circumstances. Like a warning that the defendant is free to refuse to consent, a warning that the defendant is free to leave is only one of the totality of circumstances bearing upon voluntariness.

4. Threat of a Warrant

Sometimes police officers inform suspects that, if they do not consent to a search, the officers simply will obtain a warrant. Whether such a threat renders the consent involuntary depends on the facts of the case.

a. **False Statement Concerning the Possession of a Warrant Renders the Consent Involuntary**

In *Bumper v. North Carolina*, 391 U.S. 543, 88 S.Ct. 1788, 20 L.Ed.2d 797 (1968), the police told the defendant's grandmother that they had a warrant to search her home although they did not possess one. The grandmother subsequently consented to the search. The Supreme Court held that where the police falsely claim that they have a search warrant and the person consents to the search because of this claim, the evidence must be suppressed because the police have actively misinformed the person as to his situation. A similar result must also occur where the police received consent after incorrectly asserting or intimating that they have the right to make a warrantless search under the circumstances.

b. **Genuine Expressions of Intent to Obtain a Warrant Do Not Render Consent Involuntary**

If the threat to obtain a warrant is factually correct as opposed to an empty threat, then it does not render the consent involuntary. For example, in *United States v. White*, 979 F.2d 539 (7th Cir. 1992), the police sought consent from the defendant's wife to search their home, and threatened to obtain a search warrant if she refused to agree to the search. Noting that "[b]aseless threats to obtain a search warrant may render consent involuntary," the court found that the expressed intention to obtain a warrant does not vitiate consent when it is genuine, i.e., where the police have probable cause. The court found that White's wife freely consented to the search, as the police had probable cause to search the premises and there was no indication that they were making an empty threat.

5. Use of Force

If the police use force while requesting consent, citizens may legitimately feel that they do not have a right to refuse. But whether use of force vitiates the voluntariness of consent is determined on a case-by-case basis. For example, in *United States v. Kelley*, 953 F.2d 562 (9th Cir. 1992), an armed F.B.I. agent ordered a woman to lie prone on the ground while her children were crying and running about nearby. The court found her subsequent consent to be voluntary because the police requested her consent after she was allowed to stand up, she was informed that she was not under arrest, and her children had stopped crying. On the other hand, if the officer beats the suspect in order to obtain consent, the court will of course determine the consent to be involuntary.

6. When the Suspect Is in Custody

The fact that a person is in custody and under police control is relevant but not determinative of the voluntariness of consent. In *United States v. Watson*, 423 U.S. 411, 96 S.Ct. 820, 46 L.Ed.2d 598 (1976), the Supreme Court applied the principles of *Bustamonte* and held that the fact of custody alone is not enough to demonstrate that consent was coerced. The Court in *Watson* found the defendant's consent to be voluntary where he "had been arrested and was in custody, but his consent was given while on a public street, not in the confines of a police station." According to the Court, "to hold that illegal coercion is made out from the fact of arrest and the failure to inform the arrestee that he could withhold consent would not be consistent with *Schneckloth*."

Watson has been extended to permit consent searches that are obtained at the police station. So long as there is no other indication that the suspect's will was overborne, the mere fact that the consent was obtained at the police station does not render the consent involuntary. *See, e.g., United States v. Smith*, 543 F.2d 1141 (5th Cir. 1976) (holding that "[t]he fact that Smith gave his consent when he was in custody at the police station, while another factor in the overall judgment, does not justify a departure from the totality of circumstances approach established in *Schneckloth* and *Watson*").

7. Requests for Consent

Requests by police officers are less coercive than demands. Thus, whether the police request or demand consent is a relevant factor in determining the voluntariness of consent. In *United States v. Mendenhall*, 446 U.S. 544, 100 S.Ct. 1870, 64 L.Ed.2d 497 (1980), the defendant agreed to accompany police officers to their airport office and to allow them to search her purse and her person. Holding that the consent was voluntary, the Court noted that the police simply asked her to accompany them to the office and she was not threatened or physically forced. Also, she was informed twice that she was free to decline consent. In contrast, in *United States v. Jaras*, 86 F.3d 383 (5th Cir. 1996), the court refused to find a valid consent search when officers opened the defendant's suitcases without even asking permission. The fact that the defendant appeared to "acquiesce" was not enough: consent could not be "inferred from Jaras's silence and failure to object because the police officer did not expressly or implicitly request Jaras's consent prior to the search."

8. The Character and Emotional State of the Suspect

The character of an individual and his susceptibility to police coercion may help determine whether his consent was voluntary.

a. Suspect's Lack of Education Relevant to Involuntariness

For example, in *United States v. Jones,* 846 F.2d 358 (6th Cir. 1988), the court held that the defendant, who was a convicted felon, did not voluntarily consent to a search of his home when he was stopped by three police cars, was not informed of his right to refuse consent, and had no formal education. In holding the consent involuntary, the court stressed that the defendant only possessed a fourth grade education. *Compare United States v. Lattimore,* 87 F.3d 647 (4th Cir. 1996) (voluntary consent found; court emphasizes that the defendant was "29 years old, had a high school education, and held employment with the United States Postal Service").

b. Suspect's Impaired Mental or Emotional Condition Does Not Necessarily Render Consent Involuntary

In *United States v. Hall,* 969 F.2d 1102 (D.C. Cir. 1992), the defendant claimed that she did not voluntarily consent to the search of her bag because she possessed an IQ which, according to her expert witness, placed her in the borderline range between low-average and mild retardation. In addition, the defendant testified that she only received a ninth grade education, she attended special education programs from the fourth through the ninth grades, and she received counseling for certain psychological problems during that time period. She also stated that the police did not inform her of her right to refuse consent. The court stated that the "voluntariness inquiry turns not on whether a reasonable person in the defendant's position would have felt compelled to consent to a police officer's request to search, but, rather, on whether the *accused herself* actually felt compelled to consent." Therefore, it was relevant that the defendant was mentally impaired. But the court stressed that the defendant's mental impairment did not preclude her from giving voluntary consent.

Reviewing the "totality of the circumstances," the court noted that the level of pressure applied to the defendant by the officers was minimal and that the defendant demonstrated a capacity to make autonomous decisions in the face of police questioning. The court thus found that the defendant's consent was voluntarily obtained.

9. The Suspect's Belief That Evidence Would Be Found

Defendants sometimes argue that their consent could not have been voluntarily obtained because they knew before the search that the police officers would find incriminating evidence. The contention is that no person could voluntarily consent to a search that would uncover incriminating evidence. But acceptance of such an argument would result in suppression of the evidence found in most consent searches. In *Mendenhall*, discussed *supra*, the Court categorically rejected the argument that a search could not be voluntary if the suspect knew that evidence would be found. The Court stated that although a suspect may later regret having given consent, "the question is not whether she acted in her ultimate self-interest, but whether she acted voluntarily."

10. When Evidence Is Well–Hidden

Conversely, the fact that evidence was well-hidden has been considered by most courts to be relevant to the voluntariness of the consent. The rationale is that the suspect is more likely to consent voluntarily if he has the expectation that evidence is so well-hidden that it will not be found. *See, e.g., United States v. Gonzalez–Basulto*, 898 F.2d 1011 (5th Cir. 1990), (finding that "Gonzalez may well have believed that no drugs would be found because the cocaine was hidden in boxes toward the front of the trailer and there was little crawl space in the trailer").

B. Third Party Consent

A third party may consent to the search of an area in which a suspect has an expectation of privacy, if the third party voluntarily consents to the search and has authority to consent to the search of the area. *United States v. Matlock*, 415 U.S. 164, 94 S.Ct. 988, 39 L.Ed.2d 242 (1974).

1. Rationales for Allowing Third Party Consent

Third party consent is justified on two grounds. First, if third parties have access or control over a private area, they have an *independent privacy interest* in that area and an independent right to forego such interests. Second, because the suspect has granted a third party access to a private area, the suspect has *assumed the risk* that the third party may consent to a search.

Example: In *Frazier v. Cupp*, 394 U.S. 731, 89 S.Ct. 1420, 22 L.Ed.2d 684 (1969), the Supreme Court upheld the search of the defendant's bag when his cousin consented to the search. The defendant's cousin was a joint user of the bag. Although the cousin possessed authority to use only one compartment of the bag, the Court upheld the search of the remainder, stating that it would not "engage in such metaphysical subtleties." The Court stated that by allowing his cousin to use the bag, the defendant assumed the risk that his cousin would consent to a search.

2.   Limited Access May Restrict Authority to Consent to a Search

In some circumstances, a third party's access to an area may be limited or conditional. When access is granted for such limited purposes, the third party may not possess the authority to consent to a search, or the grant of access may restrict the authority to consent. For example, in *United States v. Brown*, 961 F.2d 1039 (2d Cir. 1992), the defendant's landlady had access to his apartment to turn off the electricity when the power would short-circuit. Noting that "authority granted for a limited purpose does not translate into a general authority to authorize a search," the court held that the evidence obtained as a result of the landlady's consent should have been suppressed.

a.   Areas of Access

A third party's access may also be limited by location. If a third party possesses common authority as to only part of the premises, this factor does not imply authority to consent to the search of the entire premises. For example, roommates in a shared apartment or house may have areas of exclusive control, as to which the other person may not consent. Or, a passenger of a car may have placed his suitcase in the driver's trunk—the fact that it is placed there does not in itself give the driver the authority to open it. *See United States v. Jaras*, 86 F.3d 383 (5th Cir. 1996) (search of passenger's luggage could not be justified by voluntary consent of the driver).

b.   Marital Relationships

In marital relationships, most courts have held that there is a presumption of common authority over premises jointly occupied by both spouses. *See United States v. Harrison*, 679 F.2d 942, 947 (D.C. Cir. 1982) (upholding consent of defendant's wife as the wife had full "common authority" over storage area in the basement); *United*

States v. Stone, 471 F.2d 170, 173 (7th Cir. 1972) (holding that where husband and wife have equal rights to the use of the premises, wife's voluntary consent to search is binding on husband). According to these courts, where a defendant's spouse consented to a search of a particular area, the burden is on the defendant to show that the consenting spouse was denied access to that area.

Example: In *United States v. Duran*, 957 F.2d 499 (7th Cir. 1992), the defendant's wife consented to a search of an old farmhouse on their property. The defendant argued that his wife did not have joint access to or control of the farmhouse, and thus had no authority to consent to its search. Leaving open the possibility that one spouse may maintain exclusive control over certain portions of the family homestead, the court held that "a spouse presumptively has authority to consent to a search of all areas of the homestead; the non-consenting spouse may rebut this presumption only by showing that the consenting spouse was denied access to the particular area searched." Applying this standard to the facts in *Duran*, the court held that the defendant failed to rebut the presumption of common authority. The wife's testimony indicated that although she never entered the barn, she *could have entered* the barn if she had desired. According to the court, "[o]ne can have access to a building or a room but choose not to enter."

c.   Consent by Parents and Children

Cases involving third party consent by parents and children raise the issue of whether the parent or child possessed the authority to consent to a search of a particular private area. Some courts have held that parents with control over the entire premises may validly consent to a search of the premises, unless there is a part of the premises which is clearly and exclusively reserved for a child. *See, e.g., United States v. Peterson*, 524 F.2d 167 (4th Cir. 1975) (holding that mother of one defendant was vested with sufficient authority to consent to a search of a bedroom occupied by that defendant and his two brothers in his mother's home); *In re Scott K.*, 24 Cal.3d 395, 155 Cal.Rptr. 671, 595 P.2d 105 (1979) (holding that where locked toolbox belonged to minor and minor refused to consent, consent obtained from minor's father violated the Fourth Amendment). But courts have been reluctant to allow minor children to consent to searches of homes. *See, e.g., Padron v. State,* 328 So.2d 216 (Fla. App. 4th Dist. 1976) (holding that defendant's 16-year-old son did not share common authority with defendant over the premises and therefore could not consent to a search).

3. Retention of Ownership Interest

Authority to consent to a search may stem from an ownership interest in the property. For example, in *United States v. Davis,* 967 F.2d 84 (2d Cir. 1992), police officers received consent to search a footlocker from defendant's friend, Cleare, who told the officers that he had given the defendant a key to his apartment and that the defendant had left some belongings in Cleare's footlocker. Holding the third party consent valid, the court noted that Cleare obviously had access to the trunk as he lived in the apartment and kept the trunk, which belonged to him, in his own bedroom. Although Cleare allowed the defendant to store items in the footlocker, they never agreed that Cleare could not look inside. In addition, Cleare had a substantial interest in the footlocker as he owned the trunk and kept many of his possessions there. According to the court, Cleare possessed common authority over the footlocker even though the defendant had the only key that opened it. *See also United States v. Wright,* 971 F.2d 176 (8th Cir. 1992) (holding that "Smith possessed authority to consent to a search of his own home, including the guest bedroom where [the defendant] spent the evening").

4. Presence of Defendant and Defendant's Refusal to Consent

If the defendant is present and objects when the police ask for consent to search, many courts have held that any third party consent obtained by the police is invalid. *See, e.g., United States v. Impink,* 728 F.2d 1228 (9th Cir. 1984) (holding no third party consent is possible where the defendant is present and objecting). Other courts have held, however, that one party may consent to the search even where the other party is present when the consent is sought, and objects to such a search. *See People v. Cosme,* 48 N.Y.2d 286, 422 N.Y.S.2d 652, 397 N.E.2d 1319 (1979) (holding search reasonable upon third party consent even though defendant is present and objecting).

5. The Third Party Must Possess Actual or Apparent Authority

The Supreme Court has held that third party consent is valid if the third party possesses actual or apparent authority.

a. Actual Authority: *United States v. Matlock*
   In *United States v. Matlock*, 415 U.S. 164, 94 S.Ct. 988, 39 L.Ed.2d 242 (1974), the defendant was arrested in front of a house. A woman allowed the police to enter and search the house, stating that she shared the house with the defendant. The Supreme Court held that the search was a valid consent search, because the woman had actual authority to consent to a search of the premises. The Court stated that "the consent of one who possesses common authority over [the] premises * * * is valid as against the absent non-consenting person with whom that authority is shared." According to the Court, "the authority which justifies the third-party consent does not rest upon the law of property * * * but rests rather on mutual use of the property by persons generally having joint access or control for most purposes." *See United States v. Butler*, 966 F.2d 559 (10th Cir. 1992) (holding that third party had joint access to the searched premises, inasmuch as she had lived with the defendant and shared the same bedroom and was thus in a position to give effective consent to a search).

b. Apparent Authority: *Illinois v. Rodriguez*
   In *Illinois v. Rodriguez*, 497 U.S. 177, 110 S.Ct. 2793, 111 L.Ed.2d 148 (1990), the Court considered an issue it left open in *United States v. Matlock*. The third party in *Rodriguez* was Rodriguez's woman friend, who had, unknown to the officers, moved out of his apartment a month before the search and retained a key without permission. The Court observed that the friend did not have actual authority to consent to a search of the apartment, as she had no joint access or control of the premises after moving out. But the Court held that the officers' *reasonable belief* in the friend's authority to consent (i.e., apparent authority) would validate the entry.

c. Distinguishing Between Consent Searches and Waivers of Fourth Amendment Rights
   Rodriguez argued that, if a reasonable belief of common authority could validate a search, the third party would in effect be making an unauthorized waiver of defendant's Fourth Amendment rights. But the Court responded that this argument confused the standard of waiver of constitutional rights with the standard for voluntary consent searches established by *Schneckloth v. Bustamonte*. Consent does not constitute a waiver of Fourth Amendment rights, but rather satisfies the Fourth Amendment requirement that a search be reasonable.

d. Question of Authority Is Governed by the Standard of Reasonableness

Because *Bustamonte* requires only that consent searches be reasonable, the officers who obtain consent from a third party are entitled to make reasonable mistakes concerning that party's authority to consent. Therefore, under *Rodriguez,* third party consent is valid where an officer would have possessed valid consent to search if the facts were as he reasonably believed them to be. *See United States v. Englebrecht,* 917 F.2d 376 (8th Cir. 1990) (applying this standard and finding apparent authority for third party consent where "an individual who had been living in the same farmhouse with as well as working for Englebrecht consented to the search of the vehicles, which were parked near the farmhouse"). *See also United States v. McAlpine,* 919 F.2d 1461 (10th Cir. 1990) (holding that police could have reasonably believed that woman who reported that she was being held against her will by two men who had been sexually assaulting her was qualified to give effective consent to search of entire trailer where she had been held for two months).

e. Police Officers Must Make Reasonable Inquiries to Determine Whether Third Party Possesses Apparent Authority

The Court in *Rodriguez* stressed that the police could not presume third party consent merely upon the assertion of the third party that he has common authority. The surrounding circumstances could be such that a reasonable person would doubt the truth of such an assertion. If the facts demand further inquiry, and more facts would be relatively easy to ascertain, then a duty of inquiry will be imposed under the Fourth Amendment standard of reasonableness.

Examples: In *United States v. Rosario,* 962 F.2d 733 (7th Cir. 1992), police officers responded to a call by a motel clerk that a marijuana odor was present outside of a motel room. The officers knocked on the door and claimed that a man, later identified as Rubin Vilaro, opened the door and consented to their entry. The defendant argued that "compared to the police in *Rodriguez,* the officers in the instant case had no information regarding Vilaro's authority to consent to the search of [the defendants'] room." The court held that the police officers obtained enough information during their brief encounter with Vilaro to make a reasoned judgment about his authority to admit them into his room. "Nothing about Vilaro's speech or mannerism suggested that he needed to obtain someone else's approval to permit the entrance of the officers." In addition, the court found that "[b]y allowing Vilaro unfettered access to the door, the appellants also gave him discretion to decide whom to admit, thereby sacrificing some degree of their privacy." The court noted, however, that in the absence of sufficient facts, officers have a duty to seek further information to determine whether they may reasonably infer that the third party has actual authority to consent to the search or entry.

A case in which further inquiry was found necessary is *United States v. Salinas–Cano*, 959 F.2d 861 (10th Cir. 1992). There, the police received consent from the defendant's girlfriend to search her apartment after informing her that they were particularly interested in the defendant's belongings. The girlfriend consented to the search of the defendant's unlocked suitcase, which he had left at the apartment. The court rejected the Government's argument that the girlfriend possessed apparent authority under *Rodriguez* to consent to the search of the suitcase. The court stated that "[t]he information known to the officer was insufficient to support a reasonable belief in [the girlfriend's] authority."

f. **Third Party Consent May Be Based on Actual or Apparent Authority**

After *Rodriguez*, a third party consent search can be supported by *either* actual or apparent authority. Although the *Rodriguez* fact situation concerns apparent but not actual authority, a consent search would be equally reasonable if based upon actual but not apparent authority. *See, e.g., United States v. Chaidez*, 919 F.2d 1193 (7th Cir. 1990) (holding that although it was unreasonable to infer authority when person consenting to search said that she did not live in the house and was there only to do laundry, the fact that she had actual authority from the owner justified the search).

g. Difference Between Mistakes of Fact and Mistakes of Law

In *Stoner v. California*, 376 U.S. 483, 84 S.Ct. 889, 11 L.Ed.2d 856 (1964), the Court held that a warrantless search of the defendant's hotel room could not be based on the consent of the desk clerk. Rejecting the Government's argument that the officers properly relied on the apparent authority of the clerk, the Court stated that "the rights protected by the Fourth Amendment are not to be eroded by unrealistic doctrines of apparent authority." Although the holding in *Rodriguez* seems to contradict *Stoner*, the cases can be distinguished because the error by the officers as to the third party's authority in *Rodriguez* was one of *fact*, while the error by the officers in *Stoner* was one of *law*.

The officers in *Stoner* knew that the third party was a desk clerk and that the room was rented. They could not have reasonably believed that the clerk had the authority to allow entry into the room, because, as a legal matter, a hotel clerk does not possess the authority to allow entry into the room of a paying tenant. A mistake of law does not come within the apparent authority doctrine, as the Court in both *Stoner* and *Rodriguez* recognized.

6. Third Party Consent Where the Defendant Is Present and Objecting

In *Georgia v. Randolph*, 547 U.S. 103, 126 S.Ct. 1515, 164 L.Ed.2d 208 (2006) the defendant was arrested for drug possession after police found cocaine in his home. The police did not have a warrant to search the home, but the defendant's wife consented to the search. The defendant was present at the time of the search, however, and objected to the police request to search. The Supreme Court held that when two co-occupants are present and one consents to a search while the other refuses, the search is not constitutional.

The dissent emphasized that the Court's holding was somewhat random in its application, noting that the defendant in *Matlock* was in a squad car not far away and the *Rodriguez* defendant was actually asleep inside the apartment when third parties consented to the searches in these cases. According to the dissent, the Court's holding would protect a co-occupant who just happened to be at the same location as the other occupant but not a resident who was in the next room napping. The majority acknowledged that it was "drawing a fine line" and that its decision was somewhat formalistic. Nonetheless, the Court asserted that this formalism was justified as long as the police did not remove potentially objecting tenants from the scene to avoid a possible objection.

C. Scope of Consent

Even if the consent is voluntary—whether from the defendant or from a third party with actual or apparent authority—the consenting party may place limitations on the scope of the consent. A search is not a valid consent search if a reasonable person would conclude that it exceeds the limitations established by the consenting party. *See, e.g., United States v. Towns,* 913 F.2d 434 (7th Cir. 1990) (holding that consent for entry into an apartment to look at defendant's identification did not permit a thorough seven hour search of the apartment).

1. Officer Must Reasonably Believe That the Defendant Consented to the Area Searched

In construing the scope of consent, the question is whether a reasonable police officer would believe that the defendant consented to the search of the area that the officer searched. Reasonable mistakes as to the suspect's consent are therefore permitted.

a. *Florida v. Jimeno*

In *Florida v. Jimeno,* 500 U.S. 248, 111 S.Ct. 1801, 114 L.Ed.2d 297 (1991), the Court held that an officer reasonably concluded that when a suspect gave general consent to a search of his car, he also consented to a search of a paper bag lying on the floor of the car. According to the Court, "the scope of a search is generally defined by its expressed object." In *Jimeno,* the officer told the defendant that he was looking for narcotics in the car. Jimeno consented and did not explicitly limit the scope of the search. The officer thereupon searched the car and found a bag in the passenger compartment. He searched the bag and found narcotics. The Court found that "a reasonable person might be expected to know that narcotics are carried in some form of container" and therefore that the search of the bag was within the scope of the general consent to search the car.

b. Distinguishing Between the Bag Found in the Car and a Locked Briefcase

In *Jimeno,* the Court distinguished the facts of the case from a situation where an officer received consent to search a trunk and pried open a locked briefcase found inside. The Court noted that "it is very likely unreasonable to think that a suspect, by consenting to the search of his trunk, has agreed to the breaking open of a locked briefcase within the trunk, but it is otherwise with a paper bag."

2. Ambiguity Regarding the Scope of the Consent Is Construed Against the Citizen

The *Jimeno* decision generally establishes that any ambiguity in the scope of the consent is construed against the citizen. So long as the officer's interpretation of an ambiguous or general consent is at all reasonable, the resulting search will be deemed within the scope of the consent, even if the citizen did not intend the consent to reach that far. It is up to the suspect to clarify the scope of an ambiguous consent. This can be done by imposing specific limitations at the outset, or by terminating the search if it proceeds to areas which the suspect wishes to keep private.

Examples: In *United States v. Berke*, 930 F.2d 1219 (7th Cir. 1991), the defendant, when asked by the officer if he could "look" into his bag, said yes. The officer proceeded to search the bag thoroughly, and discovered narcotics hidden at the bottom of the bag. The defendant argued that consent to "look" did not permit the officer to rummage through the bag. The court rejected this argument and held that the defendant's consent permitted a thorough search of the bag because the officer could reasonably believe that "look" meant "search." The court noted that the defendant did not ask for clarification of what the officer meant when he said he wanted to "look" inside.

In *United States v. Jackson*, 381 F.3d 984 (10th Cir. 2004), a DEA agent approached Jackson on an Amtrak train, identified himself as a DEA agent, and asked if he could search Jackson's luggage for narcotics. Jackson gave him permission to do so, and the DEA agent looked through Jackson's bag where he found a shaving kit. The agent opened the shaving kit and found a baby powder container. The agent removed the lid of the container and found cocaine. The court found that the scope of Jackson's consent to the search was not exceeded since the DEA agent told Jackson that his purpose was to search for narcotics and that Jackson's consent to the search "could be reasonably construed as consent to search any containers within the bag which could have held narcotics, such as the baby powder container." Additionally, the court held that Jackson, who was standing next to the DEA agent throughout the search, had the opportunity to object to the search but did not do so. Finally, the court held that the scope of the consented search was not exceeded because the container of baby powder was not destroyed or rendered useless by the agent's actions and any amount of powder that spilled onto the floor was a minimal amount.

3. Consent to Search Does Not Permit the Destruction or Mutilation of the Area Searched

Because *Jimeno* distinguished the officer's opening of a paper bag from a case where an officer pries open a locked briefcase, courts have held that a search which requires mutilation or destruction of property or premises is beyond the reasonable scope of a general consent. *See, e.g., United States v. Strickland*, 902 F.2d 937 (11th Cir. 1990) (noting that the general consent to search a car did not permit the slashing of defendant's tire).

a. Removing Car Door Panels May Be Within the Scope of Consent
Some courts have upheld the removal of door panels by police officers pursuant to a general consent to search the car. *See United States v. Torres*, 32 F.3d 225 (7th Cir. 1994) (holding that search was reasonable where the police officer opened a side panel compartment of a hatchback pursuant to general consent to search the car, as defendant did not limit consent, knew officer wished to search for weapons and narcotics, and officer did not pry open or break the panel).

4. Construing the Scope of Consent for Body Searches After *Jimeno*

Jimeno establishes that ambiguities regarding the scope of consent are construed against the suspect. Suppose an officer obtains a general consent to a search of the suspect's person, and proceeds to search private areas, such as the genital area, for drugs. Can the search of a "person" reasonably be construed to extend to such areas? After *Jimeno*, some courts have found such searches valid unless the defendant specifically places a limitation on the scope of the search. *See United States v. Rodney*, 956 F.2d 295 (D.C. Cir. 1992) (upholding the search of defendant's crotch area as within the scope of consent where defendant consented to a search of his person). Other courts have disagreed. *See Davis v. State*, 594 So.2d 264 (Fla. 1992) (holding that voluntary consent to search of one's person did not encompass search of groin area). Note that the search in *Rodney* was essentially a frisk of the suspect's crotch. The court in *Rodney* stated in dicta that a general consent to a body search could not be reasonably construed to permit a body cavity search.

D. Revoking Consent

Since the defendant has the right to refuse consent and to control the scope of consent, it follows that he has the right to *revoke* a consent once given. Of course, consent cannot be revoked retroactively after the officer has found incriminating information. But it is clear that the officer's right to engage in a consent search can be terminated by the defendant or by a third party if the officer is relying on third party consent. *See United States v. Springs*, 936 F.2d 1330 (D.C. Cir. 1991) ("[E]ven after consent to search is initially given, a person may subsequently limit or withdraw that consent.").

1. Withdrawal or Limitation of Consent

Suppose that an officer obtains voluntary consent to search a home and then, when he is about to enter a closet, the defendant revokes consent and forbids entry to the closet. Can the officer consider the defendant's actions as proof that there is something incriminating in the closet? As with limitations on the scope of consent, courts have answered in the negative. As one court put it: "The constitutional right to withdraw one's consent would be of little value if the very fact of choosing to exercise that right could serve as any part of the basis for finding the reasonable suspicion that makes consent unnecessary." *United States v. Carter*, 985 F.2d 1095 (D.C. Cir. 1993). However, in *Carter*, the court held that the police officer could take Carter's " 'peculiar' way of retracting consent" into account, independent of the withdrawal of consent, "as part of the totality of the circumstances." Carter snatched a paper bag from the officer and rolled it up after the officer retrieved the bag from a larger container that Carter had permitted the officer to search.

2. Refusal to Give Written Consent Does Not Revoke an Oral Consent

A suspect can withdraw a previously given consent, but as with limitations on the scope of consent, the withdrawal must be clear to be effective. It often occurs that a suspect orally consents to a search and yet, when an officer gives the suspect a consent form to sign, the suspect refuses to sign it. The courts have uniformly held that a refusal to sign a written consent does not, without more, operate to revoke the oral consent. *See United States v. Lattimore*, 87 F.3d 647 (4th Cir. 1996) ("a refusal to execute a written consent form subsequent to a voluntary oral consent does not act as an effective withdrawal of the prior oral consent").

XI. Electronic Surveillance

A. The Law on Electronic Surveillance Prior to *Katz*

Before the landmark case of *Katz v. United States*, 389 U.S. 347, 88 S.Ct. 507, 19 L.Ed.2d 576 (1967), the Court held that Fourth Amendment limitations on electronic and other surveillance were determined by whether officers physically invaded a private area.

1. *Olmstead v. United States*

In *Olmstead v. United States*, 277 U.S. 438, 48 S.Ct. 564, 72 L.Ed. 944 (1928), the Court held that a wiretap placed on the telephone lines of a suspect's house was not a search or seizure within the confines of the Fourth Amendment. The majority reasoned that the officers did not actually *trespass* on the premises of the defendant. The Court stated that conversations overheard by officers illegally upon the premises of a suspect would be suppressed; but this was because the premises were protected from an illegal entry, not because the communications themselves were protected. The Court concluded that verbal communications were not "persons, houses, papers, [or] effects," and thus, their seizure was beyond the purview of the Fourth Amendment.

a. Dissent in *Olmstead*

The dissent strongly objected to the majority's "unduly literal construction" of the Fourth Amendment which excluded wiretapping from the Amendment's protection. Justice Brandeis urged "[t]hat the makers of our Constitution * * * conferred, as against the government, the right to be let alone—the most comprehensive of rights and the right most valued by civilized men," and so "every unjustifiable intrusion upon the privacy of the individual, by whatever means employed, must be deemed a violation of the Fourth Amendment." Justice Holmes noted in a separate dissent that "it is a less evil that some criminals should escape than that the government should play an ignoble part."

2. Development of Trespass Doctrine

The Court used the *Olmstead* trespass rationale to permit the use of various other types of electronic surveillance equipment. For example, in

Goldman v. United States, 316 U.S. 129, 62 S.Ct. 993, 86 L.Ed. 1322 (1942), the Court upheld the use of evidence obtained from a detectaphone "bug" that Federal officers placed against the outer wall of a private office. There was no Fourth Amendment problem because the officers installed the bug without physically entering the private office. In *On Lee v. United States,* 343 U.S. 747, 72 S.Ct. 967, 96 L.Ed. 1270 (1952), the Court upheld the use of testimony obtained from a wired informer who transmitted through a hidden microphone his conversation with the defendant to a Government agent stationed outside the premises. In *On Lee,* the informant had physically entered the presence, but had done so with the permission of the defendant, so again there was no trespass.

B. *Katz* "Reasonable Expectation of Privacy" Doctrine

In *Katz v. United States,* 389 U.S. 347, 88 S.Ct. 507, 19 L.Ed.2d 576 (1967), Federal agents, acting without a warrant, placed a listening bug on the outside of a public telephone booth which they suspected the defendant was using to conduct an illegal gambling operation. The Court suppressed the evidence obtained through the bug, holding that its use was a search which required a warrant.

1. Reasoning in *Katz*

Although there was no trespass upon private property, the Court held that the trespass "underpinnings" of *Olmstead* and *Goldman* were no longer controlling. The Court stressed that the prohibition against unreasonable searches and seizures was to protect "people, not places" and, thus, "the reach of [the Fourth] Amendment cannot turn upon the presence or absence of a physical intrusion into any given enclosure."

2. Electronic Surveillance After *Katz*

After *Katz,* electronic surveillance, as a constitutional matter, is treated the same as any other police investigative technique. If the police, in conducting electronic surveillance, obtain information as to which a person has a legitimate expectation of privacy, then a warrant based upon probable cause is presumptively required. In addition, Title III of the Omnibus Crime Control and Safe Streets Act imposes substantial statutory limitations on electronic surveillance. The statute sets forth minimum standards for Federal and state surveillance. Its requirements for a wiretap authorization arguably provide more protection than that mandated by the Fourth Amendment. Most electronic surveillance litigation therefore concerns statutory rather than constitutional interpretation.

a. Publishing Illegal Communications

In *Bartnicki v. Vopper*, 532 U.S. 514, 121 S.Ct. 1753, 149 L.Ed.2d 787 (2001), the Supreme Court examined whether a communication intercepted in violation of Title III may be published by someone who did not take part in the illegality. The Court held that an individual violates Title III if she intentionally discloses an electronic communication that she knows or has reason to know was intercepted illegally. However, the Court held that the First Amendment protected the disclosures by the defendant in this case because he was a radio commentator who broadcast communications on a matter of public interest.

b. The USA PATRIOT ACT

United States Congress passed the Uniting and Strengthening America by Providing Appropriate Tools Required to Intercept and Obstruct Terrorism Act of 2001 ("USA PATRIOT ACT") in response to the terrorist attacks of September 11, 2001. This Act amends Title III and the Foreign Intelligence Surveillance Act to make it easier for law enforcement agents to obtain authorization for electronic surveillance and to expand the categories of surveillance. The PATRIOT Act has been widely criticized because of its potential threat to the constitutional guarantees of the Fourth Amendment. Civil liberties organizations have expressed particular concern about the lower standard for obtaining warrants to conduct surveillance and the potential invasion of the privacy rights of innocent individuals. Despite these concerns, the Foreign Intelligence Surveillance Court of Review validated the Act's broad surveillance powers in *In Re: Sealed Case*, No. 02–001, 2002 WL 31546991 (F.I.S.Ct. 2002).

The PATRIOT ACT was reauthorized in 2006 with several amendments, including greater judicial oversight over roving wiretaps and government access to business records under FISA. The reauthorization also limits the delay of notification for "sneak and peak" warrants to no more than 30 days.

c. The Foreign Intelligence Surveillance Act

In 1978, Congress passed the original Foreign Intelligence Surveillance Act ("FISA") to authorize the interception of communications pertinent to foreign intelligence. FISA eliminated the need to show probable cause; the government merely needed to show that the "target of the surveillance is a foreign power or agent of a foreign power." Requests for an order are made to one of 11 federal district judges selected by the Chief Justice of the Supreme Court. If there are "exigent circumstances," the original Act allowed the government to conduct interceptions without a court order for up to 72 hours for an individual and up to a year for foreign governments. The PATRIOT ACT amended FISA to permit electronic surveillance in investigations whose primary purpose is criminal prosecution.

Congress passed the FISA Amendment Act of 2008 on July 9, 2008. This Act significantly broadens the government's wiretap powers in a number of areas, including permitting "emergency" wiretaps without a court order for up to seven days, rather than the 72 hour limit of the original Act. The new Act allows the government up to seven days to conduct surveillance on U.S. citizens without a court order if there is probable cause to believe the citizen is linked to terrorism, and under certain circumstances permits surveillance of U.S. citizens reasonably believed to be outside the United States. One of the most controversial sections of the Act provides immunity to electronic communication companies that cooperated and assisted the government by providing customer information for use in wiretapping.

C. Use of Secret Agents

Some electronic surveillance cases involve the recording of conversations by law enforcement where neither party involved in the conversation is aware of police observation. *Olmstead, Goldman,* and *Katz* were such cases. Other cases involve use of secret informers and undercover agents in which one party to a dialogue is conscious that communications are being recorded.

1. Assumption of Risk

In *Lewis v. United States,* 385 U.S. 206, 87 S.Ct. 424, 17 L.Ed.2d 312 (1966), an undercover narcotics agent posed as a buyer of drugs in order to gain entry to the defendant's home where suspected drug transactions were taking place. Lewis invited the agent inside to purchase drugs, though of course he did not know that the ostensible purchaser was in fact an undercover agent. The agent, upon entry, obtained substantial evidence of drug activity. The Court held that the agent's conduct did not violate the Fourth Amendment. It emphasized that the agent did not "see, hear, or take anything that was not contemplated and in fact intended by petitioner as a necessary part of his illegal business," and that there is no reasonable expectation of privacy in illegal activity. Justice Brennan, in a concurring opinion, also noted that "the agent, in the same manner as any private person, entered the premises for the very purpose contemplated by the occupant and took nothing away except what would be taken away by any willing purchaser." *See also Hoffa v. United States,* 385 U.S. 293, 87 S.Ct. 408, 17 L.Ed.2d 374 (1966) (use of informant does not violate the Fourth Amendment where defendant voluntarily gave informant access to incriminating information; the Fourth Amendment did not protect the defendant's "misplaced confidence that [the informer] would not reveal his wrongdoing"); *United States v. White,* 401 U.S. 745, 91 S.Ct. 1122, 28 L.Ed.2d 453 (1971) (statements made to wired Government informant were legally obtained; Fourth Amendment does not protect the defendant's mistaken assumption that "a person to whom he voluntarily confides his wrongdoing will not reveal it"; the Court concludes that "one contemplating illegal activities must realize and risk that his companions may be reporting to the police").

2. Limitation on Assumption of Risk

The *Lewis* Court distinguished an earlier case, *Gouled v. United States,* 255 U.S. 298, 41 S.Ct. 261, 65 L.Ed. 647 (1921), in which a business associate of the defendant working undercover for the government, gained entry to a house by pretending to stop by on a social visit. When Gouled excused himself for a few moments, the informant conducted a search of Gouled's home office. The Court held that this search violated the Fourth Amendment, reasoning that the search exceeded the risk assumed by Gouled in inviting the informant into his house. In contrast, the agent in *Lewis* remained within the reasonable boundaries of the risk assumed by the defendant—he was invited to enter the premises to buy drugs, and he did so. Lewis assumed the risk that the undercover agent would have access to information that a real buyer of drugs would have. But Gouled, by merely inviting his "friend" into his home, did not assume the risk that the "friend" would rummage through his home in his absence. If the "friend" had seen incriminating information plainly visible upon entry to Gouled's house, there would have been no Fourth Amendment violation under *Lewis*.

IV

Remedies for Fourth Amendment Violations

■ **ANALYSIS**

IV. **"Collateral Use" Exceptions to the Exclusionary Rule.**
   A. Introduction.
   B. Grand Jury.
   C. Sentencing.
   D. Forfeiture Proceedings.
   E. Deportation Proceedings.
   F. Civil Tax Proceedings.
   G. Parole Revocation.
   H. Habeas Corpus Proceedings.
   I. Impeachment.
   J. Subsequent Perjury Trials.

V. **The "Good Faith" Exception to the Exclusionary Rule.**
   A. The *Leon* Case.
   B. Objective Reasonableness.
   C. Exceptions to the Good Faith Exception.
   D. Unreasonable Execution of the Warrant.
   E. Reliance on Unconstitutional Legislation.
   F. Mistakes by Court Clerical Personnel.
   G. The Good Faith Exception and Warrantless Searches and Seizures.
   H. Reasonable Reliance on a Warrant Based on Illegally Obtained Information.

I. Introduction

The Fourth Amendment provides the right to be free from unreasonable searches and seizures, but it says nothing about what should happen if a person's right is violated. Courts and legislative bodies have crafted various remedies for a violation of Fourth Amendment rights. If no evidence is recovered in the illegal search or seizure, then the remedy most often employed is a civil action for a violation of the plaintiff's constitutional rights. See 42 U.S.C.A. § 1983; *Anderson v. Creighton*, 483 U.S. 635, 107 S.Ct. 3034, 97 L.Ed.2d 523 (1987) (Federal civil rights action for alleged violation of Fourth Amendment rights). Far more frequently, the illegal police activity uncovers evidence that is later offered in the criminal trial of the person whose rights were violated. The remedy sought by the defendant in these cases is *exclusion* of the evidence. For these situations, the courts have established an *exclusionary rule.* Broadly stated, the rule provides that evidence obtained in violation of the defendant's Fourth Amendment rights must be excluded from trial. The remainder of this section focuses on the exclusionary rule.

A. Historical Development

The exclusionary rule was not born contemporaneously with the Fourth Amendment. For over a century after the adoption of the Fourth Amendment, virtually the only remedies available to victims of illegal searches were civil suits in trespass or in replevin for return of the goods seized. The replevin action had no chance of success, however, if the evidence seized was contraband or the fruits or instrumentalities of crime, since those items were considered forfeited to the state regardless of the legality of the seizure. The trespass remedy often provided very limited damages recovery, because while an intrusion into privacy may have been great, the actual act of trespass may well have been minor.

1. The *Weeks* Rule

The Supreme Court created an exclusionary rule to operate in the Federal courts in *Weeks v. United States*, 232 U.S. 383, 34 S.Ct. 341, 58 L.Ed. 652 (1914). The Court declared that, if illegally obtained evidence could be used against the defendant in his trial, "the protection of the Fourth Amendment declaring his right to be secure against such searches and seizures is of no value, and, so far as those thus placed are concerned, might as well be stricken from the Constitution."

a. Rationale

The Court in *Weeks* articulated two rationales for excluding illegally obtained evidence. One was that the exclusionary rule is the only meaningful way to assure that officials respect the Fourth Amendment rights of the people. The other was that the interest in judicial integrity requires that the courts not sanction illegal searches by admitting the fruits of illegality into evidence.

b. Fruits

In *Silverthorne Lumber Co. v. United States,* 251 U.S. 385, 40 S.Ct. 182, 64 L.Ed. 319 (1920), the Court employed the *Weeks* analysis to prohibit the copying of illegally seized documents, and the use of the copies as the basis of a subpoena for the originals, where the originals had been returned to the defendant because they had been illegally seized. The Court stated that the exclusionary rule should apply not only to the illegally obtained evidence itself (i.e., the originals) but to the fruits of the illegally obtained evidence as well (i.e., the copies). It concluded that "the essence of a provision forbidding the acquisition of evidence is not merely that evidence so acquired will not be used before the court but that it shall not be used at all."

2. *Wolf v. Colorado*

The Court in *Weeks* specifically rejected the notion that the exclusionary rule should apply to violations by state or local police; indeed, at the time of *Weeks* it was established that the Fourth Amendment itself applied only to the actions of Federal officials. Subsequently, in *Wolf v. Colorado,* 338 U.S. 25, 69 S.Ct. 1359, 93 L.Ed. 1782 (1949), the Court confronted two questions: 1. whether the Fourth Amendment was such a fundamental right that it should be incorporated into the Fourteenth Amendment's Due Process Clause and hence applicable against the states; and 2. whether the exclusionary rule should similarly be applicable to the states through the Fourteenth Amendment's Due Process Clause. The Court held that the security provided by the Fourth Amendment was "basic to a free society" and "implicit in the concept of ordered liberty" and as such was enforceable against the states through the Due Process Clause. However, the Court held that "the ways of enforcing such a basic right raise questions of a different order." It stated that the *Weeks* rule "was not derived from the explicit requirements of the Fourth Amendment" and therefore that the exclusionary rule was not a constitutional requirement. So while the Fourth Amendment was a fundamental right, the exclusionary remedy was not a fundamental guarantee.

a. Dissent in *Wolf*

The dissenters in *Wolf* thought it anomalous that the Fourth Amendment could be considered so fundamental as to apply to the states when, without the exclusionary rule, it was essentially denied the force of law.

b. Due Process Violations

Wolf provided that a state court could constitutionally admit evidence obtained in violation of the Fourth Amendment. However, the Due Process Clause itself, even before *Wolf*, provided protection against police activity which "shocked the conscience." In *Rochin v. California*, 342 U.S. 165, 72 S.Ct. 205, 96 L.Ed. 183 (1952), officers broke into the defendant's home and used force in an unsuccessful attempt to keep the defendant from swallowing capsules which he had placed in his mouth. They then took the defendant to a hospital and directed a doctor to pump his stomach, forcing the defendant to vomit up the capsules. The Supreme Court held that the capsules must be excluded because the conduct of the officers was so egregious that the defendant's right to due process was violated. Thus, after *Rochin,* the exclusionary rule is a constitutionally required remedy for evidence obtained in violation of the Due Process Clause.

3. ***Mapp v. Ohio***

In *Mapp v. Ohio,* 367 U.S. 643, 81 S.Ct. 1684, 6 L.Ed.2d 1081 (1961), the Court overruled *Wolf* in part and held that "all evidence obtained by searches and seizures in violation of the Constitution is, by that same authority, inadmissible in a state court." The majority in *Mapp* reasoned that the Fourth Amendment would be little more than a "form of words," and deprived of the force of law, if illegally obtained evidence could be freely admitted in a criminal trial. Also, experience since *Wolf* had shown to the Court that remedies other than the exclusionary rule had proved "worthless and futile."

a. Dissent in *Mapp*

The dissenters in *Mapp* argued that *Wolf* had been based on a "sensitive regard for our federal system and a sound recognition of this Court's remoteness from particular state problems" and that nothing had changed since *Wolf* to warrant imposing the exclusionary rule on the states.

B. The Exclusionary Rule Is Not Required by the Fourth Amendment

The Court in *Mapp* had stated that the exclusionary rule was "part and parcel of the Fourth Amendment's limitation upon governmental encroachment of individual privacy" and "an essential part of the Fourth and Fourteenth Amendments." Recently, however, the Court has taken the position that the exclusionary rule is merely a *"court-made rule"* designed to deter violations of the Fourth Amendment, and that a court is *not constitutionally required* to exclude illegally obtained evidence. *See United States v. Calandra*, 414 U.S. 338, 94 S.Ct. 613, 38 L.Ed.2d 561 (1974) (The exclusionary rule is "a judicially-created remedy designed to safeguard Fourth Amendment rights generally through its deterrent effect, rather than a personal constitutional right of the party aggrieved.").

1. Rationale

The Court's most recent exposition of its rationale for concluding that the exclusionary rule has no constitutional basis is contained in *United States v. Leon*, 468 U.S. 897, 104 S.Ct. 3430, 82 L.Ed.2d 677 (1984). The Court gave the following reasons for its position:

— There is *nothing in the language* of the Fourth Amendment which refers to the exclusionary rule as a required remedy.

— An examination of the origin and purposes of the Fourth Amendment makes clear that the use of illegally obtained evidence at trial "works no new Fourth Amendment wrong." The Fourth Amendment is violated *when the illegal search or seizure occurs*, not when the evidence is admitted at trial. Therefore the subsequent admission of the evidence cannot be part and parcel of the Fourth Amendment wrong. This is unlike a violation of the Due Process Clause, where the admission of unfairly obtained evidence *at trial* is the wrong that is addressed; in contrast to a Fourth Amendment violation, a Due Process violation occurs when the evidence is admitted at trial, and there is therefore a constitutional right to have it excluded.

— Since the Fourth Amendment violation is fully complete upon the search or seizure, the exclusionary rule "is neither intended nor able to cure the invasion of the defendant's rights which he has already suffered."

— Therefore, the rule can only be justified as a judicially-created remedy designed to *deter future violations* of the Fourth Amendment.

2. Response

In *Leon*, Justice Brennan's dissent attacks the majority's holding that the exclusionary rule is not constitutionally required. He makes the following points:

— The fact that the exclusionary rule is "court-made" is not dispositive, since "many of the Constitution's most vital imperatives are stated in general terms and the task of giving meaning to these precepts is therefore left to subsequent judicial decisionmaking." In fact, the Bill of *Rights* does not establish an explicit remedy for any of the rights set forth. But it cannot seriously be argued that the Framers intended that the Bill of Rights would be hortatory only. The Framers did not envision such a thing as a Bill of Rights without meaningful remedies.

— The argument separating the officer's wrong from the subsequent admission of the evidence at trial is an unacceptably narrow view of Government. According to Justice Brennan, the Fourth Amendment "restrains the power of the government as a whole," and "the judiciary is responsible, no less than the executive, for ensuring that constitutional rights are protected."

— The majority's separation of the search from the admission of evidence at trial also reflects an unduly narrow conception of the search and seizure process. As Justice Brennan put it: "Because seizures are executed principally to secure evidence, and because such evidence generally has utility in our legal system only in the context of a trial supervised by a judge, it is apparent that the admission of illegally obtained evidence implicates the same constitutional concerns as the initial seizure of that evidence."

3. Applicability to the States

If the Constitution does not require the exclusion of evidence obtained in violation of the Fourth Amendment, it may be difficult to justify the Supreme Court's ruling in *Mapp* that the state courts must apply the exclusionary rule. Unlike the Federal courts over which the Supreme Court has supervisory authority, the Supreme Court's power over state courts is limited to questions of Federal constitutional law and other Federal law. Yet the Court, while rejecting *Mapp's* assertion that the exclusionary rule is required by the Fourth Amendment, has never rejected *Mapp's* holding that state courts must apply the exclusionary rule whenever a Federal court must do so. The Court has not chosen to explain its source of authority over state courts to impose an exclusionary rule without a constitutional basis.

4. Possibility of Congressional Action

If the exclusionary rule is not constitutionally required, then it can be abrogated by legislative action. There have been proposals in Congress to replace the exclusionary rule with a tort recovery, in which the government would pay damages for any Fourth Amendment intrusion, but the illegally obtained evidence would be admissible at trial. While none has been adopted at the time of this writing, it seems clear that Congress has the power to abrogate the exclusionary rule, so long as Congress provides an alternative remedy for a Fourth Amendment violation.

C. The Cost–Benefit Analysis of the Exclusionary Rule

Since the Court has held that the exclusionary rule is not required as a matter of constitutional law, the viability of the exclusionary rule depends upon weighing the costs of the rule against the benefits it provides by deterring Fourth Amendment violations. The application of the cost-benefit analysis has sparked considerable debate about the validity and usefulness of the exclusionary rule.

1. Arguments Against the Exclusionary Rule: The Costs Outweigh the Benefits

Those who oppose the exclusionary rule argue that the cost of the rule outweighs the benefits it provides in deterring Fourth Amendment violations. The following points are most frequently made against the exclusionary rule:

— The cost of the rule is the loss of reliable evidence, such as narcotics illegally seized in the search of a car. The exclusion of reliable evidence is a substantial cost because it may allow "the guilty to go free because the constable blundered."

— The exclusionary rule also imposes a cost in the loss of public respect for the criminal justice system. When guilty criminals are set free on what the public may view as a "technicality," the integrity of the criminal justice system suffers in the eyes of the public.

— In terms of benefits, the exclusionary rule only protects those who are by definition guilty, and provides no meaningful protection to those who are innocent. For example, if an officer wants to conduct an illegal search simply to harass an innocent person, and is neither seeking nor expecting to find evidence, the threat of exclusion provides no meaningful deterrent effect.

— Even in the context of a criminal investigation, the exclusionary rule is not a meaningful deterrent in most cases. The rule "does not apply any direct sanction to the individual official whose illegal conduct results in the exclusion of evidence." *Bivens v. Six Unknown Named Agents,* 403 U.S. 388, 91 S.Ct. 1999, 29 L.Ed.2d 619 (1971) (Burger, C.J., concurring). The fact that evidence is excluded from a trial months and even years after the officer's misconduct will have no meaningful effect on the wrongdoing officer.

— The Fourth Amendment, as applied by the courts, is not clear enough in most cases to warrant a sanction for its misapplication by officers in the field. In some cases, for example, evidence is excluded by a divided appellate court on a close question. Opponents of the exclusionary rule argue that deterrence is particularly attenuated in such circumstances.

— Because the costs of exclusion are so high, a court might be reluctant to find a Fourth Amendment violation in the first place, whereas it might be willing to find the violation if the remedy was other than exclusion of probative evidence. Thus, Fourth Amendment rights become perversely diluted, rather than strengthened, by operation of the exclusionary rule. This would not be the case, say opponents of the exclusionary rule, if the exclusionary rule were replaced with a meaningful tort remedy.

2. Arguments in Favor of the Exclusionary Rule: The Benefits Outweigh the Costs

Those who favor the exclusionary rule generally make the following arguments in its support:

— The cost of the loss of illegally obtained but reliable evidence is not imposed by the exclusionary rule, but rather by the Fourth Amendment itself. If the officer had complied with the Fourth Amendment, the evidence would never have been obtained in the first place. The Fourth Amendment *does* allow some guilty people to go free, because an officer who follows the law may be prevented from conducting some searches and seizures which could uncover evidence against a guilty person. But, as Justice Traynor stated, any argument about that cost to society was rejected when the Fourth Amendment was adopted. *People v. Cahan*, 44 Cal.2d 434, 282 P.2d 905 (1955).

— Even if the cost is considered the loss of reliable evidence, that cost is overrated because the vast majority of suppression motions are denied. The fact that so few suppression motions are granted is testimony to the fact that the exclusionary rule has been effective in shaping police conduct and conforming it to the law.

— Even if evidence is illegally obtained, it does not follow that "the guilty go free." In many cases, the guilty defendant's conviction is upheld because the admission of the illegally obtained evidence is found to be harmless error. Other rules such as independent source and inevitable discovery are often invoked to allow admission of the evidence even though the officers acted illegally.

— The exclusionary rule does not protect only the guilty any more than the Fourth Amendment itself protects only the guilty. The guilty defendant is allowed to invoke the exclusionary rule in order to protect innocent persons from unlawful police activity. *See Arizona v. Hicks,* 480 U.S. 321, 107 S.Ct. 1149, 94 L.Ed.2d 347 (1987) ("There is nothing new in the realization that the Constitution sometimes insulates the criminality of a few in order to protect the privacy of us all.").

— The argument that the exclusionary rule imposes no meaningful punishment of the offending officer misperceives the nature of the deterrent effect provided by the exclusionary rule. The rule is calculated to prevent, not to punish. The rule is designed to destroy the practical value of illegally obtained evidence. If illegally obtained evidence is of no practical use, police officers (and police departments, which are unlikely to encourage officers to engage in futile actions) will have no incentive to engage in illegal activity; they would have such an incentive if not for the exclusionary rule. It is in this broader sense that the exclusionary rule can have, and does have, significant deterrent effect.

— The evidence shows that the exclusionary rule has had a positive effect on law enforcement. Some indicators are: a significant increase in the number of search warrant applications; more aggressive efforts to educate police on the laws of search and seizure; and increasing cooperation between police and prosecutors to ensure that evidence is legally obtained so that it can be used at trial. *See* Orfield, *Deterrence, Perjury, and the Heater Factor: An Exclusionary Rule in the Chicago Criminal Courts*, 63 U.Colo.L.Rev. 75 (1992).

— Even if the exclusionary rule has limited practical effect, it has significant symbolic effect. As Chief Justice Burger stated, in the absence of some "meaningful alternative," the exclusionary rule should not be abolished lest "law enforcement officials were suddenly to gain the impression, however erroneous, that all constitutional restraints on police had somehow been removed." *Bivens, supra.*

— A tort remedy against the government is not an acceptable alternative to the exclusionary rule. For one thing, many of the citizens harmed by illegal police activity are unsympathetic, and thus unlikely to achieve much recovery. For another, it is wrong to allow the government to "pay its way" out of a constitutional violation.

3. Current Supreme Court Position

The Court has refused to abandon the exclusionary rule, even though it has expressed doubts about its efficacy and has often alluded to the costs imposed by the rule. Part of the reason for its adherence is that the Court is of the view that there is currently no effective replacement for the rule. Nonetheless, the Court has often chosen to create exceptions to the exclusionary rule for situations in which the Court views the costs of the rule to significantly outweigh the deterrence benefits that the rule would provide.

4. Alternatives to the Exclusionary Rule

The Court has indicated that it will not abolish the rule in the absence of a "meaningful alternative." The efficacy of proposed alternatives is as hotly debated as the exclusionary rule itself.

a. Civil Damage Actions

The civil damage action is the most frequently cited alternative to the exclusionary rule. Currently, a person whose Fourth Amendment rights have been violated has a civil cause of action under state tort laws, as well as a Federal cause of action under 42 U.S.C.A. § 1983 (if the violation is by a state or local official) or *Bivens, supra* (if the violation is by a Federal official). Plaintiffs in such actions generally have encountered three major, often insurmountable problems which may render the possibility of a civil action an ineffective deterrent. First, victims of illegal searches and seizures are often criminals, and thus are not sympathetic plaintiffs; also, current doctrines of immunity often preclude recovery. Second, even if a jury would grant recovery, the monetary award for most Fourth Amendment violations would probably be quite small— often too small to justify bringing the case. Third, under current law, the governmental entity is often not liable for the judgment even when it is determined that the police officer acted unconstitutionally. This means that plaintiffs are usually left to attempt recovery from individual officers, who are often unable to pay.

In *Hudson v. Michigan, infra,* the Supreme Court rejected the use of the exclusionary rule for a violation of the knock-and-announce rule. The Court suggested that 42 U.S.C.A. § 1983 was a viable remedy for this Fourth Amendment violation. Its observation that this statute was not available at the time *Mapp* was decided seems to signal that the Court may consider 1983 to be a viable alternative to the exclusionary rule for other Fourth Amendment violations.

b. **"Fortified" Tort Remedy**
On several occasions, Congress has considered a "fortified" tort remedy that its sponsors believed would be an effective replacement for the exclusionary rule. Under this proposal, the Government would be made liable for an officer's illegal behavior; liquidated damages would be available in cases where actual damages are minimal; and evidentiary rules would be employed to protect the plaintiff from the jury's possible assumption that the plaintiff is unworthy of recovery.

c. **Criminal Prosecution of Offending Officers**
Some have suggested that criminal prosecution of an officer who conducts an illegal search or seizure would be an effective replacement for the exclusionary rule. Proponents contend that this would impose a meaningful deterrent on police officers, rather than the more diffuse deterrent effect claimed by the exclusionary rule. Critics of this alternative argue that it will not be a meaningful alternative because juries would be unlikely to convict a policeman of a crime merely because the officer conducted an illegal search or

seizure. Also, a criminal prosecution would require some showing of intent, which would mean that many violations of the Fourth Amendment standards of objective reasonableness would go unpunished and undeterred.

d. Police Regulations and Departmental Discipline

Another proposed alternative is to have police departments establish rules of conduct to comply with the Fourth Amendment, and to require the departments to sanction rule violators by way of internal discipline. Critics of this proposal argue that it would be unwise to trust police departments with the job of self-regulation, and that in the absence of the exclusionary rule, there would be no assurance that departments would meaningfully seek to comply with Fourth Amendment standards.

II. Standing to Invoke the Exclusionary Rule

When a criminal defendant invokes the exclusionary rule on the ground that evidence was obtained in violation of the Fourth Amendment, there is a question of whether the defendant is a proper party to assert the illegality and to obtain exclusion, i.e., whether the defendant has "standing" to assert a Fourth Amendment violation.

A. Fourth Amendment Rights Are Personal

Fourth Amendment rights are personal rights, and the standing requirement assures that a defendant does not obtain exclusion of evidence unless his own personal Fourth Amendment rights were violated. *See Jones v. United States,* 362 U.S. 257, 80 S.Ct. 725, 4 L.Ed.2d 697 (1960) (exclusionary rule does not apply if the defendant claims that he was prejudiced "only through the use of evidence gathered as a consequence of a search or seizure directed at someone else.").

1. Deterrent Effect

On several occasions, the Court has recognized that the exclusionary rule would have a greater deterrent effect if it were applied in all cases in which illegally obtained evidence is offered against a criminal defendant. Before the search, the officer would know that the evidence obtained would be inadmissible not only as to the person whose rights would be violated, but as to any other person against whom the evidence would be relevant. But the Court has rejected the notion that this incremental deterrent effect is worth the substantial cost of exclusion in cases where the defendant's personal rights have not been violated. For example, the Court in *Alderman v. United States,* 394 U.S. 165, 89 S.Ct. 961, 22 L.Ed.2d 176 (1969), held that the defendant could not object to evidence obtained from an illegal wiretap of another co-defendant's conversation. The Court was not convinced that "the additional benefits of extending the exclusionary rule to other defendants would justify further encroachment upon the public interest in prosecuting those accused of crime and having them acquitted or convicted on the basis of all the evidence which exposes the truth."

2. Supervisory Power

The Court held in *United States v. Payner,* 447 U.S. 727, 100 S.Ct. 2439, 65 L.Ed.2d 468 (1980), that Federal courts may not exercise their supervisory power over the conduct of litigation to exclude evidence in situations where the standing requirement is not met. In *Payner,* IRS agents investigating Payner stole the briefcase of another person and photocopied hundreds of documents. These were all offered in Payner's trial. The district court invoked its supervisory authority to exclude the evidence even though Payner had no standing. The court relied on the blatant and intentional nature of the Fourth Amendment violation. But the Supreme Court reversed, concluding that the balance of deterrence and cost that was reached in establishing the standing requirement did not change simply "because the court has elected to analyze the question under the supervisory power instead of the Fourth Amendment. In either case, the need to deter the underlying conduct and the detrimental impact of excluding the evidence remains precisely the same."

B. Reasonable Expectation of Privacy

In *Jones v. United States,* 362 U.S. 257, 80 S.Ct. 725, 4 L.Ed.2d 697 (1960), the Court held that a defendant who is "legitimately on the premises" where a search occurs, had standing to challenge its legality. Later, however, in *Rakas v. Illinois,* 439 U.S. 128, 99 S.Ct. 421, 58 L.Ed.2d 387 (1978), the Court asked itself "whether it serves any useful analytical purpose" to consider the standing question "distinct from the merits of a Fourth Amendment claim." The *Rakas* Court concluded that "the better analysis forthrightly focuses on the extent of a particular defendant's rights under the Fourth Amendment, rather than on any theoretically separate, but invariably intertwined concept of standing." Accordingly, "standing" questions are now resolved by substantive principles of Fourth Amendment law. The question is no longer whether a person is legitimately on the premises, but whether a person has a legitimate expectation of privacy in the area or thing that is searched or seized.

1. Two–Pronged Test

Under *Rakas*, there is a two-pronged test to determine whether the defendant has standing to invoke the exclusionary rule. The two requirements are identical to the requirements established under *Katz* and its progeny to determine whether a search has occurred at all. See the discussion of *Katz, supra.* First, the person challenging the search must demonstrate a *subjective expectation* of privacy in the place searched or a possessory interest in the thing seized. Second, the person must demonstrate that this subjective expectation is one that society accepts *as reasonable.*

2. Burden on Defendant

The defendant "bears the burden of proving that he had a legitimate expectation of privacy that was violated by the challenged search and seizure." *Rawlings v. Kentucky,* 448 U.S. 98, 100 S.Ct. 2556, 65 L.Ed.2d 633 (1980).

3. Different Application From *Katz* Situation

While the *Rakas* test for "standing" is identical to that applied under *Katz* for whether a search has occurred, the analysis for the two questions will differ somewhat. The question traditionally labelled as standing—whether the defendant's personal rights were violated—is not identical to the question of whether any Fourth Amendment search or seizure has occurred at all. For example, the police may have violated a legitimate expectation of privacy (e.g., by entering a house), thus engaging in a search, and yet the defendant would not have standing to object if he had no legitimate expectation of privacy in the premises. In other cases, such as with an aerial overflight, there will be no search at all and therefore the court will never reach the question of "standing." It follows that the question of whether a defendant's personal rights have been violated is still a separate question from whether a search has occurred, even though both questions are governed by the same two-pronged test.

4. "Legitimately on the Premises" Test Rejected

Applying its "legitimacy of expectation" test, the Court in *Rakas* rejected the rule in *Jones,* which had provided that a person had standing to object to a search so long as he was legitimately on the premises. *Rakas,* which is discussed in greater detail *infra,* denied standing to a passenger who attempted to challenge an automobile search—even though the passengers were legitimately in the car. The Court reasoned that a person legitimately on the premises may well not have a reasonable expectation of privacy in the particular area that is searched. For example, the "premises" test would permit a "casual visitor who has never seen, or been permitted to visit the basement of another's house, to object to a search of the basement if the visitor happened to be in the kitchen of the house at the time of the search." Clearly such a person would not have the right to object to a search under the expectation test adopted by *Rakas*, since the visitor would have no legitimate expectation of privacy in an area where he had never even entered or had access. The *Rakas* Court concluded that the "legitimately on the premises" test was overbroad and inconsistent with the principle that Fourth Amendment rights are personal rights.

5. Target Theory Rejected

The Court in *Rakas* rejected the notion that a person has standing to object to a search merely because he is the person against whom the search is directed. A person may be a target of police activity, and yet the illegal search may not violate the target's expectation of privacy. An example is *Payner, supra,* where Payner was the target of police activity, but the privacy interest invaded was that of Payner's lawyer.

Deterrent Effect

The defendants in *Rakas* argued that without target standing, officers may decide to engage in illegal searches of third parties, knowing that the evidence could be used against their target, and unconcerned about the fact that it could not be used against the third party whose rights were violated. But the Court in *Rakas* responded that sufficient deterrent effect remained because the third party whose rights are violated "may be able to recover damages for the violation of his Fourth Amendment rights." So while the exclusionary rule would not deter the misconduct, the threat of civil sanction would operate as a substitute deterrent. The Court also noted its reluctance to extend the "substantial social cost" of the exclusionary rule by allowing it to be invoked by an enlarged class of persons.

6. Application of Expectation Test to the Facts of *Rakas*

In *Rakas*, police stopped a car in which the defendants were riding as passengers. The officers suspected that the vehicle was connected with a recent robbery. The officers searched the passenger compartment of the car and found a sawed-off shotgun under the front passenger seat and a box of shotgun shells in the locked glove compartment. The defendants did not own the car, and they never asserted a property interest in the shotgun or shells. The Court held that a person does not have a legitimate expectation of privacy in areas underneath the seat or in the glove compartment merely on the basis of being a passenger in the car.

a. Result in *Jones* Remains Sound

While the *Rakas* Court rejected the rule from *Jones* that standing is automatically conferred on a person legitimately on the premises, the Court noted that the *result* in *Jones* was correct. This was because the defendant in *Jones* had a legitimate expectation of privacy in the premises, beyond merely being present. In *Jones,* the defendant was arrested in the apartment of an absent friend, and drugs were found in the apartment. The friend had given Jones the right to use the entire apartment, and Jones had a key with which he could come and go. Moreover, with the exception of his friend, Jones had "complete dominion and control over the apartment and could exclude others from it." As such, *Jones* involved "significantly different factual circumstances" from those presented by the passengers in *Rakas;* Jones had a legitimate expectation of privacy in the premises while the defendants in *Rakas* did not.

b. Standing to Contest the Seizure

Defendants in *Rakas* sought to contest the legality of the search of the car. They did not contend that the *stop* of the car was illegal. Lower courts have made it clear that a passenger has standing to object to the stop of a vehicle, since every passenger suffers personal inconvenience when the vehicle is seized. *See United States v. Eylicio–Montoya,* 70 F.3d 1158 (10th Cir.1995) (passenger in car had standing to object to stop of car, but not to a search, since she claimed no ownership interest in the car or in the property seized).

7. **Owners**

Under *Rakas,* an owner of a car will generally have standing to object to a search of the car even if he is not present at the time. *United States v. Jenkins,* 92 F.3d 430 (6th Cir.1996) (owner of truck does not lose standing simply because he allowed an employee to drive it). But the same is not true with respect to a stop of a car. For example, in *United States v. Powell,* 929 F.2d 1190 (7th Cir.1991), a car owned by the defendant and containing drugs was being driven across country to the defendant's home in Illinois. The defendant was waiting for the car at home, but the car was stopped en route. The driver of the car consented to a search, and drugs were discovered. The court found that while the stop of the vehicle was illegal, the defendant lacked standing to object to it. The court held that standing to object to a stop of a car is generally limited to those who were actually stopped with the car—it is they who are inconvenienced. The fact that the defendant owned the car did not give him standing to object to the stop, since he was not at the scene and was not personally inconvenienced by the stop. The court noted that at some point, a detention of the vehicle may implicate the owner's right to use the property, whether or not he is at the scene—for example, if it was seized for an extended period of time while the owner was waiting to use it. But this was not the case with a momentary stop when the defendant was 1000 miles away. The court therefore concluded that the owner of the car had standing to object to the search but not the seizure. However, since the *search* was legal due to valid consent, the evidence was properly admitted against the defendant.

8. Permissive Use

If property is used with the permission of the owner, then the user will ordinarily have an expectation of privacy in the areas for which permission is granted. *See United States v. Rubio–Rivera*, 917 F.2d 1271 (10th Cir.1990) ("Where the defendant offers sufficient evidence indicating that he has permission of the owner to use the vehicle, the defendant plainly has a reasonable expectation of privacy in the vehicle and standing to challenge the search of the vehicle."). The scope of the user's expectation of privacy will depend on the scope of permissive use granted by the owner. For example, in *United States v. Pena*, 961 F.2d 333 (2d Cir.1992) the defendant, who borrowed a car with the permission of the owner, challenged the search of the door panels of the car. The court remanded to determine whether the scope of the permitted use extended to the right to "lift off the door panel and slip items into the door cavity." If not, the defendant would have no standing to object to the search of that area. (Of course, on remand, it is unlikely that Pena could meet his burden of showing that the permissive use extended to the interior of the door panels.). *See also United States v. Riazco*, 91 F.3d 752 (5th Cir.1996) (driver of rental car had no standing to object to its search; the driver was not on the rental agreement, and that agreement specifically prohibited use of the car by anyone not on the agreement).

9. Overnight Guests

Minnesota v. Olson, 495 U.S. 91, 110 S.Ct. 1684, 109 L.Ed.2d 85 (1990), concerned a previously unresolved issue of standing: whether an overnight guest in a home has standing to object to his own warrantless arrest. Police had probable cause to arrest Olson, and probable cause to believe that Olson was located in the home of a friend where he had been staying. Without a warrant, the police entered the friend's home and found Olson and arrested him. Olson challenged the legality of the entry into the apartment to arrest him. The question for the Court was whether Olson had a legitimate expectation of privacy in the third party's home; the Court held that he did. The Court stressed that a person's "status as an overnight guest is alone enough to show that he had an expectation of privacy in the home that society is prepared to accept as reasonable." It noted that overnight guests are unlikely to be confined to certain areas of the house, and are likely to have a measure of control over the premises. The Court specifically rejected the State's argument that a place must be one's home in order to have a legitimate expectation of privacy there.

10. "Business" Guests

In *Minnesota v. Carter*, 525 U.S. 83, 119 S.Ct. 469, 142 L.Ed.2d 373 (1998), the Court declined to extend Fourth Amendment protection to individuals visiting a home for business purposes only, for a short period of time. In *Carter,* a police officer went to an apartment building to investigate a tip from a confidential informant. The officer looked through a gap in the closed blind of a window and saw individuals sitting at a table, putting white powder into bags. He remained near the apartment while other officers sought a search warrant. When two of the individuals seen bagging the white substance left in a previously identified Cadillac, police stopped the car and saw a gun in the car. The two men were arrested. A later search of the car and apartment produced 47 grams of cocaine and an assortment of drug paraphernalia. The defendants claimed that the officer's observation through the apartment window evidence was an illegal search and that the evidence should be suppressed as the "fruit of the poisonous tree."

a. Rationale
    The Court noted that the respondents were neither overnight guests, as in *Olson*, nor were they simply "legitimately on the premises," as in *Jones* but ultimately concluded that the circumstances were closer to the *Jones* scenario. Applying the *Rakas* "legitimate expectation of privacy" analysis, the Court held that an individual with no previous connection to a homeowner who visits the home for a relatively short period of time solely to conduct a

commercial transaction is not entitled to Fourth Amendment protection. Because the Court determined that the respondents had no legitimate expectation of privacy in the apartment, it did not reach the issue of whether the police officer's observation through the window constituted a search.

b. Dissent

Justice Ginsburg's dissent, joined by Justices Breyer and Souter, focused on the right of an individual to share her home and associations with whomever she chooses, regardless of the length or nature of the visit. She expressed concern that the majority's opinion would tempt police officers to pry into private dwellings without a warrant on the chance that they might find incriminating evidence against someone who is a temporary visitor. Justice Ginsburg also suggested that the Court's opinion was inconsistent with *Katz*, noting that it suggests that "we have a more reasonable expectation of privacy when we place a business call to a person's home from a public telephone booth on the side of the street than when we actually enter that person's premises to engage in a common endeavor."

11. Possessory Interest in Items Seized Is Insufficient

In *Rakas*, the Court mentioned in the course of its analysis that the defendants had not claimed a possessory interest in the gun and the shells. But it does not follow that a defendant has standing to contest the search of an area merely because the items *seized* in the search are owned by the defendant. This was made clear in *Rawlings v. Kentucky*, 448 U.S. 98, 100 S.Ct. 2556, 65 L.Ed.2d 633 (1980). In *Rawlings* police searching for evidence of drugs forced Ms. Cox to empty her purse. The purse contained narcotics, which Rawlings claimed were his. Rawlings testified at the suppression hearing that shortly before the police arrived, Cox had agreed to carry the drugs for him in her purse. The Supreme Court held that Rawlings had no legitimate expectation of privacy in Cox' purse. The Court reasoned as follows: 1. prior to the "sudden bailment", Rawlings had never sought or received access to Cox' purse; 2. Rawlings had no right to exclude other persons from access to Cox' purse; 3. other individuals had in fact rummaged through the purse; and 4. the "precipitous nature of the transaction hardly supports a reasonable inference that petitioner took normal precautions to maintain his privacy." Thus, while ownership ordinarily justifies a reasonable expectation of privacy as to an area searched, it does not necessarily justify standing to object to a search merely because of ownership of the property ultimately seized. In *Rawlings*, the area searched was Cox's handbag— she would have standing to object to that search on the basis of ownership, but Rawlings did not.

a. Bailment Relationships

In *Rawlings*, the Court emphasized the "precipitous" nature of the bailment relationship, and the fact that others had access to the purse, as reasons to conclude that Rawlings lacked a legitimate expectation of privacy in the purse. *Rawlings* does not preclude a finding of a legitimate expectation of privacy for more ordinary bailment relationships. *See United States v. Alberts*, 721 F.2d 636 (8th Cir.1983) (defendant has standing where she stored her belongings in closed, opaque containers at the residence of another with that person's knowledge and permission, and there was no general access to the containers by other individuals); *United States v. Most*, 876 F.2d 191 (D.C.Cir.1989) (defendant had standing to object to the search of a bag he checked with a store clerk; the court states that *Rawlings* did not "establish any general rule that an individual forfeits his reasonable expectation of privacy in his belongings simply by entrusting them to the care of another").

Conversely, a bailee of property may be able to establish a legitimate expectation of privacy in the property, despite the lack of an ownership interest. Similar to the overnight guest in *Olson, supra*, a bailee has the right—and often the duty—to exclude others from property entrusted to him. *See United States v. Perea*, 986 F.2d 633 (2d Cir.1993) (defendant who was delivering another person's duffel bag had standing to object to its search: "a person transporting luggage as a bailee, or at least with the permission of the owner, has a reasonable expectation of privacy that society would recognize").

b. Objecting to the Seizure

While Rawlings had no right to object to the search of Cox's purse, he would have a right to object to the *seizure* of his property contained in the purse. A seizure would implicate Rawlings' personal Fourth Amendment possessory interest in the item seized. So for example, if police seized Rawlings' diary, or knife, from Cox's purse in the absence of probable cause, Rawlings would have standing to object to the seizure and the items could be subject to exclusion. Under the facts of *Rawlings*, however, the defendant's right to object to the seizure did him little good, since the items seized were obviously narcotics, and the officer clearly had probable cause to seize these items under the plain view doctrine.

12. Disassociation With the Object of the Search

Where a defendant disavows any knowledge of or interest in property that is being searched or seized, such an action is inconsistent with a reasonable expectation of privacy, and the defendant will not have standing to object to the police activity.

a. Express Disassociation

The defendant's disavowal of an interest may be express. For example, in *United States v. Rush,* 890 F.2d 45 (7th Cir.1989), the defendant met a traveler at a train station and carried the suitcase that the traveler brought with him. When approached by police officers, the defendant disclaimed ownership of the suitcase and the traveler admitted ownership. The court held that the defendant had no standing to object to the search of the suitcase.

b. Disavowal by Conduct

A defendant may by his conduct be deemed to have disavowed an expectation of privacy. An example of this proposition is *United States v. Boruff,* 909 F.2d 111 (5th Cir.1990). Boruff bought a truck for use in a drug-smuggling scheme. He put the title, registration and insurance in the name of his co-conspirator, Taylor. Boruff added improvements to the truck, and it was understood that, if the truck were sold, the proceeds would go to Boruff. Taylor drove the truck to Mexico, followed closely by Boruff, who was driving a rented car. A suspicious border patrol agent stopped the truck and searched it. Boruff kept driving and was apprehended shortly thereafter. Boruff sought to exclude the evidence obtained in the search of the truck, but the court held that Boruff had failed to establish an expectation of privacy in the truck. The court reasoned that despite his actual ownership of the truck, "Boruff did everything he could to disassociate himself from the truck in the event it was stopped by law enforcement officials." *See also United States v. Lehder–Rivas,* 955 F.2d 1510 (11th Cir.1992) (where defendant left a locked suitcase with another and promised to pick it up within three months, but had still not picked it up 14 months later, he no longer retained an expectation of privacy in the suitcase).

13. Co–Conspirator Standing

Standing cannot be found simply because the defendant is a member of a conspiracy that owns the property searched or seized. In *United States v. Padilla*, 508 U.S. 77, 113 S.Ct. 1936, 123 L.Ed.2d 635 (1993), the Court reasoned that to permit standing merely because the defendant was a co-conspirator with managerial responsibility for the venture would be inconsistent with the *Rakas* requirement that the defendant must have a personal expectation of privacy implicated by the search. A joint venture does not itself establish that each party to the venture has a legitimate expectation of privacy when another party, or another party's property, is searched.

C. Automatic Standing

Up until the 1960's, a defendant attempting to establish standing at a suppression hearing was confronted with a dilemma. In order to establish standing, the defendant would often testify that he owned or possessed the item which he sought to have suppressed, or that he owned or controlled the area in which the item was found. But this suppression hearing testimony was itself an admission of guilt, which could thereafter be admitted against the defendant at the trial. To assert his Fourth Amendment rights, the defendant often found it necessary to incriminate himself. To rectify this problem, the Supreme Court developed the doctrine of *automatic standing* in *Jones v. United States*, 362 U.S. 257, 80 S.Ct. 725, 4 L.Ed.2d 697 (1960).

1. Rationale of *Jones*

The Court in *Jones* reasoned that "to hold that petitioner's failure to acknowledge interest in the narcotics or the premises prevented his attack upon the search, would be to permit the Government to have the advantage of contradictory positions as a basis for conviction." On the one hand, the Government could have the evidence admitted on the ground that the defendant did not prove a possessory or ownership interest. On the other hand, the Government could argue to the trier of fact that the defendant had a possessory or ownership interest in the drugs. The Court therefore held that, if the Government sought to convict a defendant on the basis of possession or ownership, this would eliminate the defendant's obligation to prove standing.

2. *Simmons* Rule

After *Jones*, the Court decided *Simmons v. United States*, 390 U.S. 377, 88 S.Ct. 967, 19 L.Ed.2d 1247 (1968). The defendant in *Simmons* could not benefit from the *Jones* rule because he was charged with bank robbery, a non-possessory offense. But the Court recognized that the defendant had the same dilemma as one charged with a possessory offense: to establish standing, he had to admit possession of the incriminating evidence that was seized; and this testimony could be used against him at trial. In *Simmons*, the Court established a general rule that a defendant's suppression hearing testimony cannot be used against him at trial as an admission of guilt. The Court found it "intolerable" that in order to assert his Fourth Amendment rights, a defendant would have to surrender his Fifth Amendment right not to incriminate himself.

3. Automatic Standing Doctrine Abolished

In *United States v. Salvucci*, 448 U.S. 83, 100 S.Ct. 2547, 65 L.Ed.2d 619 (1980), the Court abolished the automatic standing doctrine. The Court concluded that in light of *Simmons*, the reason for the rule had been eliminated, because *Simmons* "grants a form of use immunity" to defendants who assert their Fourth Amendment rights at a suppression hearing.

a. Prosecutorial Inconsistency

The Court in *Jones* had been concerned about the fact that the Government could take contradictory positions at the suppression hearing (i.e., that the defendant did not have a possessory interest) and at trial (i.e., that the defendant did have a possessory interest). The Court in *Salvucci* stated that it did not need to decide whether this risk of self-contradiction was weighty enough to support an automatic standing rule in the absence (after *Simmons*) of any risk of self-incrimination by the defendant. Rather, the Court concluded that after *Rakas* and *Rawlings*, "a prosecutor may simultaneously maintain that a defendant criminally possessed the seized good, but was not subject to a Fourth Amendment deprivation, without legal contradiction." The Court explained that "a person in legal possession of a good seized during an illegal search has not necessarily been subject to a Fourth Amendment deprivation."

b. Risk of Impeachment

The defendant in *Salvucci* argued that an automatic standing rule was required even after *Simmons*, because *Simmons* did not necessarily prevent a defendant from being *impeached* with his suppression hearing testimony, should he decide to testify at trial. The Court responded that it had not been decided whether *Simmons* precludes the use of suppression testimony for impeachment purposes, but that the danger of impeachment was an issue "which more aptly relates to the proper breadth of the *Simmons* rule, and not to the need for retaining automatic standing." Subsequently, lower courts have held that *Simmons* does not prevent the use of suppression hearing testimony for impeachment purposes. *United States v. Beltran–Gutierrez,* 19 F.3d 1287 (9th Cir.1994) (defendant's statements at a suppression hearing can be used to impeach him if his trial testimony is inconsistent with them). The Supreme Court has not specifically decided this question.

III. Exclusion of "The Fruit of the Poisonous Tree"

A. Introduction

In most cases in which the exclusionary rule is invoked, the defendant seeks exclusion of the very evidence that was found in the illegal search or seizure. For example, if the officer conducts an illegal search of a car and discovers narcotics, the defendant will invoke the exclusionary rule to exclude the narcotics. The narcotics are termed the "direct" or "primary" evidence of the illegal search. In many cases, however, the defendant challenges evidence which was *derived from* an initial illegality. For example, suppose that officers conduct an illegal search of a car and find a list of homes where drugs are stored. They proceed to those homes, and their surveillance indicates evidence of drug trafficking. They obtain warrants to search these homes and seize the drugs they find. In this case, the list seized from the car is the primary evidence in relationship to the illegal search, while the subsequently discovered drugs are the derivative evidence. In these situations, it must be decided whether the exclusionary rule should be applied to exclude derivative as well as primary evidence or, as the Court has put it, whether the exclusionary rule should apply to the "fruit of the poisonous tree."

B. Exclusionary Rule Applies to "Tainted" Evidence

In *Silverthorne Lumber Co. v. United States,* 251 U.S. 385, 40 S.Ct. 182, 64 L.Ed. 319 (1920), officers illegally seized some documents from the Silverthornes. A court ordered the documents returned, but before doing so, the prosecutor made copies, and then caused the grand jury to issue a subpoena for the very same documents that had been seized. The Court found that the subpoenas were invalid, reasoning that the exclusionary rule applies not only to the evidence originally obtained in an illegal search, but also to all evidence derived from the evidence obtained in the illegal search. The derived evidence is "tainted." It is "fruit of the poisonous tree." In *Silverthorne,* the prosecutor clearly used information from the illegally seized documents (indeed, the information was a copy of the document) in order to obtain the subpoena.

Standing Requirement Must Be Met

A defendant can successfully challenge derivative, tainted evidence only if he has standing to object to the original illegal search. In the previous example, where officers conduct an illegal search of a car and discover a list of drug locations, those who live at the drug locations, but have no privacy interest in the car, cannot argue that the subsequent searches are tainted by the illegal search of the car. To permit them to challenge the initial search would mean that they could assert the Fourth Amendment rights of another (i.e., the owner of the car), and this is not permitted under *Rakas, supra.* If the subsequent search is *itself* illegal (e.g., if it is conducted without probable cause), then those who live at the location would have the right to challenge that search. But, in the example given, the subsequent searches satisfy the Fourth Amendment requirements of warrant and probable cause. Only those with standing to object to the initial search can contend that evidence found in an otherwise legal search must be excluded because it is tainted by an earlier illegal search.

C. Attenuation

In some cases, the link between the illegal search or seizure and the evidence obtained is so attenuated that the evidence can no longer be meaningfully considered "tainted" or the "fruit of the poisonous tree." When evidence is so attenuated from the illegality, courts reason that the deterrent effect of the exclusionary rule is equally attenuated and therefore the cost of excluding reliable evidence outweighs the negligible benefit of deterrence.

1. *Wong Sun*

The Court's leading case on attenuation is *Wong Sun v. United States*, 371 U.S. 471, 83 S.Ct. 407, 9 L.Ed.2d 441 (1963). The facts of *Wong Sun* are complicated, because there are several pieces of evidence, and the attenuation doctrine applies with different results to each. Federal narcotics agents broke into Toy's apartment without probable cause, and handcuffed him. Toy immediately made a statement implicating Yee in the sale of narcotics. The agents went immediately to Yee, who surrendered heroin to them upon the officers' order to do so. Yee stated that he had bought the drugs from Toy and Wong Sun. Wong Sun was then illegally arrested, and both he and Toy were arraigned and released pending trial. Several days later, Wong Sun came to the offices of the

Bureau of Narcotics, and was interrogated there. He was warned of his right to remain silent and his right to have a lawyer. Wong Sun confessed.

a. Possible "Fruits" in *Wong Sun*

There were two illegal police actions in *Wong Sun:* the entry into Toy's apartment, and the arrest of Wong Sun. There were three pieces of evidence which Toy and/or Wong Sun sought to exclude as tainted: 1. Toy sought to exclude the statement he made immediately after the illegal entry of his house; 2. Toy and Wong Sun both sought to exclude the drugs obtained from Yee; 3. Wong Sun sought to exclude his confession.

b. Test of Causation

The test set forth by the *Wong Sun* Court to determine whether there is a sufficient connection between the illegality and the evidence to justify exclusion is as follows: "whether, granting establishment of the primary illegality, the evidence to which instant objection is made has been come at by exploitation of that illegality or instead by means sufficiently distinguishable to be purged of the primary taint." It is clear that the Court rejected a "but for" test of taint. For example, there was little doubt that Wong Sun would never have come to the officers and confessed but for his prior illegal arrest. Nonetheless, the Court rejected the proposition that "all evidence is fruit of the poisonous tree simply because it would not have come to light but for the illegal actions of the police." Thus, the confession could not be excluded as tainted unless the prior illegality was *exploited* in some meaningful way. The Court felt that the cost of excluding all evidence which has even a minimal "but for" connection to an illegality would outweigh the benefit of deterrence that such a rule would provide.

c. Application to the Facts of *Wong Sun*—Toy's Statement

The Court found that Toy's statement was subject to exclusion as fruit of the poisonous tree. The statement was made right after the illegal entry into his house (and in fact it was made while the illegality was continuing), and the Court noted that the intrusion was a serious violation of the Fourth Amendment, one that was likely to have had a significant effect on Toy. The Court rejected the argument that the taint of the illegal entry was "purged" by Toy's voluntary decision to confess. Given the fact that the confession was made during the course of an egregious illegal intrusion, the Court concluded that it was "unreasonable to infer that Toy's response was sufficiently an act of free will to purge the primary taint of the unlawful invasion." See also *United States v. Leake*, 95 F.3d 409 (6th Cir.1996) (witness statements were tainted when officers asked the witnesses questions based on information obtained in an illegal search). Note that the Court did *not* hold that Toy's confession was involuntary. If it were, it would have been excluded without regard to the illegal arrest. Rather, the Court held that the confession was not sufficiently voluntary to purge the taint of the illegal arrest.

d. Use of Narcotics Against Toy

The Court also held that the drugs turned over by Yee could not be used against Toy. The seizure of the drugs was the direct result of Toy's statement, which had already been held tainted by the illegal entry of Toy's apartment. Since one event followed immediately upon the other, the Court found no break in the chain of causation between the illegal entry of Toy's apartment and the drugs turned over by Yee.

e. Use of Narcotics Against *Wong Sun*

Even though the narcotics were tainted by the illegal entry into Toy's apartment, the Court found that they were admissible against Wong Sun. This was because, as discussed previously, a defendant's Fourth Amendment rights must be violated by the initial illegal search before he can object to the introduction of derivative evidence. Wong Sun had no legitimate expectation of privacy in Toy's apartment, and thus lacked standing to object to the entry of that apartment. As the Court stated, "the seizure of this heroin invaded no right of privacy of person or premises which would entitle Wong Sun to object to its use at his trial."

f. Use of Confession Against *Wong Sun*

Even though Wong Sun had initially been arrested without probable cause, the Court found that his subsequent confession was attenuated from this illegality. The Court reasoned that Wong Sun had been released for several days, and had returned voluntarily to the officers to make his statement. The Court therefore concluded that "the connection between the arrest and the statement had become so attenuated as to dissipate the taint." *See also United States v. Boone*, 62 F.3d 323 (10th Cir.1995) (causal chain broken where defendant, after an illegal search of his car, jumps into his car, speeds away, and throws drugs out the window: "We view the defendant's decision to discard evidence as independent and voluntary, and sufficient to cut the link to Officer Barney's car search.").

2. Confessions and *Miranda* Warnings

In *Wong Sun,* the Court discussed the relationship between a Fourth Amendment violation and a subsequent confession. In *Brown v. Illinois,* 422 U.S. 590, 95 S.Ct. 2254, 45 L.Ed.2d 416 (1975), the Court returned to the same question but under radically different facts. Brown came into his apartment and found two policemen pointing guns at him. He was informed that he was under arrest for murder, handcuffed, and driven down to the police station. While at the station, Brown was twice given *Miranda* warnings and twice confessed. The first confession occurred 90 minutes after the arrest, the second occurred seven hours after the arrest. The lower court found that Brown had been arrested without probable cause, but held that the *Miranda* warnings broke the causal chain so that any subsequent statement was admissible so long as it was itself legally obtained. Brown did not claim that his confessions were themselves involuntary or illegally obtained. Rather, he claimed that they were tainted by the illegal arrest and that the *Miranda* warnings did not purge the taint.

a. *Miranda* Warnings Do Not Per Se Break the Chain of Causation

The Court in *Brown* held that both confessions were the tainted fruit of the illegal arrest and thus were improperly admitted at Brown's trial. It rejected the argument that recitation of the *Miranda* warnings, in and of itself, is sufficient to purge the taint of an illegal arrest. The Court reasoned that such a rule would substantially diminish the deterrent effect of the exclusionary rule: "Any incentive to avoid Fourth Amendment violations would be eviscerated by making the warnings, in effect, a cure-all, and the constitutional guarantee against unlawful searches and seizures could be said to be reduced to a form of words."

b. *Miranda* Warnings Are Relevant

While the Court in *Brown* held that *Miranda* warnings were not dispositive in dissipating the taint of an illegal search or seizure, it recognized that the warnings would be relevant in assessing the connection between the illegality and the subsequent confession. A case-by-case approach is required. The Court stated that the *Miranda* warnings are an "important factor, to be sure" but that other relevant factors included "the temporal proximity of the arrest and confession, the presence of intervening circumstances, and, particularly, the purpose and flagrancy of the official misconduct."

c. **Application to the Facts in *Brown***

The Court held that both of Brown's confessions were tainted by the illegal arrest. The first confession occurred less than two hours after the arrest, and "there was no intervening event of significance whatsoever." This was in marked contrast with Wong Sun's confession, which occurred several days after he had been arrested and *released.* The Court also relied on the fact that the illegal arrest was a serious violation of the Fourth Amendment, and thus the taint could not be easily dissipated. According to the Court, "the impropriety of the arrest was obvious" and the detectives willfully engaged in the illegal arrest in order to frighten and confuse Brown so that he would confess. Accordingly, the deterrent purpose of the exclusionary rule would be well-served by excluding the subsequent confessions. As to Brown's second confession, the Court concluded that it "was clearly the result and fruit of the first." Again there were no intervening acts such as consultation with counsel, release, or arraignment by a magistrate.

d. **Burden on Government**

The Court in *Brown* made it clear that once an illegal search or seizure is established, the Government has the burden of proving that the causal chain is sufficiently attenuated to dissipate the taint of the illegality. *See also United States v. Brady,* 842 F.2d 1313 (D.C.Cir.1988) (prosecution has burden of proving that defendant's abandonment of property was not tainted by illegal seizure).

e. **Progeny of *Brown***

Brown was held controlling in *Dunaway v. New York,* 442 U.S. 200, 99 S.Ct. 2248, 60 L.Ed.2d 824 (1979), where the defendant was arrested without probable cause, brought down to the station, and confessed after receiving *Miranda* warnings and waiving his rights. The Court rejected the notion that officers could "violate the Fourth Amendment with impunity, safe in the knowledge that they could wash their hands in the procedural safeguards of the Fifth." The Court also rejected the argument that the confession should be admitted because it was voluntary. The Court explained that the question of taint is *not whether the derivative evidence is itself illegally obtained*. If it were itself illegally obtained, the evidence would be clearly inadmissible and a fruit of the poisonous tree question would not arise. Rather, the question is whether the confession, though voluntary, was obtained by *exploitation* of the previous Fourth Amendment violation. *See also Taylor v. Alabama*, 457 U.S. 687, 102 S.Ct. 2664, 73 L.Ed.2d 314 (1982) (confessions made six hours after an arrest without probable cause found inadmissible; *Miranda* warnings held insufficient to purge the taint).

The Supreme Court confirmed *Brown* and *Taylor* in *Kaupp v. Texas*, *supra*. Kaupp was removed from his home in the middle of the night, partially dressed, and transported to the sheriff's headquarters where he was interrogated. The Court held that Kaupp was arrested without probable cause and noted that there was no indication of any appreciable lapse in time between his removal from his home and the confession. The Court cited *Brown* for the proposition that Miranda warnings in and of themselves, cannot break the causal connection between the illegality and the confession.

f. *Rawlings*

In *Rawlings v. Kentucky*, 448 U.S. 98, 100 S.Ct. 2556, 65 L.Ed.2d 633 (1980), the Court distinguished *Brown* and found that a confession was not the fruit of an illegal arrest. This was so even though the time between the confession and the arrest was just 45 minutes. The Court emphasized that temporal proximity was only one factor in assessing the taint of an illegal arrest, and that a taint may be purged in a relatively short period of time if the circumstances of the detention are not severe. In *Rawlings*, the detention was at a residence and occurred without a show of force, and the statements were spontaneous reactions to the discovery of evidence rather than the product of the illegal detention.

3. **Confession Made Outside the Home Is Not the Fruit of a *Payton* Violation**

The Court distinguished *Brown*, *Dunaway*, and *Taylor* in *New York v. Harris*, 495 U.S. 14, 110 S.Ct. 1640, 109 L.Ed.2d 13 (1990). In *Brown*, *Dunaway*, and *Taylor*, the Court excluded confessions as the fruit of arrests unsupported by probable cause. In contrast, Harris confessed after an arrest made with probable cause, but without a warrant. Since

Harris was arrested in his home, the lack of an arrest warrant violated *Payton v. New York*, 445 U.S. 573, 100 S.Ct. 1371, 63 L.Ed.2d 639 (1980). The challenged confession was made at the station an hour after the illegal entry into Harris' home. Harris argued that, under the previous cases, the confession was not attenuated from the illegal arrest and therefore should be excluded as the fruit of the poisonous tree.

a.   Analysis in *Harris*

The *Harris* Court held that a confession made outside the home cannot be the fruit of a *Payton* violation, and thus that Harris' confession was not tainted. The Court reasoned that, unlike the prior cases, Harris was not unlawfully in custody when he made the confession. The violation of *Payton* constitutes an illegal *search* of the home, but not an illegal arrest; and while evidence obtained in the search of the home in violation of *Payton* is subject to exclusion, there is no necessary connection between that search and a subsequent confession outside the home.

b.   No Retreat From *Brown*

Harris does not in any way question the fruits analysis in *Brown, Dunaway*, and *Taylor*. In those cases, the arrest was itself illegal because it was made without probable cause. *Harris* merely makes the point that a *Payton* violation does not even result in an illegal arrest. Rather, it is an illegal *search* of the home, which has no necessary connection with a confession that is subsequently given outside the home.

c.   Seizure of Evidence in the Home in the Course of a *Payton* Violation

In *Harris*, the *Payton* violation turned up no evidence. Where the *Payton* violation does produce evidence (seen by the officers in the course of entering the home without a warrant) and is followed by a stationhouse confession that is *influenced* by the seizure of the tainted evidence, then the fruit of the poisonous tree doctrine may be applicable. There is thus a distinction between a confession which is the product of the *Payton* arrest (because the arrest itself is not illegal) and one which is the product of the *Payton* search (which is illegal). See *United States v. Beltran*, 917 F.2d 641 (1st Cir.1990) (noting that if the defendant was rattled into a confession, not by a warrantless in-home arrest, but by the fact that the police found cocaine during that arrest, *Harris* would not apply and the confession could be tainted by the *Payton* violation).

d. **Confessions in the Home**

Unlike the facts of *Harris,* there will be a connection between the *Payton* violation and the confession if the defendant makes the statement in the home during the arrest. For example, in *United States v. McCraw,* 920 F.2d 224 (4th Cir.1990), a warrantless arrest in a hotel room in violation of *Payton* was followed by incriminating statements and a consent to search, which defendant gave immediately after the arrest and while still in the hotel room. Distinguishing *Harris,* the court suppressed the statements and the evidence, stating that "[a]ssuming that the consent to search and hotel room statements were voluntary by fifth amendment standards, the proximity in time and place between the arrest and the search and the statements and the absence of intervening circumstances nevertheless require suppression of this evidence to protect the physical integrity of the home and to vindicate the purpose of the Fourth Amendment."

4. **Abandonment During the Course of or After an Illegal Search or Seizure**

A taint question often arises where a defendant, after an illegal search or seizure, tries to surreptitiously dispose of evidence, which is subsequently retrieved by the officers. Of course, the mere fact of abandonment in these circumstances does not mean that the evidence is admissible, any more than the voluntariness of a confession following an illegal arrest guarantees admissibility. If the abandonment was tainted by the illegal search or seizure, then it is subject to exclusion as fruit of the poisonous tree. *See United States v. Wilson,* 953 F.2d 116 (4th Cir.1991) (where defendant runs away from an illegal stop and throws drugs away while being chased, the drugs are not admissible because "Wilson's action was clearly the direct result of the illegal seizure, and it follows that the recovered drugs were the fruit of the illegality and must be suppressed.").

a. **Calculated or Spontaneous**

The question of whether abandoned property is tainted by a prior illegal search or seizure depends on whether the defendant has had sufficient time and opportunity to make a calculated decision, or whether instead the decision to abandon the property was a spontaneous reaction to the illegal activity. For example, in *People v. Boodle,* 47 N.Y.2d 398, 418 N.Y.S.2d 352, 391 N.E.2d 1329 (1979), the defendant was illegally arrested when a police officer told him to get into the patrol car to answer some questions. During the long drive to the station, Boodle threw a gun out the window. The court held that the taint of the illegal seizure was dissipated because the defendant's attempt to discard the gun "was an independent act involving calculated risk." The court concluded that Boodle's independent decision broke the causal link between the illegality and the recovery of the gun, so the evidence was held admissible.

In contrast, in *United States v. Wood*, 981 F.2d 536 (D.C.Cir.1992), the defendant was followed into a dark passageway by two officers who ordered him to "halt right there." Wood froze in his tracks, and dropped a gun between his feet. The officers handcuffed Wood, and then picked up the gun. Wood said, "that's not mine; I was just carrying it." The officers had no reasonable suspicion to stop Wood, and so the stop was found illegal. But the Government argued that the gun was admissible because Wood's act of discarding the gun was wholly independent of the illegal stop. The court rejected this argument and held that Wood's abandonment of the gun was a "spontaneous reaction to a sudden and unexpected confrontation with the police." The court stated that "unlike the defendant in *Boodle*, for example, Wood did not attempt to hide the gun on his person and then throw it out of the car window on the way to the police station." The court noted that "no time elapsed and no intervening events occurred between the commencement of the seizure and the dropping of the gun." Accordingly, the court held that the abandonment and the gun itself were tainted by the illegal seizure, and that the gun and Wood's statement were improperly admitted at trial.

5. Criteria for Attenuation

While the determination of attenuation is a case-by-case approach, there are several factors that have been deemed relevant by the courts. Many of these factors are derived from the Supreme Court cases discussed above.

a. Impact of the Illegality on the Defendant

The greater the impact on the defendant, the more likely it is that subsequently discovered evidence—such as a confession or contraband found after consent—will be tainted. For example, in *Brown*, the Court found it relevant that the officers made the illegal arrest to surprise and upset Brown. The arrest thus clearly influenced Brown's subsequent confessions.

b.   Intervening Circumstances
Circumstances such as *Miranda* warnings, change of location, delib-
erative acts by the defendant, and acts by third parties are relevant
in determining whether the chain of causation has been broken. As
Brown teaches, however, no single intervening factor can be deemed
automatically to purge the taint of an illegal search or seizure.

c.   Temporal Proximity
Obviously, the shorter the time between the challenged conduct and
the discovery of the evidence, the more likely it is that the evidence
will be found tainted. In particular, if the illegality is continuing at
the time the evidence is discovered, it is extremely likely that a court
will find the evidence to be fruit of the poisonous tree.

d.   Purpose and Flagrancy of the Misconduct
The more serious the misconduct, the more likely it is that it will
taint subsequently obtained evidence. Also, courts reason that
applying the exclusionary rule to derivative evidence is more likely
to deter serious misconduct than it is to deter marginal misconduct.
Thus, the Court in *Brown* noted that the officers had flagrantly
violated Brown's rights by arresting him in his home, without
probable cause, under intimidating circumstances.

6.   **Insufficient Connection Between Knock-and-Announce Violation
and Evidence Found in the Home**
In *Hudson v. Michigan*, 547 U.S. 586, 126 S.Ct. 2159, 165 L.Ed.2d 56 (2006),
the Supreme Court held that a violation of the knock-and-announce rule
did not justify the exclusion of the evidence. Police, executing a search
warrant, knocked and waited three to five seconds before entering
Hudson's house. After entering, the police found large quantities of
drugs and a loaded gun. Hudson argued that the evidence should be
suppressed because the early entry by the police violated his Fourth
Amendment rights. The trial court found that the actions of the police
did violate the knock-and-announce rule and granted Hudson's motion
to suppress the evidence. On interlocutory review, the Michigan Court of
Appeals reversed, holding that the exclusionary rule was an inappropriate remedy for a violation of the knock-and-announce rule. Hudson
was convicted and renewed his claim on appeal. The Court of Appeals
affirmed the conviction, as did the United States Supreme Court.

According to the Supreme Court, the knock-and-announce rule serves
the interests of protecting the "life and limb" of the officers, preventing

destruction of the resident's property, and preserving the privacy and dignity of the resident. The Court noted, however, that the rule does not protect an individual's interest in preventing the government from seizing evidence described in a search warrant. It further noted that the exclusionary rule is not required simply because a constitutional violation was the "but-for" cause of obtaining the evidence. In this case, it was not the "but-for" cause, but according to the Court, even if it had been, "but-for" causation can be too attenuated to justify exclusion of the evidence. Finally, the Court explained that the police conduct could be deterred by other remedies, including civil rights lawsuits and internal police discipline.

7. Testimony of Live Witnesses

An illegal search or seizure may in some cases lead the police to the discovery of witnesses who can give testimony against the defendant. Generally, courts have held that the witness' voluntary decision to testify purges any taint from an illegal search or seizure.

a. *Ceccolini*

The leading case on whether witness testimony is the fruit of the poisonous tree is *United States v. Ceccolini*, 435 U.S. 268, 98 S.Ct. 1054, 55 L.Ed.2d 268 (1978). In *Ceccolini*, an officer stopped to talk with a friend who happened to be in Ceccolini's flower shop. While there, the officer opened up an envelope, and he found money and gambling slips. He then learned from his friend, who did not know of the officer's discovery, that the envelope belonged to Ceccolini. The officer relayed this information to the FBI, who contacted the officer's friend who had happened to be in the flower shop. The FBI agent did not mention the discovery of the gambling slips. The friend expressed a willingness to testify against Ceccolini, and did so at the grand jury and at Ceccolini's trial.

b. Willingness to Testify Is Likely to Purge the Taint

The *Ceccolini* Court held that, even though the path from the illegal search of the envelope to the testimony of the friend was "straight and uninterrupted," the testimony was nonetheless so attenuated from the illegality as to not justify its exclusion as fruit of the poisonous tree. The Court stated that the "exclusionary rule should be invoked with much greater reluctance where the claim is based on a causal relationship between a constitutional violation and the discovery of a live witness than when a similar claim is advanced to support suppression of an inanimate object." This is because a live witness usually makes a voluntary decision to testify, which is likely to break the chain of causation. The Court also noted the cost of excluding the testimony of a live witness as tainted fruit. It would mean that a witness would be perpetually disabled "from testifying about relevant and material facts, regardless of how unrelated such testimony might be to the purpose of the originally illegal search or the evidence discovered thereby." Against this cost, the deterrent effect of the exclusionary rule was found to be minimal in the ordinary case, because an officer would be very unlikely to conduct an illegal search in order to find witnesses. Accordingly, the Court concluded that the exclusionary rule should only apply if there was an extremely close and direct link between the illegality and the witness' testimony.

c. Application to the Facts of *Ceccolini*

The Court found that the link between the illegality and the testimony in *Ceccolini* was far from extremely close and direct. It relied on the following five factors: 1. the testimony of the witness was an act of free will and was not induced by official authority as a result of the illegal search; 2. the information in the envelope was not used in questioning the witness; 3. four months elapsed between the illegal search and the F.B.I.'s contact with the witness; 4. both the identity of the witness and her relationship with Ceccolini "were well known to those investigating the case"; and 5. there was no evidence to indicate that the officer initiated the search "with the intent of finding a willing and knowledgeable witness to testify against" Ceccolini. See also *United States v. McKinnon*, 92 F.3d 244 (4th Cir.1996) (witness statement admissible, even though witness was discovered through the use of illegally obtained information; court emphasizes the fact that the witness "freely and immediately cooperated with the police").

d. No Per Se Rule

Despite its reluctance to find that an illegal search will taint the subsequent testimony of a witness, the Court in *Ceccolini* declined to adopt a rule that the testimony of a live witness could never be excluded as the fruit of an illegal search or seizure. After *Ceccolini*, some live witnesses have been excluded from trial when there is an extremely close relationship between the illegality and the testimony— especially where the officer *exploits* the illegality to obtain the testimony.

Example: In *United States v. Ramirez–Sandoval,* 872 F.2d 1392 (9th Cir.1989), an officer conducted an illegal search of the defendant's van, which uncovered a list of names and numbers. Defendant was driving the van. One name on the list belonged to a man in the back of the van. The officer asked him what the number next to his name meant, and the man replied that he was an illegal alien and the number was the amount of money he had paid the defendant to be illegally transported to the United States. Defendant was tried for offenses involving harboring and transporting illegal aliens, and sought to exclude the testimony obtained from interrogation of the alien. The court found that the testimony of the alien was tainted by the illegal search of the van. The court distinguished *Ceccolini* on four grounds: 1. the illegally obtained list was used by the officer to question the witness; 2. no time elapsed between the illegal search and the initial questioning of the witness; 3. "the identities of the witnesses were not known to those investigating the case"; and 4. while the testimony was not coerced, the witness did not come forward of his own volition and his testimony "was induced by official authority as a result of the illegal search."

8. Identifications

In *United States v. Crews,* 445 U.S. 463, 100 S.Ct. 1244, 63 L.Ed.2d 537 (1980), a defendant was arrested without probable cause, brought down to the station and photographed. He was then released. One of the victims of the crime subsequently identified the defendant's picture in a photo array, and he was re-arrested. At the trial, the victim identified the defendant as the perpetrator, and he was convicted. The defendant argued that the in-court identification was tainted by the illegal arrest, but the Court rejected this argument. The Court reasoned that there are three distinct elements of a victim's in-court identification: 1. the presence of the victim to testify at trial; 2. the ability of the victim to reconstruct the crime in his or her mind; and 3. the physical presence of the defendant, so that the victim can compare the defendant's appearance to the "picture" of the perpetrator in the victim's mind. Five members of the Court in different opinions concluded that an in-court identification should never be excluded as the fruit of an illegal arrest. For these Justices, none of the elements of in-court identification are affected by the arrest itself. Therefore, a person brought to trial following an illegal arrest can be identified, so long as the identification itself is not tainted by impermissible police suggestiveness.

D. Independent Source

Evidence will not be excluded as the fruit of the poisonous tree if the Government can show that it was derived from an independent legal source. The independent source exception operates to admit the fruits of illegally obtained evidence, when such fruits are also found by *legal means unrelated to the original illegal conduct*. For example, suppose that officers conduct an illegal search of a car and find a list of names and addresses. They obtain a warrant to search the premises at one of these addresses through use of the illegally obtained information. But simultaneously, other officers involved in an independent investigation were conducting an undercover drug buy at the address. The undercover agent believes that his cover has been "blown" and signals the back-up officers to enter the premises. The information discovered in this search is admissible even though the officers with the "tainted" warrant may discover the same information. This is because a legal means independent of the car search (i.e., a search based on probable cause and exigent circumstances) was conducted.

1. Rationale

The Supreme Court's most recent explication of the independent source exception is *Murray v. United States*, 487 U.S. 533, 108 S.Ct. 2529, 101 L.Ed.2d 472 (1988). The Court explained that the basis of the exclusionary rule is to *deter* police misconduct, and not to punish the police. Therefore, the exclusionary rule puts the police "in the same, not a *worse*, position than they would have been in if no police error or misconduct had occurred." Where the challenged evidence has an independent legal source, application of the exclusionary rule would place the officers in a worse position than they would have been absent any violation. If no violation had occurred, the evidence would have been admitted due to the operation of the independent legal source.

2. Search With a Warrant After an Illegal Entry

In *Murray*, police made an initial, admittedly illegal entry into defendant's premises. In the course of this illegal search, the police saw incriminating evidence, which they left in place. The police then obtained a warrant to search the premises. The illegally obtained information was not included in the warrant application, and thus did not affect the magistrate's decision to issue the warrant. The police then searched the premises pursuant to the warrant and seized the very evidence that was originally discovered in the illegal search. The Government sought to introduce, and the defendant sought to exclude, the evidence discovered in the initial illegal search. The question in *Murray* was whether the independent source exception could apply to *primary evidence,* directly obtained from the illegal search, as well as to *derivative evidence,* indirectly obtained from the illegality.

a. Rediscovered Evidence Can Be Admissible

The Court in *Murray* held that the exclusionary rule did not prevent the admission at trial of *rediscovered* evidence obtained through independent legal means. As with derivative evidence, the exclusion of the evidence initially discovered in the illegal search would put the officers in a worse position than if the search had never been conducted. If the illegal search had not been conducted, the police officers would have initially discovered the evidence in the course of a lawful search pursuant to a warrant. So the fact that it was actually *rediscovered* through independent legal means did not lead to a different result. Of course, the evidence would have to be excluded if the warrant was issued on the basis of illegally obtained information. In that situation the warrant would not provide an independent legal source for obtaining the evidence.

b. Danger of Confirmatory Searches

The Court in *Murray* held that the mere showing that the warrant was issued on independent, legally obtained information could not in itself be enough to invoke the independent source exception for "rediscovered" evidence. The Court was concerned that a mere showing of independent information would not be sufficient to deter illegal "confirmatory" searches.

Example: Suppose that officers have probable cause to believe that drugs are in a warehouse. This does not mean that the officers will actually find drugs in the warehouse, because the probable cause standard is only a fair probability, not a certainty. If there are actually no drugs in the warehouse, the warrant application would end up to be a waste of time for the officers. There is a possibility, therefore, that the officers might wish to conduct an illegal warrantless search, to "confirm" whether there are any drugs in the warehouse before seeking a warrant. If the officers only had to show that probable cause pre-existed the illegal search, they would have nothing to lose and everything to gain by doing a "confirmatory search." If they found something, it would still be admissible due to the information the police had prior to the entry, and the obtaining of the subsequent warrant. If they found nothing, they could avoid the bother of obtaining a warrant. But of course, in conducting the search, the police would have illegally invaded the privacy of an innocent person.

c. Protection Provided by *Murray*

To protect against the danger of a confirmatory search, the Court in *Murray* stated that the Government has the "onerous burden of convincing a trial court that no information gained from the illegal entry affected * * * the law enforcement officers' decision to seek a warrant." This burden could not be met simply by showing that the magistrate was not presented with illegally obtained information. The officer's decision to obtain a warrant could still have been affected by information uncovered in the illegal search. The Court in *Murray* therefore mandated an inquiry into the subjective intent of the officer. See *United States v. Restrepo*, 966 F.2d 964 (5th Cir.1992) ("unlike the objective test of whether the expurgated affidavit constitutes probable cause to issue the warrant, the core judicial inquiry * * * is a subjective one: whether information gained in the illegal search prompted the officers to seek a warrant").

d. Officer's Assurance Not Sufficient

The Court in *Murray* stated that the officers' mere assurance that the original search was not confirmatory in nature would not be dispositive. It declared that "where the facts render those assurances implausible, the independent source doctrine will not apply." Thus, *Murray* imposes two requirements for applying the independent source exception to "rediscovered" evidence: 1. an officer must have a "plausible" explanation for why the original illegal search was conducted other than that it was to confirm whether there was any evidence worth seizing; and 2. information obtained in the illegal entry cannot be any material part of the basis for issuing the warrant.

e.   **Application to the Facts of *Murray***

In *Murray,* the district court credited the officers' explanation that they entered the premises in an effort to apprehend anyone who might have been inside, and to guard against the destruction of evidence. That explanation was accepted by the Supreme Court, which stated that, while the officers "may have misjudged the existence of sufficient exigent circumstances to justify the warrantless entry * * * there is nothing to suggest that they went in merely to see if there was anything worth getting a warrant for." In other words, the explanation for the search did not mean that it was legal, but it was sufficiently close that the explanation was not implausible. The officers were wrong as to exigent circumstances but not so wrong as to render their motivation suspect. The officers were guilty of misjudgment, not bad faith.

f.   **Dissent in *Murray***

Justice Marshall, joined by Justices Stevens and O'Connor, dissented in *Murray.* He contended that the majority had not done enough to deter officers from conducting confirmatory searches. According to Justice Marshall, it will be the rare case in which an explanation such as that accepted in *Murray* will be so far wrong as to be implausible. Circumstances showing some slight risk of destruction of evidence will almost always exist—especially in drug cases where contraband can be quickly destroyed. So long as the police were not completely unreasonable, their explanation that they thought they were acting legally will be considered plausible. Justice Marshall concluded that "the litigation risk" that a court may find an illegal confirmatory search "seems hardly a risk at all; it does not significantly dampen the incentive to conduct the initial illegal search."

g.   **Direct/Indirect Distinction Rejected**

The defendant in *Murray* argued that it was inappropriate to apply the independent source exception to evidence discovered as a *direct* result of the illegality. According to the defendant, this was an impermissible expansion of the independent source exception, which had traditionally applied only to permit the introduction of evidence that would otherwise have been excluded as fruit of the poisonous tree—not to the evidence found as a direct result of the illegal search.

The Court in *Murray*, however, rejected any primary/derivative or direct/indirect distinction insofar as the independent source exception was concerned. The Court explained that "this strange distinction would produce results bearing no relation to the policies of the exclusionary rule." If exclusion of direct evidence would place the officers in a worse position than they would have been absent their misconduct, the Court found no reason to exclude such evidence merely because it could be labelled "direct."

h. Mixed Affidavits

Suppose that in a case like *Murray,* the officers include information obtained in the illegal search in their warrant application. Under *Murray,* the independent source exception should not permit the introduction of the evidence obtained in the search pursuant to a warrant, if the magistrate relied upon tainted information when the warrant was issued. But what if the officers included enough legally obtained information so that probable cause existed to issue the warrant without consideration of the illegally obtained information? What if the tainted evidence is surplusage? Courts after *Murray* have held that the independent source exception can apply where the warrant application contains information *sufficient for probable cause apart from the illegally obtained information.* Otherwise, the police would be put in a worse position than if the illegal search had not occurred: if the illegal search had not occurred, the evidence would have been obtained with a warrant based upon legally obtained information sufficient to establish probable cause. *See United States v. Herrold,* 962 F.2d 1131 (3d Cir.1992) ("If the application contains probable cause apart from the improper information, then the warrant is lawful and the independent source doctrine applies, providing that the officers were not prompted to obtain the warrant by what they observed during the initial entry."). The question is whether a neutral magistrate would have issued the warrant even if not presented with information that had been obtained during an unlawful search. *See also United States v. Dessesaure,* 429 F.3d 359 (1st Cir.2005) (reviewing court must excise information obtained pursuant to an illegal search and evaluate whether what remains is sufficient to establish probable cause).

i. Independent Source Must Be "Legal"

In *United States v. Johnson,* 380 F.3d 1013 (7th Cir.2004), the defendant was sitting in a parked car with two others when police officers, without any legal basis, ordered them to get out of the car. One officer searched underneath the defendant's seat and found drugs while the other officer searched the two passengers and found drugs and counterfeit money. The officers then searched the trunk of the car and found more incriminating evidence. The defendant moved to suppress the evidence found in the trunk on the basis that the officers had no justification for the initial seizure and search under his seat. The district court denied the motion on the rationale that Johnson did not have standing to challenge the illegality of the searches of the passengers and that the evidence found on them established independent probably cause to search the trunk. The court of appeals reversed, holding that an illegal search of someone other than Johnson could not be legitimately used to produce evidence against Johnson under the independent source doctrine because the doctrine mandated that the independent source be a *legal* independent source. The court noted that "the government's view would deprive the exclusionary rule of any deterrent effect."

E. Inevitable Discovery

The inevitable discovery exception allows the fruits of illegal activity to be admitted at trial if the Government can show that the challenged evidence would inevitably have been discovered through means completely independent of the illegal activity. For example, suppose that police illegally obtain a letter in a search of the defendant's apartment. The letter indicates that the defendant has a sawed-off shotgun stored in a closet, which is a few feet away from where the defendant has been arrested and is being detained. Operating on that information, the police enter the closet and seize the gun. While the gun is a fruit of the poisonous tree, it is nonetheless admissible if the Government can show that it would have been inevitably discovered anyway in a routine search incident to arrest. *See People v. Fitzpatrick,* 32 N.Y.2d 499, 346 N.Y.S.2d 793, 300 N.E.2d 139 (1973) (where the court on these facts held the gun admissible under the inevitable discovery exception). In essence, the inevitable discovery exception is a "hypothetical" independent source exception.

1. Rationale

The Supreme Court adopted the inevitable discovery exception to the exclusionary rule in *Nix v. Williams,* 467 U.S. 431, 104 S.Ct. 2501, 81 L.Ed.2d 377 (1984). The Court's reasoning was identical to that employed in adopting the independent source exception in *Segura* and *Murray, supra:* the exclusionary rule is applied to deter police misconduct, and not to punish the officers by making them worse off than if the illegality had not occurred. If the challenged evidence would have been inevitably discovered in the course of legal police activity anyway, then exclusion would indeed place the officers in a worse situation than if the illegality had not occurred.

2. Inevitability Must Be Shown by a Preponderance

In *Williams* the Court held that the exception would be applicable if the Government could prove by a *preponderance of the evidence* that the discovery would have inevitably occurred through legal means. This standard was found to be met under the facts of *Williams*. Williams was arrested and charged with the murder of a young girl. Her body had not been found. An officer illegally obtained a confession from Williams, which led them to the location of the body. Meanwhile, a search party had been organized to find the body, and searchers were systematically covering the area in which the body was found by the officers who interrogated Williams. The officers, acting upon the illegally obtained confession, got to the body before the search party. The Court held that evidence from the body and its location were admissible under the inevitable discovery exception to the exclusionary rule, because the state proved by a preponderance of the evidence that the search party would have found the body shortly after it was actually found by the offending officer.

3. Applies to Fourth Amendment Violations

The Court in *Williams* applied the inevitable discovery exception to evidence that was obtained as the result of a violation of the Sixth Amendment (a confession obtained after indictment in the absence of counsel). But it is clear that the inevitable discovery exception applies to evidence obtained from violations of the Fourth Amendment as well. See *Murray, supra* (discussing the inevitable discovery exception in the context of Fourth Amendment violations); *United States v. Jackson*, 901 F.2d 83 (7th Cir.1990) (evidence obtained as a result of search based on involuntary consent was admissible because it would have been inevitably discovered in a *Terry* frisk).

4. Primary Evidence

In *Murray, supra,* the Court held that the independent source exception applied to primary evidence, i.e., the very evidence directly obtained in the illegal search or seizure. Thus, the independent source exception is not just an exception to the fruit of the poisonous tree doctrine, but rather a more general exception to the exclusionary rule, allowing the admission of any evidence if it was obtained from a source independent of the illegal activity. In contrast, where the state invokes the inevitable discovery exception, the courts are in conflict as to whether the very evidence uncovered by the police misconduct can be admitted. This question frequently arises when the police illegally search an automobile. Suppose the police properly stop an automobile and arrest the driver for speeding. Then, without probable cause, the police search the trunk and find drugs and a drug ledger. This warrantless search is illegal, since it is beyond the scope of the search incident to arrest exception, and it is unsupported by the probable cause necessary to invoke the automobile exception to the warrant requirement. Nonetheless, the Government argues that all of the evidence found in the trunk is admissible under the inevitable discovery exception since, after the arrest of the driver, the car would have been impounded, and the trunk would have been opened and searched pursuant to a standard inventory search.

If inevitable discovery can in fact be shown, then all courts would admit the evidence indirectly derived from the illegal search. In our example, this would include witnesses, locations and physical evidence obtained by following leads contained in the drug ledger. The question is whether the *primary evidence of the illegal search*, such as the drugs or the ledger itself, is equally admissible. On this question there is dispute.

a. Open Question
    The Supreme Court has not yet explicitly decided whether the inevitable discovery exception applies to primary as well as secondary evidence. *Nix v. Williams* is not definitive on the application of the inevitable discovery exception to primary evidence, since evidence concerning the body in *Williams*, and which the Court held admissible, was clearly derivative evidence. The primary evidence, directly obtained from the officer's illegal questioning of Williams, was the confession itself, which the Government did not offer at trial.

b. One View—*Williams* Analysis Requires Application of Inevitable Discovery Exception to Primary Evidence
    Many courts have held that after *Williams*, the inevitable discovery exception must apply equally to primary as well as derivative evidence. *See United States v. Andrade*, 784 F.2d 1431 (9th Cir.1986)

(accepting the Government's argument that primary evidence—drugs found in the trunk of an automobile—was admissible under the inevitable discovery exception, since an inventory of the illegally searched automobile would have been conducted). These courts read *Williams* as prohibiting application of the exclusionary rule where it would place the officers in a worse position than if the illegal search or seizure had not occurred. With primary as well as secondary evidence, exclusion is punitive if the evidence would have been inevitably discovered through legal means; the officers are in either case put in a worse position for having conducted an illegal search or seizure. Consequently most lower courts have held that the inevitable discovery exception applies equally to primary and derivative evidence.

c. Contrary View—Primary Evidence Must Be Excluded Even if It Would Have Been Discovered Through Legal Means

A contrary position is taken by some courts, which have excluded evidence found during an illegal search or seizure even if it would have been discovered through legal means. These courts limit the inevitable discovery exception to *fruits* of the illegally obtained evidence, and refuse to apply it to the illegally obtained evidence itself.

Example: In *People v. Stith,* 69 N.Y.2d 313, 514 N.Y.S.2d 201, 506 N.E.2d 911 (1987), the State argued that a gun uncovered in an illegal search of a truck would inevitably have been discovered in a lawful inventory search, and thus was admissible. The court held that the inevitable discovery exception should be applicable only to secondary, derivative evidence—"evidence obtained indirectly as a result of leads or information gained from that primary evidence." According to the court in *Stith,* if the exception were to apply to primary evidence, it would rob the exclusionary rule of all deterrent effect. For example, with respect to automobile searches, the police would never have an incentive to comply with the limitations imposed by the probable cause requirement, or with the spatial and temporal limitations of the search incident to arrest doctrine. They would know that, even if they violate those limitations, the evidence uncovered will nonetheless be admissible because they could argue that they would have conducted an inventory search pursuant to police department guidelines, and that such inventory search would have been legal. As the court in *Stith* stated: "applying the inevitable discovery rule in these circumstances, and effecting what would amount to a *post hoc* rationalization of the initial wrong would be an unacceptable dilution of the exclusionary rule. It would defeat the primary purpose of that rule, deterrence of police misconduct."

d. **Distinction From Independent Source Exception**

Those courts which refuse to apply the inevitable discovery exception to primary evidence find it necessary to distinguish the independent source exception, which after *Murray* clearly applies to admit the very evidence found during the illegal search or seizure. The distinction proffered is that with the independent source exception, a legal search is *actually conducted at some point*. In contrast, no legal search is ever conducted when the inevitable discovery exception is applied. This means that no warrant is ever obtained. Thus, if the inevitable discovery exception applies to primary evidence, the police could argue that their illegality should be excused because they *would have obtained a warrant—even though they never bothered to get a warrant*. Courts which refuse to apply the inevitable discovery exception to primary evidence are thus concerned that application of the exception would lead to the demise of the warrant requirement. See *United States v. Mejia,* 69 F.3d 309 (9th Cir.1995) ("To apply the inevitable discovery doctrine whenever the police could have obtained a warrant but chose not to would in effect eliminate the warrant requirement."). In contrast, the application of the independent source exception to primary evidence can at least be justified because, as in *Murray*, a warrant was in fact obtained.

5. **Inevitability, Not Possibility**

For the inevitable discovery exception to apply, the Government must show that the challenged evidence would have been inevitably discovered through legal means that would actually have been used. For example, where the Government argues that evidence obtained in an illegal automobile or container search would have been inevitably discovered in an inventory, the Government must show that an inventory search is a standard practice that is routinely conducted. The mere possibility that an officer may have conducted an inventory search is not enough. *See United States v. Gorski,* 852 F.2d 692 (2d Cir.1988) (Government's argument that evidence would have been inevitably discovered in an inventory search was rejected because the record "reveals no evidence that such searches were an invariable, routine procedure in the booking and detention of a suspect at the particular FBI office involved").

Focus on What Would Have Been Done

For the inevitable discovery exception, the question is not what the police could have done or should have done, but what they actually *would* have done to reach the evidence by independent legal means. As one court has stated: "An investigation conducted over an infinite time with infinite thoroughness will, of course, ultimately or inevitably turn up any and all pieces of evidence in the world." *United States v. Feldhacker,* 849 F.2d 293 (8th Cir.1988). The court in *Feldhacker* concluded that "while the hypothetical discovery by lawful means need not be reached as rapidly as that actually reached by unlawful means, the lawful discovery must be inevitable through means that would actually have been employed."

6. Legal Means Must Derive From Facts Independent of Illegal Search or Seizure

Where the Government points to a hypothetical independent source which arises from facts learned in the illegal search or seizure, the inevitable discovery exception cannot apply. *See United States v. Ibarra,* 955 F.2d 1405 (10th Cir.1992) (rejecting the argument that evidence found after an unlawful impoundment of a car would have been inevitably discovered in an inventory search: "no inventory of the contents of defendant's vehicle could have been conducted but for the unlawful impoundment of the vehicle"; the court notes that a different result would have been reached if the officers engaged in an illegal *search* of a car that would have been legally impounded and inventoried regardless of the search).

7. Active Pursuit

A few courts have imposed the requirement that, in order to invoke the inevitable discovery exception, the police must be *actively pursuing* the lawful means at the time the illegal search is conducted. For example, in *United States v. Khoury,* 901 F.2d 948 (11th Cir.1990), the court rejected the argument that evidence obtained in an illegal search of a car would have been inevitably discovered in an inventory. The court reasoned that at the time of the illegal search, an inventory had not yet begun, and therefore that the active pursuit requirement was not met. Other courts have refused to apply an active pursuit requirement; in these courts, active pursuit is one way, but not the only way, to meet the state's burden of proof on inevitability. *See, e.g., United States v. Thomas*, 955 F.2d 207 (4th Cir.1992) ("a situation other than a second investigation might make discovery inevitable").

IV. "Collateral Use" Exceptions to the Exclusionary Rule

A. Introduction

Even if the prosecution is proscribed by the exclusionary rule from admitting illegally obtained evidence as part of its case-in-chief at trial, there are several other possible uses to which such evidence could be put. The Supreme Court has considered whether the exclusionary rule ought to apply to a wide variety of uses of illegal evidence outside the context of the prosecution's case-in-chief. With one notable exception, the Court has consistently held that illegally obtained evidence can be used for collateral purposes. The rationale generally given is that sufficient deterrence of illegal searches and seizures will flow from the exclusion of illegally obtained evidence from the prosecution's case-in-chief, and therefore that the minimal benefits of preventing collateral uses of such evidence are outweighed by the costs of exclusion.

B. Grand Jury

In *United States v. Calandra*, 414 U.S. 338, 94 S.Ct. 613, 38 L.Ed.2d 561 (1974), agents illegally seized certain documents located at Calandra's place of business. The documents related to loansharking activities. A grand jury was convened to investigate these activities, and Calandra was subpoenaed to appear so that he might be questioned on the basis of the information obtained from the illegally seized documents. Calandra moved to suppress the documents and refused to answer the grand jury's questions. The Supreme Court held that Calandra had no right to refuse to answer the questions, because the exclusionary rule did not apply to grand jury proceedings.

1. Rationale

The Court in *Calandra* reasoned that exclusion would be especially costly because it would "seriously impede the grand jury" and "delay and disrupt grand jury hearings." Against this cost, the Court found that the benefits of deterrence from an "extension of the exclusionary rule" were "uncertain at best." The Court declared that the threat of exclusion of illegally obtained evidence from the criminal trial provided the principal deterrent effect of the exclusionary rule, and that it was "unrealistic to assume" that there would be a significant incremental deterrent effect from excluding evidence from consideration by the grand jury. According to the Court, an officer would be unlikely to violate the Fourth Amendment with the sole intent to obtain an indictment from the grand jury; that would make no sense, because the evidence upon which the indictment was based would be eventually excluded from trial.

2. Dissent

Justices Brennan, Douglas and Marshall dissented in *Calandra*. They argued that the exclusionary rule was necessary to ensure that "the government would not profit from its lawless behavior" and that, under the majority's approach, the Government would be able to profit from its own wrong because the illegally obtained evidence would be of some use.

C. Sentencing

The Supreme Court has not considered whether the exclusionary rule is applicable to sentencing proceedings. However, lower courts have consistently held that the exclusionary rule is generally inapplicable to the trial court's consideration of evidence for purposes of sentencing. *See United States v. Robins*, 978 F.2d 881 (5th Cir.1992). This view has been unchanged by the advent of the Federal Sentencing Guidelines. Courts reason that a district court imposing sentence under the Guidelines *must* ordinarily consider relevant, illegally obtained evidence. This is so even though the Guidelines remove a great deal of judicial discretion from sentencing and, in drug cases, impose a sentence based in large part on the quantity of the drugs associated with the defendant. As a result, "consideration of illegally seized evidence at sentencing is likely to result in increased penalties." *United States v. Tejada*, 956 F.2d 1256 (2d Cir.1992) (refusing to apply the exclusionary rule despite the changes wrought by the Guidelines, and holding that to avoid disparities in sentencing, the district judge must consider relevant, illegally obtained evidence).

1. Rationale

The courts refusing to apply the exclusionary rule in sentencing proceedings have reasoned much the way the Supreme Court did in *Calandra*. According to these courts, the principal deterrent effect of the exclusionary rule is attributable to exclusion of illegally obtained evidence from the prosecution's case-in-chief; and the incremental deterrent effect of excluding the evidence from consideration at sentencing would ordinarily be minimal. Against this limited benefit, the exclusionary rule would impose a substantial cost, by limiting the information that a judge could consider in assessing an appropriate sentence.

2.   Search or Seizure for Express Purpose of Enhancing a Sentence

While illegally obtained evidence is not ordinarily excluded from consideration at sentencing, courts have acknowledged an exception to this principle where the defendant makes a showing "that officers obtained evidence expressly to enhance a sentence." *United States v. Tejada, supra.* Courts reason that where it appears that the evidence has been illegally obtained *for the purpose of using it at sentencing* (rather than in the case-in-chief), then the exclusion of the illegally obtained evidence would have a deterrent effect sufficiently strong to outweigh the costs of exclusion. For example, in *United States v. Gilmer*, 814 F.Supp. 44 (D.Colo.1992), the defendant was properly arrested for drunk driving, and indicted for weapons and drug offenses on the basis of the evidence properly seized during the course of his arrest. After the indictment, officers illegally searched Gilmer's residence; this search turned up more drugs and weapons. This evidence was excluded from trial, but the Government urged the court to consider the illegally obtained drugs and weapons for sentencing purposes. Under the Sentencing Guidelines, this would have resulted in a substantial sentence, even though the defendant's actual conviction was for a relatively minor possessory offense. Under the Guidelines, the court must consider all "relevant conduct" in assessing sentence, including in many cases the possession and distribution of drugs other than those for which the defendant was charged and tried.

The *Gilmer* court held that under the circumstances, exclusion of the illegally obtained evidence from the sentencing hearing was required. The court found it likely that the second search was conducted to find evidence with which to enhance the sentence, and not for use at trial. It reasoned that at the time of the second search, the agents knew that they had a solid case based on the grand jury indictment; they made no effort to undertake a legal search which would produce admissible evidence; and they were indifferent concerning the legality of the search. The court concluded that "the circumstances demonstrate an unacceptably high incentive for the officers to violate the Fourth Amendment."

D. Forfeiture Proceedings

In a case decided before *Calandra*, the Supreme Court held that the exclusionary rule was applicable to forfeiture proceedings. *One 1958 Plymouth Sedan v. Pennsylvania,* 380 U.S. 693, 85 S.Ct. 1246, 14 L.Ed.2d 170 (1965). Under the *Calandra* balancing test, it may be questioned whether the minimal deterrent effect of exclusion outside the context of criminal prosecution justifies the costs of excluding reliable evidence from a forfeiture proceeding. However, the holding in *Plymouth Sedan* has never been revisited by the Supreme Court, and therefore the courts have applied the exclusionary rule to forfeiture proceedings even after *Calandra*. *See United States v. $277,000.00 U.S. Currency,* 941 F.2d 898 (9th Cir.1991) (exclusionary rule applied in civil forfeiture proceedings directed at illegally seized vehicle and the money found within).

1. Proof of Criminal Violation Through Other Means

Plymouth Sedan was a case in which the illegally obtained evidence was used to prove a criminal violation; the criminal violation was a predicate to the forfeiture of an automobile. If the forfeitable nature of the object seized can be proven through other, legally obtained evidence, it does not matter that the object came to the authorities by way of an illegal search or seizure; forfeiture proceedings are not terminated merely because the Government came by the property illegally, any more than criminal proceedings are terminated merely because the defendant was illegally arrested. *See United States v. United States Currency $31,828,* 760 F.2d 228 (8th Cir.1985).

2. Owner Not Entitled to Return of Contraband

Plymouth Sedan concerned the forfeiture of an automobile, which was not inherently contraband. If the property illegally seized is *contraband per se* (such as narcotics), the exclusionary rule does not demand their return to the owner. According to the Court in *Plymouth Sedan*, the return of contraband per se, merely because it was illegally seized, would frustrate "the express public policy against the possession of such objects." *See also United States v. Bagley,* 899 F.2d 707 (8th Cir.1990) (convicted felon not entitled to return of guns illegally seized from him).

E. Deportation Proceedings

In *I.N.S. v. Lopez–Mendoza,* 468 U.S. 1032, 104 S.Ct. 3479, 82 L.Ed.2d 778 (1984), officers illegally seized Lopez–Mendoza and obtained inculpatory statements concerning his status as an illegal alien. These statements were later used in civil deportation proceedings, and served as the basis for Lopez–Mendoza's deportation. He argued that the fruit of the illegal seizure should have been excluded, but the Supreme Court held that the exclusionary rule is inapplicable in a civil deportation hearing.

1. Rationale

In *Lopez–Mendoza*, the Supreme Court did not purport to use its ordinary analysis, i.e., that the exclusionary rule should not apply to a collateral proceeding because sufficient deterrence flowed from excluding the evidence from a criminal prosecution. The Court recognized that a deportation proceeding was not "collateral" in this sense, because INS law enforcement efforts are geared specifically toward deportation proceedings rather than toward criminal prosecutions. Nonetheless, the Court found that the benefits of deterrence were outweighed by the costs of exclusion. The benefits of deterrence were found minimal because "deportation will still be possible when evidence not derived directly from the arrest is sufficient to support deportation" and because "it is highly unlikely that any particular arrestee will end up challenging the lawfulness of his arrest." The Court also relied on the fact that "the INS has its own scheme" of training and discipline designed to deter Fourth Amendment violations, and that alternative remedies such as declarative relief are available to challenge systematic violations of the Fourth Amendment by the INS. On the other hand, the Court found the costs of excluding evidence in deportation proceedings to be particularly substantial. The Court emphasized that an illegal alien is engaged in an "ongoing violation of the law" and that it would be inappropriate for courts to "close their eyes" to such continuous violations by applying the exclusionary rule. This was in contrast to criminal trials, where the defendant is being tried for a past transgression.

2. Dissent

The four dissenters argued that "the costs and benefits of applying the exclusionary rule in civil deportation proceedings do not differ in any significant way from the costs and benefits of applying the rule in ordinary criminal proceedings." This was because civil deportation proceedings were the prime objective of the INS officials who made the illegal seizure.

F. Civil Tax Proceedings

In *United States v. Janis*, 428 U.S. 433, 96 S.Ct. 3021, 49 L.Ed.2d 1046 (1976), local police officers illegally obtained cash and betting records from Janis. This information was passed on to the IRS, which made an assessment against Janis on the basis of betting income, and levied on the seized cash in partial satisfaction of the assessment. Janis sued in federal court to recoup the illegally seized cash, and the Government counterclaimed for the remainder of the assessment. The Supreme Court held that the exclusionary rule could not operate against the Government in civil tax proceedings, and therefore that the cash could be levied upon and Janis could be assessed for the remainder.

1. Rationale

The Court found the deterrent effect of the exclusionary rule to be "attenuated" where evidence is illegally obtained by a state law enforcement officer and subsequently used in a proceeding "to enforce only the civil law of the other sovereign." Coupled with the fact that sufficient deterrence flows from excluding the evidence from a criminal prosecution, the Court concluded that exclusion in a Federal tax proceeding "is unlikely to provide significant, much less substantial, additional deterrence" because the tax proceeding "falls outside the offending officer's zone of primary interest." The minimal deterrent effect was found to be outweighed by the cost of excluding reliable evidence from the Federal civil tax proceeding.

2. Search by Same Sovereign

The search in *Janis* was conducted by local officials and the evidence was ultimately used in a federal tax proceeding. In a footnote in *Janis*, the Court indicated that the exclusionary rule might have more deterrent effect if the search were conducted by officials of the same sovereign which ultimately used the evidence. However, the courts confronted with this question have generally refused to apply the exclusionary rule even where the search and the subsequent civil tax proceeding are both conducted by the same sovereign. For example, in *Tirado v. Commissioner,* 689 F.2d 307 (2d Cir.1982), the court found it "unsound to invoke the exclusionary rule on the assumption that officers of one federal agency have such a strong motivating interest in all federal law enforcement concerns that broad application of the rule will achieve significant marginal deterrence." The court thus found the Federal tax proceeding to be outside the "zone of primary interest" of the Federal narcotics officer. The only exception to this principle would be where the searching agency has "a pre-existing agreement to share with the IRS information obtained during a search." *Grimes v. C.I.R.,* 82 F.3d 286 (9th Cir.1996) (finding no such agreement on the facts).

G. Parole Revocation

In *Pennsylvania Board of Probation and Parole v. Scott*, 524 U.S. 357, 118 S.Ct. 2014, 141 L.Ed.2d 344 (1998), the Supreme Court held that the exclusionary rule is inapplicable in parole revocation proceedings. Parole officers searched Scott's residence without a warrant and discovered firearms and other illegal weapons. Scott was prohibited from owning or possessing weapons as a condition of his parole. When the parole officers sought to introduce the weapons as evidence at his parole revocation hearing, Scott objected, claiming that the search of his residence was unreasonable under the Fourth Amendment.

1. Rationale

The Court repeated its "cost-benefit" analysis, and held that the costs of applying the exclusionary rule in parole revocation proceedings out-weighed the potential benefits of deterring law enforcement misconduct. Citing *Calandra*, *Janis*, and *I.N.S. v. Lopez–Mendoza*, the Court noted that it had repeatedly declined to extend the exclusionary rule beyond the criminal trial context. The Court discussed the costs of excluding evidence in the parole revocation context, noting that the costs are "particularly" high in the parole context because the State has a great interest in returning parolees to prison if they violate the conditions of their release since parolees are more likely to commit future crimes than "average citizens." The Court went on to note that application of the exclusionary rule is incompatible with the flexible, informal format of most parole hearings. Finally, the Court found the exclusionary rule to have little deterrent value in the parole context because most law enforcement officers would not know that the subject of his search is a parolee, and would be deterred from illegal conduct on the belief that the evidence would be introduced at a criminal trial.

2. Dissent

Justice Souter dissented, joined by Justices Ginsburg and Breyer, arguing that the costs of applying the exclusionary rule in the parole context are no greater than the costs of applying it in a criminal trial. As far as the benefits are concerned, Justice Souter noted that the deterrent value would be significant because parole revocation proceedings often take the place of a criminal trial. If parole is revoked, the parole may be sent back to prison for a significant period of time, thereby eliminating the need for a separate prosecution. In these instances, the parole revocation hearing is the only proceeding where illegally obtained evidence would be used against the parolee, and thus would be only opportunity to deter future illegal conduct.

The Court did not address the applicability of the exclusionary rule in probation revocation hearings, and at least one lower court has distinguished *Scott* in the context. See *State v. Scarlet*, 800 So.2d 220 (Fla.2001).

H. Habeas Corpus Proceedings

In the 1960's and 1970's, the Supreme Court decided several important Fourth Amendment issues in cases which were brought to the Court through collateral attack of a finalized state court conviction; the procedural device for such an attack is ordinarily a *habeas corpus* proceeding brought in Federal court to challenge the constitutionality of a finalized state conviction. However, in *Stone v. Powell*, 428 U.S. 465, 96 S.Ct. 3037, 49 L.Ed.2d 1067 (1976), the Court held that a habeas petitioner could *not ordinarily invoke the exclusionary rule* to challenge evidence seized in violation of the Fourth Amendment.

1. Rationale

As in previously discussed cases, the Court in *Stone* employed a cost-benefit analysis and found that the costs of applying the exclusionary rule in habeas proceedings outweighed the benefits in deterrence that exclusion would provide. The Court found that sufficient deterrence existed from exclusion at trial or on direct review, and that officers would be unlikely to "fear that federal habeas review might reveal flaws in a search or seizure that went undetected at trial and on appeal." On the cost side, the Court emphasized that the costs of exclusion were more substantial in the context of collateral attack than they would be at trial or on direct review. Allowing a remedy on collateral attack would impose greater burdens on the Government in a retrial, since finalized convictions are generally older than those appealed on direct review. Thus a retrial may be significantly more difficult due to the possible loss of witnesses and proof. Moreover, a Federal court's invalidation of a finalized state conviction, through use of the exclusionary rule, raises Federalism concerns and creates the cost of uncertainty associated with lack of finality of judgments.

2. Full and Fair Opportunity

The Court in *Stone* declared that "where the State has provided an opportunity for full and fair litigation of a Fourth Amendment claim, a state prisoner may not be granted federal habeas relief on the ground that evidence obtained in an unconstitutional search or seizure was introduced at trial." It follows that the exclusionary rule *will* be applicable in habeas proceedings where the state has not provided a "full and fair opportunity" to litigate the Fourth Amendment claim.

a. Definition of Full and Fair Opportunity

The Court in *Stone* did not define what it meant by a "full and fair opportunity" sufficient to preclude application of the exclusionary rule. Subsequent lower court cases have set forth the following requirements that must be met by the state courts in order to preclude a collateral attack on Fourth Amendment grounds: 1. there must be a *procedural opportunity* to raise a Fourth Amendment claim, including an opportunity for meaningful appellate review; 2. where material facts are in dispute, they must be determined by a *fact-finding court*; and 3. the state courts must recognize and *cannot willfully refuse to apply* the correct Fourth Amendment standards.

b. Narrow Exception

It certainly does not follow, however, that a Fourth Amendment claim can be brought on habeas merely because the state courts wrongly decided a Fourth Amendment question. The lack of "full and fair opportunity" exception to *Stone* is intended to be extremely narrow. *See Pierson v. O'Leary*, 959 F.2d 1385 (7th Cir.1992) (it was sufficient that the state court stated the appropriate standard and applied it to the facts).

c. Ineffective Assistance

If the defendant's Fourth Amendment claim is lost in the state courts because counsel was *ineffective* in presenting it, then the ineffective assistance of counsel is a separate constitutional violation. Unlike a violation of the Fourth Amendment, a violation of the standards of effective assistance is cognizable in habeas proceedings. *See Kimmelman v. Morrison*, 477 U.S. 365, 106 S.Ct. 2574, 91 L.Ed.2d 305 (1986) (rejecting the argument that "*Stone's* restriction on federal habeas review of Fourth Amendment claims should be extended to Sixth Amendment ineffective assistance of counsel claims which are founded primarily on incompetent representation with respect to a Fourth Amendment issue").

I. Impeachment

In a series of cases, the Supreme Court has held that the exclusionary rule does not prevent the prosecution from using illegally obtained evidence to impeach the defendant's testimony. The first case to recognize an impeachment exception was *Walder v. United States*, 347 U.S. 62, 74 S.Ct. 354, 98 L.Ed. 503 (1954), where the defendant, charged with narcotics sales, testified on direct examination and again on cross-examination that he had never bought, sold, or possessed narcotics. The prosecution was allowed to question the defendant about heroin that was illegally obtained from his home two years earlier; the judge gave a limiting instruction that the evidence could only be considered in assessing the defendant's credibility as a witness. The Supreme Court held that the illegally obtained evidence was properly admitted for impeachment purposes, concluding that "there is hardly justification for letting the defendant affirmatively resort to perjurious testimony in reliance on the Government's disability to challenge his credibility."

1. Rationale

In adopting the impeachment exception, the Supreme Court has applied the basic cost-benefit analysis that it has utilized to develop other exceptions. On the cost side, the Court has found that an application of the exclusionary rule to prevent impeachment would not only impose the substantial cost of excluding reliable evidence; it would also give the defendant a license to commit perjury. On the benefits side, the Court has concluded that the principal deterrent effect of the exclusionary rule lies in the exclusion of illegally obtained evidence proffered in the prosecution's case-in-chief, and that the incremental deterrent effect of exclusion for impeachment purposes as well would be minimal. *See Harris v. New York*, 401 U.S. 222, 91 S.Ct. 643, 28 L.Ed.2d 1 (1971) ("The impeachment process here undoubtedly provided valuable aid to the jury in assessing petitioner's credibility, and the benefits of this process should not be lost, in our view, because of the speculative possibility that impermissible police conduct would be encouraged thereby.").

2. Impeachment of Testimony First Brought Out on Cross– Examination

The defendant in *Walder* made a statement on direct examination that was in flat contradiction with the illegally obtained evidence. In *United States v. Havens*, 446 U.S. 620, 100 S.Ct. 1912, 64 L.Ed.2d 559 (1980), the Supreme Court extended the impeachment exception to a situation where the defendant successfully avoided contradiction with the illegally obtained evidence on direct examination, but was nonetheless impeached with the evidence due to his answers on *cross-examination.*

a. Facts of *Havens*

Officers stopped McLeroth and Havens coming off a flight. They illegally searched Havens' suitcase and found a shirt from which a pocket had been torn out. When McLeroth was searched, the officers found a pocket sewn into his clothing. This pocket matched the shirt found in Havens' suitcase. Cocaine was found in the makeshift pocket. McLeroth pleaded guilty and testified against Havens; he admitted to having cocaine on his person. Havens took the stand and after acknowledging that he heard McLeroth's testimony, was asked by his counsel whether he had ever "engaged in that kind of activity with Mr. McLeroth." Havens answered in the negative. On cross-examination, Havens was asked more pointed questions—whether he had anything to do with sewing pockets into McLeroth's clothing and whether he had a shirt in his suitcase with the pocket missing. He answered both questions in the negative, and was impeached by the shirt and by testimony about its discovery.

b. Analysis in *Havens*

The Court stated that in terms of the impeachment exception, there is "no difference of constitutional magnitude between the defendant's statements on direct examination and his answers to questions put to him on cross-examination that are *plainly within the scope of the defendant's direct examination*." The Court found that the questions put to Havens were fairly within the scope of direct. They were simply more pointed questions intending to pin down Havens' general testimony that he had nothing to do with McLeroth's cocaine trafficking.

c. Dissent in *Havens*

The dissenters in *Havens* argued that the majority had inappropriately extended the impeachment exception so that it was now in the control of the Government. The dissent concluded that the only way for a defendant to avoid impeachment with illegally obtained evidence after Havens would be to "forego testifying on his own behalf." This practical consequence would mean that the impeachment exception would give police officers an incentive to violate the Fourth Amendment. Officers would know that evidence obtained illegally would have a positive effect in litigation—it will either keep the defendant from testifying, or it will be used as powerful impeachment evidence should he decide to testify.

3. **Exclusionary Rule Prevents Impeachment of Defendant's Witnesses With Illegally Obtained Evidence**

In *James v. Illinois*, 493 U.S. 307, 110 S.Ct. 648, 107 L.Ed.2d 676 (1990), the Court refused to extend the impeachment exception to allow impeachment of the defendant's *witnesses* with illegally obtained evidence.

a.   Facts of *James*

James told police officers that he had changed his hair color and style on the day after taking part in a shooting. The trial court suppressed this statement because it was the fruit of an arrest without probable cause. Prosecution witnesses at trial identified James, though they admitted that his hair color and style at trial was different from that of the perpetrator at the time of the shooting. James called a family friend, who testified that just before the shooting, James' hair color and style was the same as it was at trial, thus creating an inference that James had never changed it. The trial court, relying on the impeachment exception to the exclusionary rule, allowed the prosecution to introduce James' suppressed statement, to the effect that he had changed his hair, in order to impeach the credibility of the defense witness.

b.   Analysis in *James*

The majority in *James* found a compelling distinction between impeachment of a defendant's own testimony and that of defense witnesses. According to the Court, the impeachment exception keeps perjury out of the trial and allows truthful testimony in, thus furthering in both ways the search for truth. In contrast, the Court asserted that there would be a loss of truthful testimony if the prosecution could impeach defense witnesses with illegally obtained evidence. It reasoned that the fear of impeachment of one's witnesses likely would chill some defendants from even presenting the testimony of others. Unlike the defendant, who could carefully tailor truthful testimony to avoid reference to illegally obtained evidence, the defendant's witnesses could not be so easily controlled: "Defendants might reasonably fear that one or more of their witnesses, in a position to offer truthful and favorable testimony, would also make some statement in sufficient tension with the tainted evidence to allow the prosecutor to introduce that evidence for impeachment."

Applying a cost-benefit analysis, the Court stated that the deterrent effect of the exclusionary rule would be substantially diminished if illegally obtained evidence could be used to impeach not only the defendant but the defendant's witnesses. This is because "expanding the impeachment exception to all defense witnesses would significantly enhance the expected value to the prosecution of illegally obtained evidence." The court therefore concluded that the benefits of exclusion, in terms of deterrence, were substantial, and the cost of exclusion, in terms of the loss of reliable evidence, was minimal.

c. Dissent in *James*

The four dissenters in *James* found no legitimate distinction, in terms of the policies of the exclusionary rule, between impeachment of the defendant and impeachment of defense witnesses. The dissenters argued that impeachment is even more vital for attacking untruthful testimony of a defense witness than it is for attacking the defendant; the defendant's self-serving testimony will be given limited weight by the jury anyway, whereas "testimony by a witness said to be independent has the greater potential to deceive."

J. Subsequent Perjury Trials

The Supreme Court impeachment cases hold that evidence obtained in violation of the Fourth Amendment may be used to impeach the defendant at trial. But the Supreme Court has not decided whether such evidence may be used against the defendant in a subsequent prosecution for perjury. However, the lower courts have relied on the impeachment cases and have consistently held that illegally obtained evidence may be admitted in a prosecution for perjury. *See, e.g., United States v. Varela*, 968 F.2d 259 (2d Cir.1992) (statements made during an illegal arrest can be used to show that the defendant was lying when he subsequently contradicted himself during grand jury testimony).

1. Rationale

According to the courts, it is unlikely that an officer investigating one crime would violate the law in order to obtain evidence that could only be used in an unrelated prosecution for perjury—especially since the perjury prosecution would be contingent on the defendant's decision to contradict, under oath, the illegally obtained evidence. As the court stated in *Varela:* "We refuse to ascribe such clairvoyance to law enforcement officers; at the time of Varela's arrest, the possibility of subsequent perjurious testimony was too remote to serve as a motivating factor to * * * officers bent on breaking up a suspected cocaine importation scheme." On the cost side, the courts note that suppression of illegally obtained evidence from a perjury trial would "convert the exclusionary rule into a license to commit perjury."

2. Search Following the Perjured Testimony

The cases which refuse to apply the exclusionary rule to perjury trials have dealt with facts in which the illegal search precedes the perjured testimony. In these circumstances, the likelihood that an illegal search would be conducted to obtain evidence for a perjury trial is remote. The argument for deterrence is stronger, however, when the search occurs after the defendant gives perjured testimony. Then the contingency of the defendant's decision to lie under oath has been lifted, and the possible use of the evidence in a subsequent perjury trial is more easily predicted by the officer. Therefore, courts have stated that "if the unlawful arrest or seizure followed the perjured testimony—instead of preceding it—law enforcement officials would have the requisite incentive to engage in Fourth Amendment violations to obtain convictions of those suspected of perjury." *Varela, supra.* In this situation, the exclusionary rule *will* apply.

V. The "Good Faith" Exception to the Exclusionary Rule

A. The *Leon* Case

In the previous section on "collateral" uses of illegally obtained evidence, the courts assumed that the illegally obtained evidence would be excluded from the prosecution's case-in-chief. But in *United States v. Leon,* 468 U.S. 897, 104 S.Ct. 3430, 82 L.Ed.2d 677 (1984), the Supreme Court held that "the Fourth Amendment exclusionary rule should be modified so as not to bar the use in the prosecution's case-in-chief of evidence obtained by officers acting in reasonable reliance on a search warrant issued by a detached and neutral magistrate but ultimately found to be unsupported by probable cause."

1. Facts of *Leon*

In *Leon,* a confidential informant of unproven reliability informed police officers of drug activity at 620 Price Drive. He stated that he had personally observed a sale of drugs at that residence five months earlier. The police investigated, and found that some of the cars parked at the Price Drive residence belonged to persons who had been arrested for drug offenses. Officers also witnessed people often going into the house and then exiting with small paper sacks. Further investigation indicated that the suspects were associates of Leon, who had also been previously arrested on drug charges. Leon's house was then put under surveillance, and officers witnessed comings and goings consistent with drug activity. Based on these and other observations summarized in an affidavit, officers prepared an application for a warrant for the Price Drive residence, Leon's house, and another house associated with the suspects. A facially valid search warrant was issued, and the searches uncovered drugs and other evidence at each of the locations. The lower courts, while recognizing that the case was close, concluded that the affidavit was insufficient to establish probable cause. They reasoned that some of the information was fatally stale; that the informant's credibility was not established; and that the corroboration was not sufficient to shore up the defects in the informant's tip. One judge on the court of appeals dissented.

2. Holding in *Leon*

The Court concluded that the exclusionary rule should not apply because "the officers' reliance on the magistrate's determination of probable cause was objectively reasonable, and application of the extreme sanction of exclusion is inappropriate." The Court based its finding of objectively reasonable reliance on the fact that the officer's "affidavit related the results of an extensive investigation and, as the opinions of the divided panel of the Court of Appeals make clear, provided evidence sufficient to create disagreement among thoughtful and competent judges as to the existence of probable cause." Thus, while probable cause did not *in fact* exist, the question was close enough that the officers could reasonably rely on the magistrate's determination that probable cause did exist.

3. Rationale—Officer Who Did Nothing Wrong Cannot Be Deterred

The majority in *Leon* reasoned that the exclusionary rule would have no deterrent effect where an officer, "acting in objective good faith, has obtained a search warrant from a judge or magistrate and acted within its scope." Where the warrant in these circumstances is issued without probable cause, it is the *magistrate,* and not the law enforcement officer, who is in error. It is the magistrate's responsibility to determine whether probable cause exists. As the Court put it: "Penalizing the officer for the magistrate's error, rather than his own, cannot logically contribute to the deterrence of Fourth Amendment violations."

4. Can the Magistrate Be Deterred From Issuing Invalid Warrants?

The majority's analysis in *Leon* focuses on who made the error, and whether the exclusionary rule could have a deterrent effect on the state actor who made the error. Where an officer relies on a facially valid warrant that lacks probable cause, the error is ordinarily exclusively that of the magistrate. The question then is whether application of the exclusionary rule would *deter magistrates* from issuing warrants in the absence of probable cause. The majority in *Leon* concluded that the exclusionary rule would have no "significant deterrent effect on the issuing judge or magistrate." According to the Court, the magistrate has no stake in the outcome of a particular criminal trial, since she is a neutral judicial official. Therefore there is no incentive for the magistrate to allow officers to obtain evidence in violation of the Fourth Amendment; and the exclusionary rule cannot be an effective means of destroying an incentive (to violate the law) which does not exist. This is in contrast with the law enforcement officer, who does have an incentive to violate the Fourth Amendment in order to obtain evidence more easily, because he is in the "competitive enterprise of ferreting out crime" and thus has a significant stake in the outcome of a criminal trial; this incentive can be destroyed by application of the exclusionary rule. The majority asserted that magistrates could be more effectively deterred from erroneous decisions by simply informing them of their errors in the course of a written opinion; that is, the magistrate's "professional incentives" will assure future compliance with the Fourth Amendment when a reviewing judge declares the warrant invalid, whether or not the evidence is excluded.

5. Dissent in *Leon*

Justice Brennan argued that application of the exclusionary rule was necessary to encourage officers to act more carefully in the warrant process, and to caution them against blind reliance on the act of a magistrate. Justice Brennan was concerned that "the good faith exception will encourage police to provide only the bare minimum of information in future warrant applications." That is, the police would know that they could take the path of least resistance to obtaining a warrant and yet remain protected from judicial review. In a separate dissent, Justice Stevens expressed concern that under the good faith exception, officers may submit a warrant application to the magistrate even if they know that probable cause is lacking, on the chance that the magistrate may "take the bait. No longer must they hesitate and seek additional evidence in doubtful cases."

B. Objective Reasonableness

The term "good faith" exception is really a misnomer, because the Court in *Leon* does not purport to allow illegally obtained evidence to be admitted simply because the officer had a *subjective good faith* belief that what he did was legal. The *Leon* exception *does not depend on the subjective state of mind of the officer.* Rather, the Court stated that the test is *purely objective:* "the officer's reliance on the magistrate's probable cause determination and on the technical sufficiency of the warrant he issues must be *objectively reasonable.*"

1. Room for Reasonable Minds to Differ

In cases where a warrant is found invalid, the good faith exception will apply so long as reasonable minds can differ on the validity of the warrant. Where no reasonable argument can be made that the warrant is valid, then the good faith exception will not apply. Thus, the good faith exception is similar to the standard used for reviewing jury verdicts in civil cases. The standard is not whether the jury was correct or whether the reviewing court would have decided the case another way; rather, a verdict is only reversed if *no reasonable person* could have decided the way the jury did. So long as there is room for argument, then, the good faith exception will apply.

2. Clearly Established Law

Another useful analogy to the good faith exception comes from the qualified immunity cases decided under the civil rights statute, 42 U.S.C.A. § 1983. Qualified immunity means that even if the plaintiff's constitutional rights are violated, there is no liability unless the officer violated *clearly established law*; if the law was not clearly established at the time of the conduct, then there is room for argument as to whether the officer's conduct was lawful. By analogy, in *Leon*, the officers could reasonably rely on the warrant even though it lacked probable cause; the probable cause question was close enough that reasonable minds could differ.

C. Exceptions to the Good Faith Exception

The Court in *Leon* took pains to *reject* a broad holding that the exclusionary rule would never apply when the officer acts in reliance on a warrant. Rather, the Court stated that "the officer's reliance on the magistrate's probable cause determination and on the technical sufficiency of the warrant he issues must be *objectively reasonable*. It is clear that in some circumstances the officer will have *no reasonable grounds* for believing that the warrant was properly issued." Where all reasonable people would agree that a warrant is invalid, then the officer will be in error in relying on that warrant; and because it is the officer (as well as the magistrate) who makes the error in relying on an obviously invalid warrant, the exclusionary rule is presumed to have some deterrent effect in assuring future compliance with the Fourth Amendment.

The Court in *Leon* set forth *four situations* in which an officer's reliance on a warrant would be unreasonable. These are the four exceptions to the good faith exception.

1. Misleading Information

If the magistrate who issued the warrant "was misled by information in an affidavit that the affiant knew was false or would have known was false except for his reckless disregard of the truth," then the error in issuing the warrant was that of the *officer,* not the magistrate. The presumption in *Leon* is that officers can be deterred by operation of the exclusionary rule, though magistrates cannot. *See Dolliver v. State,* 598 N.E.2d 525 (Ind.1992) (no good faith exception where the officer's affidavit "flagrantly misrepresented" the nature of the informant's knowledge). This exception includes not only affirmative misrepresentations by police officers, but also a failure to impart information adverse to a finding of probable cause. *United States v. Reilly,* 76 F.3d 1271 (2d Cir.1996) (good faith exception inapplicable where affidavit was based upon visual observations of officers, who failed to inform the magistrate that they were on the defendant's curtilage when they made the observations).

2. Abandonment of Judicial Role

The Court in *Leon* stated that where the issuing magistrate "wholly abandoned his judicial role," then "no reasonably well-trained officer should rely on the warrant." Again, the officer has made an error which can be deterred. In *Lo–Ji Sales, Inc. v. New York,* 442 U.S. 319, 99 S.Ct. 2319, 60 L.Ed.2d 920 (1979), the Court, in a pre-*Leon* case, found that a magistrate had abandoned his neutral role when he issued the warrant and then *participated in the search.* The Court in *Leon* cited *Lo–Ji* as an example of a case in which the warrant could not reasonably be relied upon.

a. Abandonment Must Be Known by Police

Since *Leon* focuses on deterrence of police misconduct, it follows that the officer's reliance on a warrant issued by a magistrate who has abandoned his judicial role is not fatal unless the officer knew or had reason to know of this abandonment. For example, in *United States v. Breckenridge,* 782 F.2d 1317 (5th Cir.1986), a judge admitted that he had issued a warrant without reading the warrant application; he stated, however, that he made it *look like* he was reading the application to the officer who was applying for it. The court held that the officer could reasonably rely on the warrant even though it was invalid.

b. Abandonment Other Than by Participation in the Search

It is clear that the magistrate can be found to have abandoned his judicial role other than by participating in the search. Thus, in *Breckenridge, supra,* if the officer had reason to know that the magistrate had not even read the warrant application, then the good faith exception would not be reasonable. *See United States v. Decker,* 956 F.2d 773 (8th Cir.1992) (good faith exception does not apply where it was clear to the officers that the magistrate signed the warrant without even reading the warrant application).

3. **Affidavit Clearly Insufficient to Establish Probable Cause**

The Court in *Leon* stated that an officer could not reasonably rely on a warrant issued on the basis of an affidavit "so lacking in indicia of probable cause as to render official belief in its existence entirely unreasonable." In other words, if all reasonable minds would agree that the information set forth in the affidavit did not constitute probable cause, then the officer could not reasonably rely on the magistrate's issuance of a warrant based on such flimsy information.

Example: The Court in *Leon* gave the "barebones affidavit" as an example of an affidavit so lacking in probable cause that it cannot reasonably be relied upon. The Court cited *Nathanson v. United States,* 290 U.S. 41, 54 S.Ct. 11, 78 L.Ed. 159 (1933), as an example of an impermissible, barebones affidavit. In *Nathanson,* the affiant stated that he had "cause to suspect and does believe that" illegally imported liquor was located on certain premises. An officer cannot reasonably rely upon a warrant issued on the basis of such a conclusory assertion. The Court noted that the warrant held defective in *Leon* "clearly was supported by much more than a barebones affidavit" and thus could reasonably be relied upon. The affidavit in *Leon* related the results of an extensive investigation, rather than a bald conclusion. *See United States v. Weaver,* 99 F.3d 1372 (6th Cir.1996) (good faith exception inapplicable where the warrant contained only "boilerplate" conclusory assertions, without any underlying factual information).

4. **Facially Deficient Warrant**

The Court in *Leon* stated that the good faith exception would not apply if a warrant is so facially deficient in failing to particularize the place to be searched or the things to be seized that an officer could not reasonably think it to be valid. If the warrant is so egregiously deficient in its particularization that all reasonable people would find it invalid, then an officer who relies on it is in error; and the Court in *Leon* presumes that the exclusionary rule can deter the errors of police officers.

a. *Sheppard*

The mere fact that the warrant is lacking certain formalities is not enough to trigger the "facially deficient" exception to *Leon*. This is made clear by the Court's decision in *Massachusetts v. Sheppard*, 468 U.S. 981, 104 S.Ct. 3424, 82 L.Ed.2d 737 (1984), the companion case to *Leon*. In *Sheppard*, the judge issued a warrant on a form that authorized a search for "controlled substances;" but the warrant was issued to enable a search for evidence of a murder. The judge attempted to modify the form, but failed to incorporate an affidavit stating the items that could be sought by the searching officers. The judge assured the officers, however, that all the necessary clerical corrections had been made. The Court held that the evidence concerning the murder was properly admitted despite the defect in the warrant. It reasoned that the officers had done everything that could reasonably be expected of them, and that an officer is not required "to disbelieve a judge who has just advised him, by word and by action, that the warrant he possesses authorized him to conduct the search he has requested." *See also United States v. Russell*, 960 F.2d 421 (5th Cir.1992) (where the warrant failed to include an attachment listing the items to be seized, this was a clerical error attributable to the judge and officers could reasonably rely on the warrant).

b. Lack of Particularity

It is clear that the mere existence of an overbroad description of the place to be searched or the things to be seized does not preclude an officer's objective good faith reliance on the warrant; there may still be room for reasonable argument as to whether the description is in fact overbroad. Thus, the "facially deficient" exception applies only where no reasonable argument can be made that the descriptions in the warrant are sufficiently particular.

Examples: In *United States v. Buck*, 813 F.2d 588 (2d Cir.1987), a warrant included a catch-all clause allowing the seizure of items related to suspected terrorism. The court found that the seizure of evidence pursuant to that clause violated the Fourth Amendment's particularity requirement because many items could be linked to "terrorism" in the broad sense. But the evidence seized pursuant to the clause was nonetheless admissible under the good faith exception. The court explained that "what the officers failed to do was to anticipate our holding today that the particularity clause of the Fourth Amendment prohibits the use of a catch-all description in a search warrant, unaccompanied by any list of particular items or any other limiting language." The court noted however, that *subsequent* use of such catch-alls would not trigger the good faith exception, because the court had just *clearly established* the proposition that such language was insufficiently particular.

In contrast to *Buck*, the court in *United States v. Spilotro*, 800 F.2d 959 (9th Cir.1986), found the good faith exception inapplicable to an overbroad description in a warrant. The warrant authorized the search of a jewelry store for "stolen gemstones and other items of jewelry," and gave no indication that all the jewelry in the store was stolen. The court found the description in the warrant to be *so overbroad that no reasonable officer could think it was sufficiently particular.* Therefore, the warrant was facially deficient and the good faith exception could not apply.

D. Unreasonable Execution of the Warrant

The Court in *Leon* cautioned that application of the good faith exception "assumes, of course, that the officers properly executed the warrant and searched only those places for those objects that it was reasonable to believe were covered by the warrant." Improper execution of a valid warrant is an error properly attributed to the officer rather than to the magistrate. So for example, if the warrant authorizes a search of a certain hotel room and the officers extend the search to an adjoining room, this error in execution is not excused by the good faith exception. See the discussion earlier in this outline on execution of warrants.

E. Reliance on Unconstitutional Legislation

In *Illinois v. Krull*, 480 U.S. 340, 107 S.Ct. 1160, 94 L.Ed.2d 364 (1987), an officer conducted a warrantless inspection of an automobile wrecking yard. The officer relied on an administrative inspection statute that was subsequently held to be unconstitutional. The Supreme Court held that the evidence obtained in the inspection was nonetheless admissible under the good faith exception.

1. Rationale

The Court's reasoning in *Krull* was similar to that employed in *Leon*. The majority stated that where the officer reasonably relies on a statute that is subsequently held unconstitutional, the officer has not committed a wrong and thus cannot be deterred by the exclusionary rule. Rather, the wrongdoer is the *legislature*, which has passed an unconstitutional law. The Court reasoned that, like the magistrate in *Leon*, the legislature cannot be meaningfully deterred by an application of the exclusionary rule. The Court explained that legislators are not like law enforcement officers, who have a stake in a particular criminal prosecution and who can therefore be deterred from misconduct by a threatened exclusion of evidence.

2. Dissent

Justice O'Connor wrote a dissent for four Justices. She expressed concern that legislatures could pass laws authorizing unconstitutional searches, with the assurance that at least some of the evidence obtained by such searches would be admitted—exclusion would not occur until the unconstitutionality of the statute was clearly established by the courts. She concluded that "providing legislatures a grace period during which the police may freely perform unreasonable searches in order to convict those who might have otherwise escaped creates a positive incentive to promulgate unconstitutional laws."

3. Unreasonable Reliance on Unconstitutional Legislation

As in *Leon*, the Court in *Krull* posited certain limited situations in which it would be objectively unreasonable for an officer to rely on another party's determination that a search is legal. However, the exceptions to the good faith exception are even more limited when applied to legislative action than they are when applied to a magistrate's decision.

a. Abdicating the Legislative Role

First, "a statute cannot support objectively reasonable reliance if, in passing the statute, the legislature wholly abandoned its responsibility to enact constitutional laws." The Court, however, could not cite an instance in which a legislature has "abdicated its legislative role."

b. Statute Clearly Unconstitutional

The Court in *Krull* stated that an officer's reliance on a statute would be objectively unreasonable if "its provisions are such that a reasonable officer should have known that the statute was unconstitutional." In other words, if the legislature passes a statute which is in violation of *clearly established Fourth Amendment law*, then an officer would not be reasonable in relying on the statute, and the resulting evidence would be excluded. For example, if a legislature passed a statute authorizing police officers to enter a person's house to arrest that person even in the absence of exigent circumstances, the good faith exception would not insulate a search and arrest conducted in reliance on that statute. This is because the Court clearly established in *Payton v. New York* that an arrest warrant is required for an in-home arrest in the absence of exigent circumstances. The error in relying on the statute would be that of the officer, and the presumption is that law enforcement officers can be deterred from wrongdoing by application of the exclusionary rule.

4. **Misinterpretation of Legislation**

The *Leon/Krull* good faith exception does not apply to a police officer's reasonable though mistaken interpretation of the scope of a statute permitting a search. Such a mistake is one that is made by the *officer*, not by the legislature. So if the statute does not in fact authorize a search but the officer reasonably thinks it does, the evidence obtained in the search will be excluded unless it independently satisfies Fourth Amendment standards.

F. **Mistakes by Court Clerical Personnel**

In *Arizona v. Evans*, 514 U.S. 1, 115 S.Ct. 1185, 131 L.Ed.2d 34 (1995), the Court held that the good faith exception applies when an officer reasonably relies on information from court clerical personnel which happens to be mistaken. Officers stopped Evans for a traffic violation. They entered his name into a computer data terminal, and were informed that there was an outstanding warrant for Evans' arrest, so they arrested him. In fact, the information in the computer was inaccurate—the arrest warrant had been quashed, but court clerical personnel had failed to update the information in the data base. This meant that the arrest of Evans was illegal. A search incident to the arrest uncovered evidence, which Evans moved to exclude.

The Supreme Court, relying on *Leon* and *Krull*, applied the good faith exception to the officers' conduct. The Court noted that the officers were not in error. Rather, the error was made by court clerical personnel, who could not be deterred by exclusion of evidence. Court clerical personnel, unlike police officers, are not in the competitive enterprise of ferreting out crime—they have no stake in obtaining evidence for a trial. The Court concluded: "Application of the *Leon* framework supports a categorical exception to the exclusionary rule for clerical errors of court employees."

G. The Good Faith Exception and Warrantless Searches and Seizures

By its terms, the *Leon* good faith exception applies only where the officer reasonably relies on an invalid warrant. The good faith exception was extended in *Krull* and *Evans*, but only to situations where the officer reasonably relies on an actor who has no personal stake in a criminal prosecution. So far, the Court has applied the good faith exception only where the officer is reasonably relying on an intermediary.

Example: Suppose that an officer enters a house and seizes narcotics. He had no warrant, but he claims that he had probable cause and exigent circumstances due to the imminent destruction of evidence. At the suppression hearing, the court finds that exigent circumstances did not in fact exist because, on the facts, it was unlikely that evidence would be destroyed in the time it would have taken to obtain a warrant. But the court acknowledges that reasonable minds could differ as to the existence of exigent circumstances, and that given the presence of readily-destructible narcotics in the house, the officer's conclusion as to exigency was not so far-fetched as to be completely unreasonable. Even after *Leon*, the evidence would be excluded, because the officer's "objectively reasonable" miscalculation does not qualify for the good faith exception. *See United States v. Curzi*, 867 F.2d 36 (1st Cir.1989) ("the good-faith exception is not available" where an officer conducted a warrantless search on the reasonable but mistaken assumption that the search was consistent with the Fourth Amendment). But *see United States v. De Leon–Reyna*, 930 F.2d 396 (5th Cir.1991) (adhering to the circuit's pre-*Leon* view that the good faith exception applies to illegal warrantless searches).

1. Rationale of *Leon* May Preclude Extension to Warrantless Searches and Seizures

The Court's predominant rationale in *Leon* and its progeny is that the application of the exclusionary rule must focus on the wrongdoer, and on whether the wrongdoer can be deterred from misconduct by the threat of excluding evidence. In *Leon*, *Krull*, and *Evans*, the wrongdoers were the magistrate, legislature, and court clerical personnel, respectively. The Court posited that these parties could not be deterred by the risk of exclusion, since they had no stake in the outcome of a criminal prosecution. However, the Court assumed and stated that officers could be deterred from misconduct by the exclusionary rule. Indeed, the four exceptions set forth in *Leon* involve situations in which the officer has done wrong and therefore the good faith exception does not apply. Therefore, the rationale employed in *Leon* makes it unlikely that the Court would apply the good faith exception to reasonable but illegal activity of law enforcement officers—though it would not stop Congress from doing so.

2. Some Language in *Leon* May Be Applicable to Warrantless Search Situations

While the rationale of *Leon* would cut against an extension of the good faith exception to errors by police officers, there is some language in *Leon* which may support such an extension. Specifically, the Court stated that "when law enforcement officers have acted in objective good faith or their transgressions have been minor, the magnitude of the benefit conferred on * * * guilty defendants offends basic concepts of the criminal justice system." This language is not limited to situations where the officer has reasonably relied on an intermediary.

H. Reasonable Reliance on a Warrant Based on Illegally Obtained Information

While the good faith exception is currently limited to situations where an officer relies on either a magistrate's decision or a legislative act, a difficulty in applying this limitation arises because officers often conduct a warrantless search in the hope of discovering information with which to obtain a warrant. Before *Leon*, if a search warrant was based upon illegally obtained evidence, then the warrant itself was considered tainted and the evidence obtained upon executing the warrant was excluded as fruit of the poisonous tree. Courts after *Leon* have split as to whether the good faith exception should apply where officers reasonably rely on a warrant that is issued on the basis of evidence obtained in an illegal warrantless search.

Example: Suppose the police legally arrest a person, but then conduct a search that is somewhat beyond the spatial limitations of the incident search rule as set forth by *Chimel v. California, supra* (e.g., they search the room adjoining the room in which the defendant has been arrested). In this search they discover a receipt for a storage space, and an indication on the receipt that drugs are being kept in the space. The officers prepare an application for a warrant to search the storage space. They describe the arrest, other pertinent circumstances, and state that the receipt was found in the search incident to arrest. The magistrate issues the warrant and the officers search the storage space and seize drugs. If the good faith exception applies, then the evidence is admissible even though it is fruit of the poisonous tree—unless the warrant is clearly lacking in probable cause because the illegality of the initial search would be obvious to any reasonable person. If the good faith exception does not apply, the evidence would be inadmissible as the fruit of the poisonous tree.

Split in Courts

Some courts have held that the good faith exception applies where the officer reasonably relies on a warrant based on illegally obtained information. For example, in *United States v. Thomas*, 757 F.2d 1359 (2d Cir.1985), the court reasoned that in these circumstances "there is nothing more that the officer could have or should have done" to be sure that the initial search was legal. The court concluded that "the magistrate, whose duty it is to interpret the law, determined that the [illegal search] could form the basis for probable cause; it was reasonable for the officer to rely on this determination." In issuing the warrant, the magistrate is considered to have determined that the evidence used in the warrant application was legally obtained. And unless the magistrate is clearly wrong in that determination, an officer can rely upon it in objective good faith. This position assumes, however, that the officers have fully briefed the magistrate about the pertinent facts surrounding the initial search. *See United States v. Reilly*, 76 F.3d 1271 (2d Cir.1996) (good faith exception does not apply where officers failed to inform the magistrate that the information on which they based their warrant application was obtained through a search in the defendant's curtilage).

Other courts have stated that the good faith exception does not apply when a warrant is issued on the basis of illegally obtained information. These courts reason that the initial illegal search was made by the police officer, who can be deterred by application of the exclusionary rule; police officers should not be able to sanitize their illegal conduct by running to a magistrate to obtain a warrant. *See United States v. Vasey*, 834

F.2d 782 (9th Cir.1987) (holding *Leon* inapplicable to a search warrant based on illegally obtained information: "The constitutional error was made by the officer in this case, not by the magistrate, as in *Leon*.")

V

The Privilege Against Self–Incrimination

■ ANALYSIS

I. Introduction

The privilege against self-incrimination, as expressed in the Fifth Amendment of the Constitution, provides that "[n]o person * * * shall be compelled in any criminal case to be a witness against himself." This privilege prohibits the Government from compelling individuals to provide incriminating testimony. Although the exact origin of the privilege is unclear, the right against self-incrimination was unquestionably established in English common law by the end of the seventeenth century. A century later, this privilege was explicitly incorporated into the Constitution of the United States. *See* Leonard W. Levy, Origins of the Fifth Amendment Right Against Self–Incrimination 433 (2d ed. 1986) for a complete discussion of the history of the privilege.

A. The Policies of the Privilege Against Self–Incrimination

Many policies support the privilege against self-incrimination. The following is a list of the most commonly offered justifications for this privilege.

1. Protection of the Innocent

The privilege against self-incrimination protects innocent defendants from convicting themselves by a bad performance on the witness stand. *Quinn v. United States*, 349 U.S. 155, 75 S.Ct. 668, 99 L.Ed. 964 (1955). Some commentators criticize this justification, arguing that the privilege historically protects only guilty individuals.

2. The Cruel Trilemma

The state should not subject individuals to the "cruel trilemma" of choosing among self-accusation, perjury, and contempt of court. *Brown v. Walker*, 161 U.S. 591, 16 S.Ct. 644, 40 L.Ed. 819 (1896). Some commentators argue that this rationale only justifies the privilege at trial because contempt of court cannot be used against individuals who refuse to answer police questioning.

3. Limiting Perjury

It has been argued that if there were no privilege, people forced to testify would perjure themselves in an attempt to avoid incrimination. Some commentators state, however, that perjury is prevalent despite the existence of the privilege.

4. Unreliability of Coerced Statements

Self-deprecatory statements are not trustworthy, especially when they are the product of coercion. *Murphy v. Waterfront Comm'n of NY Harbor,*

378 U.S. 52, 55, 84 S.Ct. 1594, 1596, 12 L.Ed.2d 678 (1964). Commentators note, however, that coercion may be barred without resort to a privilege as broad as that found in the Fifth Amendment, and that untrustworthy statements could be excluded even absent a privilege.

5. **Preference for Accusatorial System**

The privilege against self-incrimination is needed to allow for an accusatorial, rather than an inquisitorial, system of criminal justice. *Murphy,* 378 U.S. at 55, 84 S.Ct. at 1596. This justification is criticized as simply a restatement of the privilege itself.

6. **Need to Deter Improper Police Practices**

As self-incriminating statements are likely to be elicited by improper practices, the privilege protects individuals from the risk of inhumane treatment and governmental abuse. *Murphy,* 378 U.S. at 55, 84 S.Ct. at 1596. Some commentators argue, however, that the due process clauses of the Fifth and Fourteenth Amendments afford adequate protection against objectionable police practices.

7. **Fair State–Individual Balance**

The privilege supports the individual's right to be free from governmental interference and it requires the government to "shoulder the entire load" during contests with the individual. *See* Wigmore, A Treatise on the Anglo–American System of Evidence in Trials at Common Law VIII, § 2251, at 317 (3d ed. 1940). Some commentators argue that the probable cause requirements for search and arrest provide adequate protection against governmental disturbance, and that the privilege is not essential to protect against overreaching by the Government.

8. **Preservation of Official Morality**

"Any system * * * which permits the prosecution to trust habitually to compulsory self-disclosure as a source of proof must itself suffer morally thereby." Wigmore, *supra,* § 2251. This rationale is criticized as being tautological; it assumes that self-disclosure is immoral. Justice Scalia, in his dissent in *Minnick v. Mississippi,* 498 U.S. 146, 111 S.Ct. 486, 112 L.Ed.2d 489 (1990), argued that self-disclosure is a positive good: "While every person is entitled to stand silent, it is more virtuous for the wrongdoer to admit his offense and accept the punishment he deserves, not only for society, but for the wrongdoer himself."

9. **Privacy Rationale**

The privilege provides an enclave in which the individual may lead a private life. *Murphy,* 378 U.S. at 55, 84 S.Ct. at 1596. Commentators argue, however, that it is immoral to suggest that a murderer is justified in withholding information because he "prefers to remain in a private enclave." Friendly, "The Fifth Amendment Tomorrow: The Case for Constitutional Change," 37 U.Cin.L.Rev. 671, 689–90 (1968).

10. First Amendment Rationale

The privilege shelters individuals from governmental intrusion and oppression concerning political and religious beliefs. Friendly, *supra,* at 696. Some commentators view the First Amendment as the appropriate vehicle for addressing this problem.

B. Scope of the Privilege

There are three basic components to the privilege against self-incrimination. Each of these components must exist in order for a person to effectively claim the privilege.

1. Compulsion by the State

First, there must be compulsion by the state. An example of such compulsion is the threat of imprisonment for contempt.

2. Witness Against Himself

Second, state compulsion is only impermissible if it forces a person to be a witness against himself.

a. Testimonial or Communicative Act

An individual only becomes a witness against himself when the state compels the individual to perform a testimonial or communicative act. Other evidence, such as physical evidence of a crime, is not protected by the Fifth Amendment privilege.

b. Legitimate Risk of Harm

Since the privilege only protects the individual from answering questions that are against self-interest, the individual must demonstrate a legitimate risk of harm stemming from the testimony.

c. Must Be Personal

The Fifth Amendment uses the term "himself." Thus, the privilege is personal and only applies to individuals. It does not protect business entities.

3. Use in a Criminal Case

The state cannot compel self-incriminating testimony in a criminal case. The privilege, however, possesses a much broader scope than this language seems to suggest.

II. Proceedings in Which the Privilege Applies

A. Compulsion in Any Proceeding Where Testimony May Be Used in a Criminal Case

The language of the Fifth Amendment seems to suggest that the right against self-incrimination only protects individuals from the compulsion of testimony, where that compulsion occurs in a criminal case. The Supreme Court has held, however, that the privilege protects individuals from answering questions in *any* proceeding, if their answers might incriminate them in a future criminal proceeding. *Lefkowitz v. Turley*, 414 U.S. 70, 94 S.Ct. 316, 38 L.Ed.2d 274 (1973).

1. Ultimate Use in a Criminal Case

The privilege may be asserted in any proceeding and at any time the Government seeks to compel a person to disclose potentially incriminating information (e.g., on a tax return, see *Garner v. United States*, 424 U.S. 648, 96 S.Ct. 1178, 47 L.Ed.2d 370 (1976)). An individual can invoke the privilege against self-incrimination in civil proceedings, administrative proceedings, etc., if the statement could ultimately be *used* against him *in a criminal case*. See *McCarthy v. Arndstein*, 266 U.S. 34, 45 S.Ct. 16, 69 L.Ed. 158 (1924) (upholding Fifth Amendment claim asserted by a party in a bankruptcy case, where the statement could have been used as an admission in criminal proceeding). It is the potential of future use in criminal proceedings that gives rise to the privilege.

In *Chavez v. Martinez*, 538 U.S. 760, 123 S.Ct. 1994, 155 L.Ed.2d 984 (2003), the Supreme Court held that a police officer's alleged coercive questioning of a suspect did not violate the self-incrimination clause of the Fifth Amendment, absent use of the suspect's compelled statements in a criminal case. Martinez was shot by a police officer during an alleged altercation and received injuries that left him blind and paralyzed. Immediately after the shooting, while Martinez was being treated in the hospital, Officer Chavez questioned him about the altercation. Chavez made incriminating statements, but was never prosecuted or compelled to be a witness against himself. Martinez filed a § 1983 action against Officer Chavez, alleging that Chavez violated his Fifth Amendment right not to be compelled in any criminal case to be a witness against himself as well as his Fourteenth Amendment substantive due process right to be free from coercive questioning. The Court held that the phrase "criminal case" in the context of the Self–Incrimination Clause of the

Fifth Amendment requires, at the very least, initiation of a legal proceeding, and does not encompass police questioning during a criminal investigation.

2. The Use of Compelled Testimony Outside of a Criminal Case Does Not Implicate the Fifth Amendment

The state may compel disclosure of information, however, for use in civil or other non-criminal proceedings. The Fifth Amendment privilege does not protect against use of a compelled statement outside of a criminal case. *See Piemonte v. United States*, 367 U.S. 556, 81 S.Ct. 1720, 6 L.Ed.2d 1028 (1961) (holding that privilege does not prevent use of compelled testimony for purposes of private retribution); *United States v. Conte*, 99 F.3d 60 (2d Cir.1996) (permitting compulsion in a probation revocation proceeding, since that is not a criminal case, and there was no risk that the statements could be used in a subsequent criminal case).

B. What Is a Criminal Case?

Thus, the question arises as to whether the proceeding in which the testimony could be used is a "criminal case." Courts are likely to uphold a legislative determination that a proceeding is "civil" in nature. *See United States v. Ward*, 448 U.S. 242, 100 S.Ct. 2636, 65 L.Ed.2d 742 (1980) (holding that a statute imposing a "civil penalty" upon persons discharging hazardous material into navigable waters was not "quasi-criminal").

1. Sexually Dangerous Persons Act

In *Allen v. Illinois*, 478 U.S. 364, 106 S.Ct. 2988, 92 L.Ed.2d 296 (1986), defendant's coerced confession was used against him in a proceeding under the Illinois Sexually Dangerous Persons Act, and he was incarcerated. The Court held that a proceeding under the Act was not a criminal case within the meaning of the Fifth Amendment, but rather was a civil commitment proceeding for treatment purposes. Therefore, the Fifth Amendment did not prevent the use of compelled testimony in such an action.

2. Legislative Intent Is Crucial

The Court in *Allen* stated that the determination of the nature of a proceeding for Fifth Amendment purposes is a question of statutory construction. In this case, the Illinois legislature expressly provided that proceedings under the Act would "be civil in nature."

3. Criminal Law Objectives

The Act in *Allen* provided that the state could not file a petition under the Act unless it had already filed criminal charges. In addition, proceedings under the Act required satisfaction of a "beyond a reasonable doubt" standard of proof, and those adjudicated sexually dangerous persons were incarcerated in prisons (though they received psychological therapy). Yet, the Court held that these traditional indicators of criminal law objectives could not outweigh the fact that the legislature had characterized the Act as "civil" in nature.

C. Foreign Prosecutions

In *United States v. Balsys*, 524 U.S. 666, 118 S.Ct. 2218, 141 L.Ed.2d 575 (1998), the Court held that the possibility of criminal prosecution by a foreign government does not constitute a "criminal case" for purposes of the privilege against self-incrimination. Balsys refused to answer questions in a deportation hearing in which the government alleged that he had committed offenses during World War II. He asserted the Fifth Amendment privilege on the ground that his testimony might be used against him in a prosecution in Israel or Lithuania. The Court analyzed the policies supporting the privilege as set forth in *Murphy, supra*, and concluded that although some applied only to domestic concerns, others might be broad enough to encompass foreign prosecution. However, the Court specifically rejected the reasoning in *Murphy* that led to a more expansive view of the privilege, noting that application of the privilege to the risk of foreign prosecution would be costly to government interests. The Court further noted that domestic courts could not enforce immunity in foreign countries.

III.   What Is Compulsion?

A. Use of Contempt Power

The state's use of the contempt power is the classic form of compulsion because it imposes substantial punishment on a witness who claims the privilege, and presents the witness with the classic "cruel" trilemma: the citizen is forced to choose among self-accusation, contempt, and perjury— each of which could lead to imprisonment.

B. Other State–Imposed Sanctions

The Supreme Court has extended the concept of compulsion to include a broader range of sanctions in addition to punishment for contempt. For example, in *Miranda v. Arizona*, 384 U.S. 436, 86 S.Ct. 1602, 16 L.Ed.2d 694 (1966), the Court found compulsion in the setting of custodial interrogation. See the discussion of *Miranda* in the material on confessions.

1. Economic Sanctions for Invoking the Privilege

In *Lefkowitz v. Turley, supra*, the state sought to interrogate public contractors about their previous transactions and to require these contractors to possibly incriminate themselves by demanding that they waive immunity. In addition, the state planned to disqualify these individuals as public contractors if they refused to testify and waive immunity. The Court held that the threat of economic sanctions imposed by the state for refusing to testify was tantamount to compulsion, because the state was attempting to impose a significant penalty for invoking the privilege. *See also Spevack v. Klein,* 385 U.S. 511, 87 S.Ct. 625, 17 L.Ed.2d 574 (1967) (Fifth Amendment prohibits disbarment of a lawyer for invoking the privilege during a lawyer discipline proceeding, where any statements could have been used in a subsequent criminal proceeding).

a.   The Fifth Amendment Does Not Protect Against the Use of Immunized Testimony Outside of a Criminal Case

If the state gave the contractor in *Lefkowitz* immunity from criminal prosecution for his testimony, however, the state could then deny the contractor public contracts for refusing to testify. This result can occur because, once the contractor is immunized, his statements cannot be used against him and could not tend to incriminate him. Thus, any invocation of the privilege would be improper, because no privilege exists in this situation. While it is improper to punish a person for a valid exercise of the privilege, it is perfectly permissible to penalize a person who refuses to testify when he has no right to refuse.

b.   Use in a Civil Case

If the witness in *Lefkowitz* had been granted immunity, the state could use his incriminating statements against him by denying him contracts based on his testimony. While these statements would be compelled, the privilege only protects individuals from the use of compelled statements in a criminal case.

2.   Compulsion in the Prison Context

a.   Clemency Hearings

In *Ohio Adult Parole Authority v. Woodard*, 523 U.S. 272, 118 S.Ct. 1244, 140 L.Ed.2d 387 (1998), the Court held that the voluntary interview provision of the Ohio clemency proceedings did not violate the Fifth Amendment privilege against self-incrimination. The law provided that the Ohio Parole authority must conduct a clemency hearing within 45 days of an inmate's scheduled execution date. Prior to the hearing, the inmate was permitted but not required to request an interview with parole board members. Woodard claimed that in order to have a chance at clemency, he was "compelled" to subject himself to an interview, which would create the possibility of incrimination on the current charge and other charges. He argued that the interview was not really voluntary because his refusal to answer questions would be construed against him in the clemency process. The Court unanimously rejected Woodard's argument, comparing the voluntary interview to other decisions defendants have to make in the criminal process, including whether to testify at trial and whether to put on a defense. In each case, there may be pressures pushing the defendant one way or the other, but the Court noted that it had specifically held that these situations do not create "compelled" testimony.

b.   Prison Treatment Programs

The Court reached a similar result in *McKune v. Lile*, 536 U.S. 24, 122 S.Ct. 2017, 153 L.Ed.2d 47 (2002). Lile was ordered to participate in a Sexual Abuse Treatment Program (SATP) a few years before his scheduled release from a Kansas prison. As part of the program, participants were required to sign an "Admission of Responsibility" form in which they were required to admit responsibility for the crimes for which they were convicted and provide details of all prior sexual activities, even if such acts constituted uncharged crimes. The information provided was unprivileged and might be used in future criminal proceedings, although no information had ever been revealed under the SATP. Inmates who refused to participate in the program faced loss of prison privileges, including curtailment of visitation rights, earnings, work opportunities, ability to send money to family, and other privileges. They also would be transferred to a potentially more dangerous maximum-security unit. The Supreme Court rejected Lile's argument that the required disclosure of his criminal history violated his Fifth Amendment privilege against self-incrimination, citing *Woodard*, and noting that the consequences in this case were far less serious. The Court noted the relevance of Lile's prison status, explaining that although "the privilege against self-incrimination does not terminate at the jailhouse door . . . the fact of a valid conviction and the ensuing restrictions on liberty are essential to the Fifth Amendment analysis."

3. **Comment on the Invocation of the Privilege**

A comment by the prosecutor or the judge on the defendant's failure to testify constitutes compulsion. *Griffin v. California,* 380 U.S. 609, 85 S.Ct. 1229, 14 L.Ed.2d 106 (1965). The Court in *Griffin* held that adverse comments to the jury on the defendant's election not to testify constitutes punishment for the invocation of silence and thus violates the Fifth Amendment.

a. Argument That Evidence Is Uncontradicted May Be Compulsion

A problem arises if the prosecutor argues to the jury that the Government's evidence is uncontradicted. Whether such an argument constitutes adverse comment on the defendant's failure to testify, as opposed to the defendant's failure to call witnesses or offer proof, depends on the facts of the particular case. *Compare Lent v. Wells,* 861 F.2d 972 (6th Cir.1988) (statement that evidence was uncontradicted violated *Griffin* where defendant was the only person who could rebut the complainant's assertion that a sexual attack occurred), *with Lindgren v. Lane,* 925 F.2d 198 (7th Cir.1991) (finding no *Griffin* violation where the prosecutor argued that the testimony of a prosecution witness was undisputed because the defense witness offered in contradiction was not believable).

b. Invited Comment

In *United States v. Robinson,* 485 U.S. 25, 108 S.Ct. 864, 99 L.Ed.2d 23 (1988), the Court held that a prosecutor may comment on a defendant's failure to testify in response to defense counsel's argument that the defendant had never been permitted to explain his side of the story. Thus, the defense may, by opening the door, allow the prosecution to comment on the invocation of the privilege.

c. Adverse Inference at a Sentencing Hearing

A sentencing court may not draw an adverse inference from a defendant's failure to testify at the sentencing hearing, according to the Court in *Mitchell v. United States,* 526 U.S. 314, 119 S.Ct. 1307, 143 L.Ed.2d 424 (1999). Mitchell pled guilty to federal charges of distribution of cocaine and conspiracy to distribute five or more kilograms of cocaine but reserved the right to contest the drug quantity at her sentencing hearing. The quantity was important in that it determined the length of Mitchell's prison term. At Mitchell's sentencing hearing, three codefendants testified that she had sold each of them various amounts of cocaine. The total amount was sufficient to enhance Mitchell's sentence to a mandatory minimum of ten years in prison. Mitchell did not testify nor did she present other evidence. The sentencing court noted that her failure to testify was a factor that persuaded him to rely on the codefendants' testimony. On appeal, Mitchell argued that the sentencing court was not entitled to draw an adverse inference from her silence. The Supreme Court agreed, noting that the reasons for prohibiting negative inferences at a trial apply with equal force at sentencing, as in the present case where the negative inference resulted in a much higher term of imprisonment. In dissent, Justice Scalia pointed out that the case law has consistently distinguished between the trial and sentencing phases of a criminal case. Examples include the Sixth Amendment confrontation clause and right to a jury trial.

d. Adverse Inference in a Civil Case

A citizen has the right to refuse to testify in a civil case, if the testimony can later be used against him in a criminal case. But can the adverse party in the civil case ask the jury to draw a negative inference from the fact that the privilege was invoked? The Court in *Baxter v. Palmigiano*, 425 U.S. 308, 96 S.Ct. 1551, 47 L.Ed.2d 810 (1976), answered yes. An adverse comment is permissible in a civil case, where it is not in a criminal case, because the "awesome power" of the prosecution is not arrayed against the citizen in a civil case. The penalty for invoking the privilege is not, therefore, the government compulsion that the Fifth Amendment prohibits.

4. **Compulsion and the "Exculpatory No" Doctrine**

In *Brogan v. United States*, 522 U.S. 398, 118 S.Ct. 805, 139 L.Ed.2d 830 (1998), the Supreme Court abolished the so-called "exculpatory no" doctrine. Before *Brogan* was decided, many of the Circuit courts had adopted this doctrine, which provided that a simple denial of guilt in response to questions from government investigators did not violate 18 U.S.C. § 1001, which criminalizes the act of making false statements to government agents. Brogan conceded that he had made a false statement to government investigators but argued that the "exculpatory no" doctrine should apply because criminalizing a simple denial of guilt violates the spirit of the Fifth Amendment, placing him in the "cruel trilemma" of either admitting guilt, remaining silent, or falsely denying guilt. The Court rejected his argument, holding that the Fifth Amendment permits a person to remain silent, but does not confer a privilege to lie.

IV. Identifying the Holder of the Privilege

A. The Privilege Is Personal

The privilege against self-incrimination belongs only to the person who would be compelled to incriminate himself by his own testimony.

1. Attorneys May Not Claim Privilege for Their Client

An attorney may not invoke the privilege by claiming that his testimony might incriminate his client. This would not be a violation of the client's privilege. Of course, the attorney-client privilege might shield such a disclosure even though the Fifth Amendment privilege does not.

2. Subpoena Served Upon Accountant to Produce Taxpayer's Records Does Not Violate the Fifth Amendment

In *Couch v. United States*, 409 U.S. 322, 93 S.Ct. 611, 34 L.Ed.2d 548 (1973), the government served a subpoena on an accountant to turn over a taxpayer's records. The accountant and the taxpayer invoked a Fifth Amendment privilege, on the ground that the compelled disclosure would incriminate the taxpayer. But the Court found that the Fifth Amendment could not operate to quash the subpoena. The taxpayer had no right to invoke the privilege, because he was not subject to compulsion—the subpoena was served on the accountant. The accountant had no right to invoke the privilege because, while subject to compulsion, the documents incriminated the taxpayer, not the accountant.

3. Subpoena Served Upon Attorney to Produce Client's Documents Does Not Violate the Fifth Amendment

Similarly, in *Fisher v. United States*, 425 U.S. 391, 96 S.Ct. 1569, 48 L.Ed.2d 39 (1976), the Supreme Court relied on *Couch* to hold that the Fifth Amendment could not be invoked by attorneys who received summonses from the IRS to produce client records, where the records would incriminate the client but not the attorneys. The Court indicated, however, that the documents would be protected from disclosure by the attorney client privilege if they would have been protected from compelled disclosure while in the hands of the client.

B. Business Entities

1. Collective Entity Rule

In *Bellis v. United States*, 417 U.S. 85, 94 S.Ct. 2179, 40 L.Ed.2d 678 (1974), the Court held that the Fifth Amendment does not protect partnerships.

It reasoned that to allow a partnership to assert a Fifth Amendment privilege would be inconsistent with the traditional rule that the privilege is a personal one. The Court relied on the language of the Amendment, which is cast in personal terms.

2. No Matter What the Entity

The Court in *Bellis* stated broadly that "no artificial organization may utilize the personal privilege." The Court was unconcerned that the partnership in *Bellis* was a law firm with only three partners and a handful of employees. It did not matter how small the entity was, only that it was an entity. The Court has subsequently held that the *Bellis* rule applies equally to corporations. Thus corporations, like partnerships, are not entitled to the protection of the Fifth Amendment. *See Braswell v. United States*, 487 U.S. 99, 108 S.Ct. 2284, 101 L.Ed.2d 98 (1988) (corporation wholly owned and operated by a single individual was not itself entitled to Fifth Amendment protection).

3. Personal Privilege

While the entity has no privilege, the individuals who work for the entity still retain a personal privilege. However, whether this personal privilege can be asserted when the entity is a target of the governmental investigation is a difficult question, which ordinarily arises when the Government subpoenas an individual for documents that will incriminate the entity as well as the individual. This problem is discussed in the section on production of documents, *infra*.

C. The Fifth Amendment Protects Sole Proprietorships

Although partnerships and corporations do not possess Fifth Amendment protection, the Court in *United States v. Doe*, 465 U.S. 605, 104 S.Ct. 1237, 79 L.Ed.2d 552 (1984), held that the Fifth Amendment protects a sole proprietorship. The Court reasoned that a sole proprietorship is not an entity that is legally separate from the individual.

V. Information Protected by the Privilege

A. Evidence Is Not Protected Unless It Is Testimonial

The Fifth Amendment applies only if the information obtained through compulsion is testimonial—i.e., the kind of information that a "witness" provides. Thus, a person can be compelled to produce incriminating physical evidence, such as a blood sample, because in doing so, the person is not forced to become a "witness" against himself. The issue is whether the fact will be proven through physical or testimonial evidence.

1. The Cruel Trilemma

The distinction between physical and testimonial evidence centers around the "cruel trilemma" that the Fifth Amendment prohibits. The Fifth Amendment says that a person cannot be compelled to make a choice between imprisonment for contempt for remaining silent, imprisonment for telling the truth and incriminating himself, and imprisonment for perjury for lying. Physical evidence, however, cannot be true or false. Thus, in producing physical evidence (e.g., a blood sample), the defendant cannot commit perjury. Physical evidence, therefore, does not place an individual in a cruel trilemma. In contrast, testimonial assertions can be true or false and thus may subject an individual to the cruel trilemma of contempt, self-incrimination, or perjury.

2. *Schmerber v. California*

In *Schmerber v. California*, 384 U.S. 757, 86 S.Ct. 1826, 16 L.Ed.2d 908 (1966), the Court found that the state did not violate the defendant's Fifth Amendment rights by withdrawing a blood sample from the defendant and subjecting it to chemical analysis despite the defendant's refusal. The Court held that the privilege only protects an accused from the compulsion of testimonial or communicative evidence.

3. Extending *Schmerber*

In several cases, the Court has reaffirmed and extended its holding in *Schmerber. See United States v. Dionisio*, 410 U.S. 1, 93 S.Ct. 764, 35 L.Ed.2d 67 (1973) (holding that state compulsion of voice-prints does not violate the Fifth Amendment); *United States v. Wade*, 388 U.S. 218, 87 S.Ct. 1926, 18 L.Ed.2d 1149 (1967) (holding that forced participation in a line-up does not violate the defendant's Fifth Amendment privilege because "compelling the accused merely to exhibit his person for observation by a prosecution witness prior to trial involves no compulsion of the accused to give evidence having testimonial significance"); *Gilbert v. California*, 388 U.S. 263, 87 S.Ct. 1951, 18 L.Ed.2d 1178 (1967) (holding that handwriting exemplars may be compelled from an unwilling defendant). Although an individual's voice and handwriting are means of communication, the sample itself, in contrast to the content of the communication, merely identifies a physical characteristic that cannot be the subject of a perjury charge and is therefore not protected by the Fifth Amendment.

4. *Pennsylvania v. Muniz*

In *Pennsylvania v. Muniz*, 496 U.S. 582, 110 S.Ct. 2638, 110 L.Ed.2d 528 (1990), the Court elaborated upon *Schmerber* and stated that the line between testimonial and non-testimonial evidence is determined by examining whether the witness faces a cruel trilemma in disclosing the evidence. Police officers arrested Muniz for drunk driving. During custodial interrogation the officers failed to give Muniz *Miranda* warnings. In response to police questioning, Muniz exhibited slurred speech, failed a sobriety test, and stated that he did not know the date of his sixth birthday. The issue in *Muniz* was whether these pieces of evidence were testimonial and thus protected by the Fifth Amendment. The compulsion aspect of the Fifth Amendment was presumed by the Court, since the Court had previously held in *Miranda* that custodial interrogation in the absence of warnings constitutes compulsion. (See the discussion of *Miranda* in the section on confessions).

a.   The Slurred Speech

The Court held that Muniz's slurred speech was physical evidence and was not protected by the Fifth Amendment. The evidence of slurred speech did not involve the content of the words but focused on the way in which these words were formed.

b.   The Sobriety Test

Muniz failed the physical performance components of his sobriety test, and this fact was admitted against him at his trial on drunk driving charges. The Court did not determine whether a person's performance on a sobriety test was testimonial because Muniz did not raise this issue on appeal. Many lower courts, however, have held that such evidence is non-testimonial under *Schmerber*, because it is offered to show only physical impairment, independent of any communication which could either be true or false.

c.   The Sixth Birthday Question

During custodial interrogation, Muniz was asked the date of his sixth birthday, and he admitted that he was too drunk to figure it out. His statement was admitted against him at trial. The Court held that this was error, because the answer to the sixth birthday question was testimonial. The Court found irrelevant the state's argument that the evidence was admitted only to show that the physiological functioning of Muniz's brain was impaired by alcohol. Although Muniz's physiological processes may have been the ultimate fact that the state wished to prove, it was trying to prove this fact *through the use of testimonial evidence.*

d. The Sixth Birthday Question and the Cruel Trilemma

The Court held that Muniz faced the cruel trilemma when asked the sixth birthday question. The trilemma laid out as follows: 1. Muniz could not remain silent, due to the pressures of custodial interrogation, as recognized in *Miranda*; 2. if he answered the question truthfully—that he did not know the date of his sixth birthday because he was too drunk—this answer would incriminate him, as in fact it did; and 3. if he tried to answer falsely, by making up the date, this answer would also have incriminated him because it would have been evidence of intoxication as well as evidence of consciousness of guilt.

5. A Statement Must Be Capable of Being True or False in Order to Be Testimonial

A compelled statement must be an express or implied assertion of fact that can be true or false in order to be considered testimonial. A statement cannot be false, and there is therefore no risk of perjury, unless the statement contains an express or implied assertion of fact. For example, in *Doe v. United States*, 487 U.S. 201, 108 S.Ct. 2341, 101 L.Ed.2d 184 (1988), the Government compelled a person to sign a form authorizing the release of bank records in a Cayman Island Bank. The Court noted that if the form had stated "I authorize the release of all my banking records" then it would have called for testimonial evidence, because it would contain an implied assertion that there were in fact bank records to be released. This fact could either be true or false, thereby implicating the cruel trilemma of contempt, incrimination and perjury if the person were compelled to sign it. However, the form in *Doe* authorized the release of bank records, *if any.* This was not an assertion that bank records existed. It was merely a direction to another person to do an act. A direction in itself cannot be true or false, and therefore when the Government compels a person to issue a direction, the Fifth Amendment is not violated.

6. Refusal to Supply Physical Evidence

Because the compulsion of physical evidence is not protected by the Fifth Amendment, an individual's refusal to supply the state with physical evidence may be used against him. If a suspect refuses to supply physical evidence, the state may bring an action for contempt. Punishment for contempt is permissible because the production of physical evidence does not present the truth-falsity-silence trilemma that is the concern of the Fifth Amendment. It follows that the defendant's refusal to cooperate may be introduced at trial as consciousness of guilt. See *South Dakota v. Neville,* 459 U.S. 553, 103 S.Ct. 916, 74 L.Ed.2d 748 (1983) (defendant's refusal to take a blood-alcohol test was not protected by the privilege against self-incrimination and thus the refusal could be used as evidence of consciousness of guilt in a criminal trial).

B. Documents

The Supreme Court held in *Boyd v. United States,* 116 U.S. 616, 6 S.Ct. 524, 29 L.Ed. 746 (1886), that a subpoena of an individual's private books violated the Fifth Amendment. However, the Court in *Fisher v. United States,* 425 U.S. 391, 96 S.Ct. 1569, 48 L.Ed.2d 39 (1976), stated that "[s]everal of *Boyd's* express or implicit declarations have not stood the test of time." The *Fisher* Court stated that the contents of documents are not protected by the Fifth Amendment if they were prepared before a Government subpoena was ever served. This is because the *preparation* of such documents is "wholly voluntary" and an act completely independent from the compelled act of *producing* the documents for use by the Government. Thus, the contents of voluntarily prepared documents do not constitute compelled testimonial evidence at the time they are prepared, and the pre-existing testimony does not itself, retroactively, become compelled when the Government orders the document to be produced. *See also United States v. Doe,* 465 U.S. 605, 104 S.Ct. 1237, 79 L.Ed.2d 552 (1984) (contents of records voluntarily prepared by a taxpayer are not protected by the privilege, since the Government did not compel the taxpayer to prepare the incriminating records).

1. Types of Testimony Compelled by a Subpoena for Documents: Content of Documents and the Act of Production

In *Fisher,* the Court looked at the types of incriminating testimony that are compelled by a subpoena for documents, and determined whether the Fifth Amendment privilege protects such testimony.

a. Content of Documents

In *Fisher,* the Court reasoned that when the Government compels the production of voluntarily prepared records, the contents of those documents are not protected by the Fifth Amendment privilege, because the Government compelled their *production, not their preparation. See United States v. Feldman,* 83 F.3d 9 (1st Cir.1996) ("The Fifth Amendment does not deal with the privacy of the contents of documents, but, rather, with the voluntariness of their preparation and production.")

b. Act of Production

When the Government serves a subpoena, it does not compel the preparation of a document, but it does compel the *production* of the document. The Court in *Fisher* recognized that the act of producing a document could have certain testimonial aspects, which would trigger Fifth Amendment protection if that information could incriminate the person producing the documents. *See also United States v. Doe*, 465 U.S. 605, 104 S.Ct. 1237, 79 L.Ed.2d 552 (1984) (privilege may be invoked where the act of production itself involves testimonial self-incrimination).

2. **What Does the Act of Production Communicate and When Is It Incriminating?**

The act of producing documents communicates that the documents exist; that they are under the *control and in the possession* of the person producing the documents; and that the documents are *authentic* (i.e., that they are in fact the documents described by the subpoena).

Example: A suspect could resist a subpoena demanding the production of "all records of illegal bets" by claiming the privilege against self-incrimination. To turn over these records would be tantamount to stating that "these are records of illegal bets." That is, the admission that such records exist is itself an incriminatory admission independent from the contents of the documents.

a. Admitting That the Documents Exist

The mere existence of documents is usually obvious and thus ordinarily is not incriminating. For example, there is nothing incriminating in the mere existence of business records or records of accounts receivable. In some cases, however, the mere fact that certain documents exist could be incriminating. For example, the mere volume of records may be an incriminating fact independent of the contents of the records. Thus, in *In re Doe*, 711 F.2d 1187 (2d Cir.1983), a doctor was suspected of dispensing drugs without a proper medical purpose. The court held that a subpoena for patient records compiled during a two-week period triggered the privilege, because the existence of the records could be incriminating: there was such an inordinate number of patient files for the period that the doctor could not have seen so many patients for any appreciable period of time. The volume of the records indicated that the doctor was not seeing the patients for a legitimate medical purpose. Thus, the existence of the records in that number was found incriminating independent of the contents of the records, which indicated that drugs were in fact prescribed.

    b.   Admitting Possession and Control of Documents

Ordinarily, there is nothing incriminating in having possession and control of a document—e.g., there is nothing incriminating in the records custodian having control over the records of the business. However, in some cases the admission of possession or control of records may itself show an incriminatory affiliation with another person or business.

    c.   Admitting That the Documents Are the Ones Demanded by the Government: Authentication

If a subpoena requires the production of an individual's own documents, the Government could use the act of production to authenticate the documents at trial. By turning the documents over in response to the subpoena, the person is admitting that the documents are what the Government says they are. *See* Federal Rule of Evidence 901.

3. Foregone Conclusion

Although the Fifth Amendment protects against compelled, incriminating acts of production, compelled production of documents will rarely be prohibited in practice. Even if the act of production is incriminating, the Fifth Amendment will not apply if existence, control, and authentication can be proven through independent evidence, such as through the testimony of other witnesses. If the admissions that are made by the act of production are cumulative of other incriminating evidence, the act of production does not create a substantial risk of incrimination. Thus, in *Fisher*, the Court held that the information communicated through the act of production (existence, control, and authenticity) did not pose a realistic threat of incrimination to the taxpayer because the taxpayer's attorney had already admitted, in discussions with the government, that the records existed, that Fisher controlled them, and that the records were authentic. Therefore the information communicated through the act of production was a "foregone conclusion."

4. Content of Personal as Opposed to Business Documents

In *Fisher* and *Doe*, the Court found that the privilege against self-incrimination does not protect the content of pre-existing, voluntarily prepared documents. Although *Fisher* and *Doe* involved subpoenaed business records, their rationale logically applies to personal documents such as diaries and love letters as well. Most courts after *Doe* have held that the Fifth Amendment privilege does not protect the contents of voluntarily prepared private documents. *See In re Grand Jury Proceedings on February 4, 1982*, 759 F.2d 1418 (9th Cir.1985); *In re Steinberg*, 837 F.2d 527 (1st Cir.1988). These courts reason that the rationale of *Fisher* and *Doe*, which separates the voluntary preparation of a document from its compelled production, applies equally to business and personal records. Some courts, however, distinguish between business and personal documents and hold that the privilege against self-incrimination protects the contents of personal documents. *See, e.g., In Re Grand Jury Investigation*, 600 F.Supp. 436 (D.Md.1984).

5. Document Production, Incrimination, and Immunity

The Court found the act of production to be incriminating in *United States v. Hubbell*, 530 U.S. 27, 120 S.Ct. 2037, 147 L.Ed.2d 24 (2000). While Hubbell was serving time for tax evasion and mail fraud, the Independent Counsel served him with a subpoena duces tecum asking for the production of volumes of documents in eleven broad categories. Hubbell appeared before the grand jury and invoked his Fifth Amendment privilege against self-incrimination. After the prosecutor granted him immunity "to the extent allowed by law," Hubbell produced 13,120 pages of documents and records, the contents of which led to a second prosecution of Hubbell, this time for mail and wire fraud and various tax-related crimes. The Court held that Hubbell's act of producing the documents clearly provided the Government with a lead to the incriminating evidence that resulted in the second prosecution. The Court rejected the Government's argument that the existence and possession of the records by any businessman was a "foregone conclusion" under *Fisher*, noting that, unlike in *Fisher*, the Government could not show that it had any prior knowledge of the existence of the documents. Justices Thomas and Scalia concurred, suggesting that "the Self–Incrimination Clause may have a broader reach than *Fisher* holds," and expressing a willingness to reconsider that decision.

6. Compelling Agents of Business Entities to Produce Documents: The Collective Entity Rule

The Fifth Amendment does not protect business entities. But production of the entity's records must come by way of an agent's testimony. What if the testimony compelled from the agent would incriminate the agent personally?

a. *Braswell*

In *Braswell v. United States*, 487 U.S. 99, 108 S.Ct. 2284, 101 L.Ed.2d 98 (1988), the Government served a subpoena on Braswell, who was the manager and sole owner of a corporation targeted for investigation by the grand jury. The subpoena was served on Braswell in his capacity as a corporate agent, and demanded the production of incriminating corporate records. Braswell argued that while the corporation had no privilege, his own act of production would incriminate him personally because by producing the records, he would be admitting that they existed, that he controlled them, and that they were authentic. (No argument was made that the content of the documents would incriminate Braswell, since the contents were voluntarily prepared, and thus not protected by the Fifth Amendment after *Fisher*). The Court denied Braswell's claim and held that he was required to produce the documents on behalf of the corporation.

b. Reasoning in *Braswell*

The Court reasoned that the custodian of corporate records holds these records in a representative capacity, and when served in that capacity, he produces the documents not as a person but as a representative of the corporation. Thus, the act of production is not "a personal act, but rather an act of the corporation." The Court found it to be inconsistent to apply a personal privilege to an act that was really done by the corporation, not by the person.

c. Nonconstitutional Agency Analysis

Under the *Braswell* analysis, the production of the entity's documents is an act of the entity and not a personal act. It follows that if the agent is subsequently brought to trial, the Government cannot introduce his act of production as an admission that he knew of the existence of the documents, or that he possessed them or authenticated them. This is because the act of production was not the agent's personal act but rather the entity's act. However, the prosecution can introduce the fact that the *entity* produced the documents, and therefore that the entity admitted existence, control and authenticity; it just cannot introduce the fact that a particular agent produced the documents on behalf of the entity. It is then up to the Government to link the agent to the entity's act of production through independent evidence. As the Court in *Braswell* put it: "the jury may draw from the corporation's act of production the conclusion that the records in question are authentic corporate records, which the corporation possessed, and which it produced in response to the subpoena. And if the defendant held a prominent position within the corporation that produced the records, the jury may, just as it would had someone else produced the documents, reasonably infer that he had possession of the documents or knowledge of their contents." The Court concluded in *Braswell* that the custodian was not incriminated by personal production of the documents, but only by corporate production, which is not protected by the Fifth Amendment.

d. Oral Testimony Distinguished

In *Curcio v. United States*, 354 U.S. 118, 77 S.Ct. 1145, 1 L.Ed.2d 1225 (1957), the Court held that the collective entity rule did not allow the Government to force a corporate agent to give *oral* testimony, where that testimony would personally incriminate the agent. The Court in *Braswell* adhered to the rule in *Curcio,* and distinguished between oral testimony and document production. The distinction between protected oral testimony and unprotected act of production was explained by one court as follows: "In drawing a line between acts of production and oral testimony, the Court appears to have relied on one fact that distinguishes these two types of testimony: the corporation owns the documents. In contrast, to the extent that one's thoughts and statements can be said to belong to anyone, they belong to the witness herself. * * * Because the documents belong to the corporation, the State may exercise its right to review the records. For Fifth Amendment purposes, oral statements are different. The government has no right to compel a person to speak the contents of her mind when to do so would incriminate that person." *In re Grand Jury Subpoena,* 87 F.3d 1198 (11th Cir.1996).

C. Required Records

If the Government requires documents to be kept for a legitimate administrative purpose, neither the content nor the act of production of these documents are protected by the Fifth Amendment. *See Shapiro v. United States,* 335 U.S. 1, 68 S.Ct. 1375, 92 L.Ed. 1787 (1948) (statute requiring the keeping of certain business records does not violate the Fifth Amendment even though the recordkeeping is compelled and could subject the defendant to a risk of incrimination). Thus, the Government can, where the exception applies, compel an individual to write down incriminating statements in the record, can penalize that individual for failing to keep these records, and can imprison that individual for lying on such records. Although this individual faces a "cruel trilemma," the required records doctrine is an *exception* to the self-incrimination privilege.

1. Legitimate Administrative Purpose

The required records exception only applies if the records are required to be kept in accordance with a legitimate administrative recordkeeping interest. If the recordkeeping requirement is targeted solely at a class that is *inherently suspected of committing criminal activity*, then the required records exception does not apply, and compulsion is prohibited. *See Marchetti v. United States*, 390 U.S. 39, 88 S.Ct. 697, 19 L.Ed.2d 889 (1968) (holding that required records exception does not apply to statute requiring individuals to provide information about illegal gambling activities). Without this limitation, the state could use the required records exception as a surrogate for criminal law enforcement and as a means to end-run the limitations of the Fifth Amendment.

2. *California v. Byers*

In *California v. Byers*, 402 U.S. 424, 91 S.Ct. 1535, 29 L.Ed.2d 9 (1971), the applicability of the required records exception to California's hit and run statute was at issue. The statute required anyone involved in an accident to stop at the scene and to leave his name and address. Byers was convicted of a misdemeanor for failing to report as required by the statute, and he sought reversal on the ground that the statute violated the Fifth Amendment. The Court held that the statute was valid under the required records exception. It noted that the statutory scheme was essentially regulatory, designed to make it more efficient to process insurance claims and accident suits. As such, the statute was directed to the motoring public at large, rather than to "a highly selective group inherently suspected of criminal activities."

VI. Procedural Aspects of Self–Incrimination Claims

A. Determining the Risk of Incrimination

In order for the Fifth Amendment privilege against self-incrimination to apply, a judge must determine whether the information demanded from a witness might possibly tend to incriminate the witness in the future. *Hoffman v. United States*, 341 U.S. 479, 71 S.Ct. 814, 95 L.Ed. 1118 (1951). If the testimony could provide a link in a chain of evidence that might be incriminating, the Fifth Amendment privilege protects such testimony. *Malloy v. Hogan*, 378 U.S. 1, 84 S.Ct. 1489, 12 L.Ed.2d 653 (1964). If an admission is purely cumulative, however, the compelled admission does not present a realistic threat of incrimination and thus the privilege does not protect against such testimony. *See Fisher v. United States,* 425 U.S. 391, 96 S.Ct. 1569, 48 L.Ed.2d 39 (1976), discussed *supra.*

1. Possibility, Not Likelihood of Criminal Sanction

A statement can tend to incriminate even if the offense admitted is rarely if ever prosecuted. For example, if a person is forced to admit to buying a small amount of narcotics from a certain person, the state may be tempted to argue that the statement does not really incriminate the witness because the state would not prosecute such a small-scale drug purchaser. But this argument would fail, because the offense admitted to is a criminal offense, and the question is not whether it is routinely prosecuted but whether it *could* be prosecuted.

2. "Stop and Identify" Statutes

In *Hiibel v. Sixth Judicial District Court of Nevada, Humboldt County, supra,* the Court held that a statute that requires an individual to identify himself upon the request of a police officer does not violate the Fifth Amendment privilege against self-incrimination. According to the Court, Hiibel's refusal to identify himself was not based on any real and appreciable fear that his name would be used to incriminate him or provide a link in a chain of evidence that might be incriminating. The Court noted that there might be a circumstance in which furnishing one's identity during a stop would be incriminating, but the mere provision of such information, without a showing of how it would incriminate the individual, does not violate the Fifth Amendment.

3. The Risk of Incrimination and Denial of Guilt

The risk of incrimination is not determined by the witness' denial of guilt, according to the Court in *Ohio v. Reiner,* 532 U.S. 17, 121 S.Ct. 1252, 149 L.Ed.2d 158 (2001). Reiner was charged with manslaughter in connection with the death of his two month old son. He blamed the babysitter, who refused to testify, invoking the Fifth Amendment privilege against self-incrimination. The Government granted her immunity and she testified for the prosecution, denying any wrongdoing. In the appeal of his conviction, Reiner claimed that the babysitter should not have been granted immunity. The Supreme Court of Ohio agreed, holding that a person who denies guilt does not have a Fifth Amendment privilege. The United States Supreme Court reversed in a per curiam opinion, reaffirming that the privilege is available to the innocent as well as the guilty and holding that a witness' assertion of innocence does not, by itself, determine the risk of incrimination.

B. Assertion of the Privilege

Whenever a person is compelled to answer questions that might tend to incriminate him, he has the right to refuse to answer. If he does answer, however, the privilege is lost with respect to the answer, and the answer can be used as evidence. *See Garner v. United States,* 424 U.S. 648, 96 S.Ct. 1178, 47 L.Ed.2d 370 (1976) (holding that a person who answered questions on his tax return, rather than invoking the privilege, had not been compelled to testify against himself).

C. Immunity

Even assuming the testimony tends to incriminate a witness, the Government may compel testimony when the witness has received immunity. This is because, when immunity is granted, the witness' testimony can no longer incriminate him, and therefore he no longer faces the truth-falsity-silence trilemma that is the concern of the Fifth Amendment. The truth "prong" of the trilemma provides no risk of incarceration in these circumstances. There are two types of immunity: transactional immunity and use immunity.

1. Transactional Immunity

If an individual receives transactional immunity, the Government guarantees that it will not prosecute him for any transaction described in the testimony. Transactional immunity is the broadest form of immunity. At one time, the court appeared to require transactional immunity to supplant the privilege against self-incrimination. *Counselman v. Hitchcock,* 142 U.S. 547, 12 S.Ct. 195, 35 L.Ed. 1110 (1892). But in *Kastigar v. United States,* 406 U.S. 441, 92 S.Ct. 1653, 32 L.Ed.2d 212 (1972), the Court held that use and derivative use immunity were coextensive with the privilege and sufficed to supplant it. Thus, transactional immunity gives greater protection than is constitutionally required.

2. Use and Derivative Use Immunity

Use and derivative use immunity prevent the use of testimony or other information obtained from a person "or any information directly or indirectly derived from such testimony or other information." The Supreme Court held in *Kastigar v. United States,* 406 U.S. 441, 92 S.Ct. 1653, 32 L.Ed.2d 212 (1972), that a grant of use and derivative use immunity is coextensive with the Fifth Amendment privilege, and therefore that a person who receives such immunity has no right to refuse to testify.

a. Prosecution Is Still Possible

The Government may grant use immunity and yet still prosecute the witness for the transaction admitted to. But in that prosecution, the government cannot use the immunized statement, nor any fruits of the immunized statement.

b. Government's Burden

To subsequently prosecute a person who has received use immunity, the burden is on the Government to prove that the evidence it proposes to offer against the witness at trial is derived from a legitimate independent source.

c. Witnesses Should Not Have Access to Immunized Testimony

In *United States v. North*, 920 F.2d 940 (D.C.Cir.1990), the court held that the prosecution did not fulfill its burden of showing that its evidence was free from taint, where Government witnesses had seen the defendant's immunized testimony on national television. A majority of the panel concluded that, if witnesses have memories refreshed by immunized testimony, their refreshed testimony is tainted, even though the prosecution was not responsible for the taint.

D. Waiver of the Privilege

Individuals can waive their privilege against self-incrimination. In addition to explicitly waiving the privilege, an individual can waive the privilege by giving testimony that is inconsistent with the retention of the privilege.

1. Subject Matter Test

If a witness testifies or supplies information as to part of a story, he cannot, under a claim of the privilege, refuse to testify about related subject matter. Testimony, whether complete or incomplete, does not, however, waive the privilege as to an unrelated topic. For example, in *United States v. Hearst*, 563 F.2d 1331 (9th Cir.1977), the defendant testified that she was under duress from members of the Symbionese Liberation Army at the time of the bank robbery with which she was charged. The court found that these comments served as a waiver of the privilege as to cross examination questions concerning a later period in which she allegedly lived with SLA members voluntarily. The court reasoned that the conditions of the defendant's confinement at two separate points in time were really part of the same subject matter—i.e., the impact of these conditions on her state of mind. *Compare Lesko v.*

Lehman, 925 F.2d 1527 (3d Cir.1991) (defendant who testifies at capital sentencing hearing concerning biographical information does not waive the privilege with respect to circumstances surrounding the crime).

VI

Self–Incrimination and Confessions

■ ANALYSIS

I. Confessions and Due Process

A. The Due Process Clause Prohibits the Admission of an Involuntary Confession

In *Brown v. Mississippi*, 297 U.S. 278, 56 S.Ct. 461, 80 L.Ed. 682 (1936), the Court held that the Due Process Clause prohibits the admission of a confession if the suspect gave that confession involuntarily.

1. Evolution of Due Process

The Court first relied on Due Process to ban the courtroom use of confessions obtained by *physical torture,* and then enlarged this ban to prohibit the use of confessions obtained by *psychological coercion.* In applying the Due Process test, the courts generally focus on *three factors: the actions of the police; the characteristics of the defendant;* and *the circumstances surrounding the confession.* A court is most likely to find a confession to be involuntary when all three factors strongly suggest the presence of psychological coercion. For example, a confession might well be involuntary if an illiterate defendant with limited mental abilities is denied contact with friends, family, or counsel, and is continuously interrogated, by a large number of police officers, for many hours, without sleep or food.

2. Little Precedential Value

Courts usually cite a large number of factual details to support a finding of involuntariness under the "totality of circumstances." Thus each precedent provides only a negative example of what police conduct is improper in a unique situation. Not surprisingly, courts have difficulty applying Due Process precedents to many new factual settings, because the definition of voluntariness is a question of "degrees." This is especially true with psychological tactics, which are much more ambiguous and case-specific than physical torture or threats of violence.

3. Reliability Is Not the Only Concern

The Supreme Court's rationale for excluding involuntary confessions originally derived from its concern about the *reliability* of this evidence. Yet it is clear that even a confession obtained by physical torture can be reliable—the person tortured may be truthfully, if involuntarily, admitting to a crime that he actually committed. Accordingly, the Court's rationale for excluding involuntary confessions expanded into a commitment to deter "inquisitorial" police methods that were incompatible with an "accusatorial" system of justice. This led the Court to invalidate confessions even when independent evidence supported the reliability of the conviction. The Court has, under this theory, disapproved of specific kinds of police conduct which it considers impermissible, such as significant untrue promises of benefit, or threats of harm, extreme forms of deception, and physical or psychological deprivations that reduce a defendant's capacity to exercise the "free will" to speak or remain silent.

It is clear, however, that deceptive police tactics do not always render a confession involuntary. Thus, confessions have been admitted where a police officer informed the defendant that his fingerprints were at the scene, when that was in fact not the case. Misstating the nature of the evidence against the defendant is relevant to whether the defendant was coerced into making a confession, but it is not dispositive.

4. Continuing Viability of the Due Process Test

Ultimately, the Supreme Court decided that lower courts and police needed more positive guidance about acceptable interrogation practices, and it established some *per se* rules for confessions in *Massiah* and *Miranda*. Most confession cases today are argued on these grounds. Recently, however, the Court reaffirmed the current vitality of the Due Process doctrine established in the pre–1964 era. *See Arizona v. Fulminante*, 499 U.S. 279, 111 S.Ct. 1246, 113 L.Ed.2d 302 (1991). Today, Due Process usually is invoked by defendants who confess after "waiving" their *Miranda* or *Massiah* rights, as well as by defendants who are not eligible for such rights.

B. The Prohibition Against Admission of a Confession That Is Extracted by Physical Coercion

In *Brown v. Mississippi*, 297 U.S. 278, 56 S.Ct. 461, 80 L.Ed. 682 (1936), the Court held that admission into evidence of a confession extracted by "brutality and violence" violated Due Process, because such a confession is not given voluntarily.

Rationale

The *Brown* Court held that the use of a coerced confession at trial violates the fundamental right to fair trial procedures. The Court acknowledged that a state has broad discretion to establish procedural rules in criminal cases, but observed that it may not substitute the "rack and torture chamber" for the witness stand. In effect, the state police and prosecutor had accomplished this in *Brown*, where it was undisputed that two defendants were whipped repeatedly, and another was strung up in a mock lynching and repeatedly choked.

C. Psychological Coercion

Soon after *Brown*, the Court decided to expand the Due Process concept of "involuntariness" to include some forms of psychological coercion. In doing so, however, the Court confronted the difficult line-drawing problem of defining "how much" psychological pressure was "too much." *Brown's* rule against physical torture provided no assistance here, as psychological coercion was so much harder to define than physical coercion. The former could be created in intangible ways, with many different combinations of coercive factors existing in different cases. As long as the Court was not prepared to ban police interrogations entirely, it was forced to rely on a case-by-case approach to measuring voluntariness in cases involving psychological coercion.

1. Case-by-Case Approach

While every case of involuntariness is fact-dependent, the Supreme Court has mentioned several factors that are indicative of impermissible coercion. For example, the Court reversed convictions where confessions were produced by 36 hours of continuous questioning, or by forcing the defendant to remain naked in jail. *See Ashcraft v. Tennessee*, 322 U.S. 143, 64 S.Ct. 921, 88 L.Ed. 1192 (1944) (continuous questioning); *Malinski v. New York*, 324 U.S. 401, 65 S.Ct. 781, 89 L.Ed. 1029 (1945) (naked defendant). The Court also reversed a conviction where the police promised the defendant that only his confession would guarantee his protection from a mob of angry people outside the jailhouse door. *See Payne v. Arkansas*, 356 U.S. 560, 78 S.Ct. 844, 2 L.Ed.2d 975 (1958). On the other hand, the Court has upheld convictions when a defendant was not abnormally vulnerable to coercion, and was treated with some consideration by the police. *See, e.g., Crooker v. California*, 357 U.S. 433, 78 S.Ct. 1287, 2 L.Ed.2d 1448 (1958) (well-educated defendant was given food and allowed to smoke).

2. *Spano v. New York*

In *Spano v. New York*, 360 U.S. 315, 79 S.Ct. 1202, 3 L.Ed.2d 1265 (1959), a unanimous Court held that a "massive" overnight interrogation of an indicted defendant violated Due Process, when police ignored the defendant's repeated requests for his lawyer, and used a "false friend" of the defendant's to tell him that his failure to confess would cause the friend to lose his job, and thereby endanger the friend's young family.

a. Rationale

The Court examined the totality of circumstances and concluded that the defendant's will was "overborne by official pressure, fatigue, and sympathy falsely aroused" by the manipulation of his friendship with the police cadet who obtained his confession. The Court cited numerous factors to support its holding. Three aspects of the defendant's vulnerability to coercion were deemed relevant: he was foreign born, had limited education, and had a history of emotional instability. Several aspects of the police conduct were cited with disapproval: 1. The police questioned the defendant continuously for eight hours, during the night, using a total of 14 officers, and using leading questions; 2. The police ignored the defendant's repeated refusals to talk, and his repeated requests to consult his lawyer, who had advised him to remain silent when he was arrested; 3. The police repeatedly used the "false friend" to tell the defendant that his failure to confess would endanger the friend's job and the friend's support of his young family; and 4. The defendant was indicted, and the police had an eyewitness, so there was no need to solve the crime by procuring a confession. Given all of these facts, the Court concluded that the confession was not voluntary. The Court also emphasized that the inadmissibility of a coerced confession was based not only on its inherent "untrustworthiness," but also on the principle that "police must obey the law while enforcing the law," because life and liberty can be "as much endangered" by illegal police actions as by the acts of criminals themselves.

b. A Proposed Right to Counsel

Four Justices in *Spano* argued that the conviction should also be reversed on an alternative Due Process ground. These Justices contended that Due Process was violated because the defendant was deprived of his right to *consult with counsel* after his indictment on a capital charge. By secretly interrogating the defendant and denying his requests to consult with counsel, the police used a "kangaroo court" procedure that denied him effective representation by counsel at trial.

c. Debate Over Right to Counsel

The analysis of the concurring Justices in *Spano* was an attempt to limit the inherent indeterminacy of the "voluntariness" standard by establishing a more bright-line right to counsel. Not all members of the Court approved of this approach to reformulating confession law, however. For it was foreseeable that once a right to counsel was created in the "secret trial of the police precinct," this right would be sought by unindicted suspects undergoing custodial interrogation. Such an expansion of this right might interfere with the ability of the police to investigate unsolved crimes and gather evidence to support convictions in many cases. Thus, the proposed counsel requirement ultimately cracked open a debate about how to reconcile the interests of the police in obtaining confessions with the interests of suspects in consulting with counsel, who were likely to advise them to remain silent. Once *Massiah* and *Miranda* were decided, this debate became quite complicated, and it has continued in opinions concerning the protections provided by the Fifth and Sixth Amendments.

3. Threats of Violence

In *Arizona v. Fulminante*, 499 U.S. 279, 111 S.Ct. 1246, 113 L.Ed.2d 302 (1991), the Court held that a credible threat of physical violence created sufficient coercion to render a confession involuntary. Fulminante made a statement implicating himself in a murder of a child, while he was imprisoned on another charge. The statement was made to an undercover informant. Fulminante had been threatened by other inmates who suspected him of being a child-murderer. The undercover informant offered to protect Fulminante from these threats, on the condition that Fulminante would tell him the truth about what happened.

a. Rationale

The *Fulminante* Court relied on the totality of the circumstances to find that the state supreme court made a "permissible" finding of coercion in a "close case." This finding was based on the threat of physical violence, the defendant's reaction to it, and surrounding circumstances that enhanced the coercive nature of the threat. In addition, the Court found that the defendant's vulnerability to coercion supported its conclusion.

b. Relevant Factors

Four aspects of the circumstances rendered the confession involuntary: 1. The defendant was a prison inmate who was in danger of physical harm from fellow inmates who suspected he was a child murderer; 2. The informant became a Government agent while in prison serving time for extortion, and he was instructed to find out about the defendant's knowledge of the murder; 3. The informant "masqueraded as an organized crime figure," told the defendant he knew about the murder rumors, and offered the defendant his "protection" only if he would confess. In making this offer, the informant relied on the fact that other inmates had been giving the defendant "rough treatment"; 4. The defendant confessed immediately in response to the threat, "in the belief that [his] life was in jeopardy" if he did not.

c. Actual Violence Not Required

The Court in *Fulminante*, relying on prior cases, emphasized that actual violence by Government agents was unnecessary to support a finding of coercion. The "credible threat of physical violence" was enough to produce the "mental" coercion to confess. Specifically, the Court held that coercion could be established when a Government agent offered protection from violence in exchange for a confession. *See Payne v. Arkansas*, 356 U.S. 560, 78 S.Ct. 844, 2 L.Ed.2d 975 (1958) (where a police officer promised protection from "an angry mob outside the jailhouse door").

D. Some Police Coercion Is Required

In *Colorado v. Connelly*, 479 U.S. 157, 107 S.Ct. 515, 93 L.Ed.2d 473 (1986), the Court held that Due Process was not violated by the admission into evidence of a confession prompted by the auditory hallucinations of a psychotic defendant. Where the police were unaware of the defendant's mental illness at the time he confessed, the subsequent interrogation of the defendant was not "coercive police activity." Thus, the defendant's confession was not involuntary, as that term is used in Due Process jurisprudence.

1. Rationale

The *Connelly* Court declared that the Due Process Clause is not violated absent police conduct "causally related to the confession." The Court observed that "coercive government misconduct" was the focus of its Due Process doctrine in *Brown*, and that all subsequent confession cases "contained a substantial element of coercive police conduct." While cases like *Spano* found that the defendant's mental condition could be a "significant factor" in the "voluntariness calculus," this factor alone never was held to be controlling. Instead, Due Process precedents revealed that there must be a "link between coercive activity of the State" and "a resulting confession."

2. Deterrence

The Court in *Connelly* declared that the Due Process "exclusionary rule" for confessions has the same purpose as the Fourth Amendment exclusionary rule, namely, the deterrence of future constitutional violations by police officers. Like its Fourth Amendment counterpart, the Due Process rule imposes "a substantial cost" on law enforcement because it proscribes the admission of "relevant evidence." The Court determined that exclusion of the confession in *Connelly* could not deter coercive police conduct in future cases (because the police had not engaged in such tactics in *Connelly*). Instead, the Court concluded that state rules of evidence should govern the question whether the confession of a mentally ill defendant is sufficiently reliable to be admitted at trial.

E. Harmless Error

In *Arizona v. Fulminante*, 499 U.S. 279, 111 S.Ct. 1246, 113 L.Ed.2d 302 (1991), the Court held that the erroneous admission of an involuntary confession may be held to be "harmless error." If the government proves that the admission of the confession was "harmless beyond a reasonable doubt," the defendant's conviction must be affirmed even though the confession was involuntary. The *Fulminante* Court cautioned, however, that a reviewing court must exercise "extreme caution" before holding that the admission of a confession is harmless. It noted the "profound impact" that any confession has upon the jury.

F. An Involuntary Confession Is Not Admissible at Trial for Any Purpose

In *Mincey v. Arizona*, 437 U.S. 385, 98 S.Ct. 2408, 57 L.Ed.2d 290 (1978), the Court held that a coerced confession may not be admitted either in the state's case-in-chief, or during the state's cross-examination of a defendant whom the state wishes to impeach when she takes the stand. The *Mincey* Court rejected the state's argument that coerced confessions should be treated the same way as confessions that violate *Miranda*, which are admissible to impeach a defendant who takes the stand. Admission of an involuntary confession for any purpose is unconstitutional, since the Due Process Clause is violated at the point when the evidence is admitted.

II. The Special Federal Standard for Confessions

A. Delay in Presentment: The *McNabb–Mallory* Rule

During the same era that the Court was developing the case-by-case "voluntariness doctrine" under Due Process, it took a step towards creating a per se "exclusionary rule" for confessions obtained by Federal agents during prolonged detention of suspects following arrest. In *McNabb v. United States*, 318 U.S. 332, 63 S.Ct. 608, 87 L.Ed. 819 (1943), the Court held that confessions obtained from federal defendants convicted of murder were improperly admitted because the defendants were detained for three days of interrogation, instead of being taken to a judicial officer.

1. **Rationale**

   The *McNabb* Court invoked its "supervisory authority" over Federal courts in order to justify its exclusionary rule, and explained that admission of confessions obtained during illegal detention "would lead to the misuse of the law enforcement process."

2. **Nature of Delay**

   The *McNabb* rule required the Court to decide what sort of delay in making a prompt appearance before a judicial officer would be improper. In *Mallory v. United States*, 354 U.S. 449, 77 S.Ct. 1356, 1 L.Ed.2d 1479 (1957), the Court relied on Rule 5(a) of the Federal Rules of Criminal Procedure to require that Federal agents take arrested suspects to court "without unnecessary delay." In *Mallory*, the confession was held to be inadmissible because agents delayed the rape suspect's court appearance from the time of arrest in the early afternoon until the next morning. The *McNabb–Mallory* rule did allow for "necessary" delays, of course, so that lower courts could accept confessions that were obtained during a time when no magistrate was available, or when other special justifications existed.

3. **Demise of the *McNabb–Mallory* Rule**

   The Court never elevated the *McNabb–Mallory* rule to the status of constitutional doctrine. In 1968, Congress moved to abolish the *McNabb–Mallory* rule by enacting 18 U.S.C. § 3501. This statute provides that a confession should not be excluded from evidence *per se* because of a delay of up to six hours after arrest, and that any delay "need not be conclusive" on the issue of the voluntariness of the confession. *See United States v. Pugh*, 25 F.3d 669 (8th Cir.1994) (18 U.S.C. § 3501 supersedes the *McNabb–Mallory* rule). This statute is discussed immediately below.

4. **Relationship to *Miranda***

   In its time, the *McNabb–Mallory* rule served the function of allowing the Court to invalidate Federal confessions based on clear-cut police failure to follow a procedure designed to reduce the risk of police coercion of arrested suspects. In this way, the rule foreshadowed the Court's later adoption of the *Miranda* rules, which were animated by a similar search for clear-cut safeguards to protect suspects from the coercive pressures of interrogation. The Court did not employ the *McNabb–Mallory* rule after 1968, perhaps because it found that *Miranda* provided superior safeguards. *See also United States v. Payner, supra,* where the Court rejected the exercise of the supervisory power of the federal courts to suppress otherwise admissible evidence.

B. The Congressional Approach: 18 U.S.C. § 3501

Congress became concerned that the Court in *McNabb* and *Mallory* had focused too much on delay in presentment, and too little on whether a suspect's confession was in fact voluntary. Congress passed 18 U.S.C. § 3501, which provides that voluntary confessions "shall" be admissible, and lists several factors as pertinent to the voluntariness inquiry, including: 1. Delay in presentment to a judicial officer; 2. Whether the suspect knew the charges against him; 3. Whether the suspect was advised of his right to remain silent and his right to counsel; and 4. Whether counsel was present when the suspect confessed. The statute further provides that a confession shall not be inadmissible solely because of delay in presenting the suspect to a judicial officer, and it also provides a six-hour "safe harbor" period in which no delay in presentment can be presumed. The relevance of this statute in light of *Miranda* is discussed in the sections on *Miranda* and *Dickerson, infra.*

III. Confessions and the Sixth Amendment Before *Miranda*

A. The Prohibition on "Deliberate Elicitation" of Incriminating Statements From Indicted Defendants

In *Massiah v. United States,* 377 U.S. 201, 84 S.Ct. 1199, 12 L.Ed.2d 246 (1964), the Court held that the Sixth Amendment was violated when the Government used an informant, who had been indicted along with Massiah, to elicit incriminating statements from him while the two were free on bail and awaiting trial. The Government relied on this evidence to obtain Massiah's conviction, and the Court reversed.

1. Rationale

The Court borrowed the rationale of the concurring opinions in *Spano v. New York,* 360 U.S. 315, 79 S.Ct. 1202, 3 L.Ed.2d 1265 (1959), and held that all indicted defendants possess a Sixth Amendment right to consult with counsel when police are deliberately trying to obtain information from them. The Court extended this rule to defendants who were interrogated by secret agents, because "if such a rule is to have any efficacy, it must apply to indirect and surreptitious interrogations" as well as those conducted by police.

Critical Stage

The *Massiah* Court reasoned that after indictment, a defendant is "entitled to a lawyer's help," and to a trial in an "orderly courtroom" protected by "all the procedural safeguards of the law." Therefore, such a defendant must be given the aid of counsel in the "extrajudicial proceeding" of post-indictment police interrogation, or he will have been denied effective representation "at the only stage when legal aid and advice would help him."

2. **Need for Undercover Activity**

The Government in *Massiah* argued that it needed to use secret agents to conduct continuing investigations of indicted defendants, and that any rule prohibiting deliberate elicitation of statements in this situation would bring undercover investigations to a halt. In response, the Court declared that "it was entirely proper" to investigate a defendant's criminal activities. But, the Court insisted, the defendant's own incriminating statements could not be used against him at his trial. Implicitly, the Court suggested, such statements could be used to convict others, and could be used against the defendant himself in an unrelated trial.

3. **Dissent**

The *Massiah* dissenters found no compelling reason to extend the Sixth Amendment "to out-of-court conversations" obtained "without counsel's consent or presence." They accused the *Massiah* majority of requiring counsel's presence in order to ensure that counsel "would foreclose any admissions at all." To the dissenters, this was "nothing more than a thinly disguised" preference for prohibiting the use of out-of-court confessions entirely, which policy would have "a severe and unfortunate impact" upon most criminal cases.

B. **"Deliberate Elicitation" of a Confession From an Unindicted Suspect Who Asks to See His Retained Counsel**

In *Escobedo v. Illinois*, 378 U.S. 478, 84 S.Ct. 1758, 12 L.Ed.2d 977 (1964), the Court appeared to extend the Sixth Amendment right to counsel to an unindicted suspect in custody. It held his confession to be inadmissible because officers denied his request to consult with his retained counsel during interrogation. While the Court appeared to rely on *Massiah* and the

Sixth Amendment, this reliance was dubious because *Escobedo* had not been indicted at the time of his confession. The Sixth Amendment provides a right to counsel for the "accused." After *Escobedo*, the Court held, in another context, that a person is not "accused," and therefore has no Sixth Amendment right to counsel, until he has been formally charged by the state by way of indictment or some other formality. *Kirby v. Illinois*, 406 U.S. 682, 92 S.Ct. 1877, 32 L.Ed.2d 411 (1972) (no Sixth Amendment right to counsel at a line-up, where defendant had not yet been indicted). Ultimately, *Escobedo's* substance lost all its Sixth Amendment content when the Court reinterpreted it as a "Fifth Amendment" case. *See Moran v. Burbine*, 475 U.S. 412, 106 S.Ct. 1135, 89 L.Ed.2d 410 (1986).

Escobedo is noteworthy today because it illustrates the Court's readiness before *Miranda* to require police to honor a suspect's request to consult with counsel during interrogation. The *Miranda* right to consult counsel on request is the right most consistently honored by the Court today. *See, e.g., Minnick v. Mississippi*, 498 U.S. 146, 111 S.Ct. 486, 112 L.Ed.2d 489 (1990); *Arizona v. Roberson*, 486 U.S. 675, 108 S.Ct. 2093, 100 L.Ed.2d 704 (1988).

IV. Confessions and the Fifth Amendment

A. *Miranda v. Arizona*

In *Miranda v. Arizona*, 384 U.S. 436, 86 S.Ct. 1602, 16 L.Ed.2d 694 (1966), the Court held that a confession made during custodial interrogation is inadmissible unless the suspect receives four "warnings" describing his rights, and then gives a "knowing, intelligent, and voluntary" waiver of these rights. A police officer also must cut off questioning if a suspect invokes his right to silence or his right to consult counsel, even if this invocation follows a waiver of rights.

1. Rationale

The Court reasoned that the *Miranda* rules were required in order to safeguard a suspect's Fifth Amendment right to remain silent from the *inherently coercive pressures of custodial interrogation* by police in the absence of such safeguards. The Court's opinion first explained its rationale and holding in four parts. Then it applied its new rules to the facts of four cases, and found the confessions in all of them to be inadmissible.

a. Custodial Interrogation Constitutes Fifth Amendment Compulsion

The *Miranda* Court expressed its disapproval of the "police-dominated" atmosphere of modern custodial interrogations, and the "evils" it can bring. The Court noted that "third degree" techniques of physical abuse by interrogators were "sufficiently widespread to be the object of concern." Likewise, psychologically-oriented techniques were viewed as creating "intimidation" of suspects that was "equally destructive of human dignity." Thus, judicially-created "protective devices" were necessary in order to "dispel the compulsion inherent in custodial surroundings."

b. Interrogation Techniques

The Court relied on police manuals on interrogation techniques to describe modern practices used by police to undermine a suspect's will to remain silent. These techniques included the following: placing the suspect in isolated and unfamiliar surroundings; displaying an air of confidence in his guilt; minimizing the seriousness of the offense; interrogating persistently in order to "overwhelm" the suspect; using the "Mutt and Jeff" routine where one officer acts friendly and the other hostile; placing the suspect in a fraudulent lineup where he is identified as the wrongdoer; telling the suspect that his silence indicates he has something to hide; and advising the suspect to save himself and his family the expense of a lawyer and "handle this" by himself.

c. Not Involuntary Under the Due Process Clause, but Compelled Under the Fifth Amendment

The Court noted that such intimidating police techniques may produce a confession that is not "involuntary" under Due Process standards. Nonetheless, the Court found such techniques to be "menacing" and full of "potentiality for compulsion." Even without police use of such techniques, the "very fact" of custodial interrogation "exacts a heavy toll on individual liberty and trades on the weakness" of suspects. Therefore, the Court found the practice of incommunicado interrogation to be "at odds" with the Fifth Amendment privilege against self-incrimination. Without "safeguards" to dispel the compulsion inherent in this practice, the Court declared that *no confession* "can truly be the product" of a suspect's "free choice." Thus, the *Miranda* Court established a bright-line rule that a confession made in response to custodial interrogation in the absence of specific warnings was compelled self-incrimination, and automatically inadmissible.

d. The Fifth Amendment Privilege Against Self–Incrimination Applies to Custodial Interrogation

The Court declared that the "foundation" underlying the Fifth Amendment privilege is the requirement that Government must accord "dignity and integrity" to its citizens. The privilege is "fulfilled" only when a person is guaranteed the right to remain silent, not only at trial, but also during custodial interrogation.

The Court determined that the policies underlying the existence of the privilege at trial include the need to maintain a "fair state-individual balance" by requiring the Government to prove its case by its own "independent labors." This form of proof, rather than the use of compelled confessions, establishes "respect for the inviola-bility of the human personality." The Court concluded that the "principles embodied in the privilege" apply equally to both the formal compulsion of testifying unwillingly against oneself at trial, and to the "informal compulsion" of custodial interrogation by police.

2. **The *Miranda* Safeguards**

The *Miranda* Court established two objectives for its safeguards. The first was to "adequately and effectively" apprise a suspect of her rights. The second was to insure that "the exercise of those rights" was "fully honored" by police. The Court held that the fact of "custodial interro-gation" automatically requires the police to comply with *Miranda* safeguards.

a. The Warnings

A suspect must be apprised of her rights through warnings of the right to remain silent, and of the fact that anything she says "can and will be used" against her in court. The suspect must also be informed that she has the right to "consult with a lawyer and to have the lawyer" with her during interrogation, and that if she is indigent, "a lawyer will be appointed to represent" her. The warnings about the rights to silence and counsel are *"absolute prerequisites to interrogation."* The warning about the appointment of counsel must be given "when there is any doubt at all" about a suspect's ability to retain counsel.

b. Functions of the Warnings

The *Miranda* Court declared that the warnings would help to overcome the "inherent pressures of the interrogation atmosphere."

First, they inform the suspect of her rights and enable the suspect to make an "intelligent decision" as to the exercise of these rights. Also, the warnings would "show the suspect" that the police were prepared to honor her rights. They also would make her "acutely aware" that she was "not in the presence of persons acting solely" in her interest.

c. **Second–Tier Safeguards**

The *Miranda* Court held that the warnings alone would be insufficient to protect a suspect's exercise of the Fifth Amendment privilege. In addition, a suspect needed an opportunity to consult with counsel, because the atmosphere of custodial interrogation could "operate very quickly to overbear" her will, even after warnings were given. The procedural requirements imposed by *Miranda* in addition to the warnings are known as the second-tier safeguards, and are essentially designed to guarantee that the rights described in the warnings will be respected if the suspect decides to invoke them.

d. **Honoring the Suspect's Rights: The Right to Silence**

Under *Miranda*, a suspect may invoke her right to silence "in any manner, at any time prior to or during questioning." When she does, "the interrogation must cease." If police obtain an incriminating statement after invocation after the right to silence is invoked, it "cannot be other than the product of compulsion."

e. **Honoring the Suspect's Rights: The Right to Consult Counsel**

If a suspect says that she "wants an attorney," the interrogation "must cease until an attorney is present." When the attorney is present, the suspect "must have an opportunity to confer" with counsel, and to have counsel *present during any subsequent interrogation.*" If police want to interrogate an indigent suspect, they "must make known" to her that "a lawyer will be provided" for her "prior to any interrogation." If a suspect asks for counsel, a lawyer need not be provided for "a reasonable period of time" while police continue to investigate. However, police may not question the suspect during this time.

f. **The *Miranda* Right to Counsel Distinguished From the Sixth Amendment Right to Counsel**

The right to counsel provided by *Miranda* must be distinguished from the Sixth Amendment right to counsel in interrogations established by the Court in *Massiah.* The *Miranda* right to counsel is a procedural safeguard designed to provide protection for the defendant's right to remain silent in the fact of custodial interrogation. Moreover, the *Miranda* right to counsel does not come into play unless the suspect decides that he needs this protection and *invokes* the right to counsel. In contrast, the Sixth Amendment right to counsel applies *automatically,* whenever an indicted defendant is subject to deliberate elicitation by a Government agent. The indicted defendant does not have to invoke his Sixth Amendment right—as shown by the facts in *Massiah,* who did not even know that he was speaking to a Government agent and hence had no reason to invoke his right to counsel. However, while the *Miranda* right to counsel is not automatic and must be invoked, it is in one sense broader than the automatic Sixth Amendment right to counsel: it applies *before indictment,* in any situation of custodial interrogation.

3. Waiver of *Miranda* Rights

The *Miranda* Court stated that if the police obtain a confession through custodial interrogation, the state must bear the "heavy burden" of meeting the "high standard" of proving that a suspect "voluntarily, knowingly and intelligently" waived her rights to silence and counsel.

a. Sufficient Proof of Waiver

The *Miranda* Court noted that an express statement that the suspect "is willing" to talk and "does not want an attorney," followed closely by an incriminating statement, "could" constitute a valid waiver.

b. Insufficient Proof of Waiver

Under *Miranda,* a waiver may not be presumed from a suspect's silence after warnings. Nor may a waiver be presumed from the "fact that a confession was in fact eventually obtained." There must be evidence in the record that the suspect "understandingly rejected the offer" of counsel. Moreover, a suspect may invoke her rights after answering some questions, and thereby withdraw any waiver given at the outset.

c. Evidence That Negates Waiver

The Court in *Miranda* mentioned certain circumstances which would clearly cut against a finding of waiver. These include "lengthy interrogation or incommunicado incarceration," or "any evidence" the suspect was "threatened, tricked or cajoled" into a waiver.

4. Triggering of the Safeguards

The *Miranda* safeguards attach only when a suspect is subjected to *custodial interrogation* by police officers. The safeguards are not applicable to general "on-the-scene questioning as to facts surrounding a crime" or to other "general questioning of citizens in the fact-finding process."

5. *Miranda* Is Not a "Constitutional Straightjacket"

The Court recognized that Congress and the states had the power to establish "alternatives for protecting the privilege" that are as effective as the *Miranda* rules. The Court emphasized that it did not want to "handicap sound efforts at reform" by creating a "constitutional straightjacket" that would hamper the creation of these alternatives. It also noted that the Constitution does not require "adherence to any particular solution" for dispelling the inherent compulsion of custodial interrogation. But in the absence of "equally effective" procedures for protecting the rights of suspects, *Miranda* safeguards "must be observed."

6. The *Miranda* Requirements and Law Enforcement Goals

The *Miranda* Court rejected arguments that its rules would result in harm to law enforcement. The Court refused to find that "the end" of obtaining confessions justified "the means" of ignoring the suspect's rights, because this was "pernicious doctrine" that would allow the Government to be a "lawbreaker." The Court acknowledged that confessions "may play an important role in some convictions," but noted that in other cases this role was overstated. In the four cases under review "considerable" evidence of guilt had been acquired independently of each defendant's confession. The Court also rejected the argument that "unfettered" police discretion to detain suspects would be beneficial to innocent people, who could "clear themselves" by talking. Such a person would be "better able" to do so "after warnings and with counsel present," declared the Court.

7. Dissent

Four Justices dissented in *Miranda*, and three filed dissenting opinions.

a. Justice Clark's Dissent

Justice Clark advocated a compromise, somewhere between the positions of the majority and three other dissenting colleagues. He proposed that the Court rely on Due Process to require the police to give the *Miranda* warnings, and to prove waiver under the "totality" of the circumstances. Under Justice Clark's "voluntariness inquiry," the failure to give warnings would be only one relevant factor in determining whether Due Process was violated.

Justice Clark proposed his compromise because he argued the majority's doctrine was going "too far too fast," in the absence of empirical knowledge about "the practical operation" of the *Miranda* requirements.

b. Justice Harlan's Dissent

Justice Harlan was joined in his dissent by Justices Stewart and White. Justice Harlan argued that the *Miranda* majority's new rules were unsupported by precedent, and were unwise and dangerous as a matter of policy.

First, Justice Harlan voiced disapproval of the *Miranda* majority's extension of the Fifth Amendment to the interrogation process. He advocated that the Due Process doctrine should remain the sole standard for judging confessions, as neither Fifth nor Sixth Amendment precedents supported the Court's ruling. Justice Harlan praised the case-by-case Due Process doctrine as "elaborate," "sophisticated," "sensitive," "judicial," and "flexible." He saw nothing wrong with its lack of predictability, and found that disagreements about its interpretation were "usually confined to that borderland of close cases where it matters least." He found that Due Process precedents gave proper recognition to the value of confessions as a tool of law enforcement.

Justice Harlan found the Court's expansion of the privilege to cover custodial interrogation to be unwarranted for several reasons. First, the Due Process standard already incorporated a "protective concern" for suspects and an emphasis on "adversarial values." Second, Fifth Amendment precedents never condemned "all pressure" to incriminate oneself, and Justice Harlan found no reason for the Fifth Amendment to prohibit "the relatively mild pressure" that the Due Process doctrine permitted. Finally, he argued that no precedent required "precise knowledge of one's rights" as a prerequisite to the loss of Fifth Amendment protections.

Justice Harlan also criticized the *Miranda* decision on policy grounds. The rules would not deter "blatant" coercion, because police could lie about warnings and waivers as readily as they could lie about brutality, and get away with it. Moreover, the rules would "markedly decrease" the number of confessions. Justice Harlan viewed confessions as important for "crime control," and found that the social costs of crime were "too great" to justify the Court's "hazardous experimentation" with society's welfare.

c.   Justice White's Dissent

Justice White was joined in his dissent by Justices Harlan and Stewart. Justice White argued that *Miranda's* logic violated "common sense," because it required confessions elicited by a *single question* to be treated as "compelled," but allowed spontaneous confessions with the same custodial pressures to be treated as voluntary. Justice White found it "irrational" to believe that either the *Miranda* warnings, or the presence of counsel could make coercion "disappear"; he also found it paradoxical that the defendant's *waiver* of rights could be accepted as voluntary under *Miranda*, even though it occurred in the "inherently coercive" setting of interrogation.

In Justice White's view the *Miranda* majority had three goals: to give suspects a right to silence that would be invoked in most cases, to give the state "a severe, if not impossible" burden of proof of waiver, and to forbid interrogation except in the presence of counsel "for all practical purposes." Therefore, *Miranda* was not confined to protecting the Fifth Amendment privilege, but focused on creating a "Fifth Amendment right to counsel." Justice White found "no warrant in the Fifth Amendment" for "installing counsel as the arbiter of the privilege."

In addition to the deleterious effect on law enforcement, Justice White predicted that the ambiguity of certain *Miranda* rules would impose a cost of "judicial time and effort" in interpreting these rules in future litigation. He identified four open questions that would require case-by-case definition: whether a suspect is "in custody"; whether she is under "interrogation"; whether she has "waived" her rights; and whether particular evidence is an inadmissible "fruit" of a *Miranda* violation. Given the uncertainties concerning *Miranda's* application, Justice White rejected the notion that its rules would provide a "bright line" for police to determine whether interrogation "may be safely pursued."

B. Perspective

Miranda was a closely-divided case, and *Miranda* issues are hotly debated both within and outside the Court today. Before examining the major areas of law-making under *Miranda*, it is useful to consider how the *Miranda* opinions created the foundation for the modern debate about its meaning.

1. *Miranda* as the Definitive Solution for the Problems Presented by Custodial Interrogation

The *Miranda* rules established a new regime for judicial review of confessions, yet the Court's opinion was ambiguous concerning the evolution of that regime in the future. Some critics argue that the Court did not go far enough in *Miranda*, because the warnings alone could not "dispel" much of the coercion created by interrogation, and because the right to consult counsel would not protect suspects who "waived" their rights before consulting a lawyer. These critics complain that *Miranda* incorrectly rejected the argument that a person subject to custodial interrogation "needs a lawyer to waive the right to a lawyer." They argue, as did Justice White, that *Miranda* is inherently contradictory because it presumes that a person is coerced in the milieu of custodial interrogation, but then permits the person to "voluntarily" waive the rights that would protect him in that very situation.

Arguably, the *Miranda* Court left the door open to imposing further restrictions on custodial interrogations, and in later cases the Court was faced with claims that *Miranda* should be extended to create new rules that would effectuate its policies. *See, e.g., Colorado v. Spring,* 479 U.S. 564, 107 S.Ct. 851, 93 L.Ed.2d 954 (1987) (claim that suspect should be informed of the subject of the interrogation prior to waiver); *Moran v. Burbine,* 475 U.S. 412, 106 S.Ct. 1135, 89 L.Ed.2d 410 (1986) (claim that suspect should be informed, prior to waiver, that an attorney wants to talk to him). In resolving these and other claims, however, a majority of the Court usually chose to treat *Miranda* as the definitive solution for dispelling the "coercion" of the interrogation process, and to reject the need to expand the requirements established in *Miranda* itself.

2. The Need for Further Judicial Definition of *Miranda* Concepts, and for Case-by-Case Application of These Definitions

Justice White's dissent identified four open questions after *Miranda*, namely, the meaning of "custody," "interrogation," "waiver," and "fruits." Other major issues would require the Court's attention in later cases as well, including: the propriety of impeaching a defendant with evidence obtained in violation of *Miranda;* the scope of permissible ambiguity in the *Miranda* warnings; the propriety of the resumption of interrogation after invocation of rights; the need for a "public safety" exception to the suspect's right to receive warnings; the relevance of the nature of the offense to the *Miranda* requirements; and the role of *Miranda* in under-cover activity by police.

Usually, the application of each *Miranda* concept to a given factual setting was held to require consideration of a "totality" of factors. The Court's own applications of its *Miranda* concepts to the facts of given cases often signaled to lower courts that restrictive interpretations of the scope of *Miranda* rights were acceptable, in light of the vital role confessions play in the system of law enforcement. Thus, the spirit of the *Miranda* dissents came to occupy a place of prominence in post-*Miranda* jurisprudence.

3. The *Miranda* Compromise

If the *Miranda* Court had followed through on its premise that custodial interrogation was inherently coercive, and that counsel was a necessary safeguard in dispelling this coercion, it would have reached the logical conclusion that all confessions made in the absence of counsel (which is to say, almost all confessions) are inadmissible. The Court, however, rejected this radical proposal, because it was not prepared to rule that confessions had no place in law enforcement. So the Court compromised. *Miranda* provides a right to silence and to counsel, but the decision whether to invoke these rights (and conversely whether to waive them) are made in the same coercive atmosphere that the Court was so concerned about. In subsequent cases, the Court has held steady to this "compromise," which is designed to provide some protection to suspects, without severely impinging on law enforcement interests.

C. Is *Miranda* a Constitutional Rule?

1. Interpreting the Language of *Miranda*

Language in *Miranda* suggests that its safeguards are not constitutionally required. Clearly, there is no language in the Fifth Amendment or any other part of the Constitution that even vaguely resembles the *Miranda* warnings. Further, the Court explicitly disclaims any intent to create a "constitutional straitjacket" and invites Congress and state legislatures to develop their own safeguards, consistent with *Miranda.* Before its decision in *Dickerson v. United States,* 530 U.S. 428, 120 S.Ct. 2326, 147

L.Ed.2d 405 (2000), the Court had from time to time referred to the "non-constitutional" status of *Miranda* as it justified restrictive interpretations of the scope of the rules, at least in some doctrinal areas. (*See, e.g., Oregon v. Elstad*, 470 U.S. 298, 105 S.Ct. 1285, 84 L.Ed.2d 222 (1985) (holding that when police violate *Miranda* during an interrogation, a confession following a subsequent proper interrogation is not an inadmissible "fruit" of the initial violation)); *New York v. Quarles*, 467 U.S. 649, 104 S.Ct. 2626, 81 L.Ed.2d 550 (1984) (establishing a "public safety exception" to the requirement that police give *Miranda* warnings).

2. **A Congressional Attempt to Overrule *Miranda***

Shortly after the *Miranda* decision, Congress passed 18 U.S.C. § 3501, discussed *supra*. That statute provided that voluntary confessions shall be admissible. It further stated that there was no absolute requirement that the defendant be informed of his right to silence and to counsel, noting that these factors were relevant in determining voluntariness, but were not dispositive. 18 U.S.C. § 3501 clearly contradicted *Miranda*, and although the government never argued that § 3501 overruled *Miranda*, at least one member of the Court expressed an interest in considering the issue. *See Davis v. United States*, 512 U.S. 452, 114 S.Ct. 2350, 129 L.Ed.2d 362 (1994) (Scalia, J., *concurring*).

3. ***Dickerson v. United States*: *Miranda's* Constitutional Status**

In *Dickerson v. United States*, 530 U.S. 428, 120 S.Ct. 2326, 147 L.Ed.2d 405 (2000), the Court held that *Miranda* is a constitutional rule, which could not be overruled by an Act of Congress. The Court declined to overrule *Miranda*, and affirmed that it will continue to govern the admissibility of statements made during custodial interrogation in state and federal courts.

a. Procedural History

The case came to the Court in a very unusual posture. The Fourth Circuit, in *United States v. Dickerson*, 166 F.3d 667 (4th Cir.1999), held that 18 U.S.C. § 3501 overrules *Miranda*. The government did not argue the applicability of the statute since the Justice Department had always taken the position that *Miranda* governed the admissibility of statements. Instead, two organizations representing law enforcement and crime victim interests filed an amicus brief urging the court to rule that § 3501 superceded *Miranda*. The Fourth Circuit's decision and the Supreme Court's decision to grant certiorari re-ignited the debate over § 3501 and *Miranda*.

b. Congress' Authority

The Court addressed whether Congress had the authority to pass § 3501. It noted that Congress may amend or set aside any judicially created rule of evidence or procedure that is not required by the Constitution. Thus, the Court's decision hinged on whether the *Miranda* Court announced a constitutional rule. The Court held that it did and that § 3501 was unconstitutional. The Court then went on to discuss several factors in support of its holding.

c. *Miranda's* Applicability to the States

First, the Court noted that *Miranda* and two of its companion cases applied the rule to proceedings in state courts. It further noted that since that time, it consistently has applied *Miranda* to state courts. Since the Court's authority over state courts is limited to interpreting constitutional issues, the Court reasoned, *Miranda* must be a constitutional rule.

d. The Language of *Miranda*

The Court next turned to the language of *Miranda* itself in support of its holding that *Miranda* announced a constitutional rule, pointing out that the opinion was "replete with statements indicating that the majority thought it was announcing a constitutional rule." One such statement was the Court's pronouncement at the beginning of the *Miranda* opinion that it granted certiorari "to explore some facets of the problems * * * of applying the privilege against self-incrimination to in-custody interrogation, and to give concrete constitutional guidelines for law enforcement agencies and courts to follow." The Court explained its statement in *Miranda* that it did not intend to create a "constitutional straitjacket" simply meant that the constitution did not require the precise warnings suggested in *Miranda*, and that legislative bodies were free to create alternative procedures as long as they were just as effective in protecting a suspect's Fifth Amendment privilege against self-incrimination.

e. Post–*Miranda* Cases

The Court addressed the Fourth Circuit's reliance upon cases decided after *Miranda* in which the Court made exceptions to the rule that *Miranda* warnings be provided before questioning a suspect. These cases include *New York v. Quarles* and *Harris v. New York*, discussed *infra*. The Court stated that these cases do not undercut the constitutional status of *Miranda*, but simply illustrate the principle that no constitutional rule is immutable and that modifications of a rule are a normal part of constitutional law. The Court further noted that several of its post-*Miranda* decisions refer to *Miranda's* constitutional underpinnings.

f. *Miranda* Affirmed

Congress did not have the authority to overrule *Miranda*, and the Court declined to do so, citing the principle of stare decisis and *Miranda's* status in law enforcement practices and in the national culture. The Court noted that instead of undermining *Miranda's* doctrinal underpinnings, its post-*Miranda* cases have reduced the impact of the *Miranda* rule on law enforcement while reaffirming the decision's core ruling.

g. Dissent

Justices Scalia, joined by Justice Thomas, dissented, citing language in the post-*Miranda* cases relied upon by the Fourth Circuit. Justice Scalia stated that the language in these cases, including *Tucker, Hass, Quarles,* and *Elstad*, discussed *infra*, explicitly confirmed the non-constitutional status of *Miranda* and that the language was central to the holdings in these cases. Finally, Justice Scalia argued that *Miranda* should be overruled in favor of a totality of the circumstances voluntariness standard, as set forth in § 3501.

D. *Miranda* and Impeachment

The actual holding in *Miranda*, strictly read, was that it was error for the prosecution to admit Miranda's confession as proof of his guilt. This left the question whether a *Miranda*-defective confession could be used for other purposes. The most important "other purpose" possibility is that a *Miranda*-defective confession could be used to impeach the defendant if he takes the stand and testifies inconsistently with the previous confession.

1. *Miranda*-Defective Statements May Be Used to Impeach a Defendant Who Takes the Stand at Trial

In *Harris v. New York*, 401 U.S. 222, 91 S.Ct. 643, 28 L.Ed.2d 1 (1971), the defendant testified that he sold baking powder, not heroin, to an undercover agent. In his post-arrest statement to the police, he claimed to have acted for the agent in buying heroin from others; this statement was obtained without *Miranda* warnings, and the prosecution made no attempt to introduce it in its own case. However, the prosecution did introduce these statements on cross-examination of the defendant, in order to show that his trial testimony was inconsistent with his previous statement. The Court determined that the *Miranda*-defective statements could be used to impeach the defendant, where the jury was instructed that the post-arrest statements could be considered in judging the defendant's "credibility," but not as evidence of guilt.

2. Rationale

The Court valued the benefits of the impeachment process in *Harris* over the benefits to be obtained by excluding *Miranda*-defective statements on cross-examination. The Court found that the defendant's right to testify did not "include the right to commit perjury," and that sufficient deterrence of police misconduct could be achieved by exclusion of *Miranda*-defective statements from the state's case-in-chief. The "possibility" of further deterrence was found to be no justification for shielding the defendant from exposure to cross-examination about his prior inconsistent statements.

3. Consequences of Analysis in *Harris*

It is useful to highlight the main elements of the *Harris* majority's thinking, as its analysis created a tradition of restrictive interpretation of the *Miranda* opinion. First, the Court treated the truth-finding function of the trial as superior to the Fifth Amendment values protected by the *Miranda* safeguards. Second, the Court embraced a rule that permitted the erosion of *Miranda's* rights in practice. For, even though *Harris* prohibited the use of illegal statements to "prove guilt" during cross-examination, the jurors' awareness of these statements could lead them to infer guilt when rejecting the defendant's "credibility." Finally, the Court assumed that exclusion of *Miranda*-defective confessions from the case-in-chief would sufficiently deter *Miranda* violations, and therefore that application of an exclusionary rule in any context beyond the case-in-chief would provide a benefit too minimal to justify the cost of excluding reliable evidence.

4. Continued Affirmation of the *Harris* Rule

In *Oregon v. Hass*, 420 U.S. 714, 95 S.Ct. 1215, 43 L.Ed.2d 570 (1975), the Court held that the *Harris* rule applied to statements obtained where a police officer violated *Miranda* by interrogating a defendant after he received warnings and invoked the right to counsel. At trial, the defendant testified to a minor role in a burglary, but in post-arrest statements (after invoking and being denied the right to counsel) he had admitted taking the property himself. The Court held that it was proper for the prosecutor to cross-examine Hass about the inconsistencies between his two versions of the crime.

a. Rationale

The Court held that the reasoning of *Harris* justified the prosecutor's use of the illegal statements in *Hass* to impeach the defendant, even though the nature of the *Miranda* violation was different—i.e., *Harris* involved a failure to give warnings while *Hass* involved a failure to abide by them. The Court conceded that a police officer who gave accurate warnings might be tempted to interrogate a defendant improperly after the defendant made the decision that he would not talk. But the Court concluded that whatever difference might exist between the "incentive" to seek impeachment evidence in *Harris and Hass,* "the balance was struck in *Harris,* and we are not disposed to change it now."

b. Dissent

The dissenters in *Hass* argued that the majority had gone "beyond *Harris* in undermining *Miranda.*" They concluded that *Hass* left police with "almost no incentive" to abide by *Miranda* by honoring a suspect's invocation of his rights. At least under *Harris*, there is an incentive for police to give warnings—the officer doesn't know whether the defendant will confess, and without warnings, the confession would only be admissible for impeachment. However, once the warnings have been given and the defendant invokes his rights, it is apparent that the defendant will not confess. The officer therefore has nothing to lose by failing to respect the second-tier *Miranda* safeguards—the worst that can happen is that a confession will be obtained that would not otherwise be obtained, and that confession can at least be used for impeachment.

5. *Miranda*–Defective Confessions Cannot Be Used to Impeach Defense Witnesses

In *James v. Illinois*, 493 U.S. 307, 110 S.Ct. 648, 107 L.Ed.2d 676 (1990), the Court held that the fruits of a Fourth Amendment violation may not be used to impeach a defendant's witnesses, even though they may be used to impeach the defendant. Presumably, this means that the illegal fruits of a *Miranda* violation cannot be used to impeach a defendant's witnesses. This is because the Court now treats the "impeachment exception" for both Fourth Amendment and *Miranda* violations as being governed by the same principles. For further treatment of *James*, see the discussion of the impeachment exception to the Fourth Amendment exclusionary rule, *supra*.

6. Involuntary Confessions Cannot Be Used for Impeachment

If a confession is obtained from the defendant involuntarily, then the Due Process Clause is violated when the confession is admitted at trial. The Court has held that if the defendant confesses involuntarily, the confession cannot be admitted even for the limited purpose of impeaching the defendant at trial. *See Mincey v. Arizona*, 437 U.S. 385, 98 S.Ct. 2408, 57 L.Ed.2d 290 (1978) (distinguishing *Harris* as involving a *Miranda*-defective confession, as opposed to a confession the admission of which would violate the Due Process Clause).

7. Impeachment With Post–*Miranda* Silence

In *Doyle v. Ohio*, 426 U.S. 610, 96 S.Ct. 2240, 49 L.Ed.2d 91 (1976), the defendants testified that they had been "framed" by another participant in a drug sale. However, they did not mention this excuse when they had been arrested and given *Miranda* warnings. The prosecutor sought to impeach the defendants with their post-arrest silence, arguing that it was inconsistent to be silent at that point, if they really had an excuse for their conduct. The Supreme Court held that this impeachment was improper.

a. Rationale

The Court reasoned that it would be unfair to penalize a defendant for relying on the assurance in the warnings that he has "the right to remain silent," by allowing the prosecutor to use his silence for impeachment purposes. The Court found that while the *Miranda* warnings "contain no express assurance that silence will carry no penalty," this assurance is implicit; it would be "reasonable" for anyone to assume that the "right to remain silent" means that silence cannot be penalized. Thus, the *Doyle* rule rests on "the fundamental unfairness of implicitly assuring a suspect that his silence will not be used against him and then using his silence to impeach an explanation subsequently offered at trial."

b. Due Process, Not Fifth Amendment

The Court did not rely on the Fifth Amendment to prohibit the prosecutor's use of the defendant's silence in *Doyle*. The Court simply noted that the *Miranda* warnings were a "prophylactic means of safeguarding Fifth Amendment rights," and relied on Due

Process for its holding. Under the Due Process Clause, it was fundamentally unfair to provide an assurance in the *Miranda* warnings, and then to renege on that assurance at trial.

c. Dissent

The three dissenters argued that the majority erroneously created a "presumption" that any defendant's post-warning silence "was the product of reliance on the *Miranda* warning." The dissent concluded that "the risk that a truthful defendant will be deceived by the *Miranda* warning" and be unable to explain his "honest misunderstanding" at trial, was "much less" than the risk that the *Doyle* rule "will merely provide a shield for perjury."

d. Limitations of Due Process Analysis

The Due Process rationale employed in *Doyle* made the Court's decision restrictive in a certain way. As *Doyle* was not grounded in *Miranda* doctrine, it could not be used to justify broad interpretations of the need to give "accurate" warnings to suspects, or to protect a suspect's implicit reliance on the privilege in other cases. Also, the Court's Due Process analysis focused on the implied guarantees in the *Miranda* warnings, and on the unfairness of withdrawing those guarantees at trial. This analysis has no application where *Miranda* warnings have not even been given.

e. Continued Affirmation of *Doyle*

In *Brecht v. Abrahamson,* 507 U.S. 619, 113 S.Ct. 1710, 123 L.Ed.2d 353 (1993), the Court affirmed the vitality of the *Doyle* rule. The Court stated that *"Doyle* was not simply a further extension of the *Miranda* prophylactic rule. Rather * * * it is rooted in fundamental fairness and due process concerns. However real these concerns, *Doyle* does not overprotect them." The Court concluded that "due process is violated whenever the prosecution uses for impeachment purposes a defendant's post-*Miranda* silence" and that *Doyle* "does not bear the hallmarks of a prophylactic rule."

f. *Doyle* and the Insanity Defense

In *Wainwright v. Greenfield,* 474 U.S. 284, 106 S.Ct. 634, 88 L.Ed.2d 623 (1986), the Court held that under *Doyle* a prosecutor may not use the defendant's post-warning silence in order to rebut an insanity defense at trial. In *Wainwright,* the prosecutor sought to introduce evidence of the defendant's silence in order to prove that the defendant engaged in rational behavior upon arrest, which was inconsistent with his insanity defense to the charge of sexual battery. The Court held that *Doyle* barred the use of post-warning silence in insanity cases because "the implied assurance contained in the *Miranda* warning" is that silence will not be used for any purpose, including impeachment at trial. The Court noted that the state could introduce evidence of the defendant's rational "behavior" during arrest, as long as the prosecutor carefully "avoided any mention of the defendant's exercise of his constitutional rights."

g.   **Post–Warning Statements Inconsistent With Later Trial Testimony**
In *Anderson v. Charles,* 447 U.S. 404, 100 S.Ct. 2180, 65 L.Ed.2d 222 (1980), the Court held that *Doyle* did not apply to a case where a defendant waived his rights following the *Miranda* warnings, and gave police a statement before trial; this statement was far less complete than the account given by the defendant at trial, and the prosecutor used the statement as proof that the elaborations in the defendant's trial testimony were not credible. The Court held that a prosecutor can cross-examine a defendant concerning any inconsistencies between omissions in his pre-trial statement and his trial testimony. The defendant in *Anderson* did not exercise his right to remain silent, because the omissions in his post-waiver statement did not constitute "silences." So it was not unfair to use the statement (and its omissions) against him because the warnings specifically informed him of that possibility. *Doyle* bars only the use of "silence maintained after receipt of governmental assurances" contained in the warnings.

h.   **No Evidence of Silence**
In *Greer v. Miller,* 483 U.S. 756, 107 S.Ct. 3102, 97 L.Ed.2d 618 (1987), the Court held that no *Doyle* violation occurred when a prosecutor's attempt to inquire about post-arrest silence was cut short by a defense objection, and the jury was instructed to "ignore" the prosecutor's question. On these facts, no evidence concerning silence was heard by the jury, and no further question or argument about silence was heard.

8.   Impeachment With Pre-*Miranda* Silence

a.   **Silence Before Arrest**
In *Jenkins v. Anderson,* 447 U.S. 231, 100 S.Ct. 2124, 65 L.Ed.2d 86 (1980), the Court held that the use of pre-arrest silence to impeach a

defendant violated neither the Fifth Amendment nor the *Doyle* rule embodied in the Due Process Clause. Therefore, the prosecutor in *Jenkins* was allowed to impeach the defendant's testimony concerning his claim of self-defense to a murder charge, by asking him why he failed to report the homicide to anyone for two weeks before he turned himself in.

b. Rationale

As to the Fifth Amendment, the Court conceded that the *Jenkins* defendant might feel compelled to forgo the privilege before arrest "if his failure to speak later can be used to impeach him." But this form of compulsion did not violate the Fifth Amendment because it did not impair "to an appreciable extent" the policies behind the privilege. It did not rise to the level, for example, of the custodial interrogation found to be compulsion in *Miranda*.

As to the Due Process Clause and *Doyle*, the *Jenkins* Court found that Due Process is violated only when "governmental action" induces a defendant to remain silent. In *Jenkins*, the defendant's silence occurred before *Miranda* warnings were given, and so his silence was not caused by the implicit assurance in the warnings that his silence would not be penalized. Since the Government had given Jenkins no promises, it had not reneged on any promises by using his silence against him at trial.

c. Dissent

The dissenters argued that the *Jenkins* rule violated Due Process because the defendant's failure to report the crime "was not probative of the falsity of his testimony at trial." Thus, it was "fundamentally unfair" to allow the jury to draw the inference of falsity from his silence. They also argued that the *Jenkins* rule violated the Fifth Amendment, because it replaced the privilege against self-incrimination "with a duty to incriminate oneself," and thus created a "substantial" burden on both the privilege and the decision "to exercise the right to testify in one's own defense."

d. Silence After Arrest

In *Fletcher v. Weir*, 455 U.S. 603, 102 S.Ct. 1309, 71 L.Ed.2d 490 (1982), the Court held that *Doyle* does not apply when a defendant is impeached with silence that occurs after he is arrested but *before he receives Miranda warnings*. The Court reasoned that the event of arrest is not "governmental action which implicitly induces" a defendant to remain silent. *Doyle* applies only when the Government induces silence "by implicitly assuring the defendant that his silence would not be used against him"—i.e., by giving the *Miranda* warnings. Thus, the prosecutor in *Fletcher* could impeach the defendant by asking him about his failure to tell the police about his claim of self-defense before he received *Miranda* warnings. *See also United States v. Frazier*, 394 F.3d 612 (8th Cir.2005) (the use of defendant's post-arrest, pre-Miranda silence during the government's case-in-chief did not violate his Fifth Amendment rights because "there was no governmental action at that point inducing his silence," and "therefore he was under no government-imposed compulsion to speak.")

E. The Admissibility of the Fruits of *Miranda*–Defective Confessions

The *Miranda* Court held that a defendant's confession was inadmissible if police violated the *Miranda* rules, but did not determine whether "fruits" of confessions were inadmissible as well. For example, a defendant's inadmissible confession can lead police to a witness who incriminates the defendant, or to incriminating physical evidence. Or, a defendant's inadmissible confession may lead police to question him further; even if police observed the *Miranda* rules during the second interrogation, it is possible to view a second confession as the "fruit" of the first one.

Before *Miranda*, the problem of such derivative evidence was addressed in Fourth Amendment law by the use of the "fruit of the poisonous tree" doctrine, which required the exclusion of fruits of Fourth Amendment violations that were the products of police exploitation of the original violation. However, the Court has ruled that the fruit of the poisonous tree doctrine does not apply to the fruits of a *Miranda* violation. Originally, this ruling was based on the theory that the *Miranda* warnings are merely prophylactic safeguards, not constitutional rights. But after *Dickerson*, the rationale for the admissibility of fruits of a *Miranda* violation is simply that the court has created an exception to the constitutionally-based *Miranda* rule.

1. Identity of a Witness as a Fruit of a *Miranda* Violation

In *Michigan v. Tucker*, 417 U.S. 433, 94 S.Ct. 2357, 41 L.Ed.2d 182 (1974), the defendant identified a witness who would support his alibi to a rape charge, during an interrogation that violated *Miranda*. When the police contacted the witness, he provided information that incriminated the defendant. At trial, Tucker's statement about the alibi witness was excluded as a statement obtained in violation of *Miranda*. But the witness' statements implicating Tucker were not obtained by violating *Miranda* because the witness gave them voluntarily. If these statements were to be excluded, it would have to be as "fruits" of the "poisonous" *Miranda*-defective confession. But the Court refused to apply the fruits doctrine, held that the witness' testimony at trial was properly admitted, and affirmed the defendant's conviction for rape.

Because the fruit of the poisonous tree doctrine did not mandate exclusion for the fruit of a *Miranda* violation, the *Tucker* Court undertook a balancing of costs and benefits to determine whether exclusion, while not mandated, was nonetheless *appropriate.* The Court observed that the benefit provided by the *Miranda* exclusionary rule is the deterrence of future police illegality. The Court believed, however, that the exclusion of Tucker's confession itself provided all the deterrence necessary to safeguard Fifth Amendment rights, and that exclusion of the witness's testimony would have little "extra" deterrent effect. Thus, the benefits of exclusion were minimal. In contrast, the cost of exclusion was severe, because the witness' testimony was reliable—it was not coerced in any sense. Therefore, a cost-benefit analysis mandated admission of the fruit of the *Miranda*-defective confession.

2. **Subsequent Confession as the Fruit of a *Miranda* Violation**
Tucker did not specifically address whether the fruits doctrine could be used where the "fruit" involved was not an independent witness, but a defendant's own admissions, or physical evidence. Some of these loose ends were taken up in *Oregon v. Elstad*, 470 U.S. 298, 105 S.Ct. 1285, 84 L.Ed.2d 222 (1985). Elstad confessed without being given *Miranda* warnings. Thereafter, he was given the warnings and confessed again. The first confession was excluded from trial, but the second one was admitted. Elstad argued that the second confession should have been excluded as the fruit of the *Miranda*-defective first confession. But the Court held that the initial failure to administer *Miranda* warnings did not "taint" a subsequent confession which itself complied with *Miranda*. Where no "deliberately coercive or improper tactics" accompanied the initial *Miranda* violation, a subsequent administration of the warnings was held to "cure" any lingering compulsion from the first interrogation.

a. The Fruits of Involuntary Confessions Are Excluded
The Court in *Elstad* specified two circumstances in which a second confession must be excluded even though the officers properly give *Miranda* warnings before that confession. One situation is where the

first confession is *actually involuntary*, in the sense that it was obtained against the defendant's free will. Officers who have obtained an involuntary confession have violated the Due Process Clause to which the "fruit of the poisonous tree" doctrine is fully applicable. So if the first confession is involuntary, the second confession must be excluded if derived from the first under the principles established in *Wong Sun*. (See the discussion of the fruit of the poisonous tree doctrine in the section on the Fourth Amendment exclusionary rule, *supra*).

b. **Subsequent Confession Excluded if It Is Obtained Involuntarily**

The second situation in which a second confession may be excluded after *Elstad*, even though the officers gave *Miranda* warnings, is where the second confession is itself involuntarily obtained. The giving of *Miranda* warnings does not foreclose the possibility that a confession may be involuntary. The police officers might use coercive tactics to force a defendant to waive his *Miranda* rights and confess. If that is the case, the confession is inadmissible under the Due Process Clause. Similarly, the police might incorrectly tell the defendant that he has already "let the cat out of the bag" by confessing, and that a subsequent confession is a mere formality, where in fact the initial confession is inadmissible because it is *Miranda*-defective. While a single bit of misinformation may not be enough to render the confession involuntary, it may contribute to other circumstances to support a finding that the defendant's confession was coerced.

c. **Second Confession Not Involuntary in *Elstad***

In *Elstad*, the Court found that the defendant's second confession was not involuntarily obtained, because, among other things, the officers did not deceive Elstad into thinking that he had let the "cat out of the bag." If Elstad was under the misimpression that he had done so, then that was a mistake of his own making, and the Due Process Clause does not provide for exclusion of confessions when they are not attributable to affirmative police misconduct. See *Colorado v. Connelly* in the discussion on confessions and Due Process. In *Elstad*, the administration of the *Miranda* warnings at the stationhouse served to "cure" the defendant's inability to exercise the privilege intelligently, and to make the second confession "an act of free will." The Court found that whatever subtle form of pressure might exist in the defendant's mind from the revelation of his "guilty secret" was very different from traditional "official coercion" flowing from "physical violence or other deliberate means calculated to break the suspect's will."

d. **"Cat Out of the Bag" Warning Not Required**

The Court in *Elstad* rejected the proposal that police inform suspects that their prior admissions may not be admissible evidence, and that they have not let the "cat out of the bag" where they might mistakenly believe that they had. The Court found that such a warning requirement would be likely to decrease the number of confessions; thus, it would impose a "high cost" on "legitimate law enforcement activity," and permit "highly probative evidence" to be "irretrievably lost" to the fact-finder at trial.

e. **Balancing Approach**

As in *Tucker*, the *Elstad* Court, after finding that the fruit of the poisonous tree doctrine did not mandate exclusion, employed a cost-benefit analysis to determine whether it was appropriate to exclude a properly warned second confession that was obtained after the defendant had already confessed without warnings. The Court found that the benefit of deterring *Miranda* violations by applying the exclusionary rule was attenuated in these circumstances, because the risk of exclusion of the first confession was a sufficient deterrent. Against the minimal deterrent effect resulting from exclusion of the second confession, the Court weighed the cost of excluding a reliable confession, obtained voluntarily after *Miranda* warnings; the Court concluded that the costs of exclusion outweighed the benefits.

f. **Dissent**

The dissenters argued that *Elstad* gave officers an incentive to obtain an unwarned confession, due to the likelihood that a suspect would then confess a second time after being given *pro forma* warnings.

g. **Other Types of *Miranda* Violations**

A question raised by *Elstad* is whether its rationale can be applied to *Miranda* violations other than a failure to warn a suspect in custody. For example, suppose that police fail to obtain a valid waiver before continuing an interrogation, and obtain an inadmissible statement; or, suppose that police persist in interrogating a suspect who has invoked the right to silence or counsel, and obtain an inadmissible statement. If *Elstad's* reasoning were applied to these cases, police would need only to give fresh warnings and secure a waiver, in order to make a subsequent statement a "voluntary" and admissible fruit. Thus, *Elstad's* rationale has the power to restrict *Miranda* rights significantly, if it is extended by the Court in the future to other types of *Miranda* violations. Some lower courts have extended *Elstad's* reasoning in this way. *See Greenawalt v. Ricketts,* 943 F.2d 1020 (9th Cir.1991) (applying *Elstad,* and holding a second confession admissible, where first confession was excluded because police improperly obtained a waiver of *Miranda* rights).

3. Post-*Dickerson Elstad* Jurisprudence

Since its decision in *Dickerson, supra,* the Supreme Court has decided two cases that address previously unanswered questions about the fruits of a *Miranda* violation.

a. The Fruit of an Intentional *Miranda* Violation

In *Missouri v. Seibert,* 542 U.S. 600, 124 S.Ct. 2601, 159 L.Ed.2d 643 (2004), the Supreme Court held that a police strategy deliberately designed to elicit a confession, provide a *Miranda* warning, and then elicit another confession, thwarted the protections of *Miranda* and rendered the post-warning confession inadmissible. In *Seibert,* police officers questioned Seibert about her involvement in a first-degree murder without *Miranda* warnings for thirty to forty minutes. After obtaining a confession, the officers gave Seibert a twenty-minute coffee and cigarette break, provided her with *Miranda* warnings, and then obtained a signed waiver of rights from her. The same officer resumed questioning, and after being confronted with her pre-warning confession, Seibert confessed again. The Court determined that the intentional policy of questioning first and warning later failed to effectively warn the suspect as *Miranda* requires. Distinguishing *Elstad,* the Court emphasized the close temporal connection between the pre-warned confession and the post-warned confession, the continuation of the interrogation in the same location by the same officer, the overlapping content of the two statements, and the failure to warn Seibert that the first confession could not be used against her. These facts led the Court to find that a reasonable person in Seibert's shoes could not have made an informed choice about whether she should continue to talk, thereby making the *Miranda* warnings ineffective.

Lower courts have interpreted *Seibert* to mean that a confession made after a *Miranda*-defective confession is not admissible if the officers acted in bad faith in not giving the warnings before the first confession and if the second confession proceeded directly from the first. However, if the failure to provide warnings was not in bad faith, courts have applied *Elstad* and found the statements admissible. *See United States v. Mashburn*, 406 F.3d 303 (4th Cir. 2005) (the admissibility of Mashburn's statements was governed by *Elstad* since there was no evidence that the agents' failure to give *Miranda* warnings was deliberate or intentional). *See also United States v. Kiam*, 432 F.3d 524 (3rd Cir.2006) (applying *Elstad* rather than *Seibert* because the officers did not engage in a "deliberate attempt to sidestep Miranda.")

b.   Physical Evidence as the Fruit of a *Miranda* Violation

In *United States v. Patane*, 542 U.S. 630, 124 S.Ct. 2620, 159 L.Ed.2d 667 (2004), decided the same day as *Seibert*, the Supreme Court held that the failure to give Miranda warnings does not require the suppression of the physical fruits of a suspect's unwarned but voluntary statements. Law enforcement officers went to Patane's home based on allegations that he had violated a restraining order prohibiting him from contacting his ex-girlfriend and that he was in illegal possession of a firearm. When one officer arrested Patane for violating the restraining order, the other officer attempted to advise him of his *Miranda* rights. The advising officer got no further than the right to remain silent when Patane interrupted him and stated that he knew his rights. Neither officer attempted to complete the warnings. One officer then asked Patane about the firearm, and after persistent questioning, Patane told him it was in his bedroom and consented to its retrieval. Patane appealed the court's denial of his motion to suppress the pistol as the fruit of an unwarned statement. The Supreme Court held that police do not violate a suspect's constitutional rights by failing to provide *Miranda* warnings. The potential violation occurs only if the unwarned statements are admitted into evidence. Citing *Chavez*, *supra*, the Court noted that exclusion of the statements is a complete and sufficient remedy for such violations and that there is no need to apply *Wong Sun*'s "fruit of the poisonous tree" doctrine to physical evidence obtained as a result of the violation.

F. The "Voluntary, Knowing, and Intelligent" Waiver of *Miranda* Rights

The *Miranda* Court required the state to prove that a suspect "waived" his rights before police obtained a statement during custodial interrogation. Twenty years after *Miranda*, the Court provided a definition of the critical elements of a "voluntary, knowing, and intelligent" waiver:

First, the relinquishment of the right must have been voluntary in the sense that it was the product of a *free and deliberate choice* rather than intimidation, coercion, or deception. Second, the waiver must have been made with a *full awareness* both of the nature of the right being abandoned and the consequences of the decision to abandon it. No waiver can be considered knowing and intelligent in the absence of *Miranda* warnings. *Moran v. Burbine,* 475 U.S. 412, 106 S.Ct. 1135, 89 L.Ed.2d 410 (1986).

The Court's waiver rulings establish the *Miranda* warnings as the definitive solution for the problem of inherent coercion and lack of information during custodial interrogation. Therefore, the police do *not need to provide additional information* that would help the suspect decide whether to exercise the privilege, such as information concerning the subjects of the interrogation, the inadmissibility of prior admissions, or an attorney's desire to consult with the suspect.

1. A Waiver Need Not Be "Express"

In *North Carolina v. Butler,* 441 U.S. 369, 99 S.Ct. 1755, 60 L.Ed.2d 286 (1979), the Court rejected a defendant's claim that his waiver of *Miranda* rights was invalid because he did not explicitly state that he waived his right to assistance of counsel. The defendant received written warnings, and was asked to sign a waiver form. He replied, "I will talk to you but I am not signing any form." He then made incriminating statements, and was convicted of kidnapping, armed robbery, and assault. The Court held that an express written or oral waiver of his right to counsel was not an absolute requirement for a valid waiver, and remanded the case to the state court for resolution of the waiver issue.

a. Rationale

The Court determined that *Miranda* did not hold that an "express written or oral statement" was indispensable to a waiver, and that such an "inflexible" per se requirement did not accord with the policy behind the *Miranda* safeguards. The *Butler* Court interpreted *Miranda* as holding only that waiver could not be "presumed" from silence. However, silence "coupled with a course of conduct" consistent with abandonment of *Miranda* rights would support a finding of waiver.

b. Dissent

The three dissenters in *Butler* criticized a rule that would allow "courts to construct inferences from ambiguous words and gestures." They also argued that the *Butler* rule would lead lower courts to reach inconsistent results when faced with difficult cases where a defendant's words and actions had "uncertain meaning." By contrast, an express waiver rule would eliminate "these difficulties" and would impose no significant burden on the police.

2. The Government Has the Burden of Proving Waiver

a. Insufficient Proof of Suspect's Understanding of Warnings

In *Tague v. Louisiana*, 444 U.S. 469, 100 S.Ct. 652, 62 L.Ed.2d 622 (1980), the Court summarily reversed a conviction for armed robbery, because the state had not proven that the defendant's confession, following *Miranda* warnings, was taken after a valid waiver of rights. The police officer claimed at trial to have recited the *Miranda* warnings, but could not remember the rights himself, "could not recall" whether he asked the suspect whether he understood the rights, and "couldn't say yes or no" as to whether the suspect was literate or capable of understanding the rights. The *Tague* Court held that a suspect cannot be presumed to understand the *Miranda* warnings. *Miranda* emphasized that the government has the burden of proving a waiver; in *Tague*, "no evidence at all" supported a finding of waiver.

b. Proof Required That Suspect Understood His Rights and Voluntarily Waived Them

In *Colorado v. Connelly*, 479 U.S. 157, 107 S.Ct. 515, 93 L.Ed.2d 473 (1986), the defendant explained that he waived his *Miranda* rights and confessed after hearing voices from space telling him to do so. The Court held that the defendant's mental illness did not negate his ability to *voluntarily* waive his rights. However, the Court remanded the case to determine whether the defendant's mental state rendered him unable to *understand* the rights he was waiving.

c. Voluntariness Aspect of Waiver Is the Same as the Due Process Test for Confessions

The *Connelly* Court determined that the voluntariness inquiry "in the *Miranda* waiver context" should be the same as the voluntariness inquiry in the Due Process context. Therefore, the "voluntariness" of a waiver depended on "the absence of police overreaching." This was especially warranted in the *Miranda* context, since the sole concern of the Fifth Amendment is "governmental coercion." In *Connelly*, where police did not know of the defendant's severe mental illness at the time he waived his rights, the defendant's waiver was voluntary because there was no police coercion.

d. The Mentally Ill Defendant's Ability to Make a "Knowing" Waiver

Lower courts after *Connelly* have held that a mentally ill defendant cannot "knowingly" waive her *Miranda* rights. *See, e.g., Smith v. Zant*, 887 F.2d 1407 (11th Cir.1989) (en banc). Unlike the voluntariness aspect of waiver, which is dependent on a finding of police misconduct, the knowledge component of waiver requires a capacity on the part of the suspect to understand the importance of the *Miranda* warnings. The suspect's capacity for understanding is a factor independent from police wrongdoing; thus, if the suspect fails to understand the warnings, a waiver cannot be found even if the police have properly given the warnings.

3. A "Conditional" Waiver May Be "Knowing and Voluntary"

In *Connecticut v. Barrett*, 479 U.S. 523, 107 S.Ct. 828, 93 L.Ed.2d 920 (1987), the Court held that if, after receiving the warnings, a defendant makes a conditional waiver of *Miranda* rights, a subsequent confession is admissible so long as police comply with the suspect's condition. In *Barrett*, the defendant, after receiving the warnings, stated that he was willing to "talk" to police, but that he would not make a written statement. The police let him talk, and his statement was admitted at trial by the testimony of the officers who heard the confession. The Court held that where the suspect made his intentions "clear" and the police honored them, his statements made after the "conditional waiver" were admissible.

4. The *Miranda* Warnings Give the Suspect All the Information That Is Necessary to Make a Knowing Waiver

In a series of three cases, the defendants each argued that their waivers, made after the warnings were given, were not sufficiently "knowing" because the warnings did not contain certain information that the defendants thought to be critical to the waiver decision. In each case, the Court rejected this argument and held that the *Miranda* warnings, as a matter of law, impart information sufficient to establish a knowing waiver on the part of a person with the capacity to understand the warnings. The fact that it might be helpful for the suspect to know other facts and circumstances has been held irrelevant to the waiver question, since *Miranda* does not require that the waiver be "brilliant" or "made with a knowledge of all possibly relevant information." All that is required is that the defendant know and understand that he has the right to silence and to the assistance of counsel, as well as the consequences of waiving those rights.

a. A Suspect Need Not Be Informed of All the Subjects of the Interrogation Before Making a Waiver

In *Colorado v. Spring,* 479 U.S. 564, 107 S.Ct. 851, 93 L.Ed.2d 954 (1987), the Court held that police could obtain a valid waiver from a suspect without telling him that the subject of the interrogation would concern both the firearms crime for which he was arrested, and an unrelated murder. The defendant claimed that his confession concerning the murder was not admissible, because he had not "knowingly" waived his rights concerning that crime when he signed the waiver after his firearms arrest. The Court found that the suspect was warned that "anything" he said could be used against him, and held that this warning adequately conveyed "the consequences of abandoning the privilege." Therefore, the Court found that the defendant's waiver was valid, and his confession admissible; his murder conviction was affirmed.

b. A Suspect Need Not Be Informed That a Prior Unwarned Confession Would Be Inadmissible at Trial

In *Oregon v. Elstad,* 470 U.S. 298, 105 S.Ct. 1285, 84 L.Ed.2d 222 (1985), the Court held that a suspect was able to make a "knowing" and "intelligent" waiver, even though he was unaware that his incriminating statement during a prior interrogation was inadmissible at trial. The defendant in *Elstad* admitted his involvement in a burglary during brief questioning in his home. He argued that his later waiver preceding a stationhouse interrogation, and after receiving the *Miranda* warnings, was based on his belief that he had nothing to gain by silence, because "his fate was sealed" by his first admission. The Court rejected his claim that the police should have given him "an additional warning" at the stationhouse concerning the inadmissibility of his earlier statement, because such a requirement was "neither practicable nor constitutionally necessary."

The Court found that the requirement of additional warnings concerning possible violations of *Miranda* during an initial interrogation was not "practicable," because such violations might not be identified by police until after a second confession was obtained during a later interrogation. Nor was the warning constitutionally necessary, because the *Miranda* warnings sufficiently informed the defendant that his second confession could be used against him at trial.

c.   A Suspect Need Not Be Informed That an Attorney Is Trying to Consult With Him

In *Moran v. Burbine*, 475 U.S. 412, 106 S.Ct. 1135, 89 L.Ed.2d 410 (1986), the Court held that the defendant's waiver after *Miranda* warnings was valid, even though police deliberately failed to inform him that an attorney retained by his sister was calling the police station, and asking to be present during his interrogation. In *Burbine*, the police also told the attorney that the defendant would not be interrogated, and then proceeded to interrogate him in her absence. The Court found that the police treatment of counsel was irrelevant under *Miranda*, because *Miranda* rights must be invoked by the suspect. The Court also found that the suspect's waiver of *Miranda* rights was sufficiently knowing, even though he was not informed that counsel wanted to see him. The *Miranda* warnings sufficiently informed the suspect that he had a right to counsel. The Court rejected the claim that an event "occurring outside the presence of the suspect" could be relevant to his "capacity to comprehend and knowingly relinquish a constitutional right." Once the defendant had received *Miranda* warnings, he had all the information required by *Miranda* to produce a valid waiver.

d.   Upsetting the *Miranda* Compromise

In *Burbine*, the Court explained its reluctance to require more warnings than are already required by *Miranda*: it would cause an increase in the number of suspects who would invoke the privilege. This, in turn, would impose a "substantial cost" on society's "compelling interest" in securing confessions and punishing criminals. The Court found that *Miranda* had struck a fair compromise between the interest of citizens to be free from coercion, and the interest of the state in obtaining reliable evidence. This delicate balance would be upset if police were required to give a suspect more warnings than required by *Miranda*.

e. Affirmative Misrepresentation

The Court in *Burbine* distinguished between an officer's deliberate failure to impart information that the suspect might find useful from an *officer's affirmative misrepresentation* that gives the suspect mistaken information. Affirmative deception makes it less likely that the suspect knowingly and voluntarily waived his rights, though it is not dispositive on the point. So for example, if the officers had stated to Moran that his counsel had called and left a message that he was not coming by and that Moran ought to just confess, then the Court might have found a subsequent confession to be involuntary. Likewise, if the officers had told Elstad that he had already let the cat out of the bag and might as well sign a waiver form and confess, the subsequent confession might be found involuntary.

However, it must be noted that police deception does not *automatically* render a subsequent confession involuntary. Deception is only one relevant factor in a totality of circumstances inquiry. *See Green v. Scully*, 850 F.2d 894 (2d Cir.1988) (confession voluntary even though police deceive the defendant into thinking that his palm print was found at the crime scene). It must also be remembered that an officer's mere nondisclosure of information which the suspect might find helpful (as opposed to an affirmative misrepresentation) is not relevant at all to the waiver inquiry after *Burbine*.

f. Deceiving the Attorney, and the Attorney's Role in *Miranda*

The *Burbine* Court rejected the claim that *Miranda* should be "extended" to invalidate a confession where the police deceived an attorney concerning a suspect's ongoing interrogation. Again, the *Miranda* Court had created a compromise between the interests of citizens and the state. The compromise was struck by granting citizens some safeguards from custodial interrogation, but with the proviso that it is *up to the suspect* to invoke the rights provided. This delicate balance would be upset if an attorney were given the right, independent of the suspect's wishes, to be kept informed and to consult with the suspect. Consequently, the attorney has *no role to play* under *Miranda* until the suspect decides to invoke the right to counsel.

5. **Preponderance of the Evidence**

In *Colorado v. Connelly*, 479 U.S. 157, 107 S.Ct. 515, 93 L.Ed.2d 473 (1986), the Court held that a state did not have to prove a waiver by "clear and convincing evidence," but only by a "preponderance" of the evidence. It determined that the state should have the same burden for proving waiver as for proving that a confession is "voluntary."

a. Rationale

The Court concluded that the determination of a waiver, like the voluntariness determination, had "nothing to do with the reliability" of verdicts. Therefore, the Court borrowed the rationale of *Lego v. Twomey*, 404 U.S. 477, 92 S.Ct. 619, 30 L.Ed.2d 618 (1972), where it adopted a "preponderance" standard for the state's burden of proving the voluntariness of a confession. The Court found it was "doubtful" that a "clear and convincing evidence" standard would increase the deterrent effect of *Miranda's* exclusionary rule, compared to the "preponderance" standard. Moreover, whatever increase might occur would be outweighed by "the public interest in placing probative evidence before juries" for the purpose of reaching accurate verdicts. The Court reasoned that if constitutional Due Process protections could be enforced through a "preponderance" standard (as is the case under *Lego*), then a waiver of the "auxiliary protections" of *Miranda* "should require no higher burden of proof."

b. Dissent

The two dissenters in *Connelly* reasoned that police control over interrogations in the *Miranda* context made it "appropriate to place a higher burden of proof" on the state to demonstrate waiver of *Miranda* rights.

G. Waiver and the Resumption of Questioning After Invocation of Rights

The waiver cases just discussed all dealt with fact situations in which the suspect was given warnings and then made a decision to speak to the police. More difficult questions arise where the suspect receives warnings, decides to invoke his right to silence or to counsel, and then *changes his mind* and decides to speak to the police. Obviously, it is more difficult for the state to prove that the suspect waived his rights after invoking them than it is when the suspect simply confessed without ever invoking his rights. Something must account for the suspect's change of heart—something other than police coercion or an official disrespect of the suspect's invocation of his rights.

1. Police May Obtain a Waiver From a Suspect Following His Invocation of the Right to Remain Silent

In *Michigan v. Mosley*, 423 U.S. 96, 96 S.Ct. 321, 46 L.Ed.2d 313 (1975), the Court held that *Miranda* did not create a *"per se* proscription of indefinite duration" upon police interrogation following a suspect's invocation of the right to remain silent. Instead, *Miranda* requires only that the "right to cut off questioning" must be "scrupulously honored."

a. Rationale

The Court found that *Miranda's* mandate concerning the right to "cut off questioning" was ambiguous, and interpreted it to mean that "interrogation after a momentary cessation" would be impermissible. This did not mean that questioning could never be resumed. The goal of *Miranda* was to require police to respect a suspect's invocation, and to give the suspect control over the time of the interrogation, its subject, and its duration. A resumption of interrogation after invocation does not necessarily undermine these goals—so long as the officers show that they are scrupulously honoring the right to remain silent.

b. Momentary Cessation

The Court in *Mosley* cautioned that the continuation of interrogation "after a momentary cessation" would "frustrate the purposes of *Miranda*," because it would allow "repeated rounds of questioning to undermine the will" of the suspect. *See Charles v. Smith*, 894 F.2d 718 (5th Cir.1990) (no waiver where interrogation resumed two minutes after right to silence invoked). *Compare Grooms v. Keeney*, 826 F.2d 883 (9th Cir.1987) (officers scrupulously honored the suspect's invocation of the right to silence where interrogation was resumed after a four-hour "cooling off" period). Thus, continuation of interrogation shortly after the right to silence is invoked cannot be considered "scrupulously honoring" the suspect's right to remain silent. Most courts have found the most important factor in determining whether an officer has "scrupulously honored" a suspect's invocation of silence to be the sufficiency of the "cooling off" period. *See United States v. Rambo*, 365 F.3d 906 (10th Cir. 2004) ("Whatever else *Mosley* might require, it is clear that some break in the interrogation must occur.")

c. Applied to Facts of *Mosley*

On the facts, the Court found that the defendant's invocation was "scrupulously honored." When he refused to answer any questions about the robberies, questioning ceased. Two hours later, a different officer gave new *Miranda* warnings, and successfully obtained a knowing and voluntary waiver.

d. *Mosley's* Application to Different Factual Settings

Mosley's holding emphasized a number of factors: the fresh warnings, the two-hour break between interrogations, the different subject of the second interrogation, the different identity of the officer, and the immediate cessation of interrogation following the original invocation. The Court has not provided further guidance concerning *Mosley's* application to cases where one or more of these factors are absent. The lower courts have generally focused on whether the defendant has been given a sufficient "cooling off" period before re-interrogation has been attempted; also, lower courts have refused to find that the right to silence is scrupulously honored where multiple re-interrogations have been attempted. *See, e.g., Charles v. Smith*, 894 F.2d 718 (5th Cir.1990) (re-interrogation impermissible after two-minute break); *Vujosevic v. Rafferty*, 844 F.2d 1023 (3d Cir.1988) (re-interrogation impermissible after four attempts to renew questioning).

e. Knowing and Voluntary Waiver Must Still Be Found

The *Mosley* Court made clear that the "scrupulously honor" requirement which arises after the suspect has invoked his right to silence is a requirement in *addition* to that which applies to any *Miranda* waiver question, i.e., that the suspect knowingly and voluntarily waived his *Miranda* rights. The government makes a stronger case on the general waiver issue if the officer gave a fresh set of warnings upon re-interrogation. Otherwise the state is subject to an argument that the defendant forgot about the warnings or forgot about the consequences of waiving *Miranda* rights during the cooling off period.

2. **The Right to Silence Must Be Clearly Invoked**

What if the suspect's statement in response to the warnings is so ambiguous as to be reasonably construed as either an invocation of the right to silence or as a willingness to talk. For example, what if the suspect says, "I probably shouldn't tell you anything, my brother will be mad." The Supreme Court, in the analogous context of the invocation of the *Miranda* right to *counsel*, has held that the right must be clearly and unambiguously invoked. *Davis v. United States*, 512 U.S. 452, 114 S.Ct. 2350, 129 L.Ed.2d 362 (1994). Lower courts after *Davis* have applied the same "clarity" requirement to the defendant's invocation of the right to silence. Under this view, if the suspect's statement carries any doubt as to whether he has invoked his right to silence, the questioning may continue. The confession will be admissible so long as the defendant makes a knowing and voluntary waiver; there is no additional requirement that the officers must cease interrogation and scrupulously honor the defendant's right to silence. *See United States v. Banks*, 78 F.3d 1190 (7th Cir.1996) (relying on *Davis*, the court holds that a suspect's statement that he "had nothing to say" was ambiguous, since it might have meant he was simply angry about an officer's placing a form in front of him; because the right to silence was not clearly invoked, there was no requirement that the questioning cease).

Request to See a Third Party Is Not an Invocation of the Right to Silence

In *Fare v. Michael C.*, 442 U.S. 707, 99 S.Ct. 2560, 61 L.Ed.2d 197 (1979), the Court held that a juvenile's request to have his probation officer present during the interrogation was not the equivalent of an invocation of the right to silence. The Court found that the juvenile's request "might well be consistent with a desire to speak to the police."

3. Waiver After the Invocation of the Right to Counsel

In *Edwards v. Arizona*, 451 U.S. 477, 101 S.Ct. 1880, 68 L.Ed.2d 378 (1981), the Court held that once a suspect invokes the right to counsel, a "valid waiver of that right cannot be established by showing only that he responded" to renewed police-initiated interrogation, even if that interrogation follows new *Miranda* warnings. Thus, the mere fact that the suspect's waiver could be found knowing and voluntary under the circumstances is not enough, if the suspect has invoked the right to counsel and the police, as opposed to the suspect, have initiated interrogation. In *Edwards*, the defendant had invoked his right to counsel by saying, "I want an attorney before making a deal." The police ceased interrogation, and then returned in the morning to renew interrogation. The police gave the defendant new *Miranda* warnings, told him they wanted to talk to him, and ultimately obtained a confession. There was no showing that Edwards did not understand his rights, nor that his will was overborne. Nonetheless, the waiver was held invalid because of the police-initiated re-interrogation, and his confession was held inadmissible.

a. Rationale

The Court relied on *Miranda's* mandate that "the interrogation must cease until an attorney is present," once a suspect invokes the right to counsel. The Court reasoned that when police claim that a suspect waived his right to counsel after invocation of the right to counsel (i.e., that the suspect changed his mind for some reason), "additional safeguards" were necessary beyond the giving of new *Miranda* warnings prior to re-interrogation. Therefore, the Court determined that police cannot obtain a valid waiver from a suspect who invokes his right to counsel, unless the suspect "initiates further communication, exchanges, or conversations with the police" or unless counsel is provided.

b. **Distinction From *Mosley***

The Court in *Edwards* emphasized that different "procedural safeguards" were triggered by the invocation of the right to counsel than by the invocation of the right to silence. The reason was that if the suspect invokes only the right to silence, he may later decide on his own that it is in his interest to talk to the police; presumably, then, there is no harm in approaching him after a while and asking him if he has changed his mind. But if the suspect invokes his right to counsel, this indicates that he feels overmatched and is unwilling to deal with the police without legal assistance. It is unlikely that such a person would then unilaterally change his mind and decide that he was fully capable of dealing with the police without any assistance. Therefore, stricter procedural safeguards are required—no interrogation, ever, unless the suspect initiates it—where counsel is invoked.

c. **Bright–Line Rule**

The *Edwards* "no re-interrogation until the suspect initiates" rule is a *per se*, bright-line rule. A confession is automatically excluded under *Edwards* if the police initiate re-interrogation of the suspect after he has invoked his right to counsel—even if the state can make a convincing argument that the defendant knew his rights and voluntarily waived them. So for example, if the defendant invokes the right to counsel and two hours later an officer approaches him politely, asks him if he has changed his mind, and gives fresh warnings, the subsequent confession is inadmissible even if the suspect, when approached, says "I have changed my mind; I was just about to tell you about it when you came to me." The *Edwards* Court adopted a bright-line rule for ease of administration and to give police clear guidance, and also to *overprotect* the rights of a person who has invoked the right to counsel. The Court determined that a prophylactic safeguard was necessary to protect a person in such a vulnerable position from being badgered by police into confessing without counsel.

d. Two Step Approach

The *Edwards* Court made clear that the bright-line initiation requirement is in addition to the general requirement that all *Miranda* waivers must be knowing and voluntary. Thus, even if the suspect initiates renewed interrogation, the state must show that the suspect understood his *Miranda* rights and voluntarily waived them. The state will find it easier to prove a knowing and voluntary waiver if the officer gives fresh warnings at the time of the re-interrogation.

4. **When Does the Suspect "Initiate" Re-interrogation?**

The *Edwards* Court did not define what it meant by "initiation." The concept of initiation is crucial since without it, a defendant who has invoked his right to counsel cannot be interrogated.

a. A Suspect's Request for a Polygraph Examination Constitutes Initiation

In *Wyrick v. Fields,* 459 U.S. 42, 103 S.Ct. 394, 74 L.Ed.2d 214 (1982), the Court held that a soldier's waiver of rights was valid when it was made prior to a polygraph examination which he requested, after consultation with counsel. As the defendant "initiated" the polygraph examination, it was proper for the polygraph examiner to seek a waiver of rights, which the defendant signed. This waiver indicated that the defendant did not want counsel during the examination, and the Court found that he also implicitly waived his right to counsel during "post-test" questioning by the examiner. Thus, statements made during this questioning were admissible, as well as later statements to police, and the defendant's conviction for rape was affirmed.

b. Suspect's Desire for Generalized Discussion About the Crime

In *Oregon v. Bradshaw,* 462 U.S. 1039, 103 S.Ct. 2830, 77 L.Ed.2d 405 (1983), the defendant invoked the right to counsel, and then in the course of being transported from the police station to the jail, asked an officer: "Well, what is going to happen to me now?" A plurality of the Court held that Bradshaw's statement to the officer constituted initiation, and therefore made it possible for the officer to discuss the investigation, and later obtain a valid waiver when the defendant received fresh warnings and made incriminating statements.

The *Bradshaw* plurality reasoned that some inquiries by suspects are so routine that they cannot be assumed to represent a desire to discuss the investigation. Such inquiries would include a request "for a drink of water," or a request "to use the telephone." However, the inquiry in *Bradshaw* was found to be a request for generalized discussion of the investigation, as evidenced by the police officer's response. The suspect invoked his right to counsel at the police station; he was being taken on a trip to the county jail when he asked what was going to happen next. The police officer responded by saying, "You do not have to talk to me," and "You have requested an attorney and I don't want you talking to me unless you so desire," and "Since you have requested an attorney, you know, it has to be at your own free will." The plurality noted that generalized discussion ensued only after the defendant told the officer he "understood." Thus, there was no *Edwards* violation.

c. Knowing and Voluntary Waiver

After finding that the first "initiation" step of *Edwards* was satisfied, the Court in *Bradshaw* found the defendant's written waiver to be valid under the totality of the circumstances. The waiver occurred the day after the initiation when the defendant agreed to take a polygraph test, at the suggestion of the officer who discussed the case with him the day before. As there was no evidence of "threats, promises or inducements to talk," and the defendant changed his mind about his invocation "without any impropriety on the part of the police," the waiver was voluntary. It was also knowing, because the defendant had been informed of his rights with fresh warnings and understood them.

d. Dissenting View

The dissenters in *Bradshaw* argued that an "initiation" occurs only when the suspect communicates explicitly about the "subject matter of the criminal investigation." In the dissenters' view, Bradshaw's question sought only "to find out where police were going to take him." This conclusion could be drawn from several circumstances: the defendant had invoked his rights only minutes earlier, he was put in a police car, and he had the "normal reaction" of wanting to know where he was going. The dissenters complained that the plurality's interpretation of "initiation" allowed police to "capitalize on the custodial setting," and to re-interrogate based on responses that suspects typically have to a "loss of control over their freedom of movement."

e.   Post–*Bradshaw* Applications of the "Initiation" Rule

While neither the broad nor the limited definition of "initiation" commanded a majority of the Court in *Bradshaw,* (each view was held by four Justices, with Justice Powell concurring in the judgment on other grounds), the lower courts have followed the plurality's broader definition, meaning that more inquiries from suspects will be considered initiation rather than fewer. *See United States v. Velasquez,* 885 F.2d 1076 (3d Cir.1989) ("initiation" was communicated when suspect asked, "What is going to happen?"). These courts reason that the plurality's test is a reasonable compromise between individual and state interests and that the dissenters' test "might convert the prophylactic value of the initiation requirement into an overly stringent substantive hurdle." The courts also point out that the suspect is not bereft of protection under the plurality test: questions by a suspect that are clearly attendant to custodial issues will not be considered initiation, and even if initiation is found, the state must still prove that the defendant's waiver was knowing and voluntary.

5.   **Ambiguous "Invocation" of the Right to Counsel**

What if the suspect, after receiving *Miranda* warnings, refers to counsel, but does not clearly invoke the right to counsel? For example, what if the suspect says to the officer, "Maybe I should talk to a lawyer." Must the interrogation cease and await initiation by the suspect under *Edwards*? Or can the officer continue the interrogation in the hope of obtaining a knowing and voluntary waiver? In *Davis v. United States,* 512 U.S. 452, 114 S.Ct. 2350, 129 L.Ed.2d 362 (1994), the Court held that a suspect must clearly and unequivocally invoke the right to counsel in order to trigger the protections of *Edwards.* If the invocation is ambiguous or equivocal, police questioning can continue; and the questioning need not be limited to that necessary to clarify the suspect's desire with respect to counsel. The Court found that Davis' statement—"Maybe I should talk to a lawyer"—was not a sufficiently explicit request for counsel. *See also Fare v. Michael C.,* 442 U.S. 707, 99 S.Ct. 2560, 61 L.Ed.2d 197 (1979) (a juvenile's request to have his probation officer present during the interrogation did not constitute an invocation of the right to counsel).

6. Interrogating on Unrelated Crimes After a Suspect Invokes His Right to Counsel

In *Arizona v. Roberson*, 486 U.S. 675, 108 S.Ct. 2093, 100 L.Ed.2d 704 (1988), the Court held that when a suspect invokes the right to counsel, the *Edwards* rule bars police from initiating an interrogation about a crime different from the one for which he was arrested and invoked his right. Thus, a suspect's Fifth Amendment invocation of the right to counsel is *not "offense-specific."* When the police officer in *Roberson* sought to interrogate Roberson in custody concerning a burglary, the officer did not know that Roberson had invoked his right to counsel three days earlier during his arrest for an unrelated burglary. Roberson was given new warnings, voluntarily waived his rights and confessed to the unrelated burglary. But he had not initiated the interrogation. The defendant's statements made during the second interrogation were held to be inadmissible in the absence of initiation by the suspect, and his conviction for the second burglary was reversed.

a. Rationale

The Court held that the benefits of a "bright-line" application of *Edwards* to all interrogations after the invocation of counsel outweighed the burdens imposed on the police by the requirement that they honor a suspect's invocation of counsel. A suspect's request for counsel expressed "his own view that he is not competent to deal with the authorities without legal advice." Nothing about the context of custodial interrogation supports the idea that a suspect's invocation of counsel is "investigation-specific."

b. Information Permissible

The state in *Roberson* complained that the application of *Edwards* to unrelated investigations would bring many of these investigations to a halt. In order to interrogate the suspect, the suspect would have to initiate; but if the investigation is unrelated to what the suspect has been arrested for, initiation is especially unlikely because the suspect has no reason to know that the state is even interested in an unrelated crime. The Court responded to this concern with two points. First, the police had no need to speak to the suspect in order to inform him about the existence of such investigations; the police could simply inform counsel. Second, when the police have decided "temporarily not to provide counsel," they are free "to inform" the suspect about a separate investigation, so long as this "communication does not constitute interrogation."

c. Dissent

The *Roberson* dissenters argued that "the problems to which *Edwards* was addressed" were not present when police seek to interrogate the suspect about an unrelated crime. The dissenters believed that a suspect's rights would be sufficiently protected by requiring the police to re-advise him of his *Miranda* rights and seek his consent to the interrogation concerning the different crime. They contended that most suspects who invoke their rights "will want the opportunity" to learn about the existence of a separate investigation, and to calculate their interests anew "to decide to speak" to police "with or without representation."

7. **Request for Counsel at an Initial Appearance in Court**

In *McNeil v. Wisconsin,* 501 U.S. 171, 111 S.Ct. 2204, 115 L.Ed.2d 158 (1991), the Court held that a defendant's request for counsel at "an initial appearance on a charged offense" was not an invocation of the *Miranda* right to counsel; therefore, the *Edwards* rule did not prevent the police from initiating an interrogation. In *McNeil,* the defendant asked for counsel at his initial appearance in court on an armed robbery charge, and was given appointed counsel. He was interviewed later that night by police concerning crimes unrelated to that with which he had been charged. He was given the *Miranda* warnings, he waived his rights at this interview and during three further interviews, and confessed to these unrelated crimes. The Court found that the *Roberson* rule did not apply, that McNeil's waiver of *Miranda* rights was knowing and voluntary, and therefore that McNeil's confessions to unrelated crimes were admissible at the trial for those crimes.

a. Rationale

The Court reasoned that in order for a suspect to invoke his *Miranda* right to counsel, both *Miranda* and *Edwards* require, "at a minimum, some statement that can reasonably be construed" as a request for counsel's assistance "in dealing with custodial interrogation by the police." The "ordinary meaning" of a request for counsel at an initial appearance does not satisfy this definition. Rather, a request in these circumstances is more sensibly seen as a request for *trial* counsel, protected by the Sixth Amendment. The Court refused to interpret a defendant's Sixth Amendment invocation of trial counsel as implying an invocation of counsel under *Miranda*, because to do so would "seriously impede law enforcement."

The Court declared that under *Edwards*, the purpose of invoking the *Miranda* right to counsel is to protect "the desire to deal with the police only through counsel." By contrast, the purpose of invoking the Sixth Amendment guarantee is to receive protection at "critical confrontations" with the "expert adversary" at or after the commencement of adversary judicial proceedings. Thus, when the defendant in *McNeil* invoked the "Sixth Amendment interest" at the initial judicial proceeding, he did not invoke "the *Miranda–Edwards* interest."

    b.   Dissent
The three dissenters in *McNeil* argued that the Court's decision would "have only a slight impact on custodial procedures," because competent counsel could circumvent *McNeil* by having their clients specifically invoke the *Miranda* right to counsel at arraignment. Nonetheless, the dissenters disapproved of the Court's reasoning in principle, because it would cause "confusion" and "undermine the protections" of the adversarial system.

    c.   Anticipatory Invocation of the *Miranda–Edwards* Right to Counsel
The *McNeil* Court did not resolve the question whether a defendant could invoke her *Miranda* right to counsel by specifically referring to *Miranda* during a first court appearance. As discussed above, the dissenters argued that this would be possible and that it would therefore provide an easy evasion of the Court's restrictive interpretation of the invocation of the right to counsel at a judicial proceeding. In dicta, however, the Court rebutted the claim by the *McNeil* dissenters that such a strategy would be an adequate invocation under *Edwards*. The majority noted that most rights "must be asserted when the government seeks to take the action they protect against." Implicitly, this means that *Miranda* rights cannot be invoked "anticipatorily, in a context other than custodial interrogation." Lower courts after *McNeil* have held that the *Miranda* right to counsel cannot be invoked at a court appearance—rather, it can only be invoked when the suspect is being subjected to or threatened with custodial interrogation. *See Alston v. Redman,* 34 F.3d 1237 (3d Cir.1994) (*Miranda* right to counsel is a "shield" that can be "interposed only when state action actually threatens").

8. **Police–Initiated Interrogation After the Suspect Has Consulted With Counsel**

In *Minnick v. Mississippi*, 498 U.S. 146, 111 S.Ct. 486, 112 L.Ed.2d 489 (1990), the Court held that *Edwards* prohibits police from initiating an interrogation with a suspect who has invoked his right to counsel, unless counsel is actually present during the interrogation. This rule applies "whether or not" the suspect "has consulted with counsel." Minnick's conviction was based on a confession obtained by police after he consulted with counsel several times, following his invocation of his *Miranda* right to counsel. Even though Minnick's attorney told him not to talk to anyone or sign any waivers, Minnick did waive his rights and confess when a police officer visited him in jail, and talked to Minnick first about "how everybody was" back home, and then about the crime. The Court held the defendant's confession to be inadmissible under *Edwards*.

a. Rationale

The Court found that the protection of *Edwards* should not be "terminated or suspended by consultation with counsel," because the total prohibition of police-initiated questioning protects suspects from police "badgering," and provides the "clarity and certainty" of a "bright-line rule" for police and lower courts. The Court rejected the state's proposal that a suspect's consultation with counsel should terminate the protection of *Edwards*. It reasoned that "consultation is not a precise concept," so that the government's proposed rule would be fraught with ambiguity. Moreover, consultation with counsel does not "remove the suspect" from the "coercive pressures" of custody, once that consultation has terminated.

b. Dissent

The two dissenters in *Minnick* argued that once a suspect consults with counsel, he "knows that he has an advocate on his side," and that the police "will permit him to consult that advocate." He also should have a "heightened awareness" of his right to remain silent, based on counsel's advice. Therefore *Edwards* should have no application to a case like *Minnick*, because the situation of the suspect has changed; an "irrebuttable presumption" that his confession is based on ignorance or "coercion" at this point has "no genuine basis in fact." The dissenters contended that the *Minnick* rule would significantly "constrict" law enforcement, by creating a "perpetual irrebuttable presumption" that prevents police from initiating waiver discussions about any crime, or even asking whether a suspect has "changed his mind" about his invocation.

H. Incomplete or Ambiguous *Miranda* Warnings

The *Miranda* opinion set forth the warnings that must be given to suspects who are being interrogated while in custody. The Court did not state that the warnings set forth in the opinion had to be recited word for word. A question arising after *Miranda* is whether warnings given in a particular case are clear and complete enough to satisfy the *Miranda* safeguards.

1. The *Miranda* Warnings Need Not Inform a Suspect Explicitly of the Right to Have an Attorney Appointed Before Further Questioning

In *California v. Prysock*, 451 U.S. 1301, 101 S.Ct. 1773, 68 L.Ed.2d 185 (1981), the Court held that a defendant was adequately apprised of his *Miranda* right to counsel when police told him, in separate warnings, that he had the "right to talk to a lawyer before you are questioned, have him present with you while you are being questioned, and all during the questioning," and that he also had the "right to have a lawyer appointed to represent you at no cost to yourself." The Court rejected the argument that these warnings were too ambiguous and incomplete to comport with *Miranda*.

a. Rationale

The Court held that *Miranda* stated that the warnings described in the Court's opinion, *or their "equivalent,"* must be given to suspects subject to custodial interrogation. Thus, no particular "talismanic incantation" of the warnings is required to satisfy *Miranda*. The warnings in *Prysock* did not mischaracterize the right to counsel; for example, the warnings did not state that there was a right to appointed counsel only at "a future point in time after police interrogation." While the two warnings at issue were not given in succession, but were separated by the recitation of two other warnings, this fact did not make the warnings "inadequate" under *Miranda* since there is no requirement that the warnings be given in any precise order.

b. Dissent

The three dissenters argued that the defendant was not "adequately" informed of his right to counsel, because he was not given the "crucial information that the services of the free attorney were available *prior to* the impending questioning." The last warning was particularly unclear, because "lawyers are normally appointed by judges, and not by law enforcement officers," and so the reference to "appointed" counsel "could have been understood to refer to trial counsel."

2. Warnings Need Only Reasonably Convey the Necessary Information

In *Duckworth v. Eagan*, 492 U.S. 195, 109 S.Ct. 2875, 106 L.Ed.2d 166 (1989), the Court held that *Miranda* warnings need only "reasonably convey" the *Miranda* rights to a suspect, and that under this standard it was acceptable for the police to tell the suspect that counsel would be appointed for him "if and when you go to court." The warnings, in their totality, apprised the defendant of his right "to have an attorney present if he chose to answer questions."

a. Rationale

The Court found that the "if and when you go to court" language accurately described the procedure for appointment of counsel, and anticipated the "commonplace" question of a suspect as to when counsel would be appointed.

b. Prophylactic Rules

The Court in *Duckworth* emphasized that the warnings "are not themselves rights protected by the Constitution." Therefore, the Court declared that reviewing courts need not scrutinize *Miranda* warnings "as if construing a will or defining the terms of an easement."

c. Totality of Warnings

The Court found that the warnings in *Duckworth* did not impermissibly link the reference to appointed counsel to a "future point in time after the police interrogation," because other statements in these warnings made reference to the suspect's right to counsel "before" he is interrogated, and to the right to stop answering questions until he talks to a lawyer. Thus, "in their totality" the warnings adequately apprised the defendant of his rights.

d. Implying That Appointed Counsel Is Optional With the Authorities

In *United States v. Connell*, 869 F.2d 1349 (9th Cir.1989), the officer's oral warning to the suspect was that "if you cannot afford a lawyer, one *may* be appointed for you." He also received written warnings which stated that if he could not afford a lawyer, "arrangements will be made to obtain one for you in accordance with the law." The court held these warnings to be misleading and therefore found that the resulting confession was obtained in violation of *Miranda*. While the court recognized that a flexible approach to the warnings was permissible after *Prysock,* it stated that the oral warning was affirmatively misleading because it implied that the right to appointed counsel was optional with the authorities. Nor did the written warning sufficiently cure this misinformation, because it provided for a right to counsel in accordance with the law, and a suspect "is not required to know what the requirements of the law are." The court reasoned that the whole purpose of the warnings was to convey the requirements of the law, and this the warning did not do. Thus, the court drew a line between a merely *ambiguous* warning, as in *Prysock,* and an *affirmatively misleading* warning. Compare *United States v. Frankson,* 83 F.3d 79 (4th Cir.1996) (warnings not defective merely because they did not specify that the defendant's statements could be used *in court*; as the general warning reasonably conveyed that the defendant's statements could be used anywhere, it sufficed to fulfill the requirements of *Miranda*: "Given the common sense understanding that an unqualified statement lacks qualifications, all that police officers need to is convey the general rights enumerated in *Miranda*.").

I. The Meaning of "Custody"

The *Miranda* Court held that its safeguards were required when *two conditions were present simultaneously*—custody and interrogation. Thus, *Miranda* does not apply to a suspect who is interrogated outside of custody. The *Miranda* Court stated that "by custodial interrogation, we mean questioning initiated by police officers after a person has been taken into custody or otherwise deprived of his freedom of action in any significant way." In cases after *Miranda*, the Court has endorsed a definition of custody that required either formal arrest, or "restraint on freedom of movement of the degree associated with arrest." The Court stated that in determining whether a person is in custody, a court must employ a totality of circumstances approach.

Lower courts have come to identify a number of factors as relevant to the custody inquiry. These factors include: 1. the *purpose* of the police investigation; 2. the *place and length* of the interrogation; 3. the suspect's *awareness of her freedom to leave*; 4. the suspect's *actual freedom from restraint*; 5. the *source of initiation* of the contact with the suspect; 6. the use of *"coercive stratagems"* by the police; and 7. the similarity of the setting to the *"police-dominated"* atmosphere of the stationhouse. Essentially, the courts have equated the test for custody with the test for whether a defendant is under arrest for Fourth Amendment purposes. *See California v. Beheler,* 463 U.S. 1121, 103 S.Ct. 3517, 77 L.Ed.2d 1275 (1983) (custody is determined by whether there is a "formal arrest or restraint on freedom of movement of the degree associated with a formal arrest"). Thus, it is useful to refer to the section on *Terry, supra,* where the distinction between stops and arrests is discussed.

1.   Custody Outside the Stationhouse

In *Orozco v. Texas,* 394 U.S. 324, 89 S.Ct. 1095, 22 L.Ed.2d 311 (1969), the Court held that a defendant was effectively "in custody," when he was awakened at 4:00 a.m. and questioned in his bedroom by four police officers. One of the officers testified that the suspect was not free to go, but was "under arrest," even though there was no evidence that the defendant was so informed. The police questioned the defendant as to his name, his presence earlier that night at a restaurant where a homicide was committed, whether he owned a gun, and the location of the gun. As the defendant was not given *Miranda* warnings, his statements were held to be inadmissible, and his murder conviction was reversed.

Rationale

The Court held that it was not necessary to "extend" *Miranda* to find custody in *Orozco,* because *Miranda* held that warnings were required when a person was "deprived of his freedom in any significant way." The Court rejected the state's argument that a custodial situation could not be found because the defendant was "in his own bed, in familiar surroundings."

2.   When Custody Does Not Exist Outside the Stationhouse

In *Beckwith v. United States,* 425 U.S. 341, 96 S.Ct. 1612, 48 L.Ed.2d 1 (1976), the Court held that agents of the Internal Revenue Service were not required to give warnings to a defendant who consented to a three-hour interview with them, in his private home, concerning his Federal income tax liability over a five-year period. The agents told him that one of their functions was to investigate the possibility of criminal tax fraud. The Court held that an "interview with a government agent" possessed none of the "inherently coercive" elements of the stationhouse interrogations at issue in *Miranda*; therefore, the Court found that the defendant's statements were admissible, and affirmed his conviction. *See United States v. Hurtado,* 899 F.2d 371 (5th Cir.1990) (interrogation not custodial where defendant invited officers into her home, officers never brandished weapons, did not threaten her or restrict her movement, and she was not told she was under arrest; the psychological pressure that defendant experienced because she feared her illegal activity might be discovered is irrelevant to the determination of custody, which focuses on objective factors of police coercion). *See also United States v. Courtney*, 463 F.3d 333 (5th Cir. 2006) (defendant not in custody when she met with investigators in public restaurant of her choice, was never told that she had to talk to them, and was allowed to leave after the interview).

3. **"Focus" on the Suspect Does Not Equal Custody**

The Court in *Beckwith* rejected the defendant's argument that because he was the "focus" of an investigation, he was under "psychological restraints" during his confrontation with the I.R.S. agents, which constituted the "functional equivalent" of custody. The Court explained that *Miranda's* rationale was grounded entirely in concerns with "custodial" interrogation and its "compulsive" atmosphere, not with the "strength or content of the government's suspicions" at the time the questioning was conducted. *Compare United States v. Griffin*, 922 F.2d 1343 (8th Cir.1990) (custody found where two officers were waiting for the defendant when he came home, told defendant's parents to leave, interviewed him for two hours, and told defendant that he could not leave the room unless an officer accompanied him).

4. **Objective Test**

The Court in *Stansbury v. California*, 511 U.S. 318, 114 S.Ct. 1526, 128 L.Ed.2d 293 (1994), made it clear that the test for custody under *Miranda* is an objective one—whether a reasonable person would feel that he was free to leave. Thus, the subjective state of mind of the officer is "irrelevant to the assessment whether the person is in custody." The only relevance of the officer's state of mind is if the officer's beliefs "were somehow manifested to the individual under interrogation and would have affected how a reasonable person in that position would perceive his or her freedom to leave." Thus, if an officer thinks that a suspect is under arrest, he might well act like a suspect is under arrest—but it is the actions that count.

5. **Custody in Prison**

In *Mathis v. United States*, 391 U.S. 1, 88 S.Ct. 1503, 20 L.Ed.2d 381 (1968), the Court held that a person who was interrogated while in jail, serving a sentence on a charge that was unrelated to the interrogation, was, under the circumstances presented, in custody for *Miranda* purposes.

a. Rationale

The Court held that the "whole purpose" of *Miranda* was to protect the Fifth Amendment rights of a person in custody, and that the reason for a defendant's custody was irrelevant to his need for *Miranda* protection.

b. No Automatic Rule

The Court in *Mathis* did not hold that every interrogation of a prisoner would trigger *Miranda*. Rather, the prison environment was one factor in the totality of circumstances which indicated that the defendant in *Mathis* was in custody while he was being interrogated. So for example, in *United States v. Conley*, 779 F.2d 970 (4th Cir.1985), the defendant was suspected of involvement in a knife fight in prison. He was escorted to a conference room in the prison control center to await transfer to the infirmary for treatment of his wound. He was handcuffed, and when a correction officer asked him in a friendly manner what had happened, Conley gave an incriminating statement. The court noted that, if the custody rule were applied literally, "every question directed to a prison inmate in connection with what ultimately may prove to be criminal activity" would trigger *Miranda*. The court rejected the notion that *Mathis* established a *per se* rule of custody for prisoners, reasoning that such a position "would seriously disrupt prison administration by requiring, as a prudential measure, formal warnings prior to many of the myriad informal conversations between inmates and prison guards." The court was unwilling to "torture *Miranda* to the illogical position of providing greater protection to a prisoner than to his nonimprisoned counterpart." *See also Garcia v. Singletary*, 13 F.3d 1487 (11th Cir.1994) (finding a prisoner's incriminating statement to be admissible where a guard's question imposed no additional restraint on the prisoner such as would cause the prisoner to believe that his freedom of movement had been *further* restricted).

c. More Than Usual Restraint

When a prisoner is subject to interrogation, the court, in assessing whether the circumstances were custodial, determines "whether the inmate was subjected to more than the usual restraint on a prisoner's liberty." *Conley, supra.* The court in *Conley* found that the defendant was not in custody for *Miranda* purposes, because the questioning was brief, and it was standard procedure to handcuff prisoners who were being transported to the infirmary in the maximum security facility in which Conley was incarcerated. The court concluded that "Conley's freedom of movement cannot be characterized as more restricted than that of other prisoners to and from the facility, either by virtue of his confinement or the nature of the questioning by prison personnel." Therefore, *Miranda* warnings were not required.

6. **No Automatic Rule of Custody for Stationhouse Interrogation**

In *Oregon v. Mathiason*, 429 U.S. 492, 97 S.Ct. 711, 50 L.Ed.2d 714 (1977), the defendant, a parolee, was given a message to call a police officer, and then was asked to meet with the officer at the stationhouse in order to "discuss something." After the suspect arrived, he was interviewed about a burglary, told that he was a suspect and that his truthfulness would "possibly be considered" by a judge or prosecutor, and falsely told that his fingerprints were found at the scene. A few minutes later, the defendant confessed, received warnings, and confessed again. He was then allowed to leave the stationhouse; his unwarned confession was admitted against him at trial. Evaluating the totality of circumstances, the Court held that the defendant was not in custody at the time of his confession.

a. Rationale

The Court rejected the idea that a "coercive environment" alone could trigger the need for *Miranda* warnings, because "any interview" with the police will have "coercive aspects," and because police should not be required to administer warnings "to everyone they question." The Court found it most important that Mathiason came of his own accord to the stationhouse to be interviewed. *Compare Dunaway v. New York*, 442 U.S. 200, 99 S.Ct. 2248, 60 L.Ed.2d 824 (1979) (suspect was under arrest when he was put in a police car and brought to the stationhouse against his will, and then interrogated at the stationhouse).

b. Dissent

The three dissenters in *Mathiason* argued that the Court had given insufficient attention to the coercive environment of the stationhouse, and to the fact that the defendant was a parolee, whose presence at the station at police request could hardly be deemed voluntary.

c. When a Suspect Is Asked to Accompany Police to the Stationhouse

In *California v. Beheler*, 463 U.S. 1121, 103 S.Ct. 3517, 77 L.Ed.2d 1275 (1983), the Court held that under *Mathiason*, no *Miranda* warnings were required when a defendant was interviewed at the stationhouse, after he "voluntarily agreed to accompany the police" there. The defendant initially called the police to report a murder, and then consented to a search of his yard, where police found the suspected murder weapon. Later in the evening, the police returned and asked him to accompany them to the stationhouse, while advising him that "he was not under arrest." After he confessed during his interview, he was released. On these facts, *Mathiason* was held to be controlling, so that no finding of custody was justified. The Court found it irrelevant that Mathiason had driven himself to the station while Beheler had been driven by officers. In each case, the defendant voluntarily consented to come to the station. This factor was significant in dispelling the coercive atmosphere that the stationhouse might otherwise provide.

d. When a Suspect Is Driven to the Stationhouse by His Parents
In *Yarborough v. Alvarado*, 541 U.S. 652, 124 S.Ct. 2140, 158 L.Ed.2d 938 (2004), the Court reinstated a state court's finding that a 17 year old boy was not in custody when he was questioned at a stationhouse for two hours without *Miranda* warnings after his parents drove him to the stationhouse in response to a detective's request. Alvarado's parents waited in the lobby while he was questioned. The Court noted that factors supporting a finding of custody included the length of the interview, the fact that the officer did not tell Alvarado he was free to leave, and the fact that his parents asked to be present and were rebuffed. Factors suggesting a finding that he was not in custody included the fact that police did not transport him to the stationhouse, the absence of police threats or suggestions that he would be placed under arrest, his parents' presence in the lobby, and the fact that he was allowed to go home with his parents after the interview ended. The Supreme Court held that the state court did not unreasonably apply clearly established federal law by finding that Alvarado was not in custody. The Court noted that fair-minded jurists could reasonably disagree over whether Alvarado was in custody in light of its prior custody decisions.

7. **Custody Does Not Exist Simply Because a Suspect Is Required to Meet With a Government Official or Body**
In *Minnesota v. Murphy*, 465 U.S. 420, 104 S.Ct. 1136, 79 L.Ed.2d 409 (1984), the Court held that a defendant on probation was not in custody when he was summoned to the office of his probation officer, to discuss

a "treatment plan" for his probationary term. The probation officer had uncovered evidence of Murphy's admissions to crimes committed seven years earlier, and she planned to relay any incriminating statements he made in the meeting to the police. When Murphy arrived at her office, the officer told him that he needed a treatment program because of these crimes, and the defendant admitted his guilt. As a probationer, he was required to be truthful with the probation officer "in all matters," upon penalty of probation revocation. The Court held that the defendant was not in custody during his interview, and therefore that the probation officer was not required to give him *Miranda* warnings.

Three Distinguishing Factors

> The Court observed that three factors served to distinguish the probationer's interview from stationhouse interrogation. First, an interview would not convey the message that the defendant had "no choice but to submit" to the will of the probation officer, and confess. Second, it would not thrust the defendant into an "unfamiliar atmosphere" created for the purpose of "subjugating his will." Third, no compulsion was created in the defendant's interview by suggestions that the interrogation would "continue until a confession" was obtained. The only pressure the defendant "might have felt" was based on his awareness that if he left, his probation status might be jeopardized. The Court explained that this pressure was not "comparable" to the coercion of custodial interrogation where a suspect "literally cannot escape a persistent" examiner.

8. Custody Does Not Exist When a Person Is Called to Testify Before a Grand Jury

In *United States v. Mandujano*, 425 U.S. 564, 96 S.Ct. 1768, 48 L.Ed.2d 212 (1976), the Court held that a prosecutor did not have to give *Miranda* warnings to a suspect who was called to testify before a grand jury, and interrogated concerning his involvement in narcotics traffic. The Court noted that *Miranda's* rationale was based on the need to negate the "compulsion" inherent in informal interrogation where police may abuse their powers. Such a rationale could not be extended to questioning "under the guidance of a judge" before a grand jury. Thus, the "marked contrasts" between the grand jury setting and post-arrest interrogation justified a finding that grand jury witnesses were not entitled to *Miranda* warnings.

9. **Custody Does Not Exist During a Normal Traffic Stop**

In *Berkemer v. McCarty*, 468 U.S. 420, 104 S.Ct. 3138, 82 L.Ed.2d 317 (1984), the Court held that the roadside detention of a motorist pursuant to a traffic stop does not constitute "custody" under *Miranda*. The seizure in *Berkemer* was a *Terry* stop as opposed to an arrest. Therefore, the officer was not required to give warnings before questioning the driver as to whether he had been "using intoxicants," or before administering a "field sobriety" test.

a. Rationale

While a motorist is not "free to leave" a roadside detention, the Court decided that *Miranda* should be enforced "only in those types of situations in which the concerns that powered the decision are implicated." The Court found that the pressures of detention inherent in a *Terry* stop do not approach the "inherent coercion" of post-arrest interrogation, because a driver expects a traffic stop to be brief, temporary, and conducted in the safety of the public eye. Thus, a traffic stop is not "police-dominated" in the same way as a post-arrest interrogation.

b. More Coercive Activity May Lead to a Finding of Custody

The Court in *Berkemer* did not purport to hold that all detentions and interrogations made in the course of a traffic stop would be free from *Miranda* constraints. If police, in the course of effectuating a detention for a traffic violation, engage in coercive activity associated with a formal arrest, then any interrogation will trigger *Miranda* protections. The Court acknowledged that the custody definition is not a "bright-line" rule, but found that it was preferable to a *per se* requirement that warnings be given to all motorists. That requirement would "substantially impede the enforcement" of traffic laws, and do "little to protect citizens' Fifth Amendment rights."

c. Applied to the Facts

On the facts of *Berkemer*, the Court concluded that no custodial "restraint" existed, based on several factors. The traffic stop was of short duration, the driver was not informed that his detention was for the long term, or that the officer had decided to arrest him, and the police officer only asked a "modest" number of questions. The defendant was only asked to perform a "simple" test within view of passing motorists. This treatment was "not the functional equivalent of formal arrest."

J.   The Meaning of "Interrogation"

The concept of interrogation is a critical one in *Miranda* doctrine. Even if a suspect is in custody, police do not need to give warnings, unless they interrogate him. It is the combination of custody and interrogation that triggers the inherent coercion that requires the *Miranda* safeguards. The Court in *Miranda* did not specifically define what it meant by "interrogation;" this matter was left to subsequent cases.

1.   Police Tactics Reasonably Likely to Elicit an Incriminating Response

In *Rhode Island v. Innis*, 446 U.S. 291, 100 S.Ct. 1682, 64 L.Ed.2d 297 (1980), the defendant was arrested for the shotgun murder of a cab driver at 4:30 a.m., and placed in custody in a police car for the drive to the station. One of the officers said to another, within the defendant's hearing, "there's a lot of handicapped children running around in this area [because of a nearby school], and God forbid one of them might find a weapon with shells and might hurt themselves." The other officer said they should continue to search for the weapon. At this point, the defendant interrupted them, and offered to show them where the shotgun was, near the scene of the arrest. The Court found that the defendant's statements concerning the shotgun were properly admitted, as they were not the product of any interrogation by the officers—the statements by the officers concerning the gun were not "interrogation" within the meaning of *Miranda*.

a.   Definition of Interrogation

The Court held that "interrogation" by police under *Miranda* should be interpreted as "express questioning or its functional equivalent." This includes words or actions that police *should have known were reasonably likely to elicit an incriminating response from an average suspect.*

b.   More Than Express Questioning

The *Innis* Court rejected a narrow interpretation of *Miranda* that would limit the definition of "interrogation" to express questioning. The Court was concerned that such a limited definition would create an incentive for police to devise indirect methods of interrogation in order to obtain admissible statements. The Court noted that the "concern" of the *Miranda* Court was not limited to the need to protect a suspect from the coercion of express questioning. For example, the use of fraudulent line-ups and other psychological ploys was condemned in *Miranda*, because these are coercive forms of interrogation.

c. **Relevance of Police Intent**

The Court decided that *Miranda* safeguards were designed to protect suspects from "coercive police practices, without regard to objective proof of the underlying intent of the police." Therefore, a definition of interrogation should focus "primarily upon the perceptions of the suspect," and include acts that are likely to "elicit an incriminating response from the suspect." The intent of the police is relevant, though, because an officer who intends to elicit an incriminating response is more likely to in fact elicit one than an officer who has no such intent. But police intent itself is not dispositive—the question is whether the police activity was reasonably likely to elicit an incriminating response.

d. **The Average Suspect and Peculiar Susceptibility**

The Court in *Innis* stressed that police "cannot be held accountable for the unforeseeable results" of their actions; thus, interrogation should include only behavior that police "should have known" would be *"reasonably likely"* to elicit a response from an *average suspect*. The police activity must be assessed by its effect on an average suspect, because police are not required to predict an individual, idiosyncratic, subjective response. On the other hand, if police know or have reason to know that the suspect has a "peculiar susceptibility" to a certain tactic, ploy, or statement, then an officer must be held accountable for using a tactic that is reasonably likely to play on that susceptibility. For example, if the officer knows that the suspect is a religious fanatic, then statements concerning religion may be found to have an effect on such a suspect where they would not have the same effect on an average suspect. *Cf. Brewer v. Williams*, 430 U.S. 387, 97 S.Ct. 1232, 51 L.Ed.2d 424 (1977) (where the defendant was suspected of murdering a young child and hiding the body, the officer's statements that the child deserved a "Christian burial" were impermissible where the officer knew that the defendant was a religious fanatic).

e. **Applied to the Facts**

On the facts of *Innis,* the Court found that the police dialogue was not the "functional equivalent" of interrogation, for four reasons.

Not reasonably likely to elicit confession from an AVG suspect

First, the officers had no indication that the suspect was *"peculiarly susceptible"* to an appeal to his conscience concerning the safety of handicapped children. Second, the Court noted that it was "understandable" that police should share their concerns about the children with each other; thus, there was no indication of an intent to elicit incriminating information, which would have made it more likely to have done so. Third, the dialogue consisted of "a few offhand remarks," not a "lengthy harangue." Finally, the police comments were not "particularly evocative," even though they happened to "strike a responsive chord" in the defendant. The Court concluded that the officer's statement was not reasonably likely to elicit incriminating information from the *average suspect.* That Innis actually did respond was therefore an unforeseeable event that did not warrant exclusion under *Miranda.*

f.   Justice Marshall's Dissent in *Innis*

Dissent classic interrogation technique to appeal to emotions

Justice Marshall agreed with the Court's definition of interrogation, but declared that he was "utterly at a loss to understand" its application of this definition to the facts of *Innis.* The defendant was in handcuffs in a patrol car with three officers, driving away from the scene of the arrest, when one officer began "almost immediately to talk about the search for the shotgun." Justice Marshall identified the officer's speech as a "classic interrogation technique" of appealing to a suspect to confess "for the sake of others," in order to "display some decency and honor." Justice Marshall declared that it verged on "the ludicrous" to conclude that an appeal to protect the lives of handicapped children would not be expected to have an effect on the defendant, "in the absence of some special interest" in this subject. Given all these circumstances, he concluded that interrogation occurred even though the officer's remarks "were nominally addressed" to another police officer. Justice Marshall expressed concern that the Court's vision of an "average" suspect was of a person who was impervious to appeals to conscience or decency; therefore any such appeal would never be interrogation because it was not reasonably likely to elicit an incriminating response from an "average suspect."

Interrogation ≠ hope suspect might incriminate himself

2.   Mere Possibility That the Suspect Might Incriminate Himself Does Not Mandate a Finding of Interrogation

In *Arizona v. Mauro,* 481 U.S. 520, 107 S.Ct. 1931, 95 L.Ed.2d 458 (1987), the Court held that the police decision to allow a wife to talk to her husband in custody was not the kind of "psychological ploy" that was the "functional equivalent" of interrogation. In *Mauro,* the defendant had confessed to killing his son, and then invoked his right to counsel. His wife was "adamant" in insisting on speaking to him, and no secure interview room was available. Therefore, the police allowed the two to meet in an office, and told them that their conversation would be recorded by an officer in the room. The tape recorder was in plain view. The defendant, in attempting to console his wife, made incriminating statements. The Court held that the police action did not rise to the level of "interrogation" under *Innis,* therefore, the defendant's recorded statements were held to be admissible, and his murder conviction was affirmed.

a. Rationale

The Court held that the purpose of *Miranda* was to prevent police from "using the coercive nature of confinement to extract confessions" that would not be given in "an unrestrained environment." The police actions in *Mauro* did not meet this description. As the defendant was not subjected to "compelling influences, psychological ploys, or direct questioning," no interrogation occurred. The Court declared that police do not interrogate a suspect "simply by hoping that he will incriminate himself."

b. Relevant Factors

The Court relied on several aspects of the facts in *Mauro* for its conclusion that the police acted "reasonably and lawfully" by allowing Mauro's wife to meet with him. First, the officer who was present during the meeting asked the defendant "no questions about the crime or his conduct." Second, there was no evidence that the officers sent Mrs. Mauro in for the purpose of "eliciting incriminating statements." The police testified that they advised the wife not to talk to her husband, but that she was "adamant" about doing so. Third, there were legitimate security reasons for taping the meeting and for having a police officer present, which were "not related to securing incriminating statements." The police testified that they were concerned for the wife's safety, and concerned whether she might smuggle in a weapon for an escape attempt from the non-secure office. They also were concerned that the two spouses "might cook up a lie or swap statements with each other." Finally, examining the situation from the defendant's perspective, the Court doubted that a suspect would feel "that he was being coerced to incriminate himself in any way," simply by being told that his wife would be allowed to speak with him. The defendant was "fully informed" at the time the meeting began that an officer would be present, and would tape record the conversation. He was not forced to talk to his wife, because he "could have chosen not to speak," given his knowledge that the police were listening.

3. Confrontation With Incriminating Evidence as a Form of Interrogation

In *Edwards v. Arizona*, 451 U.S. 477, 101 S.Ct. 1880, 68 L.Ed.2d 378 (1981), the Court found that interrogation occurred when the police offered to play a tape of an accomplice's confession to a suspect who invoked his right to counsel. The suspect asked them to play it, and made an incriminating statement after listening to it. The Court cited the *Innis* test without discussion. One reading of this result is that an average suspect who is confronted with incriminating evidence is reasonably likely to make a statement; and even an explanatory statement intended by the suspect to exculpate himself is excluded under *Miranda* where offered against the defendant at trial to show consciousness of guilt.

a. Distinction From the Ploy in *Innis*

In *Innis*, the Court held that an appeal to a person's conscience or decency is not reasonably likely to elicit a response, in the absence of some peculiar susceptibility to such a ploy. In contrast, *Edwards* held, without discussion, that confronting a person with incriminating evidence is likely to elicit an incriminating response from the average suspect. The difference in result can be explained by the Court's apparent view of an average suspect as a person who is impervious to appeals to the welfare of others, but who is very sensitive to his own situation in a criminal investigation. *See also People v. Ferro*, 63 N.Y.2d 316, 482 N.Y.S.2d 237, 472 N.E.2d 13 (1984) (interrogation found where officers placed the fruits of Ferro's crime in front of his jail cell).

b. Not a Universal Rule

Perhaps because the Court in *Edwards* concluded without discussion that Edwards had been interrogated, the lower courts do not always find that confronting a suspect with incriminating evidence constitutes interrogation per se. *See, e.g., United States v. Jackson*, 189 F.3d 502 (7th Cir. 1999) (agent's statement to defendant that he knew defendant had sold cocaine to undercover officers on previous occasions did not constitute interrogation); *Shedelbower v. Estelle*, 885 F.2d 570 (9th Cir.1989) (telling the defendant that he was identified by eyewitness, which was false, was not interrogation). *See also Easley v. Frey*, 433 F.3d 969 (7th Cir.2006) (officer's statement that another individual had identified defendant as one of the perpetrators of the murder and that he might be subject to the death penalty did not constitute interrogation).

4. Direct vs. Indirect Statements

The conversation in *Innis*, held not to be interrogation, was ostensibly a private conversation between the police officers. It was not obviously directed at Innis. As such, it was less likely to call for an incriminating response by Innis. In contrast, if the officer addresses a comment directly to the suspect, it is more likely to call for an incriminating response and hence more likely to constitute interrogation. *See United States v. Soto*, 953 F.2d 263 (6th Cir.1992) (accusation of misconduct, made directly to the suspect, constituted interrogation).

5. Questions Attendant to Custody Are an Exception

The Court in *Innis* held that express questioning constitutes interrogation, but provided an exception for necessary questions that are merely "attendant to custody." In *Pennsylvania v. Muniz*, 496 U.S. 582, 110 S.Ct. 2638, 110 L.Ed.2d 528 (1990), the Court held that a defendant may be interrogated, without *Miranda* warnings, concerning "biographical data necessary to complete booking or pretrial services." When a suspect is arrested, police typically ask her name, address, age, and other such questions during the booking process. The Court thus created an exception to *Miranda* for questions that are pertinent to the suspect's custodial status.

a. Applied to the Facts

In *Muniz*, the defendant was arrested for drunken driving, and taken to a booking center, where police asked his "name, address, height, weight, eye color, date of birth, and current age." He did not receive *Miranda* warnings before giving answers, which were incriminating because he stumbled over the answers and gave incorrect information on some points; his answers were offered as evidence of drunkenness at trial. The Court decided that police did not need to give *Miranda* warnings before interrogating a defendant concerning the subjects involved in these seven questions. Thus, the defendant's statements were held to be admissible at trial.

b. Limits of the "Booking Exception"

The *Muniz* Court stated that a question will not come within the "booking questions exception," if it is "designed to elicit incriminatory admissions." In *Muniz* the police asked an eighth question during the booking process: "What was the year of your sixth birthday?" Muniz could not figure out the right answer, and this was used at trial as evidence of his drunkenness. The state did not argue that this question fell within the booking questions exception. If the state had made this argument, the Court undoubtedly would have treated the sixth birthday question as one "designed to elicit incriminatory admissions." *See United States v. Jesus Mata–Abundiz*, 717 F.2d 1277 (9th Cir.1983) (in-custody questioning by INS agent regarding citizenship not within booking exception).

6. Instructions and Questions Necessary for Custodial Procedures

In *Pennsylvania v. Muniz*, 496 U.S. 582, 110 S.Ct. 2638, 110 L.Ed.2d 528 (1990), the defendant was told to perform three tests after his arrest for drunken driving. The officers and the defendant had a short discussion concerning how the tests were to be conducted. In the course of these discussions, Muniz made incriminating statements concerning his intoxicated state. The Court held that these statements were not the product of interrogation, and therefore, that no *Miranda* warnings were required as part of the police instructions. Thus, the defendant's statements were held to be admissible at trial.

a. Rationale

The Court found that the police words and actions directing the defendant in the performance of the sobriety tests "were not likely to be perceived as calling for any verbal response." As to any follow-up questions and conversations, police statements were "limited and carefully worded inquiries" as to whether the defendant understood their instructions. Thus, they were necessarily "attendant to" a legitimate police procedure, and did not fall within the *Innis* definition of interrogation.

b. Scope

After *Muniz*, explanations concerning custodial procedures, such as fingerprinting, transportation, and inventorying, will probably not be considered interrogation even though the defendant makes incriminating statements during the process. Even direct questions about an arrestee's understanding of these procedures will not be interrogation, because these questions are reasonably "attendant to" the processes themselves.

K. The Application of *Miranda* to Undercover Police Activity

In *Illinois v. Perkins,* 496 U.S. 292, 110 S.Ct. 2394, 110 L.Ed.2d 243 (1990), the Court held that *Miranda* warnings are not required "when the suspect is unaware that he is speaking to a law enforcement officer." Therefore, an undercover agent posing as a fellow prisoner may elicit incriminating statements from an incarcerated suspect without violating *Miranda*. In *Perkins,* two informants posed as inmates, in order to uncover evidence of the defendant's involvement in a murder. They invited him to help plan a jail break, and one of them directly asked him if he had ever "done" anybody. The defendant then supplied them with the details of his involvement with the murder; the Court held that his unwarned confession was admissible at trial, and affirmed his murder conviction.

1. Rationale

The Court held that when a suspect is talking to someone whom he does not know is a police officer, the "coercive atmosphere" of police interrogation is missing. Therefore, questioning by undercover agents does not "implicate the concerns underlying *Miranda*." Although the defendant in *Perkins* was in "custody," this fact alone did not mandate *Miranda* warnings. The Court observed that there must be "interplay" between custody and police interrogation to trigger the *Miranda* protections.

2. Dissent

Justice Marshall dissented, and argued that the Court's new "exception" to *Miranda* improperly interpreted that decision as being concerned solely with police "coercion." Instead, he argued that *Miranda's* concern was with "any police tactics that may operate to compel a suspect in custody" to make incriminating statements; he believed that undercover activity was one such tactic.

L. Misdemeanors and *Miranda*

In *Berkemer v. McCarty,* 468 U.S. 420, 104 S.Ct. 3138, 82 L.Ed.2d 317 (1984), the Court held that *Miranda* protections apply to suspects who are arrested for misdemeanor traffic offenses, as well as to those arrested for more serious crimes. Once the defendant in *Berkemer* was in custody for drunken driving, the police could not interrogate him at the stationhouse and obtain a confession without giving him *Miranda* warnings. Therefore his unwarned answers to police questions as to whether he had been drinking or using drugs were inadmissible at his trial.

Rationale

The Court rejected the state's argument that an "exception" to *Miranda* should be "carved out" for misdemeanor traffic offenses. It concluded that a "misdemeanor exception" would "impair the simplicity and clarity" of police enforcement of *Miranda*. In order to invoke such an exception, police would be required to "guess as to the nature of the criminal conduct at issue" before interrogating a suspect. For example, it might turn out that a collision was the result of a misdemeanor, such as drunk driving, or a felony, such as negligent homicide, or both. At the time of an arrest, the crimes involved in some accidents might be unknown or unknowable. This kind of vagueness is at odds with the bright-line approach to custodial interrogation embraced in *Miranda*.

M. The "Public Safety Exception" to *Miranda*

In *New York v. Quarles*, 467 U.S. 649, 104 S.Ct. 2626, 81 L.Ed.2d 550 (1984), the Court held that police may ask questions "reasonably prompted by a concern for public safety" without first advising a suspect in custody of the *Miranda* warnings. In *Quarles*, the police arrested and handcuffed a rape suspect at 12:30 a.m. in a supermarket, based on a tip from a victim who described the suspect and said he was armed. Before the arrest, a police officer chased the defendant to the back of the store, and lost sight of him briefly before he caught him, frisked him, and discovered that he was wearing an empty shoulder holster. The Court held that it was proper for the officer to refrain from giving the *Miranda* warnings, and to ask the defendant, "Where is the gun?" When the suspect said, "The gun is over there," it was also proper for the officer to retrieve it from an empty carton. Both the defendant's statement concerning the location of the gun, and the gun itself, were held to be admissible in the prosecution's case-in-chief.

1. Rationale

The Court determined that the "doctrinal underpinnings" of *Miranda* did not require its application in a case where police questions were "reasonably prompted by a concern for public safety." The warnings might "deter" a suspect from answering such questions, and the Court found that the "need for answers" to these questions outweighed the "need" for *Miranda's* protection of the Fifth Amendment privilege.

a.   Cost–Benefit Analysis

The *Quarles* Court interpreted *Miranda* as holding that the "possibility of fewer convictions" was an acceptable price to pay for the benefit of protecting the Fifth Amendment privilege through the requirement of the *Miranda* warnings. The Court reasoned that the cost-benefit calculus of *Miranda* should be different, however, in a case where there is "danger to the public," and where the warnings may deter a suspect from giving information to the police that is necessary to protect the public in an emergency circumstance. In this situation, the costs of the *Miranda* rule of exclusion are more significant—not only will there be fewer convictions because of the warnings, but there will also be an imminent risk of harm to the public because of the suspect's refusal to disclose important information. This added cost led the Court to conclude that, where public safety is at stake, the costs of the *Miranda* exclusionary rule outweighed the benefits in deterrence that the rule would provide.

b.   Going Away From the Bright–Line Rule

The Court in *Quarles* conceded that its new "exception" would "lessen the degree of clarity" of *Miranda's* application. However, it predicted that the *Quarles* rule "would not be difficult for police officers to apply" because they "can and will distinguish almost instinctively" between permissible "public safety" questions and impermissible interrogation.

c.   Applied to the Facts

On the facts of *Quarles,* the Court found that the situation and the police questioning came within the scope of the "public safety exception." The police were confronted with "the immediate necessity" of ascertaining the whereabouts of the gun, which they "had every reason to believe" had been removed from the empty holster and discarded in the supermarket. If the gun were not located it posed several dangers to the public safety: "an accomplice might make use of it," or a customer or employee might find it. Finally, the police officer asked "only the question necessary to locate the missing gun" before giving the defendant the *Miranda* warnings.

2.   **Justice O'Connor's Opinion**

Justice O'Connor disagreed with the majority's adoption of a public safety exception to *Miranda*. She argued that the "public safety exception" was unjustifiable because it would blur "the clear strictures" of

Miranda; therefore, she determined that the defendant's statement, "The gun is over there," should not be admissible evidence. Justice O'Connor agreed with the result as to the admissibility of the gun itself, however. In her view, the gun was a "fruit" of the *Miranda*-defective confession, and she argued that the exclusionary rule does not apply to physical evidence that is the fruit of a *Miranda*-defective confession. (See the discussion of the fruit of the poisonous tree doctrine, *supra*.)

3. Dissent

The three dissenters in *Quarles* argued that a public safety exception to *Miranda* was unjustified on the facts presented. The dissenters noted that the police "could easily have cordoned off the store" and searched for the gun. The defendant was not believed to have an accomplice, and the store was deserted, except for the clerks at the checkout counter. The defendant had been reduced to "powerlessness," and the police were confident enough of their safety to "put away their guns." Thus, there was no danger to the police, to the employees of the store, to customers, or to the public generally, that justified the need to ask, "Where's the gun?"

4. Exigent Circumstances

In *Quarles* the majority found a sufficient public safety problem from a loose gun accessible to the public. The Court pointedly did not require more imminent circumstances (e.g., a bomb that is about to go off within minutes), nor did it require more grave consequences (e.g., mass destruction). The courts after *Quarles* have generally equated the *Miranda* "public safety" exception with the exigent circumstances exception to the Fourth Amendment warrant requirement. That is, if the circumstances present a sufficiently imminent risk to excuse a warrant, they also pose a sufficient risk to excuse the *Miranda* warnings. *See United States v. Simpson,* 974 F.2d 845 (7th Cir.1992) (warnings not required before asking about the location of a gun in an apartment where officers are responding to a domestic disturbance). *Compare United States v. Mobley,* 40 F.3d 688 (4th Cir.1994) (public safety exception not applicable: no "immediate need" to ask about the location of a gun where the defendant was arrested in his home for a narcotics offense, and officers had already determined that no one else was in the home). *See also United States v. Brathwaite,* 458 F.3d 376 (5th Cir. 2006) (public safety exception did not apply where police performed two sweeps of the home, all the occupants were handcuffed, and the public had no access to the home).

5. Subject Matter Limitation on Questioning

The Court in *Quarles* held that the officer's questioning was sufficiently within the public safety exception because he asked the suspect only about where the gun was, and did not ask him about the rape for which he was suspected. Presumably, then, if the officer had asked about the rape without giving the warnings, then any statement made by the defendant about the rape would not have fallen within the public safety exception and would have been excluded. Sometimes, however, it is difficult to determine which questions fall within the subject matter of public safety and which fall outside the scope of the exception. Courts after *Quarles* have allowed officers considerable leeway to ask questions which could be construed as either addressing the public safety problem or as addressing the underlying crime.

Example: In *Fleming v. Collins,* 954 F.2d 1109 (5th Cir.1992), officers were responding to a bank robbery, when they came upon a person whom they knew to be a local used car salesman; the salesman had a person later determined to be Fleming pinned to the ground, and he was holding a gun to Fleming's head. Fleming had already been shot. The officers intervened, picked Fleming up, and asked him three questions, none of which were proceeded by the *Miranda* warnings. The first question was, "Who shot you?" to which Fleming replied, "The man at the bank." The second question was "Where is your gun?" to which Fleming replied, "I dropped it." The third question was, "Who was with you in the robbery?" to which Fleming replied, "Nobody. I did not get any money, either."

The court held that all three questions were permissible under the public safety exception. It reasoned that *Quarles* provided flexibility to officers and authorized officers to rely on their instincts in applying the public safety exception. It concluded that it was not the role of a court to carefully parse out each question asked by the officers in an emergency situation. Thus, unless the officer's questioning went clearly and exclusively to the substantive crime rather than to a public safety matter, it would be permissible in the absence of warnings under *Quarles*. Applying this analysis to the facts, the court found that the first two questions were clearly pertinent to a safety concern. The third question was more doubtful, because it referred to the robbery. But even this question was within the public safety exception, because the officers may have been concerned about armed and dangerous accomplices in the area, and because the questioning was related closely enough to the gun left somewhere by Fleming.

V. Confessions and the Sixth Amendment After *Miranda*

After *Miranda* was decided, the Court did not revisit its doctrine concerning the Sixth Amendment right to counsel under *Massiah* for many years. But since *Massiah*, the Sixth Amendment has been held to prohibit the government from deliberately eliciting incriminating information from a formally charged defendant in the absence of counsel. This section discusses the development and current status of the Sixth Amendment right to counsel as it relates to confessions.

A. *Brewer v. Williams*: Deliberate Elicitation of Incriminating Statements From a Formally Charged Defendant

In *Brewer v. Williams*, 430 U.S. 387, 97 S.Ct. 1232, 51 L.Ed.2d 424 (1977), the Court held that the Sixth Amendment right to counsel was violated when police deliberately elicited incriminating statements from a defendant who had been arraigned for murder. This violated *Massiah v. United States*, 377 U.S. 201, 84 S.Ct. 1199, 12 L.Ed.2d 246 (1964), because the defendant had not waived his Sixth Amendment right to counsel by "intentionally relinquishing" it before police obtained his statements.

1. Facts of *Brewer*

The defendant was suspected of murder, and he fled from Des Moines to Davenport; he surrendered to the police in Davenport on advice of counsel in Des Moines. He was arraigned in Davenport. The Des Moines police promised his counsel that the officers who were sent to Davenport to pick up the defendant would not question him during the drive back to Des Moines. Counsel told the defendant of this promise, and advised him not to talk to the police until after consultation with him. At his arraignment in Davenport, the defendant conferred with another attorney, who also advised him not to talk to the police until he saw his counsel in Des Moines. When the Des Moines police arrived in Davenport, the local attorney urged them to carry out their promise not to interrogate the defendant, but the police expressed "reservations," and they refused to allow the attorney to accompany them back to Des Moines.

The defendant was given *Miranda* warnings upon arrest, at arraignment, and then again by the Des Moines detectives before they embarked on their 160–mile journey. During the ride, the defendant informed the police repeatedly that he would talk to them after he saw his lawyer. However, one police officer knew that the defendant was deeply religious, and was a former mental patient. Not long after leaving Davenport, he made a speech to the defendant concerning the importance of finding the body of the murder victim, in order to give her a "Christian burial." He then told the defendant, "I don't want you to answer me. I don't want to discuss it any further. Just think about it as we're riding down the road." After the police car had traveled another 100 miles or so, the defendant made incriminating statements about the location of evidence, and led the police to the body. He was convicted of murder.

The Court declined to consider whether the police violated *Miranda*. Instead, the Court reversed the murder conviction on Sixth Amendment grounds, because the police violated *Massiah*.

2. Rationale

The Court held that the Sixth Amendment right to counsel attached at the initiation of the "judicial proceedings" at arraignment, and was not "intentionally relinquished" by the defendant before the police "deliberately elicited" statements from him in violation of *Massiah*.

a. Deliberate Elicitation After a Formal Charge

Relying on *Massiah*, the Court in *Brewer* held that the Sixth Amendment prohibits police from *deliberately eliciting* incriminating information in the absence of counsel, when a suspect has been formally charged. The police officer in *Brewer* engaged in deliberate elicitation by making the "Christian burial speech." The officer knew that the defendant was being represented by two lawyers, and yet "purposely sought" to "obtain as much incriminating evidence as possible" during the defendant's imposed isolation in the police car on the way to Des Moines.

b. No Waiver

The Court found "no reasonable basis" for finding a waiver of the right to counsel on the facts of *Brewer*. The mere fact that the defendant confessed was not enough to prove the defendant's "intentional relinquishment or abandonment" of this right. The

Court noted that Williams had secured attorneys "at both ends" of the trip, and they acted as his agents in telling the police that no interrogation would be allowed on the journey. Williams consulted with these attorneys four times, and was assured by them that the police would not question him. Finally, he clearly expressed his desire for the presence of counsel before interrogation by stating that he would talk to police after he met with counsel in Des Moines. Thus, the defendant both expressly and implicitly asserted his right to counsel repeatedly throughout his encounter with the police.

3. Unethical Behavior as the Touchstone of Sixth Amendment Analysis

In a concurring opinion, Justice Stevens used a somewhat different approach to the problem of deliberate elicitation of statements from an accused (one who has been formally charged with a crime). Justice Stevens noted that the defendant's lawyer trusted the police to "honor a commitment" made during negotiations for the defendant's surrender; the state in *Brewer* "could not be permitted to dishonor its promise" to the defendant's lawyer by deliberately eliciting information from the accused in the absence of counsel. Thus, in his view, the confession was properly excluded because the officers acted unethically.

Indeed, in the later case of *Rhode Island v. Innis, supra,* the Court distinguished the Sixth Amendment from *Miranda* on ethical grounds. According to the Court in *Innis, Miranda* protects the suspect from the compulsion that is inherent in custodial interrogation. Thus, its focus is on whether the suspect has been *pressured* by police activity, rather than on whether such activity is unethical or in bad faith. In contrast, the Sixth Amendment focuses on whether the state has acted unethically by deliberately approaching a defendant for information, in the absence of his counsel, after a formal charge has been filed. In this respect, the Sixth Amendment is analogous to Lawyer's Code of Professional Responsibility DR 7–104, which prohibits a lawyer in the course of a matter from contacting an opposing party in the absence of counsel. (Rule 4.2 of the Model Rules of Professional Conduct is to the same effect). The theory of the *Massiah–Brewer* line of cases is that litigation begins when a formal charge has been filed; at that point it is inappropriate for the state-government lawyer or police officer—to approach the adversary for information in the absence of counsel. *See also United States v. Johnson,* 954 F.2d 1015 (5th Cir.1992) ("Once the government has brought formal charges against an individual the adversary relationship between the parties is cemented * * *. The government may not try to circumvent the protection afforded by the presence of counsel during questioning. The vice is not deprivation of privacy, but interference with the parity required by the Sixth Amendment.")

4. **Affirmation of the *Brewer–Massiah* Rule**

In several cases after *Brewer,* the Court affirmed the validity of the *Brewer–Massiah* rule. For example, the Court held that a state psychiatrist may not interview an indicted defendant in order to discover information to be used against him at a capital sentencing hearing. *See Estelle v. Smith,* 451 U.S. 454, 101 S.Ct. 1866, 68 L.Ed.2d 359 (1981) (no interview without a waiver of the defendant's right to consult with counsel); *see also Powell v. Texas,* 492 U.S. 680, 109 S.Ct. 3146, 106 L.Ed.2d 551 (1989) (defendant may not be subjected to a psychiatric examination and examined on the issue of future dangerousness without notice to counsel).

5. **Must Be Formally Charged; Having Counsel Is Not Enough**

The Court in *Moran v. Burbine,* 475 U.S. 412, 106 S.Ct. 1135, 89 L.Ed.2d 410 (1986), declined to expand the protections of *Brewer* and *Massiah* to a defendant who had not been indicted, but whose family had retained counsel on his behalf during his custodial interrogation. According to the Court, Sixth Amendment rights are triggered by a formal charge (such as arraignment or indictment), rather than by actual retention of counsel. Thus, merely having a retained counsel does not trigger Sixth Amendment rights prior to a formal charge. Conversely, if the defendant has been formally charged, his right to counsel is violated if the state engages in deliberate elicitation, even if the defendant has not established a formal relationship with a lawyer. *See United States v. Henry*, 447 U.S. 264, 100 S.Ct. 2183, 65 L.Ed.2d 115 (1980) (right to counsel applies automatically when officers engage in deliberate elicitation after a formal charge).

In *Rothgery v. Gillespie Cty.,* ___ U.S. ___, 128 S.Ct. 2578, 171 L.Ed.2d 366 (2008), the Court held that a criminal defendant's initial appearance before a magistrate judge, where he learns the charge against him and his liberty is subject to restriction, marks the initiation of adversary judicial proceedings that trigger attachment of the Sixth Amendment right to counsel. Attachment does not also require that a prosecutor (as distinct from a police officer) be aware of that initial proceeding or involved in its conduct.

6. "Deliberate Elicitation" Distinguished From "Interrogation"

In *Fellers v. United States*, 540 U.S. 519, 124 S.Ct. 1019, 157 L.Ed.2d 1016 (2004), the Court distinguished Sixth Amendment "deliberate elicitation" from Fifth Amendment "interrogation." After a grand jury indicted Fellers, police officers arrested him at his home. During the arrest, Fellers made inculpatory statements and later repeated these statements after receiving *Miranda* warnings at the jailhouse. His jailhouse statements were admitted at trial, and he was convicted of conspiring to possess with intent to distribute methamphetamine. The Eighth Circuit held that since Fellers had not been interrogated in his home, his Sixth Amendment right to counsel under *Patterson v. Illinois*, *infra*, did not apply. It further held that the jailhouse statements were property admitted under *Elstad, supra*. The Supreme Court reversed, holding that the officers' deliberate elicitation of statements from Fellers, after indictment and in the absence of counsel, violated his Sixth Amendment Right, whether or not there was an "interrogation." The Court further noted that it had not yet decided the issue of whether the *Elstad* "fruits" analysis applies in the Sixth Amendment context and remanded the case to the Eighth Circuit to decide this issue in the first instance.

B. Sixth Amendment Waiver

The Court in *Brewer* held that a waiver of Sixth Amendment rights could not be found merely because a defendant was warned of his rights and subsequently confessed. The Court in *Brewer* did not purport to decide all Sixth Amendment waiver questions, however—the most important question being whether waiver under the Sixth Amendment should be decided under the same standards applied to determine waiver of *Miranda* rights.

1. Waiver After Invoking the Right to Counsel at Arraignment

In *Michigan v. Jackson*, 475 U.S. 625, 106 S.Ct. 1404, 89 L.Ed.2d 631 (1986), defendants in two cases challenged the admissibility of statements made during post-arraignment questioning by police. At arraignment, each defendant had asked that counsel be appointed to assist him. After arraignment, police approached each defendant, gave them *Miranda* warnings, and obtained voluntary waivers and incriminating statements. The Court held that the purported waivers of Sixth Amendment rights to counsel were invalid, because the defendants did not "initiate" contact with the police after invoking their rights. Thus, the Court concluded that the bright-line "initiation" rule of *Edwards* was applicable to an invocation of Sixth Amendment rights, and so it did not matter that the waivers may actually have been voluntary under the totality of the circumstances.

a. Rationale

The Court reasoned that *Edwards* should be applied to an invocation of a Sixth Amendment right to counsel, because this right required "at least as much protection as the *Miranda* right to counsel." The Court stated that after the initiation of adversary judicial proceedings, a defendant has a right to rely on counsel as an exclusive "medium" for communication with the police. The Sixth Amendment right is so important that, once it attaches, police are prohibited from certain investigatory techniques that are permissible in the pre-attachment stage. Therefore, the Court concluded that the "legal differences" between the Fifth and Sixth Amendment contexts only strengthen the justification for requiring the protection of the *Edwards* rule in the post-arraignment setting.

b. Lack of Police Knowledge Irrelevant

The Court in *Jackson* rejected the state's argument that the *Edwards* prohibition on police-initiated interrogation should not apply where an officer does not know that an accused requested counsel at an arraignment. Once the Sixth Amendment right attaches, the state must honor it; this requirement disables the police from claiming ignorance of requests made to a judge.

c. Dissent

The three dissenters argued that the *Edwards* rule did not "make sense" in the context of the Sixth Amendment. They observed that the *Jackson* holding applied *Edwards* only to defendants who expressly invoked the right to counsel; this limitation contradicted Sixth Amendment precedents which held that the right to counsel *does not depend upon its invocation,* but upon the initiation of adversary judicial proceedings.

2. **Police–Initiated Interrogation Where the Accused Does Not Invoke the Sixth Amendment Right to Counsel**

In *Patterson v. Illinois,* 487 U.S. 285, 108 S.Ct. 2389, 101 L.Ed.2d 261 (1988), the Court held that *Jackson* implicitly held that invocation of the right to counsel was necessary to trigger the protection of *Edwards.* If this were not so, the *Jackson* decision to borrow the *Edwards* rationale would have been "unnecessary," because the police would have been barred per se from initiating interrogation after arraignment. Like the *Miranda* right to counsel, which exists during custody, but is not protected by the *Edwards* rule until invocation, the Sixth Amendment right to counsel exists upon attachment, but is not protected by the *Jackson* rule prohibiting police-initiated interrogation, until the accused invokes the right to counsel. *See also Montoya v. Collins*, 955 F.2d 279 (5th Cir.1992) (*Jackson* does not apply where the magistrate told the defendant that counsel was being appointed for him, and defendant said nothing; while not rejecting counsel, defendant never sought to consult with counsel; police can therefore initiate interrogation and obtain a voluntary waiver).

3. Sixth Amendment Right to Counsel Is Offense–Specific

In *McNeil v. Wisconsin*, 501 U.S. 171, 111 S.Ct. 2204, 115 L.Ed.2d 158 (1991), the Court held that a defendant's request for the assistance of counsel at a "first appearance" before a judicial officer encompassed only a request for assistance concerning *the offense with which he was charged*. Therefore, the police could approach him to seek a waiver of *Miranda* rights as to a crime unrelated to the charge. The defendant in *McNeil* was charged with armed robbery; he requested counsel, and was represented at his initial appearance by an attorney from the Public Defender's Office. Later that evening, the police interviewed the defendant in jail concerning their separate investigation of a murder, attempted murder and armed burglary. The defendant was given *Miranda* warnings and voluntarily signed a waiver; then he made statements about the crimes unrelated to that with which he was charged.

a. *Jackson–Edwards* Rule Against Police–Initiated Interrogation Held Inapplicable

If the *Jackson–Edwards* rule were applicable to the facts in *McNeil*, the confession would have been inadmissible, because McNeil had not initiated the contact with the police after invoking his rights. But the Court declined to extend the *Jackson* rule to cover police interrogation concerning crimes unrelated to those charged against the defendant. And the *Edwards–Roberson* rule (prohibiting police-initiated interrogation even as to unrelated crimes) was inapplicable because McNeil had invoked only his *Sixth Amendment* rights and not his *Miranda* rights in his initial appearance. (This aspect of the opinion is discussed in the section on *Miranda, supra*). Therefore, the defendant's statements were held to be admissible, and his convictions for these other crimes were affirmed.

b. Rationale

The Court held that a defendant's invocation of the right to counsel cannot embrace a request for assistance in future unrelated investigations, because "adversary judicial proceedings" have not been initiated for such prosecutions. As the Sixth Amendment right is "offense-specific," the *Jackson* "effect" of an invocation of that right must be "offense-specific," too. The "offense-specific" nature of Sixth Amendment rights has been well-established since *Massiah*, where the Court stated that it was permissible for officers to obtain information from a charged defendant concerning uncharged crimes, and to use such statements in later trials on those unrelated charges.

4. Sixth Amendment Right Inapplicable to "Closely Related" Charges

In *Texas v. Cobb*, 532 U.S. 162, 121 S.Ct. 1335, 149 L.Ed.2d 321 (2001), the Supreme Court declined to extend the Sixth Amendment right to counsel to offenses that are closely related factually to the offense charged. Raymond Cobb was charged with burglary after confessing to the offense and was appointed an attorney to represent him on that charge. While Cobb was free on bond, his father contacted the sheriff's office and reported that Cobb had confessed to killing a woman who lived in the home he had previously burglarized. Cobb was arrested and advised of his *Miranda* rights. Shortly thereafter, he confessed to murdering Margaret Owings and her 16–month-old daughter, who were present in the home during the burglary. Cobb claimed that under *Jackson*, *supra*, the police were required to secure the permission of his lawyer before questioning him about the murders. The Court of Criminal Appeals reversed Cobb's conviction, holding that "once the right to counsel attaches to the offense charged, it also attaches to any other offense that is very closely related to the offense charged."

a. Rationale

In a 5–4 decision, the Court reversed the judgment of the Court of Criminal Appeals and affirmed its holding in *McNeil* that the Sixth Amendment right to counsel is offense-specific. The Court rejected Cobb's argument that the offense-specific rule will "permit law enforcement officers almost complete and total license to conduct unwanted and uncounseled interrogations." The Court noted that the requirements of *Miranda* and *Dickerson* would continue to protect suspects from compulsory self-incrimination. It further pointed out that the Constitution does not prevent law enforcement agents from talking to witnesses and suspects, even those charged with other offenses.

b.   Applying the *Blockburger* Test

The Court acknowledged that the definition of an offense is not necessarily limited to the four corners of a charging document. It applied the test used in *Blockburger v. United States*, 284 U.S. 299, 52 S.Ct. 180, 76 L.Ed. 306 (1932), where the Court defined the scope of the Fifth Amendment's Double Jeopardy Clause, which prevents multiple or successive prosecutions for the same offense. There the Court held that "the test to be applied to determine whether there are two offenses or only one, is whether each provision requires proof of a fact which the other does not." Thus, the Court held that "when the Sixth Amendment right to counsel attaches, it does encompass all offenses that, even if not formally charged, would be considered the same offense under the *Blockburger* test." The Court applied the *Blockburger* test to the facts of the case and concluded that burglary and capital murder were not the "same offense." Under Texas law, burglary required "entry into or continued concealment in a habitation or building" while the applicable provision of capital murder required "murder of more than one person during a single criminal transaction."

c.   Dissent

Justice Breyer dissented, joined by Justices Stevens, Souter, and Ginsburg. The dissenters argued that the Court's decision significantly undermined *Jackson*, noting that criminal codes contain "overlapping and related statutory offenses" that permit prosecutors to easily charge "a startlingly numerous series of offenses from a single * * * criminal transaction." After describing several examples of how a single criminal act can result in numerous criminal charges, the dissenters discussed the difficulty of administering the *Blockburger* test, noting the disagreement among judges, lawyers, and law professors on how the test should be applied. The dissenters suggested that police officers in the field would find it even more difficult to apply the test when deciding whether to interrogate a suspect.

5.   **The *Miranda* Warnings Adequately Inform an Indicted Defendant of the Sixth Amendment Right to Counsel**

In *Patterson v. Illinois*, 487 U.S. 285, 108 S.Ct. 2389, 101 L.Ed.2d 261 (1988), the Court held that the *Miranda* rights provide the "sum and substance" of the rights provided by the Sixth Amendment; no extra warnings are required to establish a knowing and voluntary waiver of Sixth Amendment rights. The defendant in *Patterson* was indicted, but did not invoke his right to counsel at arraignment, and thus did not qualify for *Jackson's* protection from police-initiated questioning. Police gave him *Miranda* warnings in custody, and sought and obtained a waiver, as well as incriminating statements. Patterson did not deny that he understood the warnings, but he argued that the warnings were insufficient to inform him of his Sixth Amendment right to counsel, as opposed to his rights under *Miranda*. The Court decided that the value and function of counsel was the same during pre-indictment and post-indictment custodial interrogation, and therefore, that no "extra" information about the Sixth Amendment right to counsel was needed for an indicted defendant to be adequately apprised of this right.

a. Rationale

The Court reasoned that in order to give a "knowing" waiver, a defendant must be made aware of the "usefulness of counsel" and the "dangers" of proceeding without counsel. It was evident to the Court that the *Miranda* warnings sufficed to communicate these aspects of the Sixth Amendment right to counsel to a defendant. The Court noted that the state's decision to begin formal "adversarial judicial proceedings" against a defendant did not "substantially increase the value of counsel" at questioning, or "expand the limited purpose" that counsel served at questioning. Therefore, no different warnings, and no "more searching inquiry" was needed for a Sixth Amendment waiver than for a Fifth Amendment waiver.

b. Distinction From Waiver of Counsel at Trial

The *Patterson* Court acknowledged that a "more searching inquiry" was needed for the waiver of the Sixth Amendment right to counsel *at trial. See Faretta v. California*, 422 U.S. 806, 95 S.Ct. 2525, 45 L.Ed.2d 562 (1975) (valid waiver requires a searching examination of the defendant and extensive warnings concerning the value of counsel at trial). But this was because the "dangers and disadvantages of self-representation" at trial are more substantial, and less obvious to the accused, than the comparable dangers and disadvantages of self-representation during interrogation. Put another way, the consequences of a waiver of counsel at trial were more complex, more wide-ranging, and less obvious than the consequences of a waiver of counsel for police questioning. At trial, counsel has a variety of important functions, whereas at questioning, counsel's sole and obvious function is to protect the defendant from saying anything that could incriminate him.

c. Dissent

The four dissenters in *Patterson* argued that *Miranda* warnings alone were insufficient to make an indicted defendant aware of the disadvantages of waiving the right to counsel at that point. Such disadvantages included the defendant's limited ability, without counsel, to examine the indictment before submitting to interrogation, and to negotiate a plea bargain skillfully before interrogation. The dissenters contended that "at least minimal advice is necessary" concerning these disadvantages, and determined that it must include advice that goes beyond the *Miranda* warnings.

d. Indictment Warning

The defendant in *Patterson* knew of his indictment before he waived his right to counsel, and so the Court did not reach the issue whether a suspect should be told of his indictment before a Sixth Amendment waiver can be sought by police. Lower courts have relied on the broad rationale of *Patterson* to find that it is not necessary for police to provide such information before seeking a waiver of the Sixth Amendment right to counsel. *See, e.g., Riddick v. Edmiston*, 894 F.2d 586 (3d Cir.1990).

6. Two Exceptions Where Waiver Standards May Differ

The Court in *Patterson* held that where a defendant has been charged and has not invoked his Sixth Amendment right to counsel, the waiver of Sixth Amendment rights is governed by essentially the same principles as the waiver of *Miranda* rights. The Court, however, described two exceptions where an accused would not have waived his Sixth Amendment rights, "even though the challenged practices would pass constitutional muster under *Miranda*."

a. Lawyer Trying to Reach an Indicted Defendant

The Court in *Patterson* stated that where police know that an indicted defendant's lawyer is trying to reach him, the police must inform the defendant of that fact before there can be a knowing waiver of Sixth Amendment rights. This is in contrast to *Miranda*, where a knowing waiver can be made even though the suspect is not told that his lawyer is trying to reach him. *See Moran v. Burbine, supra.* The reason for the distinction is that *Miranda* rights are concerned with pressure on the suspect, and no pressure can be created by information about which the defendant is unaware. In contrast, the Sixth Amendment is concerned with preventing government officials from engaging in the unethical activity of intruding upon the attorney-client relationship once formal litigation has begun. Thus, in the Sixth Amendment situation, a defendant who is waiving the right to an attorney-client relationship is entitled to know an important factor of that relationship—that counsel is seeking him out.

b. Undercover Activity

Another difference between the Fifth and Sixth Amendment arises where the state employs an undercover informant to obtain information. *Miranda* does not apply to undercover activity (*see Illinois v. Perkins, supra*) whereas the Sixth Amendment does (*see United States v. Henry, infra*). The Court in *Patterson* pointed out that the standard waiver rules cannot apply in the undercover context. That is, a defendant could never be found to have waived his Sixth Amendment rights when questioned by an undercover agent, because by definition he does not even know that he is talking to a Government official. *See United States v. Johnson*, 954 F.2d 1015 (5th Cir.1992) (accused must "know he is being questioned by the government before he can knowingly waive his right not to be interrogated by the government without his lawyer").

C. The Meaning of "Deliberate Elicitation"

The Sixth Amendment obviously does not prohibit all contact between a state official and an indicted defendant in the absence of counsel. For example, the Sixth Amendment does not require the state to provide a bunk for counsel next to an incarcerated defendant who is awaiting trial, on the off-chance that the defendant might say something incriminating during the course of the day. It is only when the state "deliberately elicits" information from the accused in the absence of counsel that the Sixth Amendment is triggered. In these instances, the state is acting unethically by interposing itself between the accused and his counsel during the course of litigation. In several cases, the Court has sought to define the parameters of "deliberate elicitation."

1. Obtaining Information Through Jailhouse Informants

In *United States v. Henry*, 447 U.S. 264, 100 S.Ct. 2183, 65 L.Ed.2d 115 (1980), the defendant was indicted for armed robbery, and refused to talk to police while in custody. A government agent learned that a paid informant was housed in the same cellblock as the defendant, and told him to "be alert" to any statements Henry made about the armed robbery. The agent also warned the informant "not to initiate any conversation with or question" Henry about the crime. The informant testified at trial that he had "an opportunity to have some conversations" with the defendant, where incriminating statements were made. The Court found that the government, through the informant, had deliberately elicited incriminating information from Henry, in violation of Henry's Sixth Amendment right to counsel.

a. Rationale

The Court found deliberate elicitation on the basis of three factors. The jail inmate acted *"under instructions as a paid informant"*; he pretended to be nothing more than a "fellow inmate"; and he engaged an incarcerated, indicted defendant in conversation *about the crime charged.* The *Henry* Court reaffirmed *Massiah's* mandate that the Sixth Amendment "must apply to indirect and surreptitious interrogations as well as those conducted in the jailhouse."

b. Conduct Likely to Elicit Incriminating Information Is Deemed Deliberate

The Government in *Henry* argued that the police officials "did not intend" that the informant would take "affirmative steps to secure incriminating information," though that is in fact what happened. The Court responded that even if the agent lacked specific intent to have the informant elicit information, the agent "must have known" that the "propinquity" of the informant and the defendant in the same cellblock, and the fact that the informant would be paid for any information provided, would be "likely" to lead to the result in *Henry.* Thus, where the informant's own testimony revealed that he was not a "passive listener," but an active participant in conversations with the defendant, this conduct was sufficient to satisfy *Massiah's* deliberate elicitation requirement.

After *Henry,* "deliberate" elicitation does not focus on the subjective intent of the officer but rather on whether a *reasonable person would find it likely* that a planned course of conduct would lead to the elicitation of incriminating information from a formally charged defendant. Officers are deemed to intend the reasonably foreseeable consequences of their actions.

c. Undercover Activity; Distinction From *Miranda*

Miranda focuses on the pressure imposed on suspects in the course of custodial interrogation. It is thus important to consider whether the defendant knew that the questioning party was a police officer; if not, there is no pressure on suspects created by the interplay between custody and police interrogation that is the concern of *Miranda. See Illinois v. Perkins, supra* (*Miranda* does not apply to undercover activity). In contrast, the Sixth Amendment focuses on whether the Government has unethically interposed itself between the defendant and his counsel during the course of litigation (i.e., after a formal charge has been filed). That intrusion is unethical whether it occurs through police questioning or through undercover activity. It is for this reason that the Sixth Amendment is applicable to post-charge undercover activity, but *Miranda* is not.

2. Meeting Initiated by the Indicted Defendant

In *Maine v. Moulton*, 474 U.S. 159, 106 S.Ct. 477, 88 L.Ed.2d 481 (1985), a police officer asked the co-defendant informant to wear a "body wire transmitter" to a meeting with the defendant, where the two men planned to discuss their upcoming trial. The meeting was initiated by the defendant, and the officer suspected that the defendant would enlist his co-defendant in a plan to kill prospective trial witnesses. The Court found that the government's recording of the informant's conversation with Moulton was a "knowing exploitation" of "an opportunity to confront the accused without counsel being present." The Court held that this government act provided sufficient proof under *Henry* that the agent "must have known" that the informant was "likely to obtain incriminating statements" from the defendant in the absence of counsel. As in *Henry*, the Court ruled that "deliberate elicitation" could be found even though the officer had no specific intent to elicit information from the defendant about the charged crime. The officer is deemed to have intended the natural consequences of his planned activity. Both *Massiah* and *Henry* established the state's "affirmative obligation not to act in a manner that circumvents" the right to counsel; neither precedent turned on the identity of the actor who "initiated" the encounter between the informant and the defendant.

3. Use of a "Listening Post" Does Not Constitute Deliberate Elicitation

In *Kuhlmann v. Wilson*, 477 U.S. 436, 106 S.Ct. 2616, 91 L.Ed.2d 364 (1986), the Court held that the Government does not violate *Massiah* when a jailhouse informant makes no effort to "stimulate conversations" about the crimes with which an incarcerated defendant is charged, but merely listens to the defendant's incriminating statements. In these circumstances, there is no "elicitation" barred by the Sixth Amendment. In *Kuhlmann*, the defendant was arraigned for robbery and murder, and the government "planted" an informant in his cell to listen to his conversations. The defendant initiated a conversation where he admitted his presence at the robbery, but denied knowing the robbers. The informant responded by telling him that this explanation "didn't sound too good." Later the defendant changed the details of his story, and ultimately admitted guilt to the informant. The Court held that the informant's single remark did not suffice to change his "passive" posture, and that *Henry* was not violated. Therefore, the defendant's statements were held to be admissible, and his convictions for robbery and murder were affirmed.

a. Rationale

The Court reasoned that the primary concern of *Massiah* and its progeny is to prohibit attempts to *extract* information from defendants who have been formally charged, in the absence of counsel. Such activity constitutes an affirmative intrusion into the attorney-client relationship. However, when an informant takes no action, besides "merely listening," his activity may be "deliberate" but there is no "elicitation" of a confession, and no affirmative evasion of the defendant's right to the assistance of counsel. A Sixth Amendment violation does not occur where the government obtains a defendant's statements "by luck or happenstance" after the right to counsel has attached. Under *Henry*, the defendant must prove that "the police and their informant took some action" that was deliberately designed to *elicit* incriminating statements.

b. Applied to the Facts

On the facts of *Kuhlmann*, the Court found no Sixth Amendment violation. The informant asked no questions, and listened to the defendant's "spontaneous" and "unsolicited" remarks. The informant's one remark, reacting to the defendant's initial story, did not transform their interaction into a situation where the "action" of the informant was designed to elicit further incriminating remarks. *See also United States v. York*, 933 F.2d 1343 (7th Cir.1991) (informant did not elicit incriminating statements where he simply responded with neutral comments when incriminating topics were brought up by the defendant; informants are not required to reveal their status by refusing to participate in the natural flow of prison conversation).

c. Dissent

The three dissenters found the case to be "virtually indistinguish-able" from *Henry*, because the government "intentionally created a situation in which it was foreseeable" that the defendant "would make incriminating statements without the assistance of counsel." The dissenters concluded that the informant in *Kuhlmann* behaved like the one in Henry, because he "encouraged" the defendant to talk about the crime, by "conversing with him on the subject" over the course of several days. The informant even explicitly commented on the defendant's first exculpatory story, and told him that he had better come up with a better explanation.

4. Defining the Scope of the Government's Agency Relationship With an Informant

If a private individual obtains information from an indicted defendant, and then unilaterally refers it to the government, there is no Sixth Amendment violation. This is because there is no impermissible state action in obtaining the information. (See the analogous discussion of private searches in the section on the Fourth Amendment). However, if the private individual is acting as a state agent in obtaining information (such as the informant in *Henry*), then the agent's activity is attributable to the government. The Court in *Henry* and *Kuhlmann* did not describe the kind of government relationship with an informant that makes it "accountable" for the informant's acts. In both cases, no question concerning the informant's status arose, because both informants entered into express agreements with a government agent concerning their surveillance of the defendants.

Lower courts have found that an agency relationship may exist even when there is no express agreement with the informant. *See United States v. Johnson*, 196 F.Supp.2d 795 (N.D. Iowa 2002) where the court held that an informant acted as a "government agent" when he elicited incriminating statements from a murder defendant even though there was no express instruction to obtain information from the defendant. In *Johnson*, the government knew, given the informant's prior behavior, that he was likely to seek incriminating statements on the assumption that he would be rewarded; the government placed the defendant in a small cell with the informant, and took no action to limit the informant's contacts with the defendant. *Compare United States v. Watson*, 894 F.2d 1345 (D.C.Cir.1990) (no agency relationship existed even though informant was in regular contact with the DEA, because he was only a private "entrepreneur;"

therefore the fact that the informant was paid for his information *after* giving it does not indicate that he was acting as a state agent while obtaining the information).

D. Deliberate Elicitation and Continuing Investigations

In *Maine v. Moulton*, 474 U.S. 159, 106 S.Ct. 477, 88 L.Ed.2d 481 (1985), the Court rejected the government's claim that because its investigation concerned "new" crimes that the indicted defendant might be planning (i.e., killing witnesses to the charged crime), any statements that were obtained during such an investigation should be admissible in the trial for the crime with which he was originally charged. The Court found that *Massiah* prohibited the use of any statements that concerned the pending charges.

1. Rationale

The Court reasoned that it could not create an exception to the *Massiah* rule "whenever the police assert an alternative, legitimate reason for their surveillance" of an indicted defendant. Such an exception would invite police abuse in the form of "fabricated investigations" and create a risk of "evisceration" of *Massiah* rights. *Massiah* established a "sensible solution" for the problem of the government's need to continue to investigate "the suspected criminal activities" of indicted defendants. That solution was to allow the evidence gained in these investigations to be used at a subsequent trial on the crimes that were uncharged at the time the statements were made. Statements pertaining to pending charges, however, are inadmissible when they are obtained in violation of *Massiah*—even if the purpose of the investigation was to obtain information about uncharged crimes.

2. Deliberate Elicitation Found From Likely Consequences

The State in *Moulton* argued that there was no Sixth Amendment violation, because the informant was instructed to obtain information only about crimes for which Moulton had not yet been charged. Moulton was charged with theft and the state received a tip about his intent to kill a witness. Officers sent Colson, Moulton's co-defendant who had agreed to cooperate with the Government, to meet with Moulton and obtain information about the plan to kill witnesses. They instructed Colson to talk only about eliminating witnesses, and not about the underlying theft charges. In the course of the conversation about eliminating witnesses, Colson led Moulton into talking about their theft activities, and it was these statements that were offered at Moulton's theft trial.

The *Moulton* Court rejected the argument that deliberate elicitation could not be found because the officer instructed Colson to talk only about witnesses. The Court reasoned that the agents *should have known* that despite their instructions, a conversation between co-defendants about killing witnesses was likely to touch upon the underlying crime on which the witnesses were to testify. The Court noted that "direct proof of the State's knowledge will seldom be available," but that "proof that the State must have known that its agent was likely to obtain incriminating statements" suffices to establish a Sixth Amendment violation. Thus, as in *Henry,* the Court held that deliberate elicitation can be found even if there is no showing that officers affirmatively intended to obtain incriminating information; officers are deemed to intend the natural consequences of a plan that they have deliberately set into motion.

E. The Sixth Amendment Exclusionary Rule

The Supreme Court has not decided the constitutional status of the Sixth Amendment exclusionary rule, which operated to exclude the illegally obtained confessions in *Brewer, Henry,* and *Moulton.* This question is of some importance because if the Constitution requires the exclusion of evidence obtained in violation of the Sixth Amendment, then certain exceptions that have been applied to *Miranda*-defective confessions would not be applicable in the Sixth Amendment context unless the court decides to make the same exceptions to the Sixth Amendment rule as it did to the Fifth Amendment rule in *Dickerson.* For example, there might be no "public safety" exception to the Sixth Amendment; there might be no impeachment exception; and there might be no exception which would allow the fruits of Sixth Amendment violations to be admitted.

1. A Statement Obtained in Violation of a Prophylactic Rule May Be Used to Impeach a Defendant's Credibility at Trial

In *Michigan v. Harvey,* 494 U.S. 344, 110 S.Ct. 1176, 108 L.Ed.2d 293 (1990), the defendant invoked his right to counsel at arraignment, thereby triggering the protection of *Michigan v. Jackson,* which prohibits the police from initiating an interrogation of a defendant who has invoked his Sixth Amendment right to counsel. The police then violated *Jackson* by initiating an interview with Harvey, during which he received *Miranda* warnings, waived his rights, and made incriminating statements. Harvey's waiver may well have been knowing and voluntary, but his statements were nonetheless excluded from the case-in-chief because they were obtained in violation of the bright-line *Jackson* initiation requirement. But the Court held that while the *Jackson*-defective statements could not be used in the case-in-chief, they were nonetheless admissible to impeach the defendant when he testified at trial. The Court held that the *Jackson* rule was derived directly from *Edwards*, and represented only a transposition of the "prophylactic standards" of the *Miranda* doctrine into the Sixth Amendment context. Therefore, the rule permitting impeachment with *Miranda*-defective confessions should also be transposed from the same *Miranda* template.

a. **Constitutional Status of Sixth Amendment Exclusionary Rule Left Open**

The Court in *Harvey* did not address the defendant's argument that the police conduct in *Harvey* violated the "core values" of the Sixth Amendment, or his argument that such a violation would make his statements inadmissible for impeachment purposes. The record concerning the defendant's waiver was insufficient for the Court to make an independent determination whether it was knowing and voluntary. Thus the Court decided that it could not "consider the admissibility for impeachment purposes of a voluntary statement obtained in the absence of a knowing and voluntary waiver of the right to counsel."

2. **Does the Constitution Require Exclusion of a Confession Obtained in Violation of the Sixth Amendment?**

Harvey dealt with a prophylactic rule that was not itself required by the Sixth Amendment. Some lower courts have held that a confession actually obtained in violation of the Sixth Amendment cannot be used for impeachment purposes, because the Sixth Amendment's exclusionary rule is constitutionally based. *See, e.g., United States v. Brown*, 699 F.2d 585 (2d Cir.1983). In the view of these courts, the violation of the Sixth Amendment occurs when the incriminating information is admitted *at trial*. It is at that point that the right to counsel is effectively vitiated, because it is at that point that counsel's role in effectively defending the defendant is impaired. This is in contrast to the Fourth Amendment, where the violation occurs at the time of the illegal search, not at the time the evidence is admitted at trial.

Other courts have, consistent with this analysis, required exclusion of the fruits of a Sixth Amendment-defective confession at trial. *See, e.g., United States v. Kimball*, 884 F.2d 1274 (9th Cir.1989).

VII

Constitutional Limits on Identification Evidence

■ ANALYSIS

I.   Introduction

This chapter examines the dangers associated with identification evidence, and the safeguards that the Supreme Court has fashioned to assure that witness error will not irreparably taint criminal litigation. Although both courts and commentators believe eyewitness testimony to be frequently questionable and susceptible to "post-experience suggestion," juries often find the probative value of such evidence at trial to be extremely high. In order to protect a suspect's right to a fair trial, the Supreme Court has imposed constitutional limitations on admissibility of identifications by witnesses.

II.   Post–Charge Identifications

The Court decided in 1967 that identification after indictment, or an equivalent formal proceeding, triggers a defendant's Sixth Amendment right to counsel. *United States v. Wade*, 388 U.S. 218, 87 S.Ct. 1926, 18 L.Ed.2d 1149 (1967); *Gilbert v. California*, 388 U.S. 263, 87 S.Ct. 1951, 18 L.Ed.2d 1178 (1967).

A.   The *Wade–Gilbert* Rule

In *Wade*, the defendant was identified in court by two bank employees present during a bank robbery. After Wade had been indicted, and seven months after the robbery, the witnesses picked him out in a line-up. Wade did not have the assistance of counsel at the line-up. The Court found that a post-indictment line-up conducted in the absence of a lawyer, and without a valid waiver, violated the defendant's Sixth Amendment right to counsel.

1.   Critical Pre-trial Stage

Although the post-indictment line-up in *Wade* took place before trial, the Court held that in light of modern criminal procedures, the Sixth Amendment right to counsel applies to *critical pre-trial stages* as well as at trial. "Critical stage" analysis developed in earlier cases such as *Massiah v. United States*, 377 U.S. 201, 84 S.Ct. 1199, 12 L.Ed.2d 246 (1964), where the suspect, after being arraigned and released on bail, was surreptitiously monitored in conversation with an accomplice who was working with the police. The *Massiah* Court held that the Sixth Amendment prohibited deliberate elicitation of incriminating statements from a charged defendant.

In both *Massiah* and *Wade*, the Court was concerned that a defendant's right to a fair trial would be compromised if the prosecution could bring forward evidence obtained absent counsel. The Court reasoned that the right to counsel at trial means the right to effective counsel. In order to guarantee that counsel is effective at trial, the Court decided that counsel must be present at these critical pre-trial stages to avoid any prejudice arising from particular confrontations during the prosecution's gathering of evidence. Although the Government characterized the line-up as a "mere preparatory step" in the gathering of evidence—similar to analyzing blood and clothing found at a crime scene—the Court found identification evidence to be "peculiarly riddled with innumerable dangers and variable factors which might seriously, even crucially, derogate from a fair trial." The Court noted that "once a witness has picked out the accused at [a] lineup, he is not likely to go back on his word later on, so that in practice the issue of identity may * * * for all practical purposes be determined there and then, before the trial."

2. Observer Status of Counsel

While the *Wade* Court held that the presence of defense counsel was required at post-indictment line-ups, it was unspecific about the role that counsel would play at the line-up. Subsequent cases, however, have held that counsel is to be present in a "passive" observer status. Although "passive," the role of counsel is considered critical in reconstructing the line-up at trial. The defendant's presence and observations during this process are only minimally helpful in determining whether prejudicial or suggestive procedures were used during his line-up. The defendant is undergoing an emotionally charged experience, possibly behind bright lights or a one-way mirror, without any schooling in the detection of suggestive influences by the police. Furthermore, the jury is apt to regard the defendant's statements about the pre-trial line-up as self-serving, if, indeed, the defendant chooses to take the stand and possibly open himself up to cross-examination regarding prior convictions. The attorney, on the other hand, is generally more skilled in the detection of suggestive influences, both through experience and familiarity with case law. The attorney observes the questioning of witnesses by police during the line-up. Notes and observations of the proceedings allow the attorney to *effectively cross-examine the identification witnesses* at trial, and to demonstrate any prejudicial or suggestive conduct, intentional or not, present during the pre-trial line-up.

3. Substitute Counsel

The *Wade* majority mentioned in dictum that substitute counsel could satisfy the requirement of counsel's presence at the line-up. However, counsel is not a sufficient "substitute" if he is at the line-up representing the defendant's accomplice. *See United States ex rel. Burton v. Cuyler,* 439 F.Supp. 1173 (E.D.Pa.1977).

B. "Per Se" Exclusion

In *Wade,* the prosecutor had not elicited the pretrial identification in the Government's case-in-chief. It was brought out by defense counsel. Thus, the *Wade* decision only involved the question of whether the *in-court* identification upon which the Government relied was tainted by the line-up. In *Gilbert,* a companion case, the Court faced the question of whether a post-indictment, pre-trial identification in the absence of counsel could be used as evidence in the prosecution's case-in-chief. The Court adopted a per se rule of exclusion as a remedy for post-indictment out-of-court identifications that take place absent counsel: *exclusion was required even if the state could show that the identification was in fact reliable.* The Court, concerned about the consequences at trial of improper identification procedures, held that only the extreme sanction of per se exclusion would effectively deter police violations of the defendant's constitutional rights during a critical pre-trial stage. As a result, this exclusion applies even if the line-up was conducted so scrupulously that counsel's presence would be (theoretically) meaningless. The evidence from such line-ups is excluded whether or not there is a question of improper police procedure. *See Frisco v. Blackburn,* 782 F.2d 1353 (5th Cir.1986) (if counsel was not present at a line-up conducted after a preliminary hearing, then evidence of the identification is automatically excluded and "the state is not entitled to an opportunity to show that the testimony had an independent source").

1. In–Court Identification and Independent Source

Although evidence regarding the out-of-court identification at a line-up conducted without counsel is per se excluded from trial, it does not automatically follow that an *in-court identification* by the same witness is excluded as well. The *Wade* Court held that the in-court identification would be excluded if it was *tainted* by the previous, illegal line-up—i.e., if it is the fruit of the poisonous tree. The Court reasoned that the mere exclusion of an illegal pre-trial identification would be an insufficient protection of the right to counsel if the prosecution could merely call the witness to the stand to make an in-court identification that was derived from the illegal line-up.

On the other hand, it is not *necessarily* true that the in-court identification stems directly from the excluded out-of-court line-up. The Court held that the in-court identification would be admissible if it stemmed not from exploitation of the out-of-court identification but, instead, from an independent source "sufficiently distinguishable to be purged of the primary taint." Thus, the prosecution must prove that, under the totality of circumstances, the in-court identification was not a result of the improper pre-trial line-up. *See McKinon v. Wainwright*, 705 F.2d 419 (11th Cir.1983) (where the illegal pre-trial identification is not itself admitted at trial, "the at-trial identification constitutes reversible error only if it is based on, influenced by, or tainted from the earlier unconstitutional identification").

2. Relevant Factors

Certain factors are relevant in determining whether an in-court identification is based on a source independent from an illegal pre-trial identification. The independent source would of course be the witness' view of the suspect at the time of the crime, or at some time other than during the illegal line-up. The question, then, is whether the witness' in-court identification stems from a different opportunity to view the suspect, or rather whether it stems from the illegal line-up. Some relevant factors considered under the Court's test are: the extent of the *prior opportunity to view* the defendant other than at the illegal line-up; discrepancies, if any, between the witness' description of the suspect before the line-up was conducted, and the defendant's actual appearance; the *certainty* of the witness' identification at the line-up or, conversely, the witness' failure to identify the defendant with certainty; the *lapse of time* between the initial opportunity to view the perpetrator and the line-up identification; and the *degree of suggestiveness* employed in the tainted pre-trial line-up.

Example: Suppose that a kidnap victim escapes from his captor after three months in captivity. The captor is placed in a line-up, where the victim identifies him certainly and immediately as the perpetrator. However, defense counsel was not present at the line-up. This means that the pre-trial identification is excluded. However, the victim may permissibly identify the captor at trial, because the identification stems from a source clearly independent from the illegal line-up; the identification is based on the long-term, close-quarters captivity. *See McKinon v. Wainwright*, 705 F.2d 419 (11th Cir.1983) (at-trial identification admissible where the witness had known the defendant long before the crime and had spent several hours with him on the day of the crime).

3. Dissent

The judges dissenting in both *Wade* and *Gilbert* were concerned with the far-reaching effects of such a broad prophylactic rule of *per se* exclusion. They contended that the risk of unreliable identifications could be adequately regulated by allowing the defense to introduce the facts and circumstances of pre-trial line-ups in order to impeach the credibility of in-court identifications.

III.   Pre–Charge Identifications

The line-ups that took place in *Wade* and *Gilbert* were post-indictment procedures. Although the Court did not emphasize the timing of the line-ups in these cases, in subsequent cases it refused to extend the *Wade–Gilbert* exclusionary rule to counsel-free out-of-court identifications that occur prior to indictment or formal charge. The Court drew the line between pre- and post-formal charges in *Kirby v. Illinois,* 406 U.S. 682, 92 S.Ct. 1877, 32 L.Ed.2d 411 (1972).

A.   *Kirby*

In *Kirby,* a witness identified two suspects at a police station show-up. The show-up occurred before the suspects had been formally charged with the crime; counsel was not present during the identification. The witness then testified at trial, referring to the identification he made at the station house show-up, and also identifying the defendants in court. The Court held the testimony admissible, declaring that the Sixth Amendment right to counsel applied only to "criminal prosecutions" and thus was triggered only after formal adversarial proceedings had begun against the defendant.

1.   Rationale

The Court stated that it would not transform a "routine police investigation" into an "absolute constitutional guarantee," reasoning that the "initiation of judicial criminal proceedings is far from a mere formalism." It is only when charges have been brought that the government has committed itself to prosecute, and only then that the adverse positions of government and defendant have solidified. Since the Sixth Amendment by its terms applies only to "criminal prosecutions," it follows that the Sixth Amendment right to counsel set forth in *Wade* and *Gilbert* could only arise after a criminal prosecution (as opposed to a criminal investigation) has begun.

2.   Adversarial Proceedings

The Court in *Kirby* distinguished investigatorial proceedings from adversarial proceedings. Adversarial proceedings are begun when the

state formally accuses the defendant of having committed the crime. This is generally done through *indictment, arraignment, preliminary hearing,* or *information.* Thus, if a line-up is conducted after these events, the *Wade* right to counsel will apply. For criminal proceedings brought by the states, the Court looks to state law to determine when criminal proceedings have commenced. *See Meadows v. Kuhlmann,* 812 F.2d 72 (2d Cir.1987) (line-up held after filing of formal complaint in New York is governed by *Wade* rule).

3. Dissent

The dissenting judges in *Kirby* argued that the "initiation of adversary judicial criminal proceedings" was "completely irrelevant" to the question of whether a defendant would be afforded effective assistance of counsel at his trial. The impact of an uncounseled line-up is the same at trial, whether it is conducted before or after indictment.

B. Application of the Sixth Amendment Right to Counsel After *Kirby*

The *Kirby* Court was concerned about extending the *Wade* rationale into "routine police investigations." Many identifications are made on the street only minutes after the crime. Application of the *Wade* rule in these circumstances would obviously create problems; the delay resulting from waiting for counsel to arrive may perversely decrease the reliability of the identification due to the fading memory of witnesses.

The vast majority of identification procedures are conducted before a formal charge has been filed. Indeed, most are conducted to obtain evidence with which to bring a formal charge. Thus, the *Kirby* decision significantly reduced the number of cases to which *Wade's* exclusionary rule would apply.

1. Delaying Indictment

Although the *Kirby* Court stated that the right to counsel would apply only after formal proceedings had been instigated against the defendant, courts have held that if adversary proceedings, such as the filing of an indictment, are *"deliberately delayed"* in order to evade the *Wade* rule, the resulting uncounseled identification will be invalidated. *See United States ex rel. Burbank v. Warden,* 535 F.2d 361 (7th Cir.1976). However, it is quite difficult to prove that an indictment was deliberately delayed. *See United States ex rel. Hall v. Lane,* 804 F.2d 79 (7th Cir.1986) (no evidence that delay was caused by bad faith).

2. Charge–Specific

Even after a defendant has been formerly charged, the *Wade* exclusionary rule only applies to line-ups conducted to obtain evidence as to the crime charged. It is permissible to hold a counsel-free line-up for an indicted defendant as to a different crime, since being indicted on one charge is not a "criminal prosecution" as to any other. *See, e.g., United States ex rel. Hall v. Lane*, 804 F.2d 79 (7th Cir.1986) ("The fact that appellant was in custody for an unrelated offense at the time of the line-up has no bearing on [the right to counsel] since the government had not committed itself to prosecute appellant for this offense at the time of the line-up.")

C. Photographic Identification

In *United States v. Ash*, 413 U.S. 300, 93 S.Ct. 2568, 37 L.Ed.2d 619 (1973), the Court further restricted the *Wade* exclusionary rule, and held that a defendant has *no right to counsel at a photographic identification* conducted either pre- or post-indictment.

1. Rationale

The Court distinguished *Wade* by noting that photo displays do not require the actual presence of the defendant, and concluded that the presence of counsel was unnecessary to protect the defendant from an adversarial confrontation. The Court saw photo displays as a mere preparatory step in the gathering of evidence where the defense counsel had an "equal ability * * * to seek and interview witnesses himself." Justice Stewart, concurring in the result, concluded that "a photographic identification is quite different from a line-up, for there are substantially fewer possibilities of impermissible suggestion when photographs are used, and those unfair influences can be readily reconstructed at trial."

2. Dissent

The three dissenting judges argued that the right to counsel issue should not turn on whether photographic identifications included the corporeal presence of the defendant but, instead, on whether exclusion of defense counsel at such displays could result in a denial of effective assistance of counsel for the defendant at trial. The dissenters believed that the same "inherent suggestibility" of pre-trial line-ups existed in photographic identifications, and as both the defendant and defense counsel were not present during the displays, there was even "less likelihood that irregularities in the procedure [would] ever come to light."

3. Video Identifications

The lower courts have held that *Ash* and not *Wade* applies to post-charge video identifications. They reason that the identification of a suspect on a video tape is more like a photo display than an actual line-up, and that, as in *Ash,* the defendant is not physically present, so there is no adversarial confrontation requiring counsel's assistance. *See United States v. Amrine,* 724 F.2d 84 (8th Cir.1983). *See also United States v. Barker,* 988 F.2d 77 (9th Cir.1993) (counsel not required where a witness identifies the indicted defendant from a photograph of a line-up).

IV. Due Process Limitations on Suggestive Identifications

The Court in *Kirby* took pains to note that, in holding that the right to counsel was inapplicable to pre-charge identifications, it had not freed such identifications from all constitutional scrutiny. Where the Sixth Amendment right to counsel does not apply to an identification procedure, the identification must still satisfy the requirements of the Due Process Clause. The Court has held that the Due Process Clause requires exclusion of evidence of an identification if *police suggestiveness created a substantial risk of mistaken identification. See Stovall v. Denno,* 388 U.S. 293, 87 S.Ct. 1967, 18 L.Ed.2d 1199 (1967) (applying due process standards to an identification not controlled by *Wade*). The Court has reasoned that it is fundamentally unfair to convict a defendant on the basis of unreliable identifications that are manufactured by police suggestiveness.

A. Two–Factor Test

The Court has stressed that the defendant has the burden of proving a due process violation. This burden is satisfied only if the defendant can prove two independent factors. First, the defendant must show that the identification procedure was *impermissibly suggestive.* If so, the defendant must then show the identification was *unreliable* under the *totality of circumstances. See Foster v. California,* 394 U.S. 440, 89 S.Ct. 1127, 22 L.Ed.2d 402 (1969) (one-on-one show-up combined with unduly suggestive line-ups render Government's identification procedures so impermissibly suggestive as to create a substantial risk of mistaken identification; witness was uncertain about the identification and only got a fleeting glimpse of the perpetrator at the time of the crime).

1. Exigent Circumstances

The Supreme Court has held that exigent or extraordinary circumstances allow for "permissible" suggestiveness. In other words, certain circumstances could make suggestive police procedures necessary and, thus, permissible. One example of such a case is *Stovall v. Denno,* 388 U.S. 293, 87 S.Ct. 1967, 18 L.Ed.2d 1199 (1967). In *Stovall,* a vicious attack upon a married couple resulted in the death of the husband, and the hospitalization of the wife who had been stabbed eleven times. Due to the witness' serious injuries and proposed surgical procedure, a suspect in the attack was brought to the hospital for a one-on-one show-up. The Court held that the show-up procedure, while suggestive, was permissible due to the near-death condition of the witness. Indeed, the Court called attention to the flip-side of such suggestive confrontations by pointing out that the witness "was the only person in the world who could possibly exonerate Stovall."

a.   Rarely Applied Exception

Although the Government occasionally argues that there is a legitimate excuse for employing a suggestive procedure, the courts are usually not inclined to find the circumstances so exigent as to allow the state to conduct a suggestive identification. *See Neil v. Biggers,* 409 U.S. 188, 93 S.Ct. 375, 34 L.Ed.2d 401 (1972) (argument that one-on-one show-up was necessary due to defendant's "unusual physical description" was rejected; but evidence ultimately found admissible as reliable under the totality of circumstances).

b.   Street Identifications

Impromptu identification procedures held immediately after a crime (often termed "street identifications"), are considered necessary even if suggestive, and thus not violative of due process. As the court stated in *United States v. Bautista*, 23 F.3d 726 (2d Cir.1994) (a case in which the suspects were presented in handcuffs to be identified by an informant immediately after a drug raid): "A prompt showing of a detained suspect at the scene of an arrest has a very valid function: to prevent the mistaken arrest of innocent persons." *See also United States v. Martinez*, 462 F.3d 903 (8th Cir.2006) (identification of handcuffed defendant at scene of bank robbery admitted where witness had adequate opportunity to observe and gave a prior identification of the robber, and the show-up was conducted a short time after the robbery).

2.   The Linchpin of Reliability

Even if the police have employed unnecessarily suggestive police procedures, it does not necessarily follow that the resulting identification is unreliable. The identification may be reliable *despite* police suggestiveness. *See Manson v. Brathwaite*, 432 U.S. 98, 97 S.Ct. 2243, 53 L.Ed.2d 140 (1977) (identification of a photo, without an array of similar photos, was impermissibly suggestive and yet the identification was reliable because the witness would have made the same identification even if there had been an array). Thus, *suggestive* procedures—such as one-on-one show-ups, distinctively standing out in line-ups (i.e., tallest, heaviest, only black defendant in line), and individual or repetitive pictures—are considered in light of all the circumstances in determining whether an independent source exists for a reliable identification.

B. Relevant Factors in Determining the Reliability of an Identification

Where impermissibly suggestive police practices have been used, an identification will still be admissible if it would have been made *despite* the police suggestiveness. In *Manson v. Brathwaite,* the Court rejected the argument that an identification should be automatically excluded whenever the police have employed impermissibly suggestive procedures. An identification is admitted despite police suggestiveness where the witness had a "picture" of the perpetrator in his mind before the suggestive identification, and this picture was so firmly established that it was unaffected by the attempts of the police to put their own "picture" of the perpetrator in the witness' mind, through the use of suggestive tactics. In other words, if the witness has an *independent source* for the identification outside the suggestive identification, then the police have not caused an unreliable identification, and exclusion is unwarranted. According to the *Manson* court, in cases where the identification is reliable despite an unnecessarily suggestive identification procedure, exclusion of the identification is "a Draconian sanction."

Thus, the test for whether an identification is admissible despite police suggestiveness is the same as the test applied for whether an in-court identification is admissible despite the fact that the police have conducted a post-indictment line-up without the presence of counsel. In either case, if *the illegal police activity had no effect on the proffered identification, then the identification is admissible.* The factors used to determine whether impermissible suggestiveness affected the identification were set forth by the Court in *Manson:*

1. Degree of Police Suggestiveness

The more suggestive the police procedure, the more likely it is to have an effect on the resulting identification. For example, a one-on-one show-up is much more likely to have an effect on the witness than is a photo array where the photos may be dissimilar, but where the witness is at least presented with more than a single option.

2. Opportunity to View

If the witness had a substantial opportunity to view the suspect before the identification—for example by getting a good look at the perpetrator when the crime was committed—then the witness will have a stronger picture in his mind; and this picture will be less subject to change through police suggestiveness than would a vague picture obtained with a poor opportunity to view the suspect. For example, if the witness was the store clerk in a robbery, and looked straight at the robber for five minutes in a well-lighted store, then the witness' identification is less likely to be affected by police suggestiveness than if the witness had been outside the store and got a fleeting glimpse of the robber from 40 feet away in an unlighted parking lot.

3. Degree of Attention

The opportunity to view the perpetrator before the identification means little if the witness made little of that opportunity because her attention was focused on other matters. If the witness paid little attention to the perpetrator, then the picture of that person in her mind is a vague one, and thus susceptible to the effects of police suggestiveness.

4. Accuracy of the Description

Ordinarily, a witness describes the perpetrator before an identification is made. The correlation between the description and the ultimate identification, or the lack thereof, can tend to show the effect of police suggestiveness on the identification. For example, if the witness describes the perpetrator as six feet tall, 200 pounds, and then picks a person 5'6" and 150 pounds after a one-on-one show-up, there is strong evidence that the witness was affected by police suggestiveness. Conversely, if the witness describes a unique physical characteristic before the identification (e.g., a facial scar), and the witness picks a person with that characteristic in a one-on-one show-up, then there is strong evidence that the police suggestiveness had no effect on the identification. Finally, if the pre-identification description is overly general (e.g., a tall man with light complexion), then there is ample room for the police to fill in the details of that picture through police suggestiveness; but this is not as strong a possibility if the pre-identification description of the witness is finely detailed.

5. Level of Certainty

The Supreme Court has indulged the presumption that the more certain the witness is when making the identification, the more likely it is that the identification proceeds from a source independent from the police suggestiveness. *Compare Manson supra* (witness' "positive assurance" that the photo was that of the perpetrator indicated that the identification was unaffected by police suggestiveness), *with Foster v. California*, 394 U.S. 440, 89 S.Ct. 1127, 22 L.Ed.2d 402 (1969) (Due Process violated where the witness remained uncertain that the defendant was the perpetrator even after a one-on-one show-up). Some courts are not as confident that the witness' certainty is an indication that the identification is unaffected by police suggestiveness. *See Rodriguez v. Young*, 906 F.2d 1153 (7th Cir.1990) (court views reliability of "certainty" factor with skepticism as it might simply reflect the "corrupting effect of the suggestive procedures themselves").

6. The Time Between the Pre-identification Opportunity to View and the Identification Itself

It is well accepted that memory of a person or event fades over time. Thus, the witness' mental "picture" of the perpetrator becomes more vague and fuzzy as time passes—and more susceptible to suggestive police influences. Therefore, an identification made shortly after the witness' original opportunity to view the suspect is more likely to be free from the taint of police suggestiveness than an identification made a long time thereafter. *See Manson supra* (photographic identification made two days after the crime is unaffected by police suggestiveness: "We do not have here the passage of weeks or months between the crime and the viewing of the photograph.")

7. Character of the Witness

If the witness is the type of person who is easily led, or who has a need under the circumstances to make an identification regardless of whether it is correct, then it is more likely that police suggestiveness will have an effect on that witness. *See United States v. de Jesus–Rios*, 990 F.2d 672 (1st Cir.1993) (identification unreliable where the witness was told that his boat would be released from impound if he identified the person involved in the smuggling of drugs on the boat). Conversely, if the witness is the type of person who would not be affected by police suggestiveness, a due process violation is less likely to be found. Thus, in *United States ex rel. Hudson v. Brierton*, 699 F.2d 917 (7th Cir.1983), a one-on-one show-up did not cause a mistaken identification, where the witness had chased fleeing armed bank robbers in his car for several miles. The court found it extremely unlikely that the witness "would be affected by the suggestive identification procedure in light of his serious attitude and diligence with respect to the episode."

C. Totality of the Circumstances

The determinative question under the Due Process Clause is whether unnecessary police suggestiveness has created a substantial risk of mistaken identification. Thus, as the Court in *Manson* stated, "reliability is the linchpin in determining the admissibility of identification testimony." Reliability of the identification is determined by a totality of circumstances test, in which all of the above factors are relevant, and none are dispositive.

In *Neil v. Biggers,* 409 U.S. 188, 93 S.Ct. 375, 34 L.Ed.2d 401 (1972), the victim of a rape identified the defendant in a one-on-one show-up conducted more than seven months after the crime. Obviously, the time between the crime and the identification, as well as the inherently suggestive nature of a one-on-one show-up, were factors that cut against the reliability of the identification. But the Court concluded that "the identification was reliable even though the confrontation procedure was suggestive." The Court relied on the following factors: the witness had refused to identify others who had been placed before her in show-ups and line-ups, which indicated that she was not very susceptible to police suggestiveness; she was with her assailant for a half-hour at the time of the crime; she faced him directly and intimately at that time in a well-lighted environment; she was "no casual observer" but rather quite attendant to the circumstances; her description of the perpetrator before the identification "might not have satisfied Proust but was more than ordinarily thorough;" she had no doubt at the time of identification that the defendant was the perpetrator; and the problem of faded memory was alleviated to some extent by the fact that she stated that there was something about the perpetrator's face that she could never forget.

1. If Pre-trial Identification Is Excluded, Trial Identification Is Excluded as Well

If the pre-trial identification is unreliable because it is caused by police suggestiveness, then the Due Process Clause requires that it be excluded from trial. *Foster v. California, supra.* It also follows that the taint of police suggestiveness extends to any at-trial identification. If the prior identification was caused by police suggestiveness, there can by definition be no independent legal source for the in-court identification. If there were such a source, it would have served to admit the pre-trial identification as well. *See Dispensa v. Lynaugh,* 847 F.2d 211 (5th Cir.1988) (identification caused by police suggestiveness requires exclusion of both pre-trial and at-trial identifications).

2. Trial Identification Governed by the Same Due Process Standard

Identifications at trial are subject to the same concerns about unreliability as pretrial identifications. Trial identifications are tantamount to one-on-one showups. Courts have therefore held that the Due Process Clause operates to exclude unreliable in-court identifications. What this means is that the witness must have an independent source upon which the in-court identification is based. Thus, the same considerations that bear upon admission of a pre-trial identification under *Manson* will also determine the admissibility of an in-court identification. *See United States v. Hill*, 967 F.2d 226 (6th Cir.1992) (holding that the *Manson* analysis applies to in-court identifications "for the same reasons that the analysis applies to impermissibly suggestive pre-trial identifications," but that the in-court identification was admissible in this robbery trial because the witness viewed the perpetrator head-on, from a few feet away, during the robbery).

D. Examples of Due Process Identification Cases

1. Identifications Excluded

It is the rare instance where an identification will be excluded on the ground that it is tainted by impermissible police suggestiveness. One example is *Foster v. California, supra.* In *Foster,* an eyewitness was shown a three person line-up where the defendant, standing in the middle and the only person dressed similarly to the alleged perpetrator, was approximately half a foot taller than the two other men. The witness was unable to positively identify the defendant. Foster was then brought into an office for a one-on-one show-up with the witness, who still could not make a positive identification. One week later, the witness was brought in for a second line-up where Foster was the only suspect that remained from the previous week. At this point, the witness positively identified Foster. At trial, the witness testified to his pre-trial identification and also made an in-court identification. However, the Supreme Court found that the "suggestive elements in this identification procedure made it all but inevitable that [the witness] would identify petitioner whether or not he was in fact the man," and that the procedure "so undermined the reliability of the eyewitness identification as to violate due process."

Another rare instance of due process exclusion is *United States v. Eltayib*, 88 F.3d 157 (2d Cir.1996). An informant identified Eltayib as one of the persons loading cocaine from one boat to another. The witness was a passenger on the receiving boat. The witness was hit in the head with a large package of cocaine thrown from the other boat, and was knocked to the ground. When he staggered up, somewhat dizzy, he saw a man he described only as having "bushy-type afro hair." He was shown a photo array; the defendant's picture was included with seven others, but the other pictures were cropped to make it appear that their hair was short rather than bushy; only the defendant's picture was a full head shot. The court held that the police suggestiveness caused an unreliable identification. It noted the following factors: 1. The level of suggestiveness was high, given the way that the officers cropped the other photos in the array; 2. The witness' opportunity to view was limited, since he "stood on the deck of a bobbing ship in the middle of the night, nervous, and possibly dazed" after being hit with the flying cargo; 3. The witness' description of the perpetrator dealt only with his hair; 4. The witness admitted that he was not paying really close attention to the man in the other boat; and 5. The fact that the witness was certain when he made the identification would actually tend to prove untrustworthiness, "given the suggestive nature of the array."

2. Identifications Found Reliable Under the Totality of Circumstances

United States ex rel. Hudson v. Brierton, 699 F.2d 917 (7th Cir.1983), provides a typical approach to admitting identification testimony under the Due Process Clause. In *Hudson*, a witness engaged armed bank robbers in a high speed automobile chase, at one point coming within about half a foot of the robbers' car. Although the witness eventually lost the robbers, he was subsequently called down to the police station and identified the defendant, who was handcuffed and locked in a jail cell. In assessing the reliability of this identification, the court balanced factors such as the witness' close proximity to the robbers' car versus the distraction of being fired upon at close range while speeding along a highway. While noting the highly suggestive identification procedure, the court concluded that the character of the witness was such as to make it extremely unlikely he "would be affected * * * in light of his serious attitude and diligence with respect to the episode." Like the witness in *Biggers*, the witness in *Hudson* had demonstrated that he was not the type of person to be affected by police suggestiveness. *See also United States v. Zolicoffer*, 92 F.3d 512 (7th Cir.1996) (driver who chased fleeing bank robbers got a close enough look at them to have an independent source for making an identification; his description was accurate, he was paying close attention, and he was a professional photographer and thus "likely to be particularly aware of visual details").

VIII

The Right to Counsel

■ ANALYSIS

I. The Basic Right to Counsel

The Sixth Amendment provides that "[i]n all criminal prosecutions, the accused shall enjoy the right * * * to have the Assistance of Counsel for his defence." The Sixth Amendment applies directly to the Federal Government, and applies to the states through the Fourteenth Amendment. *See Gideon v. Wainwright,* 372 U.S. 335, 83 S.Ct. 792, 9 L.Ed.2d 799 (1963). The right to counsel includes not only the right to retain one's counsel of choice if one can afford it, but also the right to have the state appoint counsel if one cannot afford it.

A. The Right to Retained Counsel of Choice

The intent of the Sixth Amendment's Framers was to ensure that criminal defendants could be represented at trial by their retained counsel. Under English law, attorneys were prohibited from appearing on behalf of defendants in felony cases. The Sixth Amendment reversed this rule, and made counsel's assistance available to all who could afford to hire a lawyer.

1. Qualified Right

The Court recognizes a Sixth Amendment right to retained counsel of choice, but holds that it must sometimes yield to overriding state interests. One such interest is the state's use of forfeiture statutes to restrain a defendant from spending potentially forfeitable assets on counsel. *Caplin & Drysdale, Chartered v. United States,* 491 U.S. 617, 109 S.Ct. 2646, 105 L.Ed.2d 528 (1989) (upholding federal forfeiture statute against Sixth Amendment attack). The Court in *Caplin* held that the forfeiture provision was constitutional, even though it might render a client destitute and thus without funds to pay his counsel of choice. The right to retained counsel of choice is a qualified right, and one major qualification is that it is dependent on the ability to pay. The Court held that a defendant had no right to pay counsel with assets that were the forfeitable fruits of illegal activity.

Another interest that can override the qualified right to chosen counsel is the prosecutor's right to object to defendant's use of a counsel who has potential conflicts of interest. *Wheat v. United States,* 486 U.S. 153, 108 S.Ct. 1692, 100 L.Ed.2d 140 (1988) (upholding trial judge's discretion to disallow representation in such cases, even if the defendant wants to proceed with conflict-laden retained counsel of choice).

2. Violation of Right to Counsel of Choice Never Harmless

In *United States v. Gonzales–Lopez,* 548 U.S. 140, 126 S.Ct. 2557, 165 L.Ed.2d 409 (2006), the defendant argued that he was denied his right to counsel of his choice. The government conceded that the defendant was denied this right but argued that his conviction should not be reversed because he could not show that he was prejudiced by the actual representation he received. In other words, according to the government, the error was harmless. However, the Supreme Court held that once the denial of defendant's right to chosen counsel was established, the violation of defendant's right to counsel was complete and no showing of prejudice was required. Further, according to the Court, given the disparities in defense attorneys' approaches and strategies in representing defendants, the consequences of the denial of defendant's right to counsel of choice were not quantifiable and harmless-error analysis in such a context would constitute pure speculation.

B. The Right to Appointed Counsel for Indigent Defendants

Indigent defendants have the right to appointed counsel in *all Federal prosecutions. Johnson v. Zerbst*, 304 U.S. 458, 58 S.Ct. 1019, 82 L.Ed. 1461 (1938). Indigent defendants also have the right to appointed counsel in all *state felony* prosecutions. *Gideon v. Wainwright*, 372 U.S. 335, 83 S.Ct. 792, 9 L.Ed.2d 799 (1963). In *misdemeanor* or petty offense cases, counsel must be provided only if the defendant receives an actual *jail sentence. See Argersinger v. Hamlin*, 407 U.S. 25, 92 S.Ct. 2006, 32 L.Ed.2d 530 (1972) (extending the right to counsel to these defendants) and *Scott v. Illinois*, 440 U.S. 367, 99 S.Ct. 1158, 59 L.Ed.2d 383 (1979) (limiting the right to these defendants). The defendants who are thus excluded from Sixth Amendment protection include those who are charged with a minor crime for which jail is not an "authorized" penalty, and those charged with a minor crime for which jail is authorized but who receive only a fine as the actual penalty. However, a defendant who has not been afforded the right to counsel may not be sentenced to a term of incarceration even if the sentence is immediately suspended and he is placed on probation. *Alabama v. Shelton*, 535 U.S. 654, 122 S.Ct. 1764, 152 L.Ed.2d 888 (2002).

1. The Definition of "Indigency"

The Court has not prescribed a constitutional standard for indigency. It has left the definition to the state and Federal courts. These courts base their decisions to appoint counsel on indigency standards that vary among jurisdictions.

2. No Constitutional Right to Appointed Counsel of Choice

The Court allows state and Federal courts to decide whether to take the defendant's preferred choice of counsel into account when making appointments. Trial judges have broad discretion in this area, and a defendant's request for particular counsel may be rejected without inquiring into the merits of the request. The Supreme Court rejects the idea that a defendant has a Sixth Amendment right to a "meaningful attorney-client relationship" with appointed counsel. *See Morris v. Slappy,* 461 U.S. 1, 103 S.Ct. 1610, 75 L.Ed.2d 610 (1983) (upholding trial judge's refusal to grant a continuance which would have allowed original counsel to represent defendant at trial instead of appointed replacement).

3. The Definition of a "Criminal Prosecution" Where Counsel Rights Apply

The Court has adopted a two-part test for identifying those events that are part of a "criminal prosecution" where counsel's assistance is needed. First, the event must occur after "adversarial judicial proceedings" have begun, and second, the event must be a "critical stage" in the trial process.

a. When "Adversarial Judicial Proceedings" Begin

The formal commencement of a criminal prosecution is usually marked by the appearance of a prosecutor and a judge. A prosecutor may either file a charging document (a complaint or information) in court, or file a grand jury's indictment in court. *Massiah v. United States,* 377 U.S. 201, 84 S.Ct. 1199, 12 L.Ed.2d 246 (1964). Or, a defendant may be brought to court for arraignment or a first appearance before a judicial officer. *Brewer v. Williams,* 430 U.S. 387, 97 S.Ct. 1232, 51 L.Ed.2d 424 (1977). An event must occur at or after the commencement of adversarial proceedings in order to be part of a criminal prosecution. *Compare United States v. Wade,* 388 U.S. 218, 87 S.Ct. 1926, 18 L.Ed.2d 1149 (1967) (Sixth Amendment right to counsel attaches at post-indictment lineup), *with Kirby v. Illinois,* 406 U.S. 682, 92 S.Ct. 1877, 32 L.Ed.2d 411 (1972) (Sixth Amendment does not attach at pre-indictment lineup).

However, in *Rothgery v. Gillespie County, Texas,* ___ U.S. ___, 128 S.Ct. 2578, 171 L.Ed.2d 366 (2008), the Court held that the adversary proceedings that trigger the attachment of the Sixth Amendment right to counsel do not require the involvement of the prosecutor (as distinct from a police officer). The right attaches at the initial appearance before a magistrate judge, where the defendant learns of the charges against him and his liberty is subject to restriction, even if the prosecutor is not yet involved in the process.

b. The Definition of "Critical Stage"

A proceeding qualifies as a critical stage if it is a trial-like event, where an accused is confronted by "the procedural system" or the prosecutor, or both, in a situation where the results, without the presence of counsel, might "reduce the trial itself to a mere formality." *United States v. Gouveia,* 467 U.S. 180, 104 S.Ct. 2292, 81 L.Ed.2d 146 (1984). Critical stages include a preliminary hearing, a post-indictment lineup, a guilty plea negotiation, and a sentencing hearing; the constitution guarantees the right to counsel at each of these proceedings. *See Coleman v. Alabama,* 399 U.S. 1, 90 S.Ct. 1999, 26 L.Ed.2d 387 (1970) (preliminary hearing); *United States v. Wade,* 388 U.S. 218, 87 S.Ct. 1926, 18 L.Ed.2d 1149 (1967) (post-indictment lineup); *Mempa v. Rhay,* 389 U.S. 128, 88 S.Ct. 254, 19 L.Ed.2d 336 (1967) (deferred sentencing hearing). Events that are not critical stages include photographic identification procedures, handwriting exemplar procedures, probation revocation hearings, and administrative detention of inmates. *See United States v. Ash,* 413 U.S. 300, 93 S.Ct. 2568, 37 L.Ed.2d 619 (1973) (photographic identification); *Gilbert v. California,* 388 U.S. 263, 87 S.Ct. 1951, 18 L.Ed.2d 1178 (1967) (handwriting exemplars); *Gagnon v. Scarpelli,* 411 U.S. 778, 93 S.Ct. 1756, 36 L.Ed.2d 656 (1973) (probation revocation); *United States v. Gouveia,* 467 U.S. 180, 104 S.Ct. 2292, 81 L.Ed.2d 146 (1984) (administrative detention).

c. Confessions and the Right to Counsel

Some confessions are obtained under circumstances that violate the Sixth Amendment right to counsel. The doctrine on this subject is discussed *supra* in the section on confessions. *See Massiah v. United States,* 377 U.S. 201, 84 S.Ct. 1199, 12 L.Ed.2d 246 (1964); *Brewer v. Williams,* 430 U.S. 387, 97 S.Ct. 1232, 51 L.Ed.2d 424 (1977). Most often, confessions are obtained during post-arrest, *pre-charge* custodial interrogation, which is considered part of the investigatorial, rather than adversarial, process, and thus not covered by the Sixth Amendment. *See Moran v. Burbine,* 475 U.S. 412, 106 S.Ct. 1135, 89 L.Ed.2d 410 (1986).

II. Due Process and the Right of Adequate Access

The Supreme Court has occasionally referred to the Due Process Clause as an independent authority for guaranteeing certain rights of access to the criminal justice system.

A. Counsel for Non–critical Stages

The Due Process Clause sometimes requires counsel to be appointed on a case-by-case basis at non-critical stages. For example, counsel may be required for some defendants in parole or probation revocation proceedings. *See, e.g., Gagnon v. Scarpelli,* 411 U.S. 778, 93 S.Ct. 1756, 36 L.Ed.2d 656 (1973) (when substantial reasons make revocation inappropriate and when the reasons are complex or difficult to present without counsel).

B. The Right to Counsel on Appeal

There is a *per se* due process right to counsel on the first appeal from a criminal conviction; counsel must be provided by the state to those who are indigent. This is because the assistance of counsel is necessary to bring an effective appeal—counsel is needed to comb the record, prepare the arguments, etc. *Douglas v. California,* 372 U.S. 353, 83 S.Ct. 814, 9 L.Ed.2d 811 (1963). But there is no due process right to appointed counsel for later appeals, for the certiorari process, or for collateral attack. The reason for this is that due process only guarantees *adequate,* not perfect access to the court system. A lawyer is not required for adequate access to later stages of appeal, since the defendant will already have received the assistance of trial counsel and counsel on the first appeal. *See Ross v. Moffitt,* 417 U.S. 600, 94 S.Ct. 2437, 41 L.Ed.2d 341 (1974) (no right to counsel for later appeals and certiorari); *Pennsylvania v. Finley,* 481 U.S. 551, 107 S.Ct. 1990, 95 L.Ed.2d 539 (1987) (no right to counsel for state habeas proceedings); *Murray v. Giarratano,* 492 U.S. 1, 109 S.Ct. 2765, 106 L.Ed.2d 1 (1989) (no right to counsel for state habeas proceedings, even in capital cases). *But see Halbert v. Michigan,* 545 U.S. 605, 125 S.Ct. 2582, 162 L.Ed.2d 552 (2005), where the Court cited *Douglas* in holding that an indigent defendant has a constitutional right to the assistance of counsel in the first appeal of a conviction after a guilty plea or plea of nolo contendere.

1. The Right to Effective Assistance of Counsel on Appeal

Due process requires that counsel provide *effective* assistance on the first appeal. *Evitts v. Lucey,* 469 U.S. 387, 105 S.Ct. 830, 83 L.Ed.2d 821 (1985). Appellate counsel has no duty to argue every colorable issue, simply because the defendant wants the issues argued. *Jones v. Barnes,* 463 U.S. 745, 103 S.Ct. 3308, 77 L.Ed.2d 987 (1983) (counsel may winnow out weaker issues using reasonable professional judgment). If there is no underlying due process right to counsel, then there is no due process right to effective assistance of counsel, even if counsel is retained by the defendant. *See Wainwright v. Torna,* 455 U.S. 586, 102 S.Ct. 1300, 71 L.Ed.2d 475 (1982) (no right to effective assistance of retained counsel in second appeal).

2. The Role of Appellate Counsel Who Feels That the Appeal Has No Merit

If counsel believes an appeal is frivolous, counsel must request permission to withdraw and file a brief referring "to anything in the record that might arguably support the appeal." *Anders v. California*, 386 U.S. 738, 87 S.Ct. 1396, 18 L.Ed.2d 493 (1967). A state may require counsel to discuss why the appeal lacks merit. *McCoy v. Court of Appeals of Wisconsin*, 486 U.S. 429, 108 S.Ct. 1895, 100 L.Ed.2d 440 (1988). The requirement of filing an *Anders* brief applies only when there is an underlying due process right to counsel. *Pennsylvania v. Finley*, 481 U.S. 551, 107 S.Ct. 1990, 95 L.Ed.2d 539 (1987) (state habeas counsel need not file *Anders* brief).

C. Due Process Right to Tools With Which to Prepare an Effective Case at Trial and on Appeal

Besides the right to counsel, the Court has held that in some circumstances the state must provide technical support for an indigent person's counsel, so that an effective case or appeal can be prepared.

1. The Right to a Trial Transcript

In order for an indigent defendant to have adequate access to the appellate process, a trial transcript must be provided by the state. *Griffin v. Illinois*, 351 U.S. 12, 76 S.Ct. 585, 100 L.Ed. 891 (1956) (state must pay for a transcript even though the right to appeal is not a constitutional right).

2. The Right to Obtain Expert Witnesses for Trial

Due process requires that indigent defendants receive the basic tools of an adequate defense at trial, and this includes expert witnesses where they are necessary for an effective presentation of the case. *Ake v. Oklahoma*, 470 U.S. 68, 105 S.Ct. 1087, 84 L.Ed.2d 53 (1985) (an appointed psychiatrist is required when defendant demonstrates that sanity is to be a significant factor at trial).

3. The Rights of Indigent Prisoners to Tools for Appeal in Lieu of Counsel

Although indigent defendants have no right to counsel beyond the first appeal, they have rights to substitute forms of assistance for use in subsequent appeals and collateral attack.

a. Jailhouse Lawyers

Inmates must be allowed to have access to the assistance of other inmates who are "jailhouse lawyers." *Johnson v. Avery*, 393 U.S. 483,

89 S.Ct. 747, 21 L.Ed.2d 718 (1969) (inmates may assist others in preparing habeas corpus petitions).

b. Prison Libraries

Prison authorities must provide meaningful access to the courts for inmates by furnishing "adequate law libraries or adequate assistance from persons trained in the law." *Bounds v. Smith*, 430 U.S. 817, 97 S.Ct. 1491, 52 L.Ed.2d 72 (1977).

III. Effective Assistance of Counsel

A. Introduction

The Supreme Court has held that the right to counsel means more than merely being represented at trial by a member of the bar. Rather, the right to counsel means the right to *effective assistance* of counsel. The difficulty is in determining whether counsel's performance has breached minimum standards of effectiveness and whether, assuming counsel was ineffective, the defendant was prejudiced in some way that warrants a retrial.

1. Applies to Appointed and Retained Counsel

Both appointed and retained counsel are subject to review for ineffectiveness. Thus, the defendant does not in any way "waive" his right to effective assistance of counsel merely by choosing a lawyer who acts ineffectively. *See Cuyler v. Sullivan*, 446 U.S. 335, 100 S.Ct. 1708, 64 L.Ed.2d 333 (1980) ("Since the State's conduct of a criminal trial itself implicates the State in the defendant's conviction, we see no basis for drawing a distinction between retained and appointed counsel that would deny equal justice to defendants who must choose their own lawyers.")

2. Applies to Trial, Sentencing, and Other Critical Stages

Wherever the Sixth Amendment right to counsel applies, the right to effective assistance of counsel applies as well. Thus, the defendant has a right to effective assistance in sentencing, guilty pleas, and the first appeal of right, as well as at trial. *See Strickland v. Washington, infra* (effectiveness standards applied at capital sentencing); *Hill v. Lockhart*, 474 U.S. 52, 106 S.Ct. 366, 88 L.Ed.2d 203 (1985) (ineffective assistance in advising defendant improperly as to guilty plea); *Evitts v. Lucey*, 469 U.S. 387, 105 S.Ct. 830, 83 L.Ed.2d 821 (1985) (ineffective assistance on first appeal of right).

3. Inapplicable Where Right to Counsel Does Not Apply

Conversely, if there is no right to counsel, there is no right to effective assistance of counsel. As previously discussed in this outline, the

Supreme Court has held that there is no right to counsel for appellate review or for collateral attack beyond the first appeal of right. As a result, if counsel acts ineffectively at these stages, there is no constitutional claim of ineffective assistance. *See Pennsylvania v. Finley*, 481 U.S. 551, 107 S.Ct. 1990, 95 L.Ed.2d 539 (1987) (no claim of ineffective assistance is cognizable where counsel's mistakes occurred on collateral attack); *Wainwright v. Torna*, 455 U.S. 586, 102 S.Ct. 1300, 71 L.Ed.2d 475 (1982) (no right to counsel at certiorari stage, therefore no claim of ineffective assistance can be asserted).

B. *Strickland*

In *Strickland v. Washington*, 466 U.S. 668, 104 S.Ct. 2052, 80 L.Ed.2d 674 (1984), the Supreme Court held that the defendant must make two showings in order to obtain a reversal for ineffective assistance of counsel.

1. Deficient Performance

First, the defendant must show that counsel made errors so serious that his "representation fell below an objective standard of reasonableness" and was not "within the range of competence demanded of attorneys in criminal cases."

2. Prejudice

Second, the defendant must show that counsel's incompetent representation prejudiced him. The standard for prejudice is whether "there is a *reasonable probability* that, but for counsel's unprofessional errors, the result of the proceeding would have been different." The Court defined a reasonable probability as "a probability sufficient to undermine confidence in the outcome."

3. "Reasonable Probability" Standard

In *Woodford v. Visciotti*, 537 U.S. 19, 123 S.Ct. 357, 154 L.Ed.2d 279 (2002), the Supreme Court upheld the California Supreme Court's denial of Visciotti's habeas corpus petition based on a finding that the ineffective assistance of counsel in his case "probably" did not prejudice him during the penalty phase of his capital murder trial. The Court found that the use of the term "probable" without the modifier "reasonably" did not violate the *Strickland* standard. Reasoning that the term "probable" was shorthand for the phrase "reasonable probability" used elsewhere in the opinion, the Court determined that the California Supreme Court had not impermissibly held Visciotti to a higher standard in proving prejudice. *See also Holland v. Jackson*, 542 U.S. 649, 124 S.Ct. 2736, 159 L.Ed.2d

683 (2004) (state court did not act contrary to federal law under *Strickland*, by requiring proof of prejudice by a preponderance of evidence rather than by a reasonable probability standard, where state court had recited correct *Strickland* standard elsewhere in its opinion).

4. Strict Test

The Court in *Strickland* recognized that its two-pronged test was "rigorous" and "highly demanding," and that it imposed a significant burden on the defendant challenging counsel's performance. The *Strickland* test makes it unlikely that many claims of ineffective assistance will be successful. The Court justified its test by stating that "it is all too tempting for a defendant to second-guess counsel's decision after conviction or adverse sentence, and it is all too easy for a court, examining counsel's defense after it has proved unsuccessful, to conclude that a particular act or omission of counsel was unreasonable." The Court was concerned that "intrusive post-trial inquiry into attorney performance" would chill vigorous advocacy by making counsel reluctant to make decisions that might later be found ineffective.

C. Elements of Competence

The Court in *Strickland* noted that effective representation entails both a reasonably thorough *investigation* and a reasonably competent *presentation* of the defendant's case.

1. Investigation

In order to make strategic choices, the defense counsel must be informed of pertinent information. Ordinarily this requires defense counsel to question witnesses, investigate crime locations, interview family members, etc. Thus, courts after *Strickland* have found that a complete failure to conduct an investigation is ordinarily ineffective, since a counsel who has done no investigation will not have enough information with which to make strategic decisions such as which witnesses to call or which defense to bring. *See Foster v. Lockhart*, 9 F.3d 722 (8th Cir.1993) (defense counsel in a rape case was ineffective for failing even to discover that the defendant was impotent); *Thomas v. Lockhart*, 738 F.2d 304 (8th Cir.1984) (counsel's investigation was deficient where he did nothing beyond reading the police file); *Frierson v. Woodford*, 463 F.3d 982 (9th Cir.2006) (defense counsel who failed to present mitigating evidence or challenge witness' invocation of the Fifth Amendment at the penalty stage of capital murder trial found ineffective).

a. Information Provided by the Defendant

The Court in *Strickland* stated that the reasonableness of counsel's investigative efforts "depends critically" on information supplied by the defendant. For example, when a defendant informs counsel that a certain line of investigation would be fruitless or harmful, then counsel's failure to pursue that line cannot later be found unreasonable. *See Hance v. Zant*, 981 F.2d 1180 (11th Cir.1993) (failure to investigate defendant's background held not ineffective where defendant instructed counsel not to contact and involve the members of his family, and counsel complied with his client's instructions "because he feared that if he did not, he would lose Hance's cooperation in the defense strategy").

b. Limitations on Investigation

The Court in *Strickland* noted that at some point, an attorney's decision to end an investigation will be a reasonable professional judgment. For example, in *Burger v. Kemp*, 483 U.S. 776, 107 S.Ct. 3114, 97 L.Ed.2d 638 (1987), the defendant argued that counsel was ineffective in deciding to terminate a search for witnesses to testify to the defendant's good character at his capital sentencing proceeding. The defendant had given counsel a list of possible character witnesses, counsel had contacted the first several on the list, and each had negative things to say about the defendant. The Court concluded that under the circumstances, "counsel's decision not to mount an all-out investigation was supported by reasonable professional judgment." *See also Wilkins v. Iowa*, 957 F.2d 537 (8th Cir.1992) ("A less than exhaustive investigation is adequate for constitutional purposes if reasonable professional judgments limit its scope.")

The Court distinguished *Burger v. Kemp* in *Wiggins v. Smith*, 539 U.S. 510, 123 S.Ct. 2527, 156 L.Ed.2d 471 (2003), concluding that defense counsel's failure to investigate the defendant's social history beyond his Pre–Sentence Investigation and Department of Social Services reports constituted inadequate and unreasonable preparation for a capital sentencing hearing. Appellate counsel discovered that defendant's mother had physically abused him and that after he was placed in foster care, he was sexually abused by his guardians and gang-raped by his step-mother's sons. Trial counsel's decision to abandon investigation after discovering that defendant's mother was an alcoholic, that defendant was shuttled between foster homes, and that he and his siblings were left alone at least once without food, was unreasonable. The Court found that counsel's failure to investigate further fell short of the professional standards that prevailed in the state of Maryland at that time and that any reasonably competent attorney would have realized that pursuing such leads was necessary to making an informed choice among possible defenses.

But see Schriro v. Landrigan, 550 U.S. 465, 127 S.Ct. 1933, 167 L.Ed.2d 836 (2007) where the Court held that defense counsel's failure to conduct further investigation into mitigating evidence did not constitute ineffective assistance of counsel. Defendant had refused to allow counsel to present the testimony of his ex-wife and mother and told the judge that he did not want to present any mitigating evidence. He further told the judge to "bring on the death penalty." Under these circumstances, the Court affirmed the lower court's finding that further investigation would have been futile under the circumstances.

The Court found a duty to investigate the case file of a defendant's prior criminal trial in *Rompilla v. Beard*, 545 U.S. 374, 125 S.Ct. 2456, 162 L.Ed.2d 360 (2005). During the penalty phase of defendant's capital murder trial, the prosecutor presented evidence of several aggravating factors, including the fact that the defendant had a significant history of violent felony convictions. The Court held that when the defendant's counsel failed to examine the prior conviction file of the accused, counsel fell below the standard of reasonable competence required of defense counsel under the Sixth Amendment. The Court did not establish a per se rule that counsel must always review the case file of a defendant's prior convictions. However, in this case, where defense counsel had notice of the death penalty; the conviction file showed prior rape and assault convictions; and the file was a readily accessible public document, the lawyers were deficient in failing to examine the file. According to the Court, the undiscovered mitigating evidence might well have influenced the jury.

2. Presentation

Presentation of a defense is a function of decision-making by defense counsel. Decisions include which witnesses to call, which arguments and objections to make, whether to ask for a certain jury instruction, etc. The Court in *Strickland* stated that a reviewing court must be "highly deferential" in reviewing counsel's decisions, and that *"strategic choices made after thorough investigation of law and facts relevant to plausible options are virtually unchallengeable."* Thus, if counsel's decision, though mistaken, can be fairly considered a strategic choice, it is extremely unlikely that a court will find that counsel provided ineffective assistance. Moreover, the court must assess counsel's performance from the point of view of the circumstances known or reasonably knowable *at the time the decision was made.* The Court in *Strickland* cautioned that "every effort must be made to eliminate the distorting effects of hindsight, to reconstruct the circumstances of counsel's challenged conduct, and to evaluate the conduct from counsel's perspective at the time."

In *Yarborough v. Gentry*, 540 U.S. 1, 124 S.Ct. 1, 157 L.Ed.2d 1 (2003), the Court noted that the right to effective assistance of counsel extends to closing arguments, but stressed the importance of deference to counsel's tactical decisions. In *Yarborough*, counsel gave a closing argument which failed to highlight all potentially exculpatory pieces of evidence, highlighted defendant's bad character traits, and included only a passive request that jurors reach a verdict rather than an affirmative request for acquittal. Nonetheless, the Court held that the intermediate state appellate court's determination that trial counsel's closing argument did not amount to ineffective assistance of counsel was not an objectively unreasonable application of federal law.

Example: In *Wilkins v. Iowa,* 957 F.2d 537 (8th Cir.1992), the defendant entered a bar with a gun in his waistband under his jacket. He struck up a conversation with an ex-girlfriend, to the consternation of her fiancé. Words were exchanged, and the fiancé started moving toward Wilkins, who drew the gun from his waistband and shot the fiancé twice, killing him. A blood alcohol test showed that Wilkins had a blood alcohol content of .219. Wilkins had been depressed and was taking an antidepressant, although it was not clear that he took it on the day of the shooting. Wilkins had been seeing a psychiatrist. Wilkins' defense counsel, Walter, interviewed the psychiatrist and some of the eyewitnesses called at trial. Walter decided to focus on a defense of justification or self-defense and place less emphasis on the theories of diminished capacity or intoxication. The victim was a large man with a history of violence. At trial, Walter did not argue diminished capacity during opening or closing arguments, he did not introduce into evidence the results of Wilkins' blood alcohol test, and he did not call the psychiatrist to testify. He did, however, elicit testimony concerning the degree of Wilkins' intoxication. The trial court instructed the jury on both self-defense and diminished capacity. The jury returned a verdict of first-degree murder.

Attacking his conviction on grounds of ineffective assistance, Wilkins argued that Walter had inadequately presented the diminished capacity claim. The court, however, concluded that Walter's decision "was a valid exercise of professional judgment in formulating trial strategy, which we will not second-guess on appeal." The court found that Walter's decision to essentially forego the diminished capacity defense was reasonable, even if mistaken, on the following grounds: 1. it was appropriate to "go for broke" with the complete defense of self-defense rather than the partial defense of diminished capacity, because Wilkins was extremely reluctant to go to jail for any time at all; 2. it was appropriate to pick one defense instead of two, since Walter made a reasonable (if arguable) judgment that diminished capacity and justification are inconsistent defenses—if a jury believes the defendant was impaired, it would not find his justification defense credible, and if he could think clearly enough to respond to a threat, his diminished capacity defense would lose credibility; and 3. the justification defense was a reasonable defense to pick of the two available, since it was not only a complete defense but it was also supported to some degree by the evidence. The fact that Walter's decisions backfired was irrelevant to whether they were reasonable strategy at *the time they were made. See also Jones v. Page*, 76 F.3d 831 (7th Cir.1996) (defense counsel's failure to call the defendant's girlfriend as a mitigation witness during the penalty phase of a capital murder trial was a reasonable strategic decision; defense counsel thought that jury would negatively react to the girlfriend's necklace, which displayed the word "BITCH" in clearly visible letters, and which counsel could not persuade the girlfriend to remove).

In *Florida v. Nixon*, 543 U.S. 175, 125 S.Ct. 551, 160 L.Ed.2d 565 (2004), the Court held that defense counsel's decision to concede guilt during the guilt phase of defendant's capital murder trial did not automatically constitute ineffective assistance of trial. Defense counsel made a strategic decision to concede the defendant's guilt in light of overwhelming evidence and focus on persuading the jury to spare the defendant's life during the death phase. Counsel believed that the decision would best preserve his credibility with the jury and thus improve defendant's chance of success during the death phase. Counsel attempted to explain the strategy to defendant on at least three occasions, but defendant was unresponsive. Defendant did not explicitly agree to the strategy nor did he reject it. Under these circumstances, the Court found that defense counsel's strategy was not per se ineffective assistance of counsel. According to the Court, "[w]hen counsel informs the defendant of the strategy counsel believes to be in the defendant's best interest and the defendant is unresponsive, counsel's strategic choice is not impeded by any blanket rule demanding the defendant's explicit consent."

3. Decisions Based on Errors of Law

If counsel makes a decision based on an incorrect assumption of relevant legal standards, then the decision cannot be justified as strategic and will consequently be found ineffective. For example, in *Cave v. Singletary*, 971 F.2d 1513 (11th Cir.1992), the defendant was charged with felony murder arising from an armed robbery. Defense counsel throughout the trial *emphasized* that Cave had committed the robbery, but argued that he was not guilty of murder because he had not been the shooter. These statements amounted to a concession by defense counsel to the jury that the State had proven its case, because under the felony murder statute, commission of the robbery was sufficient to establish guilt: it was irrelevant that the defendant had not been the shooter. At the hearing after the conviction on the ineffectiveness claim, defense counsel argued that "she understood the concept of felony murder, but deliberately misstated the law throughout the trial in an attempt to confuse the jury." Her stated strategy "was to attempt to separate in the jurors' minds the robbery and the murder, then confuse the jury about the elements of felony murder so that they would acquit Cave of the murder charge."

The court found that counsel had rendered ineffective assistance. It stated that "the mere incantation of the word strategy does not insulate attorney behavior from review." The court was convinced that counsel "completely misunderstood the law of felony murder, which is a concept that often confuses lay people, but should be within the grasp of lawyers." Thus, the court disbelieved counsel's post-hoc explanation of strategy. But the court pointed out that "even if counsel's misstatements of the law were strategic in nature, we would not consider such a strategy to be reasonable under the circumstances because defense counsel may not encourage the jurors to ignore the court's instruction and apply the law at their caprice." So even if counsel understood and misstated the law of felony murder, she made a mistake of law (which could not be deemed strategic) as to the jury's duty to follow the judge's instructions. *See also Kimmelman v. Morrison,* 477 U.S. 365, 106 S.Ct. 2574, 91 L.Ed.2d 305 (1986) (counsel was ineffective for failure to file a timely suppression motion because he had conducted no discovery, laboring under the mistaken notion that the State was required to turn over all inculpatory evidence to the defense).

D. Prejudice

The prejudice standard is designed to assess whether it is worthwhile to retry a case in which ineffectiveness occurred. As such, it performs the same function as the "harmless error" test applied to constitutional violations.

1. Strength of the Government's Case

To apply the prejudice standard the reviewing court must assess the strength of the prosecution's case and the significance of defense counsel's error. It is obvious that, no matter how fundamental counsel's error, a conviction would still be reasonably probable if the prosecution's evidence is overwhelming. For example, in *Cave v. Singletary, supra,* the court found that defense counsel was ineffective for arguing to the jury, in a felony murder case, that her client was clearly guilty of robbery but not of murder. Nonetheless, the court refused to reverse the conviction because the evidence that Cave had actually committed the robbery was overwhelming. Cave had confessed to the robbery and other witnesses to the crime had identified him. Thus the court concluded that "in this case, Cave has not demonstrated that there is a reasonable probability that, but for counsel's incompetence, the result of the trial would have been different." *See also Woodford v. Visciotti, supra,* where the California Supreme Court found the strength of the aggravating factors presented by the government in a capital murder case to be so strong that the lack of mitigation evidence did not prejudice the defendant's case. The

Supreme Court reversed the Ninth Circuit's finding of prejudice, holding that the California Supreme Court's decision that trial counsel's assumed inadequate representation did not prejudice petitioner was not objectively unreasonable.

2. Weakness of the Government's Case

Conversely, the weaker the Government's case, the more likely it is that defense counsel's unprofessional conduct will have an effect on the outcome. Thus, in *Atkins v. Attorney General of Alabama*, 932 F.2d 1430 (11th Cir.1991), defense counsel failed to object to the introduction of a fingerprint card which was offered at trial to make a comparison between Atkins' fingerprints and those found at the scene of the crime. The card included a printed notation of a prior arrest that would not have been admissible against Atkins. The court found that the failure to object to clearly inadmissible evidence constituted ineffectiveness, and that without the error there was a reasonable probability that the outcome of the proceeding would have been different. The court stressed that the evidence against Atkins was barely sufficient to support the jury's verdict. While Atkins' fingerprints were found at the scene, this was explainable because the victim testified that Atkins had worked for him at the house two days prior to the crime. Also, there was no other physical evidence to tie Atkins to the crime. Under these circumstances, the court found that the evidence of the prior arrest could have had "an almost irreversible impact on the minds of the jurors." *See also Burnett v. Collins*, 982 F.2d 922 (5th Cir.1993) ("a verdict strongly supported by the record is less likely to have been affected by counsel's errors than one with only weak support").

3. No Right to a Lawless or Improper Verdict

The defendant cannot be "prejudiced" from defense counsel's refusal to persuade the jury to decide the case in an improper manner; nor can he be prejudiced if defense counsel decides to make an improper argument but does so ineffectively. Thus, in *Nix v. Whiteside*, 475 U.S. 157, 106 S.Ct. 988, 89 L.Ed.2d 123 (1986), the defendant complained that he was denied effective assistance of counsel because his lawyer threatened that if Whiteside lied on the stand, the lawyer would disclose the perjury to the trial court. The Court noted that under *Strickland*, the defendant must prove prejudice, and that Whiteside had "no valid claim that confidence in the result of his trial has been diminished by his desisting from the contemplated perjury." The Court reasoned that even if the jury had been persuaded by the perjury, "a defendant has no entitlement to the luck of a lawless decision maker." *See also Lockhart v. Fretwell*, 506 U.S. 364, 113 S.Ct. 838, 122 L.Ed.2d 180 (1993) (no prejudice where counsel fails to make argument at trial on basis of then-existing law, where the law had been changed by the time of review; question of prejudice is not solely one of result-orientation).

4. Per Se Prejudice

In *United States v. Cronic*, 466 U.S. 648, 104 S.Ct. 2039, 80 L.Ed.2d 657 (1984), the Supreme Court declared that there are certain limited circumstances in which ineffectiveness and prejudice are *presumed*, because "the likelihood that any lawyer, even a fully competent one, could provide effective assistance of counsel is so small that a presumption of prejudice is appropriate *without inquiry into the actual conduct of the trial."*

a. Limited Exception

The Court in *Cronic* stressed that the *"per se* reversal" exception to the two-pronged *Strickland* test was extremely limited, to egregious circumstances in which ineffective representation and prejudice were all but a certainty—i.e., where misconduct and prejudice is so likely that the "cost of litigating" the question would be unjustified. The limited nature of this exception is shown by the facts of *Cronic*, where the court *refused* to presume ineffectiveness and prejudice despite the following factors: 1. Cronic was charged in a complex fraud involving a check-kiting scheme; 2. Cronic was given a young lawyer with a real estate practice and with no prior trial experience; and 3. the court allowed counsel only 25 days to prepare the defense, even though it had taken the Government over four years to investigate and prepare its case. Despite these factors, the Court found that a presumption of ineffectiveness and prejudice was unjustified. Among other things, the Court noted that "every experienced criminal defense attorney once tried his first criminal case," and that the underlying historical facts to be proven at trial were not in dispute. The Court concluded that "when there is no reason to dispute the underlying historical facts, the period of 25 days to consider the question whether those facts justify an inference of criminal intent is not so short that it even arguably justifies a presumption that no lawyer could provide the respondent with the effective assistance of counsel required by the Constitution."

b. Total Denial of "Counsel"

The *Cronic per se* reversal exception to the general *Strickland* test has generally been limited to cases in which counsel was not even a lawyer properly admitted to the bar, or was subject to some other incapacity by which he could not function as "counsel" within the meaning of the Sixth Amendment. *See Solina v. United States,* 709 F.2d 160 (2d Cir.1983) (per se reversal where defendant's trial counsel held himself out as an attorney but had never passed a bar exam; counsel cannot be "counsel" as that term is defined in the Sixth Amendment where he was "engaging in a crime" during the representation of the defendant). *See also United States v. Novak,* 903 F.2d 883 (2d Cir.1990) (per se reversal where defense counsel had obtained admission to the bar by fraud); *Pilchak v. Camper,* 935 F.2d 145 (8th Cir.1991) (per se reversal where defense counsel was suffering from Alzheimer's disease during the course of the trial). On the other hand, if defense counsel was disbarred, suspended or incapacitated subsequent to the representation, or if defense counsel's failure to maintain a license to practice is merely a ministerial oversight, then a presumption of ineffectiveness and prejudice is unwarranted. *See United States v. Rosnow,* 981 F.2d 970 (8th Cir.1992) (no per se reversal where counsel was suspended *subsequent* to most of the material representation of the defendant, and defendant was represented by co-counsel as well); *Reese v. Peters,* 926 F.2d 668 (7th Cir.1991) (no per se reversal where defense counsel's license was suspended for failure to pay dues). In *Cronic,* the Court identified two other situations in which prejudice should be presumed: where "counsel entirely fails to subject the prosecution's case to meaningful adversarial testing," and "where counsel is called upon to render assistance under circumstances where competent counsel very likely could not."

c. Ineffectiveness and Prejudice May Still Be Found on the Facts

If a court holds that a presumption of ineffectiveness and prejudice is unwarranted, it has not held that the defendant received the Sixth Amendment right to effective assistance of counsel. Rather it has held that the defendant has the burden of showing ineffectiveness and prejudice *on the record.* For example, on remand in *Cronic, supra,* the court of appeals held that Cronic's counsel had in fact performed ineffectively, and that counsel's errors were in fact prejudicial to Cronic. The court found that counsel's stated strategy of "clouding the issues" could not be a satisfactory explanation for the selection of a defense, and that counsel failed to object to inadmissible evidence due to a misunderstanding of the statute under which Cronic was tried. These errors were found prejudicial given the weakness of the case against Cronic.

Subsequently, in *Bell v. Cone*, 535 U.S. 685, 122 S.Ct. 1843, 152 L.Ed.2d 914 (2002), the Court declined to find prejudice when an attorney in a capital case failed to present mitigating evidence and waived closing argument after the penalty phase of the trial. Cone claimed that *Cronic* applied because his lawyer failed to subject the prosecution's case to meaningful adversarial testing. However, the Court applied *Strickland* rather than *Cronic* because in *Cronic*, the Court held that the defendant must show that his attorney totally failed to oppose the government's case. Cone claimed that this failure only occurred during specific points of the penalty phase. Applying *Strickland*, the Court held that the state court's determination that Cone's lawyer did not perform deficiently did not involve an unreasonable application of clearly established federal law sufficient to support grant of federal habeas relief.

E. Multiple Representation

The standards for ineffectiveness and prejudice are different when the defendant's claim is that defense counsel labored under a conflict of interest arising from multiple representation of clients in related matters. Multiple representation may create a conflict because defendants may have different interests at stake, so that the attorney cannot zealously represent both or all the clients. For example, one client may be more blameworthy than another; an attempt to shift blame from a less culpable client to a more culpable client would obviously present a conflict of interest. *See Holloway v. Arkansas*, 435 U.S. 475, 98 S.Ct. 1173, 55 L.Ed.2d 426 (1978) (multiple representation may "prevent an attorney from challenging the admission of evidence prejudicial to one client but perhaps favorable to another, or from arguing at the sentencing hearing the relative involvement and culpability of his clients in order to minimize the culpability of one by emphasizing that of another").

1. Per Se Reversal if No Hearing Held After Risk of Conflict is Brought to the Judge

The Court in *Holloway v. Arkansas*, 435 U.S. 475, 98 S.Ct. 1173, 55 L.Ed.2d 426 (1978), made it clear that multiple representation of criminal defendants is not a per se violation of the right to effective assistance. The Court reasoned that in some cases, a common defense by a single counsel may be the most appropriate and vigorous defense. On the other hand, where the trial judge, after timely motions, *refuses to even consider* whether multiple representation poses a risk of a conflict, *per se* reversal is required. It would be unfair to require the defendant to show retroactively that his representation was impaired by a conflict, when he was denied a hearing on the issue at a time when the conflict could have been averted.

2. Limited Presumption

In *Cuyler v. Sullivan,* 446 U.S. 335, 100 S.Ct. 1708, 64 L.Ed.2d 333 (1980), the Court stated that, when a trial court inquires into a possible conflict, it "may assume that multiple representation entails no conflict or that the lawyer and his clients knowingly accept such risk of conflict as may exist." However, because of the potential risk of ineffective assistance arising from multiple representation, the Court held that a defendant would be entitled to a reversal if he could demonstrate that "an *actual conflict of interest adversely affected his lawyer's performance.*" Thus, the Court created a *limited and conditional presumption of prejudice.* Prejudice is presumed, but only if the defendant establishes that counsel "*actively represented conflicting interests*" and that "*an actual conflict of interest adversely affected his lawyer's performance.*" If the defendant can show that counsel acted in conflict to the defendant's detriment, he need not make the further *Strickland* showing that counsel's error had some reasonably probable effect on the outcome. *See United States v. Winkle,* 722 F.2d 605 (10th Cir.1983) ("A defendant who shows that a conflict of interest actually affected the adequacy of his representation need not demonstrate prejudice in order to obtain relief.") Thus, even if the prosecution's case is overwhelming, the defendant is entitled to a retrial if defense counsel had an actual conflict and harmed the defendant's case *in some way* as a result of the conflict. *See Strickland, supra* (discussing the limited presumption of prejudice where counsel is burdened by a conflict of interest, and noting that "it is difficult to measure the precise effect on the defense of representation corrupted by conflicting interests").

Example: In *Nealy v. Cabana,* 782 F.2d 1362 (5th Cir.1986), defense counsel represented both Nealy and his brother, who were being tried separately for the same crime. The evidence against Nealy was overwhelming, but Nealy wanted to call his brother to the stand to testify to some mitigating factors. Defense counsel decided not to call the brother, and testified later that he was motivated by the fact that the testimony could be used against the brother in his trial. The court reversed Nealy's conviction, finding that defense counsel had labored under an actual conflict of interest, and that the decision not to call the brother adversely affected the lawyer's performance. Consequently, the strength of the Government's case against Nealy was irrelevant. *See also United States v. Martin*, 965 F.2d 839 (10th Cir.1992) (reversal required where counsel employed "united we stand, divided we fall" theory of defense in a drug conspiracy case, claiming that no conspiracy existed, and vehemently opposed the defendant's wish to testify that he had withdrawn from the conspiracy and thus was less culpable: "Defendant has presented the classic conflict situation in which, in order to reduce the degree of his own culpability, he would have to testify in contravention of his co-defendant's theory of the defense.")

In *Mickens v. Taylor*, 535 U.S. 162, 122 S.Ct. 1237, 152 L.Ed.2d 291 (2002), the Court applied the *Cuyler* rule to a case where the attorney representing a defendant in a capital case had previously represented the victim. In *Mickens*, the Court held that, in order to demonstrate a Sixth Amendment violation when the trial judge knew or reasonably should have known about a potential conflict of interest, the defendant must show that the conflict adversely affected the lawyer's performance.

In *Whiting v. Burt*, 395 F.3d 602 (6th Cir. 2005), the court applied *Strickland* rather than *Cuyler*. The defendant claimed that because the same attorney represented him during his trial and on direct appeal, there was an inherent conflict of interest and prejudice was presumed. The Sixth Circuit held that the district court improperly applied the Sullivan standard to the inmate's claim and noted that after *Mickens*, no lower court had applied the *Cuyler* standard outside the "concurrent joint representation context." The court found no prejudice and remanded the case to the district court.

3. Conflict May Be Waived

A defendant may waive his right to conflict-free counsel by choosing to proceed to trial with an attorney who has an actual conflict of interest.

That is, the defendant might decide that even though the lawyer has divided interests, the lawyer is better than any other lawyer he could get. This waiver must, however, be knowing, intelligent, and voluntary, and must be established by clear and unequivocal language. *See United States v. Petz*, 764 F.2d 1390 (11th Cir.1985) (waiver ineffective where defendant was never expressly informed of his right to separate, conflict-free counsel); *United States v. Rodriguez*, 982 F.2d 474 (11th Cir.1993) (waiver valid where the defendants were informed of their right to separate counsel, were asked whether they believed that there was or could be a conflict of interest, were informed that the Government had more evidence against one of the defendants than against the other two, and were made aware that counsel could not, because of the multiple representation, employ a shifting blame strategy).

A few courts have held that there are certain conflicts so serious that they cannot be waived. They reason that a waiver could not really be knowing and voluntary in certain egregious circumstances where the risk of ineffectiveness due to conflict of interest is insurmountable. *See United States v. Fulton*, 5 F.3d 605 (2d Cir.1993) (waiver not possible where the defendant in a drug prosecution was being defended by a lawyer who bought drugs from the prosecution's star witness).

4. Waiver Does Not Bind the Court

If the defendant validly waives the right to conflict-free counsel, the trial court may constitutionally permit the multiple representation. However, the trial court is not *required* to permit multiple representation when there is, or may be, an active conflict of interest. The client's waiver does not bind the trial court because the court may consider the actual or potential conflict to have a negative impact on the integrity of the trial, or on the effectiveness of the representation. In *Wheat v. United States,* supra, the defendant argued that the trial court violated his constitutional right to chosen counsel when the court disqualified defense counsel against the defendant's wishes. The trial court reasoned that counsel's multiple representation could create an active conflict of interest and refused to abide by the waiver. The Supreme Court held that the trial court did not err. It concluded that the Sixth Amendment right to chosen counsel is "circumscribed" by the "independent interest in ensuring that criminal trials are conducted within the ethical standards of the profession and that legal proceedings appear fair to all who observe them."

Judicial Discretion

The Court concluded that the trial court "must be allowed substantial latitude in refusing waivers of conflicts of interest," even if it ultimately turns out that multiple representation would not have actually created an active conflict. The question is whether, at the time the decision to disqualify is made, there is an *indication of "a serious potential for conflict."* If so, the court will not be in error in disqualifying defense counsel even though the defendant has waived his right to conflict-free counsel.

F. Ineffective Assistance Through No Fault of Defense Counsel

In some cases, the defense counsel may perform ineffectively not because of his own malfeasance, but rather because of some state-imposed limitation. Thus, in *Herring v. New York,* 422 U.S. 853, 95 S.Ct. 2550, 45 L.Ed.2d 593 (1975), the Court stated that the right to effective assistance of counsel "has been understood to mean that there can be no restrictions upon the function of counsel in defending a criminal prosecution in accord with the traditions of the adversary fact-finding process." In *Herring,* the Court invalidated a statute which gave the judge in a non-jury trial the power to deny defense counsel the opportunity to make a closing argument. Likewise, in *Geders v. United States,* 425 U.S. 80, 96 S.Ct. 1330, 47 L.Ed.2d 592 (1976), the trial court prohibited defense counsel from consulting with the defendant during a 17–hour overnight recess between the defendant's direct and cross-examination. While recognizing that the trial court had a legitimate concern that the defendant would be "coached," the Court decided that this draconian method of preventing coaching violated the defendant's right to the effective assistance of counsel.

1. Per Se Reversal

The Court in *Herring* stated that if state interference deprives counsel of "the opportunity to participate fully and fairly in the adversary fact-finding process," then the defendant's right to effective assistance is violated, and reversal is *automatic.* The Court does not inquire into whether counsel's performance absent the interference was adequate, and no actual prejudice need be shown. Even a single instance of interference can result in *per se* reversal, as indicated by both *Herring* and *Geders.*

2. Line–Drawing

Not every state interference with defense counsel is so fundamental as to deprive counsel of the opportunity to participate fully and fairly in the adversary proceeding. Thus, in *Perry v. Leeke,* 488 U.S. 272, 109 S.Ct. 594, 102 L.Ed.2d 624 (1989), a state trial judge refused to allow the defendant to consult with counsel during a 15–minute recess between his direct and cross-examination. The Court held that this interference was not so fundamental as to deprive the defendant of effective assistance of counsel, and distinguished the interference from that in *Geders,* where the trial court refused to allow counsel to confer with the defendant during an overnight recess. As the dissenters in *Perry* pointed out, the difference between state-imposed interference during a 15–minute recess and state-imposed interference during an overnight recess is one of degree rather than kind.

IV. The Right to Self–Representation

A. *Faretta*

In *Faretta v. California,* 422 U.S. 806, 95 S.Ct. 2525, 45 L.Ed.2d 562 (1975), the Court held that a criminal defendant has a right to represent himself, which is guaranteed by the Sixth Amendment. The Court recognized that the Sixth Amendment's guarantee of a right to counsel did not plainly state that there is also a right to waive counsel. However, the Court reasoned that the Sixth Amendment "grants to the accused personally the right to make his defense" and that it is the defendant who "suffers the consequences if the defense fails." The Court concluded that "the right to self-representation—to make one's own defense personally—is thus necessarily implied by the structure of the Amendment."

1. Policy Arguments Supporting the Right to Self–Representation

The Court in *Faretta* was clearly aware that it is usually a mistake to proceed without a lawyer. However, the Court set forth two policy arguments which it felt outweighed the negative consequences of self-representation.

a. Right of Free Choice

First and most importantly, the option of self-representation respects the personal autonomy of the defendant. As the Court stated, those who wrote the Bill of Rights "understood the inestimable worth of free choice." Imposing counsel against the defendant's plain desire to represent himself renders the right to free choice in this context a nullity. The Court concluded that "to force a lawyer on a defendant can only lead him to believe that the law contrives against him," and that although the defendant "may conduct his own defense ultimately to his own detriment, his choice must be honored out of that respect for the individual which is the lifeblood of the law."

b.   Strategic Benefit

The *Faretta* Court stated that "in some rare instances, the defendant might in fact present his case more effectively by conducting his own defense." This could occur where forced representation by counsel may render the defendant disillusioned and uncooperative, or where the defendant representing himself may receive some sympathy from the jury in being matched against overwhelming prosecutorial forces.

2.   Dissent

The three dissenters in *Faretta* complained that the majority had found a right to self-representation "tucked between the lines of the Sixth Amendment." The dissenters were also concerned about the effects of self-representation on the criminal justice system. They stated that a widespread exercise of the "newly discovered" right of self-representation would result in added congestion for the courts and would have a negative impact on the quality of justice.

B.   Self–Representation Requires Knowing Waiver of Right to Counsel

After *Faretta*, a defendant simultaneously has a right to counsel and a right to self-representation. Obviously, one of these mutually exclusive rights must be elected and the other waived before a trial can proceed. Thus, the defendant must be fully advised of the consequences of proceeding without counsel before he can be found to have invoked his right to self-representation. *But see Iowa v. Tovar*, 541 U.S. 77, 124 S.Ct. 1379, 158 L.Ed.2d 209 (2004) where the defendant represented himself at a plea hearing. Tovar claimed that the Sixth Amendment right to counsel required the trial court to 1) warn him that an attorney might provide an independent opinion on the wisdom of pleading guilty and 2) that without an attorney he risked overlooking a defense. The Supreme Court rejected Tovar's claim, holding that the Sixth Amendment did not require a rigid and detailed warning about the usefulness of an attorney. According to the Court, the constitutional requirement is fulfilled when the trial court informs the accused of the nature of the charges against him, of his right to be counseled regarding his plea, and of the range of allowable punishments.

1.   Invocation of Right to Self–Representation Must Be Unequivocal

Most courts have held that in addition to being informed about the consequences of self-representation, the defendant must "unequivocally" waive his right to counsel and invoke his right to represent himself. Any ambiguity in the defendant's statements about his willingness to forego counsel will be construed against the invocation of his right of self-representation. *See Meeks v. Craven,* 482 F.2d 465 (9th Cir.1973) (defendant, when asked whether he wanted to represent himself, said "yes, I think I will"; held, not an unequivocal demand for self-representation because " 'I think I will' hardly meets the constitutional criteria for waiver of counsel"). *See also Stano v. Dugger,* 921 F.2d 1125 (11th Cir.1991) ("The right of self-representation must be manifested to the trial court by an oral or written request in order to be recognized and to trigger the requisite examination by the court.")

2. **Tension Between Rights to Counsel and Self–Representation Requires an Unequivocal Waiver of Counsel**

The "unequivocal request" requirement has been developed by the courts to resolve the tension between the mutually exclusive rights to counsel and to self-representation. Requiring that the request for self-representation be unequivocal ensures that the defendant does not inadvertently waive the right to counsel "through occasional musings on the benefits of self-representation." *Adams v. Carroll,* 875 F.2d 1441 (9th Cir.1989). Also, the requirement protects the courts by preventing the defendant from taking advantage of the mutual exclusivity of the rights of counsel and self-representation. As the court in *Adams v. Carroll* put it: "A defendant who vacillates at trial between wishing to be represented by counsel and wishing to represent himself could place the trial court in a difficult position." This is because if counsel is appointed, the defendant could argue on appeal that he really wanted to represent himself; but if he does represent himself, he could argue that he really wanted counsel. The requirement of unequivocality "resolves this dilemma by forcing the defendant to make an explicit choice. If he equivocates, he is presumed to have requested the assistance of counsel." *Id. See Meeks v. Craven, supra* ("An unequivocal demand to proceed pro se should be, at the very least, sufficiently clear that if it is granted the defendant should not be able to turn about and urge that he was improperly denied counsel.")

3. **Need Not Know Rules of Evidence and Trial Practice**

In *Faretta,* the trial judge, after questioning Faretta about the hearsay rule and state law governing the challenge of prospective jurors, ruled that Faretta had not made "an intelligent and knowing" waiver of the right to counsel. The Supreme Court held that this was error, and concluded that Faretta's "technical legal knowledge, as such, was not relevant to an assessment of his knowing exercise of the right to defend himself." Rather, the question is whether the defendant 1) was warned of the consequences of a waiver of counsel, 2) made a voluntary decision, 3) was competent and understood his rights, and 4) unequivocally stated that he wished to represent himself.

4. Defendant Must Be Competent

Besides receiving sufficient warnings about the consequences of waiving the right to counsel, it must be shown that the defendant is competent to waive that right. The Court in *Godinez v. Moran,* 509 U.S. 389, 113 S.Ct. 2680, 125 L.Ed.2d 321 (1993), held that the standard for competency to waive counsel is the same as the standard for competency to stand trial. It must be shown that the defendant has a "reasonable degree of factual understanding" and a "rational as well as factual understanding of the proceedings against him." It is permissible for the state to impose the burden of proving incompetency on the defendant. *Medina v. California,* 505 U.S. 437, 112 S.Ct. 2572, 120 L.Ed.2d 353 (1992).

But see Indiana v. Edwards, ___ U.S. __, 128 S.Ct. 2379, 171 L.Ed.2d 345 (2008), where the Court held that a state may deny a severely mentally ill defendant the right to self-representation even when he is found competent enough to stand trial. Edwards was the subject of several competency proceedings and had a lengthy record of mental illness. The court concluded that Edwards was competent to stand trial but not competent to defend himself a trial. The Court distinguished *Godinez* as a case involving a borderline-competent defendant whose ability to conduct a defense at trial was not at issue because Godinez was only seeking to enter a guilty plea, not conduct trial proceedings, which involves a significantly higher level of "technical legal knowledge."

C. Limitations on the Right of Self–Representation

The right of self-representation is not absolute. In *Faretta* and later cases, the courts have recognized that certain conditions can be imposed on the defendant's right to proceed pro se, where such conditions are necessary to further legitimate and countervailing state interests.

1. Disruption of the Trial

The Court in *Faretta* recognized that "the right of self-representation is not a license to abuse the dignity of the courtroom." Thus, if the defendant is disrupting courtroom proceedings, using the courtroom as a "soapbox," or in some other way imposing a substantial burden on the proceedings through self-representation, then the court may appoint counsel even against the defendant's wishes. *See Savage v. Estelle*, 924 F.2d 1459 (9th Cir.1990) (defendant with a severe speech impediment was found unable to "abide by rules of procedure and courtroom protocol"; therefore, the right to self-representation was properly denied).

2. Treated Like a Lawyer

The Court in *Faretta* cautioned that if the defendant opts to represent himself, he can be held to the same standards as would apply to a lawyer handling the case. The Court stated that the pro se defendant was subject to all "relevant rules of procedural and substantive law."

3. Standby Counsel

While the pro se defendant is subject to all pertinent courtroom rules, it is obvious that many such defendants are unfamiliar with those rules and that this unfamiliarity may impair the progress of the trial. Also, it could happen that the pro se defendant becomes disruptive or simply gives up in the middle of trial and asks for counsel; it would clearly present a problem of trial management for counsel unfamiliar with the case to be appointed at that juncture. The Court in *Faretta* therefore stated that a court can appoint standby counsel "to aid the accused if and when the accused requests help, and to be available to represent the accused in the event that termination of the defendant's self-representation is necessary." The Court made it clear that standby counsel could be appointed "even over objection by the accused."

a. Limits of Standby Counsel

The limits on standby counsel were explored by the Court in *McKaskle v. Wiggins*, 465 U.S. 168, 104 S.Ct. 944, 79 L.Ed.2d 122 (1984). Wiggins contended that his standby counsel violated his right to self-representation by essentially taking over the case. Counsel argued with Wiggins over his choice of strategy, made objections to the judge at sidebar concerning Wiggins' handling of his defense, openly assisted Wiggins in handling courtroom rules, and occasionally interjected objections and comments while witnesses were testifying.

The Court in *Wiggins* stated that standby counsel must act within the limits of the two policy arguments supporting the right of self-representation: that the defendant has a personal right to make his own decisions, and that the defendant may have a strategic interest in obtaining jury sympathy through self-representation. Accordingly, standby counsel cannot seize *actual control* over the defendant's case, or else the right of personal autonomy would be violated. Nor can standby counsel *appear to the jury* to be running the case, or else the strategic interest supporting self-representation would be undermined.

The *Wiggins* Court noted that "participation by standby counsel outside the presence of the jury engages only the first of these limitations," and that the personal autonomy aspect of *Faretta* was satisfied so long as the defendant is allowed to "address the court freely" and "all disagreements between counsel and the pro se defendant are resolved in the defendant's favor whenever the matter is one that would normally be left to the discretion of counsel." Thus, standby counsel can press any arguments he wishes to the judge, so long as the defendant has the final say.

b. Procedural Problems

The Court in *Wiggins* held that standby counsel may assist the defendant in overcoming routine procedural and evidentiary problems, even against the defendant's wishes, without undermining the defendant's appearance to the jury as a person defending himself. On the facts of *Wiggins,* the Court concluded that "counsel's unsolicited involvement was held within reasonable limits" and that Wiggins had made the key strategic decisions and generally appeared to the jury to be representing himself.

c. No Right to Standby Counsel

Faretta recognizes that the trial court may appoint standby counsel, as a procedural device to protect the integrity of the trial. But it is clear that the defendant has no *right* to standby counsel should he decide to represent himself. It is evident from cases like *Wiggins* that some courts may be reluctant to appoint standby counsel, lest by doing so they give the defendant a possible argument on appeal that the standby counsel rendered ineffective assistance. While the defendant has no right to claim ineffective assistance if he represents himself, he does have the right to claim that standby counsel was ineffective. *See Wiggins.*

d.   No Right to Hybrid Relationship of Counsel and Self–
     Representation

What if a defendant wants counsel to do certain things at trial, such
as question certain witnesses, and yet want to represent himself as
to other functions that the lawyer would ordinarily undertake, such
as closing argument? Is the court constitutionally obligated to
satisfy this request?

The courts have consistently held that the only constitutional rights
guaranteed by the Counsel Clause of the Sixth Amendment are the
right to have counsel and the right to proceed without counsel. The
Sixth Amendment cannot be read to provide a right to "hybrid"
representation or to a "co-counsel" relationship between the lawyer
and the defendant. *See United States v. Stevens*, 83 F.3d 60 (2d
Cir.1996) (noting the "critical difference" between a defendant
seeking to represent himself and a defendant asking to serve as
co-counsel in his defense; the latter request does not invoke a
constitutional right, and the decision whether to grant the request is
totally within the discretion of the trial judge). Thus, if the defendant invokes the right to counsel, it is counsel who undertakes and
has authority for conducting the trial. If he invokes the right to
self-representation, then he has the authority to run the defense,
subject to permissible input by standby counsel.

4.   Election Must Be Timely

Another qualification on the right of self-representation is that the
defendant must make the decision to represent himself sufficiently
before trial so that the court can adjust accordingly. *See Horton v. Dugger*,
895 F.2d 714 (11th Cir.1990) (request for self-representation, made on the
first day of trial, held untimely); *United States v. Stevens*, 83 F.3d 60 (2d
Cir.1996) (once the trial has begun, the decision whether to honor a
request for self-representation is a matter of discretion for the trial
judge).

D.   *Faretta* Violation Cannot Be Harmless

Suppose the defendant is denied the right to self-representation after an
unequivocal invocation of that right, and he is convicted. Can the government argue on appeal that the defendant was actually well-represented by
defense counsel and that counsel did a far better job than the defendant
would have done had he represented himself? In other words, can a *Faretta*
violation constitute harmless error? The Supreme Court in *Wiggins* answered

in the negative. The Court reasoned that a violation of *Faretta* means that the defendant has been deprived of his *choice* to represent himself, regardless of the probable negative consequences to his case. It is therefore no answer to say that the counsel imposed upon the defendant against his will did a better job than the defendant could have done. The Court in *Wiggins* concluded that the right to self-representation "is either respected or denied; its deprivation cannot be harmless."

Criminal Procedure—Sample Examinations

EXAM 1

Homer J. Simpson (a/k/a "H.J.") was driving his brand new silver Jaguar down North Capitol Street in Washington, D.C. He was waiting at the traffic light when a man in a Toyota Pathfinder hit his rear bumper. H.J. was furious. He jumped out of his car, ran back to check out the damage, and noticed a small dent in the bumper. H.J. ran to the driver's side of the Pathfinder, yanked open the door, and pulled the driver out by the collar. He punched the driver in the face and drove off. The driver called the police on his cell phone and gave a complete description of H.J. and his car as well as the license plate information (UMUSTAQUT).

The following day, Officer Lawman was driving his police cruiser around the circle in front of Union Station. He received a radio transmission that there was a warrant out for a white male in a silver Jaguar with license plate UMUSTAQUT who had assaulted a driver during a road rage incident the previous day. Shortly after turning onto Massachusetts Avenue, he saw H.J. driving a car that fit the description, turned on his siren, and pursued the suspect. He caught up with H.J. at 2ⁿᵈ Street and signaled for him to pull over. H.J. looked at Lawman briefly and sped off. Lawman pursued H.J. in a high-speed chase. When H.J. reached his townhouse on 7ᵗʰ street, he jumped out of the car, ran into his house and locked the door. Lawman jumped out, ran behind him, and kicked open the door. When he didn't see H.J. in the front room, he walked straight back to the kitchen and saw him headed for the back door. Lawman seized him, placed him under arrest, handcuffed him to the kitchen table and called for additional officers to assist with the arrest.

While Officer Lawman was waiting for the other officers to arrive, he looked around in all of the rooms of the house, including all of the closets. He didn't open any containers in any of the rooms. While in H.J.'s bedroom, Lawman saw some white powder on a silver dish on the bedside table. Based on his experience working in the narcotics division, Lawman recognized the powder as cocaine and placed it in a plastic evidence bag that he conveniently kept in his pocket.

By the time Lawman went back downstairs, the other officers had arrived. Lawman showed the officers the cocaine and told them where he found it. He suggested that one of the officers go to get a warrant to search the entire house. While the officer went for the warrant, Lawman decided to look around some more. He went back up to H.J.'s bedroom and opened the drawer of the bedside table. Inside the drawer, he found ten small bags of white powder that appeared to be cocaine and a small handgun. Lawman closed the drawer without removing the evidence.

The backup officer came back with a warrant authorizing a search of the entire house, including any containers where powder cocaine may be found. Lawman stayed with H.J. in the kitchen while the other officers conducted a search of the entire house. He did *not* tell the officers what he had found while they were away. During the search, the officers found the additional cocaine and handgun in the side table in H.J.'s bedroom.

Officer Lawman placed H.J. in a transport vehicle and drove him to the police station. When they arrived at the station, Lawman read H.J. his *Miranda* rights. H.J. said he wanted to speak with his lawyer before making any statements. The officer did not question H.J. and placed him in a holding cell to wait for transportation to court. After about an hour, H.J. called for Lawman and asked, "What's going to happen when I go to court tomorrow?" Lawman told him that his lawyer would be in court to advise him, but that it would be much better for him if he would give a statement that night. H.J. agreed and told Lawman that the cocaine on the side table was his, but that he didn't know anything about the cocaine and handgun in the drawer.

The next day, H.J. was taken to court and formally charged with possession with intent to distribute cocaine and possession of a handgun. In a separate charging document, he also was formally charged with simple assault. H.J. specifically invoked his right to counsel in both cases. H.J.'s lawyer was successful in convincing the court to release H.J. on bond pending his trials.

A week later, Officer Lawman went back to H.J.'s house and told him that he wanted to talk to him about the fact that he might be charged with some additional offenses. When H.J. asked what these additional charges were about, Lawman asked him if he would come down to the police station. H.J. agreed. When they arrived at the station, Lawman read H.J. his complete *Miranda* warnings and H.J. agreed to answer questions without an attorney present. Lawman then told H.J. that when he yanked open the man's car door during the "road rage" incident, he had broken the door. Lawman also informed H.J. that the driver's jaw was broken so badly that he suffered permanent damage. He further stated that H.J. would probably be charged with destruction of property (for the broken door) and malicious disfigurement (for the permanent damage to the driver's face). Lawman asked H.J. if he had anything he wanted to say about these new charges. H.J. said, "I can't help it if the guy had a glass jaw and a cheap car. That's what he gets for hitting my Jaguar!"

The government will attempt to introduce all of the cocaine, the handgun, and H.J.'s statement about the cocaine as evidence at the trial on these offenses. At his separate trial for simple assault, malicious disfigurement, and destruction of property, the government will attempt to introduce H.J.'s statement about the jaw and the car.

H.J.'s lawyer filed several motions to suppress the evidence and statements. Discuss all possible legal grounds in support of each of the following motions, the government's responses, and the court's likely rulings:

1) Motion to suppress the cocaine on the silver dish and the cocaine and handgun found in the drawer

2) Motion to suppress the statement about the cocaine

3) Motion to suppress the statement about the jaw and the car

EXAM 2

Marilyn and Tipper are students at State University, the largest state controlled university in the State. Both are computer whizzes and often refer to themselves and their friends as "hackers." They take great pride in being able to find ways around security protections which computer owners install to protect confidential information. On one occasion, they used a small personal computer and a modem (a device which permits one computer to speak to another over telephone lines much the way a Lexis or Westlaw terminal can communicate with a database) to circumvent the security codes in the University President's computer system and left him a happy birthday message on his screen which he saw when he arrived at the office on his birthday.

The State has become alarmed in recent years about the activity of some computer hackers. In some instances, hackers have been responsible for viruses which have destroyed computer data. In other instances, hackers have been blamed for pranks, like changing the grades in the registrar's office at a community college. And, in one widely reported case, hackers found their way into computerized data at a military base and leaked confidential information contained in the database to the press. As a result, the State has adopted a law, the Computer Protection Act, which reads as follows:

> It shall be a class 5 felony, punishable by up to two years in prison and a $10,000 fine, for any person to knowingly intercept, receive, record, copy, or examine any data stored in a computer database or network if it would appear to a reasonable person that the person or persons who control such database or network have sought to exclude by means of passwords, codes or other mechanisms persons not expressly authorized to use the database or network from access to it.

The statute has not discouraged all hackers, and it certainly has not discouraged Marilyn and Tipper.

In fact, Marilyn and Tipper have vowed to each other and to their friends that they will demonstrate the folly of the statute and show the State that it cannot and should not attempt to use the criminal law to deal with a minor irritant like hackers. After considerable thought about how best to get the attention of lawmakers, Marilyn told Tipper that they should use their computer to tap into the judicial database of the state and to erase all of the computer records relating to persons convicted of criminal acts. Tipper expressed some concern about the plan and suggested that it might be more of a demonstration than was needed, and also that it might be difficult to carry out the plan. After some discussion, Tipper agreed that they would see how difficult it would be to tap into the database and then decide whether to carry out the plan.

Marilyn and Tipper have two friends, Barbara and Hillary, who are law clerks for a state court of appeals judge. In the course of general conversations, Marilyn and

Tipper obtain sufficient information from Barbara and Hillary to tap into the state judicial system computer. They find that access to the judicial database requires use of a password and an identification number. To the surprise of Marilyn (and to the relief of Tipper), it is not easy to crack the security system and to obtain access to the data and their efforts fail.

Unbeknownst to Marilyn and Tipper, the administrator of the judicial database has installed an innovative device called "telephone number identification." This device identifies and records the telephone number used by anyone seeking access to the judicial database. The device works well, and each of the efforts which Marilyn and Tipper have made to contact the database have resulted in their telephone number being recorded. Each morning the administrator examines the telephone numbers which have been recorded in order to determine how the database is being used, who are the most frequent users, and whether the security of the system is intact. For two mornings in a row, the administrator has seen several contacts with the database from a number which she does not recognize. Her records show that a number of calls have been made from the same number and that the database indicates that in each instance "entry was refused." Concerned about the possible invasion of the security of the database, she calls the state police and asks if they can contact the telephone company and find out some information about the number. The state police make a visit to the offices of the phone company and learn that the telephone number is listed to Marilyn Bird, at 16 Massachusetts Ave., on the campus of State University.

The state police report what they have learned to the administrator who asks that the police continue to conduct an investigation. Two officers, Cagney and Lacey, arrange a meeting with the President of State University. They tell him about what the court administrator discovered and that they have learned that a telephone listed to Marilyn Bird was used to contact the judicial database. They ask whether the President can help them in their investigation. The President tells them about the happy birthday greeting that he found on his computer and telephones the Dean of Students to ask the Dean to speak with the officers. The Dean of Students knows Marilyn and Tipper well and tells the officers that Tipper is Marilyn's roommate. The Dean then provides the officers with class schedules for Marilyn and Tipper and goes with the officers to one of the classes to point out Marilyn and Tipper. The Dean also tells the officers that Marilyn and Tipper belong to the University's computer club which meets that afternoon and every Wednesday afternoon. The two officers, dressed in casual clothes, decide that they will attend the meeting and pretend that they are college students interested in computers. The meeting begins on time and is attended by approximately 40 people, including Marilyn and Tipper. The discussion is confined to how "Windows" can be used with Lexis and Nexis, and the officers have no understanding of what is being discussed.

When the meeting ends, Cagney strikes up a conversation with Tipper, and Cagney pretends to be interested in buying a personal computer. Cagney asks Tipper what she uses, and Tipper offers to show her the IBM clone she and her roommate use. Cagney walks with Tipper to 16 Massachusetts Ave. and enters a two bedroom apartment. Tipper shows her a computer which sits on a desk in the living room which the two entered as they walked through the front door. The two talk for a while, until Tipper excuses herself to use the restroom. As she begins to exit the living room, Cagney asks "Can I try the computer?" Hearing a "yes, help yourself," Cagney sits down at the desk and turns the computer on. As it warms up and runs some programs which set forth a menu, Cagney leafs through some papers on the desk and comes upon a note that reads, "court database, 333–3275." Recognizing the number as the number of the judicial database, Cagney puts the papers back as they were. On the menu, Cagney recognizes some files that can be used in connection with a modem to communicate with other computers. When Tipper comes back, Cagney asks whether the computer has a modem, and Tipper indicates that an internal modem is contained inside the computer.

Cagney decides to ask to use the restroom in order to be able to look around the apartment. After obtaining Tipper's permission, Cagney walks to the restroom which is located between two bedrooms. Looking left and right, Cagney is able to see into both bedrooms. She notices a bunch of computer paper on the bed in one room. When she returns from the restroom, Cagney asks whether she can use a mirror in one of the bedrooms in order to fix her hair. Tipper agrees, and Cagney walks into the bedroom with the computer paper, picks up the paper and sees a printout of a list of words, including the following: judge, justice, court, clerk.

While Cagney deals with Tipper, Lacey is on the campus talking with Marilyn. Lacey asks Marilyn whether anyone in the club ever engages in computer pranks, and Marilyn states "some of us do, and we have a monster job that Tipper and I are working on." Although Marilyn does not know it, Lacey is secretly taping the conversation with a small recording device that she has hidden in her bag.

Cagney leaves the apartment and meets up with Lacey, and the two exchange the information they have obtained. They agree that Cagney will seek a warrant to search the apartment and that Lacey will seek the help of the University President in gathering evidence. But, before they seek the warrant, the officers decide to do some further investigation. They go to an electronics store and purchase a box of diskettes and they hide a small voice transmitter in the diskette box. They drive over to the apartment where Tipper had taken Cagney and Cagney goes to the door. She knocks and Tipper answers. Cagney tells Tipper that she just bought some new diskettes and asks whether Tipper would be willing to format them for her. Tipper agrees, Cagney leaves the box, and agrees to return that morning. Later that day, Cagney and Lacey overhear Tipper and Marilyn having a discussion in which Tipper says, "Well, why don't we try the database again tomorrow night."

Early the next morning, Cagney submits to a State Magistrate–Judge an affidavit which reads as follows:

"My name is Sharon Cagney, I am a State Police officer and have served in the State Police for seven years. During this time I have had occasion to investigate all manner of crime, including computer crimes. I submit this affidavit under penalty of perjury.

"Earlier this week, the Administrator of the judicial database informed myself and my fellow officer, Janet Lacey, that someone had been seeking entry into the database. This person or persons had no way of knowing that the database is protected with an identification system that identifies and records all numbers from which calls are made into the system. Lacey and I followed up on this information and visited the phone company. We learned that the telephone number is listed to Marilyn Bird at 16 Massachusetts Ave. on the campus of State University. We visited the University, spoke to the President, met Marilyn Bird and her roommate, Tipper. I personally visited the apartment in which the two live. In that apartment I saw a computer with a modem, and I also saw a piece of paper that contained the telephone number of the judicial database. I also saw a computer printout with various words on it, including 'Judge,' 'justice', 'court,' and 'clerk.' While I was in the apartment, Officer Lacey had a conversation with Tipper in which she stated that she and Marilyn were in fact trying to break into the database. Furthermore, Officer Lacey and I overheard a conversation in which Tipper stated to Marilyn that they should try again to break into the database tomorrow night.

"On the basis of the facts set forth above, I believe that Marilyn and Tipper have violated the statute protecting the confidentiality of computerized information, known as the Computer Protection Act, which is a class 5 felony and that they are in possession of relevant evidence that would demonstrate their violation of the statute. Based on these facts, I seek a search warrant for the apartment at 16 Massachusetts Ave. to search for and seize all computers, computer paper, disks, and any other records that might relate to the crime identified herein."

The State Magistrate–Judge issues a search warrant which contains the following language: "This warrant commands the State Police to search the apartment at 16 Massachusetts Ave. belonging to Marilyn Bird and her roommate, Tipper, and to locate and seize all computers, computer paper, disks, and any other records that might relate to the Computer Protection Act." Cagney and Lacey take the warrant to the apartment. They knock, and when Tipper answers, they state that they are police officers with a search warrant. Tipper opens the door, the officers enter, and they begin their search. They examine every closet, drawer, file, and space in the apartment and seize the computer on the desk and a printer, all diskettes (both the 5¼" floppies and the 3½" floppies which are near the computer). They also take checkbooks, calendars, phone bills, and papers found on the desk near the computer.

When the search is over, Cagney tells Tipper she is under arrest. Tipper asks why, and Cagney tells her she is charged with violating the Computer Protection Act. Cagney handcuffs Tipper and searches the handbag which she had near her. In the handbag she finds some additional computer disks, another checkbook and a handwritten note containing the telephone number of the judicial database. She shows the note to Lacey, and Tipper, seeing the two reading the note, states, "It was a stupid idea, a really stupid idea. I'm sorry." "Sorry about what?" Lacey asks. "You know, the judicial records. I'm sorry," Tipper answers. "Where's your roommate?" Lacey asks. Tipper says she is not sure, but she might be at school. Lacey asks whether Marilyn has a car, and Tipper answers that Marilyn drives a black Honda Accord with the license plate "Hack."

Cagney telephones the President of the University to inform the President that Tipper is arrested and to ask for help in locating Marilyn. The President promises help, asks the Dean of Students to find Marilyn, and waits for the Dean to look for her. The Dean finds Marilyn and brings her to the President, who says, "Marilyn, this is awful. Tipper has been arrested. The police are looking for you. The University is embarrassed. Now, I demand that you tell me exactly what you two have been up to. You can consider yourself suspended, and depending on how much you cooperate, you might or might not be expelled." Marilyn answers, "Well, we were going to break into the judicial database and erase some records. It was really Tipper's idea." The President responds, "Well, the police are on their way."

Marilyn runs from the President's office, gets her car, and drives off. Cagney and Lacey, with Tipper in the car, see Marilyn driving toward them, turn on their lights, and stop Marilyn's car. With gun in hand, Lacey places Marilyn under arrest, handcuffs her and places her in the patrol car with Tipper. Lacey drives

Marilyn's car to the State Police station while Cagney drives Marilyn and Tipper in the patrol car. The officers book the two arrestees and take them before a Magistrate–Judge. The Magistrate–Judge tells them that they are charged with violating the Computer Protection Act and that each must post $10,000 bond in order to be released. Neither has that much money, but Marilyn calls her parents who agree to post bond for the two the next day. Marilyn and Tipper spend the night in jail waiting. After the appearance before the Magistrate–Judge, Lacey does a complete search of the car and in the trunk finds a briefcase. Inside is a piece of paper with the words, "Destroy the records!" written on it in large type.

Before Marilyn's parents arrive, Cagney takes Marilyn from her cell and says, "I got a call from the President. He told me what you said and that you claim it was all Tipper's fault. If that is true and you cooperate, things might go better for you. It's up to you." Marilyn responds, "It was all her fault, and I will cooperate, but I want to talk to a lawyer first. Is that alright?" "Sure!" responds Cagney.

When Marilyn's parents arrive, Cagney tells them about his conversation with Marilyn and says that "any information you can find out will help us and your daughter." As they are leaving the station, Marilyn's mother says to Cagney that "Marilyn told me that they were going to erase all the records of people convicted. I hope that helps."

Two days later, the grand jury indicts Marilyn and Tipper for violating the Computer Protection Act. After hearing of the indictment, Tipper calls Cagney on the phone and states, "I never wanted to break into the database. Can't you help me?" Cagney responds by saying, "I'll do what I can, but I'm not sure that I can help at this point. But, if you want me to try, come on down and we can talk." Tipper arrives at the station, tells Cagney everything that happened, and asks for a break.

YOUR LAW FIRM HAS BEEN RETAINED BY BOTH MARILYN AND TIPPER. ALTHOUGH YOU HAVE INFORMED THEM ABOUT THE CLEAR POSSIBIL-ITY OF A CONFLICT OF INTEREST, THEY HAVE DECIDED THAT IT WOULD BE USEFUL AT THE OUTSET TO HAVE ONE FIRM GIVE THEM A PRELIMI-NARY ANALYSIS OF WHETHER ANY OF THE EVIDENCE OBTAINED AGAINST THEM MIGHT BE SUPPRESSED. YOUR FIRM HAS BEEN GRANTED COM-PLETE ACCESS TO THE INVESTIGATORY FILE, AND YOU HAVE INTER-VIEWED YOUR CLIENTS, THE STATE POLICE OFFICERS, THE COURT ADMINISTRATOR AND THE UNIVERSITY PRESIDENT. YOU KNOW ABOUT ALL THE STATEMENTS MADE BY EITHER TIPPER OR MARILYN AND ABOUT THE EVIDENCE SEIZED FROM THEM. YOUR TASK IS TO WRITE A MEMORANDUM DISCUSSING ALL REASONABLE MOTIONS TO SUPPRESS,

THE RESPONSE THE STATE WILL MAKE TO THE MOTIONS, AND THE LIKELY RESOLUTION OF EACH MOTION.

Remember that clarity is important. Your answer should make clear each motion to suppress you believe is reasonably available to Marilyn and/or Tipper, the arguments in support of and against these motions, and the most probable resolution. The "most probable resolution" is the least important part of your answer. If your analysis of the strengths and weaknesses of each motion is adequate, the "most probable resolution" is likely to emerge almost automatically. You may use the names of important and familiar cases without full citations or even full titles. For example, if you are relying on Mapp, you can just use this shorthand reference to the case.

APPENDIX B

Criminal Procedure—Sample Answers

ANSWER FOR EXAM 1

QUESTION 1

The police obtained a valid warrant for HJ's arrest based on probable cause. The warrant described HJ as a white man in a silver Jaguar with a specific license plate number, which was sufficient detail for Officer Lawman to identify HJ and seek to execute the arrest warrant against him.

HJ's lawyer, in a motion to suppress the cocaine on the silver dish and the cocaine and handgun found in the drawer, will first argue that the officer entered HJ's home improperly by failing to knock and announce his presence before using force to enter the home. However, the government is going to argue that the officer was not required to knock and announce his presence because the officer was in hot pursuit. In *Wilson v. Arkansas*, the Court held that there are countervailing circumstances that might permit an unannounced entry, including hot pursuit. In *Richards v. Wisconsin*, the Court held that a police officer may enter without knocking and announcing his presence if doing so would be dangerous, futile, or would inhibit the effective investigation of the crime. According to the hot pursuit doctrine as established in *Warden v. Hayden*, an officer is not required to obtain a warrant if he/she is in hot pursuit of the suspect, for the same reasons *Wilson* and *Richards* permit entry without knocking and announcing. Here, Officer Lawman had a warrant *and* he was in hot pursuit of HJ. The hot pursuit of HJ began when he noticed the officer trying to pull him over, glanced at the officer, and then sped away. When HJ drove to his house, ran inside, and locked the door, the officer was not required to knock and announce his presence. The purposes of the doctrine—protecting the officer and others from violence, protecting privacy rights, and protecting against destruction of property—would not have been served since the officer had a warrant and HJ clearly knew that the officer was trying to reach him.

Once the officer entered the house, he lawfully seized HJ and placed him under arrest, based on the warrant issued. HJ's lawyer will argue that the search that followed HJ's arrest was illegal because 1) the officer's search exceeded the permissible area for a search incident to arrest; and 2) the officer unlawfully opened containers in the home. *Chimel v. California* established the permissible boundaries for a search incident to a lawful arrest. The Court held that the police may not search an entire house incident to an arrest warrant but only the suspect and any area within his immediate control, or, in other words, the suspect's "grabbable" area. After Officer Lawman arrested HJ, the suspect was confined to the kitchen area. The cocaine in the silver dish and items in the drawer were found in the suspect's bedroom, far beyond HJ's grabbable area.

The government will argue that Lawman lawfully seized the cocaine in the silver dish because it was in plain view during a lawful protective sweep. *Maryland v. Buie* established that an officer is permitted to conduct a protective sweep of the premises incident to arrest when the officer has reasonable suspicion that other persons could be hiding on the premises that may place the officer in danger. Thus, the officer is permitted to look in places throughout the premises where a person could be hiding. Officer Lawman conducted a permissible protective sweep by looking in all rooms of the house, including closets, and by not opening any containers in the house. It was while he was sweeping through the suspect's bedroom that he saw the drugs in the silver dish. HJ's attorney will argue that *Maryland v. Buie* did not apply because the officer did not have reasonable suspicion to believe that another person was hiding on the premises.

The government will argue that the officer was permitted to seize the cocaine that he saw in plain view on the silver dish. *Horton v. California* held that an officer is allowed to seize evidence whose incriminating character is immediately apparent as long as he is legally in the space where the item is seen by way of a valid warrant or exception to the warrant requirement. The government will argue that Lawman was legally in the room during the course of conducting a protective sweep and that the officer immediately recognized that the powdery substance was incriminating because of his experience in the narcotics division of the police force.

When Officer Lawman saw the cocaine in plain view, he sent another officer to obtain a warrant to search the whole house. He then returned to the bedroom and opened a drawer of the bedside table and saw ten small bags of cocaine and a small handgun. HJ's lawyer will argue that this was an illegal search because the officer was searching in an area outside of the suspect's grabbable area, the evidence in the drawer was not in plain view, and the officer had no warrant to search the drawer. The government, on the other hand, is going to argue that the evidence should be admitted under the independent source rule.

In *Murray v. U.S.*, the Court allowed evidence to be admitted because the evidence was discovered through an independent source. In *Murray*, officers observed men they had under surveillance go into a warehouse and later leave. The men turned their vehicles over to other individuals who were followed and ultimately arrested. Several officers forced entry to the warehouse and discovered burlap-wrapped bales that were later discovered to contain marijuana. The officers left and obtained a search warrant, but did not mention the prior unlawful entry or rely on any information obtained during that entry. The Court upheld the search and seizure of the drugs found in the warehouse because the officers had a legal independent source to obtain a warrant and did not mention the illegal search of the warehouse when they obtained the search warrant.

Similar circumstances existed in HJ's case. Because of the drugs in plain view, the officers had probable cause to get a warrant to search the entire house. Even though Officer Lawman illegally searched the drawer and found the evidence, he did not tell the officers about this illegal search, so the warrant was based on an independent, legal source. The officers found the drugs in the drawer based on a legal warrant untainted by the prior illegal search.

Overall, the government will likely succeed in defeating the motion to suppress evidence based on the hot pursuit doctrine, the plain view doctrine, the protective sweep rule, and the independent source rule.

QUESTION 2

HJ's lawyer will file a motion to suppress the statement about the cocaine, alleging a violation of *Miranda v. Arizona. Miranda* only applies to custodial interrogation and requires officers to warn a suspect of his/her rights before beginning an interrogation. The warnings must include the right to remain silent, that anything said can be used against the suspect in court, the right to an attorney, and the right to have that attorney present during the questioning. The suspect may waive these rights, as long as the waiver is knowing, intelligent, and voluntary.

In this case, HJ was definitely in custody when he was arrested and transported to the police station. Officer Lawman properly gave the *Miranda* warnings to HJ before beginning any questioning. HJ invoked his right to counsel and Officer Lawman did not question HJ. In *Edwards v. Arizona*, the Court ruled that once a suspect invokes his 5th amendment right to counsel, he may not be questioned again unless the suspect initiates the communication. Officer Lawman properly refused to question HJ after this right had been invoked. However, an hour after Lawman put HJ in a holding cell, HJ asked for Lawman and said to him, "What's going to happen when I go to court tomorrow?" Officer Lawman then advised HJ that it would be better for him to talk to the officer, and HJ gave an incriminating statement about the cocaine in the silver dish. HJ's lawyer will argue that the officer violated the requirements of *Edwards v. Arizona* when he questioned the suspect after he had invoked his 5th amendment right to counsel. The lawyer will argue that HJ could not be questioned again after he asked for counsel.

In response, the government will argue that Officer Lawman acted properly and was allowed to question HJ because HJ initiated the conversation by asking the officer what was going to happen to him in court. HJ's lawyer will argue that by asking the officer what was going to happen in court, HJ was in no way initiating communication about the crimes for which he was under suspicion and simply wanted to know what procedures he would be subjected to when he went to court the next day. The government will rely on *Oregon v. Bradshaw* to argue that the question asked by HJ was sufficient to initiate communication and allow the officer to question him. In *Bradshaw*, the suspect was being transported to the police station, was given his rights, and invoked his 5th amendment right to counsel. As they were traveling to the police station, the suspect asked the officer, "What is going to happen to me now?" The officer then gave Bradshaw new *Miranda* warnings, and he proceeded to give an incriminating statement. The Court ruled that Bradshaw had initiated the communication and knowingly and voluntarily waived his rights thereafter, permitting the officer to question him. The government will argue that HJ's question was identical to the question asked by Bradshaw, thus showing that HJ initiated the conversation, which then allowed Officer Lawman to question him. On the other hand, HJ's lawyer will attempt to distinguish *Bradshaw* because the officer in that case gave the suspect new *Miranda* warnings after the communication had been initiated. Here, Officer Lawman did not give HJ new *Miranda* warnings after HJ asked him a question.

Overall, the Court is likely to rule in favor of the government. The *Bradshaw* case is strong support for the government because of the near identical questions posed by both Bradshaw and HJ. Although HJ's lawyer has a good argument that HJ was not again advised of his rights, the Court is likely to find in favor of the government. HJ did appear to fully understand his rights the first time he was advised because he immediately invoked the right to counsel after the warnings were given and before the officer could ask him one question. For this reason, the Court is unlikely to be persuaded that HJ did not understand his rights when the officer later questioned him.

QUESTION 3

The 6th Amendment provides the right to an attorney once a suspect has been formally charged and adversarial proceedings have commenced. HJ was taken to court and formally charged with possession with intent to distribute cocaine and possession of a handgun. He was also charged in a separate document with simple assault. HJ invoked his 6th Amendment right to an attorney and was released on bond. A week later, Officer Lawman asked HJ to come down to the station because he wanted to talk to him about possibly being charged for other offenses.

HJ's attorney will cite *Michigan v. Jackson* and argue that the officer violated HJ's 6th Amendment right to counsel since he had been formally charged and had already appeared in court. In *Michigan v. Jackson,* the Court held that if a defendant invokes his right to counsel after formal charges, any subsequent waivers are invalid because police may not question the defendant unless he initiates contact with the police. HJ will argue that the officer violated *Jackson* by questioning him about the destruction of property and malicious disfigurement charges because these crimes are directly related to and grew directly out of the simple assault, with which HJ had already been charged. HJ will argue that the government's theory is that the damage to the car and injury to the man's jaw happened because HJ assaulted the man and were a consequence of his crime of simple assault. Thus, because the officer questioned HJ about the closely-related crime of simple assault, the officer violated his 6th Amendment right to counsel and the statement about the jaw and car cannot be used against him.

In response to HJ's claim of a Sixth Amendment violation, the government will cite *McNeil v. Wisconsin.* In *McNeil,* the Court determined that the invocation of the 6th Amendment right to counsel is offense specific and the attorney appointed or hired is the attorney only for the crime or crimes charged. As a result, the Court held that an officer may question a defendant about any other crimes except those with which the defendant is charged. The government will argue that there was no 6th amendment violation because Officer Lawman was permitted to question HJ about the destruction of property and malicious disfigurement crimes since they are separate crimes for which HJ had not been charged. The government will rely on *Texas v. Cobb*, which permits an officer to question a defendant about other crimes even if they are closely related to other crimes with which the defendant is already charged. In *Cobb*, the court held that the *Blockburger* test would determine whether the new charges would be considered the same offense for purposes of the Sixth Amendment right to counsel. Under the *Blockburger* test, there are two separate offenses if each crime requires proof of a fact which the other does not. Relying on *Cobb*, the government will argue that the crimes of destruction of property and malicious disfigurement are separate crimes, and that the officer was permitted to question HJ about the new charges.

Based on the Court's recent decision in *Texas v. Cobb*, the court is likely to rule in favor of the government on the motion to suppress HJ's statement about the jaw and the car.

ANSWER FOR EXAM 2

■ I. PROBABLE CAUSE

It is probably true that—despite all of the evidence that the police have gathered—Tipper and Marilyn are not guilty of any criminal act. The statute provides that it is a felony for any person "to knowingly intercept, receive, record, copy or examine any data" stored in a computer under circumstances in which a reasonable person should know that the person who controls the database is trying to exclude everyone except those who are specifically authorized to examine the data. It is clear from the totality of the facts that neither Tipper nor Marilyn actually decided that they would intercept, receive, record, copy or examine anything in the database. They agreed to examine the difficulty of tapping into the database and *then and only then* to decide whether to go forward with a plan of erasing criminal records.

It is difficult to argue that Tipper and Marilyn have conspired with each other or done anything amounting to an attempt. They have, at most, decided to explore whether or not they will engage in acts which, if undertaken, would be criminal.

It is not a crime under the statute to use a modem to contact a database. It is not a crime to experiment. Thus, when all is said and done, it appears that, when all the facts are known, Marilyn and Tipper are not guilty of violating the statute. Indeed, if the police had all the facts at the time they obtained the warrant, they would not have had probable cause for an arrest or search.

But, the question is not whether Marilyn and Tipper are actually guilty. Rather, the question is whether there was probable cause to believe them to be guilty at the time that the police and the magistrate judge engaged in their official acts. It is, after all, possible to have a valid arrest and valid search of people who, in hindsight, are determined to be innocent. Probable cause is not certainty. It is assessed on the basis of information in the hands of governmental actors at the time they act, not afterward.

■ II. REASONABLE EXPECTATIONS OF PRIVACY

Marilyn and Tipper may argue that the "telephone number identification" violates the reasonable expectation of a caller that she is not being recorded. The Government's response surely will be that caller I.D. is widely enough known that there can be no reasonable expectation of privacy. Moreover, the Government will further argue that any security precautions which the Government takes with respect to its own database cannot be unreasonable when imposed upon outsiders. It will be difficult for Marilyn and Tipper to prevail on this argument.

Similarly, Marilyn and Tipper may seek to challenge the use of undercover officers who lie about their true motives and their identities, especially when they use falsity to obtain entrance into a house (which is as we know neither a database nor a car). But, the Government's response that people have no expectation that others with whom they deal are not cooperating with the Government is surely likely to prevail. The Supreme Court's decisions in *Lopez* and other cases indicate that the Court does not protect people from misplaced confidence in others, so long as those others are acting within the scope of the misplaced confidence.

Tipper and Marilyn may consider a challenge to the obtaining of their telephone number by the police from the telephone company. But, cases involving bank records and telephone pen registers suggest that Government agents may obtain information from third parties who possess it without violating any expectations of privacy on the part of persons to whom the information relates.

Another claim that has little chance of success is Marilyn's challenge to Lacey's secret recording of their initial conversation. The Government can argue that people assume the risk that those with whom they speak might be recording the conversation. In view of the Supreme Court's recent expectation of privacy cases, the Government is likely to win.

■ III. THE SNOOPING BY CAGNEY

Although Cagney's entrance into the apartment was consented to by Tipper, who cannot successfully make a reasonable expectation of privacy argument based on Cagney's undercover status, Cagney's actions inside the apartment cause problems. Cagney has consent to use the computer. Thus, what she finds when she uses it is in plain view. Her question to Tipper about the modem is valid, as is Tipper's answer. Any challenge to the question based on *Miranda* will lose because this is not custodial interrogation and Tipper does not know she is talking to a police officer. *(Perkins)*

When Cagney "leafs through some papers" on the desk without consent, she invites an *Arizona v. Hicks* challenge, because she goes beyond the scope of her invitation. One question is who has standing to raise the challenge. Marilyn is not home. It might turn on whether the papers belong to both women, or only to one. Assuming that both have standing to make a challenge, the Government will argue that there was consent or that the papers were in plain view. The Government will likely lose, just as it did in *Hicks*. This may be a small search, but *Hicks* indicates that a small search is still a search. Thus, there might be a chance to suppress evidence of the telephone number of the judicial database.

Similarly, when Cagney asks to use a mirror to fix her hair, she engages in questionable conduct. Here too, standing is a question. It might be that only the person whose room was examined has standing. We don't have enough facts to offer a definitive opinion. Tipper will urge that Cagney was feigning having to use the bathroom and to fix her hair. The fact is, however, that the Government will win any challenge to the observations that Cagney made on the way to the bathroom and while standing in the bedroom. Anything observed was in plain view in places which Tipper had consented to have Cagney present. The fact that Cagney had an ulterior motive is not disqualifying. When Cagney picked up the computer paper off the bed, arguably she violated *Hicks* again. This too looks like a little search, but a search nonetheless. It is possible that Tipper and Marilyn may manage to suppress the evidence of the words appearing on the computer paper.

■ IV. THE DISKETTES

Under *Knotts and Karo*, it seems that the police may buy a box of diskettes and place anything that they want in the box. They own it, and they can do with it as they please. A problem arises, however, when they offer the box to Tipper in what is the equivalent of her home. This raises a question whether the special privacy interests of the home are violated. In the "beeper" case, the Court refused to approve the warrantless monitoring of beepers inside a house. This might suggest that electronic surveillance of conversations would be even more likely to be condemned because it is more intrusive. However, the Government will argue that Tipper never purchased the diskettes and at all times understood that she was receiving the property of another. Having chosen to receive it, may Tipper still claim she had a reasonable expectation of privacy that it did not contain anything but diskettes? This is a tough issue based on the few precedents that exist. If Marilyn and Tipper prevail, their statement will be suppressed. If not, the statement will be admissible evidence.

■ V. THE WARRANT

Marilyn and Tipper will argue that the warrant is the fruit of illegal searches and that there was no probable cause to support it. On the probable cause point, the Government will argue that a magistrate could have concluded that there was an apparent attempt to violate the law. Given the identification system employed by the judicial database and the other evidence obtained by the police, it certainly could have appeared to a reasonable magistrate that the suspects were involved in a conspiracy to violate the Computer Protection Act. There was probable cause on the face of the affidavit.

But, Tipper and Marilyn will be able to raise serious fruit of the poisonous tree questions. Assuming that the two *Hicks* violations discussed above taint the information in the affidavit that Cagney saw the judicial database telephone number in the apartment and saw a computer printout with various words upon it, Tipper and Marilyn will have an argument that, if this evidence were excluded, the warrant would not have issued. The Government will respond that there was sufficient remaining evidence to establish probable cause.

The Government's response will trigger a claim by Tipper and Marilyn that two of the statements contained in the affidavit were false, and on this point they are correct. Cagney's affidavit is absolutely false to the extent that she claims that Tipper told Lacey that she and Marilyn were trying to break into the database. This statement is not only false, but it is also difficult to find any reasonable explanation for it. One problem with the alleged statement is that Lacey was talking to Marilyn while Cagney was with Tipper. Thus, the reference to Lacey's talking to Tipper was certainly wrong. It is possible, however, that this is a typo and that Cagney meant to put "Marilyn" in place of "Tipper." The fact remains, however, that the conversation that is described did not occur. Cagney does not fairly summarize what Marilyn told Lacey. The other statement that is false is Cagney's statement that she and Lacey overheard a conversation in which Tipper stated to Marilyn that they should try to break into the database tomorrow night. There was no such conversation. Instead, the officers overheard Tipper say, "why don't we try the database again tomorrow night." Tipper did not say that the two should try to break in. We know from the facts that Tipper and Marilyn agreed not to decide whether to break in until they were sure that they would be able to do so if they wanted to.

Thus, Tipper and Marilyn have a *Franks v. Delaware* issue. The Court will disregard all statements made perjuriously or with reckless disregard of the truth. The first false statement appears to be of this type. It creates a conversation that never occurred. It is difficult to know how this can be deemed to be an honest error. The second statement is more problematic. Cagney will assert that she believed she heard the statement she reported, and that she reported it as she remembered it. This might well be a case of negligence, and negligently included information is not disregarded in the warrant application. Thus, the issue is whether, assuming the first statement cannot be relied upon but the second can be, there is sufficient evidence remaining to establish probable cause. If the *Hicks* violations exclude the evidence of the telephone number and the computer paper, and if the first Franks statement is excluded, Tipper and Marilyn's chances of success in having the warrant invalidated improve. Moreover, if the hidden mike in the diskette box is deemed to have been an intrusion into a reasonable expectation of privacy, the second Franks statement would be suppressed and the warrant application would have little left to support it.

Of course, the Government will argue good faith and cite *Leon*. *Leon* will excuse police who rely on a warrant issued by a magistrate when the warrant is not bad on its face. The Courts are divided on whether *Leon* applies to a warrant based on information obtained in violation of the Fourth Amendment. But at any rate, the officers would have to clearly describe the circumstances under which the *Hicks*-defective evidence was obtained in order to reasonably rely on the magistrate's implicit determination that it was obtained legally. Moreover, to the extent the warrant was based on a lie by the officer, the good faith exception obviously does not apply. If the evidence discussed in the several paragraphs immediately preceding is suppressed, the only remaining evidence will be the identification of Marilyn's telephone number by the secret identification system, the fact that the telephone number is listed to Marilyn, the observation of the computer and the knowledge of a modem. Is this enough to establish probable cause? Marilyn and Tipper will argue that it is not, and the Government will argue that it is. The Government's argument will not be strong at this point.

If the warrant is invalid, and not excused by the good faith exception, the search conducted pursuant to it will be invalid. If the warrant is valid, or excused by the good faith exception, the search is valid, up to a point. The point is the overbreadth of the warrant. Marilyn and Tipper will cite *Andresen* and claim that the language "any other records" is overbroad. The Government will cite the same case and argue that the language is similar to that approved by the Court. Marilyn and Tipper have the stronger argument. In *Andresen* the warrant was limited, according to the Supreme Court, to documents involving Lot 13T in a particular subdivision. The officers' discretion was therefore limited. No such limitation exists in the warrant described here. Many lower court decisions condemn such broad language. However, under the good faith exception, the warrant must be so overboard that no reasonable person could rely on it. It is not likely that the court would find the description so overbroad as to preclude the use of the good faith exception.

Assuming that the language is that so overbroad as to be beyond the protection of the good faith exception, Marilyn and Tipper might be able to suppress the checkbooks, calendars, phone bills and other papers seized. Standing will rear its head again, however. Each can only suppress the items as to which she had a reasonable expectation of privacy.

■ VI. THE ARREST OF TIPPER

If the warrant is invalid as lacking in probable cause when all of the fruits of the poisonous tree are excluded, the arrest of Tipper is invalid for two reasons. First, the entry into the home would be pursuant to an invalid warrant, making the arrest of Tipper in the home invalid under *Payton*. Second, if there was no probable cause to search, there would appear to be no probable cause to arrest; the bulk of the evidence would be tainted.

If the arrest is invalid, the search incident thereto is invalid, and the fruits thereof would be suppressed. The fruits would include the statement made by Tipper. The Government might argue that an invalid arrest in the home does not require suppression of evidence (*Harris*), but it would lose as to evidence obtained in the home as a result of an illegal search and arrest.

■ VII. TIPPER'S STATEMENT

If Tipper was validly arrested, she will nevertheless claim that the statement she made to the officers should be suppressed because she was in custody. The

Government will argue that she volunteered the statement and that like *Connelly* the Government does not have to stop a person from volunteering. The Government will likely prevail.

Tipper may argue that the question, "Sorry about what?" amounted to interrogation. But, the Government will claim that Tipper initiated the entire conversation. At some point, the Government must administer *Miranda* warnings but probably not at the time a person is confessing.

It might be that the question about the whereabouts of Marilyn is Government initiated. But, it is difficult to find anything incriminating in the answer. Tipper might have a decent *Miranda* issue, but her statement is not likely to help the Government very much. Marilyn lacks standing to complain.

■ VIII. MARILYN'S STATEMENT TO THE PRESIDENT

The President of a state university is a Government official. When he confronts Marilyn and tells her she is suspended and might be expelled, Marilyn will rely on *Lefkowitz* to argue that any statement she made was compelled in violation of the privilege against self-incrimination. The Government will respond that the threat was less substantial than in *Lefkowitz* and that this was not custodial interrogation. Marilyn will win. Any threat that compels testimony is prohibited, and *Lefkowitz* is not dependent on the existence of custody. Thus, Marilyn will be able to suppress her statement. Tipper has no standing.

■ IX. THE ARREST OF MARILYN AND SEARCH OF HER CAR

Marilyn can challenge her arrest on the basis of the absence of probable cause. No warrant is required under *Watson* for a public arrest. If the evidence discussed in connection with Tipper's arrest and the search warrant is suppressed, it is possible that Marilyn's arrest will be invalidated and that all of the evidence that flows from it will be deemed fruit of the poisonous tree.

Even if Marilyn's arrest is valid, she will challenge the search of her car on the ground that it was warrantless. The Government will rely on *Belton* and *Acevedo*. The Government will lose. *Belton* does not allow the search of a trunk. And *Acevedo* does not excuse probable cause as the minimum standard for an auto search. There is nothing in the facts presented to demonstrate probable cause to search the car. The paper seized in the trunk of the car will be suppressed, unless the search can be deemed to be a valid inventory search. The police would have to show that they routinely search cars, look in the trunk and examine papers. If the police can show a routine practice, the evidence can be admitted in some courts under the inevitable discovery exception, even if the actual search conducted was not an inventory search.

■ X. MARILYN'S STATEMENTS

Once Marilyn and Tipper are informed of the charges against them by a magistrate-judge, their *Massiah* rights, as defined in *Brewer v. Williams,* kick in. Any attempt to deliberately elicit statements from either, absent a valid waiver of the *Massiah* right, will be condemned. Thus, Marilyn will move to suppress her statement to Cagney. It appears that the statement is obtained in violation of both *Massiah* and *Miranda,* since it involves custodial questioning of a person after a formal charge has been leveled and without a valid waiver under *Patterson.* This is not an *Edwards* or *Jackson* situation because there is no indication that Marilyn invoked her right to counsel until after she made a statement. Still, waiver cannot be found in the absence of warnings and a knowing and understanding relinquishment of the right. Under *Miranda,* her statement can be used for impeachment. Whether it can be so used under *Massiah* is still open. Because this is not a *Jackson* case, the *Harvey* rationale (that a violation of a prophylactic rule is not a violation of the constitution) is not directly applicable.

Apparently, the police have sought to enlist Marilyn's parents to assist them. Marilyn's parents become agents of the police under *Massiah* (but not *Miranda* because those protections only apply if the suspect knows that he is talking to a police officer) when they obtain a statement from Marilyn and relay it to the police. Marilyn will move to suppress under *Massiah.* The Government will cite *Mauro* and claim that they did not force the parents to ask any questions or Marilyn to answer any. But, *Mauro* is not on point. It is a *Miranda* case in which the Mauros were permitted to talk with each other only if a police officer was present. The officer put a tape recorder in plain view. The instant case is a *Massiah* case, and the facts presented are akin to *Massiah* itself, since Marilyn did not know she was dealing with parents who had been directed by the Government to seek information. Her motion to suppress her statement is likely to be granted.

■ XI. TIPPER'S STATEMENT

Tipper will move to suppress the contents of her telephone conversation with Cagney. She will urge that her *Massiah* rights were violated. But, she volunteered the first part of the statement. It is difficult to say that Cagney deliberately elicited anything. When Cagney suggests that Tipper come to the station, the situation may change.

Tipper will argue that this is deliberate elicitation. The government will respond that it is all part of what Tipper initiated. This is a close question.

■ XII. THE INDICTMENT

Tipper and Marilyn might move to dismiss the indictment on the ground that it is the fruit of the various illegalities set forth above. Should they prevail on many of their claims, little admissible evidence would exist. Yet, the *Calandra* case indicates that challenges to grand jury action on the basis of illegally seized evidence are not likely to succeed.

APPENDIX C

Glossary

A

Administrative Search: As there is a reduced expectation of privacy in commercial property (as opposed to an individual's private residence), the Court allows for warrantless administrative inspections of pervasively/closely regulated industries if the warrantless inspection furthers a substantial governmental interest, and statutes provide constitutionally adequate substitutes for a warrant (e.g., notification, scope, limitation of inspector's discretion.) See Special Needs Analysis

Arrest: To deprive a person of his liberty by legal authority based on probable cause for the purpose of holding or detaining him to answer a criminal charge. All that is required for an "arrest" is some act by an officer indicating his intention to detain or take a person into custody and thereby subject that person to the actual control and will of the officer; no formal declaration of arrest is required. See Custodial Interrogation, *Miranda* Rights

Arrest Warrant: A written order of the court which is made on behalf of the state, or United States, and is based upon a complaint, or the filing, and is issued pursuant to statute and/or court rule and which commands a law enforcement officer to arrest a person and bring him before a magistrate. The warrant is issued by a "neutral and detached magistrate" (as opposed to police officers who are engaged in the often competitive enterprise of ferreting out crime) who is capable of determining whether probable cause exists. The warrant must be signed by the magistrate and must contain the name of the defendant or, if his name is unknown, any name or description by which he can be identified with reasonable certainty. Although an arrest warrant is not necessary for arrests made in public, an arrest warrant must be issued for an in-home arrest in the absence of exigent circumstances. An arrest warrant founded on probable cause implicitly carries with it the limited authority to enter a dwelling in which the suspect lives when there is reason to believe the suspect is within.

Attenuation: Under the totality of circumstances, if "fruit" from an illegal search or seizure did not come through the exploitation of that illegality, but instead, by means sufficiently distinguishable to be purged of the primary taint, then the evidence is admissible at trial and is not subject to the exclusionary rule. The egregiousness or flagrancy of the initial violation will be an important factor in the court's determination of whether or not the fruit is tainted. See Fruit of the Poisonous Tree Doctrine

Automobile Exception: An automobile can ordinarily be searched without a warrant, so long as there is probable cause to believe that evidence or contraband is located in the area to be searched. This exception does not require that the car actually be in motion at the time the officers obtain such probable cause. If the police do not perform an immediate search, the car may be seized and held without a warrant, and a subsequent warrantless search is ordinarily valid.

B

Border Search: Search conducted by immigration or customs officials at borders of the country to prevent and to detect illegal entry, whether or not there is any suspicion of illegality directed to the particular person or thing to be searched. The border search is a longstanding, historically recognized exception to the warrant and probable cause requirement. It effectuates the Government's strong interest in protecting American borders and regulating goods flowing into the country (i.e. narcotics, explosives, illegal aliens, communicable diseases.) "Routine" border searches—any search at a level below a body cavity or full strip search—require no suspicion at all; non-routine border searches require reasonable suspicion. To qualify as a "border search" a search must occur at the border or its functional equivalent.

C

Consent Search: A warrantless search made by police after the subject of the search has voluntarily consented as determined by the totality of the circumstances. "Voluntary" consent means that it was not the result of duress or coercion, express or implied, or any other form of undue influence exercised against the defendant. As consenting to a search is not considered a *waiver* of a right, the test is merely whether consent was voluntary. There is no requirement that the suspect be informed of the right to refuse consent. The state has the burden to prove "voluntariness" by a preponderance of the evidence. Furthermore, it is up to the suspect to limit and define any ambiguities regarding the scope of the consent.

Custodial Interrogation: Custodial interrogation, within the *Miranda* rule requiring that the suspect be advised of his rights to silence and counsel, means questioning initiated by law enforcement officers after a person has been taken into custody or otherwise deprived of his freedom in any significant way. Custody can occur without the formality of arrest and in areas other than in a police station; basically it is a question of whether the police officers are controlling the situation in a manner that would lead a reasonable person to believe that he is under arrest. See Interrogation

D

Deliberate Elicitation: After the suspect has been formally charged, a police officer may not "deliberately elicit" a response from a defendant without an attorney present, or a valid waiver of counsel. In the context of Sixth Amendment Right to Counsel, "deliberate elicitation" can be shown when the officer's statements are reasonably likely to elicit a response. "Eliciting" a response can be accomplished in ways more subtle than simply questioning the defendant. "Elicitation" occurs when the officer causes information to be drawn out of the defendant; this requires an affirmative effort, an active attempt, by the officer or Government agent. Simply listening to the defendant speak is not enough to trigger the "elicitation" element in the Sixth Amendment right to counsel.

E

Encounter: An encounter occurs when the contact between police officers and citizens is at a level where a reasonable, innocent person, in view of all the circumstances surrounding the incident, would believe he was free to decline the officers' requests or otherwise terminate the encounter. An encounter is not a "seizure" of a citizen and, indeed, is considered totally consensual; therefore it does not need to be justified by any standard of proof. Compare Stop and Frisk, Arrest

Exclusionary Rule: Where evidence has been obtained in violation of the search and seizure protections guaranteed by the Fourth Amendment of the Constitution, the illegally obtained evidence cannot be used in the case-in-chief against the defendant, and this rule has been held to be applicable to the States. However, since this remedy is a court-created rule, and not explicitly required by the Constitution, the illegally obtained evidence can be used at the trial to impeach the credibility of the defendant, as well as in numerous other proceedings—i.e., civil litigation, sentencing, and parole and probation revocation hearings. See Good Faith Exception, Fruit of the Poisonous Tree Doctrine

Exigent Circumstances: Emergency conditions which excuse the warrant requirement.

F

Fruit of the Poisonous Tree Doctrine: Evidence which is spawned by or directly derived from an illegal search or illegal interrogation is generally inadmissible against the defendant because of its original taint, although knowledge of facts gained independently of the original and tainted search is admissible.

G

"Good Faith" Exception to the Exclusionary Rule: Provides that evidence is not to be suppressed where it was discovered by officers acting in good faith and in reasonable, though mistaken, belief that they were authorized by a magistrate or by the legislature or by facts derived from court clerical personnel, to take those actions.

H

Habeas Corpus: A collateral proceeding instituted to determine whether a defendant is being unlawfully deprived of his or her liberty; a means by which to challenge the constitutionality of a decision after all appeals have elapsed. It is not an appropriate proceeding for appeal-like review of discretionary decisions of a lower court; it tests the state court's application of the law *at the time* of the case. Claims based on the Fourth Amendment cannot ordinarily be entertained in habeas corpus actions.

I

Independent Source: An exception to the exclusionary rule which allows evidence to be introduced if it can be traced to a source independent from an illegal search or seizure.

Inevitable Discovery: A "hypothetical" independent source exception to the exclusionary rule, which permits evidence to be admitted in a criminal case,

even though it was obtained unlawfully, when the Government can show by a preponderance of the evidence that discovery of the evidence by lawful means was inevitable. A minority of courts have limited the inevitable discovery exception by requiring the police to be "actively pursuing" lawful means at the time that the illegal search is being conducted.

Interrogation: Questions asked by an officer (other than those attendant to booking and other custody matters) as well as any comments or ploys which are "reasonably likely to evoke an incriminating response" from the average suspect. See Custodial Interrogation

Inventory Search: An inventory search is an administrative step following arrest and preceding incarceration, or following the valid seizure of property. No warrant or probable cause is required for an inventory search. This community caretaking function requires regulations and police procedures to be in place in order to control discretion of the officers. "Inventory" is a detailed list of articles of property, containing a designation or description of each specific article.

Invocation: For Fifth Amendment purposes, a defendant must affirmatively invoke his *Miranda* rights to silence and counsel (as opposed to his Sixth Amendment right to counsel which is triggered merely by the arraignment process or a similar formal proceeding). If a defendant waives his right to silence after an invocation, the Government can prove the "voluntary" waiver prong by showing that the officers "scrupulously honored" defendant's rights by giving defendant a cooling off period after he cut off questioning, as well as proving the defendant knowingly and voluntarily waived his rights. If a defendant invokes his right to counsel, the police officers are not allowed to interrogate the defendant unless his counsel is there or the defendant himself initiates the interrogation, and knowingly and voluntarily waives his rights. See Waiver

L

Legitimate Expectation of Privacy: "What a person knowingly exposes to the public, even in his own home or office, is not subject to Fourth Amendment protection. But what he seeks to preserve as private, even in an area accessible to the public, may be constitutionally protected." Police activity does not constitute a search unless it intrudes upon a legitimate expectation of privacy.

M

Miranda Rights: Prior to any custodial interrogation (that is, questioning initiated by law enforcement officers after a person is taken into custody or otherwise deprived of his freedom in any significant way) the person must be warned: 1) that he has a right to remain silent; 2) that any statement he does make may be used as evidence against him; 3) that he has a right to the presence of an attorney; and 4) that if he cannot afford an attorney, one will be appointed for him prior to any questioning if he so desires.

O

Open Field Doctrine: This doctrine permits police officers to enter and search a field without a warrant or probable cause, as there is no legitimate expectation of privacy: "Open fields do not provide the setting for those intimate activities that the Amendment is intended to shelter from government interference or surveillance." The term "open fields" may include any unoccupied or undeveloped area outside of the curtilage.

P

Plain View: Objects within the plain view of an officer engaged in legal activity are subject to seizure without a warrant, so long as there is probable cause that the object seized is or contains evidence of criminal activity.

Pretextual Search and Seizure: The practice of stopping or arresting an individual for a minor offense (such as a traffic violation) for the purpose of requesting consent to search (in the case of a stop) or conducting a search incident to arrest (in the case of an arrest) to discover evidence of a more serious crime for which the officer had neither reasonable suspicion nor probable cause. The minor offense is used as a pretext to seize the individual and/or search for evidence of a more serious crime.

Probable Cause: A fair probability of criminal activity under the totality of circumstances. It is a fluid concept turning on the assessment of probabilities in particular factual contexts—not readily, or even usefully, reduced to a neat set of rules. Probable cause to arrest exists where facts and circumstances within the officers' knowledge and of which they had reasonably trustworthy information are sufficient in themselves to warrant a person of reasonable caution in the belief that an offense has been or is being committed; it is not necessary that the officer possess knowledge of facts sufficient to establish guilt, but more than mere suspicion is required.

Prophylactic Rule: Prophylactic rules are court-made safeguards or practical reinforcements of rights protected by the Constitution.

Protective Sweep: When police officers have a legal right to enter premises, or to make an arrest outside of a premises, they are allowed to conduct a quick and limited search of the premises if they have reasonable suspicion to believe that such an inspection is necessary to protect themselves and others from potential harm.

R

Racial Profiling: Racial profiling describes the practice of stopping and/or detaining an individual because of his or her race or ethnicity (i.e. considering the person's race as a relevant factor in the reasonable suspicion calculus) based solely on the belief that individuals of that person's race are more inclined to commit crimes.

Reasonable Suspicion: The standard of proof necessary to justify a *Terry* stop, generally defined as a fair possibility of

criminal activity. Police officers must have a particularized and objective basis—based on specific and articulable facts—for suspecting the defendant of criminal activity. The relevant inquiry is not whether particular conduct is innocent or guilty, but the degree of suspicion that attaches to particular types of noncriminal acts. Compare Probable Cause, Encounter

S

Search: Visual or aural observation or physical intrusion which infringes upon a person's reasonable expectation of privacy constitutes a "search," triggering Fourth Amendment protections.

Search Incident to Arrest: A police officer who has the right to arrest a person either with or without a warrant may search his person and the immediate area of the arrest for weapons and to prevent the destruction of evidence. Often, the occurrence of an arrest results in exigent circumstances which allows for a wider, more thorough search for hidden evidence or dangerous compatriots. However, exigent circumstances must be proven by the facts of each case, and the fact of arrest, while pertinent, is not dispositive of whether there is a risk of destruction of evidence or harm to police officers. The Supreme Court has held that when a person is arrested in or near a car, police can automatically search the passenger compartment.

Search Warrant: The Fourth Amendment provides that "no warrants shall issue, but upon probable cause, supported by oath or affirmation, and particularly describing the place to be searched, and the persons or things to be seized." A search warrant is an order issued by a judicial officer, in the name of the state, directed to a sheriff, constable, or other officer, authorizing him to search for and seize any property that constitutes evidence of the commission of a crime, contraband, the fruits of crime, or things otherwise criminally possessed; or, property designed or intended for use or which is or has been used as the means of committing a crime. A warrant may be issued upon an affidavit or sworn oral testimony.

Seizure: A "seizure" of property under the Fourth Amendment occurs when there is some meaningful interference with an individual's possessory interest in that property. "Seizure" of an individual, within the Fourth Amendment, connotes the taking of one physically or constructively into custody and detaining him, thus causing a deprivation of his freedom in a significant way, with real interruption of his liberty of movement. An officer's actual physical touching or grasping of a suspect is always defined as a seizure whether or not the suspect submits to being detained. However, if an officer engages in a nonphysical show of authority, a seizure occurs only if a reasonable innocent person would not feel free to leave, and the person actually submits to authority.

Special Needs Analysis: When a search is conducted for a "special need" beyond ordinary criminal law enforcement, the Supreme Court has reasoned that the traditional requirement of a warrant based on probable cause is ill-suited to such searches. Special needs searches and seizures are permitted if they are reasonable. This "reasonableness" analysis balances the need for a particular search against the degree of invasion upon personal rights which the search entails. Special needs analysis has been applied to administrative, civil-based, and public safety searches. See Administrative Search

Standing Requirement: For Fourth Amendment purposes, an individual must show that he personally had a legitimate expectation of privacy in the area searched, or a legitimate property interest in the thing seized, in order to establish standing to object to the evidence obtained.

Stop and Frisk: Reasonable suspicion allows a police officer to stop a person suspected of criminal activity. Attendant to a stop, a frisk may be conducted if the officer has reasonable suspicion that the suspect is armed and dangerous. A frisk is conducted to protect an officer's safety, is limited to removal of possible weapons, and is not an evidentiary search. Compare Encounter, Arrest

T

Totality of Circumstances Test: Test used to determine the constitutionality of various search and seizure procedures, including the issuance of a search warrant. The test focuses on all the circumstances of a particular case, rather than any one factor.

U

Unnecessarily Suggestive: The Due Process Clause prohibits the admission of identifications where unnecessary suggestiveness has created a substantial likelihood of irreparable mistaken identification. However, an unnecessarily suggestive procedure will not taint a line-up or other identification procedure if the witness has a source independent from police suggestiveness on which to make the identification.

V

Voluntariness: Under the Due Process Clause, involuntary confessions will not be allowed as evidence at trial. Whether a confession is "voluntary" is determined by the amount of coercive police activity involved (rather than on the defendant's state of mind), and is reviewed on a case-by-case, totality of the circumstances basis. Police officers are allowed to play on a suspect's ignorance, anxieties, fears, and uncertainties; but they are not allowed to magnify them to the point where rational decision becomes impossible.

W

Waiver: The knowing and voluntary relinquishment—express or implied—of a legal right.

APPENDIX D

Text Correlation Chart

	Saltzburg & Capra 8th Edition	Kamisar, LaFave, Israel & King 12th Edition	Allen, Hoffmann, Livingston & Stuntz 2nd Edition (2005)	Johnson 4th Edition	Weinreb 7th Edition	Tomkovicz & White 6th Edition	Whitebread & Slobogin 5th Edition
ELEMENTS OF THE FOURTH AMENDMENT							
Legitimate Expectation of Privacy	37–42	254–264	349–367	52–67		3–47	121
Probable Cause	91–127	282–305	420–447	100–112	26–42	49–85	85–97, 162–171
Warrants and Particulars	127–147	307–321	447–552	86–97	13–21, 177–202	87–140	97–103, 149–193
Arrests — In House	182–188	364–369	516–517	88–93	44–51	170–186	82, 99
— Out of House	166–173	369	531–538		22–41	186	76–82
SEARCHES NOT COVERED BY THE FOURTH AMENDMENT							
Open Fields	45–47	260–263	358–360, 386		298–300	21–31	124–128
Public Access	49–59		361–378		293–298		
Only Illegal Activity	60–65	269–271			118		
Sensory Enhancement Devices	65–76	148–160, 265–276, 356–71	379–394	57–72	341–342	31–41	379–388

	Saltzburg & Capra 8th Edition	Kamisar, LaFave, Israel & King 12th Edition	Allen, Hoffmann, Livingston & Stuntz 2nd Edition (2005)	Johnson 4th Edition	Weinreb 7th Edition	Tomkovicz & White 6th Edition	Whitebread & Slobogin 5th Edition
EXCEPTIONS TO WARRANT AND PROBABLE CAUSE							
Plain view	337–342	359, 386–87	479–489	137–143	197–203	301–317	242–252
Exigent Circumstances	363–379	351, 359–364, 367–69	463–478	147–149	243–244	193–206	234–241
Inventory Searches	438–444	393–399, 350	544–550	203–06	237–242	242–263	333–336
Search Incident to Arrest — General	289–326	334–338, 350–359	531–552	185–199	204–217	144–192	195–209
— Automobile	311–322	387–92	541	194–199	214–215	214–219	206–208
Car Exception — General	344–351	371	489–508	150–157	228–242	207–242	211–222
— Movable property (Luggage/Containers)	351–363	350, 393–399	508	161–169	212–213, 235	207–242	128–129
Consent	457–466	451–58	668–683	121–134	152–177	263–300	299–313
Stop & Frisk, and the Boundaries of Reasonable Suspicion	190–289	399–434	552–589	219–271	100–136	320–425	253–295
— Roadblocking (*Sitz*)	423–434	436–437	625–641	293–309	136–143	445–465	328–332
SPECIAL NEEDS							
Administrative Searches	382–394	440–48	641–655	214	244–246, 292		315–350
Civil Based (School/Prison)	401–420	438–447	624, 641	276–292	175–176	443–445	337–340
Public Safety (Airports/Railroads)	420	437–38	571–573	292	290–291		332
Border Searches	445–456	436–37	640–641	310–316	289–290	487–497	325–328
REMEDIES							
Exclusionary Rule	493–506	218–254	336–348	2–30	143–152	833, 851	19–23, 50–52
Good Faith Exception	567–599	225–334	683–697	19–25	148–150	963–89	27–35
Standing	512–528	872–886	697–709	480–495	257–281	851–875	139–148
Fruit of the Poisonous Tree							
— Independent Source	545–551	888	709–719			880–94	46–47
— Inevitable Discovery	553–557	896–902	719–721	30	147–148	880–94	48–49
— Attenuation	529–544	886–87	709–719	500–506		900–57	40–45
— Identification of Live Witness		891			147		514–542
Impeachment	564–565	905–916	724–728		147	991–1012	36–38, 493–495, 495–497

	Saltzburg & Capra 8th Edition	Kamisar, LaFave, Israel & King 12th Edition	Allen, Hoffmann, Livingston & Stuntz 2nd Edition (2005)	Johnson 4th Edition	Weinreb 7th Edition	Tomkovicz & White 6th Edition	Whitebread & Slobogin 5th Edition
RETROACTIVITY	19–30	35–42			1219–49		902–914
SELECTIVE INCORPORATION	8–18	24–35	93–100	5–10	xiv		2–4
ELEMENTS OF THE FIFTH AMENDMENT			751–766				
Fifth Amendment Right Against Self-Incrimination (*Miranda*)	601–671	539–743	751–920	333–391	417–84, 425–39	589–624	447–452
— Public Safety Exception (*Quarles*)	735–738	629–34	891–892	414	474–478	609–612	470–471
Waiver	758–766	622–627	860–872	367–376	438–444	658–670	472–483
— after Invocation of Silence	767–769	628–637	860–872		438	672–708	978
— after Invocation of Right to Counsel	770–777	629–36	860–872		441–451	672–708	479
Custody (defined)	739–744	593–600	841–845	350–356	460–462	626–38	456–462
Interrogation (defined)	745–753	600–607	845–858	361	432–437, 439–45	638–655	463–465
Prophylactic Rule	710–717	667	890–920		429–430, 486–490	539–548	
Voluntariness	671–687	543–549	770–775	326–331	398–404	555–586	436–442
ELEMENTS OF THE SIXTH AMENDMENT							
Sixth Amendment Right to Counsel (*Massiah & Brewer*)	783–801	721–743	813, 920	435–442	404–411	729–749	444–447, 484–486
Waiver	801–811	115–132	937	435, 455	1058	658–670	990–996
*Deliberate Elicitation (defined)	793–795	593–611		526	407–408		488–489
Identification — General (*Wade/Gilbert*)	813–819	745–755	255, 257	530–552	369–377	773–786	515–517
— Limits (*Kirby/Ash*)	820–822	755–762	258	540	379–383	788–802	517–518
Due Process—Unnecessary Suggestiveness	823–841	754	255–275		377–378	807–828	520
Right to Counsel — Indigents	847–853	83–90	117–139	592–605	547–555	714–717	971–1004
— Counsel of Choice	1371–1387	206–218	238		547	711–27	997–998
Right to Self-Representation (*Feretta*)	1388–1404	115–133	215–241	634–642	1051–1060	676, 717	990–995
Ineffective Assistance of Counsel	1296–1387	139–181	168–215	621–631	1028–1051	723	1009–1045

*

APPENDIX E

Table of Cases

APPENDIX F

Index

†